TRUTH IS MY SWORD

TRUTH

IS MY SWORD

VOLUME II

INSPIRATIONAL MESSAGES AND PERSONAL TESTIMONIES TO REVEREND MOON

DR. BO HI PAK

The Holy Spirit Association for the Unification of World Christianity
4 West 43rd Street
New York, New York 10036
(212) 997-0050

First edition © 1999 H.S.A.-U.W.C.

ISBN 0-910621-93-4
PRINTED IN CANADA

DEDICATION

At age 21, I found myself in the middle of
the Korean War. Within three days of battle,
220 of my 330 classmates died. The shadow
of death was always around me. I prayed,
"God save me. You are the only one. If you
do my life is yours." Later, upon receiving
the Divine Principle and meeting Reverend
Sun Myung Moon, I felt "this is God's calling." For more than 42 years my wife and I
have followed the True Parents and have
raised our children in the tradition of the
Divine Principle. *Truth Is My Sword* is dedicated in eternal love to Reverend and Mrs.
Moon.

—Dr. Bo Hi Pak

CONTENTS

═══════════════════════

Introductions

Inspirational Messages

Appendix

PREFACE

For many Americans, the image of Reverend Sun Myung Moon that likely comes first to mind is that of a lecturer speaking dramatically and passionately in Korean, with a slightly younger man standing a step behind, inclining slightly as if to hear better, concentrating intently, and preparing to spontaneously translate the speaker's words into English. That slightly younger man, bent in intense concentration, is Dr. Bo Hi Pak.

For nearly half a century, he has literally and figuratively played the role of translator—and in some cases, mediator—between his teacher and spiritual father, Reverend Sun Myung Moon, and people throughout the world. Though he has many time professed his inadequacy for the task, the fact remains that he has been the conduit of spiritual life for a multitude of people.

An important part of this mission has been Dr. Pak's lengthy devotion and service to America. For Dr. Pak, America is much more than what we see in front of us. There is a deeper America, the historical America—the America of immigrant dreams, heroic dedication, patriots' vision, and most importantly, the hope of God. At the same time, Dr. Pak comes from Korea, and through his faith in and devotion to Reverend Moon, he taps not only the depth of Korea's roots, but the far deeper tradition of dedication to God espoused and upheld by Reverend Moon. For this reason, Dr. Pak's own sermons and talks, many of which are collected in this volume, have a unique and profound quality.

That quality also derives from Dr. Pak's tremendous enthusiasm for his subject matter—that is, life and how to properly live it. Dubbed "Mr. Bubbling Enthusiasm" early on, Dr. Pak has been just that. For example, if he cuts himself while shaving, as I have heard him explain on more than one occasion, his reponse is to say, "Great. Now I know I'm going to have a good day today." It also derives from his natural leadership. Over and over again, those working with him have seen Dr. Pak arrive on the scene, assess the situation, create an organization, and set down to work to move things forward in a good direction.

More than anything else, however, the quality of his guidance derives from his genuine love and concern for people and their families. The Unification ideal is the family ideal, and Dr. Pak and his family have sought to live that ideal and share it with others. This, of course, would be utterly impossible without the presence of Mrs. Ki Sook Pak, Dr. Pak's gracious and wonderful wife. To know Mrs. Pak is to marvel at her generosity, her faith, and her warm heart of love. Together they have reached out and helped many people to live by their ideals and particularly to apply the Unification principle in family life.

Dr. Pak encountered the Unification teaching—Reverend Moon's teaching—when he was a young army officer with a wife and small children. He was, in a word, transformed by the power of the truth. An extraordinarily dutiful and responsible man, he committed himself, and he has never turned back, even when called upon to digest, through faith, unimaginable challenges and circumstances. As more is known about Reverend Moon's life and work, the life of Dr. Pak becomes all the more remarkable. In fact, from the perspective of today, reading through the speeches in this volume and contemplating the history of the world, of America, of Korea, and of God's providence, Dr. Pak's sincerity, faith, bubbling enthusiasm, and concern for others is nothing short of overwhelming.

Like many others, I am grateful to have worked with Dr. Pak on many projects. He has always put God and True Parents before anything. He makes each project an exciting campaign to remember and cherish. But much more than that, he conveys his tradition and way of life, as taught by Reverend Moon.

Abraham Lincoln, the prairie boy who became president, ultimately gave America its greatest hero. As the American Civil War drew to a close, he gave marching orders to his soldiers to lay down their weapons and take up the healing power of love. Dr. Pak, a humble man also made great by faith and hard work, has, I believe, both cherished and embodied Lincoln's admonition to go beyond the soldiering life and become a man of peace: "With malice toward none; with charity for all . . . let us strive on to finish the work we are in; to bind up the nation's wounds . . . to do all which may achieve and cherish a just and lasting peace." But far more than that, transcending what the greatest American foresaw, the work of Reverend

Moon, assisted uniquely by men and women such as Dr. and Mrs. Pak, is bringing about a new birth of love, binding up the world's wounds, and achieving and cherishing a world of true love and true families.

To assist in this task, the talks of Dr. Pak collected in this volume provide a wealth of spiritual resources and practical guidance.

—The Editors

TRUTH IS MY SWORD

Introduction by
Dr. Aziz Sidky

Dr. Aziz Sidky served as prime minister of Egypt (1972-73). He was also ambassador to France and deputy prime minister for industry and mineral resources and minister of minerals and petroleum. He is currently chairman of the Council of Presidents of the Summit Council for World Peace.

It is my pleasure and honor to introduce this collection of _Inspirational Messages and Personal Testimonies to Reverend Moon_ by Dr. Bo Hi Pak. Upon reading these remarks I have come to know better not just the man, but also the spirit of Dr. Pak. What I have learned has impressed me greatly. Dr. Pak is one of these rare souls who has managed to live a life so full it would be enough to fill a dozen biographies.

I first met this extraordinary man in 1991. Through the recommendation of my dear friend Thomas Cromwell, publisher of the _Middle East Times_ in Cyprus, I was invited to attend the inaugural ceremony of the Federation for World Peace in Seoul, Korea. Also attending this international symposium were leaders from more than 100 nations including representatives from North and South Korea. It was amazing to see so many distinguished diplomats willing to put aside their political differences and explore our areas of commonality.

I found the background of this new world organization to be fascinating. During the summit meeting between President George Bush and President Mikhail Gorbachev in Washington, June 1, 1990, Reverend Moon conceived the idea of the formation of this global organization to promote lasting world peace based on a true value system. Upon the recommendation of Reverend Moon, a declaration stating the goals and purpose of this organization was drafted. Within a short time, more than 100,000 persons signed this document demonstrating their support.

At center stage of this ceremony was the co-chairman and secretary general of the Federation for World Peace, Dr. Bo Hi Pak. When he addressed the assembly and whenever we met in the ensuing years, he always conveyed a warmth and camaraderie that I rarely experienced in my life. Above all else, I was taken by his passion. His body and spirit are matched with a genuine focused purpose. His words are not empty or hollow. He invests himself totally in the moment, whatever the location or cause.

Since 1991, I have attended numerous programs around the world of various organizations founded by the Reverend and Mrs. Moon and presided over by Dr. Pak. Those conferences represent a very remarkable contribution to the cause of peace and harmony among our nations and the fraternal integration of our peoples. Presently, I am proud to serve as chairman of the Council of Presidents of the Summit Council for World Peace. It is an organization made up primarily of former and current heads of state and government and prime ministers who are willing to lend their expertise and wisdom to issues of peace and development. Our organization's skills and ideals were put to the test when we created the commission for Korea's reunification, on which I serve. We were proud of promoting the diplomatic breakthrough that brought the United States and the DPRK (North Korea) to dialogue in order to solve their differences regarding nuclear weapons proliferation.

I have had the opportunity to meet and break bread with Dr. and Mrs. Pak on numerous occasions. More than once, I have sought out his advice and always found his counsel intelligent and wise, but most importantly, centered on a strong faith in God. As a diplomat, I can assure the readers, this is the most important quality a leader can hope to possess. It is not enough to reach inside to come up with answers. We must also be able to reach out to heaven for divinely inspired answers.

I have read the selections in this collection and studied his life's chronology. It is most insightful and informative, not only about Dr. Pak's own exciting and full life, but also as it reflects upon his special and unique relationship with Reverend and Mrs. Sun Myung Moon, whom he considers his spiritual parents.

Although I am 10 years Dr. Pak's senior, I have watched his career and marveled at his tenacity and willingness to serve the public good. He is truly a role model for us. In 1961, when Dr. Pak first came to the United States as deputy attaché for the Republic of Korea, I was serving in my own native country of Egypt as minister of industry. In 1964, when he emigrated to the United States, I was promoted to deputy prime minister and minister of industry and mineral wealth. During the late 1960s and early '70s, Dr. Pak was busy establishing various organizations dedicated to peaceful exchange between the U.S. and Korea, namely the Korean Cultural Foundation, sponsors of the Little Angels Children's Folk Ballet, which toured the world and performed before the Queen of England and at the United Nations.

In 1970, I was promoted to deputy prime minister for production and trade and to prime minister in 1972. From 1973 to 1975, I served as personal assistant to President Anwar Sadat.

In 1976, Dr. Pak established News World Communications, which published many newspapers around the world, including the *Washington Times* and newspapers in the Middle East, Japan, Korea, and South America.

In looking back on those years, I can see how God was constantly using Dr. Pak for ever greater projects. Dr. Pak prayed, listened, and heard the call of God. He gave up a successful, promising military and diplomatic career to serve as principal assistant and interpreter to a new religious leader. Few would have taken such a path, but such is the right stuff that Dr. Pak is made. He would rather follow his faith and serve humbly than gather possessions and riches in a secular world.

From reading the collection, I believe the following excerpt from a 1985 inspirational message given to members of the Unification movement summarizes his philosophy of life, his unselfish willingness to enlighten and educate the young people, and finally, reveals the source of his boundless energy and devotion:

> While we live here on earth we are not cultivating this body; we are building our true body, our eternal body, our spiritual body. Within you now, right now, is that spiritual body. This physical body is sort of a case for the spiritual body. This physical body is like a rented vehicle for my spiritual body. When the time comes, the car rental company will say to turn it in. In our case, nature will say to turn it in. But the real body is being grown right now. You have no time to waste. You must grow your spiritual body every day. With Divine Principle and True Parents, you can reach perfection. That perfection means becoming a divine spirit. Your spiritual body will glow like a sun. That is our goal. We are investing our physical life for the perfection of our eternal life. We are

practicing this; it is not a theory. We are doing it and we have a physical central figure, who will cover millions of miles in one second. This is the kind of spiritual heritage that we have. I want to talk about other things, but this is the most important thing. You and I are the children of God. We have this kind of privilege that no money can buy. In order to have this kind of spirit, you have got to live a vibrant, very happy, rewarding life here on earth.

This collection of speeches and internal guidance is a wonderful testimony that will inspire and guide. As a long-time admirer of Reverend and Mrs. Moon, and as a friend to Dr. and Mrs. Pak, I enthusiastically offer this introduction.

INTRODUCTION
BY JULIÁN SAFI

Julián Safi is a renowned journalist with a prestigious career in newspaper editing and publishing in New York and his native country of Uruguay. He is also a businessman, an advisor, and a facilitator to both the private and public sectors in Uruguay and for international corporations. He worked closely with Dr. Pak for many years to establish, among many other publishing and commercial enterprises, the Ultimas Noticas *newspaper and the Victoria Plaza Hotel.*

A leader. I wondered how I could describe Dr. Bo Hi Pak and I concluded that the word "leader" is the most accurate, although it cannot embrace completely Dr. Pak's rich personality.

The Uruguayan writer Alicia Garcia Lopez asserted in one of her recent essays that leadership is the result of charisma, power, and a captivating personality. Dr. Bo Hi Pak has all these attributes. Among them, charisma is the most outstanding quality of this extraordinary man.

Dr. Pak, in fact, stands out for his capacity to love, for his immediate understanding of the needs of others, for his conviction (as well as being convincing), for provoking richness of values, and for being a man who generates happiness. Therefore, there is no person who has known Dr.

Pak or worked with him who has not been captivated by him and felt a deep admiration and a profound love for him.

I am included among that legion of admirers. And I think no one admires him more than I because during the 20 years that I have worked with Dr. Pak, more than having a leader, I have had a soul brother, who though his home is far from mine is always close to me. We live at opposite ends of the world in totally different cultures, but there is no distance that can separate a brotherhood like this. We have a total empathy. I know exactly how Dr. Pak thinks and what his decision would be when faced with any situation. And I know that his decisions are always the wisest, the most generous, the most visionary. I have had the blessing of having such a valuable guide in my life, and I know that I owe him in great measure for the triumphs I may have enjoyed. Dr. Pak has been the great advisor, not only through his words but fundamentally through his example.

During 20 years of work, we accomplished some incredible things together, such as the creation in a record 30 days of a Spanish newspaper, *Noticias del Mundo*, published daily in New York for the Hispanic community. After that, in my homeland of Uruguay, we created another newspaper, *Ultimas Noticias*, which became number two in the nation. We built the first five-star hotel in the country, the Victoria Plaza Hotel, that is, without doubt, the best and most luxurious hotel in Latin America. We bought a bank—yes, a bank, the Banco de Credito, which was ranked third in Uruguay after being in business for 80 years. Today it is second. And we worked together on many other ventures, such as Impresora Polo, which became the largest printing company in Uruguay, and L'Ecoile, a very refined carousel restaurant in the tallest building in the exclusive resort city of Punta del Este.

In forming these companies, we were always motivated to support the national good. More than 500 Uruguayan families—which is a very large number in a nation of three million inhabitants—live today on salaries they earn in those companies, and many thousands more indirectly benefit as suppliers of goods and services to those companies.

Thousands of memories, thousands of anecdotes, the most intense and saddest moments of my life, but also the happiest and most successful moments—these are part of the history of the 20 years since I met Dr. Pak. These years are impossible to describe adequately. No words can reflect all the sadness and deep frustration that an aborted project causes, or the overflowing joy that comes from achieving success in the face of immense difficulties. And we certainly had both!

The fact is that the achievements are here to be seen. How great it was to experience all those moments with Dr. Pak. What a road companion! How great to share good news with him from half-way across the world. And how comforting to receive his support when the news was not so good. Like a soldier who carries his wounded buddy upon his shoulders through enemy territory, Dr. Pak has supported me throughout all these years, in the midst of all the extraordinary projects we carried out. Today when I look back and see all our achievements, my admiration for Dr. Pak doubles—for his inspiration, his effort, his trust, his loyalty, his support, and his teaching.

But it would not be fair to Dr. Pak, and would not fulfill what I know are his deepest wishes, if I did not speak of the inspiration of his life, the reason for his efforts, the persons to whom he dedicates himself to serve unconditionally, in body and soul: the Reverend and Mrs. Sun Myung Moon.

One time during a brotherly talk, I expressed to Dr. Pak the admiration I had for him. He thanked me, and I know he appreciated what I had shared. But immediately he added that he was only a grain of sand in the desert, and that desert was Reverend Moon. "Imagine how he is," he said. "What I am doing is nothing compared to what he is doing. And what I do, I do thanks to his inspiration and support. Without him, nothing that we have done would have been possible. You must give him your admiration."

I heard and saw similar testimonies from Dr. Pak on many occasions. They have always reminded me of the literary technique used by Homer in his famous *Iliad* to convey the beauty of Helen of Troy. Actually there isn't any physical description of Helen anywhere in the book. Homer only mentions the effect that Helen's beauty had on others, so the reader can imagine how beautiful she must have been. In the same way, the many friends of Dr. Pak have learned to value and honor Reverend Moon through the admiration he engenders in Dr. Pak. Because if such a wonderful man as Dr. Pak, in his wisdom, experiences such strong feelings toward Reverend Moon, his outstanding virtues must be beyond our imagination, since we do not have the opportunity to share his life.

Finally, I will tell the reader that this compilation of speeches by Dr. Pak will be no doubt a wellspring of inspiration for all of us. We will be uplifted by the depth of his ideas and principles, the clarity of his concepts, the grace of his narrative, and the timeliness of his topics. With this conviction, I recommend a deep and attentive reading. You will be richly rewarded.

TRUE FELLOWSHIP

UTAH STREET CENTER, ARLINGTON, VIRGINIA
MAY 29, 1966

In March 1961, Dr. Pak came to the United States as a member of the diplomatic corps. He served as assistant military attache to the South Korean embassy in Washington, D.C. He served as a missionary part-time until his retirement from military service in 1964. Other early missionaries included Miss Young Oon Kim, who began the first mission to the United States in Eugene, Oregon, on January 4, 1959; Mr. David S.C. Kim, who came to Portland, Oregon, on September 18, 1959; and Mr. Sang Ik Choi, began a mission in San Francisco, California on November 12, 1965. The house on Utah Street was Dr. Pak's family residence and the first church center in the D.C. metro area. True Parents stayed in this home and addressed the early members there.

On the way to San Francisco I met a scientist on the plane who works with the Atomic Energy Commission. We had a wonderful conversation and discussed the troubles of the world and morality and youth. Finally we came to the topic of religion. He had his Bible on his knees. I assumed that he must be a Christian, so I asked him what church he belonged to.

Immediately, he answered, "I am a Mormon." He spoke very proudly and clearly. If he had asked me the same question, what do you think I would have said? My answer would be, "I belong to my Savior and Lord, Sun Myung Moon."

Then I came to realize how serious a business we are all engaged in today. Look back at 2,000 years ago when the Christians, the first disciples, were on the street and somebody said, "What is your faith?" They undoubtedly had the courage to answer, "I believe in Jesus of Nazareth." I know under the social circumstances of that period, 99 out of 100 would respond by laughing and say, "He is a carpenter. He is a laborer. How can you believe in him?" This is the origin of Christianity: a thorny path and road of persecution. Many people sacrificed their blood and life to witness to Jesus and say, "I believe in Jesus Christ." This is the 2,000-year history.

We should all bear witness without compromise. This family is gathered together for one purpose and one purpose alone. We share lots of fellowship. We share love. We share truth. But above all, all this love and truth and fellowship are centered upon one name and one name alone. We all are very stubborn people. I am. So is Mr. Kim. So is Mr. Choi. Otherwise they cannot walk this pioneering path. Unless they have such a strong, iron willpower, they would not have been able to walk the path they have walked. This is all of you. In one way we are so stubborn, but in the other way we are so selfless. Under the one supreme name to whom we all belong, there is nothing that we cannot do. In his name we are ready to face our death. The reason we are courageously ready to face even the valley of death is that because through him we know life. So, we are all engaged in a serious business.

On the plane, the scientist and I discussed the atomic bomb. U.S. scientists believe that Red China possesses a megaton bomb. Humanity is now capable of annihilating itself. But this scientist beautifully explained that paradise can be created by mankind by tapping into atomic energy. With infinite atomic power we could build the physical kingdom on earth. Who will make this choice? Men will make this choice. God gave Adam a commandment: The day you eat of it you shall die. Which means, obedience will bring life and disobedience will bring death. By putting atomic energy in the hands of mankind today, God is clearly telling us that obeying His law will lead to abundant life and disobeying will bring total death.

So this is a perfect time for re-creation. In human history morality has never been more important than it is today. A high standard of morals has been a good thing to have, hasn't it? But so far morality has been almost a luxury. But having this kind of power, atomic energy, in our human hands makes a moral code not just a nice thing to have but an absolute necessity. Without it, we die. This world without an absolute moral code will die.

I am really moved by this conclusion this morning. You and I have an awesome responsibility, don't we? We have the key to this moral standard. God revealed it, I don't know why, through us. And we are the ones to share this moral standard on a worldwide scale and save the world and bring the world back to God's hands. I am really serious. Once again, I realize that we are in a serious state. So our gathering has importance far beyond mere fellowship.

WHAT DOES FAMILY MEAN?

Yesterday I reported on a recent development in Washington, but that was only external. One internal development that I would like to share was in the fellowship in Washington. The brothers and sisters living together here are supposed to be a loving, unified family. We live under that name. But suddenly we came to the realization that we do not really love each other. What does family mean? Gordon, for example, said that his mother and father deserted him when he was a child, and they divorced and remarried and all kinds of things happened. He never really tapped into this infinite energy and tasted family life. So he really doesn't know what a family should be like, especially in the heavenly kingdom. We had several open-hearted sessions that sometimes lasted until two or three in the morning.

Everybody opened their heart, honestly helping each other find how we can be a truly loving family, to live up to the name Unified Family. For example, one member said, we eat together, but something is wrong in my heart. I really don't feel love in the bottom of my heart. Mr. Nishikawa discussed the beauty in this world, but to me the most beautiful thing in this world is the heart of repentance. When you give your humble heart in an effort to unite, this is the most beautiful thing—a kind of revolution. These sessions were not held because of my guidance or Miss Kim's. This atmosphere was generated among the American family members themselves. They were painful hours. But it was all locked into one great result: truly to live up to the name of the Unified Family.

I think this presents our true strength based upon this unity. The core and the bond will never break. God certainly was there. We are the Divine Principle family or the Unified Family. People in the world talk about love and good fellowship. Many social gatherings are held. But we should go one step deeper. We must be something else, which we could never find in other parts of society, something that is unique to our family. In other words, Unified Family has become the motto. This is something to present to the United States. We talk about action. The united, living example of the Unified Family is the action of this movement. This will counteract the trend of U.S. families breaking up. For this we have True Parents, we have

Father and Mother, whom we can eternally serve. So we are the only ones who can claim this true Unified Family. We are qualified, not because we are wise or intelligent, but because we are tied into this one person to whom we bear witness.

No matter how painful this thorny path may be, we must not surrender. We have got to communicate. Lack of communication brings misunderstanding. Misinterpretation creates an uncrossable gap. But once we really sit down and talk and put everything on the table, we always reach a common ground from which we can expand. And we do have already such a wonderful common ground: that one name we unite around. This is the common ground.

I would like to recall the course of history of how the Divine Principle was given to the United States. The first missionary who bore the message to this land was Miss Young Oon Kim, who came to the West Coast and started the movement. She taught the first words of the new revelation of Divine Principle in this land. She went through a tremendous ordeal, a thorny path, the road of persecution, which I do not have to go into detail about because all of us have some idea of it already. It was not safe for them to remain in Eugene, Oregon, so the first pioneer group had to move to San Francisco.

Miss Kim, to whom we all give our awe, respect, and love, is truly a dynamic spiritual champion and absolute fighter. And a very important missionary. She established a foothold in America. Then soon our elder brother, Sun Cho [David] Kim, landed in this country as a pioneer. You can see that sometimes the path of the heavenly way is ironic, because he started in the same state where we received the first persecution, Oregon. Even though Mr. Sun Cho Kim, our brother, is right here in front of me, I don't hesitate to say this. The path this elder missionary had to walk was beyond description. I don't think anyone in this room, even the family from the Northwest, can fully comprehend the thorny path he had to tread. I know some of the circumstances.

IMMIGRATION ORDEAL

The U.S. Immigration office is often a difficult place for foreign nationals. I am not criticizing this office, but you have a set of laws that all foreigners have to go through. As U.S. citizens, you never realize how painful it is. Brother Kim has no money. He has to be a student because otherwise there is no way he can stay in this country. He does not need any more education. He received his degrees in Korea. But in order to stay in this country to fulfill this great mission, he has to have some kind of student title; otherwise he cannot remain. The immigration law requires you to be a full-time student; you have to take at least 12 academic hours per semester. Of course, when English is not your mother tongue, this is not an easy task. I don't think I would ever, ever have gone through that ordeal. For seven years now he has been meeting this academic responsibility and fulfilling his great mission.

Even before I came to this country I already saw his picture along with his letter to the Master. I remember how excited I felt when I saw that picture in Korea. Unfortunately, this elder missionary is carrying the same burden even now. We all must pray that he will be free so that he will be able to devote his full strength to his mission. Here is brother Kim with us; fortunately he never gets old. That is the same face that I saw in the picture in Korea.

I arrived in this country in March 1961. But I came here in a different manner from Miss Kim or our brother Kim. It was not a coincidence that I was chosen as my nation's diplomat to this country. This time I came as a major, with my family, to serve in a foreign country as a diplomat. The rest of the military attaché posts were already full. Only this position at the Korean Embassy in Washington, D.C., was open—the only one throughout the world. Usually a colonel fills this post; only in the United States is there a major instead of a colonel.

We have 5,000 majors in the Korean army, and every one of them is eager to go abroad as a diplomat. This is really an honorable assignment. How could I ever even dream to be chosen out of 5,000? But our Leader said, "Take the exam." I had no choice. I took the exam. I really had no idea where I would end up. I just obeyed, that is all. The exam ended by noon. Of course, I dashed directly back to our church and reported to our Leader. But our Leader was not there. One of the members sitting in the room said he had some other appointment and he had left just a few minutes before. But the member told me that our Leader had been sitting down in front of the big clock at 12:00, an old-fashioned clock that rings 12 times. When that clock rang 12 times, marking high noon, our Leader looked up at that clock and said, "By now I think Bo Hi has completed the exam." Our Leader was sitting there all morning thinking of me, supporting me spiritually so that something good would happen in that exam room. I had told him 12 was the ending hour. So when the clock struck 12, he acknowledged, "Now I think his exam is over."

Without knowing the test result, I felt a sensation of confidence. I knew I would be chosen. The next day one name was revealed, and it was Bo Hi Pak. That was how I came to Washington. Certainly I was not hungry as our Brother Kim was. You know how Washington diplomatic society is. It is really luxurious. Sometimes President Johnson or President

Kennedy would give a reception and all the diplomats would be invited. This is really the highlight of Washington life. And the big spring ball is really a fantastic thing that is an obligation, I had to go. So life on the surface, to me, was fantastic.

But I have an awesome mission to fulfill: to bear witness to the Divine Principle and to our Leader. How could I, in my position? The Divine Principle is not yet the national policy of Korea. Because I represented Korea, I could not speak out officially on the Principle of Creation. Everywhere I spoke in public, it was recorded, and the State Department could examine it. The Korean government could examine what I said. So really I had no freedom of speech. Without words, how can you convey the Word? This was exactly my position.

But God worked. Worked and worked. I tried an odd and bold and risky way. I kept having a Bible study class in the basement of our home almost every week. To make a long story short, I had one critical moment when I was almost kicked out. You know how Satan works. I happened to be involved with one of the most extreme Presbyterian ministers. I was too naive. I thought I could convince him. We had some very burning discussions, but it ended up boomeranging back to our ambassador.

Anyway, this was the beginning chapter of the Divine Principle in the United States. We worked, Father worked, and the movement grew and was respected. Then last year we had a most glorious time when we welcomed our beloved Leader for the first time in this country. The movement is just beginning, and this nation is so big. We really didn't need much coordination between the three different missions that were set up. But when our Leader came to this country, we came to fully realize that our movement is moving into a new stage—from formation to growth stage. You know how excited we all were to welcome him. This is the first place he delivered his message. The first room he slept in. And he had a complete tour of the United States. Of course, each one of you had a chance to accompany him on his trip.

He was rather pleased by the accomplishments that all three groups have made, even though we thought our accomplishments were too little. Then the question of establishing some kind of national headquarters or organization arose. Our Leader gave simple instructions on this matter. He intended to have this done when he was here. When our Leader attended the farewell meeting, which was held in the basement of Arlington Center, he made two unforgettable remarks. First, he asked us all, "Would you want to see me here again? Shall I come to the United States again?" Oh yes, of course. And he said, "Where would you like to see me? Here?" And he pointed down to the basement. Everybody hesitated to say yes or no. We didn't know what his intention was. Then he said, "Shake your head like this [no]. I don't want to meet you here anymore." Which is in a way a mandate. Which means go, expand. The next time I come I don't want to have a gathering in this basement, which means I don't expect to talk to a small group here in this basement.

I AM GOING TO BE YOUR LEADER

The second memorable statement was that this first trip is a conditional trip. It was a trip where he set the heavenly condition for the future blessing of America. He said, "I observed as a third person and I have been your guest. In other words, I didn't command you this time. But next time when I come, be ready for my command. I am not going to be your guest. I am going to be your Leader. Be ready for this Leader's leadership in every way." It is true.

What is the definition of national headquarters or a national organization? I don't care what kind of definition lawyers or other people make for national headquarters, but as far as the Divine Principle movement is concerned, national headquarters is nothing more than a foundation for our Leader's leadership. In other words, this is a tool through which our Leader can express his leadership, the structure that our Leader can employ to run his business, which is to bring the kingdom on earth. To me, this is the whole definition. Nobody else is entitled to lead national headquarters except our Leader.

This is the tradition of the national headquarters in Korea and Japan's headquarters in Tokyo. This will be the tradition of the national headquarters in America and elsewhere in other countries. In other words, our Leader is the inner temple, and the national headquarters is our outer temple, so that inner and outer are fully ready to command.

Our Leader's trip was also an evaluation of the world situation from the point of view of the world movement. Our Leader made a famous remark: After I have seen the world, I am fully convinced the future world movement depends on the U.S. movement. He said, Europe is living in memories and in the past. The United States is the only country living in the future and in hope. This is, in a way, an interpretation of how our Leader felt. He made this remark when he went back to Korea. He said, I will center the movement in America. In the future, I will probably spend more time in America to run the world restoration than here in Korea. He clearly said, I have done enough for Korea. (He certainly did.) My mission is over for Korea. I am not only a Korean citizen. Now I belong to the world; now I will spend more time in America, strengthening the U.S. movement. That will bring the world together.

This is the apparent strategy of our Leader now. We are all hoping he will make his second trip soon. I know our Leader and his family will come. I don't know when, but really it depends on us, not him. Whenever we are ready I know he will come. Before he comes we should have the temple ready.

On March 10 I received the most wonderful gift. This was a letter written by our Leader himself. I have been following him the last 10 years. I never even dreamed of receiving a written letter from our Leader. Our Leader has a firm policy not to write. It was a letter—not just a few lines—in which the total scheme of the world strategy is revealed. It was not typed. Nobody took dictation for him. He, himself, wrote this long, long letter. It gave me the urgent sense that something has got to be done before we are too late.

Before March 10 I came to San Francisco because of the Little Angels tour. I met many of you, and I am sure some of you saw the Little Angels' performance. Incidentally, the Little Angels are coming back here in the fall for a four-month tour, and they are going around the world next year. They are like the apple of the eye in Korea now. It is just wonderful. Whenever the president's wife, Madame Park, has a state party for foreign guests or a head of state, she always invites the Little Angels. Our Leader was most pleased.

You just heard Mrs. Nishikawa this morning. You might not know, but I think this information is good for you. Ehwa Women's University is the world's largest university. Don't be surprised that the world's largest university is a woman's university. We are proud of that. It is a good quality school founded by the Methodists. When the Divine Principle movement spread on that campus, they overlooked it at first. But soon they discovered the force was so strong, they might be engulfed by this entire movement. They were afraid, and they began to persecute us. To make a long story short, Miss Kim and Mrs. Choi, whom you met last year during our Leader's visit, were victims. They were professors at this university, and they were kicked out. Among the students, hundreds were followers of our movement. Everyone was given the choice: Renounce your faith or get out of this school. Isn't that cruel? I don't think it would happen here. They had no other way to stop this movement.

Many people have a family tradition that would make it difficult to give up school. But 14 courageous young women said they would choose their spiritual life over their higher education, and one of them was Mrs. Nishikawa.

So that campus became a living social sadness. When we hear of Ehwa Women's University, something strikes our heart. I recently received a letter from Korea. They are celebrating the 80th anniversary of the school with a big ceremony and invited all kinds of guests. They wanted to have the best festival possible and they invited all the parents of the thousands of students, but they thought it still was not enough. They came to the Little Angels and begged and begged and begged for them to come. Isn't it ironic? This school that persecuted us so much, now they come to us, to our church, asking and begging us to come to the program. Of course, we went. We danced on the stage of Ehwa Women's University the first night.

The president of the university was so pleased. The next day she invited more guests and asked the Little Angels to perform again. Of course, we accepted. What is the greatest revenge in Christian life? Generosity. Forgiveness and love. For example, if he hits me and I forgive him, he owes me eternally. We have no time for or interest in revenge in the way of "you strike me, I strike you." It is not our way.

Ironically, the second day the president of Korea invited us to perform for their foreign guests in the Blue House. We told them the Little Angels already had a commitment to Ehwa Women's University. But the president's office contacted Ehwa University, and of course they had to yield to the Blue House. If the Blue House wants something for an official function, nothing can compete with them. So we went to see Madame Park. This is one piece of news I thought we might enjoy together.

When the Little Angels made the trip to San Francisco, I invited Miss Kim and our brother Kim to come to Washington. Both of them are my elders. Miss Kim brought me into the Principle, and I was trained by the dynamic leader in Korea. So I had a good relationship. Miss Kim accepted, but brother Kim had school obligations. But I do know that the place where our brother Kim is to operate is not here, is not in Oregon, is not Texas, and is not New York. It is national headquarters. He is talented, and his leadership is needed by the nationwide organization.

I know this will be realized if I pray fervently enough and my effort is strong enough. I know they are coming in the near future, and we will all be together in Washington. Then we can really discuss the world strategy. Of course, that does not mean we have to be in Washington all the time. It will be the base from which we work nationwide. This day is coming.

DISPENSATIONAL IMPORTANCE OF WASHINGTON

Incidentally, I overlooked one thing. Before our Leader left the country, he outlined the national headquarters and instructed us on two things. These are not my words. One, he expressed the desire to have his national headquarters located in Washington, D.C. This was done when he blessed the ground in front of the White House. After the dedication of that ground, he said quietly, this is the ground where my temple will be built. Don't misunderstand. I did not start the movement in Washington, and our Leader hasn't the slightest idea who works in Washington. He doesn't care. I approve of this idea. He only selected that piece of ground in that city for dispensational reasons. You know what I mean. Washington is today physically and realistically the nerve center of the political world and the economic world center. It is literally becoming the world capital, not the United Nations. Billions and billions of dollars are appropriated in Washington for both war and peace. All the world leaders travel back and forth from there. This is truly the city that lives up to being the center or the heart of the world. You know how our Leader values the historical dispensation. The city itself is a museum of the American people. Our Leader chose the city as the site of the Church headquarters.

Second, before he left he did one more thing. He selected Jim Fleming and Mary Fleming as architects. Our Leader recognized Jim's ability, sound judgment, and experience in management. And of course, his total dedication. Among the whole U.S. movement, it was our Master's choice to have them become the first architects of this first structure of the national headquarters. This is not my choice. This is not Miss Kim's choice. This is not Mr. Kim's choice. This is our Master's choice, which I will obey. I called Jim and Mary and conveyed our Leader's wishes, and then right after that Mrs. Choi encouraged them to accept this heavy responsibility. And our Leader said hello afterward.

So these are the two key cornerstones our Leader already laid before he departed from this country. So they started. Jim and Mary said that if they were summoned by anybody other than our Leader, they don't think they would even consider obeying because they don't consider this the type of work they can accomplish. But knowing the summon comes from the one in whom we believe and for whom we do our best, there could be no excuse. When God called Abraham and summoned him from the Chaldea, he just packed up everything and started his journey to nowhere. God didn't even tell him where to go. But Jim has a little better direction than that. They were at least told to go to Washington. They both trust our Leader, and they loaded up everything.

They made a 21-day journey and arrived in Washington, and we had a tearful prayer asking our Father for the wisdom and courage to do things right. I welcomed them and we had a prayer. After that we had a discussion night and day, drawing up a plan. But we did not draw up this plan purely out of our brains. We have samples to go by, which are the world organization and the Japanese headquarters. Of course, we never expected to come up with a perfect plan initially. But we do know something must be started. There is a Korean proverb that goes, to begin is to already be halfway done.

We regret very much not having Mr. Kim physically present. We regret it very much. At least one or two members of the Northwest family could be present. But I did the next best thing. I sent our brother Kim the minutes of what we discussed every night. Then after the plan was drawn up, before we did anything, I gave the total plan to brother Kim with my letter of explanation of many pages. And I told him not to hesitate to call me on the phone. He responded, and we had a 45-minute conversation long distance, which to me was like five minutes. I listened, took notes, and every recommendation he made I brought to the entire council, which met in Washington, and amendments were made.

For example, I initially thought that the leadership should be according to the order of arrival of the U.S. mission: Miss Kim, Mr. Kim, and myself. Since this is the very first official plan, I thought that history should somehow be reflected in the organization. So I insisted that we should have Miss Kim as head, as chairman, which is the logical thing to do. Then the rest of the board of directors can be organized. I wanted to be assistant to the two, but the unanimous opinion was that the three of us should be chairmen. So I was privileged to join as third vice chairman. This was the initial arrangement drawn up. Mr. Kim suggested, why not let the American family run the entire thing, which I thought was a wonderful suggestion. Why shouldn't we all be advisers. So we didn't want to remain on the board as initially drawn up. I put the three names in, but we immediately corrected it. So you see, our communication to you has listed three names, Miss Kim, Mr. Kim, Bo Hi Pak, as advisers to the U.S. national organization.

My dear brothers and sisters, I am not saying, by no means, that this national headquarters is completed. It is just the beginning. Many nights and days Jim and Mary sweated. But this is just the beginning. Those who make this thing perfect and make it work are not Jim and Mary. Nor is it Mr. Kim or myself. It is you, every one of you. You are the pilots. Without you it is not complete. We urgently need every resource, personal and material, and every talent to make this work. This is the task left to be done. To make it go fully, ready for our Leader's second visit. It all depends on you and me.

One of the roles I assumed during this discussion period was to communicate with our Leader. I reported every phase. Upon the completion of the initial stage, it was simultaneously reported to our Leader. Two weeks later, I received another spiritual gift. This is a second lengthy letter from our Master, which I treasure as a gift. Not to me, but to the mission of the United States. Who am I to receive this letter? He did not write to Bo Hi Pak, the individual. He touched me deeply. I have the awesome responsibility to preserve this letter, and it will be turned over to a U.S. archive, which will be created. Again, it was a very lengthy letter. First he acknowledged the entire report that I had made and approved every phase of the discussion. We are not in a position to decide anything. The commander-in-chief will decide. Until such time, nothing will be firmed up. This was my position.

And the commander-in-chief gave approval of the total plan, the organization, at least to its intent. And he gave his blessing, wishing the mission great success. The one word he used in approval was the Korean word for "great." I think you ought to be proud. But that approval is just the beginning of the letter. After that page came the mandate that the U.S. movement is to fulfill.

MANDATE TO THE NATION

He numbered the mandate. One, do this. Two, do this. And this mandate is not the things that any person or any segment can fulfill. This is a mandate to the nation. We will all sweat and labor together to accomplish it. Otherwise, we have no way to succeed. In other words, he is using this structure as a channel to fulfill his strategy before he comes.

The first mandate he mentioned was the expansion of the economic foundation. Our Leader is keenly aware the time has come for the restoration of the things of creation. Many years ago, when we were both in Korea, our Leader would keep disregarding material things. Our home church in Korea was so shabby. Everyone who has been in Korea knows that the church's main gate is extremely shabby. We said, Leader, I think we have enough money to rebuild this gate so that it looks a little better. Our Leader said, I leave it that way on purpose. He said, the leaders who will run the world movement in the future pass through this shabby gate. Isn't that meaningful?

In other words, if you have a great big building, a great big pulpit, many people come only because of that. It could attract people. But when you go through a shabby gate, you have no reason to pay attention to the shabby gate except to feel some kind of shame. But you can come courageously and stay on and on because of the truth. In other words, sacrifice. In other words, I am not coming for glory. I am coming to give myself. This is the type of person our Leader was seeking in the initial stage of his movement. But now he thinks the time is over for acquiring personal leadership. He feels he has the leadership in Korea, Japan, and the United States. Now he needs the physical container to have the leadership function rapidly. For this our Leader is very eager now to see the material world, which means the things of creation, restored to heaven.

So he emphasized business. He emphasized solid earning and he, himself, led the factory that is building one of the new, very fantastic airguns that was founded by one of our members. He invented it. It is formidable, a really wonderful air shotgun. No powder is needed, just air. Through compression of air this shotgun can fire and even burst the bullet. It is fantastic. Our Leader was here in Washington and had a sample of that gun with him. We went to a gun distribution place and demonstrated it. The gun distributor simply could not understand. Without powder it competed with the regular powder shotgun, but the penetration power of this air shotgun is greater. Our Leader really put his heart and soul into seeing this developed.

One of the instructions was to establish the U.S. headquarters of the business and obtain a U.S. patent as a new invention. The world market should be developed, for example in South America, where powder guns are prohibited. There is a vast opportunity in this air shotgun market. Even in the U.S. the training to use a powder gun is so expensive. The National Rifle Association has millions of members. They use guns for training, but powder is so expensive. So the air gun would cut down the cost of expenses for the NRA. We have the best market. But Korea is not ready to make a quantity of them. Our Leader is now directly leading the expansion of the factory so that we will have quality and quantity. And he said the U.S. movement should support this project.

In connection with this, I think our brother John Smedly should be honored. His personal name was mentioned by our Leader, who remembers every talent and potential in the U.S.

We have a job to do. I don't want to make this talk too long, but may I say this to you. Honestly and frankly, certain members among us sometimes feel a certain uneasiness between the three different groups—Northwest, San Francisco, and Washington. May I announce one campaign with you. For our movement, let us get rid of the word "group." In the sight of our Leader there is no Northwest group, no San Francisco group, no Washington group. Only the U.S. family exists. From this time on, let us exterminate the word group. We have better words to use: brothers and sisters. Portland Family. Washington Family. San Francisco Family. All together, the Unified U.S. Family.

A remark was made that I thought was very meaningful. A piece of paper means nothing. Signing a name means nothing. Mind and heart, that is what counts. I fully agree. Mind and heart are what count, not the piece of paper with a signature. But we must have a container where we can contain our mind and heart. We learned the Divine Principle so well. God, before He created inward things, always created outward things first. Isn't that so? Before mankind was created, which is the inward dwelling of the universe, God created the universe first, which is the container of man.

Before God created the spirit, God created the body in which the spirit can dwell. The external body as a container was needed before the inward spirit was created.

Before God restored men, He gave the Ten Commandments, which was the external law to obey. The Old Testament magnificently served the purpose of external restoration, outward restoration. The Ten Commandments say, you shall not kill, you shall not commit adultery. But the New Testament, which is inward, tells us, even if you harbor a lustful mind toward a woman, you have already committed adultery, which means an inward quality. Now we are going even further, into a period of heart.

Therefore, our ultimate goal is to unite heart and mind. We do start from the external things, too, as a container. Let us make it perfect. Don't you want to have national recognition? I was so sorry that national recognition of the Korean movement was delayed. That made my heart ache so deeply. This wonderful movement couldn't get recognition until recently. The U.S. has obtained national recognition before the Korean government gave recognition. Isn't your heart aching? We all, and brother Kim, cried tears many, many times over the persecution that the government directed toward us.

Don't you want to be strong nationally and united so that we can invite senators and congressmen to be our guests? We can exchange ideas. Let the guest talk from his point of view and we can give him the Divine Principle as the solution for this country. This wonderful future is just ahead of us. We have got to have a national establishment. You and you, everyone will make it be successful. I know our Leader has a plan to have one or two Northwest families become directly responsible for an important segment of the movement. Maybe he will give another mandate, like he gave Jim Fleming. You take off. Alexis, Gordon, Doris, Ted. The U.S. is a big chunk of continent, but in the eyes of our Leader, in terms of the communication of today, it is so small. It is merely like a hill.

PREPARE A SPECIAL GIFT

There is a feeling among us sometimes, why don't we wait for our Leader to come. Of course, I see the point. But why should we? The Leader's spirit is among us, isn't it? He is with us, isn't he? Don't you have, as I do, the conviction that he is walking along with us? He told us everything he has in mind for us to do. We want to be good children, children of filial piety. We all want to be loyal children, mature children. So before Father and Mother come, we can do the magnificent work, so we can present something that pleases them. Isn't that the ideal?

He can see how much we have worked. He will be so very happy to see what the children have harvested. Rather, shall we wait to find if there are solutions to all the problems? Should we wait until they come and just give him the problems as a gift? You would do this? We all want him to come to receive glory and joy, not to take care of problems. Is there any problem in the heart of our Father that cannot be solved? And he is so near. You can ask him anything. John Smedly, if you write him a letter today, he will be most eager to read whatever you send. He is so near.

The blessing is just wonderful. But his blessing will be for America. America will be blessed. We ought to be ready to be a recipient of this blessing. You know it is a matter of time. Our unity is important. It is a matter to work out. Particularly when the blessing comes, a bridge can be built. This dear brother may be Blessed with another charming, wonderful member from way on the other side of the land. Oh, this is wonderful. In our Leader's sight, he is not living in the Northwest, he is living in America. And I, Bo Hi Pak, don't think my mission will be just here in America. Maybe next year I will be summoned to tackle some mission in Korea. I am willing to be sent somewhere in another part of the world. Are we movable? Are we available? We are all Abraham.

We want to have not only a structural organization but also the symbolic organization. That is, we want to have our own building in which we must work. The building is more than just an office. Your home building is more than where you just line up your bed and sleep. Even the shape of a home means something. Every U.S. visitor who comes to Washington walks the streets, then he sees Capitol Hill—the dome of the U.S. Congress, how beautiful, how elegant, how sacred-looking it is. When you as an American citizen see that dome, what do you feel? Don't you feel a sense of pride? Don't you have a sense of gratitude? We have the same sense when we come to the Holy Ground. We are the only ones who know the value.

If we have our own monumental building somewhere, we can not only work, invite people, and teach them, but also we can light it up as a symbol of this heavenly movement. Isn't it a good dream? Sooner or later this dream will become reality. If we join together, work together, this reality will come quickly. Many hours at night I couldn't sleep when I thought of all the problems and problems and problems. I couldn't sleep. I sure want to have this thing done. My heart is so eager. I want to have it done before our Leader's second coming.

Yesterday I mentioned about our mailing service. My wife and I work after office hours until 12:00 and 1:00 and 2:00 in the morning. We keep going. Every letter we insert means one cent. Then I hope and wish and pray, and sometimes tears just run down to the machine, that God, Father, let this letter machine keep running so some kind of restoration of money can be done so we can purchase our Leader's temple here in America. Somehow. Oh, Father, please give me the kind of courage and wisdom I need. I want to give this body.

If this is everyone's wish in this room, this is the greatest power. We can do invincible things. There is nothing we cannot do. We have seen one pamphlet that the Northwest family has been using, and we recognize the quality of the brochure presenting our movement as the best one that has ever been produced. So we decided to use it in all centers. If the Los Angeles center has a talent, make it known to the whole movement. If the Northwest has a talent, it has got to be freely used by the entire movement.

Once more I invite your earnest participation in constructive criticism. It is most welcome. Your words will be heard. My testimony here this evening is that I am going to send this paper to Korea, to our Leader. I am willing to stand at the judgment seat if anything I said is wrong or anything I said is against or deviated from his own spirit. I want to be judged.

WARS AND CRISES

America has played such a monumental, instrumental role. Before you created this great country, you had to pass through many crises, the Civil War, the War of Independence. The 13 colonies united together to form the Union. And Patrick Henry spoke the immortal words, "Give me liberty or give me death." But Patrick Henry was firmly against joining the Union; he didn't want Virginia to join because he believed it would restrict freedom. So he spoke the immortal words. We quote those words in many other ways than he originally intended. He spoke these words against the Union. Now history will show how short-sighted Patrick Henry was. He was afraid of freedom and liberty. Without the Union, how would the United States enjoy liberty today? I don't think so. The American people have displayed great spirit in working together and uniting and cooperating. This is your independent spirit. This is your spirit throughout your history. Now this dynamic American spirit must be demonstrated again as we unite to accomplish heaven's work.

We are most fortunate here. Besides the three missionaries, now we have a helping hand from another great pioneer of our movement, Mr. Nishikawa. His experience, his journey, and the path he went in Japan are really monumental and symbolic to this world movement. His advice is available to us here, so we feel confident because we have the assistance of his mind and experiences. We can enlist his support, for which our Leader sent him here to America. Now we can really fulfill. Sometimes I am sure there is an American millionaire somewhere. Sometimes the economic situation has prevented us from doing so many things. If our movement had enough money, many things could have moved so much faster. We could have brother Kim fly over to Washington many times. But money prevented it. We could have had better counsel when Mr. Nishikawa is not here.

But this is one fact with which we have to live. I sure want to earn money. I want to make money, but with a different motivation. It is said there are 80,000 millionaires in America. I sure am sorry whenever I see brother Kim, knowing his separation from his family. They are one of the Blessed couples. So many years, this precious blessing that God and heaven has bestowed upon him, he just sacrificed for the mission. We want to have as firm a commitment. I want to see the day that brother Kim's whole family will be rewarded. I know God has a reward for them. But as a brother I want to do my part, too. I don't want to go any further.

This evening I earnestly express my honest feeling. I open myself to your criticism. I am ready to hear any word you speak. I am open. I helplessly and vulnerably open myself to you without defense. With my conviction I spoke the truth with heart. Let us pray.

Prayer by Bo Hi Pak:

Our loving Father, forgive us. We are so far away from your expectations. Father, so many times we spoke of your heart, but we know that we have accomplished so little toward that direction. Father, I am helplessly throwing myself on your altar for your disposal. Father, do what you want, every way you wish, any level you want. Father, all the brothers and sisters in this room, we all together come to at least one realization. We come together for one purpose: to glorify Your name and bring Your kingdom here on earth. We have the key, Father. You have given it to us. Father, let us always have a repentant heart. And Father, let us all the time ready ourselves to sit in sackcloth and ashes and to see the path, see the glorious future. Father, we want so much to do your will. Every one of us in this room wants to give our whole soul and heart for your cause, for the one purpose for which we gather. So, Father, lead us in Thy ways. We demonstrate obedience to You. Manifest Your will. The will that has been manifested clearly we will do totally. Father, thank You for this most wonderful weekend. This is such a great blessing that we, all the family in this area, can become so openly one and enjoy give and take in such a rich atmosphere. We never lose that sense of oneness, of harmony, Father. We will wholeheartedly tackle our mission in a given area. Father, please trust us. Father, we want to trust You and, Father, we want to be trusted. Throughout history so many times You have been betrayed, You have been left alone. We will not repeat this same thing. Father, our work may not be like St. Paul's work. We may not be like Peter, but Father, Peter betrayed him before his time came. He said, I don't know you. St. Paul, how great he may be, but he did not follow the living Lord before he was crucified. How poor he was. Father, we are without any qualification, yet we know the greatest name. We met him in person. Father, we communicate and have give and take with him directly. This is the source of life, source of honor. Father, for this one privilege alone, we will hold nothing back. We are willing to walk in the valley of death. Father, the world is so near to the last days. The world is so near to totally crumbling. Without your light, without your guidance and truth, this world is doomed to decline. Father, we want to realize the responsibility, too, to know the truth. Father, knowing the Divine Principle is not only a privilege but a responsibility to share. We are committed all the way. Father, we are giving glory to this name. We totally present ourselves at the altar. Take it and set your condition and we will go for fulfillment. Father, bless the rest of this hour, the rest of today and tomorrow. Father, until this journey's end, let this meeting be a most historical one that will be recorded throughout history. Father, we are so grateful for those who participated, but in the meantime those who could not come to this meeting, bless them, their hearts, wherever they are, and be with them. Father, thank you very much and all these things we pray in the name of our True Parents. Amen.

VOICE OF FREEDOM

UTAH STREET CENTER, ARLINGTON, VIRGINIA

SEPTEMBER 5, 1966

════════════════════════════

Dr. Pak returns to America after 19 historical days in Korea. He shares Father's heart toward the American members and reports about the programs and expansion of the Korean movement. He puts forth a profound new definition of the word "messiah" and talks about the need for modern heroes.

There was a great novel and movie called "Gone With the Wind." I think that to most of the Korean brothers and sisters, Bo Hi Pak seems like a man who is gone with the wind. He suddenly appears and suddenly disappears. I went to Korea August 12, telling no one, except I wrote a confidential letter to our Leader that I was coming. I did not want anyone to meet me at the airport. But a group of Little Angels was at the airport to see Ambassador Yang. When they suddenly saw my face, they said, oh my, wondering whether I was real or a ghost or something. It was a very funny situation. Some of the children burst into tears. Our Leader hadn't even told President Eu that I was coming, so no one expected me to be in Korea.

First of all, before I report what happened in Korea, I would like to convey that our True Parents and the brothers and sisters in Korea are sending their fervent love and good wishes to our beloved Miss Kim. To them, Miss Kim is a model of our Divine Principle movement. Everybody asked me about her and how she is doing. Our Leader asked many questions, which I answered. And most of your names were mentioned by our Leader. For example, he asked, how is it going with Mike, I cannot forget his laughter, his big mouth. The next thing our Leader asked was how is his appetite. So I said, his mouth is still big and his appetite is still strong, both spiritually and physically.

Then he recalled many unforgettable memories, and he particularly asked me to convey his warmest love and concern for the pioneering work that has been done by Jim and Mary who, by his direct instructions, moved over 3,000 miles and initiated the structure of Unified Family. Our Leader especially sent his best wishes and love for both Jim and Mary. He remembered practically every one of you. He mentioned Ann, how is Ann, he said. Herb, Myrtle, and Barbara and Diane. His pronunciation is very like Japanese. He asked me how much they changed. He also asked me how much taller did Barbara get. I said, she is 10 feet taller spiritually than he had seen last time.

I particularly directed his interest to the New York family. I told him that the New York center is the spearhead of the United States movement, and I told him that momentum is going to be created in New York and spread to every center throughout the country. Philip Burley he vividly remembered, and he really has high regard and praise for our brother Philip's works. Not only in New York but throughout the Divine Principle life.

All in all, I only stayed in Korea for 19 days. This trip was nothing but a miracle to me. As you know, I do not believe in miracles in terms of the 20th century. I do not believe in miracles like a person walking on water. I do not expect anybody to hit a rock and bring forth fresh water. This is not my concept of my messiah. If anybody tells me that here is a man who can walk on water, here is a man who can change a cane into a snake or bring a dead body from the tomb alive, and tells me that I must accept him as the messiah, I would shake my head like this. Because the messiah I believe in, the Lord I believe in, does not come under that definition.

Yet the Bible says Jesus walked on the water. He changed water into wine. I believe it. I do believe it. If God is willing, that could happen. But today in the modern century, God does not need to perform that type of miracle because He has given us knowledge and willpower that have developed miracles 1,000 times greater than Jesus performed 20 centuries ago. For example, astronauts have gone to the moon. This is a calculated miracle. Mankind has developed our God-given wisdom so that now we can travel to the moon.

Two thousand years ago walking on water a few feet deep was a great thing. But today mankind has conquered the ocean. We can tap the depths of the ocean, and we can stay submerged for many months if we want to. Well, 2,000 years ago the lame walked. Today, modern medical science has developed so much that they can even change the human heart. An artificial heart can replace the human heart in the living body of man. This is really a much greater miracle than what Jesus performed. In that sense, the coming messiah of the 20th century does not come as a person who only demonstrates walking on the water and flying in the sky and changing water into wine.

CHANGING DEATH TO LIFE

My definition of the messiah is this. The greatest creation of all is man and woman, and the messiah is coming to change the greatest creation from death to life. We need the messiah to ignite my heart and bring me from death to life, from Satan to God. This is the revolution for which the messiah is coming to the modern world. This is the messiah we need in the 20th century—one who comes with the truth and ignites and changes my heart and remolds and remakes this creature into a living being, an incorruptible and eternal being.

Therefore, during my trip to Korea I was not trying to find out how many lame people can now walk. I was seeking where true life is, where the change of heart is, how much this movement has progressed. This is my standard and judgment. I was deeply impressed and inspired by the progress they have made, by the struggle to which they are committed and dedicated. I have seen the birth of many heroes in the modern sense of hero, not in the sense of Napoleon or Alexander the Great. Here in America you have many modern heroes. The other day I read an editorial in the *Times* about modern heroism. No matter how modern we may be, we need heroes. John Glenn is one modern hero. Captain Scott Carpenter, who was just awarded the Medal of Honor, is another modern hero. In this sense our movement is producing modern heroes of Korea in areas that nobody can duplicate.

To go into more detail, let me say that our movement in Korea is moving from the preparatory stage into a higher stage. In other words, the long period under persecution is over. The incubation stage is over. Now our movement is on the verge of making a great impact, politically, economically, and socially. As you know, our movement never aimed at any political goal. Seeking a seat in the National Assembly is not the goal. Here in America, seeking a seat in the Senate will never be our goal. But, you know, when Kennedy was contending with Nixon in the presidential race, that he was raised Catholic was one of the most contested elements in the election. Why is that? Because whenever a big group moves, whether you like it or not, whether you accept it or not, there is always a political impact.

In Korea, it will never be our intention to get politically involved. Politics is the last thing we talk about. But knowing that our strength goes beyond the incubation stage, beyond a certain level, is truly amazing. If not a political impact, practically speaking, what kind of impact are we making? What kind of social and economic impact is this movement going to make?

Let me make a guess. Today we are engaged in a war. Whether you like it or not, we are at war. Brother Gordon just mentioned we are in a perpetual struggle against tyranny and communism, against Satan. More specifically, the two forces contending today in the world are the God-denying ideology and the God-accepting ideology. You might term one capitalism and one socialism. But I don't want to look at the world that way. I am more philosophical. We see there are two elements—those who put material as god, communism, and those God-fearing nations, such as America. Two distinct ideologies now contend. As Gordon pointed out just a few minutes ago, today's *Washington Post* clearly mentioned that Red China has now openly declared that there is war against any relation of the capitalists. China is the base of the world revolution that is working to remove all the capitalist nations from the face of the earth.

EVERYBODY'S BUSINESS

Today fighting communism is everybody's business. Every American's business, every Korean's business. It is not only the worry of President Johnson. It is his business as well as the small grocery owner's business. Then, those whose ideology or group or movement can make a tangible and visible impact with a solution for this world have to be recognized.

Today, who has the answer to communism? Everybody knows the problem exists but not many really know the answer exists. In Korea I have seen that the Divine Principle movement is giving that answer to the public, to the government. In other words, it is a new ideology that is not negative, not anti-communist. In many cases, far right-wing movements are working toward the destruction of the enemy, communists, but they do not have any blueprint for afterwards. This cannot last long. Only a positive answer can go further, to the end, to the goal.

As you know, the Divine Principle does not talk much about communism. We don't have to talk about communism. We talk about kingdom-building. We talk about the eventual and original world that God intended.

Once that world is established, there is no room for communism anywhere. In other words, we are more interested in the construction of the new world than the destruction of anything. In the process, this evil power will be eliminated. In this respect, our movement is now making great headway in Korea.

Teachers here and there are asking us to speak in universities, in colleges, in churches. Many ministers have joined the movement and speak out for the Divine Principle. A few years ago when Miss Kim and I were in Korea, we really had a cold reception. But today the churches are asking for speakers for the youth and are rolling out the red carpet. In many cases they send a truck for all the equipment and a car for the instructors.

As you know, the Republic of Korea is the foremost country in determination to stand against communism. Korea is destined to fight. It has not learned how to compromise. That has been the attitude of Korea. While I was in the Korean army, my division was the 9th ROK Division, known as the White Horse Division. I was one of the founders of that division, the 20th regiment, and fought in the White Horse Mountain campaign where that division earned such a world-famous name. Now we have sent them off to Vietnam by ship. Their morale was so high when the whole division departed for Vietnam. The Korean strength in Vietnam today is 35,000, second to that of the United States. But actually, per capita, Korea has sent more manpower than the United States. You have 180 million people here and have sent, I think, 400,000 to Vietnam. Korea only has 20 million people, but we sent 45,000 men already.

We Koreans do not know how to compromise. Even though diplomatic relations have been normalized between Korea and Japan, we do not yet feel friendly. Not because of old feelings, but only because of Japan's lukewarm attitude toward communism. Japan wants to get dollars from Red China. They are even dealing with North Korea. A few weeks ago they tried to use a North Korean technician to rebuild some Republic of Korea factories. The whole country of South Korea rebelled against that, and Japan was really condemned. We do not want a factory under those conditions. We would rather sit and starve than accept a communist technician.

But Korea, even though it stands firmly against communism, has ideological confusion and must have a positive ideology. The whole nation must understand, so they can readily fight against communism. Right now the Divine Principle, this movement, is providing this ideology.

BRIGHT SHINING FACES

When I lived in Korea we had one church and one worship service. Today Seoul church has divided into three different sections. They can no longer meet in one auditorium but have three different ones. They asked me to speak to the congregation. All right, you can't go around to three different places, so let everybody come here. Everybody gathered, but only one-third of the group could fit in the church. The rest of the people were standing outside. So they opened all the windows and, without a microphone, I really had a hard time to speak. Most of the faces were brand-new faces whom I had never seen before. And most of the faces were young. This is wonderful. They were young and their eyes were shining like the evening star, staring at me. I thought their eyesight was so strong it might make a hole in my face. They were so eager to hear something new, what's going on, some new vision from the international scene. That is what they wanted to hear. They were so eager to hear about the U.S. movement.

They have great love for all of you. Their eyes tell it. I really repented and was ashamed that we didn't do a little better to respond to their expectation. You know, don't ever think we are a minority. Don't ever think we are a small group. All of spirit world is with us, and in addition, you have so many brothers and sisters who are ready to live and die together with you.

The second impact is a social impact. We teach that man is more than just a body. Man is spirit, and that spirit will never die. Here is another point. Our true strength is not merely convincing some converts that the coming world exists and we will live in that world. If this is the only impact we are making, how are we different from other churches? How are we different from other religious institutions? Our difference is that in order to obtain this immortality of the undying spirit, we have got to be perfect. We have got to live a good life here on earth while we have flesh to be ready for the next life. So our focus, our interest, is based on you, you, you, and you and your welfare. In other words, we have a keen interest in the social problems of today. We have a keen interest that people not be hungry. We have a keen interest that people not be illiterate. We have a keen interest in each individual's welfare.

In other words, our movement is not only speaking, but our movement is acting. There is one example I can share with you. Here is a copy of the Korean-English newspaper, the *Korean Herald*, and it is reported here, "Six Jungju Teachers Shining Shoes on Seoul Streets." This is a long article, the second in a series, and pictures appear. Miss Kim knows Mr. Chong Yu Pak, who is the Divine Principle area leader. We have a district leader, and the district is divided into areas. He was assigned as one area leader four years ago. He is teaching the Divine Principle, and his heart was so touched by the bright youngsters in that area who do not have the opportunity to be educated. They cannot go to school because of economic pressures. Education is not compulsory in Korea. Parents have to pay for it. So Mr. Pak started a school.

Do you know how he started? Since there was no building to use to teach, he gathered the young people on a mountain slope and began to teach these young students who cannot go to high school. The villagers thought he was doing something awful. And instead of cooperating, they gave him real persecution. They kicked him out of the village. Then Mr. Pak almost went crazy. He was half out of his mind. He returned to the mountain slopes and began teaching the pine trees every day. At first people laughed. But a few weeks later, people just wept that Mr. Pak had so much love for their children. They said, he thinks that his students are still there, though there is nothing but pine trees; he keeps striking his blackboard and is trying to teach.

Then the villagers began changing. And they said, how awful we are that we cannot accept what he can do for our own young people. They held a meeting and decided unanimously that Mr. Pak must be accepted in the village. They provided the utmost care so he can do his work. So he started his school with the cooperation of the villagers.

After four years, this school—not heated, not air-conditioned, with no chairs like this, but with old carpet and boxes as desks—produced 500 bright young students. Among them some are applying for the university entrance tests. A high percentage of students from his school have scholarships because of their bright records. In the summertime Mr. Pak and six teachers decided they would all become shoeshine boys in Seoul City to make money to establish a scholarship fund so some of the bright students can go to college. This is the meaning of the headline, "Six Jungju Teachers Shining Shoes on Seoul Streets." These college-graduate teachers go out with shoeshine boxes and shine shoes for Seoul City.

While I was there it had been going on for one month, the month of August. It was a beautiful topic of interest, a moving topic among Seoul citizens. And when CARE in New York heard about this school, they went to that scene and took pictures and offered some financial help. Mr. Pak replied saying, we do not want your money or help at this time. We want to be ready to really appreciate and digest your financial system. Until that time, let us work toward that goal without your help. The CARE official said, I have been here for 10 years to help people, but you are the first one to reject our aid.

This newspaper article was read by President Park of the Republic of

Korea. He was so moved that he sent his own official to investigate this school. He wanted to find out what Mr. Pak is actually doing. The president was very moved by the report that came back, and he called the six teachers to his mansion and gave each one a medal. So Mr. Pak became a hero of Korean youth, a symbol of the independent Korean youth. And he clearly stated in a radio interview that his spiritual commitment and dedication comes from the Divine Principle. And it was not the first time. It was the second time. I mentioned the other day, before I went to Korea, that Mr. Han In Su was given a patriotic award by the president on inauguration day.

HEROES FOR GOD

We need modern heroes. There is a vast area where those who gather in this room can work. In a sense we are already committed to the road, whether you like it or not, to becoming heroes, both men and women. Not for the glory. Not for the praise. But for the glory of God and True Parents.

The primary purpose of my trip was to organize Radio of Free Asia. This had been my baby, really. I conceived this idea, developed it, and finally the time came that it should be started. This is a great charity and one of the biggest anti-communist projects that everybody can agree with. How much hardship, how many difficulties I went through, you have no idea. President Johnson announced that open communication with Red China must be accomplished. This is a key to peace in Asia. So actually, Radio of Free Asia is exactly what he is trying to do. But the world is not ready to move, no matter how good that idea is. It is such a simple idea that can be praised and accepted by all freedom-loving Americans and world citizens. But I had so much difficulty to go through. How much more difficulty we will face to spread the Divine Principle. The Principle is contrary to the world of people just enjoying their daily physical pleasures. In other words, this gives me an idea how difficult a task we are committed to.

Anyway, on August 9 I left America for Korea along with Ambassador Yang. The situation was precarious. At that time, the Radio of Free Asia project was virtually dying because of opposition. We could think of no other way to survive except for one last hope to go to Korea. We thought, let us do our last mission to see the president of Korea and try to get government support. That decision was not made in a simple way. It was not a happy trip by any means. I was really suffering.

We flew over to Korea. It was a really hard trip. I had only one thing to say to Heavenly Father: "I just leave everything up to you. Do whatever you want." I just kept saying that throughout the many hours of the flight. I couldn't sleep.

We arrived in Korea August 12. Our original arrival date was August 15, which is Independence and Liberation Day from Japanese rule, which is a very meaningful day. But we arrived August 12, and at this time the project had virtually died. We had three more days left. You know how I felt. We faced a negative U.S. Embassy, a negative Korean government, and these three days were a Saturday, Sunday, and Monday (the 15th is a holiday, too, so there were three holidays in a row). No government agency really worked. But a miracle occurred. Under adverse conditions, we won the complete support of the Korean government. I thought it would be wonderful if we could have some kind of agreement on the 15th of August. I never expected more than that. But on August 15 at 11:00 p.m. the voice of Radio of Free Asia was on the air.

It was a miracle. I learned that a mighty work, a miracle, will never come true until you use your last drop of blood. At 11:00 p.m. on August 15 I was lying in a hotel bed, relaxing only because I was sick. I had collapsed. Then I heard the voice of Radio of Free Asia through the powerful radio station in Seoul, 500,000 watts beamed over the entire Korean peninsula and the next day to the entire mainland of China. I cried. It was unprecedented.

VOICE OF FREEDOM

I will show you something here. This is a news report from Saigon of the Radio of Free Asia Korean-language team strategy meeting. At first, there are two languages. Soon we are going to add Vietnamese. There was publicity. First of all, the *New York Times* said the U.S.-backed radio opened in Korea. *Broadcasting Magazine* said International Radio of Free Asia started in Korea. The *Korean Herald* wrote an editorial calling it a "voice of freedom." Beautiful. Just wonderful. Radio of Free Asia is a torch of freedom. It is on the air using KGF facilities. Radio of Free Asia is a voice of hope for many. These are some of the English newspaper reports. Saigon suggested a site for our RFA broadcasting in the future. An editorial in one of the most popular Korean papers praised the creation of Radio of Free Asia.

I thought, my mission is done. I can relax a few days and I can go back to the United States. But it was too sweet a dream for me. That never happened. As soon as Radio of Free Asia was on the air, our Leader called me and said, Bo Hi Pak, do you think you came to Korea just to start Radio of Free Asia? No. To me this is very insignificant, this is very minor. Our Father said, I am pushing this project for two purposes. One, this will become instrumental in fighting against communism in Asia. There is no question about it. It is going to be a project known around the world and recognized as a very effective weapon in fighting against communism in

Asia. And it was started by this man who taught the Divine Principle. And he said, second, through pioneering this project, I can elevate my bargaining power with the U.S. government and the Korean government as the man in the role of midwife and founder of this project. They have got to look at me from a different angle. They have got to deal with me this time. And Father was right. I was really a VIP this time in Korea. The prime minister gave a party. The president gave a reception. All levels of the Korean government and businessmen were there, and I could deal with them one to one. When the movement grows, our healing power must grow, too. This is of prime importance.

Anyway, then our Leader told me, you have one other mission. You must do it right now. Actually, I don't know how I should say it. Shortly before my arrival in Korea our Leader had instructed one of his disciples to bring me home. In other words, the order for me to come back to Korea was written in a letter, ready to send. There were certain things that our Leader thought I might have a solution for. Then he received my letter that I was coming. So he thought, already spirit world communicated. He already received the order.

Anyway, our movement in Korea today is involved in a vast expansion. We have manpower ready, and we have experience ready. And we have all systems and an organization ready. But we would like to move along with the material development, too. In other words, restoration of the things of creation. We not only need spiritual power, we not only need experience, we not only need instructors who can teach, but we also need the financial strength to push things forward. This is why we are engaged in many, many important projects. We built many factories. Our brothers and sisters are really working day and night.

TEARS JUST COME

At one factory I was invited to see I was really in tears looking at their serious faces. They work from 6:00 a.m. until 11:00 p.m., then wash their body, eat supper, and go to bed at midnight. The next morning at 6:00 they come right back to that space. But their faces have an expression of joy and satisfaction. They express sacrifice and service. When I see their faces, I cannot help it, tears just come.

The world in which we live is not that honest. Whether it is in Korea, Japan, or here in America, the present system does not accept our genuine motivation. You know what I am trying to say. Therefore, in many cases we are innocent victims. You know what I mean. We are innocent victims of unreasonable authority. Intolerable things happen in many instances. There is much undeserved suffering going on because we are innocent victims of the present system of society, which we have to deal with. One area involves red tape. We need things to be done now. But red tape is involved, and that puts it off. The bureaucrats say, oh, a few months later doesn't matter; we won't get it done until next year. In the meantime, earnest intention suffers and dies. This time, I really felt that we are not only strong within the movement, but we must be strong in dealing with the society in which we live. You know what I mean.

So, this second thing our Leader asked me to fulfill was totally beyond my knowledge and beyond my ability. So again, the only thing I can expect is a miracle. And I tell you, it happened. When I came in yesterday and sat down in the chair, tears just came out of my eyes, from thinking over the last 19 days—how I lived and how I struggled and what I have accomplished. I am so deeply grateful to Father. I am so deeply gratified that I had been used as an intermediary to contribute to the overall movement. I had the feeling that I am grateful and I am ready to go on in any manner and in any place.

I learned another thing. My life seems to be not mine. Of course, I have had this feeling for a long time, but I was reassured of it. I seem to have no freedom. A long time ago all I wanted to be was a good farmer. I was a graduate of an agriculture school. I wanted to be an exemplary farmer in my village. I raised hogs and chickens in a way that no villagers had done before, a more scientific way so as to really make a profit. I started new crops. I loved hogs as much as I loved anything. Really, they were like my babies. I hugged them and kissed them. All these dozens of hogs were my hope of everything. I had so many dreams, that, oh, when this hog gets bigger I can get so much and I can increase my farm. I will have another dozen hogs and another dozen cows. This was my dream.

You know what happened one day? A hog became ill. Then one after the other they were dying. It was just like taking off one of my arms, then the other arm, next the legs. I had never tasted that much sadness. I was so sorry for the hogs and was really weeping with them. But when the last one was dying, I wasn't sad anymore. I was really mad and became crazy. I hit that hog with a club. I don't know what made me do it. I was all broken up. Then I knew that this was teaching me that God doesn't want me to be a farmer. I knew that. I learned the lesson.

Then I became a soldier. I was the most ambitious soldier in the military academy in Korea. And I was most determined to become a good soldier. I had four years of training and a degree as an engineer ahead of me. What good luck. This was going to be my life. Then what happened? Just 25 days after entering the military academy, the Korean War broke out. Three days later, two-thirds of my classmates had all died in the field. But I still never gave up the ambition to become a great soldier. I went to infantry school, and I really worked hard and graduated with honors. I had the hope that someday I would become a general or a chief of staff. I still had that ambition.

Then I learned that was not my destiny either. I ended my military career as a lieutenant colonel. All the dreams I started with and look what I became. But I don't care. I don't care what I am going to be. Because one thing is solid and sure: I am going without hesitation toward the destiny where God is leading me. I still have a great problem to worry about. But just as I faced such drastic and critical problems in the past, all I do is face it with a bold, risky idea, that Father is with me. I know I no longer can be a good Divine Principle teacher. I don't think I can teach the Divine Principle anymore. I may not be a good public speaker, but one thing helps me. After so many years in the movement, I have done away with doubt.

In the beginning I am sure many of you will share this feeling. The first day, the first year, and second year, and even after the third year of the Divine Principle, there are high moments. You're on cloud nine, you feel you are flying around in the sky. But there are also dark moments. There are always unsure moments. Yes. This is the cycle. Now, I have one reason to be grateful. As the years go by, after commitment to this life, I know one thing: No matter what and under any circumstances, no one can plant doubt in my mind. Nobody. Sometimes, yes, I allow my body to be idle, to stray away. This is in a way my confession. I do many unreasonable things that usually I wouldn't do. I am not claiming a complete sense of sainthood, so to speak. I think I am the last one to live the life of a saint. Yes, I am a sinner. I am a dirty sinner.

But I have no moment when I lose confidence and nobody can put doubt in my mind. That is one thing I can assure my Father. Father, just forget about me. You don't have to worry about me.

When I come back here and see the face of each member of our family, it is really an overwhelming joy. I know how much our Leader expects us to live up to the Principle. I know how much he really wants us to be the salt of this world and how much he wants us to share his vision so that we can be life to this world. I do know how deeply and how desperately he is asking every one of us to live up to the Principle. And after seeing him, I know he is coming. But his coming may not be as near as we thought. The reason is that so much is happening every day in Korea, and there is nothing that can be done without him. Really, his decisions are paramount. This is the only reason his departure is being delayed. In other words, this is the end of the seventh year after 1960, the consummation of a particular period. He has a certain providence in his mind to complete before the end of this year. His mind is working around the clock.

MODEL FOR WORLD RESTORATION

On the other hand, the United States is a model of the world restoration because the United States was created and designed so that all people can live in one society as one family, like a melting pot. Here in the United States we have both extremes. One is such a bright hope to bring the paradise and living kingdom here on earth. The Great Society that the United States is headed for is nothing more than a messianic project, isn't it?

Brother Jim one time told me about a joke in *Time* magazine. President and Mrs. Johnson were walking around the Potomac River and President Johnson said to his wife, "Is there any press around?" "No, I don't think there is any press around." "Shall I walk on the water then?" This implies what he is trying to do, what his project is trying to do. It is nothing but a messianic job. The poverty program, welfare, and Medicare, all these things are idealistic things. On the other hand, he has left so many open doors that there is an unclosable gap. The youth problems, crime problems, mental problems, those who shoot 30 people from a university tower. This sort of thing is unthinkable. In other words, the two extremes are right here in America.

Why? We have all the structures and systems and everything is working, but the core is missing. The truth is missing, the spirit that unites God and man and unites fellow man, that inspires duty to God and man. No brotherhood can be viable unless Fatherhood comes first. This is why our Unified Family motto is "The Fatherhood of God and the Brotherhood of Man."

This must come first. But there are problems. Segregation, for example. As one senator plainly explained, we cannot write the law saying that white, yellow, and Negro races must eat together in one restaurant. We cannot write that type of law. This comes from love between men and disregard of color. The Fatherhood of God and brotherhood of man are central to America and the axis of the world. This is what we are spreading today. We cannot ask that Congress enact any more laws. More laws complicate our lives. As for crime, we cannot expect demonstrations at the White House to bring any more result.

A quiet, calm, but real revolution must ignite the individual heart by the truth of God. We are a small group of people. In Korea today, there are thousands and thousands of members. But when Miss Kim was in Korea, the Korean movement was exactly this one-room meeting. This is no more than a one-room meeting and do not think that could only happen in Korea and not in America. The value of the individual sitting in this room is as great as the entire cosmos. Miss Kim said last night we are breathing the cosmos. Wonderful phrase, isn't it? Breathing the cosmos and communicating with the cosmos. We are cosmic beings.

Let us stand up and spearhead this group of people. We are painting the history of mankind. Thank you very much.

THE GOD AND CHRIST CLUB

PRINTED IN *THE WAY OF THE WORLD*

APRIL 1974

═══════════════════════

One of the purposes of the Celebration of Life is to revive and uplift the Christian spirit in America. Life is joy, and God intended to have us live in abundant joy. So we invite all people to come to the party!

We have felt God helping us in every detail. When people first come, they are puzzled. They don't know what to expect. But by the end of the show they are amazed. I have been in theaters before, and I myself am amazed at the production. I believe that soon we can compare with Broadway shows and win.

If there are demonstrators outside, we invite them to come in to the show. They are very surprised at the invitation, and some dramatically change their minds. After each performance we have a Rainbow Reception, where we invite guests who want to attend the workshop or join the crusade to come and meet our members. Usually 200 to 300 people come downstairs for the reception. Many people who come to the reception stand up and give spontaneous testimonies and sign up for the workshop.

I ask people to join us in the God and Christ Club. Rather than being performers first, our singers and dancers are representing God and Christ. Before they perform they often witness to the purpose of the crusade.

We want to give to everyone the most uplifting, joyous, gay, and fantastic feeling. I am determined to make the people feel like they are coming out of heaven when they come out of the hall.

In terms of our message, we are experimenting with something new. Human sound and motion are always of interest to human beings. In many cases, language is not sufficient for communication. So we also use the sound and motion of the singers and dancers. No other crusade has included dancers in its program. I also am using parachutes, fruit, trees, trains, light bulbs, and other visual aids in my presentation.

The Celebration of Life program has made our members really proud of our movement, which is gaining so much respect for such performances. In Oakland, a reporter was sent to the program by his station. Afterward, he came to the Rainbow Reception and said, "I am going to the workshop too, but not just as a reporter. I am personally interested."

We have asked people why they come to the Celebration of Life. Most people say they came in order to gain an understanding of God, better life experiences, or an understanding of the Sun Myung Moon Christian Crusade. The most frequent purpose was to gain an understanding of God.

Early Suffering, Lasting Victory

WASHINGTON, D.C.

EARLY 1974

Gleaning examples from the Little Angels Dance Troupe and the inception of the Little Angels School in Korea, Dr. Pak illustrates that the most powerful force in the universe is the power of love. He explains the vision behind the many projects he initiated in the United States.

Mike Leone couldn't find any place for sale. We couldn't rent a dormitory either, so we have secured an eight-room apartment in one building. We have to settle for that place because we couldn't find anything better. It lacks a large hall like this and a large kitchen, so I know there is a lot of inconvenience and difficulty. But still, economically and in terms of location, I felt it was the best choice. So we decided to rent that one.

But I am dreaming about building a Sun Myung Moon Christian Crusade building in New York. We have the International Training Center at Belvedere, we have Barrytown, and in Washington we have the national headquarters. Next we are looking for the Sun Myung Moon Christian Crusade headquarters, an important part of our movement. This will be equivalent to, let's say, Billy Graham's Evangelical Association headquarters. Eventually we will have our own independent sound department, our own publicity department, printing department, and public relations department. One wing will be for the New Hope Singers, another for the Korean Folk Ballet, and probably later other dancers from other parts of the world, say Spanish dancers, Mexican dancers, or African dancers. In the great cultural building in the center we will have a grand piano, musical instruments, orchestra rooms, individual practice rooms, and a dancing hall. This is my dream.

Every day I think about this. Do you know why? If you dream hard enough, long enough, the dream will come true. We have a Creator and we are the co-creators. God created you and me and gave us the power to create. Do you know where creation begins? It begins in your thoughts. The most powerful single force available in this universe is the power of thought. That is what faith and belief are all about. The message of Christ is that all things are possible. We can realize this power in our life. This is why positive thinking is very important. If you have frustrated, negative thinking in your mind you are already doing the work of destruction in your life. Destruction begins in your thoughts. Look forward, have some vision, set a goal. If you think hard enough, it will come true.

I will give you one illustration. When the Little Angels began in 1962, we didn't have even one room to practice in. So we rented a small hall in one of the suburbs of Seoul. The roof leaked when it rained, and we had to patch up the hole and make a new floor. This is how the Little Angels began.

When the Little Angels school opened, we sent advertising out to parents to send their children to be trained under our auspices. When the parents came to see the school, they were absolutely stunned. They turned around and left, never to return. It was utterly impossible for them to believe that any group could be nurtured and trained in this small cubbyhole and then go to America, England, or France and bring the Korean culture all over the world. No one would believe it. They woudn't entrust their children to us.

THREE BITTER YEARS

So I had an awfully difficult time enlisting students for the Little Angels. The only people who came were members of the church, who had faith. Unfortunately, at that time every member was struggling, so their children had not had a good education for their talent. They were like sticks. They didn't know how to move. They didn't even know how to bend their elbows. We trained these children with faith for three bitter years. I was a military attaché in Washington at that time and was trying to open up a path for the tour. I described Korea as a country with a beautiful cultural heritage, but no one believed me. So I went back to Korea and produced a very amateurish film because we didn't have money to put into a professional film. But I needed a film to explain what they could do.

At that time, when Americans heard about Korea, they first thought about the war and, second, that it is a poor country with orphans and lots of refugees and lots of communists. This was the image of Korea in Americans' minds. So when I talked about culture from Korea, they were almost thinking, how could they have such a good jewel. But the true image of Korea, as you and I know, is that it has a peace-loving culture and people who are very, very deep and are philosophical and religious.

Do you know that the major religions in Asia consummated in Korea? In other words, Asiatic religions enjoyed their golden age in Korea. Let me give you an example. Buddhism started in India but never really blossomed there. Even now Buddhism is not strong in India. Buddhism moved from India to China to Korea. In Korea, during the Shilla dynasty about 2,000 years ago, Buddhism reached its golden age. Then we exported Buddhism to Japan, and Japanese monks and scholars came to Korea to learn from Korean monks and scholars. There is now more and more evidence that the ancient Japanese culture was influenced by Korea.

This comes as a shocking revelation to the proud Japanese. Japan is such a powerful country and is a leading country of the world. But they have found that many things of the culture of Japan were given by Korea. For example, in Nara a large ancient tomb was uncovered from thousands of years ago. When that royal tomb was uncovered, they found that all the cultural elements in it, even dress, reflected Korea's heritage. This is just one instance. Many scholars say the origin of the Japanese culture was influenced primarily by Korea, so now the Japanese have many conflicting feelings. Maybe their ancient ancestors came from Korea. They feel nostalgia for how their ancestors lived. This is one reason Japanese tourists like to come to Korea. It is very difficult to get airplane reservations from Japan to Korea. In many cases they think they are visiting the ancient homes of their ancestors, particularly in the Shilla dynasty. The Shilla dynasty was truly the golden age of Buddhist civilization. We have in Korea the most fantastic temple. Many people go there and are amazed by the beauty and art and the books written in those days.

Confucianism started in China. But a great Confucian scholar was found in Korea. He deepened Confucian philosophy and developed a bible. Confucius himself didn't write too many books. Somebody had to enrich the thought of Confucius, and those who did this were Korean scholars. So the golden age of Confucius was also in Korea. This is historically accurate.

The Christian philosophy began in Asia Minor, then went all over the world, to Europe, America, Japan, and Korea. Korea has become one of the most Christianized countries in the world. Billy Graham evangelized all over the world, but no crusade could compare to the crusade he had in Korea. Even common people, not just those who are Divine Principle members, can understand the ideal of the coming of the Lord of the Second Advent in the form of True Parents. The words of True Parents are new words. Before Jesus, there were no such words as "Heavenly Father." People said the idea that God is fatherly was impossible. To the Jewish people at that time, that was the worst thing you could say. It was the worst blasphemy. How can you say God is my father? They thought it was such an insult to God. This was a revolutionary declaration.

LIFE OF SHIMJUNG

Today the word is True Parents. We are using new words, particularly the Korean word "shimjung" (heart). Heart in the Korean language is not exactly the same as heart in the American language. Shimjung is much deeper than the meaning of heart in English. It is two words—True Parents and heart—these are the terms of the new parents. Only the True Parents and Christ could bring this. This is the beginning of the new age. We are now moving into the new age of True Parents. So in this respect, due to Korea's cultural heritage and philosophical depth, there is a providential reason why Korea could be chosen as the third Israel in the modern-day dispensation. It is logical. God prepared for a long, long time. It did not just happen accidentally.

Let's go back to my main theme. The American people don't have the slightest idea about this kind of cultural and religious heritage. All American people can think about Korea is war, refugees, divided nation, and so forth. When I brought the Little Angels to this country, I had an awful time. Back home we had an awful time. Here in America we had an awful time. All over the place we had an awful time. There was no joy, no comfort, at all. But somehow the dream thrust me forward, particularly the concept of the Divine Principle.

Many people ask me how I could conceive of such ideas as the Little Angels, the Korean Cultural and Freedom Foundation, Radio of Free Asia, and the Children's Relief Fund. Normally Koreans didn't think like this. They are busy taking care of their own well-being. The country is small, and they are busy in little things. How can you even think you could reach that level? I told them, it is not me but the power of the Divine Principle. Without the power of the Divine Principle, I would be like any other Korean. The teaching of True Parents gives me a new concept of the world. The world becomes totally different. Rebirth is a real term. By myself, I am just a Korean. I always think of myself as a universal being and hopefully associated with the central dispensation of God. It was an automatic and natural thing for me to think big, at the level of the world. The world is one unit. Not Korea is one unit, not America is one unit, but the world is one unit. Naturally I can cook up what are crazy things in other people's eyes. I have dreams and constantly push those dreams forward.

In 1965 I brought the first team of the Little Angels to America, but nobody came to see them. It was a pity. Nobody came. In many cases, performers outnumbered the audience. How could I comfort the children? How could I tell the children the reason this happened? It was an awful job, and the beautiful thing was that the children trusted every word I said. They believed with beautiful, childlike, simple faith.

One week they did a Christmas show in a big theater I had rented. The first night only 12 people came, but the auditorium held 3,000 seats. I told them not to look at the people but at the seats and imagine that every one was occupied. Then I told them to think of one person as like an entire audience. In other words, you can perform in front of one person just like you perform in front of 3,000 people. Then you are real masters. The children responded beautifully. They danced and smiled. There was no sign of ending in tears. I was in the back of the theater looking at the children with tears running down my face. I was so sorry for them. I didn't know how to comfort them. But they comforted me. I didn't comfort them. They always comforted me. I felt judgment because the audience was so small and they sat there so cold. The children were working so hard.

Actually, the next morning the *Boston Globe* said Bostonians should be ashamed because they are part of a cultural people but didn't appreciate such a wonderful culture coming from a foreign land. One reporter had come to the performance and was shocked at the lack of audience for such a beautiful show. The next day everybody came. That was one big, big advertisement. I thanked God that He is so truly on our side, looking at the children and pitying them just as I did.

During that time (1965), I had a dream that one day I would like to have a beautiful cultural center, such as cannot be found anywhere in Austria or in America, not in terms of money or gigantic size but expressing some real heritage and beauty. Here in Washington there is the Kennedy Center and in New York the Lincoln Center. I wanted to create something even more unique than the Lincoln Center, something better than the Kennedy Center. The Kennedy Center cost $75 million. I don't have that kind of money, of course, but somehow even with spending only $1 million or $2 million there must be a way to make it unique and different so it can be a focal point of the world's culture. I dreamed this. Of course, we are always struggling. I expected nothing but debt, but how can you go into debt year after year? I was almost $25,000 in debt. But I did not show any sign of this to the children. I did not express any shadow of doubt. In the minds of the children they had every right to really express themselves freely. But I knew in my heart our project was in trouble.

A TIMELY CHECK

So I sent the children back and came to our Washington office, a small cubbyhole. On Christmas Day I was suffering in my office because I didn't want to show too much suffering at home. That anguished Christmas morning, a special delivery letter came from the Kenneth Allen Enterprise in New York. I opened it and a $5,000 check and a letter fell out. The letter said, I know you are in trouble, but I love the Little Angels so much. Kenneth Allen provided the first year's bookings, and managers always take their commission first. That commission came to $5,000. Of course, they didn't make any money; they spent a lot of money for promotion and so forth, but Kenneth Allen told me in his written letter that he wanted to turn over every penny, somehow hoping that this money would help save the cause. "The cause is such a beautiful one, I don't want to have that project die." I gathered everybody in my office and really cried.

Another miracle came from the *Reader's Digest* of New York. I had written 12 famous people of America a letter and explained about the Little Angels, the cause, and how beautiful they are. I selected 12 wealthy people, 11 of whom never responded. Only one response came, from Mrs. Lila Atchison Wallace, founder of the *Reader's Digest*. She read my letter and later told me she was struck by the fire and spirit that letter had. She said the *Reader's Digest* had started the same way as the Little Angels, 49 years ago. Her husband, Dwight Wallace, got the idea of digesting a vast amount of reading material and presenting it to readers in a form that would enable them to comprehend it.

As a college student, Wallace talked about his idea with some professors and writers, but everybody laughed at him. That idea wouldn't work, they said. He discussed the idea with his fiancée. She was the only one who responded to the idea and told him, if you have a dream and the conviction, then fulfill it. They printed the first issue of *Reader's Digest* in the garage of a simple farmhouse in Pleasantville, New York. You can imagine how they struggled. They really knew what it was like to pioneer, and yet 49 years later they have become a gigantic empire. Their publications go all over the world in 14 languages; 28 million copies are sold every month. The contribution they have made to the American culture and the world's culture is incredible. *Reader's Digest* is concerned with health, education, enlightenment, and entertainment.

Mrs. Wallace said the Little Angels are like another version of *Reader's Digest*. They uphold the general idea of children's purity and serve as good ambassadors through their cultural heritage. I can see your pioneering spirit and want to be part of it. She gave $25,000 without seeing the Little Angels. This is faith. So you know what I am saying. I am not just giving lip service if I say, when you really have a healthy dream and dream hard enough and long enough, a miracle comes.

PATRON SAINT

The next year the Little Angels could come here because of that gift. Mrs. Wallace came to see the Little Angels and was absolutely flabbergasted. I thanked her in a most heartfelt way. She said, don't thank me. It is sheer joy to help a project like this. Of all the many millionaires and billionaires in America, I have not seen one yet except Mrs. Wallace who is truly humanitarian, who is a wonderful spiritual person and can see value immediately. She is a wonderful Christian woman. She knows where money should be spent.

After that every year in the month of April she sent $25,000, which covered the airplane fares of the Little Angels. If we came and made no money, at least transportation was provided; we wouldn't be stranded. I wrote a two-page letter about my dream of the school. To draft that letter I spent several weeks in prayer and a few days of writing, because I was putting my heart and soul and mind into making every word shine. I wrote her about my plan to build the cultural center in Korea. Mrs. Wallace is a difficult person to see. It is not easy to invite her to dinner or even to visit her. My heart was so overwhelmed, and I was not in a position to properly describe it to her because I was so excited. I thought a letter would do the job better. She wrote me back and sent $25,000. That one person gave over half a million dollars to the Little Angels program in the last eight years. That is how the Little Angels survived.

There was only one person who did better than Mrs. Wallace. Without our Father we would never even have conceived it; construction would never have begun. But thanks to a person like Mrs. Wallace, it is well under way. The next time I go back to Korea, I will bring you beautiful pictures. The dedication ceremony of that particular building was attended by the prime minister of Korea, and the groundbreaking ceremony was attended by the first lady, Mrs. Park Chung Hee. Father blessed the building and dedicated it in prayer. He holy salted it, and the next day the prime minister came.

The first phase of construction is completed. The school is already open now. The second phase of construction is going on with Father's help, and the third phase is going to be the auditorium, where not only the Little Angels can perform but all the fine performers of the world can come to Korea to perform. It is like a state theater. President Park can come there and have a state dinner, and the Little Angels can perform. Father can give special banquets at which the New Hope Singers can perform. Yes, you will come there and perform. We have not built it yet so wait a little, but we do have lodgings. You don't appreciate these facilities in America, where they are available everywhere, but in Korea finding that kind of kitchen and that kind of facility is not easy. Refrigerators and freezers—those things are not available. I had an extra hard time creating something like this in Korea, but it is coming along. So when you come to Korea with the Korean Crusade, you are not going to stay at any hotel or small house. You are coming to our cultural center. You will be treated like royalty. It is your home in Korea. We have showers, there's no problem; you have elbow room there.

President Park gave that land amidst the children's park, which is almost 100 acres of land. We are right in the corner of the children's park, so when you look out there is a view far better than this college campus has, much more spacious, even though it is not our land. We can see the beauty of the trees and flowers. You cannot find any other place like this in Korea. This is really a heavenly spot, and President Park allocated it. Of course, we were meticulously diplomatic and worked very hard. All these years, my specialty was other people's hearts. My secret is not to have a strategy. No strategy is the best strategy. As a genuine person, you pour out your heart and soul; that is the best strategy. Just go as you are; you already are the children of God. Have conviction that you are unselfish and your dedication is clear. Like Jesus, don't worry about what to say. God will give you what to say. Just bring your genuine self without a strategy. That is always best; even with the president of Korea that worked the best. I met Mrs. Wallace once and that worked the best. I have met President Nixon, prime ministers, the queen of England, all these people, and that strategy works the best. Even in selling and witnessing, all you need really is no strategy; give your genuine entire weight to the selling or witnessing. That will bring the greatest result.

WHY CHRIST IS COMING

CELEBRATION OF LIFE—FIRST NIGHT

SEATTLE, WASHINGTON

MAY 22, 1974

Father first introduced the Sun Myung Moon Christian Crusade in May of 1974. The Crusade was originally entitled "Celebration of Joy" and its purpose was to uplift the Christian spirit in America and to teach key points of the Divine Principle. Each Crusade lasted three days. On the first night, Dr. Pak would speak about the need for the Lord of the Second Advent. On the second night, he would explain how Christ would appear again and on the third night, he would reveal the hidden meaning of the Fall of Man. The celebration included performances by the New Hope Singers and the Korean Folk Ballet, and concluded each time with a "Rainbow Reception" where guests were invited to attend Divine Principle workshops. The first crusade was held in Oakland, California, from May 15–17. The following speeches are from the second Crusade, held in Seattle, Washington, May 22–24, 1974. At each of the events, Dr. Pak was introduced to the audience by his daughter Grace (Na Kyung).

INTRODUCTION BY GRACE PAK

I have the great privilege of introducing to you Col. Bo Hi Pak and sharing with you why he feels the urgent need to speak to the American people. Today the American churches are in trouble. The Christian doctrines of the modern churches often lack rationality, and they are full of many different interpretations. Our churches face a spiritual and philosophical deadlock. Dr. Samuel Miller, dean of Harvard Divinity School, said, "Christianity may be at death's door. If religion is to have any real place in this modern world, it must undergo a revolution." But what is to bring about this revolution? What is to bring about a new spiritual awakening and revitalization of the Christian churches here in America? A new revelation from God.

We have been working for 2,000 years with the Christian ideal and yet have not succeeded in establishing the kingdom of heaven on earth. We have tried all the possible theories and ideals to break the spiritual deadlock. But our efforts have been in vain. We are at a time when we must prepare for the Second Advent. We need a new revelation now! And God has revealed it to us through Reverend Sun Myung Moon to be shared with all of mankind.

Col. Pak, as the principal evangelist and the director general of the Sun Myung Moon Christian Crusade, has the responsibility to proclaim this new revelation to America, and he is doing so with great passion and authority, thus rekindling the hearts of thousands of Americans and renewing their spirit of dedication to God and then mobilizing these young people for God.

Thus our crusade is one of true joy and happiness and the excitement of redirected life. During the crusade, members of the company nicknamed Col. Pak "God's Colonel." That is fine with him. He has noticed that throughout history colonels have the habit of breaking records and doing unusual things. Col. Charles Lindbergh, who first flew over the Atlantic. Col. Davy Crockett, who made history at the Alamo. Col. John Glenn, the first man in orbit, and of course Col. Harlan Sanders invented Kentucky Fried Chicken.

So, Col. Pak feels there is no limit to what a colonel can do. For your inspiration tonight, I present to you Col. Bo Hi Pak, God's colonel and my daddy.

Thank you, Grace. [You're welcome, daddy.] Tonight I am greatly honored to be introduced by my own daughter. After all, how many evangelists have that privilege? Not even Billy Graham. But, of course, Billy Graham does not need an introduction. One day my daughter told me, "Dad, I don't want you to be too famous like Billy Graham because then you wouldn't need me to introduce you." I told her, "Grace, you don't understand why God has called me. God chose what is foolish in the world to shame the wise. God chose what is weak in the world to shame the strong.

God chose what is low and despised in the world so that no human being might boast in the presence of God."

Tonight I feel very unworthy to stand before you. I prayed earnestly that the presence of God be with us and move each one of us tonight. When you read the Bible, in John 16:25 Jesus says, "I have said this to you in figures; the hour is coming when I shall no longer speak to you in figures but tell you plainly of the Father." That hour has arrived. Tonight the message you are going to hear is going to be a plain message. It is not in figures, not in symbols or parables. When you read further, 1 Corinthians 13:9-12 says, "For our knowledge is imperfect and our prophecy is imperfect; but when the perfect comes, the imperfect will pass away. ... For now we see in a mirror dimly, but then face to face. Now I know in part, then I shall understand fully." We will understand fully. That hour has arrived.

Tonight you are going to meet the truth face to face. Not because I am here telling you, but because God has spoken to a modern-day prophet. The Reverend Sun Myung Moon has brought the greatest message of all, for all mankind. Tonight you have a taste of that revelation. We are here at the Celebration of Life. I saw so much laughter and so many smiles and happy faces. But do you know that in a truer sense we do not have a life to celebrate? No life. Yes, no life. In the sight of God, mankind has been long dead. You read in the Bible that God created in the dawn of human history the first man Adam and the first woman Eve. Then God gave them the commandment. God said to them, "Of the Tree of the Knowledge of Good and Evil you shall not eat, for in the day you eat of it you shall die." This is the first time in the Bible that death is mentioned. The first man and first woman disobeyed God. Did they die? No. According to the Bible Adam lived another 900 years after his disobedience. Do you think God lied to them? No. God cannot lie. Then what is the death that Adam and Eve suffered in the sight of God?

In order to know the true meaning of death, I would like tonight to start by explaining the true meaning of life. I would like to use this chart for illustration. There is only one life in the universe. There is only one life and that life is God. God is life. The Bible says that in Him is life. You further read in John 5:26, "For as the Father has life in Himself, so He has granted the Son also to have life in himself." Life is something to be granted. We all need to be granted life from God.

LOST: THE SOURCE OF LIFE

I have a simple illustration here. Here is a regular electric bulb. When I turn on the switch, light comes on. This bulb has life. However, this life does not come from the bulb itself. It comes from electricity. It comes from the power plant. The source of life is the power plant, not the bulb. I have another bulb. No matter how many times I turn on the switch, this bulb does not have life. It is dead, simply because the wire is disconnected from the source. So this bulb has no way to have life. The moment Adam and Eve disobeyed God, they separated themselves from the source of life: God. This is the true death they suffered. When you read 1 Corinthians 3:16 St. Paul says, "Do you not know that you are God's temple and that God's spirit dwells in you?" Man is built as a temple of God. This body is the house of the spirit of God. This is the house where true life is to dwell.

Once this happens, then we are all to live in perfection. In this world no one truly believes in perfection. When anyone uses the word "perfection," we all say no one is perfect except God. This is a true statement. No one here on earth is perfect except God. But there is a way for man to become perfect, to become one with God, to dwell in the very source of perfection. It is when we dwell in the perfection of God that man can be perfect as our Heavenly Father is perfect. This is why the Bible says in Matthew 5:48, "You, therefore, must be perfect as your heavenly father is perfect." Did you ever think that, in a way, all men are like automobiles? God is in the driver's seat. As long as the perfect God is driving us, this automobile, this human being has no way to get in an accident.

Upon the face of this earth have we ever seen such men of perfection? Yes. One man. Jesus Christ. One day one of the disciples asked Jesus: "Philip said to him, 'Lord, show us the Father and we shall be satisfied.' Jesus said to him, 'Have I been with you so long, yet you do not know me, Philip? He who has seen me has seen the Father. ... Do you not believe that I am in the Father and the Father in me?' " [John 14:8-10] Jesus is saying that he and the Father are one. Inseparable. They are living one will. "I am in the Father and the Father in me." The two are one. It is truly the sting of perfection. Jesus was the first man who ever walked on the face of the earth as a man of perfection. The temple was perfect in him. The spirit of God was dwelling in him. He exercised the deity. Jesus was not only living on a human level, but also on a God-like level.

But God did not intend the first perfection to be in Jesus Christ. God intended that the first humans of perfection be Adam and Eve in the Garden of Eden. If they had not fallen, they would have obtained the perfection Jesus was speaking of. If Adam and Eve had obtained that perfection, what would have happened? When you read the Bible, God said to Adam and Eve, "Be fruitful, multiply, and fill the earth." This was the desire of God. God would have brought Adam and Eve, as the God-centered temples, together in heavenly matrimony so they could bring to this world millions and billions of good offspring.

HEAVEN ON EARTH

But today 30 billion people populate the world. Americans, Koreans, Indians, Eskimos—every single one of them is supposed to be a temple of God, dwelling in the perfection of God. What would you call this world if that happened? There can be only one name. The one name for this world would be the kingdom of heaven. This kingdom of heaven must be on earth because God created Adam on earth. So Adam's generation, the perfected generation, would have filled this earth. We would have seen the perfection and kingdom of God here in Seattle, here in America, and all over the world.

If that kingdom of heaven were achieved, what kind of society would that have been? Let me give you an illustration. The kingdom of heaven is like a society working like one human body. The scientists say we have more than 30 billion cells in our body, and all those cells work harmoniously without contradiction. Why? Because every single cell is under the command of one brain. My left hand cannot harm my right hand. If the left hand harms the right hand, then my brain would say ouch. The left hand is hurting himself.

One day these proud two hands may look down at my two feet and say, "You two dirty feet down there, you poor souls, all day long you have had to stay in those dark, dirty black shoes. You have never had a chance to see this beautiful world. Poor souls. Look how free I am. I am not even covered. Look how clean I am." Then the two feet could speak back to the hands, saying, "That is very true, I get dirty and smelly at night. But do you know that somebody always comes down and washes me when I get dirty? That is you. You hands." Furthermore, these two feet are saying, "Sometimes I get so dirty and so smelly even I don't want to touch myself. I am so glad somebody washes me."

But, fortunately, the hands and legs and feet don't work in our body that way. All the parts and members of the body are working for one purpose, the well-being of the entire body. This is like a heavenly kingdom because one brain is in charge of the well-being of the entire body. One heavenly God was supposed to control the entire population for the well-being and joy and happiness of the entire world. This is why the Bible says, "If one member suffers, all suffer together. If one member is honored, all rejoice together." Now you are the body of Christ, individual members of it. In this heavenly kingdom every single one of us is a member of God. A child of God. We can't hurt each other. We cannot be dishonest to each other. We cannot make each other suffer. We can only work for the well-being of God and the entire human race.

This was the kingdom God intended on earth in the Garden of Eden. But Jesus said that Adam brought death. What is death? Jesus said that everyone who commits sin is a slave to sin. And St. Paul said that the wages of sin is death. Since then, instead of dwelling in the perfection of God, we have been dwelling in corruption. We have been living in fallen nature, a world of selfishness and death. We created the kingdom of hell. We don't have to go too far to see hell.

The other day I went to the hospital. One boy there was paralyzed in the lower part of his body. He was in very poor shape. I was shocked to see that the boy's hands were tied. When I asked the nurse why she did that, she answered, "That boy does not have any sensation in the lower part of his body and when he is untied he uses a knife to cut his leg. He hurts himself and he does not feel the pain." This is exactly the situation of the fallen world. We hurt each other, we fight with each other, we drop bombs and do many terrible things, but we do not feel the pain. Our hearts are numb because we suffer from sin. Separation from God. God has been separated from mankind. In reality, we live in the kingdom of hell. This is the kingdom of hell right here on earth.

Furthermore, this kingdom is centered not on God, but on Satan. Jesus said, "You are of your father the devil." According to the words of Jesus, the god of this world is not God, but Satan. We have been sinful and subjugated in sin and chains. This is the nature of the fallen world. But this world should be centered upon God. God should serve as the nerve center. Everything should work in harmony, unity, and beauty. It was the world God intended. But instead we live in the world of hell because of the disobedience of the first man, Adam.

What is God going to do? Will God give up? No, God will not. God promised that He is going to save mankind. The will of God is salvation. What is salvation? To know what salvation is, let us ask: What does a doctor do for his patients to give them salvation? To cure a patient, a doctor needs to bring the patient back to normal health. What would you say to a drowning person in the water? All you have to do to save him, to give him salvation, is bring him out of the water onto dry land. In other words, salvation is the act of restoration.

By the same token, the salvation God is working toward is to restore fallen mankind from this kingdom of hell into the kingdom of God, the world of original goodness. The will of God, therefore, is restoration. In Isaiah 46:11 God shows His clear determination: "I have spoken, and I will bring it to pass; I have purposed, and I will do it." God did not say, I may do it or I might do it. God said I *will* do it. It is the iron will of God that the kingdom of heaven be restored on earth. God sent His son, Jesus Christ, to this world as the savior, the messiah, as a restorer, to transform hell into the kingdom of heaven. This is why Jesus said 2,000 years ago, "Repent, the kingdom of heaven is at hand." By the coming of Jesus Christ, the kingdom of God was indeed being offered to humanity. By the coming of Jesus, the kingdom was at hand.

THE CLEAR-CUT ANSWER

Do we have that kingdom here, 1,974 years later? We know we do not have that perfection. We do not yet have that kingdom here on earth. Why? The savior came 2,000 years ago. Perfection dwelled here 2,000 years ago. Why are the kingdom and perfection not here yet? This is truly the gravest question the Christian world has been asking, all humanity has been asking. Tonight you will have the clear-cut answer.

You know, 2,000 years ago when Jesus Christ came, something extraordinary happened. I would like to bear witness to this. However, instead of me doing it, let me ask some witnesses to come forward and speak to you. The first witness I would like to bring to you is Stephen. In Acts 7:51-52, Stephen said, "You stiff-necked people, uncircumcised in heart and ears, you always resist the Holy Spirit. As your fathers did, so do you. Which of the prophets did not your fathers persecute? And they killed those who announced beforehand the coming of the Righteous One, whom you have now betrayed and murdered." Stephen said that they had betrayed and murdered Jesus. When people heard this testimony their conscience hurt. They could not hear the truth anymore. So they stuffed their ears, picked up stones, and threw them at Stephen. Stephen was martyred. But shortly before he died, Stephen looked up to heaven and he saw heaven open and Jesus Christ standing on the right-hand side of God. In the Bible, Jesus is usually described as sitting on the right-hand side of God, but as a tribute to Stephen, Jesus Christ was standing and ready to receive the soul of Stephen. This was an act of approval of Stephen condemning his own people for murdering the righteous one, Jesus Christ.

My second witness is St. Peter. You know Peter as the chief disciple of Jesus. When you read Acts 3:13-15 Peter says to his own people, "The God of Abraham and of Isaac and of Jacob, the God of our fathers, glorified his servant Jesus, whom you delivered up and denied in the presence of Pilate, when he had decided to release him. But you denied the Holy and Righteous One, and asked for a murderer to be granted to you, and killed the Author of Life, whom God raised from the dead." Peter says that they killed the author of life.

Another famous witness is St. Paul. I am sure you know St. Paul very well. He was one of the most dynamic disciples of Jesus. But do you know St. Paul never had a chance to accept Jesus Christ in his own lifetime? Furthermore, St. Paul was an adversary of Jesus. He was brutally persecuting the disciples of Jesus. On the way to Damascus to kill more of Jesus' disciples, he was struck by the spirit of God. His eyes were opened. He was able to see the truth. His heart was broken, but it was too late. St. Paul says in 1 Corinthians 2:8, "None of the rulers of this age understood this; for if they had, they would not have crucified the Lord of glory." He says that if they had known who Jesus Christ was, they would not have crucified the Lord of glory. He is saying it was a mistake for Jesus to be crucified.

From these witnesses, we can see there was ignorance and blindness on the part of the chosen people of Israel. That blindness and ignorance resulted in the crucifixion. Jesus Christ did not come to die. He came to perfect the kingdom here on earth so he could truly fulfill God's will on earth. But he began his ministry at the age of 30 and he was crucified at the age of 33. It was not enough time for Jesus to build his kingdom here on earth. The chosen people of Israel did not give him a chance. This is why Jesus said that he would return so that he can complete the mission God has given to him.

Let us examine what was God's will. Many people think God sent his son Jesus Christ simply and solely to be nailed to the cross, that this was the sole purpose of His son coming. If that was the case, God did not need the chosen people of Israel. It would have been far better for God to send His son among the barbarians, disbelievers, even among cannibals. They would have crucified the son of God faster and the will of God would have been quickly accomplished. No, it doesn't fit into 20th-century logic.

GOD'S WILL FOR HIS SON

God's will was for His son to be accepted. God wanted his son to be accepted like Dwight Eisenhower was as the commanding general, in order to successfully launch the D-Day landing. Eisenhower rehearsed so many times because he could not afford to make a mistake. God sending His son to this earth was like a Normandy landing operation for God. He cannot afford any blunder. He meticulously prepared the nation and people of Israel. He sent many prophets and John the Baptist, and the mission of every single one of them was to prepare His people so when the Son of God came to that land He would be accepted. That was the will of God.

For that purpose Jesus also worked very hard to be accepted. One time a disciple asked Jesus, "What must we do to be doing the work of God?" Jesus did not say, "Crucify me on the cross, then you shall be saved by my blood." Jesus did not say that. Jesus said to them, "This is the work of God, that you believe in him whom He has sent.".Accept me. Believe in me. Unite with me, that is the work of God. Jesus desperately tried to have his people recognize him as the son of God and accept him. Jesus Christ is like the heavenly Ajax. In our home Ajax is very handy. All the stubborn stains can come out with Ajax. Jesus Christ and God came like a heavenly Ajax. They came with the power to cleanse sin. In Matthew 9:6 Jesus says that the son of man has the authority on earth to forgive sins. He has the power. No matter how stubborn the sin and stains of mankind, as long as mankind accepted, he has the power to take off the sins and bring back all of mankind whole. This is why Jesus said the kingdom will come when He is recognized and accepted as the Son of God.

But the people of Israel at that time were not of that mind. They kept rejecting him. Jesus knew these people needed something extraordinary. So Jesus worked the mighty works. Do you think Jesus performed the mighty works to show off his power like a magician? No. Jesus wanted to have people accept him as the son of God. But knowing the weak people were not ready to accept him by the word, Jesus said, even though you cannot believe me, believe my works, what I do. That is the purpose. He cleansed the lepers. He raised the dead and gave blind men sight and caused the deaf to hear. He changed water into wine to show the people that he was doing all these things by the power of God because he was the son of God. But the people were hopeless. They said to Jesus, "By the prince of Demons he casts out the demons." [Mark 3:22] Jesus, the Son of God, was compared to the Prince of Demons.

Furthermore, people said this man is a madman. He has a demon. Pick up a stone and stone him, he is a blasphemer, he deserves to be stoned. Jesus saw the hopeless signs. He truly wept and wept when he went to Jerusalem. Do you know what he said about Jerusalem? "Oh Jerusalem, killing the prophets and stoning those who are sent to you! How often would I have gathered your children together as a hen gathers her brood under her wing, and you would not! Behold, your house is forsaken and desolate." [Matthew 23:37-38] By that time Satan was actively working to bring the people to his side.

Actually Satan is holding the power and sovereignty of this earth, so the coming of the son of God is like an invasion from heaven. Satan was desperately holding his ground and trying to protect it. Initially Satan came for Jesus, but Jesus overcame the test. Satan knew he could not destroy the son of God in a face-to-face confrontation. But Satan also knew Jesus could not establish the kingdom as long as people of that time did not cooperate with him. So Satan worked actively to destroy the son of God and stop the building of the kingdom of God on earth.

That was the will of Satan, the destruction of the son of God. So Satan was working with the people of Israel so the people would prevent him from being recognized as the son of God. The Bible said Satan entered into Judas, who sold Jesus Christ. The betrayal of Jesus was not the act of God. It was the act of Satan, the Bible said. If the crucifixion was the sole purpose of God, then Judas Iscariot deserved a heavenly medal. Why? Because if only the cross would bring salvation, then somebody had to turn him over to enemy hands. Judas did. He cooperated with what so many believe was the plan of God. But Jesus said, "Woe to that man by whom the Son of man is betrayed." [Matthew 26:24] Satan exercised his maximum power, urging people into faithlessness and to send the son of God to the cross.

VICTORY OF THE RESURRECTION

However, on the foundation of Jesus' faith, loyalty, and sacrifice, God raised His son in three days from the tomb. Resurrection. That is the Christian salvation today. Resurrected Jesus. In him there is no room for Satan's power to come in. So the glorious victory was the resurrection. But you know the resurrection of Jesus did not bring the kingdom of God physically here on earth. Why? Because it was only spiritual salvation. Physical redemption of the body is still to come. Jesus gave up his body on the cross. At that time the body of the entire world and mankind was given up. Jesus, by resurrecting from the tomb, saved mankind spiritually, but, as it says in the Bible, we are still waiting to be redeemed in the physical body.

Would you like to hear what St. Paul said after being born again as a Christian? He showed anguish about our world. You and I experience anguish, but his anguish was right after the crucifixion of Jesus Christ. St. Paul said in Romans 7:24-25, "Wretched man that I am! Who will deliver me from this body of death? Thanks be to God through Jesus Christ our Lord! So then, I of myself serve the law of God with my mind, but with my flesh I serve the law of sin." We are divided of mind and spirit. We can go to heaven. We can go toward God, but our bodies and this physical world are still chained to Satan.

Ladies and gentlemen, this is why Christ is coming back to us. To make our redemption whole, both spiritual and physical. So that he can completely wipe sin from the face of this earth. So that we no longer feel any contradiction within ourselves. This is the day of hope we have been looking forward to. Tonight I am saying to you this hour has arrived. Tomorrow night you are going to hear a most extraordinary message of how Christ is coming. Christ is coming for the redemption of the spirit and body. Total salvation. In order to be the recipient of this total salvation, we must meet the Lord, the coming Christ, Jesus Christ. We cannot miss this opportunity. In order to do that you must come tomorrow night to hear how Christ is coming.

It doesn't matter where you live, what position you hold, how young or old you are, how poor or how wealthy you are. Opportunity is knocking at your door. Christ is coming to bring the kingdom that God originally intended. We must become the first citizens of that kingdom. You are eligible. You can welcome the Lord and become one with him. So please come tomorrow night.

And I will say one thing in conclusion. This is not my own theory. I am not that clever, that wise, to put together this wonderful, extraordinary message. This is a revelation from God. Only God can tell us. If any human brain could tell us, I know thousands of theologians, ministers, and clergymen would have dug out this truth a long time ago. But at this particular moment God is revealing the truth. The hour has arrived. God would not do anything without revealing His secret to His servants and prophets. And as His prophet, His servant, the Reverend Sun Myung Moon has been chosen to speak to mankind. Through him this wonderful message will be revealed. Tomorrow night you will hear plainly how the Lord is coming. Furthermore, at a later day you will have an opportunity to know when and where he is coming so you will have no way of missing this opportunity. Thank you very much.

How Christ Is Coming

CELEBRATION OF LIFE—SECOND NIGHT

SEATTLE, WASHINGTON

MAY 23, 1974

―――――――――――――

Using quotes from the Bible and insights from the Divine Principle, Dr. Pak explains how Christ will come again.

Ladies and gentlemen, this is the second night here in Seattle. I am deeply grateful and honored to have all of you here. Sit right where you are. After this message there is more exciting dancing and singing to come. Last night's message dwelled on the very important subject of why Christ is coming. My subject tonight is how Christ is coming.

Today, many people feel that we have come to a very important era. Something important will happen. The Christian world has believed in the coming of Christ for 2,000 years. And I do believe we are truly living in the most extraordinary of times. Indeed, the coming of Christ is an important subject for us to discuss tonight.

The Bible says something about the coming of Christ. When you read Matthew 24:30 it says, "They will see the Son of man coming on the clouds of heaven with power and great glory." Furthermore, in Revelations 1:7, the Bible says, "Behold he is coming with the clouds." On the other hand, 1 Thessalonians 5:2 says the day of the Lord will come like a thief in the night. The Bible seems to give contradictory testimony or prophecy concerning the coming of the Lord. If the Lord is coming with the trumpet of angels and power and glory, how can he come like a thief in the night?

Christians all over the world are focusing on the blue sky, waiting for the coming of Christ on the clouds of heaven. But this is not the only occasion that mankind has waited for somebody very important coming from the sky or clouds. There are two previous occasions in biblical history that mankind waited for an important arrival from the blue sky.

The first occasion was the return of Elijah. The prophet Malachi had foretold, in Malachi 4:5, "Behold, I will send you Elijah the prophet before the great and terrible day of the Lord comes. And he will turn the hearts of fathers to their children and the hearts of the children to their fathers." God promised the return of Elijah prior to the coming of the messiah, the son of God. The people expected Elijah to appear before the messiah could come.

Who was Elijah? He was a great prophet of Israel who lived approximately 900 years before Jesus. The Bible records that Elijah ascended into heaven in a chariot of fire. Since Elijah ascended in that manner, the people of Israel reasoned that he would return in the same way, coming down from the blue sky.

But they never heard the news of Elijah's supernatural return. Instead, one day the people of Israel heard a most extraordinary declaration, that the son of God had come. They heard Jesus of Nazareth being proclaimed to the world as the messiah.

The chosen people of Israel were puzzled. They asked, "If Jesus is the son of God, then where is Elijah?" When Jesus' disciples went out into Israel preaching the Gospel, proclaiming that Jesus was the son of God, the scribes and Pharisees rebuked them, saying, "If your master is the son of God, where is Elijah?"

The disciples could not answer that question. They were very embarrassed. So they decided to ask Jesus for help with this problem. We read in Matthew 17:10-13, "And the disciples asked him 'Then why do the scribes say that first Elijah must come?' He replied, 'Elijah does come, and he is to restore all things; but I tell you that Elijah has already come.' Then the disciples understood that he was speaking to them of John the Baptist."

This was a bombshell. Was John the Baptist Elijah? Yes. Jesus said so. Jesus speaks the truth. However, this was not convincing to the people of Israel because John the Baptist did not come from the blue sky. He was born as a man in the flesh, just like you and me. However, we read in Luke 1:17 a prophecy concerning John the Baptist before his birth. God foretold the mission with which John would go forth into the world. "He [John] will go before him [Jesus] in the spirit and power of Elijah, to make ready for the Lord a people prepared."

John the Baptist was chosen to be the harbinger of the son of God, Jesus Christ. He came to prepare the way of the Lord. Indeed, in the sight of God, John the Baptist was Elijah. God gave him the power and spirit of Elijah. John did not come from the blue sky. He was born just like anybody else, born of woman, but the prophecy was fulfilled in the sight of God. This was one occasion on which they were expecting someone important to come from the sky but that expectation was not fulfilled.

Another occasion when something was expected to come from the sky was none other than the coming of Jesus Christ himself. The people of Israel at that time thought that God's throne was up there in heaven. Therefore, Jesus Christ, son of God, the Messiah, must come from the blue sky in a supernatural manner. Daniel was a great prophet, and the Jewish people really believed the word of Daniel. Daniel 7:13 says, "I saw in the night visions, and behold, with the clouds of heaven there came one like the son of man." He saw in a vision the son of man coming down with the clouds of heaven. The Jews thought that Jesus Christ must come through the clouds of heaven.

But when Jesus came, he was born of a woman in Bethlehem. The people rejected Jesus as the son of God. They thought he was just another man. They gave great trouble to Jesus' disciples. The apostle John was so troubled he said in 2 John 7, "For many deceivers have gone out into the world, men who will not acknowledge the coming of Jesus Christ in the flesh." People were denying Jesus Christ because he was another man in the flesh. How could he be the son of God? But John said, such a one is a deceiver and antichrist. This shows how much difficulty the disciples of Jesus had. Everybody denied Jesus Christ as the son of God because he was a man. He didn't come from the blue sky. He didn't come in a supernatural way.

However, Jesus did come from God even though he was born on earth and did not come down from the blue sky. Today, the Christian world is looking up into the blue sky waiting for the second coming of Christ, just as people did in the time of Jesus. Do you have a guarantee that your expectation will not be betrayed this time? This is indeed a very serious subject.

Tonight we must have a clear-cut answer through the Bible. I would like to draw your attention to Acts 1:11, where two angels asked, "Men of Galilee, why do you stand looking into heaven? This Jesus, who was taken up from you into heaven, will come in the same way as you saw him go into heaven." For 2,000 years this particular verse, Acts 1:11, has been used as proof that the son of God will come back to us through the clouds of heaven. However, tonight, let us deeply read this passage and get the true meaning out of it. First of all, the angels are speaking to the disciples of Jesus who are looking up at Jesus who is ascending into heaven. Their hearts were sorrowful. They were troubled. Their hearts were saying, Lord, we need you. Please come back soon. Then the two angels appeared beside the disciples of Jesus and said, why do you stand looking into heaven?

Let us analyze. When you say "why do you stand looking into heaven," it has a negative connotation. The angel is almost saying, man, it is no use looking in that direction. On Christmas Day my eight-year-old son kept looking at the chimney waiting for the arrival of Santa Claus. So I said to him, why do you look into the chimney? Even though I am not saying it, I know Santa Claus will not come from the chimney and it is no use waiting for Santa Claus that way. Santa Claus will walk in the front door. Your daddy will be the Santa Claus. Even though I am not saying it, I am implying to my son it is no use looking into the chimney.

WHY ARE YOU LOOKING UP?

If Christ is returning from the blue sky and clouds of heaven, the angel would have told the men to keep looking. He will indeed come from that direction. But the angel said, why do you stand looking into heaven? It is of no use. Then the angel explained that Jesus who was taken up from you into heaven will come in the same way as you saw him go into heaven. What does that mean? First of all, we must clearly know the meaning of heaven. There are two meanings of heaven. The first heaven means sky. The disciples were looking up into the sky. But the second heaven does not mean the sky or any other physical location. This heaven means the spiritual kingdom of God, God's dwelling place, the spiritual world. And this heaven does not exist up in space.

Some years ago Moscow radio made an impressive broadcast on Christmas day. I want you to hear these remarkable words, "Our rocket bypassed the moon. It is nearing the sun and we have not discovered God. We have turned out the lights of heaven that no man will be able to turn on again. We are breaking the yoke of the Gospel, the opium of the masses. Let us go forth and Christ will be relegated to mythology."

Very impressive, but Moscow radio missed the whole point. They looked for God up in the sky. God is not up in the sky, up in space. For that matter, Neil Armstrong, on the way to the moon, didn't say he waved to Christ. Christ is not up there hanging in the sky. No. The spiritual heaven is entirely separate. It has nothing to do with this physical place. Everything there exists spiritually. Nothing exists outside the law of God.

So, when you are taken up into that heaven, it means ascension. Ascension into spiritual heaven. It does not necessarily mean a physical ascension like this. This ascension has nothing to do with physical elevation. And so does descension have nothing to do with the physical landing.

Jesus said in John 3:13, "No one has ascended into heaven, but he who descended from heaven, the son of man." Jesus is saying the son of God descended from heaven. Do you think Jesus Christ came down like an airplane landing? Let me give you a very simple illustration. This is a little parachute I borrowed from my son. Let me throw it. Did Jesus come down that way 2,000 years ago? No. Physical descent has nothing to do with the coming of Christ.

Jesus came, we know, through the natural process of birth. He came to this earth as a baby. He was born through Mary as a baby. But in the sight of God that was precisely the descent. Therefore, as soon as the descent was complete, the moment of the birth of Jesus Christ, his heaven-bound trip began. In other words the ascension began the very moment Jesus descended.

Once again, let me paraphrase this whole thing. The angel is asking the disciples why they are looking into heaven. This Jesus who entered into the spiritual world, the spiritual kingdom and the throne of God, will come, will descend in the same way you saw him come 2,000 years ago and went into heaven. This shows Christ is indeed coming once again to our world, as he did 2,000 years ago, born as a man. A man of flesh. Therefore, Revelations 12:5 says, "She brought forth a male child, one who is to rule all the nations with a rod of iron."

Who has the right to rule all the nations with a rod of iron? The president of the United States? It is a powerful nation. However, the head of state of this country does not have the right to rule all the nations. The queen of England? No. The pope in Rome? Not him either. Only one person. One man has a right to rule all the nations with a rod of iron. Christ. And the Bible says woman brought forth a male child. He is to come through a woman. She is bringing forth this male child as a man. This is so completely clear.

Once we know this much, then the Bible really starts to make sense. Tonight I cannot go through all the important quotations from the Bible, but let me recite just a couple of the very important ones. Luke 17:20: "Being asked by the Pharisees when the kingdom of God was coming, he answered them, 'The Kingdom of God is not coming with signs to be observed; nor will they say, "Lo, here it is!" or "There!" for behold the kingdom of God is in the midst of you.' " No sign. When he comes from the clouds of heaven, with the trumpets of angels, there will be a sign. Jesus said, no sign to be observed. When he comes as the son of man in the flesh, there will be no sign in the sky to be observed.

Most important of all is Luke 17:25: "But first he must suffer and be rejected by this generation." Be rejected by this generation. This is a stunning statement. Who in the world would reject him and make him suffer when he comes in glory and power and with the trumpet of angels? Would you? No. You will welcome him, won't you? When Neil Armstrong came back from the moon, there in the Pacific Ocean, the president of the United States went out to meet him. When the son of God comes from the cloud of heaven, I know the pope would be there. I know Billy Graham would be there. I know that all the ministers would be there. I don't think I can get a ticket into the welcoming ceremony. So probably, it is a great opportunity for NBC to put on a special so you can watch in your living room. Everyone will want to be there to welcome the Lord in the clouds of heaven. But Jesus said that he will suffer and this generation will initially reject him. How can the prophecy, the word of Jesus Christ, be fulfilled? It can only be fulfilled when he comes again as the son of man, in the flesh.

WILL HE FIND FAITH ON EARTH?

When you read Luke 18:8, Jesus is saying, "I tell you, he will vindicate them speedily. Nevertheless, when the Son of man comes, will he find faith on earth?" Faith is believers on earth. It is really an astounding statement. There are millions of Christians on earth waiting for the coming of Christ. Here in America alone there are thousands and thousands of churches. Jesus is saying that he will not find any faith, not even a single believer on earth. Why is this? Even though there is great faith upon the face of the earth, these faithful have already set their minds up in the blue sky. But when the Lord reappears among ourselves, as a humble man in the flesh, you know that this world, the Christian world, will be ready to throw the first stone at him, just as it happened 2,000 years ago.

There was great faith at the time of Jesus. So many faithful Jews went to the synagogue morning, noon, and night. They prayed and they obeyed the Law of Moses. But they are the ones who plotted to kill Jesus. Not a single one of them would become the follower or disciple that Jesus wanted. History shall be repeated once again. The Christian world must be very careful in order not to make the same mistake the Jewish people made 2,000 years ago.

Just one more. Matthew 7:22-23 says, "On that day [the day of the coming of Christ], many will say to me, 'Lord, Lord, did we not prophesy in your name and cast out demons in your name, and do many mighty works in your name?' And then will I declare to them, 'I never knew you;

depart from me, you evildoers.' " How could that happen? A man was loyal all his life, but Jesus will say depart from me. When will this happen? When he comes to the world once again in the flesh.

Throughout history many crimes were committed in the name of the Lord. In this present world, so much evil is committed in the name of God. During the Protestant Revolution alone, in Europe almost half a million people were persecuted because they were thought to be enemies of God. They were exterminated in the name of God. Two thousand years ago when Jesus Christ came, the Jewish people thought Jesus was a heretic, a blasphemer, an enemy of God. They not only threw stones at him, but they actually crucified him.

However, I mentioned yesterday that Christ is coming to complete salvation, to bring the kingdom of God here on earth. Therefore, he will become a lord and judge. Even though he passes through the road of tribulation, he will indeed be lifted up as the son of God upon the face of this earth. He will become the Lord of Judgment. By then the entire world will see him and know him for who he is. Those arrogant ones and evildoers who already threw stones at him will regret it, but it will be too late. The Lord will say, "Depart from me, you evildoers." We must become one of those who accept the Lord.

COMING ON THE CLOUDS

Before I give you an indication of how we could do that, let me give you the true meaning of the clouds of heaven. When Jesus said, "I am the vine and you are the branches," those words have a symbolic meaning. Jesus does not mean that he is a literal grapevine and we all are branches of a grapevine. It is symbolic. The Bible is written in symbols and parables. The spiritual facts and truth are set in a physical language so it has to be expressed in symbolic terms. The word "clouds" also has a symbolic meaning.

What is a cloud? A cloud is vaporized water. Therefore, we must know what water is first. What is water? The Bible says in Revelation 17:15, "The waters that you saw, where the harlot is seated, are peoples and multitudes and nations and tongues." The water in the Bible is a symbol of people, nations, and multitudes. Water has many foreign elements, many sinful elements. In the water there are many pollutants, particularly in this day and age. However, once that water is vaporized, it is purified into steam or a cloud. It is genuinely pure. So Christ is saying, I will come among pure, genuine people.

He will come, pick up the strong, and rule all the nations. Therefore, today this is our duty: We must know how we can become that consecrated group so that we can meet the Lord. The most important thing to know today, however, is that consecrated Christian does not necessarily mean churchgoer. It does not necessarily mean the Bible scholar or those who do many good works and charities. There is one more important thing that we must do to become consecrated. Jesus said in John 14:6, "I am the way, and the truth, and the life; no one comes to Father, but by me." When Jesus comes, this Bible is no longer needed. The living Jesus is the living Bible. He is the light.

Yesterday I explained that Jesus came as the author of life. Anybody who belongs to him has life. Anybody who does not recognize him does not have life. It is death. This is the judgment of the last days. The Bible says that the sun will be darkened and the moon will not give light and the stars will fall. But this will not happen literally. God will not destroy this earth at all. Why should He? This earth did not commit any sin. Only man committed sin. God only needs to re-create man and put him on earth and then the earth will become the Garden of Eden. There is no reason for God to destroy the environment of man. God needs to change man, judge man, separate man to bring the kingdom.

Then what are the criteria on the day of the coming of the Lord? "Accept the Lord" will be the criteria. Those who accept the coming Lord, recognize him, shall live for eternity with God. Those who do not recognize him shall go into the great fire.

AN IMPORTANT NEW TRUTH

Ladies and gentlemen, the conclusion and most important statement is: "How can you meet the Lord?" What are the criteria or qualifications to meet the Lord? Knowing the Bible is not enough. Going to church is not enough. We must do one very important thing. We must know Jesus Christ when he comes the second time. He will declare a very important new truth to this world.

Two thousand years ago Jesus Christ came not to repeat the law of Moses. He came to perfect the law. Jesus knew many new things about the law. But people at that time rejected Jesus Christ because they thought he was corrupt because he did not repeat the law of Moses. Two thousand years ago, Jesus said, "I have many things to tell you, but you cannot bear them now." One time Jesus said, when I tell you earthly things and you do not believe, how can I tell you heavenly things? The whole heavenly truth was not told in the Bible. This Bible did not carry the full truth, the complete Kingdom of God, the blueprint of heaven. Jesus brought the truth 2,000 years ago, but people were not ready to accept.

This time when he comes he brings out a new truth, a newer truth than the New Testament. We must expect a new truth and we must open our hearts, be humble and meek, so the spirit of God can speak to us. This is the criterion. This is most important. How much Bible you know is not important. How much money you have is not important. What is most important is we must remain poor in spirit, thirsting for righteousness. Open your heart so the spirit of God can speak to you directly.

Peter, the chief disciple, didn't know anything about the Old Testament. He never went to the synagogue. He never prayed before he met Jesus, but he accepted Jesus. Those harlots, those tax collectors, those lepers, those blind men, those outcasts of society saw the coming of Jesus, the son of God. Why? They were poor in spirit. Thirsting for righteousness. Their hearts were open so the spirit of God could speak to them directly.

Today, the Christian world had one warning of the time of the coming of Christ. The worst enemy of the Christian world is arrogance. Be humble and meek, then God will speak to you directly. Read Amos 3:7: "Surely the Lord God does nothing without revealing his secret to his servants the prophets." When you are ready servants, ready prophets, the time has come when God will speak to you directly. And the son of God is not coming in the clouds of heaven. He is coming as the son of man in the flesh once again because the kingdom he needs to build is on earth.

Jesus gave the key to the kingdom of heaven to Peter by saying, "Whatever you bind here on earth shall be bound in heaven. Whatever you loose here on earth shall be loosed in heaven." Heaven is OK. The error, the sin, was committed here on earth. Jesus Christ is coming as a heavenly Ajax to wipe out the stains here on earth, so he has to come here on earth where the sins are. Isn't that logical? We can have that kingdom, the sons and daughters of God here on earth, here in America. Here in Seattle. Let us be open and I must tell you the day has come.

I want to give you one invitation to come to our Celebration of Life workshop this weekend. Tonight in just 40 minutes, I can only scratch the surface of the entire content of the revelation given to Reverend Sun Myung Moon. We have prepared a most joyful workshop this weekend, a two-day Celebration of Life workshop to hear the entire message. Not only how Christ is coming, but when he is coming, where he is coming. In order to meet someone successfully, you need three pieces of information: when, where, and how. I just said how tonight. You need when and where. We invite you come to the workshop. And tonight I truly appreciate your most attentive attention. Thank you very much, ladies and gentlemen.

THE CRISIS OF LOVE

CELEBRATION OF LIFE—THIRD NIGHT

SEATTLE, WASHINGTON

MAY 24, 1974

Dr. Pak delivers the final talk in the three-part series and reveals the true meaning of the Fall of Man based on the Divine Principle.

Tonight, I would like to thank you for this wonderful gathering. Each night the excitement is mounting here in Moore Theater—more attendance, more applause. Truly you are making all our company, the Sun Myung Moon Christian Crusade, very happy. Tonight, I would like to deal with one of the most important subjects of all: love. There are many crises in our world, but there is also a crisis of love. But the root of the crisis of love was there at the dawn of human history. Tonight I want to talk about the origin of that crisis of love.

God created the world. According to the Bible, God created the Garden of Eden and in that garden God planted two mysterious trees carrying mysterious names. One tree was named the Tree of Life. The other was named the Tree of the Knowledge of Good and Evil. God also created two persons initially, one man and one woman. That man's name was Adam and that woman's name was Eve. Then God gave them the commandment. As you read in Genesis 2:17, God said to them, "But of the Tree of the Knowledge of Good and Evil you shall not eat, for in the day that you eat of it you shall die." This was the first pronouncement of death in the Bible. Adam and Eve, however, disobeyed the law. They ate the forbidden fruit. What was that forbidden fruit? Was it an apple, an orange, a banana?

A few years ago I went to Rome and had the opportunity to visit the beautiful museum in the Vatican. There was a great big painting, a masterpiece painted by the famous Michelangelo. He painted on that big wall the story of the Bible from Genesis to Revelation, from the creation to the resurrection. I looked at the section on the fall of man. Michelangelo painted an apple tree. There is a woman eating one apple and giving another one to Adam. There was also the serpent who enticed Eve. Michelangelo indeed followed the instruction of the Bible.

Do you really think that a piece of apple caused the misery of mankind and literally the kingdom of hell on earth? If an apple was the problem, I am afraid Adam had very bad teeth. He didn't even chew the apple too well. He swallowed the whole apple and that is why we all have an Adam's apple today.

The problem today, however, is that the original sin of Adam and Eve caused what must be a hereditary sin. Because the Bible says in one man, Adam, all die. The result of the fall in the Garden of Eden has now passed from generation to generation and is affecting our world today. This must be a hereditary sin. How could an apple or orange cause such a hereditary sin? Impossible. Science cannot prove that. Furthermore, Jesus said in Matthew 15:11, "Not what goes into the mouth defiles a man, but what comes out of the mouth, this defiles a man." According to the teaching of Christ, the theory of eating an apple and becoming fallen is not true.

Many Christians today believe the apple or orange was not the problem. The problem was an entirely different one—disobedience. That was the sin. God was very angry because man disobeyed Him. However, I ask you, would you test your children to find out if they are obedient to you or not by risking their lives? Would you leave a poison cookie in front of your little child and say, the day you eat of it you shall die? And then just watch? No parent would do that. But God is our Father. Our Father would never test His own children by risking their lives. If that were the case, God is indeed not a God of love. He would be a God of cruelty. So it cannot be that way.

WHO IS SATAN?

So today, we must take a serious look at what actually happened in the Garden of Eden. And there is one more important thing to discover: the identity of Satan or the devil. Jesus Christ warned of the existence of the devil in the Bible. It is a reality that the devil exists in this world. The Bible said that devil is Satan. Who is Satan? What kind of crime has Satan committed? Furthermore, day in and day out Satan is accusing man in front of God. But man cannot prosecute Satan because we do not know the identity of Satan. Furthermore, we do not know the crime of Satan. We have not yet proven what kind of crime Satan committed.

Tonight we are going to uncover the original sin and the original entity of Satan. So I would like to invite all of you to join with me in a heavenly FBI investigation. Let's go to the Garden of Eden and discover what actually happened.

First of all, I would like to invite your attention to the Tree of Life. If we know the meaning of the Tree of Life, then we know automatically the meaning of the Tree of the Knowledge of Good and Evil whose fruit God warned Adam and Eve not to eat. The Tree of Life is mentioned in Genesis, but this is not the only place in the Bible it is mentioned. In Revelation 22:14 there is another mention of the Tree of Life: "Blessed are those who wash their robes that they may have the right to the Tree of Life and that they may enter the city by the gates." And in Revelation 22:13, God says, "I am the Alpha and the Omega, the first and the last, the beginning and the end." Therefore, the Tree of Life God mentioned in the first book of the Bible, Genesis, and the last book of the Bible, Revelation, must have meant the same thing. God is an eternal God. The truth of God is unchanging. The Bible is telling the same truth cover to cover. Therefore, wherever the Tree of Life is mentioned it must be the same.

Today Christians and theologians unanimously agree that the Tree of Life in Revelation symbolizes Jesus Christ. Why? The Bible says in Revelation 22:14, "Blessed are those who wash their robes, that they may have the right to the tree of life." The Tree of Life is Christ. Then, the Tree of Life in Genesis must also be Jesus. However, as you know, Jesus was not incarnated in the Garden of Eden. When you read further, 1 Corinthians 15:45 says, "Thus it is written, 'the first man Adam became a living being'; the last Adam became a life-giving spirit." The last Adam, Jesus, came to this world as a life-giving spirit. Jesus was not in the Garden of Eden, but Adam was. Therefore, the Tree of Life in Genesis symbolizes Adam.

But there were two mysterious trees. The Tree of Life is Adam, so the other tree, the Tree of the Knowledge of Good and Evil, must have meant another person in the Garden of Eden. The only other person there was

Eve. The two trees represent Adam and Eve. We discovered a very important thing; now let us continue our FBI journey.

This time let us investigate the serpent, because the serpent caused the trouble. Let us hear what the snake, the serpent, said to the woman. In Genesis 3:4-5, after tempting her to eat the fruit, the serpent says to the woman, "You will not die. For God knows that when you eat of it your eyes will be opened, and you will be like God, knowing good and evil." This serpent in the Garden of Eden mentioned the name of God. He knew not only of God's existence but also that God gave a particular commandment to man. A snake in the field has no way to know the presence of God. Snakes are not spiritual beings; only a spiritual being can understand God. Therefore, the serpent must symbolize a spiritual being who has the ability to understand the presence of God. But Adam and Eve in the Garden of Eden cannot be the serpent because they were the victims. There is one other creation that can understand God—angels. Angels are spiritual beings. So an angel could be the serpent. Do you say "impossible"? Let the Bible answer.

THE GREAT DRAGON WAS THROWN DOWN

When you read 2 Peter 2:4, it says God did not spare the angels when they sinned. The Bible said the angels sinned. Furthermore, when you read Revelation 12:9 you find, "The great dragon was thrown down, that ancient serpent, who is called the Devil and Satan." The serpent is not really a snake. The serpent was an expression of the devil, Satan, deceiver of the entire world. And the Bible says then he was thrown down to the earth and his angels were thrown down with him, showing he had committed a crime. The angel became Satan or the devil, and he was thrown down into the nether gloom along with his own angels. So according to the Bible, Satan was an angel.

What kind of crime did that angel commit? This answer is also in the Bible. Let us read this time Jude 1:6-7, "And the angels that did not keep their own position but left their proper dwelling have been kept by him in eternal chains in the nether gloom until the judgment of the great day; just as Sodom and Gomorrah and the surrounding cities, which likewise acted immorally and indulged in unnatural lust, serve as an example by undergoing a punishment of eternal fire." The sinning angels committed the same crime or sin as those in the city of Sodom and Gomorrah, which was immorality and unnatural lust. Therefore, the fallen angels' sin must have been immorality and unnatural lust, which is adultery. The fallen angel became Satan. That angel committed the sin of adultery, according to the Bible.

Let us invite your attention to another area. Let us this time examine Adam and Eve. Genesis 2:25 says, "The man and his wife were both naked and were not ashamed." However, Genesis 3:7, after they ate the fruit, says, "Then the eyes of both were opened, and they knew that they were naked; and they sewed fig leaves together and made themselves aprons."

In Job 31:33, Job says, "if I have concealed my transgressions like Adam, by hiding my iniquity in my bosom." Job is saying that Adam in the Garden hid his sin with the apron. But if eating the apple was the sin, then the hand and the mouth must have been responsible, and Adam should have covered his hand and mouth. But the apron covers the lower part of the human body.

There is only one sin that can be committed by the lower part of the human body. That is adultery. The serpent enticed Eve, and there was a relationship between the woman and the fallen angel. Then that sin was repeated between Eve and Adam. This was the tragedy that caused God's heart to grieve.

THE SIN THAT AFFECTS LINEAGE

You know there is only one sin that can affect generation after generation. That is adultery, because it affects the lineage. God created His children to be His own pure lineage, but that lineage was stained by Satan with the original sin. And that stain, that spot, has been there, existing all through human history from generation to generation. This is why Jesus said, "You are of your father the devil." Human history started from the devil as father, instead of God.

Let me explain briefly how all this happened. God first created the angelic world. The angels are like servants. This is why the Bible says, do you not know that they are all ministering spirits. In other words, angels were ministering spirits as servants of God. God sent angels to Abraham to inform him he would have a son at the age of 100. God sent an angel to Mary to inform her she was going to bear a child. God also sent angels to Sodom and Gomorrah to demolish those wicked cities with fire and brimstone.

God created man as the children of God. We are the children, and the angels are the servants of God. A father's servants also belong to the children. In other words, we are like a prince and princess of God. The angelic world is the servant world. They not only serve God, but were supposed to serve man. This is why 1 Corinthians 6:3 says, "Do you not know that we are to judge angels?" We are even given the power to judge angels. Before the creation of Adam and Eve, the archangel named Lucifer was the center of everything. He was like the prime minister in the sight of God.

He handled every problem and distributed the love of God to the angelic world.

But when Adam and Eve were created, Lucifer saw the difference in the love God had for Adam and Eve and that God loved them more than He loved Lucifer. The ambitious Lucifer was very jealous of the position of Adam. Then he looked at Eve, and she was a very beautiful woman. Thus, he began to harbor false ambition and arrogance and to develop selfish motivation. The Bible in Isaiah 14:13 says concerning the motivation of Lucifer, "I will ascend above the heights of the clouds, I will make myself like the Most High." The servant wants to become the most high in heaven. He can think of only one way he can do that: win the heart of the daughter of God, Eve. If he could become united with Eve, then he could cast out Adam. He can place himself in the position of Adam so he can control the entire human world.

With his misdirected ambition and his burning desire for illicit love with Eve, the archangel approached Eve with a lie. He twisted the truth of God and successfully won her heart. They united in illicit love, unlawful love, and impossible love. That constituted the spiritual fall of man. When that happened, Eve received two elements. One was fear. Even though the archangel was moving toward the enticement of Eve, his heart was struggling. He was in fear, knowing that he was violating the law of God. That fear was transmitted to Eve, our original ancestor, so our world today is full of fear. Fear overtakes us. This fear was transmitted from the fallen archangel to Eve.

Eve also opened her eyes. Actually God planned to have Adam and Eve's eyes opened in the wisdom of God. But they prematurely united with the wisdom of Satan and became wiser in Satan's knowledge. Eve realized Lucifer was not her intended mate. Adam was. So she dashed to Adam and urged him to act as her husband—but without God's blessing. This was an unlawful union between man and woman—without God, separated from God, united under Satan. This constituted the physical fall. God created man in spirit and body. They fell in spirit and body. The corruption of man was thus completed.

WRESTLING WITH THE ANGEL

Now I know you have two important questions. Let me touch upon them very quickly. How is it possible for an angel to commit adultery with a human, with Eve? We have flesh, angels do not have flesh. However, the spiritual world is capable of duplicating all the physical phenomena, plus more. For example, Jacob met an angel when he was returning from Haran to his home in Canaan, at the ford of Jabbok. God sent an angel to wrestle against Jacob, and they wrestled all night. One had a physical human body, and the other had a spiritual body. But they wrestled against each other all night. Genesis 32:25 says, "When the man [the angel] saw that he did not prevail against Jacob, he touched the hollow of his thigh; and Jacob's thigh was put out of joint as he wrestled with him." The angel with his spiritual body hit the thigh bone and put it out of joint. If an angel and a man can wrestle, and an angel can dislocate Jacob's hip joint, an angel and a human are capable of doing anything together, including adultery.

Another question, probably the most important one this evening: Why did God Almighty allow such a situation to occur? How in the world could Adam and Eve, created in the law of God, and an angel also created in the law of God, derail from the principle of God?

Let me make one simple illustration. Here is a track I got from a toy shop, and here is a toy train. This train has no freedom to maneuver outside the track. The track is like the will of God, divine law. The train is like the creation, man or angel. All creation was created under the divine law of God. The apple tree cannot arbitrarily become a banana tree. It is impossible. The law of God dictates that the apple must be an apple tree. So Adam and Eve, including the angelic world, all were created within the divine law of God. In this situation it is impossible to derail from the law of God.

However, many times train accidents happen. When an even stronger power hits the train's side, then the train can derail. If in this universe some power is stronger than the law of God, then a man and angel can derail. Your question must be, is there such a power in this universe stronger than the law of God? My answer is yes. One power. One supreme power in this universe. That is the power of love. God put the power of love supreme, at the highest possible level in this universe, because God wanted to create the world of love, and God is love. He wants to manifest His infinite love to this world and receive infinite love from His creation, man. In order to have this love fulfilled, love cannot have any limitation. Love cannot be limited by boundaries and cannot be confined in a small container. Love, in order to be love, must be free. Absolutely free. The most powerful force in the universe. Even in our human world that has been proven.

There is the one power that can bring you beyond the power of death. That is the power of love. In the past and today, many patriots die for love of their country. And brides and bridegrooms on their honeymoon tell each other, "I love you more than my own life." Or, "I love you unto my death." (Then problems come and this honeymoon pledge usually doesn't last more than three days.) In any case, it is a proven power that love is supreme in this universe.

MATURITY IN LOVE

Because love is supreme, once man has reached perfection, which means maturity in love, we become a mirror of the love of God and capable of receiving the infinite love of God. Once we reach that level, because love is supreme, men and God are united in love, and nothing in this universe can separate them. This is how the perfection of love can last from eternity to eternity.

Let us hear what St. Paul said about love in Romans 8:38, "For I am sure that neither death, nor life, nor angels, nor principalities, nor things present, nor things to come, nor powers, nor height, nor depth, nor anything else in all creation, will be able to separate us from the love of God in Christ Jesus our Lord." Love is like a magnet between God and man. Nothing in this universe can separate the perfected love relationship between God and man. Perfection remains for eternity. We are to live in infinite joy and love in fellowship with God. That was the original design.

But God knew that until man reached that perfection, man needed extra protection. God knew there was the possibility of infiltration of the illicit love of the angel. That is why God gave them the commandment: Adam and Eve, my children, watch out. I want you to be pure. Maintain your purity until I let you unite in love between me and you and you two together. Guard your love. Do not misuse it. This was the commandment, and they were expected to obey this commandment. Following that commandment would keep the train on the track until Adam and Eve were mature, perfected. Once perfection was reached, that commandment would no longer be necessary, because the super power of love would unite God and man eternally.

The problem was not so much the temptation of the angel. Or the power of love. The problem was the lack of faith of the man and woman in God. What made God's heart grieve, what made God very angry, was the faithlessness of Eve. One commandment came from God. The day you eat of it you shall die. Then Satan approached her saying, no, you will not die, that is the truth, the other is a lie. And the woman believed him. And Adam fell also.

NO TRUE LIFE

Therefore, Adam could not become a life-giving spirit. Adam and Eve and all their descendants did not have true life. Therefore, Jesus said we must be born again. God initially created the Tree of Life. Adam was supposed to become the Tree of Life. However, because of uniting with Satan, Adam became the tree of death. Jesus Christ came 2,000 years ago as the Tree of Life. So he said, I am the author of life and you must root yourself in me.

All we have to do is change our root of satanic origin to the root of God's origin. Jesus Christ represented that root, that tree.

We are all expected to become grafted into the Tree of Life so we can share the one true richness of life from the true source of God. This was what Christianity is all about. This is the mission of Jesus Christ. This is what salvation is all about: that we no longer belong to that false tree but belong to the root of life. However, I tell you that the time has come for the Second Coming of Christ. For what purpose is he coming? So far we have been born into the dead tree and we must be adopted into the new tree of life. But this is still not the end of it. We are eventually to be born into the Tree of Life. Then we will no longer need a savior. This is the purpose.

The Second Coming of Christ is coming. This is the hope of mankind, that we all can be born no longer in the dead tree through Satan but through the son of God, so we are able to give birth to sinless children. That person is born in the kingdom of heaven, automatically transferred into the kingdom of heaven. This was the original intention of God and this is going to be fulfilled by the Second Coming of Christ. This is the hope. Hope for Seattle. Hope for America. Hope for all mankind.

In 40 minutes I can only very briefly touch upon the truth of the Divine Principle revealed through the modern-day prophet Reverend Sun Myung Moon. I want you to know more. The opportunity is coming tomorrow and the day after tomorrow. At a beautiful site, this crusade is conducting a two-day seminar. All you have to do is come tomorrow morning by 10:00. A bus will be waiting outside the theater at 9:00 a.m. You will have a room, a meal, wonderful fellowship. Our young people will all be there, and we are going to have a grand time. This is probably one of the most critical investments of your life. You will not regret it.

Furthermore, this is a very unique opportunity. Tonight, in my final greeting to you, I want to say that Seattle has been very kind to the Celebration of Life. I heard so many wonderful comments and encouraging remarks every day. I thank you very much for coming in this enthusiastic fashion. Someday we will come back to Seattle. But until then we are going on to other cities: St. Paul tomorrow, next week Dallas, New Orleans, Miami, and Columbus, Ohio. We are going to cover 50 cities in 50 states. Our young people are going to attract thousands and thousands of people to God and Christ. I thank you for coming.

Comforting Father's Heart

MINNEAPOLIS, MINNESOTA

MAY 31, 1974

Dr. Pak gives spiritual guidance and inspiration to the members following the first night of the Celebration of Life tour in the Minnesota region. He reminds them that their unique purpose as Unification members is to comfort the grieving heart of God and challenges each person to strive daily for spiritual rebirth and perfection through practicing honesty, purity, and selfless dedication.

Last night, about 400 people attended the Celebration of Life, not including our members. Of this number, 41 people signed up for the workshop. This is about 10 percent of all those who attended. This is a remarkable figure. In America, many direct mail campaigns are conducted to get a certain response. Usually, only 1 percent of the people contacted respond positively. But here, the ratio is now 10 percent. That means that if we can get 1,000 people to attend the Celebration of Life in one night, then we can expect 100 people to sign up for the workshop.

This auditorium has a capacity of approximately 3,000 people. If we have a capacity audience, then we could have 300 people sign up for the workshop. This is not a dream. This is within the realm of possibility. This is a goal that can be reached.

In other words, I am saying that a new era has arrived for our movement. For the last 10 years we have been having difficulty to get 10 people, five people, or even one person, to come to a workshop. Now we can expect 100 people to come to our workshop. And once people come to a workshop, there is a good chance that as many as 50 percent will join and become solid members like you are.

This new era did not come about by chance or coincidence. In order to reach this great moment that is now dawning, so many brothers and sisters have gone ahead of us, shedding their tears and their blood and their sweat here in America.

But long before this work started in America, many members shed tears, sweat, and blood in other places—Korea, Japan, and so forth. And long before any Korean or Japanese brothers and sisters shed their tears and sweat, our True Parents were already shedding their tears, sweat, and blood for decades, when absolutely no one on the face of this earth understood their tribulation.

And we must realize that before the True Parents, our Heavenly Father has been working in tears, sweat, and blood for the last 6,000 years to make this day possible.

HOW ARE WE DIFFERENT?

What is it that makes our movement different? What is truly the focal point of our movement? Why are we all here? We are here to take over the burden of our Heavenly Father. We are here to comfort our Heavenly Father's grieving heart.

Humanity has never known our suffering God, until our True Parents came upon this earth and introduced us to the suffering heart of our Father. We are the first group upon the face of this earth who has even begun to glimpse this. Every day we understand more deeply the Father's suffering heart.

Our God has not been happy. Our Father has been crying tears, because he is the bereaved Father who lost His beloved children 6,000 years ago. He has been like any parent who has witnessed the tragic death of his child. That has been the Father's heart. And no man here on earth ever even glimpsed the grieving heart of our Father.

The Divine Principle introduces to us our Father's suffering heart and makes us commit ourselves to become God's soldiers, to relieve and liberate God's broken heart. We are the troops gathered here together to mend the broken heart of the Father. Therefore, we have not come for our own glory. We want to heal Father's heart first. Then the ills of mankind will be cured. This is the order of business.

Everybody in this world is trying to be happy every day. But there can be no happiness in this world until the Father's broken heart is mended. That comes first. Then the crises of this world will see hope and will begin to be solved in a most fundamental way.

This is what we are. We are here, chosen by God, as His liberation army, to liberate the suffering heart of the Father, so that we can truly bring the first joy to our Father. And we are also here to alleviate the suffering and anguish of Jesus Christ. All the Christian world thinks we are not taking Jesus Christ seriously. That is absolutely wrong. We are the only ones who are truly taking Jesus Christ seriously. We believe all that the Christian world has believed, that Jesus Christ is the son of God, the Savior, and the messiah—and more.

We are the first people upon the face of the earth who truly understand the suffering heart of Jesus Christ. For the first time, we understand why Jesus said, "My heart is very sorrowful, even to death," in the Garden of Gethsemane. The best interpretation that the Christian world could offer for this passage has been this: Even though Jesus came to die on the cross, he was also a human being, as well as God; he prayed in the garden this way because at that moment he was tempted by his human weakness to avoid his mission. But as I said the other night, Jesus taught all of his disciples, "Do not fear those who can kill your body but not your soul. Do not fear those who can kill only the flesh."

And Stephen, Peter, and Paul—the great Christians of the early Church—as well as many great men in the modern church, have certainly lived up to Jesus' commandment. Do you think that Jesus Christ would violate his own code, his own commandment?

DON'T INSULT JESUS

You know, Terry Walton, our workshop teacher, said in his lecture that it is the greatest insult to Jesus Christ to believe this of him. And we are the ones, the first ones who truly understand the anguish and suffering of Jesus Christ. Once we know and understand, we must make ourselves ready to liberate the suffering heart of Jesus Christ. So we are truly the ones who take Jesus Christ most seriously. We do believe everything that the Christian world believes, and more! Much more! This is where we are.

Last night, six people in that audience of 400 said that they would like to join the Unification Church movement!

When our Father spoke in Washington, D.C., John Dolan, the brother who is now our state representative from Iowa was there. The very next morning, he packed up his sleeping bag and knocked on the door of the Unification Church in Washington. And nobody in the Washington

Center took him seriously. We thought he had something wrong up here. I understand that our brothers and sisters there asked him, "Did you come to a workshop, or did you learn the Divine Principle?" John said, "What is the Divine Principle? All I heard was Reverend Sun Myung Moon." Then our members said, "Well, that's better than the Divine Principle. Come in!"

So you can see that there are many people out there like John, who are ready to respond to the first touch of the spirit of God. There were six people last night. In other words, a new era has come to us, in which people will join the movement first, then begin to learn the Divine Principle!

Last night, I had a report from Seattle, Washington, from the regional commander, Reverend Reiner Vincenz. He told us that he had very happy news. He said that every night since the Sun Myung Moon Christian Crusade brought the Celebration of Life to Seattle, 20 to 30 people were coming to the center to study the Principle. Many people are anxious to learn more, and many people want to move in. He almost has to say, "Wait. Learn more first!"

So we can see that something is happening. A spiritual baby boom is taking place. After World War II, America had a baby boom. The Sun Myung Moon Christian Crusade is like a heavenly whirlwind, bringing a spiritual World War II all around America. So after the victory of this spiritual World War II, a spiritual baby boom will follow. And here in the state of Minnesota, and throughout this five-state region, I hope and I know that you will have that spiritual baby boom after the Celebration of Life.

I am very glad that the state of Nebraska brought more than 25 people—a busload—from Omaha. All our members and prospective members came together. We welcome them, because this is the way this Crusade has to be conducted. Even though the Crusade comes to only one place in a particular region, all the states of that region must take advantage of it to bring in as many people as possible. This can be one week of wonderful spiritual experiences, having a great impact on people, bringing about conversions.

A NEW CONVERSION

In a way, we have to be born again every day. I've been a member of the Unification Church for 17 years. But I must make a new beginning every morning. I must try every day to become a better person. Rebirth must take place every morning. We must not stagnate. We have to make a new beginning, a new determination, until we reach our goal, the state of perfection, complete oneness with Heavenly Father. Until we reach that goal, we cannot relax. Therefore, each day is a new day. Each day is a new conversion.

For that matter, this Crusade is not only good for the people living in St. Paul. It is good for all of us. It's good for me, because by doing this each day, I am becoming a better person in the sight of God.

I would like to conclude by giving you three important words that we have to keep in our prayers and in our minds every day and every night.

The first is honesty. The entire mix-up of human history, brought by the fall of man, started with dishonesty. The Archangel Lucifer was a master liar. Jesus said, "You are of your father the devil. ... He was a murderer from the beginning, and has nothing to do with the truth, because there is no truth in him. ... He is a liar and the father of lies." [John 8:44] This was the motivation of the fall of man, where the mix-up of human history originated, in dishonesty. This brought the fall.

So in order to restore this world into the original world of truth, we must live up to honesty in an absolute degree. We must first of all be honest with ourselves. We must be absolutely honest with our Heavenly Father. In many cases, people are very foolish, trying to hide something from our Father which He already knows. We might make a mistake honestly. This is just beautiful in the sight of God, to tell Him everything. Let Him know a second time. God will smile at you.

This world in which we live is a dishonest world. There is no trust. Therefore, this world has to change. So Jesus said, when he first came, "Repent." What does it mean to repent? Repentance means getting it out, placing everything out on the table and showing God what we are. We must show God what naked persons we are. Show Him. This is repentance. The kingdom of heaven starts right there.

We must be honest with ourselves and honest with God. Then we must be honest with our brothers and sisters. When you are weak, tell your leader you are weak. When you are troubled, tell your leader you are spiritually troubled, that you need help. This is honesty.

When you do not repent, when you try to hide, you will find that this cannot work in the movement of truth. Be like a child. Why did Jesus say we must become like little children? Because children are the same inside and outside. That is beautiful in the sight of God.

Each day we have to take off the shackles of our hiding, so that each day we become more naked in the sight of God, so that one day we will truly become the same person inside and outside. This is honesty.

The second word is purity. Tonight, I'm going to preach on the subject of the fall of man. The fall of man, this chapter of the Divine Principle, is truly a formidable weapon, a great truth. It reveals how human history began in the wrong way, through the misuse of love. Love is supreme in this universe. Therefore, God made love supreme so that through love God's ideal of creation could be fulfilled. God intended this to be a world of love. However, Satan twisted this love from unselfish giving into selfish taking. He twisted love, making lawful love into illicit love. That was the fall of man. That was the beginning of the wrongdoings of all humanity.

So we ourselves are the children born in the Garden of Eden. All men must think, "I am Adam, 16 years old." All women must think, "I am Eve, 16 years old."

While we are fulfilling the work of God, it is our duty to keep our minds, spirits, and bodies in absolute purity. On the day that the realization of the truth of the Divine Principle comes to you, that is the day of your birth. Then you don't have to worry about your past. You don't have a past! Your past is mere dust. From that day on, we all are to do our absolute best to keep our mind, spirit, and body in absolute purity. We must be pure, so that we can truly give our first love to God, our first love to the True Parents.

This is our lifeline. Then God will certainly give us the Blessing, heavenly matrimony, so that we shall truly have the magnificent power of love in all its great value. Then we shall have joy and happiness in a heavenly way. This is the Divine Principle.

The third word is dedication. If I could add one more word, it would be selfless—selfless dedication.

What is perfection? The perfection that the Bible and Jesus Christ speak of, and the perfection spoken of in the Divine Principle, is not the type of perfection where we become supermen, like Astro Boy, flying from one place to another, from England to here. It does not mean having superpowers like being able to jump across canyons or bending steel railroad tracks. That is not the type of perfection God is speaking about.

PERFECTION IN SELFLESSNESS

Perfection is a state of mind. Perfect man will not be a couple of feet taller. No, you will not change. You will look just like you are. But perfection comes in a state of mind. Perfection comes in selflessness.

In other words, when you truly forget yourself, so that only our Heavenly Father and our True Parents dwell in you, that is perfection. When you look at the grass, you would not be seeing with your own eyes. Unconsciously, automatically, you would be seeing from the Father's point of view.

Look at the trees. Appreciate those trees, the breeze, the clean air, and the blue sky not from your standpoint, not being conscious of yourself. You are not there. Rather, see from Father's point of view. Glorify His name.

This is our Father's creation. All this beauty comes from the Creator's point of view. Our life is to appreciate the Creator's beauty, the Creator's love, day in and day out, 24 hours a day. When you really live every moment from the Father's point of view, when you live Father's life instead of your own, then we are partaking of the life of God. This is ultimate perfection.

Reread the Bible. Jesus never said, "I believe in my Father." Jesus said, "I am in the Father." He did not say, "I believe Heavenly Father sent me." Instead, he said, "Don't you know that I am in the Father, and the Father in me?"

In other words, to Jesus Christ God is not the subject of belief. As long as you believe something, there is always room for disbelief. As long as we believe in God, the communists can say, "We don't believe in God," and there is nothing you can do about it. God was not supposed to be the subject of belief. God was supposed to be a matter of fact. We say there is a moon. The communists say there is a moon. They don't say, "We believe there is a moon," and we don't say, "We believe there is a moon." The moon is a matter of undeniable fact. There can be no dispute about it. Even communists cannot deny the facts.

By the same token, God was supposed to be a matter of fact, with no room for dispute. That the situation could occur, that one person could say, "I believe in God," and another person could answer, "I don't believe in God," shows that this is the fallen world. God is not yet made real to us. When we read about Jesus Christ, we know that to him God was not a subject of belief. God was a fact. His presence was real. And to our True Parents, I can see every day that for them God is not the subject of belief. God is a matter of fact, present in their lives. The Father's heart is with them.

This is our job. This is our perfection, to make God a matter of fact in our lives, so that the presence of God is so real that it is undeniable. Then we will partake in the whole universe from the point of view of God, so that we shall truly become selfless people. We will be living as a part of God. It will not be Bo Hi Pak's life, not Hugh Spurgin's life. We will all be living one life, the life of God. We will feel it, and feel as Father feels. This is the goal of perfection.

And this will come when we obtain selflessness. When that state is reached, we are no longer ourselves. We have the universe within us. And this will manifest externally as dedication.

We do have dedication. Nobody here in America can dispute the dedication of our membership. But we still have a long way to go to reach perfection. Good deeds and dedicated work alone are not enough. We must have as our spiritual motivation the realization of a selfless heart.

That has to come first. Otherwise, no good deed will be truly good in the sight of God.

PRACTICE LOVE

Honesty, purity, selflessness or dedication—when we combine all these things together, this becomes love. If we practice honesty, purity, and self-lessness, we are practicing love. We are becoming the fruit of love. We are becoming the culmination of the seed of love. Then we can disseminate the love of God all over the world.

This is my conclusion after learning the Divine Principle. One way or another, all of us who learn the Divine Principle will come to this conclusion. There is a tireless effort we must make to attain this perfection.

The human spirit has been stained and rusting for 6,000 years. Every day we must polish it up into its original shininess. And this 6,000-year stain cannot be taken off in one day or one year, or a few years. It's a life-time job. But it is a joyful thing to do.

So here we are this morning. Sometimes we get so busy and caught up with our outside tasks and responsibilities that we forget where we are. We must restore peace in the depths of our hearts. You must have a burning coal inside your heart. That is your engine. Your spiritual engine must be burning every day. This is your energy, your source of power.

This morning we have this chunk of spiritual food. Now let's go enjoy this good food for our bodies.

CHRIST IS HERE

CELEBRATION OF LIFE WORKSHOP

NEW ORLEANS, LOUISIANA

JUNE 16, 1974

Dr. Pak speaks to workshop participants following a Celebration of Life Crusade in New Orleans and divulges the good news that they are actually living at the time of the Second Coming. He speaks directly to the members, too, and entreats them not to lose faith in the face of adversity, to separate from Satan, and to commit themselves to studying the Divine Principle in order to nurture their spiritual growth.

In the next few moments I really want to make myself clear. I hope I can overcome my limitation in language. I need your eyes. I must be able to look at you. Stare at me. Even if you're staring at me so strongly it punches a hole in my face, I don't mind. Please stare at me and really penetrate my mind. With such a force you can make two holes in my face.

In the next few moments, I would like to be absolutely honest and blunt because, in a way, truth is very simple. Joe Tully concluded and Josette supported and all of our brothers and sisters already knew what proclamation we heard this afternoon: Christ is here on earth as a man among us, dwelling among ourselves. For 2,000 years, millions and millions of Christians have been waiting for that one day, to hear the declaration of the coming of the Lord, and they didn't see it. They gave their entire life, their sweat and blood, to serve Christ, and they hoped they would see the Christ in their lifetime. Even though they died in good faith and are in Paradise, they couldn't see that ultimate day.

We are going to celebrate Jesus Christ's birth on December 25. Human history is counted from the birth of Christ. Even the communists count that way. The son of God who truly changed the mode of history and brought a greater impact than any human being has ever done before, Jesus Christ, is returning to this world in your lifetime. Today, he is with us.

This is an unbelievable story, the kind of news that shocks people so much they might have a heart attack, but we are not shocked this afternoon. Why? The reason is very simple. The significance and size of the news is beyond the grasp of our imagination, beyond the comfortable human mind. Therefore, this news is the greatest shock, probably, in human history. But I promise you that a spiritual electric shock will come to you step by step as you open up your mind. The scope of your mind becomes wider and wider every day. I have been following the Reverend Sun Myung Moon for 17 years. I am still every day making an effort to make my mind more open, wider and wider, and trying to have my perception get greater so that someday God can really find His reflection in me.

Yes, you have heard the greatest news that the gospels can tell, the greatest news you can expect. The conclusion of the New Testament is focused on the coming of the Lord one day. According to the last chapters of Revelation, Jesus said, surely I am coming soon. The Apostle John responded by saying, Lord Jesus, please come. The fulfillment is here—the son of God who came to fulfill the mission described by the lecture. His name was Jesus 2,000 years ago. His name today is Sun Myung Moon. I hope I am shocking somebody. If you really know the scope of this declaration, I expect that someone, someday, will stand up and walk in front of me and slap my face. I know I will get it someday. I am going to declare this regardless, unto my death, because death is no longer meaningful to me. We are talking about the death of this physical body, but God does not see physical life as the true life.

God does not see your physical life as life. God only sees the eternal life, the spiritual life, as real. That is the only life in the sight of God. Jesus said, do not fear those who can destroy your body and who cannot do anything with your spirit, but fear God who can destroy your body and your spirit. I know many people in this world can destroy my body. One bullet is enough. But I know nobody can destroy my eternal life because I am part of the body of Christ.

This is what the Unification Church is all about. When you came to the Celebration of Life, actually you came to the most important, the most serious, moment of your life. Life or death hinges upon this meeting. This is why I said there are many great things happening to make headlines in Louisiana, but in the sight of God this is the greatest happening in the South, in the state of Louisiana, because here we make the proclamation of the son of God who came to restore the entire world as God originally intended in the Garden of Eden. You cannot deny you heard this. From this time on, it is up to you.

SPIRITUAL PYRAMID

Individually you are here, but I want you to know you are part of a spiritual pyramid, and you are the pinnacle. Let me explain. Behind you thousands and thousands of people are lined up—your entire family tree, probably hundreds of thousands of people making up the pyramid. They put you on the pinnacle. You came to listen to the Celebration workshop. Do you think you came by your will alone? No, not at all. I want you to know you are the product of history, the cream of history. Behind you there is an invisible power, a mixture of spiritual power, the power of goodness and of evil. It makes either fortune or disaster, because the day of the Lord is not only great, as the Bible said, it is also a terrible, terrible day. The Lord is coming to judge and you can be separated. One is taken up and one is left behind.

Undoubtedly the same situation will happen in this group. Therefore, it is truly a serious moment. Whether you really consider this as truth or not, it will bring serious consequences not only for your own life but for the thousands of people who were working to push you here for this occasion. You heard the Divine Principle, and many of you probably thought this is a very provoking concept with new ideas and it's very interesting. But I must tell you, the Divine Principle you heard yesterday and today is the word of Christ. If you really learn the depths of the Divine Principle, you will come to the conclusion I came to a long time ago after the first lecture I heard.

I have confirmed that conclusion many thousands of times after that. No one, no human being, can bring such truth except Christ. What the Divine Principle is all about is the Principle of Creation. This is the first time God is letting us see His original blueprint of creation, particularly the purpose of creation, which gives us a reason to live. Then the Divine Principle gives another picture: the Fall of Man. The Fall of Man is a very, very important chapter. No clever brain put together such a theory. Not at all. This Principle was fought for and gained by the living Christ, literally bought by his sweat, tears, and blood. Every word in the Fall of Man was the result of his fierce battle against Satan. The result of his victory over Satan is that the Principle is given to us freely.

You think that is cheap. Not at all. For the first time in history the true identity of Satan is uncovered. We are now able to prosecute Satan in the sight of God, which humanity has never done before. We humans didn't even know we are to judge angels. We did not believe that we are greater than angels because we had come down so low. We have been in a very menial position and have almost worshiped angels. That is what Abraham did when the angel came in. Everybody jumped. We think angels are next to God.

That is the way we thought in the fallen world, but the angelic world is to be the servant to man. We are the princes and princesses of God, and the fall of the angel and misuse of illicit love brought a tragedy that twisted God's lineage into satanic lineage, that murdered God's son and daughter and gave them another, sinful birth. This is what the Fall of Man is all about. We have been living with that wrong, sinful root ever since. The Tree of Life could never become a reality.

Reverend Moon confronted Satan. God did not help him win the battle. Do you know why? Because the messiah is man's champion. God wanted a man to defeat Satan. This man of God, Sun Myung Moon, did it and prosecuted Satan in the sight of God. He uncovered Satan's true identity. The battle in the spiritual world has already been won. In other words, Satan was already prosecuted there.

Satan is known as a snake. In one moment in 1960, Satan's head was crushed by a rock, and the rock is Christ. Christ really burst and crushed Satan's entire sovereignty. But the serpent is a slow-dying animal. Even though its head is crushed, the body wiggles and jumps and hits this and that. That is why we have the kind of world we do. This is the job we are to finish. The main battle is won. A decisive victory has been won for us. The victory is already ours. We are going to gather the crops and join the battle, deliberately sticking that body a little bit so that we participate in the victory over satanic power.

There is a lot of satanic effort in this world. But I want you to know that because of this truth, the Divine Principle, and because of the coming of Christ, Satan has been crushed. Satan is destined to die, but the slow-dying animal in its final desperation is trying to do lots of damage, trying to prolong its sovereignty here on earth. The heavenly world is already decided.

I preached only two nights here, but the first night in the Celebration of Life I usually preach about why Jesus came.

SHAKE THE CHRISTIAN FOUNDATION

When you think about it, this is a revolutionary message. Martin Luther put up his 95 theses on the door of the university, but that is peanuts compared to what Reverend Moon is saying: Jesus did not come to die. The 2,000-year-old Christian foundation is being completely shaken by what Christ is saying. Jesus did not have to shed his blood; he came down to this earth already having the power to forgive sin. He is like the heavenly Ajax. He can clean up everything. All people had to do was accept him and become one with him.

Jesus gave us so much forgiveness, raising up the dead, giving sight, cleansing lepers, making the lame walk. He did not say, I will give you a medical treatment. Jesus raised them up by the word, by saying I forgive your sins. When the sin is forgiven, the lame walk and lepers are cleansed. The Jewish people didn't have to kill him. All they had to do was accept him, then the entire nation of Israel would have been forgiven and cleansed. They would have been engrafted into the Tree of Life and become like another Christ. That was the purpose, that was the procedure, that was the process he gave.

It sounds easy when we hear it, but think of the magnitude of the declaration. Who else can say such a thing except the Christ, except the Lord of the Second Advent? Today, the Christian world is waiting for all dead bodies to rise and come out of their tombs and start to walk around. In many cases that is the resurrection that they believe in, or they conclude they don't really know what resurrection is all about. Well, Jesus said, if you believe in me you shall never die. But good Christians have been dying for 2,000 years. What are we to believe?

Christians really do not know, but Reverend Moon brought a true definition of death and a true method of resurrection.

You know, when you are given spiritual eyes, then you don't see these clothes, these eyeglasses, or hair color. You see the true you, your spirit body, your spirit man. That is what you will see when you are given spiritual sight. If you have spiritual sight now, tonight, look around the city of New Orleans and you will see the most incredible sight. First, you will actually see dead persons. They may be known as millionaires, or important government officials, or as tremendous speakers or scholars, but you may find that their spiritual part is pitch dark, that their bodies are completely distorted.

Those who suffer the heavy burden of leprosy have distorted hands and faces. It is unbearable to see. But compared to dead spirits, leprosy is nothing, absolutely nothing. You will see horrible things in the human body beneath this flesh, beneath the beautiful neckties and suits they are wearing. You will see the shape of the formation stage spirit man, but it is something like a plastic bottle with nothing in it. It doesn't make sense. It is there, you can feel it, but there is no substance in it—only the shape is there.

Then you will see another type that is beautiful. We call it a life spirit. The spirit body never ages; you stop at your prime so even if you live to be a hundred years old and have white hair, when you die you go back to your prime, even if that is 22. You are young and giving off a dazzling light. This is the life of a person who is good in Christ. This has been the goal of Christians for 2,000 years: to go to Paradise, the place where Christ is. This beautiful, loving spirit is in part tremendous love and energy and mercy, but still it gives out light reflectively. It is shining not as a radiant being but as a moon receiving light and reflecting it. This is what you see. This is truly a magnificent spirit, yet not the ultimate one.

There is one higher step: the divine spirit. The only one in history who achieved the divine spirit status in the spirit world is Jesus Christ. Jesus is like a sun. In the spirit world there is no sun coming up in the east and going down in the west. The sun is always there. The love of God shines through Jesus Christ, who is a radiant, life-giving spirit giving out a dazzling light. When Jesus appeared on the Mount of Transfiguration and met with Moses and Elijah, the three disciples saw beautiful shining light and the white gown of Jesus. At that particular moment, God gave the disciples the power to open their spiritual eyes to see the spiritual truth. What they saw in Jesus was his divine spirit shining.

Before Abraham, everybody lived in the pitch dark. In the Old Testament era, by the law of Moses we can develop up to the form spirit level, and in the New Testament era, which is the Christian era, we can become life spirits. If Jesus Christ had not been crucified, he would have pioneered the final, divine-spirit level, so that all men could be like him.

God's ultimate will is to raise us to divine spirits. We are entitled to be divine spirits like Jesus. However, because of the crucifixion, no pioneering was done. It is a wilderness. Upon the foundation of Jesus, the Lord of the Second Advent pioneered the final level and opened up this path so that all men can now follow and through becoming one with him and loving him become divine. This is your opportunity. The Lord of the Second Advent and the first heavenly family are not only the ones who opened the kingdom of heaven on earth, but they are the ones who for the first time opened the kingdom of heaven in heaven. Do you know that even Jesus Christ for the first time shall enter into the kingdom of heaven along with the Lord of the Second Advent? So far, the highest we could go was paradise.

Then why, even though the life spirit stage is available to you and this is the real form you are going to live in for eternity, are people still in pitch darkness? Because even though this is available, if you don't have faith in it, it has nothing to do with you.

GET ON GOD'S HIGHWAY

In the early days, to get from the East Coast of America to San Francisco, there was no path. Someone had to pioneer the way. Today you have super-highways, but unless you drive the car, a superhighway has nothing to do with you. Isn't that true? You will never get to San Francisco unless you actually drive there. By the same token, the path has been opened up to the life spirit stage in Christianity, but unless you have faith in Jesus nobody can go up there. This is why 95 percent of the world's population lives in pitch-dark death.

Do you know this reality? Ninety-five percent of the world's population is dying and staying in death. This is the world God is looking down upon—the world of death. How can He not grieve in His heart? Probably only about 2 or 3 percent of the world's people can reach the life spirit level. However, the time has come that, upon the foundation of Christianity, the Lord of the Second Advent is pioneering the way to perfection. The kingdom will come, and that kingdom must be established as quickly as possible.

The entire spirit world will be pushed into that kingdom, and all mankind will be saved sooner and quicker. This is your opportunity. At the time of Jesus, many faithful Jews opposed him and called him a heretic and blasphemer. I am sorry, but no matter how good they were according to Mosaic law, they pulled against the author of life. In other words, even though they had a limited light, they waged a war against a greater power coming from God. Then this little bit of light was crushed by the greater power of electricity. What happened? It burnt them up. In other words, when you push big power into a little circuit, the little circuit breaks.

Spiritually, that same process occurs, and therefore it burnt them up. The worst thing that we can think of is to misunderstand the coming of the Lord and do cruel acts and work against him. At the time of Jesus that happened, because even though they were living and dwelling in the form spirit area, they went right down to death.

The Lord is coming. Perfection is available. This perfection can come, however, only when you accept the Lord. This is truly the greatest gospel that can come to you. It is like somebody writing you a check for $10 billion. What would you think? You won't even say thank you because it is impossible. You will be laughing. Ten billion dollars? I can't believe it. Even a $1 billion check you wouldn't believe is real. The news you heard here cannot be compared to a billion dollars or a trillion dollars. Oh, I wish we could have a gift, that just for one minute God would take us all over there for a guided tour of heaven. Just one minute would be enough, but actually I don't want that, because then we would have nothing to be proud of. What God wants is our faith. Accept the truth and accept it in faith. This will become a lifetime asset for your eternal life. This is the one thing we can be proud of in the sight of the Father. Nothing else.

It is a powerful world out there. There are 120 nations and many presidents and queens and kings and colleges and universities. It is really a formidable world out there. The Unification Church contains really crazy people. This small group of crazy people is gathered together and saying, we are going to die for one man. When I die, I am going to die for this man. And my joy abounds.

Actually, my motto is this. I quote one Bible verse as my credo in my daily life. Jesus said, he who seeks to find his life will lose it and he who loses his life for my sake will find it. This is my credo. Jesus Christ died on the cross. For our kingdom of the Lord of Second Advent we need to sacrifice, too. Not necessarily be nailed down on the cross, but make a daily, living sacrifice. What the Unification Church is really living is a prolonged crucifixion. You carry a little bit of the cross every day. This is what we are doing. What we are really doing is a dying process. I am giving up this body for the purpose of Christ. What I am saying is, Christ is coming. Use me as you wish. Send me anywhere. Order me to do anything you want me to do.

DYING AND LIVING

I want to have a celebration sometime of those who have really faced persecution. We, the members of the Celebration of Life crusade, would like to prove our faith and lay down a new chapter in history. We have something to write about. Historians will find this a very difficult thing to write about because we have been taking it too easy. I am not seeking an easy way out. I would rather make this body go through a slow process of dying so my true spiritual life will be a resurrection. Every day is a dying process. My real body's living process is going up another step, another step. That is the body you are going to have for eternity, so why don't you invest your flesh for a good purpose? In return, what you get is an eternal, perfected divine spirit. This is like what Jesus said: What does it matter if you gain the entire world but forfeit your own life? Jesus wasn't talking about this earthly life but about divine spirits and life spirits.

Our Master is driving Unification Church members to go out and sell flowers, to fast, to witness to one person a month. It sounds very cruel, but if your body has the strength and courage to bear this cruel order you are blessed. Christ knows where he's leading us. This is what Jesus said 2,000 years ago. Truth remains the same. He who loses his life for my sake will find a glorious life. Many Christians in the past were martyred in glory, becoming the prey of lions. They didn't fear death because they trusted the Lord.

Unification Church members are 10 times stronger in their commitment to Christianity because we have the living Lord with us. That is the power that lets me speak today and every day. If you have this commitment, miracles will happen. The sky is the limit on what you can do if you really want to commit your life for the cause of God. What you will get is a limitless source of energy that will flow into you. You will become a channel of God. You can really change. You can do greater work than even Christ. Jesus said everyone going out in his name can do not only what he can do but can do even greater things than him. Didn't he say that? Why? Because he was a pioneer, but we can go much faster. Past pioneers could go west at only five miles per hour in a wagon. Today you can drive 60 miles per hour. Even an antichrist can go 50 miles per hour. We can even fly in a Boeing 747. We can do much greater things than his disciples did at the time of Jesus. Why? Because we have the advantage of the age.

All of heaven is focused upon you. I want you to know that. Spirit world is the world of subject. This world is the object. You don't have to win the battle in spirit world; it is already won. The entire spirit world is already on our side. So even though it looks very small, a little rock can always burst and crush Satan. By that little rock hitting a big idol, that idol is crushed to death. What is the process that we are engaged in here? This rock will grow inevitably, whether you like it or hate it. You may want to oppose it or persecute it, but even if all the Unification Church members in Louisiana are killed, it doesn't matter. We will still grow, because the subjective decision is made already. Nothing can stop us because spirit world is already on our side. Spirit world is the subject. We will grow and grow and eventually cover the entire earth.

My ambition in my lifetime is to serve and attend the True Parents as much as I can and contribute to the restoration of the world as much as I can. That is my only concern. It is only a matter of time. We can do it in 10 years, we can do it in 100 years. It depends on us. America can be restored in 10 years or 100 years, depending on you and me. God always leaves room for man to do his part. This is the whole scheme and secret. God eventually wants to give man the credit, so He leaves room for you to get the credit.

The small Unification Church group looks miserable in a way, so small that people laugh at it. But you will see that this is the group that really changes the direction of history, that changes America and the world. Then why are you and I here? Your ancestors worked, but more than that,

God chose the foolish to shame the wise. God chose the weak to shame the strong, because this is the way God will be glorified more. No one has a Ph.D. No one is a college professor, no one is a governor or a senator, congressman, or professor, but I envy you.

In your unstained youth you can give your first devotion to God. How wonderful! This is the pride you can have. Let me conclude now. For those new members, soon we are going to hand out papers. I want you to sign to become a member of this great crusade. If I said anything else, I would be dishonest. I want you to join because this is a blessing and part of the best luck I can recommend.

Many people may think, well, I only heard two days; I'm not sure, I'll look into it and study it more. You know what I did? I heard the workshop in two days like you. In cold Korea in the wintertime we ate only two meals a day. I heard all of the Principle, and the very next day I not only joined but I wanted to go to the main church and speak with Sun Myung Moon. Do you think I knew everything about the Principle? No. But I knew the magnitude of what I had heard, that indeed nobody else could have brought it except the Christ. Furthermore, I knew that in order to not accept the truth I would have to come up with a better truth. I would have to argue why this or that is wrong, why this or that is not true. I had no hope of winning this battle of truth, so as the good American saying goes, if you can't win, join them. That is precisely what it is all about.

GOD WILL TELL YOU THE TRUTH

I felt I really needed to study this, and the best way to find out the truth is to join. I trusted that God would let me know whether this was truth or not. No lie can be hidden for eternity. No matter how well planned a lie is, you know a lie when you hear one. Isn't that true? Watergate, for example. They worked everything out so beautifully, but one by one it came apart. No matter how misunderstood, truth always wins. This is the wonderful power of God. Truth always stands out eventually. So, how can you tell whether this is truth or not? Join and find out; that is the best way. I am very honest and frank. Many people may say, well maybe that is the antichrist. Or, I belong to Jesus Christ so maybe I cannot go to such a group. I have heard many things like that.

The Bible says, watch out for antichrists. It says, people will say to you, I am the Christ. In other words, today many people will make their decision whether to commit their life based on hearsay. If you are really serious about your life, what you need is firsthand information. The best way to find out if this is the antichrist or not is to join and find out. How could I be more honest than that?

Furthermore, another reason this is the only way God can fulfill his dispensation is that the antichrist today is communism. The snake that has been crushed is wiggling its whole body, trying to do as much damage as possible. Now it is working through communism, which denies God. Since the snake can no longer have this kingdom, it wants to spoil it. This is Satan's scheme. That is the evil mind: If I cannot have good things, I don't want to let anybody else have them. Satan knows he cannot have this kingdom. Even though he possesses sovereignty in the kingdom of hell, it will not be prolonged. So Satan is saying, I don't want even God to have it. I don't want God's children to have it. The true antichrist is saying no such thing as God exists.

This movement is not going up against the Presbyterian or Lutheran Churches or the Catholic Church. They are not even in our sight. Christ does not even worry about them. What Christ is really worrying about is how we can deter communism's power and truly bring the entire world into the Kingdom of Heaven. This is the only ideology that can win over communism. Since they are saying there is no God, only a positive, "yes, there is God" movement can win over communism. Many Catholic countries in South America are overrun by communism, which shows that the church has no power any more. It cannot stop communism. But we already have enough proof that the Unification Church can stop communism and even wipe it out with the help of the spirit world.

Our Leader said many times that once we create a certain foundation, then spirit world will convert many hard-core communists. Sometimes hard-core communists in Korea became the best Unification Church members. They believed in communism only because there was no good alternative. They had not been given a chance, but they are really hot people. Jesus said be either hot or cold. God abhors lukewarm people.

In America today, what I am worried about is that this country is becoming very lukewarm. American people don't care if things are either good or bad; they just don't want to be a part of it. It comes from a very selfish psychology: I don't want to be hurt, I don't want to be benefitted, and I don't want to be touched. I want to have my shell around me so no one can come in and touch me. This is the American mentality. I would rather have a positive response or negative demonstration. I really do like both of them. There's more chance for the honest truth to be professed, because the truth is going into their heart. They can become strong members.

The communist world is truly the antichrist of the 20th century, because it is trying to throw God out the window. Who is going to stop it? Tell me. The Lutheran Church or the Catholic Church? What I am asking is if Christianity in general has the power to stop communism though it has been here for 2,000 years. No. What can stop communism is this ideology centered upon the Lord of the Second Advent, knowing eternal life is so sure, knowing the Kingdom of God is upon the face of the earth, knowing we belong to this most wonderful center of the universe. I have True Parents; now I no longer have to be starved in sin and loss. This man sees communism as the enemy of God. It is my pleasure to fight and win over communism for Father. No motivation will become stronger than to do something for Father. We are fighting communism for Father. I want to do things for the glory of Father. Communists are saying your Heavenly Father is dead, is not there. I cannot tolerate that.

So all you new guests, you are no longer guests; you are members of the family and brothers and sisters. Join, every one of you, and find out. If it is not true, let me know. I will join you. You will lose nothing except the chains and bondage of sin.

DON'T LET SATAN CRAWL IN

Now I have a word for the members, our brothers and sisters. First, don't become a John the Baptist of failure. When you joined the movement, you had initial excitement, but soon this dissipates and you will see many grim realities. That is when Satan crawls in and tries to drag you out. One in 12 is going to be a bad apple. Jesus showed that example. One of the 12 disciples was a bad apple, Judas Iscariot. This will happen. I don't want you to become one of those rotten apples.

John the Baptist 2,000 years ago testified to Jesus at the Jordan River as a man of God who bears the sins of the world. John knew who Jesus was, but he never committed his life to Christ. This poor man finally asked the Lord, are you truly the one who is to come or shall we wait for somebody else? What insulting words those are. John the Baptist was beheaded not in martyrdom for Christ but for a silly love scandal of King Herod.

You like the Principle, but on the other hand so many worldly things come in. How could it be true? Why should this be this way? Why is that man so imperfect? Why is my leader giving me such a hard time? Why is that sister so ugly? Why is that man so tall and that man so fat? All kinds of things come into your mind. Become a single-minded person. I think brother Terry or Gilbert said, be bold, take an adventure. Be single-minded. That is what you need once you know this is the truth. Accept blindly at that point. In our movement we must demonstrate blind faith in Christ. That was what Ham needed when the naked body of his father was lying before him in the tent. It is natural in the common sense to be shameful of a father who is drunk and lying naked, but God wanted Ham to look at the naked body of his father and take it in blind faith. After all, Noah was the one God worked through for 120 years, the one God put His hope in while He demolished the rest of the world. That is my father. Whatever he does, he is right. That is the condition of faith that God was seeking in Ham, and he failed.

One time or another, members of the Unification Church will have that test. You will say, whatever the Lord of the Second Advent, the True Parents, desire me to do I will do. After all, he brought this message. He is changing this world, and my mind is bubbling in joy.

LOVE WITHOUT LIMITS

The second point for our members is that we have been talking for the last two days about love, love, love. What is love? Loving brothers and loving sisters, loving Father, loving God. What is love? I will give you one clue. Love is indescribable. There is no limit to your loving God and loving Christ, but I know where to start. Love must start from absolute honesty. You think you love your wife, but you have something dishonest to hide from her. I don't want to tell her something. Then do I really love her? Love starts from honesty. We must be honest with God, honest with Christ, and honest with ourselves. In many cases we don't know who we are and then lots of doubt and lots of weakness come in. You may try to put up a false front and not let other people see it. But God already knows you. Jesus said repent. Repentance is nothing but exposing your honest state to God.

Expose yourself to God. Tell God, Father, I am in this shape. God already knows all. God can say, my poor child, don't worry. I will give you strength. That is what God will say. That is everyday life. Every day is a new start. Every day we turn to God our Father. You know, I wanted to do this, but it didn't come out too well. I am in this shape. I need your help. Be honest with God, because God already knows no matter how much you are trying to hide. Expose yourself to God; then your heart is emptied out. Your burden is lessened. Christ knows what you are all about. Be honest with yourself and with your brothers and sisters. It will prevent many, many catastrophic situations if you start with honesty.

Fallen man started from dishonesty. Liar, liar, father of lies, that was Satan. He was the father of lies. That is what the fall of man is all about. So to restore the kingdom of God we must start from honesty. Second, we must preserve purity. Give your first love to God and Christ, nobody else. Preserve your purity. The fall of man was unnatural love, immorality. We are the ones to straighten things out. So I want you to be pure like snow, pure like clouds in heaven. Preserve yourself. Do not be tempted. The most important advice I can give is do not expose yourself to temptation. Dress humbly and decently; do not expose your bodies too much. Do not give others temptation. I want you to be pure in the sight of God so that God will give you a divine marriage with your eternal mate. Then the sky is the limit. Infinite joy and love will be yours. For all of eternity you are going to have love and joy.

We must keep the same commandment that God gave to Adam and Eve. Do not misuse love. We must protect our love and redirect our love to God and Christ. You know through the Principle that love is so powerful that unless you have absolute faith in this commandment you will lose the war. Many good Divine Principle members lose the war because of their weaknesses. They cannot combat the temptation of love. Divine Principle of God plus faith is stronger, true? Then every day bear the cross willingly; let us become examples of selfless devotion.

One day you will think entirely from God's viewpoint, from the viewpoint of True Parents. When I first learned English, I asked people how to learn English very well and quickly. You know what advice I got? Don't think in Korean and translate into English. You will speak one step too late. Think in English instead. But still I had great difficulty. I cannot think many jokes in English. But I am trying. I am thinking in English, and when I go back to Korea I am told I speak Korean like an American.

TRUE PARENTS' EYES

In our way of life, you must think like True Parents, look at everything from that angle. Look at a tree not with your own eyes but think that True Parents' eyes are behind your eyes and True Parents are looking at this tree from your position. If you perfect that, you are nearly at perfection. This is what perfection is all about. I lived and slept and ate and dined so many times with Sun Myung Moon. Every time during these 17 years, he struck my heart. I shake my head and think, indeed, this man is the son of God. Every time I end up saying in my heart, indeed, this man is the son of God. I can see so vividly he is thinking of God, nothing but God. Nothing else exists. If there is someone to whom he gives a hard time, I know where the anger comes from. When he is mad, he is so fierce you really taste hell in that moment.

But I have a secret how to overcome when he yells at me and really gives me a hard time. I become a little child. I hold on to his hand, smile, and say a very nice thing about Father. One time I said, your scolding is very tasty to me, thank you very much. Even Father had to smile. All you have to do when Father scolds you is love him. Show your love. Be closer to him. It's a wonderful occasion to become closer to the True Parents.

You know, Jesus Christ prayed, my God, my God, why hast thou forsaken me. In that moment God was really scolding Jesus in a way. God was saying, I don't know you. But our Father, Reverend Moon, told us the unspoken words in Jesus' heart: Father, under any circumstances I will not betray you. I will hold on to the heart of the Father. That is how Jesus died on the cross. That was his way of showing his ultimate loyalty. Many things are discouraging to you. Many things make you miserable and you taste hell. God wants you to taste everything through which your faith will be hardened. In those circumstances, I want you to know the secret to get closer to Father. The other day I said, since man betrayed God, since man kicked God out and united with Satan, God in retribution must kick man and man must not say, why did you kick me. He must not say, I don't like you, and run away from God. God has a right to kick man and betray man. Man should turn around and say, you have every right to kick me, every right to betray me, but I cannot betray you. This is restoration, right?

Sometimes you will feel so lonely that God is no longer with you. Everything seems confused. The Divine Principle seems confusing, leaders have been giving me a hard time, even Christ didn't come to me. I want you to know God is kicking you at that moment. Then if you really know the Principle, you say, hmm, I know the secret that the Principle taught me. Since we kicked God, God has the right to kick me. This is the time. I will not fail this one. Father, I will outwit you. Then turn around and show your loyalty and love.

This is sort of the conclusion for this workshop. I really enjoyed it. I heightened my spiritual state in this enrichment for two days. The Divine Principle is not just knowledge; it is food you need every day.

We need the Principle and truth every day. When I was listening to the lectures, I was deepening my understanding of the Principle even though I had heard it thousands of times. The next four days of the workshop are being planned. I want you to have a wonderful time. In the meantime, I want you to get on the bandwagon. Get into action. Do not be indecisive. As a military officer in battle I learned one great thing: No decision is worse than a bad decision. The worst commander may be trembling: I don't know what to do. Oh, oh, shall I commit this platoon or not? An indecisive commander kills everybody. Even if we make a wrong decision but a decisive one, the situation gets better. Indecision is worse than a bad decision. Of course, here you are not going to make a bad decision. What I am trying to say is that there is a time to play, a time to rest, a time to eat, a time to enjoy, a time to goof off. There is a time for everything, but there is also a time for making a decision. If you don't make a decision now and go away, next time it will be doubly difficult to commit yourself.

Remember Abraham, who was first asked to offer animals, but the next time he had to offer his son. Satan is trying to bluff you, because Satan already knows you are closer to the Divine Principle. Satan will do everything in his power to block you, so the best way to separate yourself is just to commit yourself in the sight of God and demonstrate to Satan that you no longer are afraid and no longer affected by satanic influence. He will go to somebody else, because he doesn't want to waste his energy on you if he sees he cannot separate you from the Kingdom of God. That is the best way you can separate yourself from Satan. Make a commitment. An opportunity may never come your way again. This is your opportunity.

You don't have to meet Reverend Sun Myung Moon now. If you meet him, nothing will change your decision except truth, and you learned the truth. You will just know him better. Studying the truth deeper and deeper is the only way you can get closer. Even if you live right in the same house, do you think that makes you closer to Christ? Not at all. Only knowing the truth. Yesterday and today I felt so much closer to True Parents. When I am listening to the truth, I feel so close to True Parents. You may be many thousands of miles away, but you can be so close. So when you feel weak and low, go to a workshop and study and read the Divine Principle. That is the best remedy and the best medicine to grow. Thank you very, very much. It is a special privilege to be here. Thank you! God bless you! Thank you very much!

WE ARE MAKING NEW HISTORY

PRINTED IN *THE WAY OF THE WORLD*

JAPAN 1974

━━━━━━━━━━━━━━━━━━━━━━

Dr. Bo Hi Pak speaks to the members of the Global IOWC in Japan. He reminds them that their work has no historical precedent, and that they are the champions of God and the arms and legs of the Messiah. He entreats them to give their best as they speak to the Japanese people, and to be willing to suffer in order to bring victory.

What the Global International One World Crusade (IOWC) is doing in Japan has no historical precedent. What we are doing here is making history that has never existed before. So I want to speak to you this morning on the topic "We Are Making New History." As you know, according to the Divine Principle, history started from the very beginning on the wrong track, going in the wrong direction. God wanted to build His kingdom and His ideal through the first man and woman. However, that first man and woman betrayed God. Since then, all human history has been in rebellion. God cannot approve of it.

Therefore, God's will has been for restoration, to turn man's wrong history into the right history. But, as you know, God is spirit. He does not have a body. He does not have arms. He does not have legs. He does not have a mouth to be able to communicate directly with human beings.

So God needs somebody to do His job. And that somebody is the messiah. The messiah is God's arms. Jesus came as the messiah 2,000 years ago. However, the people did not recognize the son of God. They betrayed the son of God, just as Adam and Eve had betrayed God. Therefore, God's body, the Christ, could not fulfill the mission of building God's kingdom on earth and fulfilling His ideal 2,000 years ago.

Since that time, God has been working to create another opportunity. And you and I know that opportunity is at hand. This world is falling into despair, because God must bring to an end the history of this wrong world. In order to destroy the old history of evil and create a new history, He must bring about the end of the world. We are here to be the champions of God. By himself, the Messiah cannot fulfill the entire will of God for this world. He is like a brain that needs the many cells and different organs of the body.

SPEAK FOR GOD

So when you go out in Tokyo and speak to the people, you are speaking for God. I want you to know that never before in the history of Tokyo have God's people declared the kingdom. Therefore, we are making history. We have no one from whom we can learn what to do. We must create the path. What is our most important responsibility, then? The most important mission for all of us here is to set the right tradition.

What was wrong with Adam and Eve? They distrusted God. They listened instead to the lies of Satan. Truth departed from them. That was the wrong tradition. So the first tradition we must set is to return to truth. We must trust God. How must we trust God? Jesus said we must love the Lord our God with all our heart, all our mind, and all our soul.

Suppose you have a lover. If you gave your love with all your heart, all your mind, and all your soul, what would you have left after that? There would be nothing left over. So we must set the tradition to give our entire selves—heart, mind, and soul—to God. There is another way of expressing this. If you love a person with all your heart and mind and soul, then you are literally crazy about him. That is what makes it good or bad. If you are crazy about drugs or crazy about material things, the result is bad. But when we are crazy about God, crazy about Christ, this is the life to live!

There are 23 different nationalities represented at this gathering. I speak English, and he speaks Japanese. However, some people may not understand either of these languages. I am sure you all are experiencing how difficult it is without a language to communicate with. But it was reported to me this morning that the people of Tokyo are so impressed with the way we are working, even though we do not have the language to be able to communicate. An international member and a Japanese member are going out as a pair into the city, and they are not able to talk with each other very much because they do not have a common language.

LANGUAGE OF HEART

But we have one very special language so that we can communicate regardless of nationality. That is the language of heart. Actually I am not a Korean. You are not Japanese. You do not come from Europe or America. We are all living in our Father's home as His children. So we must set the tradition to be pious sons and daughters.

Satan will never give up this world easily. We have to take it almost by force. That is why Jesus said, "I did not come to bring peace, but a sword." Without winning this divine battle, the kingdom of God cannot come to this earth. God and the messiah need soldiers, brave soldiers. And most importantly, these soldiers must be loyal and of unwavering faith. In other words, they must be pious sons and daughters who are willing to die for the messiah. And of all the peoples in the world, the Japanese people have been most prepared in that spirit. Throughout Japan's history, the Japanese culture and way of life have always emphasized loyalty and piety.

As with many other countries, Japan's history begins with a legend. That legend says that Japan is God's country. That tradition has been brought down through the emperors, from generation to generation. The people have really been unified about that central point. They have been exemplary subjects, giving their last measure of devotion and loyalty to their emperor.

During World War II, America and the Allied forces fought against the Japanese. During that time, the Americans especially had a hard time with Japan. Compared to giant America, Japan was like a peanut. But that peanut was so strong that the American people could not figure out where its power came from. During that time, America tried to find the secret of the Japanese. Well, they never found it, for it was the age-old tradition of Japan, the spirit of loyalty and piety. Even the Japanese privates, the very lowest soldiers, when they attacked an enemy camp, they always shouted mansei—banzai!—and cheered for the emperor. They knew that when they were hit by the enemy bullets they would die. They wanted to shout banzai as their last word before they died. That is an example of the Japanese spirit.

God made these people ready for one great day. When the messiah, the True Parent, comes, he needs soldiers like that. The Western countries need to learn this culture from Japan. This is our challenge.

Now I have a word for the Japanese brothers and sisters. This is your opportunity as well. What you have to learn is the idea that the world is bigger than Japan. We must learn that there are many different ways of life in this world. We must learn to adapt to, adjust to, and harmonize with different ways of life. If Japan fails to learn to work with other people, then the Japanese can never be elevated into greatness. So the Japanese brothers and sisters are faced with a new challenge and opportunity: to learn that they can contribute not just to Asia or Japan, but to the whole world. So we have a wonderful opportunity to live together and show a true example of the kingdom of God here on earth.

Japan is a small country in size, probably smaller than America's state of Minnesota. But there are almost 100 million people living in this small territory. That is almost half of the United States' population. In America, we have to move around so much to meet people. Here, we do not have to move too much. All you have to do is just turn around. When you go to the Ginza at night, it is entirely different from New York's Fifth Avenue or Washington's F Street. In the Ginza, you don't have to walk, because people will move you! All you have to do is stand facing the right direction. That is Japan.

MAKE THEM MISS US

So I want to ask you people of the IOWC to make a good impression on the Japanese people. That is our first mission, to let them feel heaven before they hear our message. When we leave Tokyo, we want the people to feel lonely without us. We want them to be looking forward to our return, anxious to see us again.

Finally, in order to set this good tradition, let us be willing to suffer. Let us be willing to go through the worst kinds of experiences. Let us be willing to shed our tears, our sweat, and our blood for the messiah. You and I must pledge, "I will not speak one word of complaint."

I have one personal credo that I am always reciting in my heart. It is taken from the Bible, the words of Jesus. He said, "He who seeks to find his life will lose it. But he who loses his life for my sake will find it." As long as you and I live by this credo, we will find our lives.

WORLD DAY

MIAMI, FLORIDA

JUNE 20, 1974

This speech was given on the second day of the three-day Celebration of Life Crusade in Miami. Dr. Pak begins by sharing victory stories from the previous night and then goes on to explain the meaning of World Day or Day of All Things. He discusses the process of restoration and reminds members that they are indeed the "lords of creation." He thanks them for their hard work and sacrifice and stresses the importance of investing their whole hearts into their work, thereby giving value to every action and every day.

First of all, I would like to reveal the victory we won last night. As you know, last night in the Celebration of Life here in Miami we broke the record. We had the greatest attendance so far. Remember, this is only the record so far. Everybody is trying to beat the record. So I would officially like to invite the members of the Crusade to give a great big hand to Reverend Martin Porter and the International One World Crusade of Region Six.

We had a guest attendance of 1,075, and a Family attendance of 110, for a total of 1,185. Immediately after the show I called East Garden to tell the True Parents, so that they would feel better on World Day. And indeed, they did.

An even more impressive record was the number of response cards turned in; 157 people turned in cards, out of which 22 signed box number one, "I would like to commit my life to God and Christ, and I want to join the Sun Myung Moon Christian Crusade and the Unification Church Movement." This is also a record.

And 70 people signed up to come to a workshop, 18 from the cards and an additional 52 people from the Rainbow Reception. So you can well see how important the Rainbow Reception is. This is truly the fishing pot. This is where we are fishers of men.

Incidentally, speaking of fishing, our True Parents have been spending a few days fishing in Barrytown, which is significant in the heavenly dispensation. Father is fishing in a very symbolic sense. The days that Father catches more fish, we catch more people fish. And last night Father caught the most fish in Barrytown. This is why we won this great victory in Miami.

Also, 21 people said, "I would like to contribute to this Crusade and this movement regularly." There were 25 people who asked for additional information and 58 positive responses, people who wrote nice things about the Crusade.

So on the initial night, we won a great victory. This is indeed a remarkable victory. And tonight, the second night, World Day, we are going to have a real World Day celebration in the form of a great victory in Gusman Philharmonic Hall. Let's aim and pray to have all 1,800 seats occupied tonight. This will be a second record.

STANDING ROOM ONLY

Tomorrow night, then, we will have a little problem. We will have to turn people away. We will have a camera installed, so that any people who cannot get into the theater will be able to stand outside and watch the closed-circuit television monitors. How wonderful! May that happen tomorrow.

As soon as I arrived in Florida, I received a detailed report from the regional commander, Reverend Porter. My heart was really aching to know the hard work that our regional teams, the IOWC team, the Florida members, and the others, have been putting into this campaign. They work from 5:00 o'clock in the morning. They usually have dinner at 11:00 p.m. They are out there all day, raising funds, distributing tickets. You have worked so hard, in such a sacrificial way. God knows, and Father knows, your hard work. This is one small way, I'm sure, that Father is giving you the reward.

I am really serious when we see our brothers and sisters going out every day, working so hard, and paying so much indemnity. There have been many accidents. Reverend Porter told me that even during the Day of Hope tour you didn't have that kind of experience. But we are paying so much indemnity now, and so many accidents are happening. My brother over there was badly injured in a car accident, but Father protected him. Come here, please. Give him a big hand, please.

Reverend Porter also mentioned to me that during this campaign, three vans were demolished. So I feel we are really paying. And Reverend Porter is such a positive thinker. I like him very much. I love him, of course. But I really love his positive way of thinking. His way of interpreting indemnity is exactly my way. Reverend Porter thinks that in order to give God a great victory, we are paying just a little bit of indemnity. We don't mind. Great victory is coming. That's his expectation. Every day he is expecting a miraculous situation. I know he will get it.

A GREAT OFFER

Another important thing happened last night. I think this is also quite significant. In Miami Beach, there is a huge convention center. I have never been there, but I'm going to go there in order to see the situation. This is probably one of the finest convention centers here in America. They are going to have an International Exposition Fair November 15 through 24. This is called "Expo '74 Florida." And last night, Mr. Don Garland, the general director and coordinator, brought his entire family to the Celebration of Life. He told me that they would like to invite the Celebration of Life to perform at the Miami Beach Convention Center during this Expo '74. They are offering us one of their largest auditoriums so that we can present our Celebration of Life program for one, two, or even three days and really proclaim the truth. They expect more than two million people to come to the center.

You know what this means. I wanted to be sure, so I asked them, "Do you want to have only the music and dancing, or do you want the whole thing, with the message of God?" He said, "The whole thing!"

Anywhere we go, we go with that condition. We are not going to just present the music or the dancing. We are going to go with the music and dancing and inspiration all together, with the proclamation of the Reverend Sun Myung Moon. This is the only way we will go. There is no other way.

Proclaiming the truth is our duty. That is our purpose for being here. The Celebration of Life is not just entertainment. It is not just songs and music and dancing. This is a proclamation. In music and song we radiate the spirit of God and the truth of God. And by the message we truly proclaim the Kingdom of God.

And this man also said that he has been in theater for 25 years. Apparently he is the kind of person who goes all over the world, seeing the best shows available and bringing those shows to conventions, arranging many shows, and so forth. He said, "I have never seen such a radiant, beautiful, professional show as you presented in Gusman Hall." I took that as a great compliment. He is a professional person, an impresario himself. A person like him commenting like that is truly meaningful.

Last night we were presented with this key from the city of Holmstead. The mayor told me he was deeply impressed and that he wants us to come to perform sometime in Holmstead. He said they would give us a "red carpet" welcome.

GOD TRUSTS US

Nothing comes easy, but the greatest things will be forthcoming. I have a great expectation every day that God will indeed bring a great miracle to us. We are not very special people who have been summoned for this great task, but God wants to use us to shame the people who think they are wise, those who think they are strong. We are summoned to really show the glory and power of God. We are not that special. But God has summoned us only because He trusts our hearts. More than anything else, what God needs is loyalty and steadfastness, and the love of the True Parents. These are the only weapons we need. Then God will provide everything else we need. God will provide us with knowledge, experience, and power.

What God is looking for in us is our heart. He is seeking from us love for the True Parents, unity with the True Parents, and loyalty and steadfastness. If we truly determine to live up to the credo that we have expressed here this morning in this important World Day celebration, if we truly live up those words—"He who seeks to find his life will lose it; and he who loses his life for my sake will find it"—if each day we are dying and bearing the cross, then we can truly live and revive this world.

This is a life of joy, a really victorious way of life. Each day we are perfecting our true life and our true body, which is our spirit man. We have been chosen to have the privilege of attaining the spiritual perfection of divine spirits. This is the highest goal of man.

Today is World Day. The literal translation of this is the Day of the Universe, or the Day of Creation. I would like to briefly go over the significance of this day, so that we can all know deeply the importance of this day's celebration. Because of the fall of man, mankind lost three major things. First, we lost the True Parents. Adam and Eve were supposed to be the True Parents of mankind. They were supposed to be the first Christ. They were supposed to be the first perfected man and woman. If they had been the True Parents, if the fall had never happened, then man would have been enjoying perfection ever since. But we lost the True Parents. Second, we lost the children. Without True Parents, how could there be true children? Third, we lost all things of creation, because they were subjugated under the satanic power. We were supposed to enjoy lordship over all creation. However, the creation has been subjugated in futility under Satan. We have never had our true lordship.

HEART OF THE FATHER

The greatest proclamations that the True Parents have brought forth into this world are the heart of the Father and restoration. We know that the Father's heart has been broken. The True Parents came to this world to proclaim the broken heart of God. Only the son of God could do that.

Today there are so many people in the world who are not even sure about the existence of God. But this group right here, our people, our brothers and sisters—we are not worrying about the existence of God, and we are not discussing the presence of God. What we are talking about is the heart of the Father. The heart of the Father was broken. But we, as His true sons and true daughters, are in a position to relieve Father's grief.

Then let us talk about restoration. Throughout history, man has not known the goal or the purpose of human history. We have not known our destination. Now we know, through the Divine Principle, the revelation of our Father that history is moving forward to achieve the purpose of restoration. Restoration comes in three major ways. First, there is the restoration of the True Parents. This came in 1960. On that day in 1960 we instituted the first Parents Day. This is a most significant day, because before the True Parents were restored, our Heavenly Father was literally living in hell. The debt of 6,000 years of sinful history had to be paid off. This is why the restoration of the True Parents was not easy. They could not just set a day and proclaim it. No, the entire history of God had to be restored. The indemnity had to be paid.

This is why our True Father and Mother walked such an agonizing way, to restore all that, to set the condition to bring all mankind to the "break even" level, in other words, to the position where we could say that the debt has been paid.

Ever since 1960, all the children of the Unification Church could come under the True Parents. You do not know how significant it is. I do not really know 100 percent how important and significant it is. But we must learn the Principle more deeply, and we must live the Principle, so that we can know what it means to have True Parents.

In other words, our citizenship has changed. We now belong to the kingdom of heaven. We are the citizens of the kingdom of heaven, and we belong to the True Parents.

During the war, Korea was divided into North and South. Some of our people were working in North Korea in the guerrilla warfare, as spies and so forth, for the nation's security. If they were discovered, they would desperately try to escape over the border to the South. The whole enemy force might be chasing them, but as soon as they crossed that boundary, they were safe in their own territory. The enemy had no more authority to pursue them.

WE BELONG TO TRUE PARENTS

Why am I saying this? Even though we may be living in the same world, we have crossed over the boundary. Our sovereignty, our citizenship has been changed. As soon as we belong to the True Parents, the satanic forces have no power to come after us. We are in new territory. We are in this world, but we are not of this world. We belong to the True Parents, which means that we now have the opportunity to be saved not only spiritually, as the Christian faith does, but we are completely saved physically as well.

In other words, when our unity with the True Parents becomes 100 percent perfect, then we shall not only be saved spiritually, but also we will be given physical salvation and the redemption of our body. In this way, we can become True Children. So in the fall of that year (on the lunar calendar, October 1), God and the True Parents saw Children's Day.

So we have restoration of the True Parents, and we commemorate this day on Parents' Day. And on Children's Day we commemorate the restoration of True Children. These are two of the most important celebrations during the year.

After that restoration was accomplished, then God could proclaim World Day, the restoration of all things of creation. This is today. Actually, it is June 1 on the lunar calendar, and this year June 20 on the solar calendar.

We are now celebrating this World Day. Actually, the True Parents wanted to come to Miami so that they could share this victory of the Celebration of Life together with us. But because there is a nationwide celebration in Belvedere and East Garden, and there are many programs on this particular day, they were unable to come. So last night Mother asked me to give each one of you their deepest love and best wishes.

I want you to understand that after the restoration of the True Parents and the True Children, we can now restore the true lordship over all things of the creation. So when we go out in Miami and look at the water and the sky, at the palm trees and the buildings, we want to be saying to them, "Take comfort from me. I am seeing you and appreciating you with Father's eyes."

FATHER, LOOK WITH MY EYES

This is what you should be able to do. When you look at beautiful things, do not just say, "Beautiful flowers! Beautiful beach! Beautiful palm trees! I have never seen such beauty before. I'm so glad I came from Korea to see this." Do not look from your own point of view. Instead, say to the palm tree, "Listen to me. I am the representative of God and the True Parents. I appreciate your beauty from the Father's point of view, with the Father's eyes." Then say, "Father, use my eyes to enjoy this tree, these flowers, this beach, this beautiful land, from your point of view."

Children praise God by saying, "Our Father in heaven." The Creator of all made this flower and this palm tree and brought this Miami Beach into existence. Praise the Lord. This is the art of the Heavenly Father. All the things of creation are the masterpieces of our Father. A child may draw a very funny-looking man. But when his parents praise the beauty of that drawing and appreciate the child's ability, then the child is comforted and encouraged. By the same token, Father has created so much beauty and glory for the appreciation of man. Then we must be in the position, through those things of creation, to return the glory to the True Parents and to our Heavenly Father.

The other day, I sat in on our workshop in New Orleans. There I made a really important proclamation in conclusion. I asked, "What is perfection?" And I told them that many years ago, when I began to study English, I asked many teachers, "How can I learn English quickly?" All American teachers advised me that there was no way but to think in English. They told me not to think in Korean and try to translate in my head and then speak in English. No matter how good a computer we may have up here, it is one step too slow if you think in Korean, translate into English, and speak in English. So they told me to think in English.

Today that advice is very meaningful to me. We are speaking in the heavenly language. We are expressing the True Parents' heart. We are speaking God's heart. We are speaking the language of the heart. So we must not think in human language and then translate into Heavenly Father's language. We must learn to think in the heavenly language. We must tune in, so that every word we speak, every sight we see, every sound we hear, every feeling we experience comes directly from Heavenly Father. This is the goal of perfection.

I want you to understand. Since we belong to the True Parents, since we are the masters of the New Age, when we go out on a boat, out on a train, out on the green grass, out in a car, I want you to know that we are going as the lords of creation. This is the significance of this day, World Day, the Day of All Things.

So, brothers and sisters, we don't just get up each day at five o'clock in the morning and come back at 11 o'clock automatically, like a machine, like clockwork. Unless we put our hearts into it, our hard work will have no meaning. We will be like machines. You know, a vending machine works 24 hours a day. It never sleeps, right? But there is no meaning to it, because it is just mechanical work. We must not be like a vending machine. We are here to represent and reflect the heart of the Father. Each moment of every day, every action we make we must give meaning, so that as a result we are bubbling with excitement and joy. Otherwise, no matter how hard you may work, it will not be to the glory of the True Parents.

For example, consider fund-raising. The great fund-raisers of our movement were asked, "How did you become such a good fund-raiser?" Some of them have made $700 or $800 in one day. They said that if they think of money, they can't raise funds. Instead, they think of Father. Then their flowers sell like hotcakes. They think of Father. I just couldn't believe that one person could sell $700 worth of flowers in one day. That means that 700 bundles had to be sold at $1 each. In 12 hours of work they had to sell 700 bundles of flowers.

But that person said, "Actually, some mysterious power came to me. I just prayed to God that I was here for Father's work, for Father's heart, and just gave out the flowers. And when I gave people the flowers, dollar bills just automatically came out." She was so busy giving out flowers that she didn't even have time to say, "Thank you."

One day this person knocked on a door and a lady answered and saw her standing there. Apparently some spiritual electronic shock was communicated before a word was spoken. She just said, "How many bundles do you have?" "Seventy bundles." "Leave them all right here. How much do I owe you?" "Seventy dollars." This woman went right in, wrote a check for $70, came back and said, "Here you are. Thank you very much."

Amazing. And Randy here was a very outstanding leader for a mobile fund-raising team and raised a tremendous amount of money. He and all the other leaders of these MFT [mobile fund-raising team] teams testified to me that they were working every day to find out how they could raise funds better. They do not think in business terms. They do not think about how much money they are making. They only think about Father's heart. They found that prayer was the key. I was really so touched by that testimony. Prayer is the key. With prayer and the Father's heart, the flowers really sell like hotcakes.

COMMUNICATE WITH NATURE

Now we have come into a different era. We can even communicate with the things of the creation. There are some people who have had some experience in the spiritual world. And those people tell us that in the spiritual heaven we can talk to trees, talk to rocks, talk to flowers—not by words, but by feeling. Certain communication is available. You can see when a tree is really joyful. It is dancing, praising and glorifying God.

All the things of creation are here for Heavenly Father's glory. And in the spiritual world everyone can see. The same thing is happening in this world; the only difference is that we cannot see it with these eyes. We do not have our spiritual senses. But our True Father tells us that this is why he loves nature so much. This is why he goes fishing. All day he is having fellowship with nature, with the water, with the scenery, and all the beauty of nature, even the fish. Those things are genuine, unstained, God's creation. There is honesty there. There is truth there. The human heart, however, is wicked. It shows one thing on the outside but is something else on the inside. Nature is not that way. Yet Paul says in Romans that all things of creation have been groaning inwardly ever since they lost the true lordship of Adam and Eve. The creation has been in agony, waiting for the day when the True Lord would come and become lord over creation.

And we are in that position. We must love all things of creation from the Father's point of view, with Father's eyes.

Let me conclude by saying just one more thing. I said that in the spiritual world flowers can talk. That is, they can communicate. Trees can communicate. Rocks, water, streams can communicate. Let's say we could give mouths to those flowers and trees, even those palm trees on the beach. Then we could ask them, "Who would you like to belong to?" Do you know what answer you would get? You would always get the same answer from the flowers, from the trees, from the water, from the rocks. Anything beautiful would always reply with the same answer. They will say to you, "I would like to belong to he who loves me most."

You could see in our pantomime last night, "The Daisy," that the flower really hated that man. That flower wanted to belong to the person who could love it, appreciate its beauty. The flower wanted to be appreciated. Then who loves this flower the most? Who loves the creation the most? Our Heavenly Father does, because He created it. Who loves a painting most? That is the person who painted it. Nobody can compete with that person's love for his painting. Take Picasso, for example. Nobody can appreciate his work more than himself.

God created this world. God loves this world most. That is why, naturally, all things of the creation belong to God. And when we become one with the heart of our Heavenly Father, we are the owners of these flowers, loving with the Father's heart, putting ourselves in Father's position. Then we can look at this flower with Father's eyes and say, "Our Father, what a beautiful thing you have created, this wonderful daisy." Then that daisy will say, "I am so lucky, so happy. I finally found someone who loves me, who appreciates me." That flower will want to be picked by that person and stay with him.

This is a great truth. By the same token, who is the true owner of America? Who truly owns this America? It is not owned by her citizens. Do you think you own it? No, God does not recognize all those papers up in City Hall. God only recognizes the hearts of men. America belongs to that man who loves America most.

This IOWC team represents 12 different nations. The New Hope Singers come from 13 different nationalities. But we are truly lords over all the things of creation here in America. We are the owners of America, in a way, in Father's sense, because we love America most. Because Father loves this country, we have come to love America as Father loves her.

By the same token, I want you to be very ambitious. You can own God, own the True Parents. How? The answer is simple: Love them most! Love God most. Then God is yours. The True Parents are yours.

ACTS OF THE APOSTLE

This is a beautiful day, World Day, 1974. And 1974 is a special year in the history of "the acts of the apostles," the history of the Unification Church, and the history of the universe. 1974 is going to be the highest year of honor. 1974 is a very special year because the True Parents have put their greatest effort into this year and have done the most extraordinary, historical things in this year. So I want you to take great pride that we have all participated in this heavenly dispensation, in the work of God's restoration in the year of 1974. I want the members of the Sun Myung Moon Christian Crusade to feel great honor that you have participated in this crusade in the year of 1974. And furthermore, you are going to perform for Father's final and most important Day of Hope tour, for banquets and speeches in eight cities.

This is going to be a very historical event. So at the end of this year we are going to make a new plaque. At the top it will say, "Sun Myung Moon Christian Crusade." Then will be listed the names of every member of the New Hope Singers, the Korean Folk Ballet, all the headquarters team, and the technical crew. Everybody's name will be inscribed on that big plaque. We want that to be shown to posterity, to history.

And the IOWC, too. Father is coming to Atlanta for the Day of Hope tour. And you will also go up to New York for the Madison Square Garden campaign. I don't want you to miss these things. After all, this is the most historical, most extraordinary event that has ever taken place in the kingdom of God. So to be part of it is a tremendous blessing.

So the year 1974 is very special. Let's make this year really special by applying ourselves to the fullest degree, giving our whole effort. Right? [Right!]

This is the message for this day. I am very, very happy to be in Miami. After all, we are the frontline soldiers. During the Korean War, I was a soldier during Christmastime. The Christmas celebration on the frontline of battle was very unique and very touching. We were in a tent, with a small, very ugly cake—because soldiers made it. We had many kinds of food, but there were no containers for them. But we had our helmets, you know, steel helmets. They are very handy. Not only do they protect you from bullets, but they serve many other purposes. In the morning, you wash your face out of your steel helmet. In the evening, you eat out of your helmet. We might even wash our feet in it at night and eat out of it the next day. It's very handy.

Anyway, we had some ugly-looking bread in our helmets. We had to cook everything ourselves, because there were no cooks to do the job. We had funny little candles, and sang Christmas carols like "Silent Night, Holy Night." We sat there with our rifles in our hands. That was a very special celebration of Christmas. The Christmas feeling was so real there on the frontline. The spirit was so real.

I want you to know that this is the frontline of heaven. We have our M-1 rifles at our side. You cannot see it, but every one of you has it: the word of God. And we are really away from home, away from our True Parents. But God is so real at the frontline. God and the True Parents are so real right here in the Sun Myung Moon Christian Crusade, and for the members of this state and region. This is where the battle is. We are the frontline soldiers. So this is a real celebration. We may not have excellent china and silver to eat from. We may not have those, but we will have a good celebration. Think of it. This is where the frontline is, where the spirit of our Father and True Parents is most apparent.

So let's have a good spiritual breakfast. I hope brother Martin Porter has a good breakfast for us. Let us celebrate, then we will go out and win a tremendous victory, and we will have a real celebration this evening. Immediately afterward I will call East Garden and let our True Parents know what a victory we have won on World Day. Right? [Right!]

ALL MY EXPECTATIONS
ARE BEING FULFILLED

PUBLISHED IN *THE WAY OF THE WORLD*

JULY/AUGUST 1974

━━━━━━━━━━━━━━━━━━━━━━━━━━━━━━━━━━

In this interview, Bo Hi Pak describes the Celebration of Life tour as a revolutionary concept in the world of evangelism—combining truth with the joy of music and dance. He reports proudly of reaching many young and non-Christian people, and talks about its positive impact on participating Unification Church members and on his own family.

What is the meaning of the Celebration of Life tour?

This Sun Myung Moon Christian Crusade, Celebration of Life, is a revolutionary concept in the world of evangelism because this is a new form of evangelism. We are bringing a free expression of joy in music and dance. We are introducing a 21st century-style formula for evangelism. This has revolutionized the world of evangelism. We are very glad that the Unification Church is doing it. We are spearheading it, we are making headway. We are becoming pioneers and champions of a new form of evangelism that will be effective in reaching out to people, particularly non-

Christian people. We will reach many, many young people, non-Christian people. Evangelism in the past was tailor-made to evangelize among Christians. This is the way we can attract many non-Christians, many nonbelievers. We come to them in a beautiful way, in a most impressive and favorable way, to introduce them to God and Christ.

Second, we are revolutionizing the teaching of the Divine Principle. In order to be able to cope with the mass media, great numbers of people and audiences of thousands, we should have a new form of presentation of the Principle. We must make the presentation of the Principle simple, fantastic, and heart-warming. That is the formula I wanted to come up with; I wanted to pioneer it. And even though I do not feel my task is complete, I do know it is working, I know the direction now. We can work harder and harder, and we can perfect it. I think it would be a powerful message for the public, for a mass convention or assembly. In other words, we are elevating it from the classroom-type presentation to mass evangelism. We are now capable of presenting it on this scale, and it becomes so powerful, because none dare compete with the truth of the Divine Principle, once we find the formula and tailor it for the public.

In this particular crusade I have picked out the three key points representative of our movement. These three points are: Jesus did not come to die; Christ is coming not on the clouds of heaven but as the son of man in the flesh; and the original sin was a misuse of love.

Would you explain the impact this can have on a church member?

Two things are primarily happening among our family members. First of all, by inviting people to the Celebration of Life, they are positively identified as people who can command respect and admiration for our movement. People want to be known by this wonderful group. We are becoming the target of envy. In many cases, our family members were like the underdog. There were many unkind things said about them, and they did not have many prospects for successful and winning days. They had to fight through many persecutions. These have been the local situations in our movement.

And now the Celebration of Life brings a different attitude. We are in a commanding position. We are so positive. Even those people who came to oppose us came and said nothing. They became completely neutralized, and in some cases they changed their minds. We are so confident, so good, so refreshing, so honest, so sincere, how could they say anything about it? We are giving new confidence, new hope, new dimensions to the world. So they see how good we can be. They feel very happy to be part of this Celebration of Life Crusade and to become pioneers together for God and Christ.

Second, they truly feel close to God and Christ, because through this presentation of the Principle, even our family members have never before experienced such joy and a realization of conversion, the truth coming into your whole being, centering on God and Christ. It brings a real heart-to-heart relationship.

What has your work on the Celebration of Life meant to you?

This has been a really rewarding experience personally. I have wanted to do this for a long time. This is the kind of thing I have been dreaming about. It is a dream which has become a reality, so I have a tremendous personal satisfaction. Through this I have come to know God and Christ in a deeper sense. I have been the one most blessed and rewarded by being part of the Celebration of Life, because I am the one that has been most uplifted. I have experienced God's kingdom and His loving heart, and so I have become closer to God. This is really a tremendous uplift on the personal side.

My family also feels the same way. By doing this, my family is becoming more happy and united. My wife is enjoying the tour, and we can share much joy together. My son will soon graduate from high school, and he would like to join. So our whole family is centered around the Celebration of Life and the work of God. I cannot think of any other way that we could better do the work of God and experience together harmony and happiness in the family.

What are your expectations for the future?

I think our future is simply great. I have great expectations. However, things will happen in a far greater and far more intense degree than anybody can envision at this time. This world may change. The world in which we live truly needs a great realization of the presence of God, because everything, all aspects of human life, are running toward a deadlock. We need a new dimension. Otherwise, the survival and the very existence of human culture are in question.

Where can we find the solutions to today's conflicts? We have tried everything, and we cannot find any ultimate solution. So the solution has to be a spiritual one, because the fundamental core of the universe is God, and God is spirit. God is the subject of the universe. No matter what we might do, the solution must come from the subject point of view, from God and from the spiritual world.

We are doing precisely that. We are not talking about the problems of the world. We are presenting the solution. We are working not on an analysis of the problem but on the cure to the problem. That is the fundamental principle of our work. About the future, only God knows. The sky is the limit. This whole world is waiting to be saved. We need help from God and from God's power, and from a spiritual awakening and enlightenment. We are providing the answer to the world.

The Celebration of Life is one segment of a great movement that will ignite millions of people and give them a fresh outlook on life. That is what we are doing. I really feel good about it. I have waited a long time for the Celebration of Life. The Sun Myung Moon Christian Crusade is going to be the greatest crusade ever launched. It is going to be a pioneer. Only history can tell what magnitude it will have. But I think this crusade will remain until the kingdom of heaven comes on earth to the full extent.

We will soon move on to other parts of the world—Europe, the Middle East, Asia, Latin America, Africa, etc.

Initially, American settlers started from the New England area and pioneered the virgin land of the West. We are doing the same way. We are like the Mayflower of heaven landing on Plymouth Rock in New England. We have tribulations and hard work to do, but that is nothing. We are pioneers, we have to take all these things. We are on untouched land. A whole new horizon is waiting to be cultivated spiritually.

God has spoken through all the ages, through many prophets, like Moses and Elijah and John the Baptist and through Jesus Christ, His Son. I think the living God is speaking to us, and I believe that Reverend Moon is the instrument of God. Through him God is speaking the most wonderful revelation concerning God's modern-day dispensation. Therefore, through him many messages are coming; the meaning of the symbols and parables of the Bible are becoming clear.

We tell people what we believe is a way of life truly centered on God and Christ. In this way we believe that true happiness and joy can be derived. Young people respond to it very well, because they can see the spirit of dedication to God and Christ in joy. We can communicate that joy to young people. Furthermore, they are very much intrigued and impressed by the love and the new expression of God and Christ. They hear the meaning of the Bible and the words of Jesus becoming relevant to their own life. They see our bubbling enthusiasm.

We have gathered members of our movement who have the highest professional skills in putting this program together. They really communicate their tremendous spirit of joy in God and Christ. This is what they are radiating. It becomes contagious. We have sessions of studying the Bible, and furthermore, we even raise the funds to support our program. It is therefore a really strenuous schedule for our young people.

They are very happy to be part of something very unique, and I am very proud of their spirit. I really feel proud to be able to do this wonderful work for God and Christ. I think it is one of the greatest things that I have ever witnessed. These young people, once they are motivated, can do things that are impossible otherwise.

Our movement, the Unification Church, is the fast-growing mother organization. The Sun Myung Moon Christian Crusade is the outreach arm of the Unification Church International. We have so many members around the world and are the fastest growing faith in our modern day. Young people have been moving away from organized churches. But our movement attracts mostly young people. I think this is really a wonderful thing.

We have missions in 40 different countries, and in three years we will go to 120 different nations. In America thousands of young people are coming to the realization of God and Christ and are centering their lives on God. This is really wonderful.

LOVE AND FAITH

PRINTED IN *THE WAY OF THE WORLD*

JULY 8, 1974

═══════════════════

Dr. Pak gives a detailed explanation of the restoration of love, highlighting the three core ingredients: absolute honesty, purity, and selfless devotion. He discusses how we can make Satan powerless and how we can strengthen our faith until we can overcome what he calls "the moment of disillusionment."

In Minneapolis I talked about how we could give love and practice love among our members and within our family. People will be changed by the vibration and by the radiant spirit within us.

Because the dawn of human history began with lying, in order to restore ourselves, we must start first with absolute honesty with ourselves and with God. God already knows everything.

Second, we must know that the most important thing in life is purity. The loss of purity brought the fall of man. For restoration, we need the presence of unstained love. We must restore love, first directed to God and Christ. As brothers and sisters we have one concern, to direct our love, unstained, to God and Christ. This is the only way we can be welded together in the body of God. This is the only way we can receive our salvation. Our movement is about a revolution of love; our entire heart and mind are to be directed to God and Christ. When you love someone with all your heart, soul, body, and mind, there is no room for anything else. If we are to be crazy about something, we should be crazy about God and Christ. We must mutually assist each other so we can direct our love to one point.

The third point is selfless devotion. Take the route of the cross. When we practice these three, we consummate our love. If you do these three for God, you are loving Him. If you do these three for Christ, you are loving him. If you do these three for your brothers and sisters, you are loving them.

When people come to Christ, they are caught up in the burning joy and excitement. But before too long, many become disillusioned and discouraged. This is in a way a natural process. We will always have that. All of us have low periods. No single one of us may be the exception. This is because nothing can progress in a straight line. It always goes in a wave. So also our faith. We have to struggle every day, up and down.

We must therefore know some secret—how to overcome ourselves when we reach a low point. How can we spring back to the high point? In our daily life, this is very much needed. If you study the Divine Principle in depth, you know the secret. The Divine Principle is always the key.

A COMPLAINING MIND

The first sign of weakness comes in the form of complaint. In the realm of God there is no room for complaint. You can complain in any position, once you start. If you are a king or a queen, you could still complain. Therefore, complaint comes from a state of mind, not from the environment. We could make a prison a place of joy even, with the right mind.

How can I diagnose my state? One symptom is complaint. Why does that person act like that? We ask, why is that person so beautiful? When you start asking those questions, I want you to know, that is an alarming sign. The true person dwelling in the love of God is always grateful.

Jesus could have said to God while on the cross, "Can't you do something about this suffering?" But he didn't. The Bible says he cried out, "My God, why have you forsaken me?" After that came an unspoken sentence. "Even if for some unknown reason you want me to die, rest assured, I will not fail you." Because of this absolute loyalty, God exercised the power of resurrection. When Reverend Moon was in the Hungnam prison camp he could have complained. Instead, he prayed, "God, don't worry about me." He always thought, "I am busy serving the Father." This is a new standard of serving God.

This is the secret to overcoming our low periods. We must know that the fall of man came by man's distrust toward God. Man turned around, leaving God alone. God did not kick man, man kicked God out. So in order to come back to God, we must go through the law of restitution. This means that before you are given the title of true sons and daughters of God, God must kick you, once. Adam and Eve said, "God, I don't know you." So in our course, God will say, "I don't know you."

At that test, many say, "You kicked me, God. Why? I'm leaving you." In the Divine Principle, however, we learn why God kicked His children. We must demonstrate our worthiness to receive God's blessing by being separated from Satan.

Take the example of Job. Job was a millionaire and a loyal worshiper of God. Satan told God, "Sure Job serves you; you have given him such great wealth. Take away his wealth and he will curse you." So Job woke up one morning and found everything he owned gone. But still he served God. So Satan said to God, "Sure he loves you, he is so healthy." So Job became leprous, his body was like the surface of the moon. When urged to curse God and die, Job said, "My life, my health, my fortune all come from God. If He takes them away, why should I complain?" Job did not curse God.

SATAN BECOMES POWERLESS

When one's faith reaches that state, Satan becomes powerless. Then, whatever God's blessing, Satan cannot accuse. God wants us to be victorious over the fallen serpent, Satan. But God cannot do this for us. By demonstrating such absolute faith we can separate ourselves from Satan and be completely free.

This is not just Job's story; this is Bo Hi Pak's story, this is your story. This is the beauty of the Bible. I want you to know that in your life, too, there will be a time when God will say, "I never knew you." When you first come to God, He is always embracing you, comforting you. But then the moment will come when God will say, "I don't know you." So you say to Him, "God, I know more than you. I know why you have to say that."

The Divine Principle is so wonderful. It teaches us how to prepare ourselves in advance. If we don't know, we can be really lonely and confused. The moment Jesus was nailed on the cross, God was saying, "I never knew you." Jesus said to Him, "Whatever you do to me, I am with you."

In the Bible there are many such moments. God gave Abraham a son, Isaac, at the age of 100. The same God later asked Abraham to offer his son as a burnt offering. Abraham could have said to Him, "Are you crazy, God?" His little boy Isaac asked, "Daddy, where is the lamb?" He had been to sacrifices before. He knew there had to be special animals.

Abraham had brought the wood and the knife, but where was the lamb? At that moment Abraham could have said, "What kind of God are you to do this to me?" But Abraham said, "My son, God will provide the lamb." He raised his knife, ready to kill his son. In another moment his son would be dead. At this very moment, if Abraham had a trace of complaint, even though he might have killed his son, the offering of his son would have been rejected by God.

So many times we do good things, but if our heart is not there, the deeds do not blossom in the glory of God. If Abraham had complained, the purpose of God's glory would not have been achieved. But when Abraham lifted his knife, there was no hesitation. God will respond to man's heart, not to his deed. Deed is the manifestation of the heart. If we do things without the right heart, it is not acceptable to God. With our heart we can separate ourselves from Satan.

Satan's temptation to Jesus was the first showdown between Jesus and Satan. Satan lost. So Satan changed his tactic: he moved into the hearts of the Jewish people. The Bible says that Satan entered the heart of Judas. He wanted to make the hearts of the people rebellious.

I want you to know, Satan is really aiming at you as individuals, searching where he can invade. He is like a disease, a germ. When you have strong enough defenses, it cannot invade. But when your defenses are weak, the germ invades. Therefore, each of us must know the secret, how to overcome the moment of disillusion.

We must be prepared, with our faith strong enough and ready enough. Then you will overcome difficulties many times over. What faith is good enough in the sight of God? What faith is deep enough that if God and Christ would say, "I don't know you; go to hell; die," you would turn around and say, "God, I am with you."

Then Satan will shake His head and say, "I can do nothing with him. He is impossible." Satan has a little black book with everyone's name in it. After such a person's name it reads, "impossible." So Satan won't even touch him. He will go somewhere else where he can work.

Through your faith, you can turn God's no to you into a yes. So let's become impossible persons in Satan's black book!

A Victory for God

PRINTED IN *THE WAY OF THE WORLD*

AUGUST 1975

═══════════════════════

Koreans think that Korea will be the next target of communist aggression after Vietnam. When you look at the Asian land mass, you can see that the Korean position is vulnerable. The communists might even feel that they don't have to do anything; they can just blow this country away into the sea. The whole Asian continent is communist. Korea is hardly even a pinpoint. Even the whole Korean peninsula is not free. It is truly an impossible game.

All the Asian countries that have remained free are now rushing into worshiping Mao Tse-tung—the Philippines, Malaysia, Indonesia, Thailand. Korea, alone, has resolved that we either die or we live in freedom. Korea is the one country in Asia trying to live up to the great cry of Patrick Henry, "Give me liberty or give me death!"

Throughout the history of God, He has manifested the power to show His own people that, with absolute trust in Him, they could make the impossible possible, creating a miracle. Moses was taught by God how, by faith, the impossible could be turned into reality and victory. Crossing the Red Sea is one example.

This is what Korea is facing. For Korea there are many Red Seas, not just one. In the north, there is Kim Il Sung, wanting to take over Korea at any time. He has built so many tunnels underground that there is no 38th parallel anymore. In the west, the giant China of Mao, with almost one billion people, can become a machine under one order from Peking. In the east, Japan is very weak. The Communist Party is legal, occupying many seats in the government. The communists believe that it is only a matter of time for Japan to fall. China and Russia even think of bypassing Korea. If Japan falls, Korea has nowhere to go. And to the south of Korea is the sea.

I met Harry Truman before he died. He said that he made two great decisions while he was president of the United States. One was dropping the atomic bomb on Hiroshima and Nagasaki. He still thought that he did the right thing, even though he devastated the two cities, because the Japanese were in no mood to stop the war. They were determined to fight to the last man, which would have brought millions and millions of casualties. The second, he said, was the commitment of forces in Korea. By doing this he saved Korean freedom. He added that if his decision had been delayed three days, there would have been no Korea, because by then all of Korea would have been thrown into the sea.

This is the Korean position. The Korean people realize more than anyone else what kind of position they are in. What boosted the morale of the 35 million people of Korea was Reverend Sun Myung Moon proclaiming that Korea is the chosen nation of God, that God will never abandon this country, and that the Unification Church International is ready to save the Republic of Korea.

Everyone thought that our activities were more intriguing than a presidential campaign. We also had a good opponent. The existing churches did not like our determined spiritual revolution. They did everything they could to make our crusade a failure. Under these mixed circumstances, the results were amazing. It was the greatest campaign I have ever seen.

HEROES IN KOREA

The IOWC members were really heroes in Korea. They were truly wonderful. The hundreds of IOWC members campaigned tirelessly, handing out brochures on street corners and knocking on all two million doors of Seoul from 7:00 in the morning until 10:00 at night. It was the greatest honor and inspiration to lead this campaign of more than 700 courageous people, the living Davids of the 20th century, in the streets of Seoul. Each IOWC member wore a big flag, making the city like a flower path. I'm very proud of them; they testified to what Reverend Sun Myung Moon stands for.

For the first time Reverend Sun Myung Moon was presented literally as having a messianic mission. This is because what Korea needs today is the hope and conviction that nothing will ever happen to Korea; that

Korea will be under the power of God; that in the name of God and with the power of God, the entire world would stand behind them and save them. This new hope is, above anything else, what is needed in Korea. United together and marching together as one fortress, they will have no reason to fear North Korean or any other communist aggression.

We know that South Vietnam did not fall because of lack of manpower or weapons. At the moment of surrender, they had $5 billion worth of weapons. They had tremendous manpower, many times that of North Vietnam. South Vietnam fell because the people did not have a purpose to fight. Without conviction and a will to fight, naturally the nation cannot stand.

This time, Reverend Moon brought a sense of purpose to defend Korea. The resolution of representatives of 60 nations to fight for Korea truly shook the entire country. The Unification Church stood as the messiah for Korea, the Salvation Army in the truest sense. In the 1950s only 16 nations defended Korea when the communists attacked. Now the Korean people could see that over 60 nations would rally around them at the outbreak of hostilities.

One day I took the New Hope Singers and the Korean Folk Ballet to the frontline, where we gave a special performance for hundreds of thousands of frontline soldiers, like Bob Hope did. We did not have just dancing and singing for them; we also had a message. That message was: "You will never be alone. Do not lose strength. Do your duty. You have lots of friends in the name of the Unification Church throughout the world. We will never hesitate to come to your aid, to fight with you side by side if anything happens." And this boosted their morale so much that many soldiers were in tears.

I want you to know that we, the Unification Church International, are not only serving as the salvation force for the Republic of Korea, we are the ones responsible to turn communist aggression away in every corner of the world. Over and over, I was so deeply impressed by the spirit and determination of Reverend Moon. He took the entire world situation upon himself. He knew that no one is responsible but himself. He knew that there is no other way for the worldwide alliance of communism to be stopped but through the Unification ideology. But on June 7, Reverend Moon branded communism as another form of religion because communism provides a philosophy and controls every action of the human body. Communism is an evil religion without God. Communism tries to pose itself as God, trying to take over God's job.

Therefore, there is only one way we can win over communism: with a better, stronger, and truer religion centered on God. A God-denying ideology can be deterred only by a stronger truth. The problem is that today's Christianity is failing to live up to this standard. Many Christian nations are giving up, opening the road to communist takeover, showing that Christianity is not really living up to God's desire.

The Unification Church is a new breed of Christianity. We are igniting the spiritual revolution so that our conviction goes beyond the communists', bringing the human race toward a strong commitment to the reality of God. In this way alone Reverend Moon has shown the world the way to conquer communism.

NOT A DROP OF RAIN

I announced to the crowd: "Look at the sky over there. The weatherman said that in five minutes those showers will come upon this island. But I want you to know that this is the beautiful strategy of God. When you stay strong even under the rain, your eloquent testimony against the threat of Kim Il Sung will be a thousand times stronger. God wants us to exhibit strong resolve to show Kim how determined we are. So do you promise that even if it showers, you won't move?" Then I introduced Reverend Moon and he began to speak his most beautiful message. I now believe the Old Testament more than ever before, because not even one drop of rain fell!

Many religious leaders gathered, eloquently testifying to what Reverend Moon was doing for the world. These people speaking on our behalf showed complete unity, which is what the government is seeking. The government is really looking at the religion that is united in a common stand against Kim Il Sung. We served that purpose so beautifully.

After this June 7 rally, the Unification Church International will never be the same. We have gained new power and recognition. More important than anything else, we became a new hope for the Korean people. Truly there is not one single Korean who has not heard about Reverend Sun Myung Moon. And they heard of him as a patriot, a prophet of God, spearheading the salvation of the Republic of Korea. There was no better way to represent him to the Korean people. I was jubilant about the outcome of the rally.

The next three years will be most important, centered on activity here in America. Yankee Stadium will be a national event, particularly in conjunction with the Bicentennial, something like a "God Bless America" rally. No religious or government leaders could lead a rally of such magnitude. Centered on Reverend Sun Myung Moon, we will. I know that Reverend Moon will say on that occasion: that America must win this important test at her 200th birthday. The test is to return to the founding spirit of America. Then the new era of America will dawn, and our young people, the decent patriots of America, will recognize that Reverend Moon is the hope and the Unification Church is the champion of God.

Our path will not be an easy one. But if you had chosen an easy way of life, you would not be assembled here. We came here to really invest our youth and life and energy and heart and soul in the best way possible to be used by God, to become the nourishment of the kingdom. That is why we are here.

And I tell you that the most exciting period is going to begin from this time on here in America. My heart is pumping in joy and excitement. We will live a life that will never be dull. What we need is just one single-minded conviction that God is with us. I am and you are His ambassadors in this new dawn of the heavenly kingdom. This time I have come back with even stronger determination to give the best of my life any way that He wants, to serve His way here in America.

What America becomes, the world shall become. Even though we won a great victory in Asia, Asia is dependent upon what America will become. The showdown is not going to be in Korea, even though the physical setup is there. We are going to create the cue-sheet, the plan of action, the power behind all things. I am confident that we have the leadership and inspiration that we need. Above all, God is depending on you, telling you: "Come my way and you will be with me and I shall be with you." Several years ago I adopted as the credo of my life: "He who tries to find his life will lose it, and he who loses his life for my sake will find it." Unless we do it, no one else will, except the communists. We have the most profound mission of the messianic era of the 20th century.

WE ARE GOING TO CREATE THE MIRACLE OF THE CENTURY

NEW YORK, NEW YORK

JANUARY 19, 1976

The Bicentennnial God Bless Amercia Festival held at Yankee Stadium on June 1, 1976, was the culmination of numerous outreach projects, conferences for parents, and a public service clean-the-streets campaign. During the months prior to June 1, Dr. Pak inspired the membership to understand the spiritual significance and importance of the rally. Dr. Pak's absolute conviction and joy is inherited by the members as he explains that the work they are doing for the God Bless America Festival will allow them to become co-creators of the universe.

This gathering is equivalent to the gathering of thousands of Unification Church members throughout the world. Truly the forthcoming God Bless America Festival is going to be created under the spiritual guidance and with the heart and soul of our True Parents. We are like a bridge to the heart, soul, life, and spirit from Reverend Moon to every nation of our movement. We know that God is with us. Father won the victory, and we are the ones to transmit that victory to all of the world.

Unification Church members think that we are the minority. Everywhere we are pushed into corners. Everywhere we meet negative people. Everywhere we are faced with negative press. This has become the daily diet of the Unification Church. So we often think that we are on the verge of being overrun. But I want you to know that this world is but a small portion of God's creation, a small portion of the cosmos. Our Parents have won the rest of it—the entire history, the entire spirit world, and entire heart of God. No matter what negativity we face, just laugh at it! Smile at it! In due course, we'll lick it. It's just a matter of time.

We are grateful that God has given us this little opportunity to claim some worthiness in His sight. If God had done everything, we would have nothing to do. We would be begging for glory. He is giving us a chance to work so that we can claim some victory on earth. Instead of begging for glory, we can be entitled to it. God wants to have worthy sons and daughters with whom He can share all His glory. You must look at it in that positive way. The whole universe has been won; a little tiny bit is left to us to finish. Let's say God is building a brick wall. Ninety-nine layers have been completed, and just one more brick will complete the wall. God wants us to pick up that one brick and put it in the right place in the wall. Then He will say: "You and I completed it." What a wonderful title God is going to give us: co-creator of the universe! Co-creator of man!

The most important thing we have to do is have absolute conviction and positive thinking. For 24 hours every day, we must be bubbling with enthusiasm. Second, we must consider that the world where we are doing battle is not the main world. The subject world is the spirit world. The destiny of the world has already been determined. In due course that victory in the spirit world will be transmitted to this world. We cannot fail. In spirit world redemption has been claimed. The head of the serpent is crushed; this world is merely the tail. There is no chance for that serpent to be revived.

We must today clearly perceive the victory. That is the first purpose of this meeting. Already the victory is there. You must see it, you must touch it, you must feel it.

My job is to give you the feeling of utmost conviction and absolute positivity. We can do it. We can win. We have already won. Your thinking can be translated into visible situations. Your thinking is everything. Father has not one dot of doubt about his mission. I've been following him for almost 20 years, and not even for one split second did I glimpse that he was doubtful about his mission. What you think is what you are; what you think will show in an external way. How much victory you conceive of shall be translated into Yankee Stadium.

For this meeting I would like to excite you with the dream of this God Bless America Festival. We must make "God Bless America" and "Reverend Moon" synonymous in the hearts of every American. If we do this through Yankee Stadium, then we have consummated our mission. Americans have heard so much about Reverend Moon but much of it is negative. Many people earnestly want to know "Who is Reverend Moon? What is he trying to do?" The Yankee Stadium crusade is going to give a clear-cut image and answer to the American public. Who is Reverend Moon? He is the one who brings "God Bless America." I never doubt for a moment that this will do it. It will present Father correctly to the American public so that he will gain acceptance from the government down. This is our purpose. Acceptance. Proclamation is not enough. Two thousand years ago there was proclamation, but no acceptance. We have proclamation; we must have acceptance. The God Bless America Festival is for acceptance of Father. Through this supernatural, superracial, patriotic, humanitarian, embracing, God-centered movement, we can do it. We can achieve the goal of acceptance. Remember the word "acceptance."

When you speak to the American public, always think, "How did I present Father's name? Did I do well? Did I increase his kingdom or close another door?" Either you are opening a door or closing a door. Which one? With our every action we must open doors. Father must be appreciated by Americans. At the end of Yankee Stadium, we want to hear the majority of Americans saying, "We need him here in America." If Americans speak this simple conclusion at the end of Yankee Stadium, we are successful.

We do not look like giants, but inside every one of us is a diamond. Our capability is shining like diamonds. All we have to do is put our diamonds together into one cohesive working harmony to bring a tremendous outcome. All together we are going to create the miracle of the century. Yankee Stadium will be the first miracle of the third century of the history of America!

Let us have great ambition for God. Ambition is a God-given gift, wrong only when it is self-centered. Father is the most ambitious man under the sun. He would like to accomplish the greatest victory possible for God before his earthly life is over. We are joining with him as co-crusaders for the greatest victory here on earth.

PREPARING FOR YANKEE STADIUM

NEW YORK, NEW YORK

FEBRUARY 1, 1976

With preparations for Yankee Stadium in full swing, Father has asked Mrs. Won Pok Choi to visit and give her testimony to the members. When she concludes, Dr. Pak shares about the value of working for God's providence, using as an illustration a meeting in the 1960s with Arthur Ford, the famous American medium.

More than anyone else, Mr. David Kim scares me! [Laughter] This morning I do not intend to give you any additional sermon of any kind. It is certainly not scheduled, it is certainly not my intention; but more important, above all, is listening to Mrs. Choi. She has such a beautiful testimony, which is stronger than any other message coming from the brain or mind. It is coming from the life she lives. There is no more powerful testimony than your own personal experiences with God and True Parents. This is why Father, before he left, personally instructed her to come. I'm very fortunate that I could be with you this morning to listen to this portion of her testimony.

Even though I lived through this period of Unification Church history and have served True Parents and Mrs. Choi for many years, this beautiful testimony revealed to me many things that were new. I'm sure I heard this testimony before in Korea. At that time, however, I wasn't spiritually mature enough to grasp its meaning. Now everything comes to me with such a bubbling new enthusiasm. It gives me a new height of understanding of God and True Parents.

How truly great our True Parents are. In one word, how great we are simply because we belong to the True Parents. Not because of our own right, but because of the Master, the son of God. Truly God is centered upon this one man. The world will change in accordance with the will of God as revealed through this one man.

No matter what America is saying against him today or how they quibble over his words and say nasty things about him, I want you to know that this is the opportunity that God has given to us to stand up for our great cause and the great Parents. So that up in heaven someday, when we all end up there in the one great family of God, we have something to say in front of our Heavenly Father. We have something to be proud of in front of the throne of God. I welcome this severe confrontation in America before Yankee Stadium, because, in a sense, it is a great blessing. It's a different form of blessing. God has given us this particular opportunity so that we can stand up for Him. He's giving us a chance to sacrifice ourselves in the name of God.

Think of it, Mrs. Choi being thrown out of her school. Despite receiving persecution and unwarranted treatment by the school, the society, and the government, she was jubilant because she had tranquility and true peace with God. There was no power that could deter her march toward the kingdom of God. She has a beautiful testimony. In future generations, she will be used by God as a living example so that everyone can really see God and His love through her life.

NO SMOOTH PATH

In our way toward heaven, we must not expect a smooth and rosy path. This is not the blessing. That would be, in a way, a curse. We must expect a hard path from God. This is where we can prove ourselves worthy of God.

Throughout my life in the Unification Church, God and True Parents have been very good to me. I'm not worthy of such treatment. I'm grateful, but at the same time it is my prayer every day that God will bestow hardship on me so I can prove myself in His sight.

The other day we had a grand strategy meeting for Yankee Stadium at the 43rd Street headquarters. I simply stated to our members gathered there, the leadership, that we must be prepared to be sacrifices for the success of Yankee Stadium. For us, we have already conquered death. Death cannot deter us or stop us. Eternity has already started. Don't expect your eternity will start the day you die here on earth. Not at all. Eternity started when we met the True Parents. And eternity is maturing every day.

So, whether the physical body drops dead someday, or even tomorrow, it doesn't make any difference; we are in eternal life. But the important thing I am praying for is, God please use this body. This particular bullet is the most useful, most effective weapon for You. I don't want to just drop dead. Father, I want to be willing to die for You for a meaningful purpose. My prayer is that Father will give me an opportunity to explode like an atomic bomb, so that it can affect millions of people at one stroke. Father, I want to die that kind of death. Father, if You can use me for that kind of opportunity, that kind of sacrifice, I'll not only be willing but it will be a great honor.

We must feel the same way. We are giants, not because we are great but because True Parents are great. God is great. Because we are so close to God, you see, we are giants. Each one of you is a radiant segment of God, the sun of the spiritual heaven, or small suns.

A SHINING SUN

When you open up your spiritual eyes, you can see that Reverend Sun Myung Moon is a shining sun. I do not have these kinds of spiritual experiences. But I do know, through my experiences and learning the Divine Principle, that this is true. I will give you one example. I do not know how much you have heard about Arthur Ford. He is deceased now, but Ford was known as the foremost American medium, with the capability to communicate between the spirit world and this world. He wrote a book about the world unseen—the fantastic phenomena that Mrs. Choi touched on. There are unseen phenomena in a reality that exists alongside this physical world.

It is pity that physical eyes just don't see this world, but that does not mean it does not exist. Actually, the visible world we think is real is not the real world. Our world is the world of shadow. The real world is the world of spirit, in which we are going to live for eternity. But there are some gifted people who can communicate with or can see that world, and Arthur Ford was indeed one.

Some years ago, in 1965, Father made his first visit to America. I was in Washington, leading the Washington center. I was a missionary in Washington, D.C., and was very honored to have Father come to our center, which was actually my home, for three months. That was a most precious opportunity. Of course, Mrs. Choi was alongside Father, assisting him at every moment. One day we visited Philadelphia to see all the historical sites that were the cradle of this nation. Then, upon an invitation, we went to meet Arthur Ford. Ford suggested he have what he called a sitting.

He wanted to communicate, to see what the spirit world would say. This is written in his book, so I'm not going into detail. I'm sure many of you have read it. The moment Ford put a handkerchief on his head, lying back in a chair and breathing deeply about three to five minutes, the atmosphere become solemn, dignified, and very strange and mysterious.

I was so curious about what was happening. I was like a three-year-old child. My eyes were popping out like this. The first word Ford spoke, his voice had changed; in other words, he was not speaking but was unconscious. He was speaking as an instrument of the medium, an instrument of the spiritual person in the other world, whose name was Fletcher. Fletcher used Ford's lips and organs, and his voice was entirely different from Ford's a few minutes before.

As Fletcher spoke, Ford's lips moved. He said, "This whole room is shining in a radiant sun. In the Bible, God ordered Moses to take off his shoes before he was given the revelation, because that was a holy place." Fletcher told all of those in the room to take off their shoes, because they were in the presence of a great master of God. He said the whole room is radiant like the sun and you would not be able to open your eyes if you really could perceive the strength of this light. You would be blinded by the light, its intensity is so strong.

When Father speaks, the entire spirit world sees that he is radiant, like a sunbeam. By living such a life—such an intense life that gives true power, energy, and life—we in turn, become radiant light. This is what the Divine Principle teaches.

When the spirit man is in formation stage, it is not quite mature, so you are like a transparent body; you can see through it. There is no real substance in it. But when you come to the growth stage, you are like a moon, becoming radiant but not yet giving off your own light. When you become a divine spirit, however, you will become a radiant sun, a life-giving soul. That is the goal of life. We want to mature into that kind of life-giving person, a radiant sun.

TALK TO GOD ALL DAY

Here in America, our movement does not talk too much about miracles, strange experiences, and so forth. But they are happening. Furthermore, the more difficulty we face, the greater the revelation will be. When our hard-working fund-raisers are out in the street, there is no leader, there is no one to speak to, no one is really friendly; you are out in the desert, one-to-one with God. All day long, you can call on the name of God: Unless You help me, I cannot accomplish my mission. This is how our brothers and sisters really discover God's presence so close. This is a wonderful blessing.

At the same time, about 300 pioneers are working in the field. I met one pioneer working in Washington, D.C., yesterday. His name was Eugene Kenedy. He was riding a bike, and he had on a heavy coat. He was moving from one street to another, witnessing from morning to night. When I saw him, he had no home, no real place to go, only a sleeping bag with him. But his face had such radiant, sparkling eyes; I have never seen a man so healthy looking. I shook hands, and we had a wonderful chat. He witnessed to me and I witnessed to him.

Yes, don't you know, even after becoming members, we must witness to each other. Do you see that? This is very, very important! Mrs. Choi this morning witnessed to you. And you witnessed to yourself or to others. We must grow and mature. Don't ever think, since I sent in my application to the Unification Church, I'm already in heaven. Not at all. That is merely a condition that you are entitled to, enter heaven, but you haven't yet.

So we must witness to each other. How beautiful it is if we meet on a street corner. Somebody approaches you, not knowing you are already a member of the Unification Church, and tries to talk about Reverend Moon earnestly, to talk about the new revelation, the new world coming, the true love of God. You will be on cloud nine instantly, just from looking at the living example.

So, we are never alone. I thought the United States was a pretty big country. Now I bump into our members on every street corner! It is not a big country after all. Really, you go out and bump into our members at every corner. Particularly, when Yankee Stadium comes closer, we will bump into each other 10 times, 100 times a day. How will you feel? Oh, one brother is already covering that corner, and my sister is covering that street corner. Over there is my elder sister. There's my leader fighting very strongly. The whole city will be covered completely, so that not even one small peanut can leak out. That kind of feeling is so wonderful. We witness to each other. So I had a chat with Eugene Kenedy on the street, with his bike. Soon we will bump into our members in every corner of this world.

I want you to know True Parents arrived safely in Korea. At the very moment of their arrival, they took up their heavy burdens. He will come back with great news. I have great anticipation. I am leaving tomorrow for Korea. I will serve him as much as I can while I am in Korea. I prepared a good report for him. Most important, I will report about this testimony, your gathering here, and so forth.

In the early days of the church in Korea, I was not the earliest member. Mrs. Choi was there, and Mr. David Kim, our dear elder brother. When I came, I was truly like a little baby; I was very young. I was a young-looking Korean officer. They said, "baby officer." I had very big cheeks. Anyway,

I came and mingled with the early pioneering church members in 1957.

In those days, there was such beautiful harmony and brotherly love. As Mrs. Choi indicated, there was pure brotherly love morning to night. It was truly heaven. We miss those days very much. However, we must re-create such scenes here in America. We are pioneering today. America is celebrating its bicentennial. Actually, the Unification Church is in the early first century of the movement in America. You are the pioneers! So, there is no reason why we cannot duplicate such a beautiful tradition such as that back in 1950, 1955, or 1957 here in America. Let's have no dull moments; there is no such thing in our life as routine. In life with God, there is no routine; there is no repetition of anything. Every day is a new creation, a new challenge.

I would like to challenge you. Until Father and Mother come back, please pray hard. Already a 120-day prayer vigil has started. Yankee Stadium is a little over 100 days ahead of us. We're getting closer. I really want you to get yourself ready until Father and Mother's return, so that they will feel that we are truly ready for the great victory in Yankee Stadium. This is your job. I'm leaving tomorrow morning for Seoul. We have a conference today, and we'll gather all the reports.

As you know, Father and Mother's birthday is January 6 on the lunar calendar. On the solar calendar, it's February 5. Literally in every word, every sentence, Father and Mother were predestined by God 6,000 years ago. They were born on the same day, although 23 years apart. God prepared it that way.

Whatever cards you make, whatever wishes you want to convey, no matter how big my package would be, I would be most happy to carry them. In addition, I will carry to Korea your spirit, your zeal, to present to the True Parents and at the same time share with the Korean brothers and sisters.

So thank you very much, once again, our dear elder brother David Kim, for giving me a very charming introduction, which I do not deserve. What he's saying is that you should live up to that introduction, so I will do my best. Meanwhile, I would like you to enjoy the testimony of Mrs. Choi in the following weeks. Do not miss this meeting. It's very, very important. By listening to her, when Father comes back you can enjoy Father's message. You can understand him far better. This is truly a great opportunity that I want you to grab. Take advantage of this particular period, and let us truly live up to our True Parents' expectation.

Thank you very much!

National Parents Conference

NEW YORK, NEW YORK
MAY 30, 1976

━━━━━━━━━━━━━━━━━━━━━━

Nine parents' conferences were held in localities through-out the United States in 1976 to provide an opportunity for parents to learn more about the teachings of the Unification Movement as well as to invite them to attend the Yankee Stadium rally. In the following text, Dr. Pak shares his personal testimony and speaks heart-to-heart to the audience.

Reverend Moon personally asked me to see you and welcome you on his behalf. As parents of members of the Unification Church, you are great people in the sight of God. You are remembered in His heart in a very special way, simply because you gave birth to a son or daughter for the purpose of God's providence. Your children would never have been in the Unification Church unless it was the providence of God. Your sons and daughters were hand-picked, chosen by God to serve a very special purpose in this critical period in God's timetable. You as parents ought to be congratulated because you are the ones who gave birth to and brought up in the world wonderful sons and daughters of God. You must have done something right, or your ancestors must have done something right.

Actually I, too, am a parent, one of you. Two of my children are in the Unification Church. One is a sophomore at George Washington University and is working side by side with your children in Harlem and the Bronx in the Yankee Stadium Crusade. I am proud of my daughter. My son is now in Korea studying the Korean language, but he has gone through the Barrytown training, and I'm proud of him, too. So I'm speaking to you as a parent with children who are giving their lives to our movement.

I owe a great deal to Reverend Moon. One parent wrote Reverend Moon some time ago and in her letter she said, "Reverend Moon, I thank you in all sincerity because you gave something to my children which as a parent I would never have been capable of giving." I fully echo the sentiments of that parent. I have four more children growing up. Having my children deposited in the hands of God, I have no worries. God is taking care of them. My four little ones are already studying the Principle. I know as long as they are within the teachings of the Unification Church, their lives are secure.

A QUESTION FOR GENERATIONS

I'm sure people around the world are asking, "Who is Reverend Sun Myung Moon?" That question will be asked a million times, but I know one thing: That question will not be answered in our time; it will go on and on for centuries and centuries. For generations to come they will be asking, "Who is Reverend Sun Myung Moon?" Just as we are still asking, "Who is Jesus Christ?" The man of Nazareth, a humble carpenter, uneducated, was crucified on the cross, but he really turned the history of mankind upside down. He is a man of mystery even now after 2,000 years. Reverend Moon is, in that sense, a man of mystery and will remain a man of mystery. Many, many dissertations will be done on him. Scholar after scholar will study him, and that study will continue.

Let me give you what I think he is. Dr. Thomas Boslooper said he is a man of God. Indeed, he is a man of God. I can only tell you who Reverend Moon is by testifying to what he has done for me. He saved my life. Without him, I don't think I would have had a chance of being here tonight. I would have been gone a long time ago.

I was a soldier in the Korean War. In combat, the shadow of death was hanging around me all the time. I was a company commander of over 200 men. I was crossing a river with the men when all of a sudden a surprise attack came from the hill in front of me. The Red Chinese Army was just waiting for our most vulnerable moment to open fire. A shower of bullets came at us and no one could escape. I was on this edge of the shore, so I instantly collapsed on the sand. I was not a Christian. I was not even a

Buddhist. My mother was a good Buddhist and my father was a follower of Confucius, but I didn't have anything. The first word that came to me was *Hananim*, God. I knew no one could save me. Buddha—impossible. Confucius—impossible. But I knew if someone could save me, it was God.

A split second later, another thought came to me. The shower of bullets kept coming. My men had completely collapsed and were destroyed and I knew I could not avoid the same fate. My second thought was, I was not ready to die. Even though I called on God, I knew He had no reason to come to rescue me. My heart was empty. I knew I was not ready to die.

The third thought that came was: If I can ever escape this desperate situation, I must find out the meaning of life. I must fill my heart with meaning so I will be ready to die.

GOD SAVED MY LIFE

All of a sudden U.S. fighter bombers appeared and fired at the Chinese soldiers. It was their turn to take cover and they had to stop firing on us. I stood up and examined my body because if I had been hit I would not have been able to escape, but my whole body was intact. I called out to my men, "This is our chance. Follow me!" Only two men could follow me, and both were desperately wounded. I was the only one without a scratch. After that incident I learned how to humble myself in the sight of God Almighty. I knew it must be God who saved my life. I determined to give my life to whoever saved me, for His purpose. My search for truth began in that moment.

In 1952 I came to Fort Benning, Georgia, to be trained at the infantry school because the Korean War was still going on. I observed America, that she was receiving blessings because of the Christian character of this nation. I came to Washington, D.C., at that time, and one thing I distinctly remember. There was a small prayer room at in the Congress building. The guide told me that the great leaders of this country, when they have an important decision to make, come into that small room and humbly kneel down to seek divine guidance. That overwhelmed my heart. I saw at that time the true greatness of America. I knew then that America deserved its blessings because of the God-centered nature of this country. So I went back to Fort Benning and was baptized at the Church of Christ in Columbus, Georgia, and I kept on studying the Bible.

But the more I tried, my heart still remained very cold. My heart was not ignited. I knew it was still empty. I was not yet ready to die. The Church of Christ minister came to me and said, "I think you have good potential to be a missionary in the future, or a minister of the church, so we'll give you a scholarship to go to the Church of Christ University in Texas, on the one condition that you become a minister of the Church of Christ."

At that time, believe it or not, I couldn't speak even one word of English. I could barely say good morning. My ambition was to come back to this country and study English someday. But after mulling it over for a couple of nights, I declined that offer. I said to the minister, "You know, I'm dying to study in America, but you set the condition that I must become a minister of the Church of Christ after I return to Korea. I cannot preach about God. Do you know why? God is not real to my heart yet. If I'm going to stand up and speak about God, I would be a liar, a hypocrite. I cannot become a minister with this heart."

My search continued. In 1957, God led me to meet Reverend Sun Myung Moon in Korea. In two days of studying the Divine Principle, all my questions were solved. I was a new man. God had become real to my heart. That's what Reverend Moon did for me and that's what he's doing for thousands of young people, including your sons and daughters, here in America, more hundreds of thousands in Japan, more hundreds of thousands in Korea, Germany, England, even in communist countries. This is what Reverend Moon is doing. He is making God real to my heart and to everyone's heart. When you know God, when you have a taste of God, no one can turn you back; no Rabbi Davis, no Ted Patrick, no power can separate me from my oneness with God.

But Reverend Moon is very humble himself. He says, "I am not doing this. I am merely a humble instrument of God." In other words, Reverend Moon is being used by God. He is starting a fire of revolution in the hearts of men, the greatest revolution of all. Military, economic, industrial revolutions are noisy, but they are not so big. The real revolution is a quiet one—the revolution of man. For that purpose Jesus Christ came. Two thousand years later, here in America and all over the world, the same vitality, the same enthusiasm that Jesus Christ brought, that same power, that same Holy Spirit is working right now in the hearts of young people around the world. It's the work of God. No one can stop it.

Many people think that kicking Reverend Moon out of America will stop the movement or that shooting him down will stop the Unification Church. Nothing is farther from the truth. It is not the work of Reverend Moon. If something like that should ever happen, millions of Sun Myung Moons will rise up until God finishes His task. Nothing under the sun can stop the march of the will of God. This is the way I feel and the way your sons and daughters feel.

I want to be very honest with you. You know the criticisms we are getting—brainwashing, mind control, even hypnotism. When Reverend Moon spoke on Capitol Hill last December he told those distinguished

Americans: "Let me ask you one question. Are you Americans so foolish as to be brainwashed by a Korean, particularly since I use an interpreter?" Later one congressman commented, "That was the most beautiful answer I have ever heard."

BECOME A NEW PERSON

What is happening today is really a revolution of man. Revolution is a basic characteristic of Christianity. What did Jesus say in the first Gospel: "Repent, for the kingdom of God is at hand." What does "repent" mean but to give up your past and become a new person. Jesus said you must be born again, or you are not entitled to the kingdom of heaven. Rebirth means to become a new creature, accepting God and making God real to your heart. This is revolution. This was supposed to have been happening for the past 2,000 years. But even Billy Graham has pointed out the rapid decline of the Western church.

About 15 years ago I picked up a *Time* magazine when I arrived in America and I turned to the religion section. I was quite interested in one remark by the dean of the Harvard Divinity School, the late Dr. Samuel Miller. He said, "Christianity may be at death's door. If religion is going to play some important role in the modern world, it has to undergo a radical revolution." Last year, in a November issue of *Newsweek*, even Pope Paul said the Christian church may be destined to decline because it has lost its appeal to the young people of our times.

Here in the Unification Church, your sons and daughters have gathered. Contrary to the testimony of Pope Paul, something has happened. Young people have ideals, courage, scientific minds, and a sense of dedication. Young people are not moved unless they are convinced. Who can brainwash your sons and daughters? You know them well. They've gotten hold of something. The revolution of man that was intended by God to take place 2,000 years ago is happening now. That is what the Unification Church is all about. Our door is open 24 hours a day. Anybody can come in and anybody can leave. Many times Reverend Moon asks people, "Why don't you leave me alone and go?" No power, no strength, no cement could bring your children into the Unification Church except the power of God. That is why I'm here.

THE POWER OF GOD

I've been faithfully serving Reverend Sun Myung Moon for 20 years. But in my mind I'm not serving Reverend Moon at all; I'm serving God and I know that by obeying and following Reverend Moon I can serve God better. It is in my interest to listen to him, not by his orders. This New Yorker

Hotel is full of young people. You have never seen Reverend Moon come here and say, "Do that. Clean up those rooms. Go out on the streets." But a miracle is happening every day. One week ago we moved into this hotel. It was almost like a bombed-out place, but one week later we are fully activated and 2,000 rooms are not enough. What power makes this possible? Only the power of God.

In our movement, miracles are happening every day, and your sons and daughters are creating them. I live every day in astonishment, watching them. No power under the sun could make such beautiful things happen except God.

I would like to tell you one more thing. Many parents are concerned about the welfare of their children. Naturally, I am too. What are their living conditions, are they getting the proper doctor's care, are they getting a proper diet? You know we didn't buy this hotel to live luxuriously. Our members do go through hardship. But no one works harder than Reverend Moon himself. I'm younger than him. I try to outdo him, but in 20 years I have never won one game. I am always defeated by him. Late at night I see Reverend Moon on his knees in prayer. I hardly see him in bed sleeping. Do you think he is going out to sea for enjoyment? No, he is going out to taste suffering, to take physical and mental torture in a way, to feel the rigors of the world. He can't stand still. The ocean becomes his competitor. It is very hard to understand, but I tell you this in all honesty and sincerity.

As parents, we realize what is good for our children—a good house, good clothing, good food, and a sports car. All the luxury in the world is available in America today. But in the Unification Church, once we become aware of the presence of God so clearly, our criteria, our sense of values change. We normally would think of our lifetime as being around 100 years, rarely more than that, so we want to be successful within that period of time. But in the Unification Church, we look at value from the true point of view.

Jesus said, you may gain the entire world but lose your own life. We see invisible values clearly. This is where the problem comes. The rest of the world does not see what we see so clearly: a different set of values. We go after those values that will remain even a million years after this chunk of dust has decayed. We believe in immortality and that the real life is our eternal one. The 100 years or so we have on this earth are a privilege, an opportunity to serve God, to learn the heart of God, to live with God. That relationship with God determines our eternal life. Jesus Christ told us that.

From the worldly eyes of the reporters of the *Washington Post* or *The New York Times*, the life of Jesus Christ was a miserable failure. A young man started out to turn the world upside down, but at the age of 33 he was hanging on a cross, dying, and his disciples all had fled. In the worldly sense, Jesus was a failure, but in the eternal sense, not at all. He lived the most victorious life ever lived by any human being on earth. So he is triumphant now and forever. His life will go on. Even communist countries calculate history according to his year of birth.

BUILD HEAVEN ON EARTH

Today, we believe in that dream for which Jesus Christ came—to turn the world into the kingdom of God here on earth. We are not going to be in heaven after we die; we are going to find our heaven here on earth. Unless we build heaven here on earth, we will never find heaven "up there." This is our way of life, and we are serious about this life. No one is more serious about the realities of life here on earth than members of the Unification Church.

How I feel is exactly how your sons and daughters feel. I want to do more for God, more for Jesus Christ. I'm just not doing enough. Every day is a new day in which I can determine myself to do more. We have to die, but when that time comes (and it can come at any age), I want to be ready to go without regret. My life here on earth is my opportunity to serve God, whatever the sacrifice.

When you know this seriousness, I hope you can understand where our movement stands and where we are going. We have been the targets of ridiculous accusations; many things have been said about Reverend Moon, even about me. As special assistant to Reverend Moon, even I became famous. They even make me out to be the head of the Korean CIA. Let me tell you about the Korean CIA business. They are trying to destroy the Unification Church by linking us with the Korean CIA, or any CIA for that matter. This deliberate attempt by a negative power is due to the fact that they do not want us to succeed, period. I tell you, if I ever had or any member of our movement ever had any association with the Korean CIA, we would not have survived up to this point.

I came to America in 1961 as a military attaché to the Korean embassy. It was an honored position for a military man. At that time my goal was to become a general. I was hand-picked out of hundreds of candidates. After I came to this country, there was a military revolution in Korea and Park Chung Hee came into power. I was not in Korea; I was already in Washington. The Korean CIA was formed after the revolution. How could I have been an agent of the Korean CIA even before its birth? I could go on and on like that, but it's not necessary for you, our courageous parents. If you had believed such nonsense, you would not have come here. I'm sure my heart will reveal a good enough testimony to answer all the accusations.

We are headed for a collision with the evil ideology of communism. Sooner or later, this country must awaken to the menace of communism. The world is being taken over by communism, inch by inch, and yard by yard, nation by nation. In less than half a century communists took over two-thirds of the population of the world. Do you think America can survive while the rest of the world is in the hands of the communists? You are wrong. America will not survive. Abraham Lincoln said that a nation cannot endure long, half-slave, half-free. In the sight of God, the world is the same. The world will never survive half-slave and half-free. America, as you will hear Reverend Moon say, has been called upon to be a champion of God like David before the Goliath of our times: communism. The Unification Church has no weapons, but we have the weapon of the truth of God. Nothing is stronger than this weapon. With the truth, we can destroy communism. Knowing that danger is coming, God called on Reverend Sun Myung Moon as His champion, to speak up.

More than anyone else, communists know the menace of the Unification Church to them, so they are out to get us any possible way that they can. God is on our side. Our march is His march. They will never win. We will win, because God is ours. Because of this, many accusations are deliberately made against us, but this morning Reverend Moon said, "Do not be concerned. Let us go on and finish our task." Yankee Stadium is one step toward our goal, but we will take many other steps, and your sons and daughters will become more courageous, more effective, and above all, more loved by God. I can assure you of that.

Your sons and daughters need your support. They may not be able to be with you all the time, but they have an important mission. They are like the Revolutionary War soldiers at Valley Forge. Their mission is that important: building a new nation, a new world. Give them your love and they will respond with their love.

TODAY IS THE REAL BEGINNING FOR YOU

NEW YORK, NEW YORK

FEBRUARY 21, 1977

═══════════════

Only two days before True Parents' Birthday, members are gathered in New York for the International Blessing of 74 Couples, and Dr. Bo Hi Pak speaks to the couples directly before the ceremony. He lovingly acknowledges their loyalty and devotion and their trials and victories. He describes the historical event as another important cornerstone of the Kingdom of God on earth, being laid this time in America.

After the evening banquet with True Parents, Dr. Pak speaks again, joyfully engaging the new couples in several games. He then invites them to express their gratitude and joy by entertaining True Parents with their many talents.

God created Adam and Eve to be the parents of mankind, and He blessed them saying: "Be fruitful and multiply, and fill the earth and subdue it; and have dominion over the fish of the sea and over the birds of the air, and over every living thing that moves upon the earth." God created man for the fulfillment of these three major blessings expressed in Genesis 1:28. The first blessing is the perfection of man. The second blessing is that of the divine marriage of perfect husband and wife to create the family. The third is lordship over all creation.

If Adam and Eve had been totally obedient to God and had united with Him, they would have become the first temples of God through their individual perfection. It was God's plan then to bring perfected Adam and Eve into heavenly matrimony, and as husband and wife, they would create the first family of man on earth. As they multiplied children, their posterity would have filled the earth, and they would have been given lordship over all the earth. That would have consummated the three blessings of God, and the joy of God would have been abundant throughout heaven and earth.

Through disobedience, however, Adam and Eve separated themselves from God and could not achieve perfection. Therefore, God could not bless Adam and Eve in heavenly matrimony, and human history started with a satanic lineage. It is truly heart-warming, though, to know that in the long 6,000 years of biblical history, God's total goal has been the restoration of mankind into His own family. He has been longing for the day of the first heavenly wedding ceremony.

THE GREATEST PRIVILEGE

It is incredible and astonishing to realize today that we members of the Unification Church are living in another messianic era. We are privileged people who are allowed to see God, not in a mirror dimly, but face to face. We are privileged people who have been experiencing the very heart of God.

Today we see 74 chosen pairs of men and women who have been handpicked by God to be Blessed in heavenly matrimony. This historical event which we are about to witness will unite the entire heaven and earth in these men and women, creating heavenly families that will be admitted into the Kingdom of God on earth and in heaven.

Although our work and the media are quiet today, the billions of citizens in the spirit world know that today another important cornerstone of the Kingdom of God on earth is about to be laid here in America. The entire spirit world is enviously looking upon these privileged men and women from 11 different nations of the world.

As members of the Unification Church International from all over the world, we bring our heartfelt congratulations to you selected champions of our movement who are participating in today's honor and glory. We extend our heartfelt congratulations upon your Blessed marriage.

We pay our deep respect and admiration to you who, through your long-standing loyalty and absolute devotion, have won today's honor to be selected as Blessed couples. We know that many of you have gone through untold tribulations and persecution. You have victoriously gone through severe tests of God in personal tragedies, and you have withstood the worst temptations. Today, you are here as victors of heaven. You are shining examples of Church members throughout the world. You have been the pacemakers of our movement, and you have set a beautiful tradition to be followed. Yet, today is the real beginning for you. All heaven and earth will watch what you do after this Blessing. We still have ground to cover to reach perfection. But I am sure you will come out final and eternal victors.

I would like to end by quoting the words of Reverend Sun Myung Moon in his message on September 11, 1974:

> What is our purpose? To become true men. We will create the true husband and wife and become true parents to give birth to children who experience love among themselves and from a loving brotherhood. And those children and parents together will create one heavenly family. That family will expand into a true society. That true society will expand into a true nation. That true nation will expand into a true world.

> God bless you all. Thank you.

[After the Blessing ceremony, Dr. Pak offered more remarks.]

Never in the history of the Blessing of the Unification members, except the first 36 families, have the True Parents granted permission for individual couples to take photographs with them. This is an extraordinary honor.

Before we receive instructions from Father, I would like to express a few words in a very informal manner. First of all, this is the first formal wedding ceremony outside of Korea. Of course, we did have wedding ceremonies in Belvedere and some of our leaders were married back in 1969. So I would like you to know that Father and Mother gave very special consideration to make this wedding ceremony possible.

As you know, the day after tomorrow is our True Parents' birthday, and this birthday in 1977 is a very special one. On the foundation of the victory of 1976 here in America, this wedding ceremony today was made possible. Therefore, Father and Mother gave us instructions to do our very best to set the tradition for future weddings and make this wedding ceremony noble, dignified, and colorful. You brothers and sisters who are not being Blessed today, your chance is coming. You must earn it.

These 74 couples are extraordinary ones in many respects. They are truly pacemakers, and the tradition has been set by them, particularly those Japanese who came here to be Blessed. Those who belong to the 777 and 1800 Couples Blessings, you have gone through personal tragedies, but you withstood them for the True Parents. Those people who were matched this time in America are the ones who were working for Yankee Stadium and Washington Monument. They had the full capability to be Blessed in the 1800 Couples Blessing, but because of the mission, they couldn't get out of America.

Among all these special people are Martin Porter, very special, and Irene Welch, the first member of the Unification Church of America. So this is a really great day for this very extraordinary group of people. All you 74 couples, your wedding was one of the most beautiful weddings I have ever seen.

And Father and Mother stayed for the pictures. This is only for you. Father and Mother have never done it before. Even I don't have a picture like that. When I got Blessed in 1961, the 36 couples were Blessed in Korea, but my wife and I were in America so we kept the same hour. Just like Mrs. Cho Sun Sook and Mrs. Sun Chum Yo, these two brides are doing the same thing. From Heavenly Father's point of view, the Pacific Ocean is nothing, it is a peanut. It makes this ceremony very, very dramatic for our brothers Ed Bolton and Keith Anderson, and for the two brides in Korea. So give them a big hand. You have great faith, not seeing your own bride. That is really a great tradition. I know the blessing of God is going to be abundant.

So this wedding is setting the pace, and much greater numbers are coming in the future. You are pioneers of great weddings of the future.

[Dr. Pak spoke again after the evening banquet.]

Are you enjoying the dinner? Are you really enjoying the dinner? How are your chopsticks? Do they work? OK. Father and Mother are enjoying watching you eat. Really, Father and Mother are enjoying watching you, and you are so slow tonight. Now I know the reason why. Well, the taste is entirely different tonight, isn't it? It is a great privilege to have True Parents come to our banquet. Again, this is extraordinary. We never had this type of banquet in the past Blessing celebrations. You are, all in all, in a very special group.

Actually tonight, I would like to initiate one game, then I will turn everything over to Martin Porter. We didn't prepare any formal celebration. The day after tomorrow we will have a formal celebration together with

True Parents for their birthday. Every one of you will have a special seat.

Furthermore, the reason we don't have a formal program tonight is Martin Porter and Mr. Matsuzaki told me there are so many wonderful talents among you. They want to show Father and Mother how good you are. It is up to you now. This can go on all night, as long as Father and Mother are happy. But it can be over in 30 minutes if you fail to satisfy Father and Mother.

All right, start with the first game. Each husband and wife look at each other. Who can watch your mate longer without blinking your eyes. Are you ready? The greater the love, the longer you would not blink. Whose love is deeper? All right, everyone get closer together, close the distance between wife and husband. Now, everybody quiet. All the serving people quiet. This is a serious game now. Close your eyes. Ready? Open your eyes.

All right, more husbands won. All right, once more. Ready—go! All right. More husbands. This time try another game. All the wives try to make the husbands laugh. All the husbands try to keep yourself from laughing. You can do anything you want, make facial expression, use your hands. Husbands should not laugh. All right. Now ready—begin! Those husbands who didn't laugh raise your hands. You poor husbands, why didn't you laugh? What kind of husbands are you? Oh boy, what cruel husbands you are.

Now husbands, make your wives mad. He upset you very, very much. Very furious. Now begin, make her laugh. All right, those who didn't laugh raise your hands. Everybody is defeated. That is great.

This is really a day for great laugher. Everybody laugh. Show True Parents how well you can laugh. Face True Parents and laugh so much you make Father and Mother laugh. Go on, you are not yet successful. What are you doing? Go on, hurry up.

FATHER TRUSTS US

═══════════════════

Drawing on his own experience, Dr. Pak explains how God is always preparing us for future missions and candidly shares about his first meeting with Father and the Unification Church.

Good morning. How are you this morning? You look great. Father, I am ready to translate. Father is here [in spirit]. Father is here with us. All I have to do is translate for invisible Father standing right here speaking to us. I still feel very strange when I stand in front of you all by myself. It doesn't feel real. Almost I feel that it is so unreal without Father.

It is a beautiful morning. We gather together every Sunday morning here at Belvedere for 5 a.m. service, ready to be with Father and pray. It is such an inspiring thing to hear your singing voices. This is truly heaven. That inspires me more than anything else. The Unification Church has many, many special features, special traditions and so forth. But as far as my experience goes, I have discovered that Father is working strongly in our movement through the singing of the Unification Church members. I am not just talking about singing here in America and at Belvedere.

I will tell you a little bit of my testimony. Back in 1957 when I first came to the movement, I was a military officer with the rank of major serving as an aide-de-camp to a U.S. general, Major General Hamilton House. He was head of all the U.S. military advisory groups in Korea. He was advising the entire Korean army, and I was hand-picked by him to be his assistant, like I am now a special assistant to Reverend Moon. You see, Heavenly Father is always preparing you. Many years before you even imagine, he puts us in the position to prepare and be ready for future missions. Now I realize Heavenly Father had a reason to put me there as an aide-de-camp to the U.S. general. My primary job at that time was to translate for him from English into Korean and vice versa. Translating Father's words is an extremely difficult task. I am sure you are very sympathetic.

AN IMPOSSIBLE TASK

Father speaks in depth, always giving a profound message. It is virtually impossible to convey 100 percent of Father's meaning in such a short time. It may take a millennium to explain even one sentence Father speaks. So how could a poor interpreter come out and say exactly what Father's spirit is? How can it be translated? From the very beginning I knew it was virtually an impossible task to be a translator to Father. So I prayed to God to help me fulfill my mission. It is not a job for a technician or a professional translator. There are a great many professional Korean translators, English translators, and all kinds of translators at the United Nations. I don't think any one of those can do the job of translating for Father because it is virtually impossible to convey Father's message absolutely correctly.

So I pray to God. God, let me translate in faith. I am desperately trying to somehow bring Father's spirit to you. Sometimes I make great blunders, errors, and many mistakes. But I feel as long as the spirit is right, as long as I can be truly in Father's spirit, then I can translate. You do not really listen to what I say. Actually you are listening to the spirit itself. Some member told me during Father's crusade, "You know, after one hour, I forget I am listening to an interpreter." I felt that was the greatest compliment.

Anyway, to go back to that U.S. general. Translating from English to Korean is equally difficult. Particularly you American people have a terrible language. I always thought Korean was terrible, but English is equally terrible and difficult. And you American people use a lot of slang and colloquialisms. Even today, I cannot understand many of the jokes that Americans tell. But this particular American general in Korea always wanted to tell jokes when speaking at big gatherings of Korean generals. He wanted to see the people laugh, to relax the mood and break the ice. That is a good American way of delivery. You want to establish rapport. But translating jokes is so difficult—boy, that kills me. That really kills me.

The general would stand up and tell a joke. I would be sweating and listening and trying to catch every word, every meaning so I can translate, so everybody can laugh and enjoy the joke. I desperately tried to hear. Sometimes it worked. Good, yes, I understood. Sometimes it didn't work. When the general started to tell an American joke, in a second I knew if I could translate it or not. Sometimes I was just full of blanks. I caught every word of it, but ... no meaning. It is not funny at all. Supposedly it is a most funny American joke, but it certainly is not funny at all in Korean.

PLEASE LAUGH FOR ME

One time when I was translating for the general, he spoke some words in good American English. Then he was looking at me, "Go ahead, translate." But his words had no meaning for me. I stepped forward, and I had to say something. The general said something, so I had to say something, but I didn't know what to say. So I just honestly confessed, speaking in Korean, "Ladies and gentlemen, you know the American general was trying to entertain you and spoke what is supposed to be a most wonderful American joke. It must be a very funny one, but it is so funny that even I do not understand it. But I do know that it is a very good American joke, a very funny one, so could you kindly do me a favor and laugh at the joke?"

That was really funny. The roar of laugher really brought the roof down. The only puzzled person was the general. Later he said, "Boy, I spoke five minutes. It took me a good five minutes to tell that joke. Your language must be wonderful, fantastic. You translated in 30 seconds and everybody laughed." Well, I confessed to the general what I had done. He said, "Well, that is OK, Bo Hi. At least your joke is better than mine."

This morning we have two television sets here. Some people might think Father is going to speak through the television. The answer is yes. Yes. Yes. Yes. We have a wonderful program for you. I want to make my testimony brief so that Father can speak to you directly through the television. How would you like that? Great, isn't it?

After all, why did God give television to America? Why did God give television to the world? God gave this modern communication technology for the sake of God. When you read the Bible, you learn that in the Last Days the word of God will flash like lightning from East to West. The entire world will know and hear about the coming of the Lord. That was the prediction.

But do you know that today our world is much smaller than an ancient village? I was living in a village back in the countryside of Korea. Let's say some important person died in that village or something happened. It sometimes would take a day for the news to travel around the village. But nowadays, with modern technology, when something happens, such as when John F. Kennedy was assassinated in Dallas, Texas, in a flash the whole world knew about it. It is an amazing world. The world is so small. Now, anything Reverend Sun Myung Moon does, he raises his voice or lifts up his arms, becomes news. In Korea, sometimes they know certain things faster than you do. What an amazing world.

But why did God give us these modern technologies? Because when the time comes when absolute truth is revealed to us, God wants to use this technology for His purpose. Not Satan's purpose. To give the world the Word of Life, so everyone can come to live in the sight of God for eternity. That is the purpose. Unfortunately, those same modern technologies are utilized by Satan as well, and television today is doing a great deal of damage, spreading immorality and violence, all kinds of things. Satanic images are being transmitted through the television tube. One nickname for a television is "one-eyed monster."

USE THE MEDIA FOR GOD

But we are going to change all that. We are going to use the television media and all other modern communication media to transmit Heavenly Father's truth to the world. We are gradually coming close to doing that. Father predicted that this year, 1977, we will begin that crusade. So the first program you are going to view today is one prepared to be telecast to the nation.

Through this program the world can see Father, Mother, the first family of heaven, and, most important, they can hear Father directly. This is the first experiment. The title of this program is "Reverend Moon in America," which primarily features the Washington Monument rally, September 18, 1976. But far more than that, this one-hour program is prepared to show Father's work and his entire life all over America. You are the first group of Unification Church members to see it. Even Father hasn't seen it. So, tonight, we are going to put everything in the car and drive to Boston to show Father. The reason we want you to see this program first is so I can bring to Father not only the program, but your enthusiasm. That is the purpose. So we will view it shortly. But first, I would like to spend an extra few moments to share with you some of my inspiration.

As I said at the outset of this talk, the singing of the Unification Church has a special meaning. When I joined in 1957, there was only a small group of Unification members. One person I met when I first came in the church was Mr. David Kim. He was there with a handful of the early pioneering group of the Unification Church. Don't you think he deserves a big hand? Think of it. Our church was only a small cubbyhole, a shack-type church. Really pioneering. But there in that shack they were talking about the unification of the world, one ideology under one God, all people as one family under one Father. Amazing

But the main point I want to make is this. I listened to the Divine Principle two nights. I was a military officer, but some beautiful young lady invited me to listen to a very important talk. She didn't tell me anything about Reverend Moon or the Unification Church. She didn't even tell me anything about religion or Christianity. She just said it is a wonderful and most attractive and interesting talk. Won't you come? Well, certainly I couldn't reject an invitation from a beautiful young lady.

But then in two days a whole new world came before me. I was a quite healthy, young, hopefully good-looking officer, strong, very proud. A major of the Republic of Korea Army, serving a U.S. general. I was a very proud person, a very strong, healthy person. I listened to the first night's lecture. It was tremendous. I was really bubbling with enthusiasm. This is something very extraordinary. Very special. So I promised I would come the next night at 7:00. And now I understand how Satan worked. All of a sudden from 5:30 on, I had a fever, I was dizzy, I couldn't get up. Amazing. I had never in my life had this experience. I was totally sick. I wanted to call the lecturer to say that I was sick and could not come to the lecture tonight, that we must postpone it. The good thing was that in Korea at that time there were not many telephones. I was lying down in my bed, and I looked at my watch, and it was 8 o'clock. In my mind I saw an empty room, a cold, wintry, February room. The person was waiting just for me, because this is not a group lecture. It is just one person to one person. That is the way we did. One person to one person.

I knew that the lady was waiting for me. The sole purpose was to teach me and I was not there. So at 8:00 I said to my wife, I must go. My wife was shocked. You are a sick person. How can you go? No. I cannot miss this appointment. So I just picked myself up and went to the lecture. I was dizzy, almost to the point of collapse. That two-hour lecture that night was so painful. I just don't know what I heard. I couldn't remember a thing because it was so painful. Nothing came to my mind. But I stayed. I was not going to be a coward. I didn't want to be looked at like a person who was weak.

She finally concluded. This was the Divine Principle lecture on the coming of the Lord of the Second Advent. She said, "Wonderful. You came and you listened to the whole thing." At that exact moment I discovered that all my illness was gone. I was like a brand-new person. So I stayed on for another two hours for a deep discussion. Then I told her that I wanted to go to her church and participate in the service. Normally, what would you say to a person who says, "I want to go to your church"? "Oh. please come." That would be the response. But she said, well, you don't have to be that quick. Amazing, the response was lukewarm.

I JUST COULDN'T WAIT

But I persisted. I wanted to go. I was a Christian, but nothing was really concrete to me about Jesus, about the Bible, nothing. But the Divine Principle was different. A complete revolution was already taking place in me. I was ready to go. But she said, wait. I persisted, don't you have a service on Wednesday? She said, yes, we do, but can't you wait until next Sunday? We have a Sunday morning service so I will invite you Sunday to the morning service. I said, why not Wednesday night? That would be the next night. She said no, we have a service but you don't have to be that quick. I am not good enough to come to your church? She was embarrassed. Then she said, yes, all right, we will think about it. I will call you tomorrow morning. She didn't give me an answer.

The next morning I called her. What about tonight? She said, all right, we will meet you somewhere and then we will go to church together. I dressed in my beautiful uniform and was there on time and she appeared and we went to church together. Later, I discovered why she was so hesitant to bring me to church. She thought, this is a good-looking, proud military officer, and I don't want to give him a poor impression of the church which might discourage him. Why? At that time the church building, as our brother David Kim and myself know so well, was a shack. The church door was a small door. You have no idea. There was no big sign saying Unification Church. No sign.

We went into one of those little alleys and into the church. It was February and it was very cold in Korea. Wooden floor and no heating. There was a stove in the center, but no heat. When I went in I joined a group of young people, about 20 or 30 young people just like you, except dark hair and brown eyes. Men on one side and women on the other, and they were singing.

The reason I am sharing this testimony is that their singing, just like your singing, was different from the singing of any other church. I was baptized in Fort Benning, Georgia, in 1952, during the Korean War. I had come to America in 1952 without speaking one word of English, but I was deeply impressed by the Christianity of this country. Also during the war I had many experiences of narrowly escaping death, and I wanted to join some kind of religion. I was desperate to hold on to some kind of religion. I wanted to become a good Christian and I was baptized in the Church of Christ in Columbus, Georgia. Thereafter, I visited many, many churches.

I heard many hymns, but nothing like the hymns I heard that Wednesday night. There was no piano, no organ, nothing. Just one leader leading and singing. Everyone was singing from their heart. The voices were coming from way down in the human soul.

That experience shook me, cleansed me. That is the Unification Church. That is our tradition. So when I hear your singing, it always brings me back to the memory of that Wednesday night. After almost 20 years, our tradition is just the same. Instead of a wooden floor, we are sitting on a concrete floor. We have a good brother playing the piano. We have a PA system. But not that much has changed. Our tradition is still the same. You are singing from your soul, from the bottom of your heart.

A HUMBLE MAN

That is the way I became a member of the Unification Church. I was totally cleansed the first night. Amazingly enough, I thought I was waiting for the leader of the church. I expected that he would come out in a very dignified manner and deliver a sermon, and then all would rise up and have a prayer. I thought some person in a robe would come out and deliver the sermon. But actually, a young man, just like you, came out and gave a testimony that night. I don't remember too much about the testimony. But what I remember most vividly was, at the end of the service, another humble man stood up, no tie, no good suit or anything like that. He was very humble, wearing a military surplus-type jacket and humble trousers, holding the Bible. He had been sitting right next to me. We had sung together and prayed together and listened to the sermon together.

That person all of a sudden stood up and came to the front and began to speak. And I was totally amazed at his power and dignity and conviction. Who was that? Father. That was Father. I didn't even know, while he was speaking, who he was. But I was so impressed, so deeply touched by his conviction and power and authority and dignity. And, of course, I had no idea I would become his interpreter a few years later. But that was Father. That is the way I met Father. He was sitting on the same floor with me, worshiping together on the cold floor. He is the one who is now shaping the world.

Today, the subject of my talk is "Father Trusts Us." You know, trust is something that nobody can give you. Trust is something that we must earn. Trust takes time to earn. "In God We Trust," you say in America. It is easy to say, but difficult to live up to. Same thing in the Unification Church. You want to be a trusted member. Trusted by your colleagues, brothers and sisters. Trusted by your leaders. Trusted by True Parents. And ultimately you want to be trusted by God.

But this is something we must earn. Trust is not given to you. Now, today, I would like to take a few moments to explain why this month of July in 1977 is a most important time. I feel that while Father and Mother are away from New York in Boston is a testing period for all of us. Actually, God and True Parents are testing how trustworthy and mature we are. Therefore, we want to earn grade "A" marks. We want to be straight "A" students in this test in this summer of 1977. This is the task and challenge ahead of us this month.

When you look at the history of the Bible, there are many times that important prophets of God wanted to trust their disciples, leave them to do the job while they went away somewhere to do something else for some providential reason. I want to cite two prominent instances in the Bible.

The first we can remember without any difficulty is the time of Moses. Moses entrusted the people to Aaron while he went up to the mountain in the wilderness for 40 days. During that time Moses was concentrating on praying to God, and he received the Ten Commandments. It took him 40 days to go up the mountain, communicate personally with God, receive the Tablets, and be ready to come down and spread the word of God to his own people on the way to the land of Canaan. Moses had already shown his people tremendous miracles. They had seen over and over again how God was working strongly with Moses. Moses truly represented God. He performed miracles that only God can perform, such as parting the Red Sea so the people could escape the Egyptian army. There was the pillar of fire during the night and pillar of cloud during the day, the plagues God used to torment the Pharaoh and all the Egyptians, tremendous miracles one after the other. The Israelites were eyewitnesses and could not miss the power of God.

Then Moses left for 40 days and went up the mountain. I would like to read from Exodus 32:1 what happened at that time.

> When the people saw that Moses delayed to come down from the mountain, the people gathered themselves together to Aaron, and said to him, "Up, make us gods, who shall go before us; as for this Moses, the man who brought us up out of the land of Egypt, we do not know what has become of him." And Aaron said to them, "Take off the rings of gold which are in the ears of your wives, your sons, and your daughters, and bring them to me." So all the people took off the rings of gold which were in their ears, and brought them to Aaron. And he received the gold at their hand, and fashioned it with an engraving tool, and made a molten calf, and they said, "These are your gods, O Israel, who brought you up out of the land of Egypt!"

Throughout history, over and over, the Bible describes how deceitful the human heart is. How unreliable. Jeremiah 17:9 says "the human heart is deceitful above all things." For this reason we are far inferior to nature. In nature there is no deceit, but man is the only creature who can tell a lie, who can change and betray. Nature doesn't. Animals do not lie. But think of it. The Jewish people saw so many great and wonderful things happen through Moses, but all of a sudden they doubted by saying "we don't know what has become of him." So they thought they needed another god. They asked Aaron to make another god to lead them to the land of Canaan.

BE CAREFUL OF PRAGMATISM

The amazing thing is that even leaders sometimes become blind. Aaron did what they asked. He did not say, didn't you see the power of God? Can't you be steadfast and faithful to God, you men of weak faith? Aaron did not scold them, but instead, directed them to make the golden calf. Very pragmatic. Today, we here in America must be very careful of these pragmatic thoughts. Many members can come up with beautiful ideas. Well, we could do it better this way. We could do this one better. That looks foolish. We don't do things that way in America. That is against our culture. And Father has said over and over, there is no such thing as American culture or Korean culture in the sight of God. We are creating a new culture, the culture of God, one unified culture.

So we are going to follow this one unified culture and unified tradition. Today, Father is away. During the summer of 1976, when we were working so hard for the Washington Monument rally, Father was primarily at sea. Many leaders had told Father, we may not have much chance to succeed in Washington. After the June 1st Yankee Stadium rally, we don't have time to prepare. We don't have money to continue campaigning. The members are tired. There are many reasons. But Father went to sea in the Atlantic Ocean. He received the heavenly Tabernacle and Father said to us, behold, you trust me. Go on. In 40 days we brought the victory of Washington.

You think you and I brought the victory. That is erroneous. Not at all. It was True Parents' faith in God, True Father's perseverance and untiring energy, and the special revelation from God he received on the ocean. That is what brought the victory of Washington Monument. We are going through this same period in 1977. From today through September 18, 1977, the one-year anniversary of Washington Monument, we are going to fulfill a miracle. If we remember that, we are not going to fail the True Parents. We are really going to show what we can do without the direct presence of Father and Mother in New York.

This is our bubbling enthusiasm. This is going to be our chance and challenge to meet Father's expectation. You know that there are many, many ex-Moonies. Some people think, how come the Unification Church has so many former members who go out and testify against you? Normally I say two things. First, it shows that no one is brainwashing Unification Church members. Second, and more important, we have a good example of an "ex-Moonie" at the time of Jesus. His name was John the Baptist.

Think of it. The Gospel of John, 1:29-34, says of John the Baptist:

> The next day he saw Jesus coming toward him, and said, "Behold, the Lamb of God, who takes away the sin of the world! This is he of whom I said, 'After me comes a man who ranks before me, for he was before me.' I myself did not know him; but for this I came baptizing with water, that he might be revealed to Israel." And John bore witness, "I saw the Spirit descend as a dove from heaven, and it remained on him. I myself did not know him; but he who sent me to baptize with water said to me, 'He on whom you see the Spirit descend and remain, this is He who baptizes with the Holy Spirit.' And I have seen and have borne witness that this is the son of God."

I have seen, and I have borne witness that this is the son of God. No one can know him any better than this one. John the Baptist clearly stated that this is the son of God. He knew who Jesus was. But that same John the Baptist became entangled with worldly affairs. When he looked at the situation from a pragmatic way, he came to a different conclusion. Let's read Luke 7:20 in which John the Baptist has sent a man to Jesus asking the following foolish question, "Are you he who is to come, or shall we look for another?" The same John, who had already borne witness at the Jordan River that Jesus was the son of God, is now asking if Jesus is the one whom God promised to send. In that moment, he became an ex-Moonie.

RESTORE JOHN THE BAPTIST

You know, once we Unification Church members lose sight, we lose everything. To Unification Church members, the greatest of all missions is to become a John the Baptist of the 20th century. Not in the fashion of John the Baptist 2,000 years ago, but a true John the Baptist who fulfills his mission. That person can say when he is dying, glory hallelujah!

When I am translating for Father, normally the first 30 minutes is the introduction. This is the time that ignites me. Then after 30 minutes I really do not know if I am in the Father or the Father is in me. I am totally on cloud nine. That is when the real message begins to flow. I am sure sometimes you sense it. I am the first to be so inspired. Why? Because every time I feel that Father is speaking right here, the words are flowing from his mouth, I am so convinced, so full of enthusiasm, full of grace, full of blessing. The innermost part of my heart is saying, God, I thank you. I thank you that, in my lifetime, I have a chance to see him. You gave me the opportunity to testify to him. You gave me the chance to be with him and live together and speak together and eat together. My beloved brothers and sisters, it is my testimony to you that in this man of God I have seen the coming of the glory of the son of God. And he is the one 1,000 times over to be the messiah and lord. That is my testimony. Every time when I translate, that is my conclusion.

Father, you are 1,000 times more than what I expected the son of God to be. And the most wonderful blessing is that he has the power to make you and me into direct children of God also. If we follow his footsteps, follow his example, we surely will become a son or daughter of God. No question about it. You must have dignity as a son or daughter of God. You cannot shame yourself. You cannot even embarrass yourself. You are the representative of God. You are the living God walking. Father made me so. Father made you so. All the sisters, all the brothers.

You and I were very narrow-minded, very trivial, small persons. But Father, in his power, has made you and me into universal persons. We are today as big as the universe. We are breathing the universe. Everything we touch, every penny we raise, every word we speak, we are doing and speaking as a universal representative, a representative of Father's direct image. If we have that feeling, that awakening, that awareness every moment of the day, then we are all right. We are truly the sons and daughters of God. No one can take us away.

So knowing Father, knowing God should not be mental work. This is not mathematics. It should be automatic. Knowing God and knowing True Parents is a language lesson in a way. It becomes automatic. When you learn English, you learn to think in English. When you learn Korean, you must think in Korean. In the same way, all Unification members must think in "Father."

WHAT IS YOUR FINAL WORD?

When something hits you, American people automatically say, ouch. What do Japanese people say when something hits you? *Hiti*. And Korean people say, *aya aya*. That is an automatic response. But from now, when something hits you, whether it's a heavy hit or a light one, your reaction should not be to automatically say ouch or *hiti* or *aya*. Your reaction must be and should be to say *Aboji*—Father. Your reaction should be to say, Father. If a good or joyful thing hits you, your reaction should be, *Aboji*, Father. If a terrible or impossible thing hits you, your reaction should be, *Aboji*. Someday, who knows, maybe a bullet will hit you. Maybe a knife will hit you. Your reaction must be, *Aboji*. When you die, the final word you speak will be, *Aboji*.

But with the final word *Aboji*, you never die. Don't you see that? You never die. The person who can react to good or bad, painful or burdensome events with Aboji will conquer death. There is no fear anymore. That person never dies, never becomes a prey of Satan. We live that kind of life. We become a different creation. You may be an American, a Korean, a Japanese, or a European, but from today we are not American, or Korean, or Japanese, or European. There is no such thing in this congregation. I see only one people here: Children of God. Children of the True Parents. We have a new breed, a new race. They call us Moonies. All right. As long as that says what we are, that is fine. In the first century, they used the word "Christian" scornfully. They would say "Oh, he is a Christian." That was a bad word at that time. It was not a respected word. But because of the deeds of Christians, today the word Christian has become a respectable word. Today Moonie is not a respectful term. But we can say of ourselves, "I am a Moonie."

One morning I was selling the newspaper, and one person said, "You Moonie. How old are you?" So I said, immediately, "I am a 20-year-old Moonie." But in my innermost heart, I said, all right, time will tell. The time will come when you will not say Moonie in a scornful way. The most respectable term under the sun will be to be known as Moonie. That is the day we will be victorious for Father. We are going to show the world how proud we are to be Moonies. We have that conviction. Our last word is going to be *Aboji*. Our every reaction to joy and sorrow and pain is going to be *Aboji*, not ouch, not *hiti*, not *aya*. *Aboji*.

But it takes real training and effort. Remember, this is not just mathematics. You cannot figure it out. It has to become automatic. Anywhere you are hit, the whole body responds with *Aboji*. Anything you do, any word you speak—*Aboji*. That is the word of the Father. You are the representative of the Father. Your whole body is an extension of the Father. So today, God and True Parents give us a chance to become real children. Real Moonies. Father wants us to prove whether we can truly say *Aboji*.

I am sure in this very hot summer, in this suffocating heat, that many people are lethargic, drowsy, and have a hard time carrying out their chores. Maybe in this room, some brother or sister might say, I just cannot go on. I am at the end of my rope. I simply cannot go on any further, not even one more step. I tell you, that is the time to say *Aboji*. That is the time to say to yourself, this is where I prove myself. When you think you are at the end of the rope, that is the moment you can prove yourself so that you can earn Father's trust.

WHAT KIND OF MOVIE WILL YOU MAKE?

Yes, you are at the end of your rope. Think about if someone is making a movie about you in the future. You don't want that movie to be dull or uninteresting, do you? Everybody who comes to watch will be dozing. No, you want to make an exciting movie. What makes it exciting? When you are able to say, this is not the end of the rope, this is the beginning. Then the heroic action comes. No hero is born in ordinary circumstances. A hero is born in emergency circumstances. Isn't that true? The movies always make it exciting and thrilling when the character hits the bottom of despair. Then a man can prove how faithful he is, how courageous and how unselfish. That is the moment a man can prove himself.

So you see, and Father sees, that we have tremendous persecution in America. I welcome it. Yes, after all, kingdom-building is not going to be done in one, two, or three years. It may not be done in our lifetime. But the important job we are all going to do as pioneers is to lay the cornerstone. This is the right condition to lay for posterity. We must leave behind us something people can pick up and be inspired about. That is the spirit of Aboji, in joy or in sorrow. In utmost stress, or utmost pain, you can say Aboji, and you can say Aboji as the last word of your life. Let's make ourselves that kind of Moonie today. This particular thing cannot be tested until your final moment comes. That is why preparation is so important. You have to prepare and prepare and prepare and prepare, and only prove it once.

This is like an intercontinental ballistic missile, an ICBM. America has tremendous ICBMs, but they cannot really test them. They cannot test an ICBM across Soviet Russia, because once it is tested that is the end of it. So, without testing, they must be sure it will work. By the same token, we are all ICBMs here, spiritual ICBMs. All of us are guided missiles. We have a million-pound spiritual warhead. Not for destruction, but for the construction of a new world, the Kingdom of God here on earth. But it is important to be sure the ICBM is really working. We must be tested without being exploded because that explosion comes only once in a lifetime. And that is the end of it.

So no one is sure. I am not sure myself really. Who knows? Therefore, today I must try to make sure. Go on with *Aboji* spirit. In pain, *Aboji*. In sorrow, *Aboji*. In joy, *Aboji*. Everything connected to *Aboji* because I am looking at things from his eyes, his point of view. I pray to God that I can explode as a heavenly ICBM when the time comes. I don't want to be a dud, a bomb that does not explode. I want to truly explode for the sake of the world and bring the Father's Kingdom here on earth.

Brothers and sisters, it is so nice to see you. Thank you very much. Let us pray.

Prayer by Bo Hi Pak:

Our most loving Heavenly Father. Thank you very much, Father, for gathering us together in this room. Those brothers and sisters who could not be here with us, let them be here with us in spirit. So that everybody joins together to pledge ourselves to be your sons and daughters. Your proud sons and daughters. Father, our True Parents are in Boston, please trust us. We want to be trustworthy and to prove ourselves in your sight, so we can truly represent you. We can show you our maturity. We are mature children, not childish in your sight. We want to be, after all, another Reverend Sun Myung Moon. I want to be another Moon. I am a Moonie, a proud Moonie. And we want to make the world envy Moonies. We want to be truly representative of your spirit, your image. We truly want to transform this world into your kingdom. Thank you, Father, we are going to now enjoy a most exciting program. Now, Father, may your spirit be with us all the way. All these things we pray in the name of our True Parents. Amen.

[After viewing the video "Reverend Moon in America," Dr. Pak continued speaking.]

Do you approve of it? [Yes!] Would you like to show it all over America [Yes!] What about all over the world? Shall we do it? Let's do it then. We will begin right here from New York, Washington, Philadelphia, Los Angeles, San Francisco. We will show it over and over and over again. Formation, growth, and perfection, so that 100 percent of Americans will see it. By Christmas time I think this program will be shown all over America and all over the world. This is just the beginning. We are going into electronic media. This is the way we can reach out to millions of people at one time. This is just the beginning. In the days to come we are going to have a tremendous program on the electronic media.

The one-eyed monster will turn into a most important instrument of God. As we sing in "The Battle Hymn of the Republic," God is marching on, truth is marching on. We must have the conviction that our march represents God's march. Our march represents the march of the truth. Today and this week we will bring more results so that we have more good reports to send to Father and Mother. I am driving up to Boston to take this video-tape to Mother and Father right after this service. Father and Mother will see it and I will convey your enthusiasm along with the program. Right! Then let's all stand and conclude the service by having three cheers that Father and Mother can hear all the way in Boston.

WHAT IS YOUR MOTIVE

BELVEDERE ESTATE, TARRYTOWN, NEW YORK

JULY 24, 1977

In this speech, Dr. Pak explains in detail the dynamics of spiritual growth, the importance of our physical bodies and our good deeds, and prompts us to remember how crucial our internal motivation is while serving and educating.

Let us greet our True Parents by turning north again. The last time Father said he heard your good morning, but it was not loud enough for Mother. So this time we'll make it really loud. Good morning, Father. Good morning, Mother. I am sure this time both of them heard us.

I would like to also welcome some representatives of our Father and Mother from East Garden. Three of the True Parents' children are here with us. Shall we welcome them. Hyo Jin Nim, In Jin Nim, and Un Jin Nim. In Jin Nim and Un Jin Nim spent time with True Parents in Boston and they caught quite a few tuna, I am sure. As a matter of fact, I spoke to Boston last night and Father has been victorious every day. Every day. Not just one giant tuna every day, but sometimes two. Three days ago he caught two tuna fish, and two days ago two tuna fish, and yesterday one tuna. Every day Father is going out to sea, battling with the sea, and winning a great victory. And I know Father is feeling that the entire membership of the Unification Church and heaven and earth and the entire spirit world and physical world are really battling together with him. Actually what Father is doing is not just fishing for tuna. It is a battle every moment of the day. I know that Father is symbolically leading the entire crusade.

The other day I went up to Boston to greet Father. Father's lips were all blistered. He goes out to sea very early in the morning, and he comes back very late sometimes. Truly Father is overextending himself. Father doesn't just look at it as tuna fishing. Many people think, well, this is summer vacation and Father is having a relaxed and easy time. Never. Never for Father. This summertime he is battling harder than anybody else. Every time when I see Father in Boston, or out there in the wild ocean, we always learn that Father is not there for fishing per se. Wherever he is, Father is battling for his kingdom. He is struggling against Satan. And he is working harder than anybody else. He wanted every one of you to share some of Father's catch. Have you enjoyed some tuna in New York? You should. If you haven't, then something is wrong. Father gave you a tuna. So I hope even brothers and sisters in Japan enjoyed it. Father wants to send the tuna he catches all over the world.

As a matter of fact, this morning shall we welcome Mr. Kuboki, president of the Unification Church of Japan. I just heard a report from Japan that Japanese family members received Father's tuna from Boston. Father shipped it by air in a huge ice box holding a 700- or 800- or 900-pound tuna. Japanese people appreciate tuna. We Americans do not so much. But the Japanese people really feel how precious that tuna meat is. Father sent it over to Japan knowing that Japanese families are so fond of it. I just got a report that every member in the whole country shared Father's tuna.

FATHER IS FEEDING THE WORLD

This is Father's feeling. He wants to feed everyone, first Unification members all over the world, but eventually every single human being on earth, physically as well as spiritually. Spiritually there is no better food than what Father is providing. This is the life-giving truth. Only with that does mankind have hope. We can be born again. Father wants to make every child of God here on earth live in accordance with the law of God. Father wants to give everyone compassion and love so that they can really be fed by Father and Mother. That is the way Father feels. He feels responsibility for every human soul. Furthermore, he is responsible for all the human souls in spirit world. I call them "upstairs people." We are downstairs people. Father is responsible for spirit world and physical world together. Father wants to see to it that every human being is protected and nurtured.

I thank the New Hope Singers this morning for their special hymn. Actually, these days the New Hope Singers are not often New Hope Singers. They are giving their utmost energy for witnessing and selling newspaper subscriptions. And many of them are fasting as you are, trying to gain results for the True Parents. Particularly as we discussed here a couple of weeks ago, while Father is away from New York, it is our chance to prove the maturity of our movement and our leadership. We want to present Father with great results. So know how hard every member of the New York church is working, including the IOWC, adjacent to New York City. The New Hope Singers don't even have time to practice. They are just going out selling and witnessing and delivering newspapers as you do. But I requested them to perform this special number and I thank you for your spirit.

This is the third week that I am giving the Sunday morning sermon, but I am praying that next Sunday Father and Mother will be here, and hopefully this prayer will be answered. Father is scheduled to come for a nationwide conference that will be held Friday and Saturday. Then I would like to tell Father: every one of us wants to see you and wants to hear you. We need your energy. We need your breath. Can I say it? [Yes!] Can I really? [Yes!] Then I really earnestly petition Father, please come spend at least one Sunday morning with us. So I will petition it, and I am sure Father will listen because of you. Not because of me. But shall I say that every one of us really wants to see you? We are dying without seeing you for three weeks. Can I say it? [Yes!] I will say it. Father, they are dying without seeing you for three weeks. But three weeks looks like three years and 30 years and 3,000 years. We cannot go on any longer like this, Father. We need you. We want you here. We need your physical presence. Can I give that earnest petition? [Yes!] All right. Then we look forward to seeing Father and Mother in one more week.

This morning I have so much to share. How can we share so much in a short time? This summer, I had the most wonderful fortune to have Hyo Jin Nim with us in Washington, and we studied the Bible and Divine Principle and Father's words together. Hyo Jin Nim and I flew back to New York last night so that we could worship together this Sunday morning in the spirit of True Parents. But I promised him one thing: that my sermon would not exceed one hour. And he said, do you promise? I told him that I could talk for three hours, but for the sake of the New York church members, who have to go out and deliver the papers and witness today, I hope that Father will give me the power and really inspire me in one hour. So I need your prayer. Hyo Jin Nim is watching me now. We have give and take going on here, some sparkling of the spirit going back and forth. I think I can make it this morning; I have one hour to make sense. Now it's 6:25 a.m., so the conclusion should come at 7:25 a.m. I don't have to watch the clock because Hyo Jin Nim is going to signal me.

This morning I would like to dwell on the subject of motivation. Some time ago, I was translating Father's speech, and even as I was speaking Father's words to you I was astounded. Father said, even though some of you are preaching the Divine Principle, it does not guarantee that everyone will end up in heaven. Suppose there are two men preaching the same Divine Principle, let's say the Principle of Creation or the Fall of Man. But Father said one can end up in heaven and the other can end up in hell. This was truly astonishing to hear. We thought the Divine Principle is everything, so preaching the Divine Principle is a noble deed. If we teach the Divine Principle, we felt that we are automatically destined for the Kingdom of God in Heaven. But Father said that is not true. Why?

MOTIVE IS THE JUDGE

The same act of the Divine Principle can be judged from the motive. What is your motive for preaching the Divine Principle? Either good or evil will result from your motivation. Good and evil, as you know through the Divine Principle, are not judged by the surface action or the visible deeds. They are judged by the invisible motive. If I am preaching Divine Principle and at the very bottom of my heart the reason I am doing it is to show myself off, then no matter how good a teacher of Divine Principle I am, it is not going to do me any good. When you are teaching the Divine Principle, if you are preaching from the heart of God, or as a representative of Father's heart, if you are really pouring out Father's energy trying to convey Father's own heart, then that act of preaching the Divine Principle is good.

So we can see that even the value of preaching the Divine Principle depends on the motivation and can turn out to be either good or evil. In following Father and the Divine Principle and living the life of a Unification Church member, I personally, over and over, have realized that ultimately what counts is motive or state of mind. I see all of you brothers and sisters here before me. The thing I cannot see is your state of mind. I cannot see your mind, what you are thinking right now. But God sees the invisible face, or invisible mind. That is what will be judged. That is the criteria. That is the real you, the invisible you.

Let me draw a very simple diagram. Don't laugh at me because I am not a good artist. When I was in school, I did everything pretty well except drawing. So I want to draw two men. Last Sunday I said that we exist in duality. You see me as one person standing here, but actually on the platform there are two persons. Here I am, the visible Bo Hi Pak. But inside there is another Bo Hi Pak. That is the spirit man of Bo Hi Pak. You are looking at two persons. So let me draw here, my head and my body. At least I have two legs. There is another Bo Hi Pak.

The Christian history of the last 2,000 years could not teach the two-man concept. But Father, in the Divine Principle, clearly teaches us one person is composed of two people. One is the physical person, which is visible. The other is the invisible spirit person. When you were born, you were born as two persons. The relation of the two persons is so important. Let me refresh you on some of the teachings you have learned in the Divine Principle. This physical man has two elements: subject and object. The subject is the flesh mind, which we call intuition. The object is the body. In order to sustain this physical body, we need certain elements: air and sunlight. Without air, which is invisible, we could not sustain our life even five minutes. Physical man also needs a physical element, food, to sustain the physical body.

The spirit man also needs to be nurtured. Because nothing that God created can be perfected at once, everything has to go through the period of growth. The spirit man also needs to grow, and he needs two elements. One we call the living life element, which is the truth of God or God's own energy. Our spirit is joined with God through the life element. The spirit man also needs the vitality element from the physical body. So in order to have this spirit man grow, it must receive from God the life element and from the physical body the vitality element. With these two elements, the spirit man will grow to perfection.

But at the same time the spirit man also returns to the physical body certain elements. These we call living spirit elements. As you can see, give and take is going on here between the physical body and the spirit body. The important thing is the relationship of the two. Which one is subject? [Spirit.] By the way, there is a young lady here whose name is Linda. Good morning, Linda. She is taking notes and I can see that she can draw a Bo Hi Pak better than I can. You draw very well. So I will concentrate on you, and if you can understand, everyone understands. Wonderful. You are my object for give and take.

So now I see two Linda's. A physical Linda and a spiritual Linda. Both need to grow. In order to grow we need to receive elements. But ultimately, our important goal is the growth of the spirit man, because your spirit man lives for eternity, not the physical part of you. This is where there is a great deal of confusion in the religious world. Today there are many, many churches. Some believe that this physical body can live for eternity. Some teach that the physical body dies after 80 or 90 years of life because of the fall of man. For example, I understand that Jehovah's Witnesses teach that we die because of the fall and that once we are restored and become one spirit with God, we will live here on earth without end. That is a real confusion. This belief is very sweet to the ears: Yeah, I want to live, I don't want to die, so let me believe this and accept Jesus Christ and God. I can live here on earth, and this physical body can sustain me on earth for eternity.

THIS BODY JUST WON'T LAST

But that is not true. God did not create man like that. Eventually there is going to be a great deal of disappointment. After 60 or 70 years, someone who believes that they can avoid physical death is going to look at the mirror and say, boy, this is not the way I was supposed to live for eternity. I have more lines and my face is getting older and older. I was supposed to live for eternity. This body was supposed to last for hundreds of thousands of years.

I am sorry to tell you but that will not happen. God never intended that. All material things are going to decay, to come to an end. Our physical body is material. It is divine law that we cannot live in the physical body for eternity.

The purpose of the physical body is to give our eternal body, the spirit body, a chance to grow. The other Sunday, I told you that the physical body is like a vehicle. We rent a car. God is running the greatest rent-a-car company on earth. We are borrowing this flesh from the car rental company. We all borrow a certain amount of dirt, in a certain shape. Where did you come from? Actually, you come from the earth. The soil. The material world. When I was born, I probably weighed about six or seven pounds. Now I've grown up and I weigh maybe 170 pounds. I don't want to weigh 190 pounds; I want to stay about 175 pounds. So I was a seven-pound baby and grew up to 175 pounds. Where did that 168 pounds come from? From nature. From the soil. From the ground. Because of the food I ate, the tomatoes, the meat, the kim chee, I grew up to 175 pounds. So actually, for the last 47 years, I borrowed from nature 168 pounds of flesh.

The purpose of this physical body is to provide the spirit man with vitality elements so that the spirit man can grow. The physical body is like a fruit tree, and the fruit we are growing is the spirit self. The spirit man can grow to perfection and that is the one that will live for eternity. That is the Divine Principle.

Another important thing is that since the fall of man, the chance for growth of the spirit man has been limited by the amount of truth that was available. The fall brought man into darkness, into a dungeon. As you know, the Divine Principle teaches clearly that the work of God is the work of restoration. God intends to restore man. The ultimate goal of restoration is to restore our spirits. During the Old Testament era, the only life element for the spirit man came through the level of truth revealed in the Old Testament. No matter what good deeds a man like Abraham did, his spirit man could grow only up to the level of form spirit. The form spirit is very translucent, like a milk bottle that you can see through.

When Jesus Christ came 2,000 years ago, he brought the New Testament, which brought a higher life element. This life element can bring the spirit man into the growth stage, which is called life spirit. The life spirit is like the moon. The life spirit has the power to reflect light. In the spirit world heaven and hell are distinguished by light and darkness. We here in the physical world have night and day, about 12 hours each. But in the higher spirit world, there is eternal day. You're worried that will make a long work day, aren't you? Don't worry. That eternal day will never be boring. It is the world of light. Father taught us that in the spirit world the air we breathe is the air of love. Not oxygen. We will breathe the air of love. The sun rays we receive in the spirit world are the love of God. Sun rays, in the form of love, make eternal day. Hell is the place where the rays do not reach; they are blocked, so it is a world of darkness.

GOING BEYOND LIFE SPIRIT

The life spirit is capable of receiving the love of God and reflecting light. So it is like the moon reflecting the sun's rays and giving life. So far the New Testament era is following Jesus Christ. By following and being obedient to the New Testament, the best level the Christian can reach is the level of life spirit. We call the place that life spirits dwell paradise. But Christianity thinks this is the final destination. True Father has declared to the world that paradise is not the ultimate destination. Paradise is not the Kingdom of God in heaven. It is like a lobby in a train station or airport. There is another gigantic step to go, that is, to grow to the perfection level.

The perfection level of the spirit we call divine spirit. First, form spirit, then life spirit, and ultimately divine spirit. A divine spirit is a shining, life-giving spirit. The warmth of love is generated by the divine spirit. The divine spirit is like the sun in the sky. It gives tremendous light. So the ultimate destination of all men, of you and me, is to become a divine spirit. In order to become a divine spirit, we must receive first the perfected life element from God in the form of truth—that is, the Divine Principle. The Divine Principle is the ultimate teaching of God. It reveals everything that we need to achieve the divine spirit stage. This is the message that only the Lord of the Second Advent can bring. Therefore, we are living in a time like the time of Jesus Christ, the transition from one age to another. We are not living in the New Testament era. We are now entering the Completed Testament era.

You can become a divine spirit by receiving the perfected life element through the Divine Principle by accepting the True Parents. This is what it is all about. The ultimate goal is to become a divine, life-giving spirit. When you read the Bible, you learn that Peter and John and James, the three major disciples of Jesus, went to the Mount of Transfiguration. All of a sudden they saw Jesus transformed into a different body. Actually, the physical body that Jesus lived in is not different from yours and mine. I don't think Jesus always wore perfumed and fragrant garments, because he worked just like our Father. He overworked himself. He did a lot of sweating. There was a lot of dust on him. He taught day in and day out. Sometimes his face looked pale. No question about it. Just like your face looks pale. Some of the New Hope Singers look pale.

But that day, Jesus' disciples for the first time saw an entirely different Jesus. All of a sudden Jesus was shining in a white garment. His entire face was shining. A halo was glowing around him. Their eyes were so disturbed by the intense light, they couldn't directly look at Jesus. Then the disciples saw that Jesus was talking with Moses and Elijah. Well, Moses and Elijah had been dead a long time, but there they were, talking with Jesus. They were also wearing white garments and their faces shone, but not as much as Jesus'. Jesus was like the sun. Christians do not understand this. What Jesus' disciples saw on the Mount of Transfiguration was the divine spirit of Jesus. The only person to achieve the divine spirit up to that point was Jesus. So when their spiritual eyes were opened, all of a sudden they could see Jesus' spirit. That is what they saw. Moses and Elijah never died—they are upstairs. They came downstairs to have a discussion with Jesus.

As you know, spirit people have to come down and work on earth because without the physical body they cannot progress in the spiritual world. They had lost their physical bodies already, so they had to come down and work through Jesus' disciples' physical bodies. Today is the same. Many Christian martyrs and holy people of great faith are coming down today to seek you out. They need to "borrow" your physical body to perfect their spirit man. Sometime later I would like to talk about reincarnation, which is the theory that we can die and go to spirit world and be born again as a baby, grow up again, and so forth. But the Divine Principle teaches that there is no such thing as reincarnation. Actually, spirit men are assisting people on earth.

So why is the physical body so important? Unless the physical body here on earth gives vitality elements to your spirit man, no matter what kind of truth you are receiving, your spirit is not going to grow. Your spirit is going to stand still. There is no way to grow. That is why the physical body is so important here on earth. That is why perfection will come here on earth first, not in the spirit world. This is why God sent his son here on earth to consummate the work of restoration. The physical body and physical life are so precious. If you pick fruit when it is still green, it can't grow into perfection, maturity. It cannot ripen. By the same token, our spirit man should stay with the physical body until it is perfected. The spirit man can reach perfection only here on earth. That is the way God planned it. So in that respect we need the physical body. That is why our physical body is very, very important.

You know, Neil Armstrong went up to the surface of the moon in a rocket. Often when I teach the Divine Principle, I use the illustration of a rocket. Let me draw one rocket. An amazing thing, this rocket. Most of the body of the rocket is the fuel. Actually there is very little on the top. This little part landed on the moon and returned to the earth. When you go to the National Air and Space Museum in Washington, D.C., you can see the Apollo 11 command module. It is a very small portion of the rocket. The rocket is built in two segments, one that reaches the destination and the other that is only needed to get the rocket out of the earth's atmosphere. When Apollo 11 was launched, most of the millions of pounds of fuel burned in the first few seconds of the flight. The first segment separated from the second. It was no longer needed. The command module and the moon spaceship kept going.

LET'S GO INTO ORBIT

This teaches us a lot of things. Most of the rocket is like a physical body. Our spirit man is like the command module. What we are trying to achieve centers on the command module. But this body is needed to put the command module into orbit. The spirit world or the Kingdom of God in heaven is like the orbit. So this rocket is thrusting the command module into orbit. This relationship is similar to the relationship between physical man and spirit man.

The reason I'm telling you this is that in order to have this physical body give vitality to the spirit man, you need to live the truth. You need to go ahead with the action of the truth. You also need the right motivation. That is what counts. Father has told us over and over in Sunday morning service that you must not complain. No matter how much you accomplish with this body, selling newspapers or witnessing or walking

100 miles a day, if your heart is a complaining heart, then no matter how good your actions are, it does not give good vitality elements to your spirit person. It is no good. God is looking at your state of mind and your motivation.

Let me read one verse from the Sermon on the Mount. Jesus was talking about the seventh commandment in the Sermon of the Mount. Matthew 5:27-28 says, "You have heard that it was said, 'You shall not commit adultery.' But I say to you that everyone who looks at a woman lustfully has already committed adultery with her in his heart." In the Old Testament era, it was good enough just not to commit adultery. That was the external restoration. But Jesus came and taught that the state of mind is also important. Therefore, it is not really the action, but the state of mind. If you look at a woman with a lustful eye, you have already, in the sight of God, committed adultery.

This shows so clearly that what counts in the sight of God is the motive. Now, when you look at another place in the Bible, Luke 21:1-4, you read, "He looked up and saw the rich putting their gifts into the treasury; and he saw a poor widow put in two copper coins. And he said, 'Truly I tell you, this poor widow has put in more than all of them; for they all contributed out of their abundance, but she out of her poverty put in all the living that she had.' " In the sight of God, it is not what size checkbook you have, how much contribution you can give; the important thing is how real is your heart, what kind of motivation you have. The two coppers in the widow's pocket are everything she has. Without any reservation she is giving everything that she has. That is far greater than giving a fat check out of your abundance.

There are so many examples. But I want to go into something even more important and spectacular. Nowadays, America's pragmatic systems are not that good for the heavenly purpose. For example, we give offerings at church and to charities, but the amount is often determined by how much of it is tax-deductible.

One time I watched a Liberace show in Las Vegas. Liberace is a flamboyant, spectacular showman. He is known as Mr. Showman. He came out with all kinds of bizarre hats and he drove out on the stage in a Rolls Royce, wearing a mink coat. "Look at my mink coat. I wore this at the Queen's command performance." I had no idea how extravagant he is. He surely deserves the title Mr. Showman. Anyway, at one point he came out wearing a very colorful suit. It was shining all over, and everybody was exclaiming. He told us that the most expensive part of his suit is not the suit but the buttons. The buttons are all diamonds. He said he really wanted to show off the buttons, but he couldn't come out just wearing buttons so had to wear a suit. Anyway, the key point is that these diamonds were so expensive that he put his initial on them, which made them tax-deductible.

What I am trying to say is the American system tends to make us concentrate on external considerations, appearances, rather than motivation. We think less about how right is my motivation with God and more about the technicalities. Is it tax-deductible? Will somebody see me? It is self-advertisement. I tell you that way of life will not help your spirit man at all.

We learn another portion of Sermon on the Mount. Matthew 6:1-4 says,

> Beware of practicing your piety before men in order to be seen by them; for then you will have no reward from your Father who is in heaven. Thus, when you give alms, sound no trumpet before you, as the hypocrites do in the synagogues and in the streets, that they may be praised by men. Truly, I say to you, they have received their reward. But when you give alms, do not let your left hand know what your right hand is doing, so that your alms may be in secret; and your Father who sees in secret will reward you.

BE RECOGNIZED BY GOD

What we need is a motivation that can be seen only by God. This is what Father is emphasizing. It is not important to be recognized by your own leader or make the headlines in any paper. The important thing is to do things with a true motivation. Today, without knowing Divine Principle, without knowing God, the world lives without the awareness of spirit man. They don't care about the spirit man. They only want to live with the physical body, whatever they see as a happy life here on earth. This is the only goal. That is the most foolish way of life here on earth, which most people do not realize. They don't care about the spirit. But ultimately what will remain, what will count, is the spirit.

I am going to recommend you read *Life in the World Unseen*. After learning the Divine Principle, I read this book a couple of times. This is really a fascinating story about the spirit world. This is how the book was written. Anthony Borgia is a British gentleman who received a special spiritual communication from the person in spirit world whose name was Monsignor Benson, who was a prominent clergyman here on earth. During his life, he taught many things he thought were right about spirit world, about spirit men, and so forth. But when he died and went into the spirit world, he discovered how erroneously he had taught here on earth. The many books he had written were totally untrue. But it was too late. He had lost his physical body. But he repented and regretted so much the misinformation his books contained. So he made a special effort and pled to the higher spirit world and received permission to communicate with his own messenger here on earth. He established a channel to be able to correct the many untruthful things he had stated before his death.

The result of that work is *Life in the World Unseen*. So actually Anthony Borgia is like a secretary, not the author. He took dictation. The author is the spirit man, Monsignor Benson, who appeared to Borgia and gave him dictation word for word. I enjoyed this book because, first, I know it is not fiction. It is truth. Because of the Divine Principle I have a way to judge this book. Second, it is fascinating because it teaches so much about spirit world and confirms the Divine Principle so eloquently. We learn the Principle, then when we read this, we can see how true it is. A word of warning for some of the people who are going to read the book: Monsignor Benson lives in the world of light, but not in the world of Jesus, not in the highest portions of Paradise, and not in the Kingdom of Heaven in the spirit world. He is in a good spirit world, but not the highest.

SPIRIT WORLD IS SO CLEAR

After reading this book, I feel I know so much more about spirit world, so much more of the truth about spirit world than Mr. Benson, even though I have never been to that place. That was a true joy to me. Why? Because of the Divine Principle. Divine Principle came from the highest truth of spirit world. When you receive the Divine Principle, you know more about spirit world than anybody else. Today I would like to read a couple of sections about the relationship between the physical world and the spirit world.

One day Mr. Benson was able to visit what they call the dark world, or hell. I learned a long time ago from Father, and this book confirms it so beautifully, that in spirit world, like a ladder, there are many, many levels. The higher you are in spirit world, the more freedom you have to go down to lower levels. You can go down to visit the dungeons of hell. That is why Jesus Christ, after his crucifixion, went first, not to heaven, but to the dungeons of hell for 40 days to work with the lower spirits. When you are in a higher level you can go down to any part of the spirit world, but you cannot go to a higher level than you are. That is a spiritual law.

First, I would like to tell you how this person, Mr. Benson, described his own death. He said that between the physical body and the spirit man, there is white cord. This cord is so elastic it can be extended for miles and miles and thousands of miles and it can come back. Many times while we are sleeping here on earth, our spirit man goes to the spirit world, wandering and looking at the many aspects of spirit world, but still connected by the magnetic cord. When this magnetic cord is cut, this is what we call the moment of death.

Mr. Benson was dying in the hospital and he was weakened by illness. At a certain moment, he felt a tremendous urge to wake up. So on the bed he woke up. But actually the person who woke up was not his physical body but his spirit body. The real him. The real Benson. So he woke up and he saw another him lying down in the bed. That is the physical man. When the time comes we leave. We cast off the physical body. So when he got up he felt in perfect health. And there was a physical body lying in his bed and everybody was gathered around, the doctors and nurses and family members. They announced that Monsignor Benson was dead. So they began to pray, and some family members were crying and mourning. But he was watching all this as a big show. He was listening and watching everything. Well, he could be amused and enjoy watching the scene of his own death. He woke up out of his own body. Actually that was the moment that the elastic white cord was cut, and the physical body and spirit body separated. After that, there is no more give and take between the two. The physical body decays and goes back to the earth.

Mr. Benson could see his own body lying there, but he himself was healthy and already he was dressed in a white garment. You don't have to go to the store to buy a suit to wear in spirit world. That is wonderful. You don't have to worry about what to wear or what to eat. There was already an escort from the spirit world.

I cannot go into this too deeply, or I will I break my promise to Hyo Jin Nim. I want to read one paragraph about how he went down to hell and met one person.

> He met one person in a lower spiritual realm. He said he had been in spirit world some years now. In his earth life he had been a successful business man. Successful, that is, as far as the earth plane judges such things. From the earthly viewpoint he was a very successful business man. He had not thought of much else than his own business. He always considered that any means were justified in gaining his own end, provided they were legal. He was ruthless in his dealings with all others, and he elevated efficiency to the level of God. In his home all things and all people were subservient to him. He gave generally to charity where there was likely to accrue the greatest advantage and credit. He supported his own religious church with vigor and regularly with fervor. He felt he was an ornament to the church, and he was much esteemed by all those connected with it. He added some new portions to the edifice at his own expense, and a chapel was named after him as a donor.

But from what Edwin, the guide, had been able to glean from his story, he had scarcely committed one decent unselfish action in the whole of his life. His motive was always self-aggrandizement. And he had achieved his purpose on earth at the absolute expense of his life in the spirit world. He, that person in spirit world, complained the church had misled him all along. Since his munificence had been received in such fashion that he believed his gift to the church would weigh heavily in his favor in the hereafter, in the spirit world, he thought, "I gave so much money to the church so I bought heaven. I have a beautiful heaven reserved." But that is not the way the law worked.

Again, he could not see that it was motive that counts and that the happy state in spirit world cannot be bought with hard cash. A small service performed unselfishly builds a greater edifice in the spirit world to the glory of God than do large sums of money expended on ecclesiastical bricks and mortar erected for the glory of men with full emphasis upon the donor.

He thought he had the highest happiness: I bought it. I gave millions of dollars. Look at the church. It has my name on it. Look what I did, I gave a pipe organ to my church. Look what I did, I gave thousands of dollars to the orphans of Vietnam. In America, frequently we think in those terms, that we can go to the great heaven. The book said that it is the motive that counts.

Now I am going to draw the conclusion. Ladies and gentlemen, what then should be our motive? We look at ourselves as Unification Church members. What is our Father teaching every day? What have we learned here in the Unification Church? You know, we learn one way of life. Alpha and omega. Alpha is Father and omega is Father. We members, knowing the Principle, know that we benefit the most by not benefitting ourselves. Unselfish motivation. You see, when you have the slightest degree of greediness and complaining heart, you need to come back to God and make up with God first. Set your state of mind straight. Make yourself straight in such a way that you are starting out the day with Father.

FATHER MUST BE THE MOTIVATION

I am emphasizing this because every Sunday morning we must initiate our every action and every move from Father. Is it Father's will? I am doing Father's work. I am bubbling with enthusiasm for Father. Whatever the result at the end of the day, it must be Father's. Alpha Father, omega Father. Start the day with Father and end the day with Father. Every action you do, witnessing, preaching, fund-raising, and selling newspapers, Father must be the motivation.

You know, I have a great admiration for Japanese people. I have learned a great deal about the Japanese spirit, and the Japanese brothers and sisters are doing really amazing things for Father. It is a great joy. One time I heard about a Japanese soldier during World War II (of course, they fought not for God but for the emperor) who was going into battle in the final assault. He ran on the battlefield when the assault order came, shouting "banzai! banzai! banzai!" Do you know what banzai means? Mansei. The Japanese word for mansei is banzai. Why did he do that? In an assault, you don't know when the final moment will come, when the bullet will strike. So if he was going to die, he wanted to die with "banzai" on his lips. He wanted the final word on his lips to be banzai for the emperor.

Even though that loyalty was centered upon the emperor, we Unification Church members can learn from this. We are running. The assault line is in New York. Every day is an assault day. We are running with the word "Aboji, Father" on our lips, crying out "Aboji," and running and running. Our banner is the Divine Principle. We are not going to kill anyone. We are going to let the people live. Our job is different. But the experience is the same. With our spirit we are running with the banner of Divine Principle every day, with the word Aboji on our lips.

Some of you sitting here look pale. You look sleepy. Some of you fasted and are undernourished. You are not dressed as well as Liberace. But I tell you, from the spirit eyes, from the eyes of God, you are the most beautiful people. You are the most shining people here on earth. God sees light. On a dark night when you fly in an airplane over the countryside, you see only pitch-dark earth. Here and there a light is shining. Those are the members of the Unification Church. God is like a pilot steering the plane going over the earth. You are there and God sees the light sparkling. It comes from the members of the Unification Church. Your face may be pale and you may be weak, but you don't care. True Parents have the power to raise us up to divine spirits. In the sight of God, we are shining like stars. When I ride in a plane at night, I go over two different kinds of areas, rural and city. When the plane is over New York, there are so many city lights. God wants to see, not darkness, but the Unification Church members shining like sparkling jewels.

Our motivation must be totally unselfish. Meeting True Father and hearing the Divine Principle is not itself real gold. This is merely an opportunity. If you are a wise man, you are going to use this opportunity to the maximum. Don't hold back. Don't save your body. It doesn't matter if you live 30 years or 50 years or 100 years. Jesus lived only 33 years here on earth, but he was a liberator. He was a savior to mankind. It doesn't matter how long you live. It does matter how you live, with the proper motive, proper vision, proper perspective, and absolute loyalty to True Parents. Do not waste the opportunity. Live for the sake of this life element, this Divine Principle, for the sake of True Parents. Knowing this much truth, if you can die for the cause, there is no greater honor that God can give you.

I would like to conclude with one verse from Jesus Christ in Luke 12:4: "I tell you, my friends, do not fear those who kill the body, and after that have no more that they can do. But I will warn you whom to fear: fear him who, after he has killed, has power to cast into hell; yes, I tell you, fear him!" Do not fear the enemy. Do not fear the government. Do not fear the soldiers. Do not fear communism. Do not fear assassins. All those can only kill your body; they can never even touch a finger to your soul. After I am gone from this physical body here on earth, whether I leave it now, or 10 or 20 years later, doesn't make any difference. The important thing is to invest my physical body completely so God can benefit. So the Kingdom of God can benefit.

Our True Parents don't teach the fear of God. We are not following God because we are fearful of Him. He is my father. You are not afraid of your father. You love him. You love him so much, therefore there is nothing you cannot do for him. That is the message.

My brothers and sisters, I may not have spoken very eloquently or expressed myself well. But I am sure you wise brothers and sisters understand what I am trying to say. What would be the truly honorable prototype of Unification Church members? With the True Parents we conquered death a long time ago. We do not taste death. We do not see death anymore. We only see one thing. I am praying for that one day. God has given me this one body as an opportunity. Thank you very much. Let us pray.

Prayer by Bo Hi Pak:

Our most loving Heavenly Father. I just cannot fully explain what you want to tell our brothers and sisters. I am sorry, Father, I am so inadequate, so incapable to transmit your heart. Particularly your agony, your anticipation, and anxiety. Father, therefore, I must leave everything to you, the end result. Father, I want you to take over. Take over the mind and heart of every brother and sister listening. Let them become your closest sons and daughters. Let them become your truly loyal subjects for your kingdom. Father, these are the people in whom you bestowed your hope. We are your hope. If we fail you, no one else can fulfill your hope, Father. When we do this, it is very serious. Today and every day, Father, we want You to give us faith, give us Your truth, and in response we give You our loyalty, our steadfastness, our dedication, our absolute life-giving life. Above all, we give our life to it. Because You have given us eternal life. We dedicate our lives to you. It is more than a pledge. More than a joy to do it. Father, thank You.

Until we welcome once again True Parents here in this room at Belvedere, I want You to stay with us all the way and live with You, walk with You, eat with You. We laugh and cry with You. We do everything with You, Father. I am Your body. We are Your body. Father, You are dwelling in us. I feel You are talking to us, speaking to us every moment of the day. So any person who feels weak this morning, let them be strengthened, Father. Let them become a giant, Father, with a new spirit and stamina and then we can surely go assault the world of Satan. With the word of Aboji on our lips every minute. Father, we want to speak Aboji as the final word, and we want to assault enemy territory, not in retreat. Thank you, Father. Until we welcome True Parents next week, protect our Father. Father, we give ourselves Your protection, Your power, Your inspiration so we can report tremendous things next week. Thank you. All these things we pray in the name of our most beloved True Parents. Amen.

WE ARE SUNNIES

BELVEDERE ESTATE, TARRYTOWN, NEW YORK

JULY 31, 1977

In this sermon, Dr. Pak expounds on his favorite Bible verse, Matthew 10:39. He also explains Father's proclamation from the state leaders' conference on the day before, where he renames Unification Church members "Sunnies."

Shall we all stand together and greet our True Parents. Let us face north. Last time I asked Father, "Did you hear the good morning from Belvedere?" And Father said, "Well, I heard only the men's voices, not the women's." This time all the women, all together, good morning, Father. Good morning, Mother. Thank you, be seated. I think this time definitely Father heard our ladies.

I really did not expect our brother, David Kim, to introduce me. Furthermore, I was embarrassed because I did not deserve what he said, and I really do not want to hear any word of recognition or praise of any kind because I know how trivial I am. How imperfect I am. How simple I am in the sight of God and how imperfect in the sight of True Parents. The only thing I can do is humble myself. None of those can apply to me really when I see God or True Parents. But I thank him anyway. He loves me. He is my elder brother. He loves me and that is good enough. He cares for me and I love him, too.

You know in our movement, to you and me here, titles and ranks have no meaning. You call me Col. Pak. You call me Mr. Pak. Well, you may call me just Pak, Bo Hi or little boy Pak, Bo Hi, it doesn't make any difference. You and I have the most important title of all. I am a son of God. You are, too. You are the daughters of God. I am a humble, small, yet proud son of True Parents. You are too. You are humble, yet proud daughters of the True Parents. That is the most important title of all, for which we are eternally grateful. I sometimes think, if I die, maybe my children will make a little tombstone on my grave. And I am working for just one little title there: "Bo Hi Pak, Son of the True Parents, who lived and died for the sake of the True Parents." If I am worthy of such a tombstone, this is the greatest honor. There is nothing more I can ask for.

I know that "Son of the True Parents" will be written on that simple tombstone because I am—and you are and you are—children of True Parents. But the next line is going to be difficult to earn. "Who lived and died for the sake of the True Parents." It is not easy. Actually, you and I today are working toward that goal, so that at the end of our lives, people can recognize us as the sons and daughters of True Parents who lived and died for the sake of True Parents. If you are confident that you have won that title, you have lived a most successful life. You are living with the greatest honor and you died with the greatest honor. So that is our challenge. I am trying today to live for True Parents. I am trying to murder my own ego. So that Christ lives, True Parents live. But actually the last day of my life is not here yet. I don't know when it will come. Who knows, it may be tomorrow. It may be a year later. It may be 10 or 20 years later. No one knows. Only God knows.

LIVE AND DIE FOR TRUE PARENTS

But the question is, can I say that I lived and died for the True Parents. It is our challenge every day. Above all, the greatest honor that I can have is that True Parents and God recognize this man as a son who lived and died for the True Parents. That is the challenge. I really humble myself. I do not know because I haven't experienced my death yet. That experience only comes once in a lifetime. You cannot die twice. For all other things, performing arts and all things, you can do a dress rehearsal. But for this one thing, death, you cannot have a dress rehearsal. It just comes, period.

So whether you can say you are living and dying for the sake of the True Parents, that is the life-long challenge. We must meet that challenge. This is the struggle. That is why last Sunday morning I gave you the example of the Japanese soldier during World War II. His sole goal was to die for the emperor. He wanted to die as a patriot. So when he assaulted the enemy territory, he didn't want to say "ouch" when the enemy bullet hit. He didn't want to say, I am dying, or, God will save me. He wanted to die for the emperor. He wanted the last word of his life to be banzai for the emperor. He cannot guarantee it. So when he was running with a bayonet on his rifle, running into enemy territory, he said banzai, banzai, banzai. Then he was guaranteed that his last word would be banzai.

This is going to be our philosophy. Our last word will be Aboji. Father. For you and me, every day is an assault. So we run, with the word Aboji, Aboji, every moment. That is the only way you can guarantee that your final word at the moment of death is Aboji. What a beautiful way of life. Neither the Metropolitan Life Insurance Company or the Equitable Life Insurance Company can guarantee your life. Only God guarantees your life. Only True Parents guarantee your life. We want to be sure that we have paid our insurance premium with God and True Parents, that our heart stays with the True Parents our entire life to the moment of death. You know, insurance companies issue a certificate. You don't have a written certificate from God or True Parents. The only certificate is written in your heart, and the manifestation of that certificate will be Aboji. If your heart is right, then your words will come out as a reflection of your heart. Your final words will be Aboji. Then God and True Parents will recognize your certificate.

FOR MY SAKE

This morning I prepared a Bible verse. Actually, I planned that Bible verse as a conclusion of this sermon, but somehow God gave me the atmosphere to use it now. God works in mysterious ways all the time. Matthew 10:39 says, "He who finds his life will lose it, and he who loses his life for my sake will find it." The entire beauty of Christianity is in this one verse of the Bible. He who finds his life will lose it. He who loses his life for my sake will find it. It is a paradox. It is contradictory. But that is the beauty. When you know the spirit world, that is the most logical truth you can find. You cannot find any truth better than that one.

The person who only lives for this world is a fool. In a way, from the worldly sense, you and I are dumb. We are fools. During the time of Jesus Christ, those who followed Jesus Christ were fools. St. Paul wrote in I Corinthians 4:10, "we are fools for Christ's sake." Today, in the eyes of the world you and I are fools. We are fools for True Parents. The world can laugh. But you know I enjoy this verse more than any other.

Today everybody, every citizen of America and the world, is trying to have luxury, a good life, good home, honor, respect. They want to be praised and cheered. They want to become president, prime minister, somebody.

The entire effort of the world is to find their life. But in the sight of God, all those mundane efforts are a losing effort. True Father recently talked about this. Everybody is trying to gain something for himself. I want to be rich. I want to be somebody. I want to be emperor. I want to be the ruler of the world. While they are chasing after this—all of human history did this way— they are losing everything. The world today is a losing world. While they are making a concerted, desperate effort to gain, the result is losing. It is pitiful.

We are foolish people. Why? Because instead of trying to gain, we are trying to lose. And thank God, True Parents push you to lose. The last couple of days True Parents held a tremendous conference with the state leaders. I have been translating for Father for two whole days. Father's emphasis is you have to lose yourself for the sake of your state, the sake of your mission. This is foolish in the eyes of the world. But the important thing is for whose sake. The Bible said "for my sake." For Christ's sake. For God's sake. In our case, for the True Parents' sake. If that is correct, then God guarantees that you will find your life. You will never lose. You will find your eternal, glorious life.

WE ARE VISITORS TO THIS PLANET

The other Sunday I talked to you about us being visitors to this planet. We just visit this planet for 100 years at the most. All of you, Unification members, I want you to live 100 years because God needs you here on earth. I want you to be strong and healthy because God needs you down here. That is the sole reason. But anyway, we are visitors. Maybe you will live 100 years or 120 years, but compared to eternity, 120 years is nothing. Far less than a peanut. That is my favorite word. Looks like a peanut. Peanut. Compared to eternity, your 120 years here on earth is a peanut. Even the very smallest peanut.

Our real life is not the life of this physical flesh, this clumsy hand. You think our body is perfect, but this body has so many limitations. You cannot fly. You can feel pain. Amazing limitation. So we are not going to live for eternity with this flesh. God gave you the perfected form of living. That is your spirit man. I told you the other day you are two persons. I see you here as one person, a physical person. I also see you as a spiritual person sitting right there. A physical person I can recognize with my physical eyes. A spiritual person I can only recognize with my spirit eyes, which I don't have now. But I do know you are sitting as two persons right there. And when you give up this body, the only body that sustains your life is your spirit man, spirit woman. That is the real you. In that respect we cannot die. No one can kill us.

The other day I quoted Jesus speaking in Luke, telling his disciples not to be afraid of those who can only kill your flesh. They are not going to be your enemy. The only one you truly have to fear is the person who can send you to hell, who can destroy your soul. No one here on earth can touch the real you. The real Bo Hi Pak, nobody under the sun can touch except God. Brother Kim mentioned about the government harassment. There are many investigations of our church, me, Father, and so forth. They can never touch me, except my flesh. That is not the real me. It is like they can come and touch only the car, but not the passengers. Think of it. The policeman comes to arrest you. The only thing he can do is to touch your car—period. He cannot open the door and drag you out. It is a rental car. I rent the car from Hertz Company or Avis or whatever. I rent the car from God. And the only thing they can do is to come and touch your car. Not the passengers. Not the real you.

A little later I am going to read from the book *Known But Unknown* by Arthur Ford. On the back of this book it says that every spiritual medium or spiritual person says, "It is not possible for men to die." It is an amazing statement. It is not possible for men to die. Not you or anybody. Why? Real death in the sight of God is not physical death. Real death in the sight of God is separation from God. That is the real death. That is what the fall of man is all about.

HOW DID THEY DIE?

Adam and Eve ate the fruit of the Tree of Knowledge of Good and Evil in the Garden of Eden. The Bible says they died, but the Bible also recorded they lived another 900 years. What does it mean? The Bible said the moment they ate the fruit they died. In the sight of God, Adam and Eve died. They no longer had anything to do with God. They were separated from God. Death occurred at that moment. But in the worldly eyes, Adam and Eve did not change even one bit, except they probably showed their anxieties. But, basically Adam and Eve didn't look any different after the fall.

However, death occurred. They fell from the light to the darkness. The real death True Parents are concerned about is not physical death but spiritual death. And everyone who died physically since the fall continues their existence for eternity. But not in light. Not in the world of God. Not in the sight of the love of God, but in the dungeons of hell, in the world of darkness, in the impossible and irrevocable unprincipled fire of hell. That existence is far worse than living. You know that. Many people would rather not exist than to exist in that spiritual hell.

What is the worst thing that Jesus said to his betraying disciple, Judas Iscariot? He did not say, I will punish you with death. He didn't say, I am going to kill you. No. In sympathy and compassion, Jesus said of Judas, it would have been better for him if he had not been born. He betrayed the son of God to the enemy. That crime is irrevocable in the sight of God. The punishment comes in eternal life. That hellish fire is going to be far worse than any type of living. Thus we are talking about the real death. That is the death God fears the most.

This world is a world of death, separated from God. That is why we need a savior, to bring us back to life. God did not want His children to suffer for eternity. God wants to restore His children out of that hellish fire. That is why God sent Jesus Christ 2,000 years ago to bring mankind out of spiritual death and back to life, one with God. But because of the crucifixion, that salvation was not completed. That is why 2,000 years later He sends another Messiah.

The world is no different from 2,000 years ago. At the time of Jesus this world was a world of death. Dead. Just a pitch-dark, dead world. And still today our world is a pitch-dark, dead world. You have been working in New York. That is a pitch-dark New York. Look at what happened. Several weeks ago there was a blackout. Yesterday True Parents and I discussed it in the car. That was a pity. New York was hit with a 24-hour blackout. Approximately 4,000 looters were arrested overnight. This is the lowest, most savage, most primitive society you can imagine. That happened right in New York. There is no law. That was a jungle. Everybody became a beast. They could do anything. They could steal things, attack a person, rape a woman, commit arson. It is ugly.

This is one sure sign that the moral decline of this nation is happening rapidly. This nation is barely supported by the pillar of law and regulations. When those regulations break down, then overnight New York becomes a savage jungle civilization. There is no pillar inside the human heart. Nothing can support society for eternity except a God-centered pillar inside the human heart.

Two thousand years ago, the situation was precisely the same. Today we are sending men to the moon, we have color television, we have communication lines all over the world, we have Polaris missiles—all kinds of wonders we have created through science. But human morality and the human heart are no better than 2,000 years ago and maybe even worse.

So we need to be liberated from bondage and come back to life spiritually. A real man was brought to earth. Actually, you and I crossed that boundary line between hell and heaven. For the time being, during the time of restoration, hell and heaven co-exist. Sometimes hell and heaven co-exist in your heart. Some days you live in hell and some days you live in heaven. There are so many Moonies who became ex-Moonies because they did not any longer see the heavenly side. They only tasted the hellish fire and they could not liberate themselves. They had no hope anymore. Everything was pitch dark. They couldn't see the vision. Then they became ex-Moonies. But if you lose sight and vision of the spiritual aspect of our movement, you are going to be a loser.

So we need a messiah. God has been preparing to send the messiah. God will send someone with unlimited power resources. We need power to illuminate ourselves here on earth. Everyone is going to become an electric bomb spiritually. All the bombs are dead, pitch dark. But once reactivated, your source of power is plugged into God, you are reunited with God, and then God's energy is flowing into you. Then we begin to glow. We are the glowing bombs.

I want you to know that of all the people who lived here on earth for the last 6,000 biblical years, not a single one died and vanished out of the universe. They exist somewhere. But there are two ways of existing: in the light or in the darkness. Once in the true life with God, they can plug in to God's power. Those who are plugged into nothing remain in pitch dark and continue their existence in hellish fire.

RAISE THE DEAD

Therefore, True Parents are proclaiming that the restoration of man is not just going to take place here on earth. God, Father, and you and I are responsible to raise those dead in the spirit world. We must liberate not only the physical hell, but also spiritual hell. The billions of people there.

So, he who finds his life will lose it, and he who loses his life for my sake will find it. "For my sake" is the key. Abraham, Moses, and the other great saints of the Old Testament era can say they lived for God's sake. But they were, let's say, 30 percent illuminated, because that was as much truth as was available in the Old Testament. They couldn't go any further. In the New Testament era, after Jesus Christ, we could illuminate ourselves probably up to 60 percent or 70 percent. It was the growth stage. In other words, we were closer to God. We could liberate ourselves from darkness and come closer to God, but we could not be one with God yet because the whole truth was not yet available yet.

Now in our time, with the True Parents and with the Divine Principle, our union with God is going to be perfect. It is all up to us now. The highway is laid and the rail is constructed. The locomotive is here. All we have to do is our five percent responsibility. That is, hang on to the locomotive.

It is amazing. The other day we went to Barrytown to go carp fishing. Did you go? Boy, carp fishing. One thing I like about carp fishing in the mud is that after about an hour everybody looks alike. You cannot tell John from

Jim. You cannot tell who is Japanese, who is Korean, who is American. You cannot tell black from white or yellow. Well, I thought, this is the world of God. God is color-blind. God does not see color. One color He can see. When we laughed, we could see each other's white teeth. I was amazed. Everybody had white teeth. Yes, that is a common thing. Teeth. The hard bone in the mouth. Everybody is the same. Well, Divine Principle is our teeth. Everybody is the same. White and hard and look alike. We live by that bone.

FATHER IS THE LOCOMOTIVE

Carp fishing taught me something else. Many times Amtrak trains go by. It is very enjoyable to watch that very beautiful silver streak go by. But more amazing was the freight train. I never realized, even though I have been in America for so many years, until the Barrytown fishing, that a locomotive can pull such a long train. One time I counted. One, two, three, four, five, six—80, 90, 100, 105, 110, one time I counted about 120 cars. Then I looked at Father. I said to myself, "Father, you are the locomotive. We are like the freight cars. Father, thank you. I don't have any energy myself. I don't have anything. I don't generate the power. But you pull and pull, and with your faith you can pull three million easy. Ten million easy. You are pulling the entire humanity."

Then I learned the lesson. All I have to do is hang on to him like the links that attach one freight car to another. All I have to do is hang on to his tail. Father, I hang on to you. That is all we need. That is our five percent responsibility. Our five percent responsibility is going to be obedience. Steadfastness. Hang on, never give up. That is our responsibility. Another thing I learned from the freight train (a lot of lessons from that freight train). Suppose you are a freight car close to the front of the train. When you lose your link, you are not only losing yourself, you are losing all the freight cars behind you. Boy, that is a fearful consequence. You are responsible for so many spiritual children directly or indirectly. It is not going to affect only you, but your spiritual children and your physical children and your descendants. We are responsible for the millions of people and billions of people who follow us. So our five percent responsibility is to be obedient. Hang on. That is our five percent responsibility.

Actually, although we begin as a freight car, Father doesn't want us to end as a freight car. What God wants and what True Parents are training you for today is to become another locomotive. Another Sun Myung Moon. So that I can pull many, many freight cars after me. I can pull the Korean freight car. You can pull the Japanese freight car. You can pull the American freight car.

You see, a fundamental differences between Christianity and Unification Church is this—we are going to perfect ourselves to be a loco-motive, to be another Christ-like man so we can act as a powerful loco-motive pulling the heavenly train. Each one of you is responsible for millions and billions of people. You must become a locomotive. That was the main message of Father yesterday to the state leaders. You are the mes-siah.

Father has been asked by the media, "Are you the messiah?" Do you know what Father said? "Yes, I am. So are you, so are you, and so are you." Such a beautiful, beautiful answer I had never imagined. My limited brain almost exploded. I couldn't take such wisdom. Are you the messiah? Yes, I am. And so are you. Eventually everyone is a messiah. Everyone eventu-ally is a son of God. Everyone eventually is a life-giving, illuminating heav-enly body. Our goal is to become a messiah.

At the time of Jesus the same question was asked of him. Are you the messiah? Are you the son of God? Jesus was very wise, and I am amazed by his wisdom. Jesus quoted from the Bible. Don't you read the Old Testament? You all believe in the Old Testament, don't you? Don't you know that the Old Testament says that every one of you is meant to be walking God, liv-ing God? So what is so unnatural about being a son of God? I thought what Jesus said was the best answer until I heard Father's answer. Everyone is des-tined to be a messiah. All we need is one prototype. One model in the cen-ter. We have a living example. If we follow him and follow his Principle, his heart, his way of life, we definitely will become another messiah. That is the essence of Father's message recently.

God and Father are not satisfied for you just to become a good mem-ber of the Unification Church. A good freight car. That does not satisfy God. It does not satisfy Father, truthfully. God wants more than that from you. True Parents are asking more than that from you. True Parents are ask-ing you to become another Messiah. You are responsible for the tribe, nation, and world.

ARE YOU READY TO BE A MESSIAH?

So, Father keeps asking if we are ready to be a messiah. That is the main thrust of the message. Father has given us so much truth. All we have to do is practice that truth and we can become a messiah. Another Sun Myung Moon. Father is not satisfied that you are good Moonies. No. Father wants you to become more than a Moonie. Father wants you to become another Reverend Moon in your area, in your respective mission.

Yesterday Father gave an astonishing proclamation at the state lead-ers conference. Father said, the world has given us a name: Moonie. I am a Moonie, you are a Moonie. Well, Father said, we didn't make that name. Why not make one name ourselves? So a new baby is being born today, and we have a new name. Our name is not Moonie, but Sunnie. If people say are you a Moonie, you say no. I am a Sunnie.

I will ask you a question. Are you Moonies? [No, we are Sunnies.] We were promoted yesterday. We went from Moonie to Sunnie. So we will make the world Moonie first, then eventually we will let them be promoted to Sunnie. Let them work for the name Sunnie. This name doesn't come easy. We have to work at it. You did and I did and I am glad. Rejoice over it. Congratulations, we are promoted.

Sunnie is a far better title than major general, or even a four-star general or even a five-star general. We are Sunnies. Why?

I will explain. Yesterday Father said you must not lose this opportunity to become a messiah. This is the only time in human history this opportunity will knock at your door. You must answer it, you must grab it. In order to grab it, Father said, first, you must not become a burden on the Unification Church or anyone else. You must not become a passive person. You must not become a burden on our church, Father, or Heavenly Father. You must become a dynamo, a power-giving, illuminating element. You must be a divine spirit. You must act upon your own initiative and spread light and heat to the world. Light is the truth, heat is love. We must spread the truth and love to the world. Therefore, your name today is Sunnie.

REFLECT LIGHT, GIVE LIGHT

There are two major heavenly bodies in the sky, the sun and the moon. The moon reflects light, but the sun gives life, light, power, energy, illumination. We must become suns. We must give our light and heat to the world. You must become an engine, dynamo, locomotive. That is why we are now called Sunnie. In Father's name, Sun Myung Moon, there is both sun and moon. Amazing. Eventually American people will call Father "Sun Moon." I know that because the clumsy American tongue can't pronounce Myung very well.

In a way, English is a very hard language. But I tell you, Korean is much more complicated. Korean has a greater variety of sounds. Americans just cannot pronounce some Korean words. It is impossible, because your sounds have a limited variety. Also, the Japanese tongue is very limited linguistically. So Japanese people have a difficult time learning English and an even more difficult time learning Korean. In Japanese, there is no L, no R, no TH, no F. So Japanese publications use Americanized Japanese and American terms with phonetic sounds. For TV, they say "tedabe." Hotel, they call "hoteru." Hilton Hotel, they call "Herton Hoteru." I thought I was pretty good at English, but I would hear a Japanese person saying something in English and think, boy, that person is really using a very difficult language; there are some crazy words. I just couldn't figure it out. But it turned out to be sometimes "Herton Hoteru." That type of sound I just couldn't catch. I'm saying all this in a very innocuous way. Of course, I have a great love for Japanese. Japanese brothers and sisters, raise your hands please. Fine, thank you.

I admire and love Japanese brothers and sisters so much. And I tell you, Japanese brothers and sisters in this new age of Father have done more for Father than any other country, including Korea. I tell you, we owe Japan a great deal. That is true. That is not flattery. We owe Japan and Japanese brothers and sisters a tremendous debt. I once went to Japan as part of an evangelical tour of 14 cities with the IOWC. Father would speak the first night, I would speak the second. I was going out there and saying in Japanese, ladies and gentlemen. My Japanese is not that good. Speaking in Japan was one of the highlights of my life.

When I learned something about Japanese history, I realized that the Japanese people have been trained for this new age for the messiah. For all their history, they have been trained for loyalty. I have never seen any people more loyal than the Japanese. To the emperor, to their lord, to their master. They have been teaching loyalty, justice, generosity for 2,000 years, and they have been waiting for the day to cash in on their training. When is that? The time of the Lord of the Second Advent. Now they have found their true subject. Up till now, the history of loyalty of the Japanese people has been a dress rehearsal. The real performance has just come. Don't you agree?

Anyway, I want to tell one joke about Japanese. A Japanese scholar was invited to be the keynote speaker at a scientific conference in London. And he was so proud. He was determined to give the speech in English. So he wrote his draft in Japanese and translated it into English. He used the most difficult words in the dictionary. He said to himself, "I am going to surprise all the western scholars. They will be shocked when they hear me." He memorized and practiced pronouncing every word until he was ready. So he went to London. When his time came, he went up there and most proudly presented a beautiful, hour-long dissertation, entirely in English, without even one mistake, totally in English. After his speech, there was a standing ovation. "Boy, I did it, by George, I did it," he thought. Then, these English scholars were talking among themselves, saying "He is very good. His Japanese is very good. And, you know, his Japanese almost sounds like English." Do you get it? He gave his entire message in English, but everybody heard it as Japanese. So they said, the Japanese language almost sounds like English. I understand that. It could happen.

Let's go back to the mainstream now. In Father's name, Myung is very difficult for Americans to pronounce. Americans say "Mi Young." One time Jean Dixon came to the Waldorf Astoria and gave an introduction of Father. Before she went up to the platform she practiced saying Father's name many times. She wanted to pronounce Father's name well. She practiced but when the time came for her to speak, she said, "Ladies and gentlemen, the Reverend Sun Mi Young." She couldn't pronounce Myung. In American culture, you use an initial for a middle name. So many newspapers have written Sun M. Moon. Good, that is all right.

Soon another book will come out about Father. The book I mentioned the other day, *Sun Myung Moon and the Unification Church*, was written Dr. Sontag. But another book is coming out soon, titled *Sun Moon*. I bet you dollars to donuts that in the future in western culture, Father will be known as Sun Moon. I told Father this and he smiled and was beaming ear to ear. Let them do that. That is all right. It doesn't matter whether we call God John or Doe, as long as you know Him correctly.

Anyway, Father's name has two heavenly bodies: Sun and Moon. But why is Father known as Reverend Moon? I thought about this a lot. This is very, very meaningful. Why is he called Reverend Moon all over the world? This shows Father's humility in the providence. The moon reflects the light of the sun. Actually, here on earth, from God's standpoint, Father is the moon. Who is the sun then? God is the sun. Eternal sun. Father is the moon reflecting the full strength of the sun to mankind. That is Father's role. From the standpoint of God, Father is the moon. This is a humble way of putting himself here on earth. And that is beautiful.

MOONIES FIRST, THEN SUNNIES

But from mankind's point of view, Father is the sun here on earth. And we all must become another sun here on earth. So that is why we should take the first word of Father's name, Sun. We shall be named from today on, Sunnies. When you think of this Sunnie, think about the sun and think about Father. And think about yourself as the image of the sun, as another Reverend Moon. Another Father here on earth. I am a Sunnie. I must be a life-giving, illuminating spirit. I must give and be an example. I cannot hide myself. This is the whole message of Sunnie. You and I are Sunnies. And we must reach out to the world and convince them first to become Moonies.

Are you Moonies? [No, we are Sunnies.] Are you ladies all Sunnies? [Yes.] You brothers, are you Sunnies? [Yes.] Boy, echo. All over. I am sure in Boston Father can hear you say Sunnie.

Yesterday I asked Father, as I promised you last Sunday, to please stay and speak to you this morning. I told him, the national leaders got to see you, but the New York members miss you very much. Father's answer was, "What are you talking about? Tell them they are Sunnies. They are the Reverend Moon. They don't need me anymore. I trust them." So now you can see Father treats you as a mature Sunnie. Father is giving you this chance to prove yourself.

So I want you to feel honored. Father trusts you and puts you in a position to prove yourself. As a matter a fact, yesterday Father was very happy to hear the report from the leaders and particularly the New York Church. Mr. Sawada gave a very moving, heartwarming report about the New York Church members and 43rd Street and all the Performing Arts members. How they are going out, day in and day out, really having a showdown in prayer. They even fast. If they don't get the expected result, they fast. If their team doesn't get the expected result, the team leader fasts. If all the teams did not get the results expected, them Mr. Sawada himself fasts.

And Mr. Sawada said to Father, "Father, you know you told us that every time we work harder than the level of the Washington Monument campaign, always God will work with us. And Father, I know what you mean. Right now the New York Church is in a position to really work harder than for Washington Monument rally. Father, I want you to trust us. We are really doing it. I, myself, for the first time see hope in New York. I thought there was no hope for a long time, but now I have something inside telling me that we can do it. And our members are demonstrating it. Those members of Performing Arts and 43rd Street, our New York Church members are brilliant. Father, I am proud of them." So Mr. Sawada represented you very well. He is a good leader. He really wanted to bring the members out in front of Father so you can be recognized. Father was very, very pleased.

LITTLE REVEREND MOON

Then the four IOWC team leaders, Reverend Vincenz, Reverend Sudo, Mr. Ron Pepper, and Dr. Bergman, each reported on how the teams are doing. And Reverend Sudo started out with a big joke. He said, "Father, we have a rumor in the New Jersey area. People are saying that Reverend Moon is being seen almost every day in the New Jersey area, that Reverend Moon is here all the time. They are saying that they always thought that Reverend Moon was quite a tall person, but he is really quite small, smaller than I expected." That was good. Reverend Sudo was very happy to be mistaken for Reverend Moon. Father said, "Then you must be responsible. You are Reverend Moon. I want you to be mistaken by the people of the world for Reverend Moon."

After the Yankee Stadium rally, I was visiting Washington, D.C., then coming back to New York. At the airport a porter came to take my luggage and he looked at me and said, "By the way, aren't you Reverend Moon?" I was shocked. I couldn't say no and, honestly, I wasn't good enough to say yes either. So I said, "How do you know Reverend Moon?" I just mumbled the question. But inside I was tickled to death. That is how good I felt. Everyone is Reverend Moon. You are Reverend Moon too. You look like Reverend Moon, I hope. At least Reverend Moon's spirit is shining through you. So we men have one privilege: we can be mistaken for Reverend Moon easier than our sisters. Oh, I pity you poor ladies.

But anyway, Reverend Sudo is mistaken for Reverend Moon, and people are saying that every day Reverend Moon is coming around this area. So soon Reverend Moon will be everywhere. Reverend Moon pops out everywhere, all over the world. I want this to happen. In the future, all of us children will take the parents' role. We'll go out and speak at evangelical meetings and Day of Hope banquets. Father wants us to do that. Then all the newspapers will come out saying, Reverend Moon is in town. I would like that. Why? So that I can have all the people come out to hear Reverend Moon. After all, when we speak, we speak with Father's spirit. We will pray, "Heavenly Father, hide myself, only manifest Father so the people can hear and see Father." We all can do that. Whether we are black or yellow, it doesn't make any difference. White, it doesn't make any difference. You can do that.

One time I saw the movie titled "Spartacus." It was very, very moving. I really enjoyed it, and I cried a lot. Spartacus, the leader of the slave revolt, and all his followers were crucified at the end, defeated. But in one scene, when the Romans had captured them, they asked which one is Spartacus. One by one, they all answered, "I am Spartacus." I know every one of you has the courage to stand up and say, "I am Sun Myung Moon." Go ahead, American government. I am Sun Myung Moon. Go ahead, communists. I am Sun Myung Moon. To the Mafia, I am Sun Myung Moon. To the gangsters, I am Sun Myung Moon.

GIVE ME WISDOM

I am very happy to hear from our brother Tim about some persecution mounting in Washington and government harassment. I am glad because here is a chance for me to stand up and say, I am Sun Myung Moon. This is my privilege, my honor, my greatest joy. I am asking God for just one thing—wisdom. God, my brain is not good enough. Give me wisdom so I can act wisely. Then I have that courage and I can stand up for Sun Myung Moon. All of us can do that. Can you do it? [Yes.]

During the conference yesterday, Father said the reason he went out to the ocean was that he wanted to be alone. He is shedding so many tears. He does not want to show his tears. The ocean is the best hiding place for Father. That is one of the reasons he is going out there so much. He asked the state leaders to pray, not dry prayers, but wet prayers. Pray to God with wet tears and pray as a responsible son, as another Sun Myung Moon here on earth.

I prepared another testimony out of this book. Since God's spirit didn't lead me in this direction, I didn't use it. Tomorrow I will meet you again, once more. While Father is absent, Father will ask us to go ahead precisely the same as if he were here. Tomorrow is the first day of the month, and I will talk about the significance of the month of August that Father explained yesterday at the conference. Also, I will read a testimony of how beautiful the spirit world is. Some of the testimony is so astounding. So I am glad this morning that Father's spirit led me in this fashion. You and I really enjoyed Father's presence. I can see his spirit all over the place. Way out there in the lawn, out on the concrete, inside the rooms. I am so glad God worked. We are so determined to become a sun and an important responsible son. We are suns, and we are another Sun Myung Moon.

So this morning's subject was "We are Sunnies." Let us pray. Thank you very much.

Prayer by Bo Hi Pak:

Our most loving Heavenly Father. Thank you for your spirit. Thank you for your truth. Thank you for your inspiration. Man is incapable of doing all this. I know that your spirit persisted, and overwhelmed this place. Your most important children's dwelling place. Your voice is strong out of your heart. Father, thank you. And Father, we have been given a new name. Father, I want to live up to it. I want to be a Sunnie. A real Sunnie. Father, as the members go out to the world, make all the people Moonies so that they recognize Reverend Moon, our Father, here on earth and so that they can someday become Sunnies with us. Father, thank you very much for this day. For this privilege. For this opportunity to work for Father and work for you, Heavenly Father. Thank you, Father. Oh, Father, our heart is so filled with your spirit. No words are adequate. So Father, please look down and look inside our hearts directly. I know you can, and that you will, and will respond to us. So Father, our True Parents in Boston are trusting us. We cannot let them down, Father. We must live up to their expectation. This week we will make a most important week. Father, we gather together tomorrow morning, so that we can renew our vitality for the month of August. Be with us all the way, Father. All the way. All these things we pray in the name of our most beloved True Parents. Amen.

Thank God for Persecution

BELVEDERE ESTATE, TARRYTOWN, NEW YORK

AUGUST 1, 1977

Here, Dr. Pak continues the talk he gave the day before and focuses on the value and necessity of persecution. Using John the Baptist as an example of someone who had the vision and lost it, he cautions Unification Church members that they will also be tested. He implores them to strive to become pillars of faith.

I would like to have the IOWC leader, Mr. Ron Pepper, lead our manseis. Let us all stand and have three cheers for True Parents.

It is through persecution alone that we can truly know the suffering heart of God. Father has described God's suffering heart. His heart is aching and broken. How can you understand the broken heart of God and be closer to him except through persecution and tasting the same suffering? So this morning I say to you, thank God we have some persecution. This gives us a brilliant opportunity to taste the heart of God, to join Him in His suffering. Thank God.

Yesterday I told you our job is to live and die for Father. Die for the True Parents. The most dramatic way of proving that you are living and dying for True Parents and God is through undergoing persecution, not through the way of glory or praise. If your heart has not been tested and you have not proven yourself, you know God only like a black and white picture. Going the way of persecution makes God more vivid and real, living color, like a color television.

Without persecution our movement cannot be tested. If we have ample money for everything, and if people serve us and salute us, do we have a great blessing? No! We are persecuted only because we are right and because we want to change from the selfish point of view. We are talking about a vision for the future of the world, the Kingdom of God. After all, for 6,000 years who has been the ruler here on earth? The Bible clearly states that Satan has been the ruler.

The Unification Church came to this satanic world like paratroopers from heaven. We landed in hostile land. We are going to take away Satan's territory and his people and transform them into the Kingdom of God. That means the satanic people must lose. Who likes to lose? Naturally, Satan reacts most violently. But to me the persecution shows clearly that what we are doing is right. We are not here for self-centered motivation. But the world comes against us because they are threatened. They know we are right. When paratroopers are coming down, how can you expect a royal welcome? Will you be ushered in politely? Can you expect that? No, sir. You can expect machine gun fire, artillery, barbed wire, land mines. When the United Nations landed at Inchon with General MacArthur, they were greeted by communist fire. That is how we are greeted. It's natural.

Father is saying, thank God we have persecution. That proves that we are doing right. That proves that we are truly the first troops to land on this hostile ground of satanic territory. We are trying to change this world to the Heavenly Kingdom. We can't expect that to be easy. Through learning the true heart of God, we will be just like him. To understand God's heart, we live it. That is what Father is doing.

PRAYING WET PRAYERS

In the early days of our ministry in Korea, most of our prayer was totally wet prayer. When the congregation prayed in Korea, the church had a very humble wooden floor. Dr. Sontag has been there and I am sure he can vividly recall. Now they have linoleum to make it better, but 10 years ago there was not even some floor cover. It was the hard, wooden floor. When we met, night and day, Father prayed and everybody prayed. Usually that prayer ended up washed in a flood of tears. There is no one under heaven, no living individual here on earth, who has shed more tears than Father. He shed the tears of God.

In Korea, Father sometimes began to pray upstairs in his own small, humble prayer room. It is a Japanese-style building, and Father would sit and pray on a tatami mat. Sometimes members would see water dripping down from the second floor. They wondered if it was raining or leaking something. But there was no rain. They went upstairs and found Father totally weeping in prayer for hours and hours. His eyes were swollen from so much weeping. Father cried out God's sorrow. Not his own sorrow, God's sorrow. He wanted to heal the broken heart of God through his tears.

Ladies and gentlemen, for the first time in history God's heart was healed, by the tears of one man, Reverend Moon. For the first time God found here on earth a friend. God found a handle he could connect to, a handle he could pull.

Actually, you and I certainly have no power to change the world. God has that power. All God needs is a handle. Look at Noah's flood judgment. How could God judge the world by flood? Because there was a handle. Noah presented his untiring and unchanging face to God, and God could pull that handle. There was a condition established here on earth, so God could pull that handle and judge the world. It is just the same today. God is looking for the handle. Reverend Moon is the handle of God. Then God will manifest his power and pull the world.

This is why sometimes when Father proclaims something that he is going to do or something that will happen it seems to be impossible. Last year, he said we will go to Moscow. Everybody in the world laughed at him. The only one who did not laugh at that statement was God. Reverend Moon made that statement, not because he believes in his own power or in your power, but because of his belief in God. He knew that we have to present the handle that God can grab with His gigantic hand. That is our job. The primary job of the Unification Church today is to change the quality of man.

THE AGONY OF GOD

If even one person out of this congregation can come near to the standard of Reverend Moon in understanding God's suffering heart, our movement would be infinitely proud. I tell you, we have so far to go. This is the agony of God. This is the agony of Reverend Moon. So, brothers and sisters, do not try to be a worldly success. Let us make spiritual success in the sight of God. Let us present ourselves as truly the one that God can say, "My son, you know me. I am glad you know me." And then we can tell God, "I will take over your mission. My Father in heaven, you suffered enough. Why don't you rest and leave the mission to us. Relax on your throne for the first time in history." God has been waiting for such a man and such a group. Reverend Moon is saying every day, God let me do it. Why don't you take a rest? And we join with him. We are saying the same thing in our prayers.

"God, my Father, you suffered enough. I am your son. I am your daughter. We can do it. You just relax and you just watch me."

The world may call you a madman or a blasphemer. The world may try to stone you to death. But you have nothing to fear. I told you already, no power can touch the real you. They can only touch your flesh, which is eventually going to go back to the earth. No power can touch the real son of God in you, the real daughter of God in you. Not the power of the whole U.S. government.

Actually, we are carrying one bomb for the satanic world. I tell you, that is this body. Our prayers should be: Heavenly Father, let me have a chance to explode greater than the atomic bomb, greater than the hydrogen bomb. We want to make an impact, not for the destruction of the world, but for the construction of the world. We want to use this one final bomb you gave us, this body. I want to invest it.

Think of John the Baptist. God sent John the Baptist ahead of Jesus to prepare the way for the Lord. He was like a pathfinder, a "recon" team, or a scout. He was to make Jesus' "landing" easier. But one of the most extraordinary proclamations of the Divine Principle is that John the Baptist was not a man of success. He failed his mission. He did not pave the way of Jesus into glory. Instead, he paved the way of Jesus into crucifixion.

John the Baptist knew he was a great prophet. When he spent 40 days in the wilderness, he ate locusts and wild honey. That was the way he survived. He did not want to eat anything—not meat, not blood. He knew his body was holy, and he could not stain it with ungodly things. He was a great man, far greater than you and me. John the Baptist was a great prophet. God gave him the vision to see Jesus as the son of God. John testified to Jesus at the Jordan River, saying, you are the son of God. I proclaim to the world, Jesus, you are the son of God.

JOHN THE BAPTIST WAS ALREADY DEAD

But before John the Baptist was beheaded by Herod, he had already died an even worse death. His spiritual death came first. His clear mind and vision that had recognized Jesus was missing. He was in prison at that time. He was tortured, not by King Herod, but by his own conscience. Something was missing. He was not sure. To John, Jesus was an enigma, he couldn't quite figure him out. He looks like the son of God, then he doesn't look like the son of God. If he is the son of God, how could he be criticized as a man of demons, and how could the world try to stone him to death? John sent two disciples to Jesus to ask, "Are you he who is to come, or shall we wait for another?"

What a contrast. John had testified that Jesus was indeed the son of God, but at the end of his life, he was asking the question, are you really the messiah, or shall we wait for another messiah? Was this was an utterance of trust or doubt? It is doubt. He died in doubt.

Unification Church members face the same danger. One of the fears we Unification Church members have is that we might doubt, at the end of the day. The end of your day, the end of my day. I don't want to be in a position to say, are you really the one or shall we wait for another Reverend Moon? That is the worst condemnation. If you are sure, every day you are living with bubbling enthusiasm and excitement that you know who he is. You not only know who he is, you are living his burden. You are weeping his sorrow. You are shedding his tears. You have been beaten to death because of him. You have been thrown into jail because of him.

American government, would you give me the greatest Medal of Honor by throwing me into prison because of Father? I would consider that the greatest medal of all. America cannot honor me any more than to send me to jail because of him. Because of the tears I shed for God. Because of the tears I shed for mankind. Because of tears I shed for True Parents. Boy. America would do me a great favor. Through persecution, God gives me the greatest blessing of all.

Brothers and sisters, let us be totally sure of one thing. We must not become a John the Baptist, asking the question, are you he who is to come or shall we wait for another? You and I are proud Moonies, and we were just promoted to Sunnies. We are Sunnies. Sunnies are ready to do anything, ready to go anywhere for His sake. For righteousness sake. That is a Sunnie. So I tell you my final word this morning is this: There can be ex-Moonies, but there can never be ex-Sunnies. Do you agree? Let us pray.

Prayer by Bo Hi Pak:

Our most loving Heavenly Father. Thank you very much. You hid me and spoke Your most precious word through this humble flesh. Our Father, thank you, thank you, that you give us the title of Sunnies. We have seen the glory of the coming of the Lord. We have seen the march of truth. Father, now we are going to live it, we are going to proclaim it, we are going to wage war against the satanic world. We are going to bring victory. Father, every year, by the time September 18 comes, we want to bring equivalent victory that matches the victory of Washington Monument last year. That is our determination this morning, the first day of August. Today we pledge to you our utmost loyalty, our heart, everything that I have got to bring that victory possible. We want to do it. Not for our own sakes. Not our own egos. Not our own fame. Not for our own honor, but for you, Father. We want to forget ourselves. We want to lose ourselves so that you can come in 100 percent. So you can run me. Run every one of us in this room. Thank you, Father. Thank you, Father. You just relax and watch what the Sunnies will perform this month, the month of August. Father, at the end of this month you will see the result. You will see our heart today and every day. We are proud of your son and daughter. All these things we pray in the name of our beloved True Parents. Amen.

A Living Marble Vase

Dr. Pak returns from a conference for European leaders and shares his insights from listening to and fishing with Father. Using the recent phenomena surrounding the selling of marble vases in Japan, he proceeds to demonstrate how the value of a thing or a person comes solely from its purpose and encourages members to become "living marble vases."

Let's face north and greet True Parents. Last Sunday I was with True Parents in Boston, and I clearly and most distinctly heard your voices. So let's make it even louder and clearer. Good morning, Father. Good morning, Mother. I am sure they heard all of us. Let's face front. Good morning, everyone.

How are you? [Great.] You sound great. You look great. Your smiles are so great. I have been away for two weeks actually. Last Sunday I couldn't be here because of the European conference in Boston. But it seems like I've been away for two years. I have been missing you very much and I wanted to be here. So I asked special permission from Father to return to Belvedere. I told him I wanted to be with you brothers and sisters on Sunday, and Father granted permission, so I was able to come back yesterday. I am here. Wonderful.

How do I look? [Great.] Father is even darker than me by now. I am not that strong a sailor or fisherman, and I am not that strong at sea. Every day this last week, we were out in the Atlantic Ocean, starting from 3:30 in the morning. After that, 5 a.m. pledge service is nothing. Every day is pledge service, but that pledge service is not on the land, it is at sea. By 5 o'clock we are already in the middle of the sea. Even now, for me, the whole Belvedere ground is shaking like this. Yesterday I was sitting at a table trying to do something and all of a sudden the table started to move. Boy, I thought it was an earthquake. I just couldn't imagine. But after one week at sea, everything is moving.

Last Sunday was my first day at sea. Practically the whole conference was conducted on the ocean. I was ready, but after one hour on the water, something funny was going on in my stomach. Something very funny, and I had a headache, and, boy, I had an awful day. The first day was absolutely hell. I really prayed, Father, Aboji, please help me. At least I was successful in keeping everything down in my stomach. I couldn't eat too much, but at least I could keep everything down.

A DESPERATE PRAYER FOR DRY LAND

That evening, I was talking to myself, "Father, I know this meeting is so important, and I hope the meeting tomorrow is on land. This meeting is so important, so I hope, Father, that you conduct the meeting in the house instead of on the sea." But that evening Father announced: "Tomorrow morning, 3:30, everybody in the boats." Boy! He said this particular meeting has a special meaning, and we will conduct it on the water.

Then, I made up my mind. Father, I may just collapse or die, or I may drown in the sea, or I might become the prey of sharks; but whatever happens, I am going to be there. I could never say to Father, I am so weak and I can't go out to sea. I will never say it. Father, I would rather collapse or be thrown into the sea and become the prey of sharks, but I will go. So the next morning I made it. I was like a kamikaze pilot. I made up my mind, and at 3:30 I got up and was first in following right behind Father. It was dark, and there is a cliff going down in a rocky area. It was very, very slippery and so rugged. I followed right behind Father, and I was on the boat right next to Father, and I made up my mind. OK, Satan, you test me. Come on.

Then, an amazing thing happened. That day I didn't feel anything funny in my stomach. I really enjoyed the second day. On the second day, God helped me in one way. The sea was very calm that day. Boy, then I really felt heaven in the sea. Very calm, like a mirror, and also that day the tuna helped me too. The tuna didn't bite, so I didn't have to move around too much. I was sitting down and listening to Father talk about different things. So that was a heavenly day. I really enjoyed the second day. I learned that everything depends on the state of mind. Now I just made up my mind to conquer the sea. I have done it.

The third day the sea was rough, and Father conducted the meeting on the boat. All the European and Korean and Japanese leaders came. Father invited everybody into the cabin, and we were all sitting very close like this, as you sit here. Father was giving them a message and I was translating. Boy, that was a real challenge. I was not just translating. I had been fighting with the sea and I had to balance myself so I would not collapse in front of Father's chair. When I would look up, I could see the window going up and down, up and down, and I looked at the sky and the next thing I saw was the sea going up and down. Father's message was so beautiful. Again, I really made up my mind that I would not give any weak sign of any kind. I would show Father that I am determined to do the mission. But, I was amazed myself. I just couldn't imagine translating for long hours. The sea was moving and the desk was moving up and down, and the faces of many of the European leaders became pale; their eyes became like this. They were just barely hanging on. The first day I looked very miserable. But second, third, fourth, and fifth days, no problem. I really have confidence following Father that I can be a good sailor and a good fisherman.

You know we heard that during the month of August Father caught 41 giant tuna. I thought tuna fishing must be somewhat easy. You just go out there and pull the tuna out of the water. I had that kind of impression. Father caught one tuna, two tuna, three tuna sometimes. Of course, we have three different boats. A small one, a little larger one, and three boats go out together. If each boat catches one, that makes three. So I thought, just go out there and pull the tuna up. But God gave me a lesson. It is not that easy. You have to really struggle. You have to really pray. You have to really go after them. It was hard work, many days. God gave me that lesson by giving no tuna the first day, no tuna the second day, no tuna the third day, even though we got up at 3:30 in the morning and didn't come back until it was almost dark. Over 15 hours out there, and no sign of tuna. Some other boats caught tuna. We were so envious. We were wondering why the tuna weren't biting. Father said because you are new people. The tuna know you are novices, newcomers, so they shy away from you. You must become friends with the tuna. Talk to the tuna, say hello to the tuna in the morning and greet them every day. Good morning, tuna. In the evening, no tuna. Good-bye tuna, we will see you tomorrow morning.

Everyday when I came back to the house, In Jin Nim would ask, did you catch a tuna? No, but I have an appointment with a tuna tomorrow morning. Then the next day she asked me, did you catch a tuna? No, I postponed the appointment until tomorrow morning. The first day, second day, nothing happened, third day nothing happened, fourth day nothing happened, fifth day nothing happened. Boy, five days. Sunday, Monday, Tuesday, Wednesday, Thursday. Now it's Friday. I have to leave to come back to see you on Saturday, so I was really desperate. I wanted to catch a tuna with Father. Father, what am I going to do? Give me just one tuna. I just want to be victorious so I have a victorious story to share with our brothers and sisters. If I go back without a tuna, what shall I tell them? I will have nothing to share. Everybody felt that way. Father answered our prayer.

FINALLY—VICTORY

Friday was a victorious day. In the morning we caught a giant tuna. Boy, the rope was going out. Calm sea, but one tuna struck. Boy, this is like a war. Everybody was shouting and running back and forth and pulling on the ropes. It was a gigantic battle, and we won it. So I came back here to report to you that we were victorious and we caught one giant tuna.

There was a second strike that day, but the tuna got away. We did see it, but it got away somehow. I felt so bad—I wanted to catch a second tuna. Two would be so much more victorious. Father said, you did catch one tuna, so you are victorious. But you also lost a tuna, so you feel very empty or miserable. The memory of the second tuna lasts longer, Father said. There is always a meaning. In any case, I am here with you and, I tell you, it is not easy to catch a tuna. Each one is such a battle. Each one requires such concentration. No good thing comes easy. You know it, I know it.

Father is working harder than anybody else. At 3:30 in the morning, Father is the first one to be up and get ready to go out to sea. During the day he meditates a lot. He looks out at the ocean and he is thinking. I see now why Father enjoys it so much. He sees nature untouched by humanity. It is not spoiled. Out there is a line waiting for the heavenly pioneer's hand. Father feels a real challenge in the sea.

During the week-long conference, many, many great lessons and messages were given. This morning I would like to share with you testimony given by some of the leaders, particularly from Japan concerning marble vases. So I brought one marble vase here to show you. This morning's message is titled "A Living Marble Vase."

By the way, all the European leaders left recharged. Every three months European leaders get together for this conference. This one in Boston was a most meaningful one because they struggled together with Father for one week, learning Father's way of life and listening to so many instructions and messages from Father. August 15 was the 32nd anniversary of Korea's liberation, so we had a special prayer at sea. The four boats gathered together around New Hope. New Hope is like the flag ship, then there is Sea Hope, a little smaller boat; then Go Hope, a little smaller even; and last there is the fast boat that is called the Flying Phoenix. So we have a heavenly fleet out there. The heavenly fleet gathered in diamond formation, like the heavenly four positions on August 15. Father gave a special prayer on the ocean and said this is the most meaningful year after the Korean liberation. We are now moving into the 33rd year since the liberation, and as you know, Jesus' ministry was consummated at the age of 33 when he was crucified. So reaching the 33rd year is very meaningful.

Speaking of tuna once again, many people come to that area, the Gloucester and Provincetown area, to fish. As you know we visited Provincetown one day. Provincetown is where the Mayflower, about 300 years ago, came across the Atlantic from Europe. Provincetown was the first place the Mayflower anchored. Then from there they moved up to Plymouth Rock and landed there. The name probably comes from Provident Town. It is the most providential town. So Father took two days out of the six-day conference to visit Provincetown. We stayed in two small cottages. Just like the MFT [mobile fund-raising team], we slept on the floor in sleeping bags and went to bed very late at night. And promptly at 3:30 we got up and were ready to go. It was a most meaningful conference at Provincetown. Father also mentioned that the reason he came to Provincetown is to make a new beginning. The Pilgrim Fathers came with the Mayflower and anchored here first. He said, let us have our new anchor from this meeting on. Let us make a new history.

There was a testimony given by Mr. Furuta, who is leading the MFT of Japan. The Japanese MFT movement is slightly different from our American-style operation, but the spirit is the same and the purpose is the same. In Japan we organize into companies that sell primarily three items: ginseng tea, marble vases, and flowers.

Mr. Furuta reported to Father and while I was translating to the European leaders, I thought that I would like to share this testimony with my brothers and sisters in Belvedere. Several years ago this marble vase I have here was manufactured in Korea out of Korean stone. It was dug up and hand-carved by our members into a vase. There are all different kinds of vases, some are taller, some are shorter. Some have this shape, and some have a different shape. Some are dark like this, some are white, green, and so forth. Different hues and shades of color. Different designs. The differences are not made by men—the nature of the stone itself brings out the different flavor of the vase.

Several years ago when the first marble vase was produced in Korea, according to Father's instruction, we exported that vase to Japan. Our MFT team went to sell marble vases, but not a single one was sold. We had a very, very difficult time selling the marble vases. Many times our members said that we would get better results with other items, ginseng tea or flowers. The marble vases were a difficult item to sell. But Father asked them to continue. Continue and persevere. Don't give up.

Then this year, 1977, after several years of continuing marble vase production and selling in Japan, an amazing thing started happening. Many, many spiritual phenomena started occurring connected to the marble vases. The members who are selling the vases are having amazing experiences. Mr. Furuta himself has been absolutely flabbergasted at the kind of reaction they are getting from people concerning these marble vases.

First of all, there are many, many spiritualists in Japan. They are not Christian, or mainline Buddhist, or anything like that. They are fortune tellers and palm readers, spiritual advisors. Nowadays in every country there are many people who are spiritually oriented. One member was going to visit some other place and a fortune teller saw him and asked him to show him the vase. The spiritualist asked, "Can I buy that? Don't even tell me how much the vase costs you. I will pay any amount of money you want." Our member was completely thrown off balance.

The vases come from different countries. Some good quality stone vases from Taiwan normally sell for about 50,000 yen, a little less than $200. But we have been selling the Korean vases for about 200,000 yen because they are very special and really beautiful, all hand-made, no machine work. This is not small money, 200,000 yen is $700. It's not easy to convince someone to pay $700 for a vase.

So the member answered the spiritualist, "Yes, I can sell you this vase, but it is a little bit expensive." Our member was ready to say that it costs 200,000 yen, but before he could say anything, the spiritualist said, "Expensive? Yes, I am sure this vase must be expensive. So I will give you one million yen. Two million yen. Even three million yen (three million yen is $10,000). Whatever the price, I will pay it."

This member was very wise. Instead of naming an exact price, he said, "I am not just selling vases. I am doing the work of God. Every yen you pay goes to the beautiful work of Heavenly Father. That is what I am doing." This fortune teller said, "I know you are doing that. I already knew before you told me. So let me pay you three million yen for the vase. Will you sell it?"

Then that fortune teller told the member that the reason he was buying the vase was that it was not an ordinary vase. "This vase has a special spiritual power," he said, "and the spirit tells me I do not deserve to own one like it. But it is such a precious treasure, not just an ornament. I can see spiritual light shining out of the vase. It is incredibly important for me to have this vase and treasure it." That man paid three million yen for the vase.

So when this member came back to headquarters and reported what had happened, all our members' eyes popped out like this, like popcorn. Each thought, boy, I want to do the same thing. So from the next day on all the members are going out and trying to locate the spiritualists. They are going after the fortune tellers, mediums, palm readers, and spiritual advisors. Amazing things are happening. Almost one out of two of these spiritual persons say, "Yes, I will buy. You are a very special person and you are doing a special work. Your vase is very precious and I will buy one." So they pay at least 200,000 yen, sometimes one million yen, because we don't put a price tag on the vases.

ASK GOD THE TRUTH

Some spiritualists or fortune tellers say, no, I don't want it. I don't need it. But now our members have so much confidence that this vase carries a special power. So, they say, "Are you really a spiritualist? Do you really have the power to communicate with spirit world?" "Yes, I can hear voices and I can see visions." "All right, then do me one favor. I will leave this vase with you and you take it to your shrine and pray about it. Ask God or whoever you are worshiping to tell you the truth about this vase."

The spiritualists can't say no, so they go to their holy place and pray. Then in almost 100 percent of the cases they come back and say something like, "You know, I was spanked by the spirit world. The voice spoke strongly and harshly, saying, 'How could you be so dumb? First of all, your spirituality is so low, you don't even deserve to own a vase like that. You must feel honored that a member came to you and offered one vase to you. It is a great honor. You better take the opportunity.' " Then they say that they will buy, whatever the price.

But even people who are not spiritualists—businessmen or professors or housewives—but who are spiritually keen people sometimes tell the most fantastic things about the vases. They sometimes see a special image in the vase. Some people say, I see Buddha's image coming out so strongly in this vase. Some Christians say they see the image of Christ in the vase. In these cases, they don't want to bargain; they feel the vase is so precious, they are determined to buy.

The Japanese people have things that they consider sacred, such as Mount Fujiyama, Japan's beautiful snow-capped mountain, and the crane, and the turtle, which they believe give good fortune. We Korean people also believe that the turtle brings long life and good fortune. My second daughter's nickname is turtle. So sometimes they see in the vases the image of the crane or a turtle or Mount Fujiyama. Then, because those images are sacred to them, they buy the vase for their home.

Our members, therefore, are getting wiser. When a new shipment of vases arrives from Korea, they examine them and try to see if there is an image of Fujiyama or a crane or a turtle. Sometimes they find nothing, just a beautiful and colorful vase, but ordinary. So they have to just promote it as an ordinary vase. One member brought an ordinary vase to recommend to a customer. But to the surprise of the member, that person saw something absolutely special, which the member couldn't see. "What do you see there?" "I see the image of my grandfather." Of course, our member had no way to know his grandfather, so we certainly didn't see anything. Some other person said, "My mother died 10 years ago. My mother was a fantastic woman and I can see her face in this vase."

On the Sea Hope boat, there was a Japanese cameraman whose brother in Japan bought one vase and wanted his father to buy another vase. He went to his parents' home and asked them, "Will you do me a great favor and buy this vase? It would be a great help to our movement. Father, I know 200,000 yen is not a small amount of money, but I know you can afford it. It will become a treasure in your home and for your children and descendants, and in the future this vase will become more valuable." But the father was very nasty and cold. "You are crazy. You want me to pay 200,000 yen for that piece of stone? Get out of here with that vase." The brother was kicked out.

The next day while his father was working in his machine shop, some metal was thrown into his face and chest. He was burned and black dots covered his chest and face. It was a very unusual accident; nothing like that had ever happened before. He was taken to the hospital and had surgery. Then the father, who is a veterinarian, found that the animals at the animal hospital all became very wild. One day he was attacked by a bull with horns. He had a big, big scare. Nothing like this had ever happened in his entire life.

This member's mother was a very sensitive person, and she could see that something unusual was happening in her house. She realized that it was because her son had asked them for a favor, not for his own sake but for the sake of the movement. He had pleaded and pleaded for the sake of our movement. He is giving himself totally to the work of God, his plea was pure, and his father so ruthlessly rejected him. The mother's conscience was hurting because they had rejected their son's request. One night the mother spoke to her husband, "We made a terrible mistake. We should have done what our son asked. But better late than never. We must repent and apologize to our son and buy one vase." The father agreed. He just could not afford another accident. So they called their son, "Please come and don't come empty-handed. Bring that vase with you." So they bought one vase. Thereafter, everything became peaceful.

This kind of news is spreading, and the most surprised people are our members. Our members just hadn't regarded the vase as that precious or important. But now they are repenting. There are so many strange and marvelous testimonies coming one after another that this vase has been named "the vase of good fortune."

The story does not end there. The people who buy these vases do not use them to put flowers in. They put them in a special place in their homes. Some women testified that when they first bought the vase they didn't see anything in them. But then several months later they were looking at the vase and, all of a sudden, an image popped up. The image hadn't been there before. The image might be of Jesus or Buddha or some monk from Japanese history. Some Japanese pray in front of this vase and then see the image of their ancestors on the vase.

There are all kinds of stories, too numerous to mention. One person who bought the vase and drank water from it reported that they were cured of a disease they had for eight years. Another person reported that he had fallen and hurt his arm and that the arm was cured after touching the vase. So our MFT vase team said, well, we should do the same. They drink water from the vase every morning. Sometimes they drink ginseng tea from the vase. Double energy.

NO MAGIC POWER

Now I am sure all these stories sound unreal and superstitious. But let me tell you that when Father heard these reports he asked, "Do you know why that phenomenon is happening in Japan at this time?" Nobody could answer. Father said that these Korean vases are not special. They are made of ordinary stone and they don't have any magic power. Not at all. These supernatural, marvelous things are happening connected to the vases because they have a special purpose. That purpose is parallel with the purpose of the universe and Heavenly Father. Therefore, the marble vases affect the entire work of restoration. To make a long story short, the vases have supernatural power simply because Father is behind it. This vase is directly connected to our True Parents' goal, which is the restoration of the universe.

What does this mean? The entire universe has a purpose and goal. When God created the universe, He had a purpose of creation. Now the time has come for the entire universal purpose and goal to be restored.

Universal restoration is coming. And God sent one person to the world to be the center and moving force of this restoration: our True Parents, True Father. The entire universe, particularly spirit world, is coming down so strongly to work, to push all the universal phenomena into the fulfillment of that goal. We have tremendous supporting power because we belong to that center. This vase, sold by any other merchant, would not have the same power, even if it came from the same stone, from the same mountain, and was processed the same. It would not be connected to the heavenly work of restoration.

This entire universe, and particularly the spirit world, is focused on one central goal, the restoration of the universe, especially the restoration of men. Therefore, our members can advance this heavenly goal by going out with a loving heart to sell this vase. Going out with an attitude of "I am not doing this for myself. I am doing it for the sake of God and the sake of humanity" really advances Father's work. That fervent desire gives such power. The supernatural power is not from the stone itself, but from its purpose. The backbone of that power is our True Parents, because True Parents are heading the central role of the restoration of the universe and mankind.

If one of these vases is just sitting in a corner getting dusty, it is shameful. The vase I have here today comes from my own office. I am sure every morning I am going to polish it. Not because I am going to get a million yen out of it, but because I want to see that this marble vase is activated with the power of God and can manifest supernatural power. And I am going to wipe the vase with the feeling of, Father, I want to become a living marble vase for you. That is the meaning of this sermon this morning.

WE ARE MORE POWERFUL

Now, you and I are far more precious than a marble vase. If even a piece of stone can manifest supernatural power because it is serving God's providence, then how much more you and I can do when our spirit and power are directly connected to the work of the True Parents. When we center ourselves on Heavenly Father and His work, when we liberate ourselves from our selfish thoughts, when we connect ourselves so intimately to Heavenly Father, when we can say, I am in the Father and the Father is in me—then you and I will become a living marble vase.

I would like to give one illustration. During the Celebration of Life tour, I always carried around one lamp. I had one important demonstration with the audience. I said, what is light? What is death? You eat a McDonald hamburger, you sleep in a bed, and wake up in the morning, but that does not mean life. According to the teaching of Jesus, even though we think we are alive, we are all dead. One day one of Jesus' disciple came to him and said, "My father is dying. Let me go and bury my father and come back and serve you." Jesus answered saying, "Leave the dead to bury their own dead." Jesus told him to leave the burial of his dead father to the dead people of the world, the people who are still in darkness. Instead of going to bury your own dead father, you must follow life. That means, follow Jesus.

We must learn the true concept of life and death. The three or four billion people in the world all think they are living. Everybody thinks they are enjoying a marvelous life. But in the eyes of God, this world is pitch dark. Particularly the communist world is pitch dark. There is no sign of life even though there is biological life. Like an insect, we can eat, we can move, we can see. This is not necessarily life in sight of God. We are dead unless we are connected to God. There is only one source of light and life in this universe and that is God. Separation from God is death. No matter how strong you are, you may be a heavyweight boxing champion, it doesn't make any difference. Separation from God, not knowing God, that is death. Knowing God is life.

Adam and Eve were supposed to live as one living entity with God. They were supposed to be a walking God, the visible form of God. God is invisible. Adam was visible. God is subject, Adam was object. That is the only difference. This is why Jesus said, "I am in the Father and the Father is in me." The Father and I are one. That was the concept of life.

I illustrate this with the lamp. It is as though you and I are light bulbs. But we give no light unless we are in the socket and the switch is on. When the switch is on, this light bulb gives light and heat and dispels darkness. This dark, gray piece of metal glows with powerful light and heat. Why? Because the source of light is coming through this wire from the source of electricity. That is the way we can give light as a living person. We are a light bulb, and when our lives are connected to the source of endless power, which is God, we become entities that give light and heat.

THE LIGHT BULB OF GOD

However, if we disconnect ourselves from the source of energy, no matter how many times you turn on the lamp, there is no light because it is disconnected from the source of power. This bulb is dead. The shape is the same. A living bulb and a dead bulb look the same. The only difference is whether it is connected to the power source. Even though all appearances are the same, this bulb is dead. No matter what, this bulb will not function, never give light, never give heat. By the same token, you and I are the light bulb of God. All of mankind since the fall has been disconnected from the source of power. Therefore, the world has been living in death. Death has reigned on the earth.

So restoration means coming back to God. Reuniting with God. That is the history of religion, particularly Christianity. In the Old Testament we began to come back to life. Our light bulb gives only about 10 watts. A dim light. In the New Testament, by coming back to God through the truth of Jesus Christ, we increase to at least 100 watts. There is light and heat, but it is limited light and limited heat. Now the New Testament era is over and we are moving into the perfected era, which we call the Completed Testament. Through the power of the Divine Principle coming through the True Parents here on earth, that new age will dawn. That will create a perfect conductivity between the energy source—the power of God—and us. Then we shall become like sunlight, 1,000 watts.

Now we are learning another important lesson. God, the source of power, is limitless. There is no end to His power. There is no power break, no power failure. The important question is how much you can become a recipient of that power. This is what determines your value. Even within the Unification Church, you can become many different types of light bulb. You can become a 100-watt bulb, but that 100 watts is limited by the bulb, not by God. You can expand the wattage to 1,000. You can expand that energy into 10,000 watts, one million watts. There is no limit. As much as you can expand your capacity to transmit light, you can become that glowing man in the sight of God. Each man is a light-giving object.

Therefore, today our goal is to become perfectly united with God and with the Divine Principle. With the advent of the True Parents, that is now possible. We have been given this challenge and this opportunity. It is our responsibility, yours and mine. It is up to us how much we take advantage of this opportunity to grow into greater wattage light bulbs.

You know August 18 was my birthday. I was born in 1930, so I just celebrated being 47 years old. Already, I am 47 years old. I don't feel like it, but it is reality. I am 47 years old and going into my 48th year. When I pray knowing that I am already going on to age 48, I have one regret: that I learned the Divine Principle at the age of 26. I was young just like you are now. Most of you are around 26. But 26 to 36, that was my prime slice of life. My regret is that I wish I had suffered more for the sake of God in those days. I wish that I had suffered more for the sake of True Parents. I wish that I had tasted prison in those days. I wish that I had even been tortured by the police in those days so that I can know God more and understand the True Parents more. My youth will never return. I will never become 26 again. I will never be 36 again.

In two more years, I will be 50 years old. The level of energy and vitality of the human body has to follow natural law, and no matter what, I cannot compete with your physical vitality. Knowing that my prime youth is gone, that is my regret, wishing that I could have done more, so that at the age of 50 I could say, "Yes, God, I have done my absolute best. No one can do better than me." I can't say that. I could have done more for God. More witnessing, more fund-raising, more fights against Satan. I could have done many things more dramatically. If I were now a 23-year-old, I think I could do more bold things and much more dramatic and gigantic and courageous things without fear.

I have greater wisdom now because I have learned more. But I wish I had that wisdom at the age of 26 or even at the age of 36. How much more I could be proud of those days. Now I tell you, my brothers and sisters, you think you are suffering. You think you are living a hard life. Yes, I know. Some MFT members here have been struggling for two and three years and in some cases under horrible conditions. Do not sag in power, saying, why should I do this. I want you to be proud, saying, I have done this because of the Father, for nobody else. I didn't do it for myself. Not for my own family. Not for my own things. I gave myself totally for the sake of the True Parents, for the sake of God, for the central purpose of the universe. I want you to keep that pride.

Do not weaken yourself. You must keep your spirit up, saying to God, I want to be really proud of my young life and being totally dedicated to Your purpose. Sometime you may falter. At the age of 26 or 30, you may even collapse and die for the sake of God and True Parents. You have been living the most successful, glorious life anyone can imagine. Jesus at the age of 33 died on the cross. But actually Jesus never died. His death on the cross crystallized his life, and a miracle came forth showing the power of God. For 2,000 years Jesus is the living star, giving light to the world.

We must be wise. If you weren't a wise man, you would never have joined the Unification Church in the first place. You did not come to the Unification Church to relax. You did not come to join a beach party. You did not come to win a big fortune and become a millionaire in the Unification Church. You did not come to be the most glorious politician of mankind. You are wiser. Your wisdom tells you that this way of life is the right way of life. It is better than anything under the sun. That is why I joined. But this way of life is not just an external one. Our real wisdom shines out, telling us that there is a more important life to live than just a hundred years here on earth. That is why we joined.

Our greatest virtue is to persevere. Revitalize yourself every morning. Pick yourself up and do not lose the vision of the Unification Church. Once you lose the vision, you have nothing, and you become men and women of miserable failure. Because once you lose vision, you have nothing to be proud of. But if you have the vision and conviction, you have everything. Even if physical death takes you, you are not a failure. You are not a loser at all. The important thing is not the suffering itself but the meaning of the suffering. Do you understand the meaning of the suffering? It is like what Jesus said, "He who finds his life will lose it, and he who loses his life for my sake will find it." The key words are, "For my sake." Not your sake, not the world's sake, not vanity's sake, but for my sake, the sake of the Christ. For the sake of the True Parents and God and humanity. That is what you are living for. You suffer for that purpose.

Our members are carrying the marble vases for many miles during the day. They are small Japanese women. Their feet are tiny. Think of it: they are carrying around several vases like this sometimes all day long. Do they say, why should I do this? Why should I be working this hard? But every moment that young lady is saying, Heavenly Father, this is your vase. Please find someone who will buy this so that person will receive the blessing; then blessing can also come to our work so we can be successful in our mission. Dear God, I want to give you my heart. This vase is carrying heavenly heart. Heavenly sorrow, heavenly tears. There is a meaning. Then a miracle comes and supernatural things happen.

DON'T FINISH YOUR LIFE WITH REGRET

Now, I tell you, my dear brothers and sisters. You and I are far greater than this stone vase. We are hand-picked and chosen to be the sons of God and daughters of God. The question is, do you realize it? That is the key. If you feel that you are really chosen and are really giving yourself for the sake of God and True Parents, then you are living a most invincible and successful life here on earth. As a person who is a little older than most of you are, it is my advice that you make sure that when you are 40 or 50 or 60 that you don't have to feel that you wish you had done more. The worst kind of life you can live is one full of regret. At the moment of your death, you want to be able to say to Heavenly Father, "Father, you know I have lived out my life without any reservation, for your sake and your sake alone. God, my Father, of course I could be better, I could have done more. But I do know, Father, I can say proudly, that I did not spare one ounce of energy, one drop of blood for any other purpose except you. You know my heart is pure. You know I did my best. You know that I have done everything I can. God, my Father, now I am returning to you. Those things I left undone I know, God, you will take it over, you will fulfill it."

Every one of us will come to that final moment, whether it be tomorrow or in 10 years or 50 years. The person who can say this when that moment comes and die without any regrets will have had the most successful life on earth.

Father said in Boston that many people see the image of their loved ones, their Buddha, in these vases. By the same token, when you are walking in the heart of God, from street to street and from town to town, people will look at you and say, I see the image of Jesus in that man. I see the image of Buddha in that man. Because you are far greater than the vase. God can manifest his power even in a vase. How much more can God manifest His power through the living sons and daughters of God. You can imagine. Unlimited power. Once your heart is right, then you become a powerful being here on earth. Walking God.

I am sure if you walk with the right heart a similar kind of story can be manifested through you over and over. I am sure many people can say yes, yes, I experienced that myself in my newspaper selling. *The News World* is not just a newspaper. It is a light-giving object of God. When you sell *The News World*, in your heart it is becoming God's object. It is becoming a powerful tool of God. I am sure you experience all kinds of situations. It is not just happening in Japan. Do not ever think the vase has some supernatural power and it is only manifested in Japan. No. Right here in New York and every part of this country and all over the world, wherever you walk in the heart of God, that power will be yours.

Next Sunday I will share more about other subjects of Father's message in Boston and this first marble vase. My conclusion is this: You and I are greater than the marble vase. Let us become a living marble vase. We are the sons and daughters of God. Once we work with one perfected united heart with God, then God will manifest through you. You become a life-giving object. You become a heat-giving object. That light will shine in the darkness of this world. And heat will warm up this entire freezing world of hell into spring of the Kingdom of God here on earth.

Thank you.

TESTIMONY TO THE POWER OF GOD

BELVEDERE ESTATE, TARRYTOWN, NEW YORK

AUGUST 28, 1977

Using examples from the life of Jesus, Dr. Pak talks with great insight about the qualifications needed to follow the Messiah. He gives one of the most extensive and honest testimonies of his own life, describing how God guided him to meet the Unification Church and True Father, and prepared him to become Father's translator. With Apostle Stephen as his guide, he also shares how he is preparing himself to come before the Fraser committee.

[A few testimonies were given at the start of Sunday service.]

I am sure many of you have had similar heartwarming experiences. I am sorry I couldn't give every one of you a chance to speak. In due course, I am sure you will have a chance to express yourself. Your time will come.

It is always beautiful to hear a testimony. The brother and sister spoke so beautifully because they are so genuine. No pretense there. This comes directly out of their hearts, so we can see where he is and where she is. It is absolutely beautiful. The beauty of spirit.

Sometimes we wonder, why am I here? The Unification Church is such a gigantic, universal, global dispensation. The work of God is mighty, and we are the destiny of spirit world and physical world. We hear such monumental things about the dispensation. Also, when we learn the Divine Principle, inevitably we come to the conclusion that a universal, historical event is happening right here. Then you look at yourself. Who am I? Am I good enough to be a part of this important mission? I am not very good. I didn't learn much. I am not that smart. I am not a Harvard Ph.D. So if God is almighty and all-capable, I am sure He could summon all the big people in the world: intellectual people, professors, ministers, politicians, and Nobel prize winners. These people are far more fitted for this place. Who am I?

So, our situation is unreal and artificial. Who am I? How do I fit into this mission? I tell you, the answer is that you are like the tip of the iceberg. You only see the visible you, just one individual. But I want you to know that each one of you sitting in this room does have an invisible you, a spiritual you. You are like a tree, and you are positioned at the top of the tree. You are the fruit of the tree. What is this tree? This is the tree of history, the ancestral tree.

Let's say your name is Jim. For Jim to come and sit in this position, there is a long, long history dating back to Adam and Eve. Literally to Adam and Eve. Because human history, after all, started from one man and one woman created by God. Jim is related to that man and woman. So he has a long history that can be made into a family tree. You are the fruit of history, the total sum or total aggregation of the family tree. So it's good that you feel that you are not worthy to be here. That is a good and humble feeling. Yes, I do feel, as you feel, that I am not worthy. But then we must attribute some greatness to our ancestors. You can say proudly that you are here because your ancestors did something right. They did something right for you. That is why you are here.

THE SOIL OF HISTORY

Take little Linda, for example. Little Linda is five years old, but her will power is far more than a five-year-old's will power. There is a long, long family tree behind her. The aggregation of good of that family appears in Linda. Linda is a little flower blossoming in the soil of history. That is what all of you are. You are very, very precious in the sight of God. Otherwise, you couldn't be here. You are not just a number. You are not just a computer number. Nowadays everybody is recognized by numbers. Here in America your name is no longer significant. Your Social Security number is more important. The two most important numbers in America are the telephone number and the Social Security number. John Doe or Bo Hi Pak or Linda so-and-so are not that important. Because machines handle numbers far better than names, the computer hates names and loves numbers. America is more and more becoming a computerized country. So each individual is becoming a number.

But not in the sight of God. In the sight of God, no number is important. Your soul, your individuality is important. You are not just you. You are the aggregation of the entire human history. That is why you are here. It is very, very important to know this so we can give tribute to our ancestors.

Another reason you are here is this: God wanted to show His almighty grace and power by having nonentities like you and me become sons and daughters of God. You can read in Luke 3:8-9: "...do not begin to say to yourselves, 'We have Abraham as our father'; for I tell you, God is able from these stones to raise up children to Abraham." God was scolding the Jews, telling them not to be proud of their heritage. Unless you are doing the will of God, that is not important. The important thing is that God can make the children of Abraham out of stone and dirt.

This is another reason we are here. You are not a Ph.D. I am so glad we are not all Ph.D.s. I am so glad we are not all college graduates. We are glad we do not come from a noble or royal family. I am so glad we are not important senators and congressmen of the country. They are very important people, yet God wanted to show His power by picking people like you and me to be the true sons and daughters of God. How much more dramatic an expression of the power of God! Jesus' disciples 2,000 years ago were not chosen from the high priests. Jesus' disciples were fishermen, even prostitutes. Those were the first followers of Jesus Christ. They came before any high priests or kings and queens of that age. That is the way God used His power.

Another important reason that God chose you and me is that we are nonentities and therefore can be humble. Over and over in history we have seen that people who are somebody lose the quality of humility before God. God will not build His kingdom on wisdom alone. On knowledge alone. On capability alone. On appearance, never. The essential quality to be chosen by God is meekness of heart. Your softness. Your humility. The worst enemy of God and the worst enemy of Jesus, the worst enemy of our Father is arrogance.

ARROGANT BEFORE GOD

Today, here in America the worst barrier that exists between Americans and the truth of God is arrogance. America is arrogant. American people feel we are first-class citizens. We have the best of everything under the sun. We don't need anything from Korea. That kind of arrogance. "Oh, I already have the truth. I am a minister of a church. I have been a theologian for so many years. I don't need any further truth. I learned the Bible from cover to cover. I became a Ph.D. of the Bible. I learned and I know God. Don't tell me about God. Why are you talking about the Divine Principle? Why are you talking about a new revelation? Why are you talking about Reverend Moon coming to teach America? We already have everything. We have beautiful churches. We are Christians." That arrogance makes a barrier between Americans and God.

You see, you and I have the privilege of worshiping together in the name of True Parents in this place because you and I at least demonstrated humility. You confess that your heart is empty. You know that you alone cannot find God. You confess you need help. Your open mind has brought God into your heart. So you are here for two reasons: your ancestors plus your humility. Our ultimate success also rests on our humility. In the Unification Church if you become arrogant, if you start building a strong wall, saying, "I learned enough Divine Principle, don't tell me any more," at that very moment your growth is stopped. So if you really learn Divine Principle, if you really learn True Parents, every day and every morning you come to the realization of how inadequate you really are. That is good thinking. How unworthy you are. How far away from understanding the True Parents. So you humbly accept more knowledge like a hungry child. Then your growth will be infinite. You can go on.

So, in speaking of Ph.D.s, there are even Ph.D.s from Harvard who think very humbly. By the way, there is one important Harvard Ph.D. who is now attending a three-day workshop in Boston. Not only one but two Ph.D.s. One of them is Harvey Cox, one of the giant theologians of the world. He is at the pinnacle of success in the world of theology. He is a professor at Harvard Divinity School and the author of many important books. But once the Divine Principle touched him, he felt something very strange. Something his own understanding could not perceive. Something greater than his knowledge. And he was intrigued by it. However, the great aspect of the personality of Harvey Cox is his humility. He has a very humble character. That is why he is open. He said he wanted to attend a workshop, so last Friday night at 6:00 he came to our Boston center for a workshop. He came just like you, without a tie, wearing a humble jacket, and, more amazingly, with a sleeping bag.

He said, I don't need any special treatment. I don't need any special chair. Just treat me as one of your students. I am willing to sleep on the floor in a sleeping bag. I will get up at the same time. If you get up at 3:30, I will get up at 3:30. If you run for morning exercise, I will run with you. I will eat the humble meal or whatever you serve, I will enjoy that. And if you make me fast, I will fast too. I want to be a Moonie. We said to him, well, you can start out a Moonie, but we want you to end up as a Sunnie.

Dr. Cox thinks the Divine Principle is a broad and revolutionary concept in theology. It is like an atomic bomb in the theological world. He wanted to set up a special course at Harvard University to teach the Divine Principle.

So a person like Harvey Cox knows the value and magnitude of the Divine Principle, how great it is. We just eat it up and receive it, not really knowing how delicious it is. We are all like that. But a person like Harvey Cox enjoys the taste of the Divine Principle. So Aidan Barry, the director of Massachusetts, is teaching all three days. He said, "I just enrolled as a student at Harvard Divinity School, and Harvey Cox was supposed to lecture to me. Now here I am standing in front of the professor and I am lecturing him. What a strange work of God." But he was a little bit nervous. And I told him, this is not you. It is not your knowledge you are going to supply to him. You are merely being used as the instrument. God is lecturing. Actually, Father is lecturing him. So when you think of that, you have nothing to be nervous about. "Yes," he said, "I feel better already."

That is really true. Divine Principle is not a theory. You are not teaching anybody. Don't ever think, I am teaching professors. Don't think, I am teaching that minister. You are wrong. You are arrogant there. All you are doing is bringing witness to the people. Witness to Divine Principle. There is one important minister who used to be a member of the Cabinet of the Republic of Korea. He came to visit and he was staying with us for several days to learn about the Divine Principle and he got to meet Father. He was so intrigued. This minister said, "I must learn the Principle." He arranged to attend our special Los Angeles Korean leaders seminar conducted by Reverend Kwak, as a student, just like anybody else. A minister and cabinet member sits there just like anybody else.

At the last meeting in Boston, the Japanese leaders reported another astonishing thing. Japan is a thriving and booming country today. In terms of money, in terms of wealth, Japan has everything. But the more they acquire materially, the more they feel that they are lacking something vital, something important. There is no spiritual vitality, no vision, no feeling of service.

One high-level Japanese industrialist began searching for answers and came to the conclusion that the only possible answer is the Divine Principle of the Unification Church. He requested that the Unification Church provide a special seminar that he organized in his own facility. Our lecturers gave a solid three-day seminar. They were Ph.D.s, learned people, and good Christians. They were not used to being lectured to; they always tell other people what to do. But within 30 minutes they found the message pouring upon them so refreshing, so logical, and so beautiful that their hearts were filled quickly. They automatically pulled out their notebooks and started writing. By the end of three days they completely filled about three notebooks.

One of the most important men in the group commented at the end of the session, "By God, knowing that Reverend Moon comes from Korea and that Korea and Japan, even though geographically we are very close, we had a difficult time for at least 36 years." One man confessed, "I heard the Korean people are very, very ingenious and they have a brilliant mind, but I didn't know the Korean people are this good." In other words, he was speaking of Reverend Moon. "I didn't know this gigantic genius can come out of Korea. I thought he was Japanese," he said. It doesn't matter, because it is not the Korean Divine Principle. That is what he misunderstood. It is God's Divine Principle. But God's Divine Principle was manifested through Korea in the person of Reverend Moon. It all it belongs to Korea, Japan, to you, to everybody.

When these people heard the power of the Divine Principle—these people who know the world, have a lot of knowledge, and know theology—their reaction was absolutely fantastic. They are going to organize a second seminar and a third seminar. They now feel that there is some purpose for the thriving economy of Japan. They want to pioneer the way. The weight and power of the Japanese economy can be used to help erect the kingdom of God here on earth.

THE SOURCE OF LIFE

Now it is your job and our job. We are going to have the same kind of Divine Principle seminar here in our country and invite Henry Ford. Invite the chairman of the board of the Rockefeller Foundation. Why not? Particularly I would like to see the day that the *Washington Post* and the *New York Times* publishers come to our seminars. Why not? With our power alone it is impossible, but with the power of God and the Divine Principle, it is more than possible and can be done. Because the important thing is, the Principle is not just knowledge, it is the source of life. There is no limit in the power of God, so don't limit yourself. Even a person like Harvey Cox comes to the Unification Church as a private or a freshman.

Since a few brothers and sisters have given their testimony, I would like to take a few moments to give my testimony. I am not sure my testimony will be as interesting as Jim's and our sister's. I feel very, very strange when I look back on my life. I came into the movement 20 years ago, at about the age of 28. A sister came to me and said that I had talked about being past my prime when I was 36. She said that she is now 36, and I make her feel very old. I said, I am sorry, I didn't mean that. I feel like I am still at the pinnacle of Unification Church life and this is the time I can fulfill more than any other. But what I said at that time was, when I look back, 10 or 15 years ago, I realize that if I had suffered more, if I had shared more with brothers and sisters, if I had had more knowledge of Divine Principle and knew Father better, then I would have worked more boldly and accumulated more wonderful things to share with you today. That is what I am saying.

So I urge you to take the experience of your elders, your seniors, and put it to work in your life. So that now while you are in your youth, you can accumulate more knowledge and power and experiences and dramatic accomplishments. Then when you are 50 or 60, you can share with your children and with all those who are going to follow after us.

I wish I had greater things to tell you about my life, but I don't. However, I would like to humbly share several important aspects of my testimony as a manifestation of the power of God and the power of the Divine Principle. Since I am 48, if I really give you my entire testimony in detail, it would take about 48 years, or 48 hours at the bare minimum. I certainly do not intend to do that. In the next 48 minutes, however, somehow I would like to bring out the highlights.

GOD PRESERVED MY LIFE

The number one thing I feel about my life, is that, long before I knew the Divine Principle, some strange power, I must say, the power of God, preserved my life. I could have been dead for a long, long time. My honest feeling is, my life is not my life. It does not belong to me. I will tell you more about it.

Second, I feel that far before I knew the Divine Principle, God already had some plan and schedule to bring me to become an interpreter for our Father. The way I learned English is very, very strange. You will be astonished. It happened in an abnormal way. I was in a position that made it virtually impossible to learn English. But somehow a strange power pushed me into learning English before I discovered the Divine Principle.

There are elders in Korea who came to the Unification Church earlier than me. Sometimes I have wished that I had been among those who were with Father in North Korea, who suffered with him, and were in prison with him. How wonderful if I could say, "I was there with Father." But this is a very greedy feeling and I repent. Now I have realized that God had a purpose in having me come to the movement in 1957 and not before. If I had come into the movement any earlier than 1957, I would not be an interpreter for Father because I would have not studied the English language enough to translate for Father. Prior to being introduced to the Divine Principle, my entire heart and soul was with English study. My ambition was to become a great military leader of the Republic of Korea.

In order to do that, I determined to learn English, not for the sake of God but for the mundane, worldly purpose.

My ambition as a young man was to become a general. That was my real ambition. To do that, learning the English language was essential. So I gave my entire self to the study of English on a 24-hour basis. But as soon as Divine Principle hit me, then my ambition was totally changed. Prior to that I was looking forward to putting a star on my shoulders. One-star general, two-star general, boy, three-star general, maybe even four-star general. Why not? Maybe someday I would be a five-star general like General MacArthur. That was my only ambition.

But as soon as the Divine Principle came into me, being a five-star general looked like peanuts; it was just nothing compared to serving God on the eternal basis. At that time, I didn't know that someday Father would go to America to make Day of Hope tours and set up our international headquarters in America and preach the gospel all over the world from the American base. I certainly did not have the kind of vision to see Father's plan. I only saw the Divine Principle. I only saw Father in Korea. As soon as the Divine Principle came into me, my ambition to learn English was totally gone. I dropped English dead on the floor. I never even looked at the English book. I only picked up the Divine Principle book.

Within two months of beginning to study the Divine Principle, I became a lecturer of the Divine Principle in Korea. I was still a major serving in the military. During the day I served in the army, and in the evening I would work in the area Father assigned me. I was lecturing every night. At that time my other ambition was to proclaim the truth in a large mass meeting. I wanted to become an evangelist. I really wanted to speak like a Billy Graham in Korea. I wanted to speak to all the Korean people. That was my ambition.

Father gave me several opportunities before I came to America. I spoke at a gigantic auditorium, and I proclaimed the Divine Principle and testified about Father. But the most important person in the entire auditorium was Father himself. I lectured to Father himself. That was a great, great privilege. That is the skeleton testimony I wanted to give you.

AMERICA WAS A DREAM

Even though I said that my hometown is Seoul, Korea, I was not born in Seoul. Borrowing Mr. Sudo's language, I was really a Korean "country pumpkin." Even though my home had a very beautiful, noble ancestral heritage, my home was never rich. I entered elementary school and did a pretty good job. I brought my father and mother great joy by doing good school work. But it was a country school about 100 miles south of Seoul in Chung

Nam Province. At that time, I heard about America, but America to me at that young age in elementary school was further away than even the sun or moon. America was the country of some dream. I never imagined that I would go to America. Even Seoul was far away to me.

When I graduated from elementary school in the sixth grade, the class made a special trip to have a tour of Seoul. This was a dream come true. So at the age of 12 I went to Seoul for three days. I was so fearful of getting lost that I followed the teacher's instructions and stayed with the group every minute. The astonishing city of Seoul touched this young boy's heart.

At that time we were under Japanese occupation, so I was speaking and learning Japanese in school. I thank God that today I can speak three languages: Korean, Japanese, and English. In those days I spoke better Japanese than Korean because that was the primary language we were educated in. We spoke it almost 24 hours a day. The last time the global IOWC team went to Japan I was able to deliver the Divine Principle sermon in Japan. Think of it, 15,000 Japanese people gathered in Budokon in Tokyo. I was there the one night Father spoke. The second night I had the mission to speak. So I delivered the sermon in Japanese to 15,000 people in 14 different cities in Japan. I did a pretty good job though, and I thank God I was educated in Japanese so I was able to do that.

Anyway, to make a long story short, the time came to move into middle school. Unlike in America, where going to junior high and high school is taken for granted, in Korea that isn't the case. You have to pay tuition to attend middle school and high school. My family was not rich enough to pay for my middle school and high school. Even though I had a pretty good record in elementary school, I couldn't go to an important middle school or high school in Seoul or another major city. But my uncle knew my intellect or talent, and he paid my tuition for three years at the local agricultural school. I learned to become a farmer. This is why I know how to raise pigs, chicken, tomatoes, and potatoes.

Also, in those days I learned to do menial work with joy. I didn't mind working with the soil and digging in the field. That was my joy. After that three years, I talked to my father and mother. They wanted to send me to higher education, but they were not able to do that. I told them, don't worry about me, I have enough education. I want to be your good son and become a farmer just like you are. I will be a very prosperous farmer in this community. So don't worry about my higher education. I made up my mind to become a good farmer and serve my father and mother well for their old age. I had learned farming, and I farmed very ambitiously. I raised chickens and hogs and plowed the fields. At that time in Korea, human waste was good fertilizer, so I went to the elementary school and they give me human waste for my fields. I carried it on my back. It was very smelly, but I thought of its purpose, so to me it was a sweet fragrance. I would think, this manure is precious for my farming. So I was ready to become a young farmer, working very hard morning to night.

Then the liberation came in 1945. The Japanese government was removed from Korea. We set up our provisional government under the supervision of the United States Army. There was a great deal of turmoil and confusion. All the Japanese schoolteachers went back to Japan. One day the school came to me and asked if I could teach in the school because there was a lack of teachers. Since the school was in my local community, I said I would be most happy to. So I became a schoolteacher at the age of 17.

THE SHY, UNEXPECTED TEACHER

In that country elementary school, some of the students were older than 17. The teacher was a young boy, and the classes had some very big boys and young ladies. The first day I went into the class and tried to teach, this shy boy teacher didn't even have the courage to look at the girls' side. I only looked at the boys' side. It felt so strange that those girls were listening to me. However, I really enjoyed the three years of my teaching and considered it my sacred duty. I became very popular among the students.

I wanted to be a farmer as well as a teacher; that was my ambition. Then when I was 21, all of a sudden, the government knew that they needed the Republic of Korea Army, so they installed a draft system, drafting people into army service. I was among the first group to be given a physical examination. I was a good farmer and I had a good, healthy, young body, so they hit me on the back, and just like that, they said, "You pass. You are now a private in the Republic of Korea army."

Then a totally different image came to me. Now that I have become a soldier, I cannot be a farmer any more; I cannot teach school anymore. So a different ambition came. If I have to go in the army anyway, why can't I be an officer? Why can't I be a leader in the Korean Army? I learned that a West Point-type military academy was being erected, and I fervently wished to go there. But my school background was not good enough. I needed at least six years of high school to quality for the military academy, but I submitted my application anyway. So this country bumpkin visited Seoul for the second time in my life to take the entrance exam. I didn't have money to pay for a hotel, so I brought a little rice with me and visited my friend's home and give my rice to them. Can you cook my meals for three days while I'm here to take an exam?

On the first day I was supposed to submit an application. That was a very crucial moment. I knew my application was not good enough to be accepted. I was pushing myself to the limit. When I looked at all the other applicants in the long line, I saw they were the best-looking high school boys wearing their school uniforms. They were from the best high schools in Seoul. They were outstanding, cosmopolitan Seoul boys, and here I was, a country bumpkin, standing among them looking very, very shabby and miserable. I looked at myself, wearing my home-made suit and very cheap shoes, with a very pale face, standing among the elite of the high school graduates of Seoul.

I waited my turn to submit my application, and finally I came to the sergeant. "Sir, here is my application." He examined it and said, "It is not accepted. You are not qualified to take the exam. Your school record is missing." "I know, sir, but can you give me a chance to just take the exam?" The sergeant said, "No. There is no exception. Next!" He shoved my application back at me and called for the next person. I didn't know what to do. I felt so despondent and discouraged. I thought about it a few minutes. I had no God to pray to. I didn't have God at that time. I was not a Christian. I didn't go to church. My mother was very close to Buddha, but I didn't know how to pray to Buddha. My Father was a very good scholar of Confucius, but I didn't know how to pray to Confucius. I just didn't know what to do. But this young man at least had some guts and will at that time, and instead of going back home I went to the back of the line, all the way to the end, and waited for another turn.

I waited and waited. The line was very long. A couple of hours later, I got to the front of the line and stood before the same sergeant. He recognized me and said, "What are you doing here? I told you that you are not qualified. Why are you making my life miserable? Get out of here. Shoo!" Again I just didn't know what to do. I was pushed out of the line. Many more people were waiting to submit their applications. I was going to have to go back home and be a private in the army. But then, even though I didn't know the Principle of formation, growth, and perfection, something told me: don't give up.

I went back and stood in the line once more. Another couple of hours passed. Then I was in front of the sergeant again. This time I was ready to fight. This time I knew what to do. "Here is my application, sir." The sergeant was so mad. He stood up and grabbed my application and said, "Are you kidding me?" I said, "Sir, all I am asking is to be given one chance to take the exam. I came all the way from Chung Nam just to take the exam. If you reject me, I am not going to go back. I am going to throw myself in the Han River. You are going to read about me in the newspapers."

GIVE HIM A CHANCE

This man was so upset. He was yelling like crazy, so loud that an officer came over and said, "What happened? What is going on here?" The sergeant reported to the officer, "This guy has been bothering me all day long. This is the third time he has come, and I keep telling him he's not qualified and to go back home." The officer said, "Let me see his application. You're right, he's not qualified." This was a really critical moment. God was really working in that moment. "He is going to flunk anyway, but let him take the exam. Don't make him throw himself in the Han River." The sergeant was amazed.

That officer changed my entire destiny in that moment. My application was accepted, and the next morning I came for the exam, which lasted for eight hours on eight different subjects. The first subject was English. I had never even heard any English at that time. Under the Japanese occupation there were no English lessons in middle school. I picked up the test paper, and I didn't even know which way to read it, which way was right side up or upside down.

My heart was aching. I was desperate to get into the military academy, but here I was in the first hour of the exam and I could not even write one word. Tears were running down my face. But I had to do something. I couldn't just sit there. I decided to do something crazy. So I turned the paper over and started to write a petition in Korean. I wrote explaining that I had not been fortunate enough to study in a good school, and I had not had a chance to learn even basic English. I promised that if I was accepted I would work 10 times, 100 times harder in every subject. I hoped someone would understand my sincerity, my earnestness, my real ambition to learn. I knew that it was impossible. Nobody would trust my word.

When the supervising officer came around, I hid my paper so he wouldn't see that I was not writing in English. I was afraid they might stop me. When he passed by, I kept writing in Korean. When the time was up, I held my paper so no one could see it and put it into the middle of the pile of papers. I didn't have the courage to put it on top.

The tests in the next hours were on Korean language, history, and geography. All these things, as a school teacher, I had taught myself very well. I wrote very well. But the mathematics test was on higher math, like algebra and geometry. I couldn't do very well. But, amazingly, the night before, my former classmate, who was a Seoul University student, had taught me several math formulas. He had said, memorize these, they may be useful. So I did. Then on the test, 50 percent of the problems were on the very things I learned the night before. At least I wouldn't get a zero in mathematics.

When I finished, I thought I did pretty well in Korean and history and geography, but I got a zero in English, maybe 50 points in math, and in chemistry I didn't do well. But overall I knew that I had not passed, especially since I could not compete with the Seoul high school students. I was despondent. I knew that I would not be accepted.

So I went back to the country and just tried to forget about it. It was not my fortune to enter the military academy. But about two weeks later a letter came. The letter, which had an official seal, said that I had been admitted to the first class of the military academy of the Republic of Korea. I cried. I really cried. On June 1 all the elementary students came to the station to say goodbye, waving flags. "My teacher has now become an officer in the Republic of Korea Army. How wonderful it is." I had a most wonderful sendoff.

When I arrived at the military academy, the first announcement was they were giving another exam. Boy, examinations made me absolutely crazy. I felt if I fail in this final minute and am not accepted, I certainly cannot go back to my hometown. I cannot say to my students, I flunked the exam and I came back. I couldn't say that. I simply couldn't say that. I determined that I would throw myself in the Han River. I would rather die. That was very serious. Somehow I passed.

On the first day, all of the new cadets got crewcuts to make a new determination. We received our military uniforms and were enrolled in the military academy—the West Point of Korea.

FROM THE CLASSROOM TO THE FRONTLINE

That is the way my military life started. But that was only for a brief time. On June 25 the Korean War came. On that day, we cadets were already in the war. We hadn't learned how to shoot a machine gun, but we were under machine gun fire from the enemy, North Korea. In the first three days, two-thirds of my classmates died in combat. A little over 100 survived. They took us to the rear area for a quick training of eight weeks. We originally were supposed to attend school for four years before we got our commissions, but because of the war we were commissioned as second lieutenants after only eight weeks of training. We went back into the battlefield and became platoon leaders. Many more died.

I was a platoon leader and then a company commander. I saw many people die. My classmates, my sergeants, my privates, my men were dying all over. I learned the seriousness of life and death in that early age, the age of 21 and 22. About a year later, 150 officers were selected to go to America to study military tactics and become instructors in the Korean Infantry School.

When I came to America in 1952, I realized that God had blessed this country. I developed tremendous respect for the American people and the American culture, because I saw that God was working so strongly in this country. I could see His abundant blessing. I knew I would be going back to the combat zone. I thought this was certainly my first and last opportunity to see America. You can imagine how I felt. A man who didn't speak one word of English was lucky enough to come to America for six months of training before going back to the war. How could I imagine that I would someday come back to America?

I wanted to see Washington and New York because I heard about those two cities. It was a dream world for me at that time. As trainees, we didn't have any vacation. The schedule was too tight. But we had three days off around the Fourth of July. I found four bold officers from among the 150 who wanted to visit Washington and New York in three days. Of course, we didn't have money to fly. Today it is easy to fly to New York and back in three days. So we went to Columbus, Georgia, and found a taxi. We didn't speak much English. The cab driver asked us where we wanted to go. We said, "Washington, D.C." That taxi driver was completely flabbergasted. Washington? Yes, Washington. How much, we asked.

THE LONGEST TAXI RIDE

I am glad we couldn't understand anything he was grumbling. Washington by taxi? It is just impossible, impossible. I repeated, Washington, how much? He kept shaking his head. Then I showed him our money. When he saw the money, well, he started to change. $250. All right. We gave him the $250. That is how we set the record for the longest taxi ride in American history, from Columbus, Georgia, to Washington, D.C.

Now, with the IOWC spirit, a trip like that is no problem. But it was a 16-hour taxi ride. After ten hours the taxi driver started dozing—boy! The car started to swerve, going this way and that way. We five officers decided we had to do something or, instead of getting killed in the Korean combat zone, we would be victims of the U.S. highway. So we took turns and did surveillance on the taxi driver. We would face the driver and constantly supply him with cigarettes and coffee to keep him awake. I am sure he drank about five gallons of coffee that day and smoked about 10 packs of cigarettes.

When we got to Washington, D.C., the first place we visited was the Washington Monument. It is very meaningful that even before I met Father I came to Washington Monument. But certainly I didn't have any idea that someday I would translate into English Reverend Sun Myung Moon's message at the Washington Monument. I had absolutely no idea.

At that time all the English I knew was "good morning," "how much," and "thank you."

Besides the Monument, what I remember about Washington is the Capitol. Our guide explained many things about the building, which is very impressive, but what touched me the most was the little prayer room. I wrote about it later in "My Tribute to America." You may not have known that there is a prayer room in the Capitol. It is a small dark room with a stained glass window that shows George Washington kneeling down in Valley Forge praying to God and asking for His help. Our friend from the Korean embassy explained that the senators and congressmen come there to pray when they have an important decision to make. That touched me. I saw the greatness of America right there. I saw the reason that God is blessing this country. In later years I made the same visit with True Parents and I explained that to Father. We went into that small prayer room, and Father prayed there.

Then we went to New York. We didn't take the taxi because the driver had to sleep. Otherwise we would definitely die on the road. So we let him sleep in Washington while we went to New York. We visited the Empire State Building and several other places, Columbia University and the Brooklyn Bridge and so forth. New York to me at that time was a city of wonder. I was sure I would never be blessed with a second chance to visit there. I felt that I had seen America. When I saw the Statue of Liberty, I saw America. I could go back to my people and tell them about America, about New York and Washington. When I went back to the combat zone, I could be killed, but so what? I had seen America.

We went back to Washington and met up with the taxi driver for another 16-hour drive. This time we were better prepared. We had gallons of coffee and boxes of cigarettes and kept feeding this taxi driver and drove for 16 hours and got back to Columbus, Georgia, after three days. Later I heard that the taxi driver said, "Boy, I met five crazy Korean officers and I lost 16 pounds on the three-day trip."

THE RIVER TURNED RED

I was deeply touched by America's standing with God. I wanted to become a Christian because I wanted to become somebody. Previously in combat I had an experience. Our entire division had collapsed, and we were retreating. I was leading a company of 200 men going back to the south. We came to the Chung Chon River in the eastern part of Korea. Other people were also retreating. About 1,000 people were following us. I asked the men to put all of their gear on top of their heads and ford the river. I was still on the river bank, watching how things were going. Hundreds of people were in the water when all of a sudden from ahead of us, at the top of the hill, machine gun fire opened up. It was totally annihilating. Everyone in the water was being killed. Within minutes the water became crimson red. We were helpless. We could not shoot our rifles because they were on top of our heads. There was no cover on the river bank. I shouted to the men not yet in the water to get down. Everybody fell to the ground. The machine gun fire continued to come like a shower of bullets. In seconds the entire river was covered by bodies and blood.

The first word that flew into my head was "God! Hananim!" I didn't know the Christian God, but in my young man's mind, I believed there was a God. That word came to me first. In the second flashing moment, what came to my heart was, I am so empty, I am not capable of calling God's name, God is not part of me. At that time I felt that I was not ready to die. My heart was absolutely empty. I had no right to call the name of God. The third flashing thought, while the machine gun fire was still coming, was: God, if you give me a chance and allow me to survive this, I will be your man. I will serve you. I will discover you. God, can you give me a chance? I am not ready to die. All these thoughts came so quickly to my mind.

Finally, as a military soldier, I knew the only thing that could save us was a miracle, that is, to have U.S. fighter bombers attack the enemy. That was my fourth thought. At that moment we heard the sound of airplane engines. Fighter bombers appeared and circled the area and shot rockets into the enemy territory. Now the Chinese Army had to take cover. So the shower of bullets suddenly stopped. This was our opportunity to escape. The first thing I did when I got up was check my body. In combat you can be hit by bullets and not even know it. So I checked to see if I was wounded. There was not even a scratch. My body was intact. I shouted out, "Follow me. This is our chance." Only two men followed me. All the rest of the 200 men were dead, and even these two who were alive were terribly wounded. So I helped these men to get away from that cliff. That was the most incredible experience.

After that, I spoke to God—not as my Father, I didn't know God was my Father at that time—God, thank you, my life is no longer mine, it is yours. I owe you my life. Anything you want to do, please do it. I want to search after you. I will do anything for you. My life is yours. From that time, I began to search for the truth about God.

There is one more experience I want to share with you about my life as a military cadet. One time, during the first three days of combat when two-thirds of my classmates were killed, we were climbing a hill. There were two seniors in front of me, and the mortar fire and machine gun fire was severe. Before this, I had never even heard of mortar fire or artillery fire. It was just incredible. I needed to take cover. You know in Korea there are tombs all over the mountains. They are not like tombs in the United States. The tombs usually have a little mountain and there is a little stone for offering. The tombs are very handy in combat for taking cover from enemy fire. I saw a tomb, and the two senior men who were ahead of me took cover behind it. I was trying to join them. I was crawling forward, short of breath, step by step, foot by foot. Then they saw me coming and they said, don't come, don't come. There are too many here. It is too crowded.

DENIED SAFETY BUT GIVEN LIFE

In that moment I was very, very disappointed. These men were telling me it was too crowded. They told me to stay where I was. There was nothing else to hide behind. The ground was flat and the enemy fire kept coming. They were senior, so I had to obey them. I stopped, but my heart was discouraged. I was very hurt. They denied me the chance to take cover. A moment later, there was a gigantic explosion in front of me. Enemy mortar fire had hit right in between the two positions. In the next second, all I could see was a big hole where they had been and their two helmets. The two men were gone. They actually saved my life. If I had kept going, by the time I arrived there, the mortar fire would have hit and I would have died with them.

I cannot enumerate all the experiences of this type that I had, one after the other. As a young man, the same age as you are now, these kinds of mysterious happenings changed me. Even without having a Christian mind and Christian God, I determined to become somebody who really served God and His purpose. There must be divine will in my salvation.

So I had come to America with all of these experiences behind me. I wanted to find God. I could see that God was working very, very strongly in this country. I wanted to become a Christian. I went to a local church in Columbus, Georgia. I became a Christian in America without knowing English. I was baptized by submersion. I was submerged in water and came out a Christian in the Church of Christ. I began to study the Bible. Two things came into my mind strongly: One, I want to become a good Christian; two, I want to master English. This is where my drive to learn English began.

SO MANY QUESTIONS

To be a Christian was not easy. I studied the Bible. I went to many churches. I had so many questions. I asked the ministers, What is the fall of man? How come eating a little apple, the fruit of the Tree of the Knowledge of Good and Evil, brought such formidable consequences? How could the action of eating bring about a hereditary sin? And I wanted to know, if God is love, how could God allow sin to creep in and then say He would save us? Don't you think that is just a little hypocritical? God is saying, I gave you a disease and now I will give you medicine to cure yourselves. I asked the same kinds of questions you had at one time. It is common sense to come up with these questions. They are not theological questions. I fired one question after another at the minister and he couldn't answer. The minister, who was a good man, said, "I don't know all these answers, but I know one thing: there is a God and we must be obedient to Him. If you are too fussy, you will not make yourself a good Christian." He was actually saying, don't ask such questions. The important thing is that my heart needed to be ignited. My heart remained cold. I was baptized, but my heart remained cold. I read the Bible, but it did not give me meaning; nothing clicked. God was unreal to me at that time.

I decided that I would keep going as a Christian, but I had no satisfaction. My heart remained cold. In the meantime I studied English. I entered the Army Language School. Getting into that school was another miracle. You know what happened? I will just give you one instance. I knew at that time that I could not learn English unless I devoted myself to it full-time. I could not cover enough ground learning from an instructor. I wanted to devote myself totally to the study of English. I needed to get into the Army Language School, but I had to get permission from the commander of the infantry school where I was an instructor. I went to the commander, General Soh, who is the Defense Minister of the Republic of Korea now. He knows me very well. The last time I went back to Korea, I met him and we talked about the good old days. I said, "General, you were very stubborn at that time; you didn't allow me to go to the Army Language School." "Yes, but you learned English anyway," he said. He is a very wonderful person, and we are close now.

I asked General Soh, "General, the instructor's life in this school is wonderful. There is no question about it. But I want to learn English. Could you kindly send me to language school where I can learn English?" He said, "Captain Pak, you are such a good instructor in our school. We need you." This was very flattering, but what he was saying was that he could not allow me to go because I was needed. So he declined by saying, "I need you. You are a good instructor in our school. Without you we will be helpless, so help me for another year. When I transfer out of this school, you will go too. That is a promise. Can you take it?" I could not say no to a general. When this happened I gave up.

I COULDN'T SIT STILL

October 1 was examination day to select the students for the language school. I cannot forget that day. Many applicants took the exam. Even though I had a promise from the general, my heart was very, very sad because I wanted so badly to learn English. He had blocked my opportunity. I was lying on the floor in my bed roll. One of my friends, Major Lim, took the exam and came back to the dorm. I said, "Don't talk to me about it." Then he said, "By the way, I have news. General Soh was transferred yesterday. He received orders from military headquarters to go to some other post." I jumped up. General Soh had promised that when he was transferred I could go to language school, but it was just one day too late. The examination was over, and I had missed a golden opportunity. I was shocked and dismayed. I just couldn't sit still. I had to do something. So I got out and I ran. Where? I ran to the examination place. Of course, nobody was there. There were empty desks. It was all over.

I saw the janitor and asked him, "Do you know where the army officer is who came from Taegu to supervise the exam? Do you know which hotel he is staying in?" The janitor said, "That hotel."

So I went there. I didn't know what I would say. My disappointment and enthusiasm were all jumbled together. I just couldn't stand still. I had to do something. I asked the hotel clerk what room the colonel was staying in. I knocked on the door, and a man answered, "Yes! Who is it?" I said, "Captain Pak, sir." He opened the door and said, "Oh, Captain Pak, how are you?" He was not in his military uniform but casually dressed. He was waiting to go back to his headquarters, his assignment completed.

After he opened the door, I didn't know what to say. He said, "Oh, Captain Pak, it has been a long time. Come on in." I looked at him and I didn't know him, but apparently he knew me very well. "It's nice to see you. You look well." (I didn't look that well.) And he said, "Sit down. Sit down. Let us talk." Still I didn't know what to say, because I didn't know who he was. I was completely lost. His name was Colonel Kim. He said to me, "Captain Pak, I know you don't remember me. There is no way you can remember all of the students you have taught. I was one of your students in Infantry School. I was in the 28th advanced class, the colonel's class." I had taught hundreds and hundreds of colonels, and certainly there was no way to remember them. He said, "I was in the 28th session of the advanced colonel's class and I was taught by you. I have been instructed by many people in the infantry school, but I never forgot you. One instructor impressed me so that I never forgot him. That man is you. I remember your face, your name, and I remember what you taught me. I even remember the jokes you told in class."

I was totally amazed. Now I felt so relaxed. I told him, "Colonel, I came for a serious talk. There may be no way you can help me. I have an ambition to learn English. I am desperate to learn English. When I went to America and saw that great country, I felt in my soul that I must somehow learn English. I want to get into this language school."

We talked about everything that happened, including General Soh's promise to me. I said, "Here I am. I don't know what to do. I missed this opportunity." Then Colonel Kim said, "Well, I am going to be your friend. I am going to give you a chance to take the exam. You can take it right now, here in my room. I happen to have an extra examination paper." He opened up the package of exam papers and pulled some out. "Here is the part on military tactics. Here is history. Here is the essay. All right, take the exam right here." Boy, what a miracle. So I sat down on the floor and spent two hours writing.

Also amazing was that Colonel Kim said that I must be tired and he ordered Coca Colas and cookies and encouraged me to have some. He said, "I merely came to supervise the exam; I did not create the test. Professors at headquarters did it. So I don't know the problems." Then he looked through all the good papers other people wrote. "Well, Captain Pak, this paper looks very good; why don't you consult it. Go ahead and use it as reference." You can imagine what I felt.

A VERY SPECIAL TEST

How could I fail such an examination? There was no way. Think of it. God works so mysteriously. If I took the regular exam, I might have failed because I have no English background. In this way, my entrance was guaranteed. That is why I was accepted into Army Language School. Other applicants were college graduates and had been English majors; others were already interpreters and were far advanced in English. They were reading *Time* magazine and *Newsweek* already. They could talk about Shakespeare and Hemingway. I was talking about a, b, c, d, e, f, g. The difference was like heaven and earth.

Only 30 people were accepted in the class. We had exams every Saturday. According to the results of the quizzes, the classes was divided into A class, B class, and C class. Those ranked one to 10 were A class, 11 to 20 made up B class, and 21 to 30 were C class. Certainly I could not keep up with the other students, so I was an honorable member of the C class. But I was really determined. I had the Unification Church spirit even before I knew the Unification Church. I knew I was there for some purpose. Twenty-four hours a day I just studied, studied, studied. For me, there was no Saturday, no Sunday. In the Japanese Navy in World War II they had a schedule: Monday, Tuesday, Wednesday, Thursday, Friday, Monday. They skipped Saturday and Sunday. So I studied with the Japanese spirit.

I memorized everything. When we were given a quiz, I knew precisely what page and what line the material came from. I have a memory book in my brain. After about six months of study, sometimes, to the amazement of the instructors, I got 100 percent on the Saturday quiz and was promoted to the A Class. Then the following week somehow my memory wasn't that good and I missed a line, then the whole result was different. When I started out on the wrong line, I ended up certainly on the wrong line. Right? So I had a blind memory. I came up with zero. Up and down, up and down went my grades.

At that time I was married and my first child had been born. Like most people in Korea at that time, we were poor. You could not live on the salary of that time. We were poverty stricken. But I was determined to study. I sent my wife and my daughter back to my wife's family home and I made a showdown to win or lose in this game. In about nine months, I went from learning my ABCs to reading *Time* magazine. I learned the entire several year curriculum in nine months and I graduated in good standing.

MY EARS DIDN'T WORK

However, I had learned from the book but not from the ear. At the graduation ceremony, the American military advisor came and gave the congratulatory message. He said, "I give you my hearty congratulations because now I can deliver my speech without using an interpreter." But I couldn't understand him. Later on I learned he had said that. At the time, I didn't know what he was saying. My ear was totally blocked. I had no comprehension. Here I was, graduating, and I couldn't comprehend even one word. An American speaking sounded very funny. The sound was different from hearing the Korean instructors speak English. My ear just wasn't open to American English. So on the day of graduation this thin pale officer was totally despondent. I had given everything for a year, and I didn't gain even a decent understanding of English. What could I do? So I made one more determination. I would go on. I enrolled in another English school where ear training was given. I played tapes recorded by Americans. I plugged the recorder into my ear and listened 24 hours a day. After three months, my ears opened. It was like a deaf person who suddenly, miraculously, could hear.

The American advisor who admitted me into the second school was totally amazed by what I had accomplished. He said, "Are you the same Captain Pak of three months ago? You can speak and understand beautifully now." Then another opportunity came to go to America, and I went back to Fort Benning, Georgia, for advanced training. I never dreamed I would come to America a second time. But this time, in 1956, I came to America without an interpreter. I studied right alongside American officers. I was determined to study not only military art but English. The first thing I did was purchase a tape recorder and I studied English by the same method which I had enjoyed so much. Unless you study English by your eyes and your mouth and your ears altogether it doesn't work. I went to church and delivered some speeches because I wanted to develop my speaking ability.

At the end of this training session, I was second in the entire class even though I was competing with the American officers. This was remarkable. The school commandant, Brigadier General Malloy, who later on became the Commander-in-Chief in Korea as a four-star general, was amazed by my record and sent it to the U.S. general serving in Korea, General Matthews. General Matthews was chief of the U.S. Military Advisory Group in Seoul. When he received my papers, he thought, this man must be pretty good, and he wanted to see me. When I reported to his office, he said, "You did a pretty good job in Fort Benning, didn't you? I have a commendation letter from General Malloy. Would you like to serve me as my assistant? I need a Korean interpreter and aide. I think you are the right man for me." All of a sudden I was given a chance to serve the U.S. general in Korea, which required daily English language in all of my work.

At that time, I was simultaneously searching all over for the ultimate truth about God. My heart was still empty. My Christian zeal was not ignited. Then a young lady from the Unification Church approached me. That was the historical moment. You can see that God built me up to being an assistant to the U.S. Army general where English had to be my daily diet. Then he brought me to the Divine Principle.

HOW COULD I REFUSE?

Since time is passing quickly, I would like to be brief. I listened to the Divine Principle in two nights. Two nights of lectures answered all my questions. I was really bubbling with enthusiasm for the day when I could proclaim the truth to the Korean people or even the people of the world. I was so astonished by the power of the truth in that two nights of lectures. Dr. Young Oon Kim taught me. She is my spiritual mother. She had invited me, "Won't you come one night to hear some wonderful philosophy?" She didn't say Divine Principle, she didn't say Reverend Moon, nothing, no mention of the Unification Church. "I will buy you a little dinner. Will you accept my invitation?" I was a very proud officer, an aide to the general. I was a very proud person. How could I refuse this invitation from a beautiful young lady?

When I arrived there I couldn't even walk upright through the door to the house. I crawled into a little room. There the most astonishing thing was revealed to me. I didn't remember what I ate. It was not the important thing. There I was searching for the possibility of knowing some great truth. I said, "I need a lecture." She gave me a two-hour lecture, all of part one of the Divine Principle. Then she invited me to come back the next day at seven o'clock. The next day I got so sick, I couldn't go. There weren't many telephones in Korea then, so I couldn't call her and tell her that I was sick. Knowing that this lady was waiting for me, I got up and said to my wife, "I must go. I cannot disappoint this young lady. I have to keep my promise." I went there and for two hours listened to part two. It was so painful to wait until the two hours were over. The amazing thing was that at the end of the lecture, I wasn't in pain anymore. I became a new man. There was no pain, no headache, nothing. Then I had a tremendous appetite to discuss more. So I stayed there until almost 12 o'clock, which was the curfew hour. We discussed, discussed, and discussed the Divine Principle. She still didn't mention Reverend Moon.

I wanted to go to her church. I asked her if they had a Wednesday worship service. She said, "Yes, we do, but, Captain Pak, you don't have to be that excited; calm down a little bit. I might invite you next Sunday." She didn't even say next Sunday was all right; she said, "I might invite you next Sunday." So I asked her, "Am I not good enough to come to your church?" She said, "No, no, that is not it. You should digest what you have heard of the Divine Principle." I said, "No, I can't wait. I want to go to tomorrow night's service at your church." She said, "No, no, there is no chance you could come." But I insisted and said, "I will find your church and I will go there anyway whether you welcome it or not." She knew that she could not win and said, "All right, you come."

I went to that church, a very humble church in Korea. It didn't look like a church. It had a wooden floor. There were young people, dressed informally, not wearing ties. It was a cold winter day—it is very cold in Korea in February. There was no heat from the stove. We sat and sang the Divine Principle hymns just as you did this morning. But there was only a handful of people, not this many people. The hymns were so powerfully inspiring to me. As I have said many times, our hymns are more inspiring than anything else. The Unification Church hymns are different, because we are singing out from the soul, not just from the lips, not just the music, not from the good melody; we are singing out from our soul. That is what we are doing. Just like you do now, it was their tradition in those days. The young people were kneeling on the floor and singing so loudly and most beautifully from the soul. It touched my heart.

Later I learned why Miss Kim was hesitating. She did not want me to see such a humble-looking church. It had no heat and no chairs. Maybe this proud officer would not like it. He might not want to join such a poor church. She was afraid that might happen. I was really searching. I was dying for the truth. I had had all kinds of experiences, which I have described to you. I had to learn some truth. I wanted to be a person who is not afraid to die. I was inspired. That first night someone delivered a sermon. I don't remember what I heard, but I was so inspired that night, sitting on the cold floor just like you do. Then at the end of the sermon, a young man stood up and came to the front. He had no tie on and was wearing a humble-looking jacket. He gave the members instruction. He had such power and grace and authority. More than anything else, what touched me was his authority.

SUCH POWER AND GRACE

Who is this man? He had been sitting right beside me. We were worshiping together. I thought he was one of the members. He sang together. He worshiped together. So he was just one of the members, I thought. Then at the end of the service he stood up and came to the front where he gave instructions with power and authority.

After the service was over, Miss Kim came over to me, smiling, and asked me if I enjoyed the sermon. She asked me if I would like to meet her leader. I said, "Yes, I am ready to meet your great leader." I thought I was going into some throne room, and I would have to bow down. I imagined that the leader must be a fantastic person. He must be so genuine and pure. He should not even be exposed to this filthy and mundane world. He must be somewhere behind a veil. I said, "Yes, I am ready to go." Then she turned around and said, "Son Sengnim, would you meet Captain Pak." Well, that was the very person speaking in front of us with authority. That was Reverend Sun Myung Moon. That is the way I met Reverend Moon.

That is the way I met Father. From that night on I stayed in the church until the curfew hour. Sometimes I stayed even after the curfew until one or two o'clock because I was a military officer and I had a military jeep. No military police stopped me, even after curfew. I took advantage of that. I stayed late listening to Father in an informal setting night after night after night. I studied the Divine Principle all day. My concern about learning English was gone. I just didn't care about English anymore. I asked myself why I didn't come to the truth much earlier. I spent so much time on English.

THOSE WERE REMARKABLE DAYS

However, because of my occupation as an aide de camp to the U.S. general, I had to speak English every day. This is the way God helped me to maintain my English ability. I went to work and just did my perfunctory duty. I just did what I needed to do. Then I studied the Principle and went to hear the lectures. At night I went to the church where I sat in a small room together with Reverend Moon and Reverend Kwak. We had a wonderful, wonderful time together. This went on day after day and month after month. Those days were truly the most remarkable days of the history of the Unification Church. Father in an informal setting gave out his heart. He spoke with such frankness, candor, and honesty in such beautiful depth about the truth. I was so inspired.

All right, this is part one of my testimony. Some day I can reveal part two, the rest of my story: how I came to America, how I came to serve in the embassy and so forth. Anyway, let us come to the conclusion because time is going so fast. Now today after 20 years, I learned why God prepared me to speak English even before I was introduced to the Divine Principle.

As you know, hopefully on September 1, Father will come back. On September 1 our longing period is over. I will stand by his side. Father will be here and I will go back to my original duty translating for him. But I tell you, when I was first given the mission to translate for Father, I knew that it was a virtually impossible job. Such abstract depths of the deep thinking of God—how can I translate this? I cannot even express what he says in Korean well, how can I do it in my limited English? So from the beginning I felt that it was an impossible task, but the order and mission were given. The only way I can do it is by faith. So I want you to know my secret of translating Father is not skill. My skill in English is still far from being able to interpret for Father well. It is impossible. But I want to do it in faith, in total obedience to Father. Somehow I want to translate his spirit. If I can convey Father's spirit somehow, then I have done my mission. It will be done.

That is the way I have felt for the last several years during the Day of Hope tours. Father never prepared a text for his speeches. He always spoke from his heart. My only preparation is prayer and then all of a sudden, 10 or 15 minutes into the speech, some rapport, a harmony is established between Father and me. Then when Father speaks I can feel his spirit so beautifully. I can speak out of his spirit, and then after one hour it doesn't matter what language I am speaking. I am elated, I am walking on cloud nine. As I experienced at Madison Square Garden, after two and one half hours, I was the one so inspired when the speech was over. That was one major rally where Father spoke without text. I felt that I was flying.

PRECIOUS GALLONS OF SWEAT

But when I go back over the translation tapes, I am ashamed of myself, ashamed of my lack of English ability. I repent all the time to Father that I am going to be judged later on in the spirit world for not doing a good job for our True Parents. I know I deserve that condemnation because my English capability is never good enough to translate for Father. The only way I can pay indemnity is to do my best and sweat more. One day I spoke to Father, "Father, you must forgive me. I have no way to do the job perfectly. I have no way to justify your words and how I translate them into English. I have made so many mistakes and blunders. I am sorry. Can you forgive me because of one thing at least: I sweated. I really poured out all my sweat, gallons and gallons, particularly, Father, during the Day of Hope tour. My underwear and even the shirt and the jacket and the trousers were soaked. Everything got so wet. Father, at least I sweat. So can you forgive me because of my gallons of sweat?" He laughed. He smiled. I hope he will say yes someday. But I repent my inadequacy to do the job well. So my apology goes to you.

Actually the words of Father that I understand are 100 times greater truth than you hear through the interpretation. I am sorry I could not give you the best of Father, total Father. I want you to understand that I will do my absolute best to translate his spirit, so that at the end of Father's sermon, I want you to be at the same level with Father's spirit. I want you to feel you are on cloud nine and know you are important and are inspired to do the job that God asks you to do. If this is the case, then I am sure there is room for me to be forgiven.

Today I determine once again I am going to restudy English and do a total English overhaul. Just as an engine needs an overhaul after being driven for 100,000 miles, I determine now at the age of 48 that I am going to overhaul my English. I am determined, especially as God has given me an opportunity to do it. So for the next several months I am going to totally refinish, retouch my English capability so that I can improve at least slowly, step by step, to better translate for Father in the days to come. That I promise.

Also, this is my supreme mission, to translate for Father. This is a more important mission than anything else you can imagine. So everything is concentrated to do that job. I need better health, for example. I want to take exercise, not for my own sake, but in order to keep up with Father's energy so that I can translate all the time up to the age of 60, 70, 80. Only God knows how long my health has to be good. As long as I am alive, I want to be in the position to translate for Father. Now I need health, a good body. So I want to take exercise.

The amazing thing about Unification Church is this. Whatever you do, if your goal is unselfish, you can do it. There are many reasons for desiring to make yourself healthy. In my case I want to keep up with Father's energy so that I can translate for Father better with energy and power. That is why I want to take exercise. I want to fulfill that mission well.

FRASER IS AFTER ME

Now here is one more opportunity, a challenge that came to me in Washington, D.C. The entire government is harassing us, trying to undermine our Father's work. As a first step, they are trying to knock me out. My brothers and sisters, all kinds of investigations of me are now going on. I know their goal is to knock me out first, then they will move on to Father. I am like a road block. If they feel they have knocked me out successfully, they can knock Reverend Moon out also. This is their scheme. I am being accused of all kinds of wrongdoings. The Internal Revenue Service is after me. The Federal Trade Commission is after me. The Justice Department is after me. The Federal Reserve Board is after me. The notorious Fraser committee is after me.

In my entire life, I tell you, I never have felt more challenged than today. I am not afraid of anything. I am not fearful of such investigations. I don't even worry about the outcome or what they might do with me. They might judge me in court. Go ahead, do that. They might throw me into jail; okay, do that. Well, if I ever go to jail, I have a beautiful plan what to do. I already have my schedule. If the Fraser committee cites me for contempt of Congress, it will mean about a one-year jail term. If they ever throw me into jail, I know I am going to have a beautiful year. I am going to have tremendous things already lined up. I am really looking forward to that.

Instead of being afraid of it, I am looking forward to it. I am not afraid. There is one thing I am afraid of. In everything I do, I want to give honor to Father and honor to God. I don't want to make a mistake. I don't want to become a coward in the sight of God, in the sight of truth, in the sight of you. I am praying everyday: God, give me your wisdom and let me do justice and bring back to you this opportunity to present Father to the entire world so the glory of God can be shown throughout the entire world.

There is one person in the Bible whom I want to be like. That person is Stephen. I want to become like him in the Completed Testament Age. We are living in the era of the coming of the Lord, the era of the True Parents. We are living at the pinnacle of history. That is in itself a great glory. I want to become somebody in the Completed Testament Age.

I want to read one paragraph from the words of Stephen, and then I will let you know why I want to be like him. If sometime you have a lack of energy, I recommend you read the Acts of the Apostles. It will truly give you energy. History is powerful. Stephen was the first martyr in Christian history. He was a very wise man. More important, though, he had the conviction to follow Jesus Christ, and in his wisdom and spirit was a great disciple of Jesus. In Jerusalem, the people could not compete with Stephen in wisdom. So they plotted against him, just like what is happening in Washington today. They cannot come squarely against us, but they are using dirty tricks, just like they did to Stephen 2,000 years ago.

In those days in the synagogues they spread rumors that Stephen was condemning God and Moses by uplifting Jesus. They said Stephen was the enemy of Moses and the enemy of God. Also, they gave out the rumor that Stephen was proclaiming that Jesus' power was going to destroy the Holy Temple. They said he was a blasphemer and must be condemned.

So Stephen was called by the council to the synagogue. The council was laying judgment upon Stephen. There was a high priest in charge, just like Fraser is today. I imagine that if Fraser ever calls me, he will be like a high priest, sitting on a big bench. I may be sitting way down there, a very small guy, trembling, and in a poor position, in the position of Stephen. All kinds of charges were brought against Stephen, just like today the Fraser committee has brought charges saying I am a KCIA agent, working secretly for the Korean government. There is no truth to it at all.

YOU BETRAYED THE RIGHTEOUS ONE

Stephen was condemned. His face was glowing with the Holy Spirit. He stood up without any fear and laid down a heavy dose of judgment on the hypocrites. You can read it in the Bible. I would like to read just one paragraph. "You stiff-necked people, uncircumcised in heart and ears, you always resist the Holy Spirit. As your fathers did, so do you. Which of the prophets did not your fathers persecute? And they killed those who announced beforehand the coming of the Righteous One, whom you have now betrayed and murdered, you who receive the law as delivered by angels and did not keep it." [Acts 7:51-53] What power! Stephen is actually saying: you, your ancestors, your fathers keep persecuting the God-sent prophets. Now you are doing just the same as your forefathers. You are the ones who murdered the Righteous One that God promised to give us, Jesus Christ.

Stephen is condemning the priests and scribes and elders and so forth as the murderers of Jesus Christ. You murdered the Righteous One. These are not things that a fearful person can say. This is a person with conviction and power who can speak up and say, you heard the message from God delivered by angels but you did not keep it, you hypocrites. People certainly didn't want to hear that. Do you know what the people did? They knew Stephen was telling the truth. They knew every word Stephen was saying was the truth. Their consciences hurt. They could not bear it. They didn't want to hear any more from Stephen, so they stuffed their ears. They stuffed their ears and dragged him outside and picked up stones and threw them at Stephen. Stephen became the first martyr.

The Bible says the moment they threw the stones at him, he looked up into the sky. He saw the heavens open. He had no fear. Jesus Christ was standing at the right-hand side of God. This is beautiful. I take a great meaning out of this phrase. In other places in the Bible, Jesus Christ is described as seated on the right-hand side of God. But at the moment Stephen was being stoned to death, the Bible said Jesus was standing. Because of such a dramatic, heroic action of Stephen, Jesus simply could not sit still. He had to stand up, ready to receive Stephen's soul. This is the greatest way of life a Christian can live.

THE GREATEST HONOR

Today you and I are following an even greater course than Stephen. This is the greatest honor we could ask for. Having Jesus and our True Parents stand up and be ready to receive our soul. Yes, we want to become sons and daughters of God who can make Jesus and True Parents stand up and make God get out of His throne and be ready to receive our soul. The final word Stephen spoke was, "Lord, do not hold this sin against them." This was the same prayer Jesus had prayed. You think attacking and killing is power, but the real power is forgiveness.

This is what the Unification Church is doing today. We are not here to stand in confrontation with the rest of the world, even with the communists. That ordinary people can do. But God's power makes us even stronger. That power will give you the power to forgive and save them and liberate them. This is our position, this is the Unification Church. Even fighting against the Fraser committee. Our ultimate motivation is not to hate at all. Our ultimate motivation is love, forgiveness, and to really liberate them from the darkness of their sin.

Someday history will record the acts of the apostles of the Unification Church. I want you to become one man and one woman whose courageous deeds and powerful deeds of forgiveness are recorded in this new acts of the apostles. That is the example we found in the New Testament. With the power of the Divine Principle, we can do just the same or more. Isn't that true? Yes.

There is one more thing I want to share with you. This may be my final session with you before Father comes. I am so glad. I have really run out of resources. Father must come so I can be filled. You need Father, not me. I am glad he is coming. I am so glad. So during this next week, you are really going to work harder to be ready to meet Father. I want you to be ready.

My conclusion is this: the kingdom of God is not going to be occupied by people with famous names, prosperous-looking big figures and so forth.

There were many great figures in the Old Testament era, high priests and scribes and elders and kings and queens and so forth. But do you know that the first one who entered the kingdom of God along with Jesus Christ was not a priest, not a scribe, not an elder, not a king, was not even an apostle of Jesus Christ. No, it was the unknown thief. He led a criminal life, a dirty life. He may have killed people. He probably stole and robbed many times. That man became the first to accompany Jesus Christ to Paradise. The thief on the right-hand side of Jesus during the crucifixion grabbed the opportunity, a once-in-a-lifetime opportunity, a most dramatic opportunity. He had the honor of being crucified next to Jesus.

Two thieves had the same opportunity, but they responded in totally different ways. The thief on the left-hand side said, if you are the Son of God, why can't you come down and save yourself. I pity you. Why can't you save yourself and save us? He scornfully laughed at Jesus.

The thief on the right-hand side heard what the other thief said as he cursed Jesus in that fashion. Of course, this thief was not a Christian or a disciple. He protested saying, you rascal, you and I deserve this death many times over, but he didn't do anything to deserve to be crucified. How can you speak in such an evil way to the most noble and divine person? He defended Jesus in a most dramatic manner on the cross. He turned to Jesus and said, "Lord! Lord! Can you remember me today? Can you remember me?" Jesus said to him, "Truly, truly I say to you, you shall be with me in Paradise." He was the first person who was accepted by Jesus and he accompanied Jesus to Paradise. He grabbed the opportunity. He gave his final devotion, final energy, final soul for the sake of Jesus. This moved the heart of Jesus.

Today you and I are almost like this right-hand side thief. There are always left-hand side thieves. The rest of the world might say the same thing to our Father. We are the ones saying, "How could you say such an awful thing to the holy one who comes to save us and is without sin?" We say like Stephen, "You were given the truth and you did not keep it." We turn around to Father and say—no matter how miserable we are, how humble we are—"Father, can you accept me? Can you forgive me? Can you take me along?" Yes, we must move the heart of the Father. We must move the heart of the Heavenly Father and the heart of True Parents. Then we will be all right. You will be most dramatically victorious. No one can doubt your victory. No victory is greater than that one. I want you to know that we will be hearing from Father in that case: "Truly, truly, I say to you, you shall be with me always, here on earth and thereafter in heaven."

BE HUMBLE BEFORE GOD

BELVEDERE ESTATE, TARRYTOWN, NEW YORK

SEPTEMBER 4, 1977

═══════════════════════════

This sermon is full of wonderful testimonies, stories, and anecdotes, all revealing great spiritual lessons and wisdom. Drawing from Father's life, Dr. Pak reminds members that God is always watching us, and that through our suffering we can learn and experience God's heart, the value of the Blessing, and develop parental love and total commitment.

I promise you very definitely this is the final Sunday I will give the sermon instead of True Father. So we will give our final greeting to our True Parents, loud and clear from the bottom of our hearts. Let's face north. Good morning, Father. Good morning, Mother. Thank you.

I am sorry. I am sure next Sunday True Father will be here. Actually, Father and Mother were here the first of September, and I thought Father would deliver the sermon then. But there were two important occasions on that day. There was the celebration of In Jin Nim's 12th birthday at East Garden, and Father summoned the state leaders to a conference. So right after Father's morning pledge service, we had a birthday celebration; then the state leaders came to East Garden and we had a conference all day long. It was very intense. After that conference, Father departed for Boston.

I knew Father would go back to Boston because this is the final week of what they call giant tuna season. Father doesn't do anything without following it to a correct or perfected conclusion. That is the way Father always is. If he is doing something, he always finishes it.

Father was already victorious in the Gloucester area and has set the record for tuna. Nobody else came near to Father's record. Last Sunday I mentioned to you that people have been spreading a rumor that Reverend Moon must have some special electronic gadget. Actually, what Father has is spiritual power. Or they even say he has the power to brainwash the tuna. So all the tuna come to Father. But Father catches tuna after a really determined fight. So I knew that Father would go back up there. By September 1 when Father was here, he had caught 57 giant tuna over 800 pounds each. Think of it. If we brought 57 tuna to this auditorium, it would look like a mountain of tuna. However, even though no one could keep up with his record, Father's standard is higher. He is going higher and higher and trying to set the record in history. So I know Father would like to be there on the final day of the tuna season. I know Father would like to finish the season by catching another giant tuna. A victorious ending. That is the way Father always works. So that very evening, after the all-day state leaders conference, Father left by car for Boston. I knew that Father would not sleep at all because he would barely arrive by 3:30 a.m. and Father is always up and out to sea by that time. In some cases, Father has already caught a giant tuna and is coming in when other boats are going out.

NO ONE CAN KEEP UP WITH FATHER

There were many, many reports during the conference, but the most astonishing testimony is Father himself. We think we work hard, but really the one who is working hard is Father. No one can keep up with Father. We don't sleep too much or eat too much. But actually Father is the one who is completely intoxicated with the mission that God gave him. He feels such desperate anxiety to restore this world. He forgets sleeping. He forgets eating. Some of the members who serve Father in Boston are here, and we all recognize how hard Father is working.

Aidan Barry from the state of Massachusetts said it was such a great honor to have Father in the state of Massachusetts for the entire summer. He had several opportunities to go fishing with Father. He said Father has been fishing all summer, every day, but Aidan just participated a few days, keeping the same pace that Father keeps all the time, and Aidan said he was totally knocked out.

Father goes out to sea at 3:30 in the morning and many days he comes back quite late. Everybody, including the seasoned sailors, like Captains

Allen, Dikon, Matsuzaki, and Gerhard, the giant German brother, are out there to support Father. But even they at their young age just cannot keep up with Father's pace. They have to sneak in some time during the day to take a little nap. Otherwise, they just collapse. Aidan said that on one particular day there were about 17 people on the boat. Everyone of them, all 16, everyone except Father, at some point sneaked into the rear cabin and slept. Just a little nap because they just couldn't go on. Allen sometimes is so tired from steering the boat he has to sleep. But only one person stays on the bridge from morning to night. That is Father.

Father is not a superman. But his heart and anxiety and desperation to do God's work keep him totally alert. He is the only one to stay on the bridge and stay awake. Father himself said to me at the conference, and all the people heard, that he is human. He has weakness, too. He sometimes feels very tired, no question about it. He is not made of iron. Many people misunderstand and think Father is an iron man. Bionic man. He is not. He is just like you and me. He has a feeble, weak body, the same as you and I do. The difference is, he has the power and determination to push himself, which we don't. The difference is the intensity of his mission, his heart.

Father explained there is a gap between God's heart and men's heart. But there is no gap between God's heart and his heart. There is no gap. He feels precisely as Heavenly Father feels. God does not want to rest for even one moment. God wants to see history moving and progressing every moment of the day, 24 hours a day, day and night. Father is reflecting that wish, so he just can't let himself rest or slow down. He has to fight sleepiness. He said he pinches himself to keep awake. Another thing Father said was, "You think you can sneak into the back cabin and sleep, and you come out and think, 'Oh good, nobody noticed, I sneaked really well and had a little nap.' You think you are very successful, but you are a fool. Don't you know the entire spirit world is watching you?" That is the way Father lives.

GOD IS WATCHING

This is a most important thing to hear. Father never thinks that only people are watching him, or only members are watching him. Most important to Father is the spirit world. The entire spirit world is watching him all the time. Moreover, God Himself is watching him. God is cheering him on. Father has a desire to never let down God and to never let down the billions of people in the spiritual world. He never wants God to feel empty because His son is lagging behind. I would never put myself in that position, Father thinks. That is his absolute determination. This is the way we all should live. You think you sneaked out for a nap and got away with something. No, you didn't. The entire spirit world watched you. So it doesn't matter whether members are watching or leaders are watching. Most important is that God is watching 24 hours a day. And God is not watching with a critical eye. God is pushing and encouraging us, trying to inspire us. Because God's work here on earth depends upon you.

Mother told me something in secret. No one else knows this, but I want to tell you because you have been longing for Father so much. Mother told me that one night Father wanted to wake up at 3:30 a.m. as usual, and, also as usual, Father didn't go to bed until 12:00 or 1:00 a.m. Mother had set the alarm and at 3:30 Father was just sleeping like a log. He looked so tired. But Mother, knowing that Father would not be happy unless he was awakened at 3:30 a.m., said, "Father, it is 3:30 now." Father answered yes, OK, and got himself up and out of the bed. Mother was in the wash room or somewhere else and she heard a big boom, the sound of someone falling down. She dashed into the room and Father was on the floor. What happened, Father? Nothing, never mind, he said. Then Father tried to get up and there was blood running down his face.

You can imagine how shocked Mother was. But Father said, "Never mind." She asked him, "Would you lie down for another 30 minutes or an hour? You don't have to get up at 3:30. Nobody told you have to be out at 3:30. Nobody will call your name at roll call, so please rest another 30 minutes." Father said, "No, God is waiting out there. I have an appointment with God at 4 a.m." That is the way Father feels. He wiped the blood off and went out to sea. I don't think even people closely serving Father knew this story, but I heard. I have a special source of information, you know. And the next time I saw Father there were two scars on his head. But just think of it. No one would be critical of Father for sleeping another 30 minutes. Everybody wants him to rest a little more. But Father said, "Mother, never mind, I have an appointment with God out there in the vast ocean. God has been meeting me all the time at 4 a.m. I must be out there." So, with that scar, Father went out at 3:30 a.m.

That is Father's life. Another morning Gerhard was on night watch. Father had gone to bed that night about midnight. Around 12:45 a.m., Father came downstairs completely ready with hat and boots, the uniform of the sea, and said, "Good morning, Gerhard. Is everybody ready?" Gerhard said, "Father, it is only 12:45 a.m." Father looked at his watch. "I thought it was 3:45." Father was really grumbling and very unhappy. Boy, it is 12:45, but I thought it was 3:45. What does this explain? It explains that Father has no concept of time. In doing the work of God, there is no concept of time. For 20 years, I have heard Father say, "Who told you you need three meals a day? Who told you that you need seven hours of sleep?

Who told you?" You see. We are accustomed to limiting ourselves. A limitation in our mind limits our capability. For 10 or 20 years, we are used to thinking that 7 p.m. is dinner time. So when 7 p.m. comes, you feel hungry because your body is accustomed and limited to that way of life.

But Father has no such preset concept. We should do this. We should eat this. We should dress this way. We should rest this long. He has no concept. He is so focused on building God's kingdom that it doesn't make any difference whether it is night, morning, or day. Father totally forgets the time. Many times Father forgets about meals. Dinner is served and Father thinks that was breakfast. He doesn't remember if we had any breakfast this morning. He forgets. Totally forgets the day.

"IS EVERYBODY READY?"

And that night in Gloucester, Father went to bed at 12 midnight. Father couldn't have been in bed any more than 30 minutes. Then he saw the clock and misread it, thinking it said 3:30. Automatically he was up. It didn't matter if it was 12:45 after only 30 minutes in bed. It didn't make any difference. Father was already up and ready to go and coming downstairs and saying, "Good morning, Gerhard. Everybody ready?" Nobody was ready. So Gerhard said, "Father, it is only 12:45. Nobody is up." Father went back up the stairs and went back to bed for another two hours. But Gerhard said Father looked very unhappy that day. Very unhappy because he had to go back to bed again.

I have been on the ocean with Father many times, and I know there are many, many reasons why Father goes out to sea. Father has told you why, and he will say more in the future. I am sure of one reason. When you go out in the ocean, there is no land around you. The ocean is so different from the land. The vast ocean is right there, unstained, as God created it. Father enjoys a genuine communication with nature. Also, Father really enjoys the fellowship with God. A lonely fellowship. Father is on the bridge, and all day long he is surrounded by the vast sky and water. Father enjoys the intimate fellowship with unstained, untouched nature, which is still as God created it. So Father can claim, this is God's sea. Therefore, this is my sea. This is my ocean. This is my world. Before anybody claims it, God, I claim this ocean as your ocean. Your world. I know that Father every day is claiming that ocean in the name of God. So, we must pray for Father now at the conclusion of his summer fishing and being with God on the ocean.

During Father's stay on the sea, many, many important things have been happening all over the world. And I am sure next week some important news will be revealed. I want you to look forward to that. There was much important news revealed through the leaders conference. Even though Father is out there, the entire world moves and is centered on this one man, because spirit world is united on this one man.

So it doesn't make any difference if Father is in Gloucester or East Garden or Belvedere. It doesn't make any difference. Centering upon this one man, there are things happening all over the world. So I assure you this is the final Sunday without Father. Next Sunday will be a happy day for me and for you. For all of us, right?

I would like to share with you a letter I received from one of our brothers, Rodney Edwards. Rodney is a black brother who always sits right here. He's always the supporting cheerleader for Father. Initially, Father did not notice. But every Sunday, consistently, Rodney would come early and sit right there. Always smiling, always ready, always enthusiastic. Supporting Father. That moved the heart of Father and Mother very, very much. Father even now recognizes his name.

"WHERE IS MY BLACK SON?"

One Sunday he just disappeared. He didn't come. And after the speech Father asked me on the way to East Garden, "Where is my black son? Where did that little son go?" "Father, he is on MFT." "Is he? I miss him," Father said. Father said, I miss him. Beautiful, Father misses him. Rodney is out there fighting very hard on MFT. I received a letter from him that I would like to share with you this morning.

> Dear Col. Pak, how are you? I heard that you are responsible for Sunday Service at Belvedere. I am sorry that I can't be there to support you.

This is beautiful. He didn't say he was sorry he couldn't be here to hear me. No, he comes on Sunday mornings to support. Beautiful. He doesn't come to receive the power or inspiration, but to support Father or to support me. He wants to come to give. You all think you come here to receive, but he comes to give, to support Father, or whoever is speaking. That is the way the spirit should be.

> I had an experience about two weeks ago. I was working fund-raising and I felt your spirit very strongly. I miss True Parents very much. I am grateful for my experience on MFT because I am able to more deeply understand Father's course and the meaning of restoration through indemnity. I had one particular experience which helped me to realize that we are "criminal" undesirable persons in Satan's world.

A beautiful expression. In the eyes of Satan we are criminals. We are treated as criminals. Jesus Christ in the eyes of Satan was the worst kind criminal. So they nailed him to the cross.

> I was forced to leave a city named Springfield because I was black and going door to door to fund-raise for God. None of the white members were brought to the police department. I realized that many people would like to have Father brought to jail because he is Korean going door to door, knocking on the closed doors of people's hearts to let God enter their lives.

Beautiful, isn't it. You see, this is the way we should live. When you suffer, when you have some unusual circumstances, you must relate that particular experience with Father and with God. Thus, you can understand and experience God's heart. This is a beautiful way to live. When Rodney received persecution, this unwarranted treatment, when he felt indignation, he related that situation with Father's position and even God's heart. So he can take that suffering not for himself, but for the sake of Father, the sake of God. This is the way we should live. You see, you are going through a tremendous ordeal. Tremendous, dramatic experiences every day. But don't go through those experiences or take that suffering meaninglessly. You must put meaning into it. Otherwise, the suffering will not do you any good. When Rodney was mistreated, he put himself in Father's position. Yes, this world hates me because I am black, going door to door, being persistent and fund-raising for God. But actually, Father is like a fund-raiser, heavenly fund-raiser himself. Our Father is Korean, scornfully looked at, but going persistently door to door trying to open the hearts of men to let God move in. That is why he is persecuted. This is the way Rodney related his experiences with Father's.

> I had another experience as well. I went to the police department to leave the names of members soliciting. I started talking to the police chief and found he was Abel-like. One day, he said, a woman called and filed a complaint against Reverend Moon because he was playing God. He thinks he is God. That was the accusation. The woman said to the police, "Reverend Moon is no good, he is playing God. He thinks he is God."

> The police chief began to tell her the story of a carpenter who left his profession and was dissatisfied with the established religion and started his own religious movement. The woman said, "I don't want to have anything to do with a person like that." The police chief replied, "Lady, the man's name was Jesus Christ." She immediately hung up the telephone. I gave the police chief some literature. He read the first paragraph and said, "I understand Reverend Moon's movement more clearly."

> Col. Pak, I just finished a 21-day MFT fund-raising competition. I understand more deeply the blessing of being in the family and know-

271

ing True Parents. I am able to see more clearly people in the fallen world are open regardless of their external circumstances. I repent that I have constantly received incredible blessing, but I give so little in exchange. I thank Heavenly Father and True Parents and everyone who sacrificed tears, sweat, and blood to lay the foundation.

I will never forget the victory celebration after Washington Monument. The Washington Monument campaign was my most difficult and desperate period in the church. I felt like a failure because I couldn't do enough for God and True Parents. I lost my position and responsibility as team captain. I felt unloved and abandoned during the Washington Monument campaign. At the Washington Monument victory celebration, however, when you reached down and selected me to dance with you, I could hardly believe it was happening.

Right after the Washington Victory Celebration, Father could not be present because Washington at that time was very tense. Therefore, Father had a separate victory celebration on October 4 in Belvedere, but we were given the opportunity by Father to go ahead and have a nice picnic and celebrate the victory. So I led that victory celebration in Washington. We went to a park and had a nice celebration. I was giving the victory message. I don't know what I said, but I was so excited. Anyway, during the speech I just couldn't talk by my word alone. I had such an urge and strong excitement. I must dance somehow. I needed a partner. There was Rodney, in front of me, supporting me, he was right there. So I picked him up. You are my partner, let's dance. So we both of just really hugged each other and embraced and danced. That is what he is talking about.

> I could hardly believe it was happening. My deepest desire when I was in front of Father at Belvedere was to go up on stage, sit in Father's lap, and give him a great big hug and kiss him.

I have given Father a really strong hug and kissed him many, many times. In a worldly sense, he smelled like sweat and someone working very hard, but the smell of Father's sweat was really heavenly—it was heavenly perfume. Rodney worked so many days so hard, day in and day out, no time to even get the laundry done. This brother may not even have had a change of underwear. So naturally he smelled of sweat and dust and so forth. But we embraced and danced and that was a heavenly fragrance.

> When you embraced me I felt the spirit of Father was embracing me. I didn't want to release the embrace of love.

The other outstanding experience was at Belvedere when Father called me his little black son. This experience I always try to recall when I am struggling to fulfill my goal. During times of persecution and abuse from people, I say to myself, he called me his little black son. I am at least worthy to be called his son. I must do as he would.

This is wonderful. There is always a time when you try to fund-raise or witness when everything goes wrong. Nothing clicks. But in those situations, Rodney remembers, yes, Father called me my little son. You are my little son. My little black son. That is a most loving term. My little son. Father called me his son. I just simply cannot let him down. I simply cannot. Impossible. That becomes a source of power and source of inspiration and pushes him on.

> Please tell Mother and Father I miss them very much. I send my love
> and prayers for their eternal happiness. I love you also very much, Col.
> Pak. In the Name of True Parents, Rodney.

Rodney also wrote a letter to Father which I did not yet read to Father. That letter is his own testimony, how he used to be an emotionally disturbed racist. He had such hatred for white people because of several experiences during his high school years when white brothers gave him a very hard time. So he grew up as an emotionally upset, violent racist. Then his life changed. He became a lover of all men. I will not read this because I only have part of it and he probably has a series. Someday, I will be able to share this letter, not only with Father, because all these things will be recorded in the Acts of Apostles in the future Bible.

TRUE PARENTS' LITTLE SONS

You are writing the same chapter. You are no different from Rodney. You are all Rodney. You are all the little black son, little white son, little yellow son of our True Parents. I told you one Sunday there is no greater title you can have than to be called the son of God, son of True Parents. President of the United States or His Excellency ambassador of so and so, Royal Highness. Whatever. Those are great titles. Duke, queen, king, emperor, prince, and princess. But there is no title that matches the height of being called the son of God. That is the title we go by. You are the son of God and daughter of God.

At the last conference, Father emphasized MFT work. As you know, our Unification Theological Seminary had a first graduation at Barrytown. The seminarians had a high expectation of what they would do after graduation. "We have a master's degree. We mastered theology. We mastered philosophy. We mastered the art of education. We mastered history. So we are somebody now. We are ready to tackle prestigious work." This is how everybody thought. But right after graduation, Father said, "You, you, you, you, you go to this state, you go to this state, you go to this state, join MFT." Everybody said. "MFT—no, that can't be. Father, we didn't waste two years here at Barrytown just to join the MFT." They didn't say it out loud, of course, but they thought like that. I am sure that some of the brothers or even the sisters grumbled inside.

But anyway, they obeyed. Some did well. Total commitment regardless. Some had a hard time, I am sure. At the September 1st meeting Father wanted to see all the records of the seminarians on MFT. Some sister seminarian had a $200 a day average. Some brother averaged $150. Then there were many brothers who made $150, $175, $125 a day, and so forth. Father hand-picked 11 seminary graduates who did well in MFT. He said, "These people met God." They always thought they were learning about God in the classroom. They never met God until they got out to the field, standing on their own feet, asking funds for the purpose of God. They looked like beggars in front of the people and took all kinds of persecution. There they really met God.

Now these people are ready for their mission. You see, God is not locked up in the classroom in Barrytown, or even Belvedere in this hall. God is out there in the forefront on the street corner, where you are witnessing, where you are selling papers, where you are fund-raising. There, if your heart is right, you meet God. God is a frontline soldier. God is always available to meet the frontline soldiers. When you become a comrade of God, God is right there. Father knows this principle so well in his own life. So 11 people have been selected and assigned as state leaders. Those state leaders who did not produce a result in the last six months have to come back for retraining, primarily MFT training.

Father explained the purpose of the MFT as part of three principles. In our movement we do things to precisely follow the principle of restoration. First, God created all things. Then God created men. And God wanted to fulfill love. These are the three primary goals of creation. So in restoration through MFT, we are actually restoring all the things that God created. That is the first step.

Then we go witnessing and there we restore humans. When we restore things and restore men, then we are going to fulfill love, which means internally you will have a right to be Blessed and become members of God's family. You can become eligible to be the master of the house. You can become the center of the heavenly kingdom. The family is the building block of the heavenly kingdom.

That is the purpose of MFT. Therefore, in the Unification Church, whether you are young or old in our membership, Father said that all the members of the Unification Church who did not have MFT training must go off to MFT because that is the quickest way to be recognized in the movement and recognized by God.

Then from here we will always come back to witnessing, to restore man. These two outstanding criteria are going to be our base for the future and for future blessing as well. As you know, on October 1, we are going to have a national Divine Principle test for all the state leaders or anybody who is ready. You must pass, either this time or next time. But by all means, you have to study the Principle, because without knowing the Principle how can you witness to others? How can you become a doctor without knowing how to diagnose a patient?

THE BLESSING ELEVATES US

So then you are eligible to fulfill love. The Blessing itself is not for our own selfish taste. Our Blessing comes as a reward, but at the same time, it is more than a reward. The Blessing comes to elevate us into greater instruments so that we can do better and greater work for God. That is the meaning of the Blessing. The Blessing is not coming for your own sake but for the sake of your spouse. Love is a giving thing, unconditional giving, together, united. To give love to Heavenly Father and to the world. When you do it together, husband and wife, you can spread a more perfect love to the world and to God. God looks at this love, husband and wife united, and sees a wholesome love. It is one unit, it is not two separate loves. One love. That is the way God accepts.

At the last state leaders conference an astonishing testimony was given which I would like to share with you. In August, one of our state centers brought 90 percent of the result in the entire United States. That was the Northern California center, located in Oakland, headed by Dr. and Mrs. Mose Durst. I am sure many of you came from that region. Raise your hands those who come from Oakland. Look at how many brothers and sisters. I want you to be proud of it. Dr. and Mrs. Durst and their members accomplished as much as the rest of the 49 states put together, including New York. And, according to Dr. Durst, last month was not too great a success. He was very apologetic to Father.

In just one month, 317 people heard the conclusion in workshop. In order to have 317 people hear the conclusion of the Divine Principle, they must have brought thousands of people to the lectures. According to Dr. Durst, practically every bus, every transportation mode there is in Northern California, particularly in the Oakland-San Francisco area, is met by our members. Every train and bus arriving at the Oakland stations is met by members. Every plane is met by our members. Think of it. Every movement of people, there are our members welcoming. The first one to meet them. Literally every day hundreds and hundreds of people are met and invited to the lectures.

Last month, 24 people moved in, but Dr. Durst was so apologetic to Father. "We are used to bringing 50 or 60 members into the center. But, this month, Father, we didn't work hard enough. We apologize. Next month we will bring greater victory."

MANY BABIES FROM BOONEVILLE

He was so humble and apologetic to Father. But many babies are on the way, he said. They are in the incubator somewhere. They are 8-½ month babies, so they need a little extra care. So many incubators out there in Northern California. They are hatching now. This morning I am sure many spring chickens are hatching. Amazing. It is a joy. Sometimes as many as 500 to 600 people come to a workshop. It used to be Booneville, but now they have an even better place than Booneville. Booneville was a farm and there was a building there used as the lecture hall called the Chicken Palace. So that makes everybody a spring chicken, doesn't it? We have all been hatched in the Chicken Palace. Right?

Dr. Sontag, who wrote the book *Sun Myung Moon and the Unification Church*, went there for a workshop. He enjoyed that chicken palace more than anything else: the smell of chickens, and there were feathers all over the place. He liked that. When Dr. Sontag heard we moved into better facilities, he said too bad. Nobody can experience the Chicken Palace any more. That was a real experience. But anyway we needed better facilities for the 500 people crowded in every week.

Last month the Northern California center also contributed 50 members to the MFT. The rest of the United States, all 49 states put together, contributed 28 members last month. Think of it. For that matter, Father said New York must be ashamed. However, I respect Mr. Sawada for his zeal, his humility, and total dedication. When Mr. Sawada was speaking to Father, I could see his sparkling shining eyes, saying, Father, just give me a chance, we will definitely deliver the results. What a beautiful thing to behold. I don't know if Mr. Sawada is here or not, but it doesn't make any difference. Of course last month, the New York area was totally concentrated on newspaper subscriptions. That is a different situation from California. California doesn't have a newspaper, but New York does. We are selling newspaper subscriptions door-to-door, so Father understands it. And I, of course, was very sympathetic to Mr. Sawada and the New York situation, but he said this month is really the month to bring in the people.

I am sure by the end of this month New York will do far better than Northern California. Father asked, do you know why this Northern California center does so well? Simply because, Father said, the leadership is right. Providentially speaking, the leadership should be man and wife. The key to success is the total unity of Dr. and Mrs. Durst, in heart, centering upon God. This is really the ideal. Heavenly Father loves to see the heavenly four positions we all learned about. Adam and Eve totally united, centering upon God, will bring the children. So naturally spiritual children will flock to Northern California. The Principle is working.

Another reason that Northern California is succeeding is the atmosphere. If you want to study, why do you need Harvard or Yale? People who go to Harvard or Yale are, of course, very bright people. But they go to these universities for the tradition and the atmosphere of study. When you go onto the campus you cannot help but be absorbed into that atmosphere. By the same token, the Dursts' center has a loving, warm, parental atmosphere. Father said that even though he doesn't go there, he can sense that the Oakland center has an atmosphere of family, with Dr. and Mrs. Durst in the father's and mother's role, embracing and giving out so much warmth and love. Each member there is not concerned primarily with their job but they are united, focused on the new members. When they come home for dinner, really hungry, their first thought is, hey, what about that new boy I brought in and that new sister someone else brought. Did they listen to the Divine Principle well today? They are most concerned about the well-being of the new members.

People surround each new member and worry and watch and pay attention if someone is listening to Divine Principle. If someone is lecturing, the person passing by is praying, God, could you make this man open his heart so the Divine Principle can reach him. Everybody is praying. So there is a totally giving, unselfish, loving atmosphere. Everyone is concerned for each other and paying attention to each other, particularly the new people coming in. All the older members are embracing them in such a way that new people become a prisoner of love. We all want to become prisoners of love. Really, I tell you what mankind is seeking is not freedom. The real thing mankind is looking forward to is bondage—that is, the bondage of love. We want to become bound by love. That is where we find real freedom and real joy.

Many people think they have freedom in the outside world. They are really in bondage. They are really enslaved. This is why in the New Testament St. Paul said we are God's servants. We are the prisoners of God. We can find real freedom when we are free from sin, free from a guilty conscience. Going out and doing everything you want is not freedom. That is real enslavement. The mind and conscience and heart know they are not doing things right. But in Oakland they are becoming prisoners of love. They just don't want to be separated from this group.

Another amazing thing is how quickly the Oakland center can train and rear spiritual babies, nurturing them with spiritual food so they grow quickly. They send them to headquarters and MFT duties and other missions. Sometimes the young members are sent out from Oakland and they find the spiritual atmosphere so cold and impersonal. They try to do their very best but they are not mature enough, and they miss their mother and father. They miss the Oakland atmosphere very much. So, sometimes they just leave, and everyone thinks they left the movement. Actually, it turns out they went back to Oakland again.

Amazing. Because love is a magnet. The love atmosphere in Oakland pulls them so much that, even though they are doing their job the best way they can, they feel the pull and leave. And people are shocked and say, "Oh, someone from Oakland is gone. He just left the movement. He is an ex-Moonie." No! He just turned up in Oakland. So the spiritual parents in Oakland embrace him and give them burning zeal and discipline and training and send him out again. Sometimes it takes two or three trips. Father asks, why is this happening? Because other centers are lacking that loving, giving, godly atmosphere. This atmosphere is everything. Father said that for New York Church to be successful each individual who comes there must feel that warmth and become intoxicated in love. Even a foreign person coming into that atmosphere must be able to sense it. When they walk into the third floor of the Tiffany building at the newspaper, people must sense the feeling of love and trust and warmth. Then there is such a strong bond nothing can disconnect it.

This shows, Father said, that Oakland center has that standard of unity and loving atmosphere, but other centers are far from that perfection. That is why results are coming in Oakland. Think of it. In the entire United States, 90 percent of the work of our movement is done by one center. If all 50 states were like Oakland center, what would happen? It all depends on the leadership.

DON'T LOSE GOD

That is why Father was not just satisfied to train members in the seminary. If we train in the seminary and send them out to the big mission with a nice suit and all they do is give Sunday sermons and get treated as a very prestigious person, then we are no different from the ordinary Christian churches. They have been doing it for 2,000 years. They have been talking about God for 2,000 years and they lost God. Amazing, isn't it? They talk about God every day, but they lost God.

So this is why Father has hand-picked seminary graduates, outstanding men and women, and sent them out for state missions. Next month it will happen more. Next year it will happen more. Each state of the United States is like one country in Europe. Each state has that potential. California, for example, is greater than Japan or greater than Germany. Far greater than Great Britain. California, one state alone, can be the ninth strongest, richest country in the world.

So here in America there are absolutely endless resources we can tap. America is a rich country. We have no idea how rich this country is. America is a powerful country. We have no idea how powerful this country is. Even the president of the United States doesn't realize how powerful this country is, how much potential it has. That is why God is centering upon this nation. Each state of the United States can be compared to our movement in Germany, Holland, England, Italy, and France.

Our movement in Japan has the power to influence all the political and economic arena. It is a wonderful movement. The CARP [Collegiate Association for the Research of Principle] movement in Japan is the strongest movement in the whole world. Right now Japan has about 2,500 regular CARP members. There is a CARP organization at every major university, and CARP is the strongest student movement in Japan. It is in a face-to-face struggle with the communist student movement. You see, the communists are always using the college campus as their fertile ground. They always infiltrate among the professors and students. They are winning the battle on college campuses. This is the way communism takes over. Communists plan very wisely.

But up until now the communists have been enjoying a honeymoon. No one has ever challenged them on the college campuses. The communist tactic is that the end justifies the means. Their message is savage, cruel, unscrupulous. In Japan, as many Japanese brothers and sisters know, there are killings in broad daylight on college campuses. It becomes a daily diet. Uncooperative professors are stabbed to death, just like that. So how can the professors speak out against communism even if they feel there is some evil in communism? They cannot speak up. No student wants to have a quarrel with a communist student because they are so cruel.

The communists use threatening tactics. That is the way they work. In Russia, Cuba, all over the world, the communist regime works at gunpoint. If people obey, they live. If they don't obey, they die. In China alone, 150 million people were killed. In Russia alone after the 1917 Bolshevik revolution, over 50 million people were killed. You have no idea how many people are suffering in Siberia and Cambodia right now. But the American press never speaks up. Hundreds of thousands of innocent people are dying in Cambodia simply because they are condemned as reactionaries. You see, how savage it is. You members might have some understanding of this, but the American people in general understand very little.

You kill a person by gun, but in Cambodia they say you don't even deserve a bullet. You are not worth even one bullet. So they beat them to death with bamboo sticks. That is the way they kill them. The communists always use terrorism. Scare tactics. That is the way they are going to take over the world. They think they can take over the world in that fashion and they have been successful because they met no resistance.

But in Japan, for the first time, they hit a real wall: the Unification Church. There is only one group of people where the bamboo spear doesn't work. The scare tactics don't work. Nothing works. Furthermore, we challenge them to come out for a philosophical confrontation. All right, if you think communism is right, come out in the open and let us discuss and let the public be the judge. And they discovered that communists don't have a theory to repudiate the Divine Principle. So they are not coming out for the confrontation. The Divine Principle for the first time in history is exposing the lies of communism. How can we make communism weak, vulnerable? We must expose their lie. They say there is no God.

COMMUNISTS ON THE DEFENSIVE

So on the college campuses for the first time they are on the defensive. The communists have always been on the offensive. But for the first time they have met resistance and this time they found themselves on the defensive. In the meantime, our college CARP organization is publishing a newspaper because our word is the truth, and the word is power. We have about 45 campus newspapers in Japan. Imagine—45 newspapers. Not just one News World. On every campus a newspaper. Also, we have organized the Professors Peace Academy, and about 400 top-notch professors have joined our crusade. So we have professors and students united. They have been supporting each other with give and take. We use the Principle, give and take. The professor without students is helpless. It is like an airplane without wings. No power. The student without the professor is also like an airplane without wings.

Our organization is strong and the membership is growing. The core membership of 2,500 will become 5,000 very soon, then 7,500, 10,000. The CARP organization is going to be a formidable organization that the communists will be afraid of.

This is happening in Japan. There is no reason why we cannot duplicate this here in America. We could do it. As I said, each state has as much potential as Japan. Think of the state of New York. How much you can do in the state of New York. But we feel so much persecution in this country, and we feel stranded and unable to work. Even with this persecution, and all kinds of misunderstandings, America is still a heavenly sanctuary. This is where God is going to make a showdown. America is where God is going to win. I just cannot see any other way. I can see more clearly than you do because I came from an outside environment. I know the Korean way of life. I know the Japanese way of life. America is a heavenly sanctuary. If we have been given this opportunity and still we cannot win, boy, we have no faith in the sight of God. Either here or thereafter in the spirit world.

Think of it. Particularly in light of the storm of persecution. I really thank God for the Constitution God gave this country. The First Amendment right—you know it—religious freedom, separation between state and church. Without protections like these, Jesus was crucified 2,000 years ago. God knew so well why His son Jesus was crucified. Not because of the lack of the word. Not because of the lack of a following. Not because of the lack of popularity. But because of the system of that age, that one man can be the ruler as well as the judge. He can put a man to death. God more than anybody else learned a lesson through Jesus Christ. So for 2,000 years God has been preparing the environment where the duplication of His son's crucifixion would never be possible. That is America. That is democracy.

GOD CAN USE DEMOCRACY

Democracy is not at all a perfect political system. But right now it is the best system for the purpose of God. God knew it, so God established it. One time Winston Churchill said that democracy is the clumsiest system under the sun, but we use it because we can't devise anything better. That was his answer. Democracy is a clumsy, wasteful system, but mankind has not yet devised anything better. But God has a different purpose. Democracy is giving God's forces the best environment to establish a beachhead for God's Kingdom here on earth, slowly but surely. As Rodney said, in the eyes of the satanic world, all we Moonies are criminals. To them, we are invasion forces.

So God has been thinking, when My forces invade the earth a second time, in the form of the Second Christ, how can I protect My son well? What system would be the best? Can you think of any better system than the present democracy? I can't. Democracy guarantees freedom of religion and thought. That is what Jesus needed 2,000 years ago, but there was no system. Today we have democracy with checks and balances, separation of powers, the three branches of government. Power comes from the people, and the truth of God is going to win the people. So once we have been successful in winning the people, then certainly God's forces will have the power here on earth to influence the nation and world to be the God-centered nation and world.

So I want you to look forward to becoming leaders of the Unification Church, but start out from the most dismal and lowest possible level. I clearly remember when I first joined the Unification Church. I was a major in the Korean Army and very proud. I am sorry that last Sunday I gave you too long a testimony. Some of you were bored, I am sure. But anyway, I was a proud major serving a big U.S. general.

As soon as I discovered the Divine Principle, I joined the Unification Church. On the first day, I was asked to give a testimony or some greeting. Actually they wanted to find out how good I was. They wanted to test me. A polite way of testing is to ask, "Will you come and speak a few words to the congregation?" So when you are given the opportunity, I want you to know that is your test. I didn't know at that time it was my test.

Anyway, I was given that test. I remember very distinctly that I said that I am proud of myself even now. I am a major, a proud officer in the Korean Army, coming out of the Korean West Point, seasoned in war, decorated heavily, and so forth. But now I join your army as a private. I hope within six months I can be promoted to PFC, private first class, when I am able to teach the Divine Principle. In the Korean army, the system is very strict. The U.S. army system is nothing compared to Korean army discipline. They really discipline you. When you salute, the senior officers come around and say, your eyes don't look right. They give all kinds of commands. Wash my stuff. He gives you very smelly laundry. First the cadets wash the seniors' socks. Then if they say the socks are still smelly, you get all kinds of punishment.

Anyway, I went through that system. I enjoyed it, as a matter a fact. God gave this opportunity to become a good PFC in the Unification Church so he gave me preparatory training first. So when I joined the church I gave that testimony. I said, I am not a major in this heavenly soldiers army. I am joining as a private. I will salute you like this, and I saluted with both hands. Because you are in the heavenly army, I salute with both hands. And I promise I will wash your socks, I will do any menial job. In the military the one thing you don't want to do is KP duty. KP stands for kitchen police. That means cleaning the kitchen. Dish washing. That is the worst chore. It is very difficult to do with a cheerful heart. But I did that. I washed very well.

So I said, I am going to wash your dishes, I am going to wash your socks. I will have one big bag here so I want you to put your dirty, smelly socks in it. Everybody laughed, and my bag always remained empty. Nobody put their smelly socks in it. I had no socks to wash in the Unification

Church. So I did something else. I got up very early in the morning. At that time in Korea everybody could not stay in the center because the center was too small. So I got up early and went to the church and I cleaned the floor, mopping the floor and working in the garden, and emptying the trash cans, and so forth. I really enjoyed that. I really wanted to become a private in that army. Anyway, this is the spirit that we all need.

By the way, Aidan Barry reported at the conference that Harvey Cox did come to the Boston center. Dr. Cox is a giant in the world of theology at Harvard Divinity School. He came and he actually slept on the floor in a sleeping bag. And everybody was trying to give him a special breakfast, but he said, no, I am your workshop trainee. An amazing thing is he didn't come by himself. He brought his own secretary to suffer with him. Together they listened to Aidan Barry's lecture, but they had a television program in New York the following day, Sunday, so he could not hear the conclusion. But he said he would come back for the second workshop. So that is the spirit. That is really beautiful. He is a man of greatness. Only great men can do that.

So we are all here starting out on MFT, looking forward to becoming stars of the movement. You see, to become a star of the movement is not necessarily to become president of the Unification Church of America. It is not necessarily to have a very famous name in our movement, but it is becoming one person who can be remembered in the heart of God and the heart of True Parents.

TAKE THE INITIATIVE TO LOVE GOD

For example, I told you about Rodney Edwards. He is our star now because he already occupied the important part of True Parents' heart. One time Father asked this question: "Would you like to become a person who loves God, or would you want to become a person who is loved by God?" Loving God is your action. You take the initiative. But to be loved by God is not your decision. It is God's decision. You cannot have control over that. So, Father said, you must become a person that deserves to be loved and remembered by God. God has distrust in His heart because throughout history, over and over and over, people betrayed God. People pierced God's heart over and over. We disappoint God when we say one thing and do something else. That has been the history of mankind.

There is no one more mistrusted than God. God over and over was exploited and used by man for their own selfish purpose and man kicked God out when He was not needed. That is the way God has been treated. So Father said, God is not going to trust you easily or too soon. You must demonstrate extraordinary fortitude, extraordinary loyalty, extraordinary heart toward God so that God can be 100 percent sure that you are indeed His son. You must earn His respect and admiration. Trust does not come as a gift. You must earn it. In the Unification Church you must earn it. I have no confidence that I have earned Father's trust or God's trust. I do not know whether I am loved by God. I have no confidence. Actually, I am scared because my time is running out. That does not mean I will finish my life tomorrow or the day after tomorrow. But I am not 20 or 30 years old anymore. My time on earth is ticking down. But still I do not have complete confidence I am a person who is loved by God. I am still working on it. I don't know if I earned God's trust or not or True Parents' trust. I don't know.

So what you can do is be humble and start all over again every day. Do your utmost. That is the only way we can be successful. That way you cannot fail. When you expect to be somebody and other people don't treat you like somebody, then you get hurt. You may be thinking, I am a leader, I have done this much, I have fund-raised this much, I raised $12,000 a month. I am a hero. But nobody recognizes me as a hero. Never mind—just remember Father's words. You may think you successfully sneaked out and had a nap without being noticed by anybody. You fool. The entire spirit world watched you. By the same token, you think no one knows your good deeds. You worry that the church doesn't recognize you. Your leader doesn't recognize you. Never mind. The entire spirit world saw all you did. The person who thinks he is somebody in the Unification Church has an inherent danger. That person can become a betrayer, the worst enemy of the Unification Church.

But you are not sure of yourself. You are not sure and you have the humility to go out again. That person—there is no way Satan can knock him out. There is no hope that Satan can pull him out. This is very, very important.

As you know, St. Paul is a saint who literally made history in Christianity. He is one of the cornerstones of Christianity. Some theologians call Christianity a St. Paul religion. St. Paul fashioned Christianity in a certain mode. It is true. But St. Paul suffered a great deal, going to Asia Minor and all over that part of the world. He could travel because he was a Roman citizen. He was not born in Rome, but he acquired Roman citizenship, and he really used his Roman citizenship most effectively for the benefit of God. I say the same thing to you.

You, as American citizens, should be proud of and cherish your citizenship because it gives you more chance to serve God, like St. Paul. Today American citizenship is your passport to the world, like diplomatic immunity. You American people are treated everywhere as first-class citizens.

Even in the communist world, you are free to come in. How wonderful. That is what St. Paul did. He used his Roman citizenship to travel anywhere he wanted. You can go to Czechoslovakia, Russia, Cuba, anywhere.

So that means the entire world is your stage, as it was for St. Paul, who made incredible evangelical tours over and over. Amazingly, St. Paul never became a burden on the church; he did his own fund-raising. He knitted fishing nets and sold them to earn money. And he had extraordinary evangelical success. St. Paul was, indeed, a shining figure, a hero of Christianity in the early first century.

ST. PAUL PASSED THE TEST

When Paul and Barnabas were on their first missionary tour, Paul performed a miracle, telling a man crippled from birth that he had the faith to be well, and the man stood and walked. When the crowds heard what had happened, they said that the gods had come down, and they wanted to worship Paul and Barnabas. This was a test for St. Paul. Paul, who was such a great man, could have become the worst enemy of God at that moment. He could have gone from one extreme to the other. If he became arrogant, he would become Satan at that point. If he became absolutely humble, he would remain as the son of God. St. Paul was absolutely furious. "Men, why are you doing this? We also are men, of like nature with you, and bring you good news, that you should turn from these vain things to a living God." [Acts 14:15] My brethren, what are you doing? I am just like one of you. You can touch me, I am a man, I am no different. I am as imperfect as you are. The only power is Jesus Christ, the power of God manifest. You can become the recipient of that power as much as I am. He humbled himself and gave praise to God instead of letting them honor him as a god.

The Divine Principle teaches that Satan was not always Satan. Satan was originally God's archangel, Lucifer. He was God's creation. He became Satan because of arrogance and jealousy. So arrogance and jealousy are satanic characteristics. Knowing this, we also know that no matter how hard you work, no matter how great your accomplishments are, the ultimate test comes on this one point: how humble you can be. Once arrogance creeps in, that is the end of leadership, the end of elder brothership, the end of elder sistership. So a true leader in the Unification Church is one who sacrifices and has a parental heart. No parent becomes arrogant in front of their children. No parent wants to become a showoff in front of their sons and daughters. Instead, it is a parental heart to want to be proud of their children. The parents want to applaud. Father and Mother want to be proud of their sons and daughters. That is Father's heart and Mother's heart.

We can continue our mission to ultimate success with this heart. I want you to know two things this morning. Never mind if you get recognition or not. You do have recognition in the world of spirit, which is the subject world. Yesterday, I was driving up from Washington with my son, who is going to college, and I talked about this subject. Many people think this physical world we live in is the only world in which we can enjoy life. That is a fallacy. That is a mistake. Actually we are living today in a very clumsy world. It is a world of shadow. The real world is the spiritual world, the invisible substantial world. It is not the world of ghosts. It is a substantial world, far more substantial than this world. This world is like the reflection in the mirror. I can see your face over there. The image in the mirror is life in the physical world, which is unreal compared to the spirit world.

I talked to my son about how imperfect this world is. First of all, in this world, everything decays. Everything has a temporary life. You lay railroad track, and you think that steel will last millions and millions of years, and even if it did, that is still not eternity. Compared to eternity, millions of years are as brief as a spark. Whatever you have in the world has no permanency. It will decay. How imperfect this world is.

NO SECRETS IN THE SPIRIT WORLD

I have another example. This world can lie. I can see you, but I cannot see the real you. I can see the shape of you, but I cannot see the real you, so you can lie to me. How imperfect. How clumsy it is. But in spirit world, that doesn't work. They don't see you externally. They see the real you, the permanent and eternal you. There is no way you can show off. It doesn't work. No contracts need to be signed in spirit world. No receipts need to be turned in. Boy, what a good world for that one thing alone. I am so glad we don't have to sign so many receipts upstairs. America is really becoming a paperwork country. Isn't it true? Tons and tons and tons of papers. Trying to prove you are not cheating, but so many papers showing how good you are at cheating. They are trying to hide behind a facade, a false exterior. They think they can enjoy their life because nobody sees. I have money, I have this life to enjoy, this relationship, how lucky I am. Actually, how foolish he is. That is the real truth. In the spirit world, there is no way you can lie. No way you can cheat. What you are is what you are.

So why did God create the corruptible material world? I explained that even after the Kingdom of God is established here on earth, there will be heartbreaks and joy and setbacks and heroism. Do you know why? That is the way God wants to train us, prepare us for the spirit world. In other words, this earthly world is going to permanently remain as a training ground. As God's workshop. Also, I like to give this example: This physical world is God's Ranger program.

I mentioned last Sunday, I was at Fort Benning, Georgia. There they have what they call Ranger training. You cross a river on a rope, looking down at the river, wondering if there are alligators down there ready to enjoy lunch or dinner. You are looking down and you have to cross. We don't have to do that, but we do push ourselves to go through challenging experiences. Why? Because that gives you discipline. By the same token, this whole world is like God's Ranger program. It shall remain so forever. Even after the Kingdom of God is established, and Satan is demolished, and all the wicked guys are gone, still there is emotional upheaval. Ups and downs, sorrows and setbacks, and heroism. Sacrifice shall remain.

Even when the Kingdom of Heaven comes, if somebody falls from the roof, that person will get hurt. If somebody falls in the water, he might drown. And someone will have to put themselves in danger to pull him out. There are all kinds of opportunities for heroism. Why? So that we can become mature, so that we have the capability to experience joy, the capability to appreciate sadness, the capability to get excited. Emotional, dramatic experiences are needed to mature our spirit. That is why God created this clumsy world as a Ranger training ground. So we must be deadly serious about this life. This 100 years, which is shorter than even a spark of light compared to eternity, is our opportunity to prepare for eternity. This is our chance, far greater than the California gold rush.

And I want you to know that you and I already are 99.9 percent successful. We are winners in life. Do you know why? Because of one simple fact: We met the True Parents. That is the one single factor that makes your life and my life 99.9 percent successful. All we have to do is one-tenth of one percent proving that we are steadfast and worthy to be called the sons and daughters of God. That is what God wants us to prove. It is such a minor, minor, minor role God wants you and me to play. That is our remaining homework, and there is only one simple way to fulfill it: become unconditional sons and daughters. Children of unconditional, absolute loyalty.

Many times I caution my son, who is going to Yale, a proud Ivy League university, not to become an intellectual fool. Intellectuals think they know everything. Academically, they are at the top of the world; they have all the science and philosophy they need. But actually, they know nothing. I told my son yesterday that the best the academic world can do using the inductive method of learning is just digging up—they cannot penetrate the physical world. What they are talking about makes sense as long as they are talking about this one little piece of the world. They are trying to devise what they call science and logic that works in this half of the world, which is the shadow world of this cosmos.

But scientific and academic reasoning will never penetrate the spiritual realm. It comes from God as a revelation. You must receive it. Man's wisdom will never crack the spirit world. God's wisdom we must have given to us and we must have a humble heart to receive it.

HIGHLY EDUCATED FOOLS

Many of today's scholars are so accomplished and distinguished, so great. They think they know everything. They are what we call intellectual fools. We must not become intellectual fools. There are distinguished professors at Harvard and Yale and Princeton, and I bet you dollars to donuts, that many of them will end up in hell because the arrogant never open their hearts to accept a greater truth than the one they know.

The academic community is fine, but they need real humility so that they are ready to receive God's revelation. The real truth comes as a revelation, not as a research paper. No institute will produce the real truth. God's revelation is greater than all those professors. The quality you need is humility, or good luck. We are lucky guys really. You and I are lucky because we got to hear and accept that revelation. So, I want you to become unconditional. Who can become the best disciple of Jesus? Once they recognized who Jesus was, the disciple who became unconditional was successful. Like Peter. Peter was not an intellectual person, he was almost dumb in a way, but he had true wisdom.

On the other hand, Judas Iscariot was a very smart man. He was trying to reason everything Jesus did, and he was the one who had charge of the treasury. One time a woman, Mary of Bethany, used expensive oil to anoint Jesus' feet. Judas objected, saying, Why do you waste such expensive oil? Why don't you go to the marketplace and sell it and give the money to the poor? He thought he was a spokesman for Jesus, but Jesus scolded him, saying, "The poor you will always have with you, but you do not always have me." [John 12:8] You can always have charity, but the son of man is here on earth just once.

Jesus approved that woman's loving act. Jesus said, she is right. That is what we need. Judas was very intellectual and looked at Jesus' deeds very critically, which led him into his betrayal. Later he was taken by evil spiritual forces and he betrayed Jesus; his conscience hurt him, and he killed himself. He did not betray Jesus for those famous 30 pieces of silver. No. It was not the money. He was the treasurer and had access to money anyway. No, he betrayed Jesus because he doubted his messiahship.

So we must not also become intellectual fools. There are many ex-Moonies out there. They talk about how this is wrong and that is wrong in the church. Of course, they can think of a thousand things wrong with the Unification Church, trying to justify themselves. But I bet you that their heart, their conscience knows that those who persist in the church are right. They know they are defeated. But they are trying to justify themselves. It does not work; particularly in the eternal world it does not work.

Today what we need is total commitment. I don't mean 99.9 percent or 99.9999 percent. But the last penny of our energy, our emotion, our love, our physical strength, our sweat and blood. This is my earnest testimony. After following Father for 20 years, I know I am in the right place. I am fortunate. Nothing I have can repay this fortune. And I know one thing, I haven't got to heaven yet. I am still working on it. Don't be boastful. Don't be arrogant. Be ready and willing to give your last penny. That is my testimony, that is my lesson. And I hope this testimony helps you to succeed together. Not for our sake, but for the sake of God and True Parents, for the sake of the Kingdom of Heaven here on earth. Let us pray.

Prayer by Bo Hi Pak:

Our loving Heavenly Father. Thank you very much for this special morning. Beautiful morning. We have the joy of gathering together with our brothers and sisters with whom we share a common goal. One goal and one purpose. We are in a different body, but we are one. Because our heart is one. Our purpose is one. Our goal is one. Our center is one. Our country is one. Our kingdom is one. Father, thank you. We want to expand this one kingdom, one heart, one God, one True Parents to the entire world. We want to expand it so that everyone, every single soul here on earth, can share that joy and that awareness and commitment. Father, thank you very much for this noble teaching of your Divine Principle. Thank you that people like us, trivial, unworthy, could somehow be hand-picked by you so we could come to this knowledge of the Principle so quickly. We thank you. We want to deserve that right. We want to preserve that right. Thank you, Father. Thank you. September is an important month. Father, until we meet True Parents here once again, to hear him give us the wonderful word of God, we want to show him also, prepare for him also, the wonderful result. The victorious result. And this week we go out and make our own preparation, our own distinguished conclusion to show Father. So be with us all the way. All these things we pray in the name of our most beloved True Parents. Amen.

WE ARE PETERS

━━━━━━━━━━━━━━━━━━━━━━━━

At this Belvedere service, Dr. Pak asks several members to give their testimonies. He then gives a sermon based on the Bible story of Peter, who denied Jesus, repented, and became the rock of faith for the Christian Church. He draws a powerful correlation between Peter's situation and our own and inspires members to transform their negativity into positivity and faith.

Good morning, Father. Good morning, Mother. Good morning, brothers and sisters. And good morning, little sister Linda. One time one sister told me that she happened to sit near Linda and she was so tired that she was dozing during Father's speech. Linda said, "Wake up." Knowing that little Linda was waking her up was the most embarrassing moment she had ever had. Ever since she is determined never to get sleepy during Father's speech. Once again, as the saying goes, "a little child shall lead them."

I have great respect for little children. They are so pure and genuine, so beautiful, and that is the one reason that I really fell in love with the Little Angels and worked with them for 10 years. It was a great pleasure and fortune, working with the children. Jesus one time said, unless you are like a child you will not be admitted into the kingdom of heaven.

When people get older, like we are, we put on certain layers, and the purity and genuineness get lost somehow. Superficiality and hypocrisy grow and that is the nature of the adult. Unless we go back to the nature of a child who has absolutely no hypocrisy, no superficiality, we cannot be admitted into the kingdom of heaven. Yes, a child makes a mistake sometimes, but they don't want to hide it. They let it be known. They are helpless out there when they make a blunder. When they are in pain, they cry. When they are hungry, they search for food. They express genuinely and purely their inward state of mind. That is a child. The first thing we must learn about the kingdom of heaven is to become like a child. That is very true. It is a great and admirable thing that a child like Linda comes here.

TO SEE HIM IS TO HEAR HIM

Even many of our brothers and sisters are missing today. Maybe there was some transportation problem because of the especially cold weather. In any case, many brothers and sisters aren't here today. We always expect people to fill up upstairs and overflow downstairs, and we feel sorry that brothers and sisters downstairs listening to Father miss a lot of the message, because many times 50 percent of Father's message is in his facial expression and body language. So that 50 percent I can't translate and I don't have to translate because you can see Father's meaning, right? But downstairs, they can't see Father, unless they all have some special medium of communication. I really do not like brothers and sisters to have to listen to Father without seeing his face. It has no spirit, like a can of beer left open for three days. It doesn't sound right, doesn't taste right.

So, therefore, our wonderful brothers in Belvedere and East Garden staff bought a new tent so we can open up this door, move this platform over there, then Father can see through to the entire congregation. There is no more basement seating from this moment on. This morning we don't have to even open up the door, and there is no one downstairs. You come such a long distance so early in the morning to really get inspired by Father's spirit. You want to go out and produce. If that is the purpose for coming to Belvedere, then you must come to the main floor, later on in the tent, so that you can have eyeball to eyeball conversation with Father. When Father speaks, I want you all to really stare at Father. This is very important. Actually, you are not hearing Father's message, or for that matter any music or any conversation, by ears alone. We hear by our eyes. Unless your eyes are directed toward the person, you never hear him truly. This is an amazing thing.

Here's a very good test. When you go to bed and people are making noise in the same room and you don't want to be disturbed, do you stop up your ears? You don't have to do that. All you have to do is close your eyes. Then you no longer hear. Amazing, isn't it? When you close your eyes, you have already closed your ears. So when you are deep in sleep, snoring, you might not even hear a bomb go off right next to you. Somebody might kick you or trip over you and you don't feel a thing.

So all you have to do to close your ears is to close your eyes. When your eyes are closed, your ears are automatically closed. Therefore, the opposite is also true. When your eyes are open and staring right at the speaker, then you are really listening and understanding that message. Please, this is very important in our movement. So, I want to use this new discovery. I am not going to patent it. I will give it to you free. Use it, tell everybody. You are listening to me with your eyes. So I want you to give me your eyes this morning, and I will give you my eyes.

Whenever Father is away for a few days, I normally come here to Belvedere to take his place, which is a very difficult job to do. Therefore, I want to give you an opportunity to hear testimonies from brothers and sisters. The most powerful thing in this world, particularly in our movement, is testimony. In the early church in Korea, when there were only a handful of people in our entire church congregation, when we gathered together, we did three things: pray, sing, and share testimony. Testimony is one of the most powerful things you can receive. You can share another person's experience through hearing their testimony.

You may feel that you are not adequate as a lecturer of the Divine Principle. Don't worry, at least you can tell your own story. Nothing is more believable than your own testimony because it is taken out of your own experience. Not theory, not philosophy, but your own life. It is your own discovery of who True Parents are to you. That is the most powerful thing under the sun.

So I want you to train yourself to give your testimony. Win over new people. You start out with your own life. People are interested in other people. Human behavior is very fascinating. We are always interested in somebody else. *The Washington Post* and the *New York Times* are great papers, but not everyone reads those papers even if they are available in their town. Do you know what they read? They read the local newspaper. Do you know why? The main reason is that they want to know what people in their neighborhoods are doing. What Joe is doing, what their mayor is doing, what Susan is doing, who died, who was born, who was married. People are very interested in all human events.

JOIN THE UNIFICATION ARMY

The U.S. Army, after a long analysis of human behavior, created a new slogan to enlist new army people: "Join people who join the Army." In other words, they describe the Army as people. Good people want to come and join people who join the Army. That is Unification power, too. We are actually saying, join people who join the Unification Church. How would you like that? Join people who join Reverend Moon. All we have to do is testify who Reverend Moon is, then let them know there are wonderful people you can be a part of.

That is the way it goes. So testimony is very important. I would like to ask one brother and one sister this morning to come out and say a few words. One brother already raised his hand. I would like to have two sisters. One western sister, one Japanese sister. We will start out with the brother.

[Dr. Pak continues after one testimony.]

Brother James spoke to us without any preparation, but I know you enjoyed it because he is so genuine. His testimony came right out of his heart. One day in Washington a young black brother, maybe 16 or 17 years old, wanted to witness. So we gave him a chance to come speak to us. Oh, he really wanted to speak. He was standing in front of everybody, but he didn't know what to say. He was just shaking and saying, "it is just great, it is just wonderful" about a hundred times. Everyone was very inspired. It doesn't take so many words. I said what a great sermon he delivered. I really admired him because he was so genuine. You could see he was totally intoxicated in the love of God, just as you could see James is in love with God. You see that he is really living in intoxication. He is drunk, literally drunk with God.

That is what we need. Then everything will come naturally. God will tell you what to do. This is why the Bible says, don't worry about what to say; just go with the right mind, right heart. Eloquent speech is not going to bring the people, but love will. People understand love. People know instantly if this person is loving me, if this person is caring for me. You know in your heart you care for him. You love him. There is the communication. That is the most powerful thing. You can stay up all night writing an eloquent speech, but that will not bring members. That will not inspire people.

That is now the state of the churches. They even prepare their prayers, don't they? In other words, they read the prayers. All night they use the dictionary, look in an encyclopedia, and check what St. Peter said, what

St. Paul said, trying to make up beautiful pages of prayers. And the next morning they read the prayer, because they cannot rely on their heart or their own conviction. They cannot rely on their own confidence and love with God. They have to rely on knowledge. In our church, you know we never prepare written prayers. We see God, close our eyes, see the face of True Parents. Then you know what to say. Maybe the grammar is poor, maybe the language is poor, but the prayer is real and powerful. That is the way it goes. Now I would like to hear the sister's testimony.

[Dr. Pak continues after a Japanese sister's testimony.]

Did you speak English when you first came from Japan? How many years ago did you come? Yankee Stadium time, which was 1976. At that time did you speak English? She came from Japan for the Yankee Stadium campaign. She really looked like a typical Japanese lady, and she did not speak English when she came, but ever since Yankee Stadium she has been learning. Listening to awkward English, Japanese-style English, really has a fresh feeling. Testimony is an amazing thing. Why did I want a Japanese sister to talk to you? Because I want to show you that not only eloquent language has power. The language of heart, genuine, with true expression is powerful. That moves other people. That is why the Japanese brothers and sisters produce more for God than anyone else even though they do not have a background in America or good language skills. They produce more in fund-raising, witnessing, organization, workshop. Why? Because they have heart even if the language is less.

[Dr. Pak continues after a sister's testimony.]

Beautiful testimony, eloquent, clear, full of heart. I really am without words.

So these are great sermons this Sunday morning. This great brother and great sisters who gave testimony this morning have given you a greater sermon than a person like me can deliver. They come right from the front-line of our mission where God works. God is not working at headquarters. God is not working in the office. God is working on the frontline; on the street corners, home church, fund-raising, MFT, and extreme frontline are where God is truly working.

This morning I would like to share with you a few thoughts. I am not going to take too much time because we really want to go out and work. However, I want you to leave with enough inspiration. So let us inspire each other so we can go out, particularly during the absence of True

Parents. This is the time we can show our maturity. Father is always telling you that you are the ones who will take over. You are the messiahs. Go ahead. Do it. Let me see it. So this is the time that we can really show that we are indeed the messiahs.

So I would like to dwell on a very important thought. My title this morning is "We Are Peters." As you know, Peter was the name of Jesus' disciple. Many people today understand that Simon Peter was the chief disciple of Jesus, but nowhere in the Bible does it say that Peter was the chief disciple. But when you read all the scriptures, Peter does seem to be the head man, the boss, the chief of staff.

WHO DO THEY SAY I AM?

What does it mean to say "We Are Peters"? Let us read the scriptures. Matthew 16:13 says, "Now when Jesus came into the district of Caesarea Philippi, he asked his disciples, 'Who do men say that the son of man is?' " In other words, who do the outside people say that I am? What do they call me? Jesus asked his disciples because, just like you going out witnessing in New York City, they were always meeting people. And the disciples answered, "Some say John the Baptist, others say Elijah, and the others Jeremiah or one of the prophets." That was their answer, but actually, the disciples were not that honest. They didn't want to say the bad things that people were saying about Jesus. What were people saying? Here is one example. Matthew 12:24 says, "It is only by Beelzebub, the prince of demons, that this man casts out demons." When Jesus performed lots of miracles, they said he was Beelzebub, which is the name for prince of demons. But that is not all. They said even worse things.

Read John 10:33, "It is not for a good work that we stone you, but for blasphemy; because you, being a man, make yourself God." People were saying, we cannot forgive you, Jesus, because you, as a man, act like God. How could you do that? That is blasphemy. You are a liar and impostor. So we are going to pick up stones and stone you to death.

Again, that is not all. You can read in John 10:20, "Many of them said, 'He has a demon, and he is mad; why listen to him?' " The people were saying Jesus is a mad man. But his disciples answered Jesus saying that people say you are Elijah. You are John the Baptist. You are Jeremiah. You are one of the prophets. But at the same time Jesus was called a prince of demons, Beelzebub, mad man, blasphemer. Think of it. The son of God, Jesus, was turned into a prince of demons.

But if at the time of Jesus there had been a *Washington Post* or a *New York Times* in Jerusalem, many more things would have been said about Jesus, I am sure. Definitely they would call him a brainwasher. Many people would say he is a demigod. Others would say he is a charlatan. They might have said he is something like Hitler, even though Hitler was not there, but something like that figure. Demon, monster. All of which today are the things that people say about Father.

Jesus came to build the kingdom of God here on earth, proclaim the word, and tell people to repent for the Kingdom of God is at hand. He was sweating day and night, just like our Father. Working and sweating and giving his entire life to lift up the world, cleanse the world, lift us up to the throne of God. Helping us receive salvation. People said to him he is a prince of demons, a blasphemer, and a mad man.

ON THIS ROCK I WILL BUILD MY CHURCH

Then Jesus goes on in Matthew 16:15-20, after hearing their answer, "but who do you say that I am?" A very critical question. Who do you say I am? What do you say about me? "Simon Peter replied, 'You are the Christ, the son of the living God.' " That was the answer of Simon Peter. "And Jesus answered him, 'Blessed are you, Simon Bar-Jona! For flesh and blood has not revealed this to you, but my Father who is in heaven. And I tell you, you are Peter, and on this rock I will build my church, and the powers of death shall not prevail against it. I will give you the keys of the kingdom of heaven, and whatever you bind on earth shall be bound in heaven, and whatever you loose on earth shall be loosed in heaven.' Then he strictly charged the disciples to tell no one that he was the Christ."

Many people today think, particularly Roman Catholics, that Jesus built the church on the person of Simon Peter. But actually, the rock means faith, the church was built on the foundation of Peter's faith in Jesus as Christ. That is the true meaning of the Bible.

Today we know what people say about Father and what the newspapers say. What do we say about Reverend Moon? What is your answer? Upon that answer the Unification Church will be built. Today many people think Reverend Moon is a good teacher, just as 2,000 years ago many people thought Jesus was a good teacher. They also thought Jesus was a prophet, and today many people say Reverend Moon is indeed a modern-day prophet. On the other hand, many people criticized Jesus; they said he was the prince of demons, and people paint Father almost as a demon. Jesus was called a blasphemer and a madman. Today people also have said that Father is a hypocrite, charlatan, and blasphemer.

But the important thing is, what do we say about Father? My confession of faith is this: Reverend Moon, Father, is indeed Christ. What is Christ? What is the definition of Christ? Christ is the person in whom the word of God is made flesh. When God created Adam, God wanted Adam to be the first Christ of mankind. Adam was supposed to be known to mankind as Adam Christ. Because of the fall of man that did not materialize. So God made His word flesh in the person of Jesus. The individual named Jesus became Christ. So we call him Jesus Christ.

However, the consummation of the mission of Adam was not seen 2,000 years ago. Therefore, the Bible prophesied there would be another coming of the Messiah. That person who comes to complete the mission of Jesus is the Christ. I am not asking you to accept my answer, but this is my confession, just like Peter's. Father is the Christ, the word of God made flesh.

These things cannot be taught. This confession must come as your hard-won realization. Father would never say to you that he is the Christ. I never heard Father say this. And did you know that Jesus himself never outright proclaimed, I am the Christ? In the entire Bible, Jesus never said it. Furthermore, Jesus never said, I am the son of God. Many times Jesus said, I will lead you to become the children of God. He never said, I am the son of God. He always said, I am the son of man. The Bible never said Jesus is the messiah. Did you know that?

THE PERFECTED ADAM

But in many places in the Bible, Jesus said he came in that capacity. For example, the last sentence we read from Matthew 16 said, "Then he strictly charged the disciples to tell no one that he was the Christ." He didn't say, I am the Christ, but he prohibited the disciples from saying it. But Jesus accepted Peter's confession of faith. This morning my confession to you, which you do not have to accept, is that Father is the Christ. And furthermore, Father is more than the son of the living God. My testimony is that Sun Myung Moon is the True Father or True Parent of mankind. In the New Testament, it is written that Jesus is the son of the living God. The Completed Testament, which is the final volume of the Bible, will say, Sun Myung Moon is the True Father of mankind, or True Parent of mankind. Another way to say it is: Sun Myung Moon is the perfected Adam.

I do believe that many of you would echo the same testimony. When Peter said, you are the son of the living God, you are the Christ, Jesus said, upon this rock I will build my church. Today, the Unification Church is built on the modern-day Peters, on the rock of faith of knowing who Father truly is. This is our privilege. Jesus at that time said the power of death shall not prevail against his church. Death has no power. By the same token, when we follow Reverend Moon in this faith, death has no power. Nothing can stop us. Upon that spirit, Christianity produced tremendous martyrs. Many people were killed because of that faith. But the power of death could not conquer them. If you have that power, that faith, if you are another Peter with that faith, then nothing, no power under the sun, can stop the spread of this movement.

That makes each one of us strong. That particular feeling made brother James, who shared his testimony today, totally intoxicated in the love of God. How can he feel the living God so strongly? Because we have something special. We have jewels, we have diamonds. No matter that other people think Father is a charlatan, a Hitler, whatever. Just like 2,000 years ago. But the followers and disciples of Jesus knew who he was. Why are we here on Sunday morning at Belvedere? Because we know something that people outside do not know. We know something that it is so precious. The power of death cannot stop it. That is why we are here.

What happened to Peter? At the time of Jesus' crucifixion, the same Peter who testified to Jesus as the son of the living God was literally scared to death. He was trembling in fear. When he was asked if he was one of the followers of Jesus, Peter said, I do not know what you mean. Then another woman in the crowd spotted Peter, saying, you were with Jesus of Nazareth. Peter denied it, saying, "I do not know the man." But yet another person said, "Certainly you are also one of them." Just as Peter denied knowing Jesus for the third time, a cock crowed, and he remembered that Jesus had predicted he would deny him. Peter came back to himself. He realized what a terrible crime he had committed. In his heart he had murdered Jesus.

At that moment Peter repented. He was so ashamed. In that dark period of his life, Peter certainly was not Peter; he was not a rock at all. He was a poor, scared individual trying to hide and stay out of danger. He was surely a bag of dirt. You know what this body is, don't you? Dirt. Just dirt. Without the spirit of God, we are reduced down to just a bag of dirt. Peter was not a Peter at all. He was not a rock at all. He was crumbling dirt.

But gradually, Peter's confession in front of Jesus came back to him. He determined to indemnify his failure. He decided to die for the cause, to die for Jesus. He wanted to die in no ordinary way so he could pay back the debt. When you read the Acts of the Apostles, Peter's faith shines out. Peter returned to his original state as Peter. He became a rock once again. He was shining out in faith, shining out in the spirit of God. Wherever he spoke, he was speaking with the authority of Christ. He inherited the spirit of Christ. He performed miracles. He healed sick people. Peter was invincible. No persecution could hold him back. Nothing outside people said or did could bother him.

If people say very negative things about Father and the Unification Church, and you lose power and become pale and totally hopeless, I want you to know that at that moment you are a chunk of dirt, not living in the spirit of Christ. But if you are living in that spirit today, just like Peter 2,000 years ago, after he found his faith again, what the outside people say will not bother you. Even more, when people say negative things about Father, it will spur you on into a greater fighting power. You can turn the negative power into positive fighting spirit. That is the way it should be. If you are in that position, you are a real Peter.

PRECIOUS BROTHERS AND SISTERS

BELVEDERE ESTATE, TARRYTOWN, NEW YORK

JUNE 4, 1978

Dr. Pak delivers this sermon in San Francisco just a few days after celebrating the second anniversary of Yankee Stadium. Using Yankee Stadium as an example, he explains that the real power and strength of the movement stems from the heart of the members themselves. He also describes his experience testifying before the Fraser committee and its effect on both America and Korea.

He testifies to the recent European Blessing of 118 Couples, and to the successful launching of the European IOWC and concludes with an exciting progress report about the Little Angels School.

Before we sit down, let us greet our True Parents. Let's see, which direction is Europe? Let's face to the east and give a loud and cordial and cheerful good morning to Father and Mother. Good morning, Father. Good morning, Mother. Good morning, everyone.

It's so nice to see you. You know I have been away too long. I almost feel like I have been away for years. Actually I have not been away that long, only for a little over one month, but I have made a complete circle of the world. I see many, many beautiful faces of our brothers and sisters here today and all the leaders are back. How are you? And familiar faces like Linda. Boy, Linda you came. Stand up and show your face; everybody wants to know you who you are. Linda, you're growing up, you lost a couple of teeth and your new teeth are growing in. Beautiful.

So here we are once again at Belvedere. I walked across the lawn to come here and truly I feel like I am coming back to heaven, coming back home, and the birds are singing, and they seem to be welcoming the coming of the Kingdom of Heaven here on earth. Truly that is my feeling. I am sure it is a beautiful time for you also when you come to Belvedere on a Sunday morning. A couple of days from now we are going to have our World Day celebration, and many preparations are going very well. So I'll be seeing you the day after tomorrow, but today primarily I am here to give you a report on what is going on in other parts of the world.

But actually there are many leaders here to report to you. Have you met Gregory Novalis from Zaire? Gregory is the missionary to Zaire where the situation is rather hot right now. However, Gregory is not here because the situation is hot, but so that he can take care of it after proper guidance. He went to the national leaders conference in San Francisco, and I am sure he gave the most heart-warming and thrilling report to our brothers and sisters. You haven't heard his report, have you? So we would like to have him give you a first-hand report, with the realistic feeling of what the front-line missionaries are doing over there.

Also our brother Mike Warder has just come back from an important international conference in the Hague and he was also in Iran. I'm sure that Mike will give us an exciting report too. So that means I must make my report rather brief, right? [No!] I have never seen such generous people as you are. Our brothers and sisters are truly generous, genuine, and pure people. Everywhere I go, that struck me, in Korea, Japan, England, all over.

A group of Korean reporters is visiting our movement here in America. However, they are not just ordinary reporters, they are the principal people behind the Korean daily newspapers. They visited our *News World* offices and our church headquarters on 43rd Street. They are coming tonight to Belvedere. Yesterday they were in Washington and they came to my home and we had a very wonderful fellowship. They want to see the real Unification Church in terms of our massiveness and strength, such as the New Yorker Hotel building, the 43rd Street building, and the Tiffany building where *The News World* is located. All these external things are indeed impressive to these Korean visitors.

REAL POWER COMES FROM MEMBERS

However, the most striking to them is not the buildings or the size of the movement, but what ordinary individual members are giving them without even knowing it. We are not consciously working to create a good image or propaganda for them. We are just living the regular Moonie's life, but they are struck by every aspect of that life. For example, they came to the World Mission Center and saw our brothers and sisters going out so early in the morning with heavy bundles of newspapers. They all have shining faces and are singing and humming songs. These Korean publishers just couldn't believe it. Where do you get your energy, they asked. How can you do all those things? They see that the real power of the Unification Church is our members.

They went to Niagara Falls, and two of our brothers were driving them all day long. These two brothers made a tremendous impact on the Korean visitors. They said, we have never seen such dedicated people; they are trying to serve us so much they make us feel awkward. These two brothers are happy to do it. One day they took everybody into a drug store, and the employees asked them where they were from. Are you Japanese? Well, these Korean visitors don't speak much English, so our young brothers stepped forward and said, no, they are Korean. And they began giving the employees a lecture on Korea and where it is and its history. And of course, the conclusion of their testimony on Korea included the name of Reverend Sun Myung Moon. The Korean visitors were utterly amazed; they almost had tears in their eyes. We Koreans could not speak with such power and pride about our country, but this American brother spoke up for Korea with strength and pride and hope. This made a deep impact on them.

This is our daily life. But every day of our life is a shining one. Sometime you feel tired, sluggish, discouraged; and so do I. Yes, we are all human beings. Yet we have an inner strength that will never let us down, the spirit of a Unificationist.

These Korean visitors came to my home in Washington and had a Korean supper with kim chee and everything. I knew that they are not particularly religious, probably not Christians. They are reporters, so I have to treat them rather casually. Of course, I have a big picture of Father in my living room, let them see it, and a big picture of our Mother on another wall, let them see it. But I didn't plan to say too much; I wanted them to enjoy their dinner. So they served themselves their dinner buffet-style, but they didn't start to eat, so I said, please, go ahead and eat. No, they said, Mr. Pak [Joong Hyun Pak of Performing Arts who was their guide] brainwashed us that we must pray before we eat. Boy, that was absolutely fascinating to me. So we prayed in the name of our True Parents. They said they are half-way through their tour schedule, so they are only half-way Moonies now, but by the time they say goodbye in Los Angeles, they are going to sign applications to be members of the Unification Church.

That is the real power, the real strength of the Unification Church. Wherever we go, it is the little things that come out of our deep innermost heart. The power is so strong the people outside can't understand. That is why they are saying we are crazy and brainwashed.

You know a couple of days ago we celebrated the second anniversary of Yankee Stadium. Of course, Yankee Stadium was not the largest of all rallies we've done—Washington Monument was the greatest rally. However, in the history of the Unification Church, Yankee Stadium is unforgettable. Yankee Stadium showed clearly our true desire to serve God and the courage and undaunted spirit of the Unification Church.

WHY, GOD?

I was in San Francisco with Reverend Kwak, Mr. Salonen, and Mr. Kamiyama for a conference, and we celebrated the Yankee Stadium anniversary in San Francisco. When I prayed at Pledge service, the tears just started pouring out. The memories of Yankee Stadium were so vivid, particularly when the rain and storm struck about 5:45, just about the time people would be leaving their homes to come to Yankee Stadium. The rain and wind washed away and ripped apart all the decorations. I am sure you have seen the videotape of all the incredible things that happened. It was like the end of the world. It became totally black and dark. We were asking, God, why is this happening? We are doing so much for you, our Heavenly Father, why couldn't you give us good weather? Why do you have to punish us in this manner with stormy weather? For a moment, everybody was thinking like that.

But the beauty and the power were immediately manifested. We were not defeated by the rain. We were not defeated by all these incredible happenings. In the pouring rain, our brothers and sisters, with flags in both hands, soaking wet, began singing out "You Are My Sunshine" from the bottom of our hearts and with all our might. That was the most beautiful song and perfect for that occasion. "You are my sunshine, my only sunshine." We were pleading with God, not in complaint, not in protest, but in joy and power, showing Father we will prove ourselves under any circumstances. This is tough but we are not going to be defeated by this test.

Every single member was standing in the rain, singing out—the band, the leaders, all the spectators, visitors from Korea and Japan and all over, forgetting that their beautiful clothes were getting wet; they didn't care. They never saw such a marvelous thing. I was half laughing, half crying. I don't think anyone could tell if I was laughing or crying, my emotions were so mixed. I was crying not so much because of the rain, but because of the joy of seeing the true strength of the Unification Church. I told God, Father, with these brothers and sisters we know we can turn the world upside down and right side up. We know we can fulfill your will. We know we will never let you down. God, thank you for giving us such strength and such precious brothers and sisters. That was the real reason for crying, not the weather.

That was Yankee Stadium. The real power of the Unification Church manifests itself when the chips are down, when there are crises, when everybody else takes cover, when everybody is trying to save their own skin. Unification members want to give their lives—that is the difference. As long as we have that spirit, no power under the sun can stop this movement. That spirit was so heavenly and so beautifully manifested in Yankee Stadium. When I was called to the Fraser committee, I wanted to have that same spirit. I wanted to represent you and True Parents. We are going courageously forward to make sure justice is done. That is the spirit.

Also, when I think of Yankee Stadium, I remember the courageous leadership that was demonstrated in those difficult days by Mr. Kamiyama. He was truly struggling from morning to night, crying out from the bottom of his heart, and leading the entire crusade, from Madison Square Garden, to Yankee Stadium, and then Washington Monument. This is a good opportunity to give our dear brother Mr. Kamiyama a big hand.

WELCOME FOR THE FIRST TIME

After the third testimony given to the United States Congress at the Fraser committee, I had the mission to go back to Korea where I stayed about three weeks, following a most hectic schedule. But unlike any other visit in the past, this time I was truly given a whole-hearted welcome by the Korean people. I had never felt my country and my countrymen so close to me and to our Father. Why? Because of the news about the Fraser committee testimony.

You know, when I went to the Congress to give testimony, I had no idea that this would have an impact back in Korea. I didn't expect it. In my testimony, I really exploded, protesting the injustice of this unfair investigation Fraser is conducting against our movement. Also, I wanted to use that opportunity to testify about Father. Finally, I wanted to defend Korea from the providential point of view, not so much the political or economic point of view. I see Korea from a providential viewpoint, as a Unification church member more than as a Korean. So actually all I did was testify with religious conviction and fervor, but the Korean people could care less that

that was given in religious fervor. What they were truly grateful for is that one Korean man stood up fearlessly. That really struck them. At last, they felt they have a champion. They realized that champion is the Unification Church, and that spirit is the spirit of Reverend Moon.

I never expected such a cordial welcome. My arrival in Korea was announced all over the radio. I had intended to go back to Korea very quietly. My purpose was to slip into the country to do a special mission for our movement. Here I was in the middle of my testimony, and I didn't want the Fraser committee or the American media to think I was trying to create some fanfare. But a reporter recognized me at the airport, and pretty soon the radio was announcing that Bo Hi Pak was coming home.

Also, I was scheduled to leave Korea on May 18, but I changed the day so I could fly to London. You know who I wanted to see there, right? True Father. So I actually was leaving on May 19, but through the grapevine everyone knew that I was leaving on May 18, and on the night of May 18, the radio and television were announcing that Bo Hi Pak had left for the United States. I heard that I had left, but I was still there.

FRIENDSHIP BETRAYED

You should know that the Korean people really feel betrayed at the treatment during the last two years by the American press and American government, especially by the Fraser investigation. The Korean people genuinely love America. For more than 30 years, the Korean people have been loyal, faithful friends to America. Korea was willing to sacrifice for the sake of America's cause, and a very good demonstration of their loyalty is that Korean forces fought in Vietnam together with American forces. The Korean forces were the finest forces in South Vietnam, because that is the way the Korean people wanted to say thank you to America. We fought in Vietnam, not so much for Vietnamese freedom, which was of course important, but more to stand side by side with America.

But the last two years of the so-called Koreagate investigation really tormented the Korean people. They feel betrayed. Furthermore, this situation was dramatized by the American press, especially the *Washington Post* and the *New York Times*. The genuine pure heart of the Korean people has been deeply disturbed, hurt, and saddened. Congressman Fraser is a symbol of the anti-Korean forces in America. The Korean people do not know much about the American system. They aren't familiar with the hundreds of committees in the Senate and Congress. The ethics committee was investigating Korea, and then there was the Fraser committee, and a Senate committee.

But the Korean people don't know all the individual committees. They think there is one Congress and one committee investigating Korea, headed by Fraser. He is the symbol of evil. Why did he try to hurt Korea? Why did he try to push Korea to be another Vietnam, when Korea is starting to thrive and survive in response to America's aid for the last 30 years? Korea is just about ready to say thank you to America. Look how much you have done for Korea. All the aid you gave was not in vain. America, look what we have done. Korea is like a child coming home with a Ph.D. saying, Daddy, Mommy, look what I have. You have done so much for me for so many years, and now I want to really appreciate you. Here is what I did, and now I want you to be happy. This was the kind of gratitude that Korean people want to show to America.

Then all of a sudden Korea sees America as a traitor, separating herself without any good reason. Betrayed. But there has been no spokesman who can speak up for Korea and tell America that we are not trying to harm you, we love you and together we are going to survive. Together we can be prosperous. We certainly have no notion of wanting to hurt America. On the contrary, we will do anything for you. That is Korea's true feeling. But nobody has spoken like that.

Instead, the Korean people have been further saddened by more betrayal of the Korean people, such as former Korean CIA director Kim Hyun Woo, who sold out the country to save his own skin. The Korean people are really ashamed. Other Korean betrayers are Choi Hyun Lee, Sun Myung Ho, and Kim Sung Kun. They thought that Tung Sung Park would be our spokesman and really speak out in defense of Korea. But Park was in so much trouble himself and had so many explanations to make, that even though he testified to the ethics committee, it was not really a defense of Korea. That is why the Korean people say they are all getting ulcers.

Then Fraser called me to testify. The Korean people were hoping that Fraser had finally made a mistake, calling a Moonie to testify. Fraser probably thought he had another Korean to make fun of, another Korean who would betray his country and maybe say the Korean government is a dictatorship. Fraser was hoping that I would try to prove the innocence of the Unification Church by criticizing the Korean government. The best way to defend the Unification Church is to testify against the Korean government, right?

FRASER'S MISTAKE

But Fraser didn't understand the Moonie position. What I have testified to the committee you already know, so I am not going to repeat it. However, the reaction in Korea to my testimony was astonishing. They said, you saved millions and millions of dollars in health care by curing the Korean people of their ulcers. In the Unification Church they found their spokesman. This wasn't by any of my effort, but God's. No matter how hard I worked to create such a situation, it would not happen.

Some portion of the testimony was aired in Korea over public television. Every word I spoke was a bitter denunciation of Fraser's motivation and showing what Korea is trying to do and what Reverend Sun Myung Moon is trying to do in America. The Korean people were intensely united in the spirit of the testimony.

At the hearing, there was a great deal of fighting over time, particularly the second and third testimonies. Mr. Fraser said, Mr. Pak, you are not going to deliver a speech. You are here to answer my questions. I said, Mr. Chairman, unless you give me a chance to deliver our side of the truth, I will not answer your questions. That was a very heated battle. Then Mr. Fraser said, no, leave your speech here and I will put it into the *Congressional Record*. But I said, Mr. Chairman, you can print the sentences of my testimony but you cannot print my feeling, my agony, my soul, my anguish. Those things cannot be translated into letters. It cannot just go into the book. You must hear it with your own ears. Then Fraser said, no, you are not going to make a speech. I insisted, no, I'm not going to answer any questions. Then he said, I'll give you five minutes. I said, no, I need 19 minutes, 45 seconds. Fraser said, no, you can't have 19; how about 10 minutes? I said, no, sir, 19 minutes, 45 seconds.

Well, Fraser just didn't know what to do. He was very nervous. He could very well have said, get out of here or you are in contempt of Congress. But he couldn't say that because all I was trying to do was make a speech. This is the nation that guarantees freedom of speech, isn't that right? I was standing on my constitutional right. So he said, all right, Mr. Pak, you turn on your stop watch; you have 15 minutes. When he said 15 minutes, I knew he couldn't stop me. Even if I went over 15 minutes, he couldn't stop me. So I looked at the clock and started reading the testimony.

THE NATION HELD ITS BREATH

The Korean people heard this conversation with Fraser. They never saw such a battle. I started reading, but the speech was almost 20 minutes long and I had to reduce it to 15 minutes, so I was reading it speedily. The Korean people's hearts were palpitating, hoping I could do it in 15 minutes, hoping Fraser wouldn't stop me. They did not understand everything I was saying, because I was speaking in English, and the Korean translation was trying to keep up with my rapid English. Their hearts were choked and they couldn't breathe very well. Then came the point when I was raising my voice, accusing Fraser as an instrument of the devil and calling him a persecutor. "Do you think history will remember you as the champion of the human rights? No, you shall be remembered as the worst persecutor in history—if history remembers you at all." At that moment I couldn't help but burst into tears. And the television showed that, so all the Koreans burst into tears.

At that moment, the barrier between the Korean people and the Unification movement was broken down. All were one. Our cause is Korea's cause, Korea's cause is our cause.

Our Father and our True Parents have been striving for that unity for the last 30 years, but the Korean people for a long time misunderstood our Father. Father's image with the Korean people was bad because they do not know him. And for all that time our Father poured out his sweat, heart, and tears for the sake of the Korean people because Korea is important for the dispensation. But our people didn't appreciate Father's work. It's like the image of the Unification Church has been hidden behind a veil, but that veil has been removed. Now we can see each other clearly face to face. They can see for the first time the true image of the Unification Church. Wow, Reverend Moon is getting so much opposition in America and elsewhere. They didn't understand the reason. They thought the Unification movement might hurt our national cause. But now they have come to realize the Unification Church is standing up for freedom and for the strong anti-communist Korea because of our belief in God. We have waited for this understanding. It is God's gift.

So this time when I came to Korea, I went to visit some dignitaries, influential people. Normally, as soon as I sit down, I show my respect and start to speak, giving many explanations. Yes, we are doing this. Yes, this is our genuine intention. Our movement is booming in this way. Our movement plan is going in this way. Reverend Moon is doing this in America and so forth. Look at this picture, look at this publication, look at this document. That is the way I am a salesman of our movement every time I go back to Korea. But this time was different. As soon as I walked in, they came to the door saying, sit down, sit down, don't speak, just let me speak to you. So I said, yes, what would you like to say? Then they said they feel wonderful, that their hearts are lighter and their ulcers are gone. So all I had to say was yes, yes, yes, and, in the end, thank you very much. That's all.

According to the Divine Principle, you know how important it is that we be recognized by the people of the world, particularly Korea, Japan, and here in America, the three providential nations. So when I went to Washington to give testimony before Congress, I didn't know what would happen. But I knew one thing: I would not shame our True Parents. As Jesus said, those who try to save their own life will lose it and those who lose their own life for my sake will find it. That is how we are living our daily life. That is what we are practicing. We want to give our life. That is our credo. There are many churches here on earth, but no church is trying to live up to that one line of Jesus' teaching like the Unification Church is. Yes, as the Bible says, he who will live like this is always the victor. If you try to save your own skin, it will bring you a greater setback and greater debt. This is our way of life and we want to perfect it.

The other day I spoke to national leaders in San Francisco and asked them, what is the real strength and power of the Unification Church? It is that we are the people who overcome the fear of death. For us, eternal life has started. We are not waiting to die to start eternal life. Our physical body will someday transform itself and go back to the earth, but our spirit body goes on for eternal life. What the world commonly calls death is a mere process of life. So eventually we'll return this body to nature, and then the real you will take off.

Right now that spirit man is within you. You are two persons, one I can see with my physical eyes, but the really beautiful you can't be seen with physical eyes. I tell you, the spirit bodies of the Unification Church members are real beauties; every single one of you can win the Miss America contest, spiritually speaking. As long as we live up to True Parents' direction and the Divine Principle way of life, we cannot help but be the best-looking man and the best-looking woman in our spiritual form. You may look miserable and pale and weak and sick, because of your hard work and suffering, but I tell you, your spiritual body is shining like the sun. When you reach the divine spirit stage, you shall be shining like the sun. Yes, ours is a beautiful life. It is not an easy or comfortable life, but I tell you it is a great life. Hang on to it; don't give it up until you get the real reward. The reward is a million times greater than what you have done for God.

That is why, to increase your reward, God sometimes allows you to go through pain. A great philosopher said that genius is the infinite capacity to swallow pain. I'm sure that Thomas Edison must have swallowed a great deal of pain, lack of sleep, and hard work. Unification Church members are expanding our capacity to swallow pain. That makes you great, that is our real greatness. Once you accept the Divine Principle, once you know who the True Parents are, then you need one more virtue to be successful—perseverance. This is my way of saying: hang on. Many times we are tempted to let go of the rope for a little while and have a little rest. Don't even think of it. Once you release it, you can never come back to that particular point later. Hang on to it. That is the secret of success.

THE EUROPEAN BLESSING

Now let me speak about London a little bit. You want to hear what Father is doing, right? Father went to London to give the long overdue Blessing to the European family. Father has not been in Europe for four years, so you know how the European family has been waiting for the coming of Father. They have been waiting and praying and praying and praying. This time that prayer was answered. Father felt strongly pulled spiritually to fulfill the responsibility in Europe. The first thing Father did is gather together the potential brides and grooms and match them. On May 21, 1978, in London in our church auditorium, 118 couples were selected, matched, engaged, and Blessed.

Out of 118 couples, 106 were international; only 12 couples were matched with the same nationality. Most of the Germans were matched with their age-old enemy, the French. You know the Germans and the French are not that friendly. Normally when French and German people are riding in a car or bus or subway, they don't even look straight at each other or say hello. The French people are, in a way, a culturally arrogant people. They have great cultural accomplishments in sculpture, painting, music. French people are very proud people. They say, we don't want to learn English, no. You English people, you German people, you Portuguese people, if you want to come to know about French culture, you have to learn French. The French language is the most romantic language, most poetic and musical. So they say, you come to learn our culture, I am not going to learn your culture. That is how the French people are. Jean Pierre, is that true or not? Particularly they do not speak highly of Germans. They say the Germans are a war-mongering people, they are aggressors, they don't know anything about art. Their life is not romantic, they are like machines.

So Father thought the very best couple under the sun would be the most romantic French and most mechanical German together. One German husband and French wife gave a testimony about their marriage. The French woman said, Father, I thank you very much for matching me with a German. I am so glad also that I don't speak German too well, and I am so glad that my husband doesn't speak French too well. Father asked why. Well, Father, she answered, I am a very excitable and talkative person. If I spoke my husband's language, I would speak too much about everything in the first night. So I want to be slowed down. I don't even have to be slowed down because I don't know the language. Father laughed and laughed.

One couple was Norwegian matched to Norwegian. The sister stood up and said, Father, I know my husband because I have been working in the center with him, and I hated him very much. He was very mean and so uncompromising. In fund-raising or witnessing he never gave us a rest or let us come in before 9:00 at night. He was a ruthless leader and I hated him. I never in my life thought about him as my husband. But then you said, this is your husband. So then, Father, I looked at him from a different viewpoint. Father, I was amazed. I found him to be so handsome. I found him to be so perfect as my husband. I knew that I had hated him because he had been so faithful to your teaching; that is why he was harsh. He was pushing me around and he was leading the members in that fashion because he doesn't want to compromise. He wants your work to proceed. He wants to have Father's mission done. So everything he did came from his unselfish heart. So when I see him now as my husband, I feel he is the greatest of all public leaders because I know he is an unselfish person; he is absolutely loyal to you. Well, that is a great testimony. She had an entirely new outlook. When I look at him as my husband, everything is so sweet, so beautiful.

NOW I SEE THE GARDEN OF EDEN

One tall Englishman, Michael Marshall, was matched with a young Korean lady. After the marriage they went for a walk in Hyde Park. He said he had been to Hyde Park probably a million times for witnessing, but until the day he walked there with In-Ku, his new wife, he never realized Hyde Park was so gorgeous and wonderful. He never realized flowers were really dancing for us or that the sun really shines with God's grace. He never realized the birds have been singing for the sake of God's children. He said, I saw the Garden of Eden. Until now I have been blind, but the moment you gave me the Blessing and gave me my wife, I saw the Garden of Eden.

Well, I tell you, the day of the matching, everybody was tense. Almost all of them were trembling inside. Everybody was pale. They looked like they all just did a seven-day fast. But every single one of them was saying, Father, whatever you wish. Otherwise they wouldn't be there. We will obey your wish. So after all the matching was done, Father was really looking at each brother and sister. From Father's point of view, he told them, you will produce tremendous children and I am looking forward to that. Your character is like this, so your wife's character should be like this, so it is a good match. Father was really giving Father's love to each couple.

After the Holy Wine ceremony, they were in their wedding dresses and marching with flowers in the wedding procession. I have never seen European people so beautiful. The day of matching, everybody looked half-starved and I didn't see any beauty. But once they were matched and moving into the ceremonial procession, I was totally amazed and I praised God and True Parents. How beautiful our brothers and sisters are. How proud I am of them. Out of the thousands of years of European history, and many revolutions, that day of May 21 was the greatest revolution of all. Father brought the greatest revolution to Europe. He broke down the barriers between the European nations. He brought all nations together. Everybody now is proud, not as a German, not as a Frenchman, not as an Englishman. They are now proud as Europeans.

There is the United States of America, then we will have the United States of Europe, United States of Africa, United States of South America. All the nations will come together under God, like the 12 tribes coming together under Moses, and create the Kingdom of God here on earth. I can see it so clearly. We are taking steps toward that goal. So the brothers and sisters here at Belvedere today who came from Europe, do not feel that you come from Germany or France or England. You must feel that you come from Europe. Europe is in Cain's position and America is in Abel's position. True Father has come to America to work with Abel for so many years. The reason Father went to London, I want you to know this very clearly, is he wants to come to Cain, the elder brother, to restore him, give him a chance to be restored. That is the purpose.

EUROPE IS SECOND FRONTLINE

Some people might even feel in their innermost heart that Father left for Europe because America failed Father. Not at all. Father spoke to the European family this way: I have been in America because America is the Abel nation. We declared New York as the frontline. Now I can leave America for the time being because America has matured. You have grown up now. I can trust America. I am sure they can become and act like another Sun Myung Moon in America. I trust them. So I came to Europe to work with Cain, who is your elder brother, so that I can declare London as another frontline, the western frontline. Father said New York is the eastern frontline. They are the western frontline. Father is opening up two frontlines. Europe must be restored before it's too late. That is the purpose.

So now the great crusade is going on in Europe. We are going to have 1,200 IOWC members gathered in London. The Go World Brass Band is there already. Also after graduation, all the seminarians will go to London, because they are the elite of America. Father wants them to be in London. Each European nation will send one-third of their membership. The German IOWC of 140 all came to London. So people are coming from all over the world. One hundred fifty brothers and sisters are coming from Japan to London.

So now you know Father is opening up another frontline. Wherever Father goes, there will be action, that's for sure. Right? Not "peanut" action, it is a gigantic action. The small island of England will be trembling, jumping up and down, because our members day in and day out will be stamping on the ground going all over England. Father said, boy, this England is good because it is so small. We can swallow it in one morning. Each day we are going to have 3,600 people come to lecture. Each person will bring in three persons to a lecture each day. Ten o'clock lecture, 2:30 lecture, 7:00 o'clock lecture. If 1,200 people are working, you know that 3,600 people will be coming to lecture each day. There will be a 40-day campaign beginning June 1. Their goal is 5,000 new members for England. If the goal is not fulfilled, then they will go on a second 40-day, a third 40-day, till we have a 120-day campaign. European brothers and sisters are just dying to see this day. They love Father.

So I want you to act like mature children now. Don't be jealous. You have been with Father so long, and now this is the time to appreciate how precious Father is during his absence. Would you like to get behind the European brothers and sisters? You must reap the trust of Father, you must bring the true victory and deliver when he comes. When Father walked in, the European brothers and sisters were so, so happy to see Father. They wanted to touch Father. Their eyes and faces were glowing, just absolutely beautiful. Now they are going to achieve the goal.

On June 1, the 40-day campaign will start all over the world, not only in Europe, but also in Japan, Korea, all countries. So we must have a special fund-raising campaign here in America and a special witnessing campaign. We want to make a new history during this time while Father is away. Father is trusting that we are mature. When Moses was away, what did the Jewish people do in the wilderness? They didn't have too much faith. They became confused and created the golden calf and worshiped it. They were immature. Father said you are mature. You are holding the eastern frontline here in New York. We must act like mature children, and there is one way of doing it. You must feel during this period, I am Sun Myung Moon, I am Reverend Moon. Yes, this is my message. We must each become another Sun Myung Moon. So whatever you do in the morning, noon, and evening, eating, witnessing, fund-raising, you must act as a principled, responsible person. If I fail, everything fails. If I succeed, everything will succeed. The mission in New York and here in America rests upon my shoulders, not anyone else's. That feeling and that kind of responsibility will bring the ultimate results. When Father returns—I promise you Father will return—we want to show him a tremendous victory. Father, look what we have done. Look at my heavenly Ph.D. degree. Father, please accept it. That is the way we must welcome Father. Not with empty hands, not with empty words, but with results.

Speaking of the European wedding, do you know Adrienne Dellas? Those who know her, raise your hands, please. Thank you. She was here in Belvedere for many years. She was an accomplished ballerina. She joined the movement and gave up her ballet career. Divine Principle became her career, and she fund-raised and witnessed and brought many spiritual children. On Sunday mornings and at some celebrations, she served Father here in Belvedere. She danced some Korean folk dance, but she gave up her career for the sake of the Divine Principle. That was a most beautiful demonstration of her faith. She thought she was giving up her career for the sake of our True Parents, but instead True Parents gave her the most magnificent chance to be a choreographer and teacher. About two years ago she was sent to Korea to work in the Little Angels school.

I'll show you the picture of the Little Angels school where Adrienne is working. Another sister, Fran Drayton [Ichijo], went to join her. Many other sisters and brothers will go as ballet teachers or English or other language teachers. We are looking for all these. Father really wants to make this school one of the finest international institutions.

Recently, the famous Royal Ballet from London was invited to come to Korea to inaugurate one of the finest theater opera houses in Seoul. This is a national theater-type opera house, with a 4,000-seat auditorium. So the Royal Ballet came to Korea and performed one week, during which time the Royal Ballet choreographer and dance master visited other Korean dancing institutions to see if there were some good students to bring over to London to have them study in the Royal Ballet school. They visited Ehwa University, one of the largest women's universities. It is a Christian-oriented university, the one that gave our movement a really hard time. But when the Royal Ballet members saw their dance department, they said, they think they are doing ballet but, in the eyes of the Royal Ballet, it is nothing. Next they went to the National Ballet company, which is government-sponsored. They thought this was a big company, but the Royal Ballet concluded after examining them that this is not a ballet, this is a joke. So they came to the conclusion that in Korea there is no ballet. Korean people are not good at ballet. They will have to look somewhere else.

ASTONISHED BY HIGH STANDARD

So then Adrienne invited the Royal Ballet dance master to our school. They saw the young students training. The ballet master just couldn't believe his eyes in the first bar practice. He was completely astonished. This is absolutely international standard. How many years did you take to train the children like this? Adrienne said two years. He said, you have done a magnificent job. Normally the Royal Ballet school takes six years to train to that level. Then they also looked around the school and said, you have a better school than the Royal Ballet. I must take a picture and send it to the Royal Ballet school superintendent so they can create a studio like this.

To make a long story short, every student in our school was accepted by the Royal Ballet School in London. The first wave of three students is going this September. In London our church will have a separate dormitory to accommodate the students from the Little Angels school. Also, it is a very interesting coincidence that the Royal Ballet School is only a five-minute walk from our Lancaster Gate center in London. So everything worked out as God had already planned.

When this thing happened, the news spread in Korea. Adrienne became a national heroine and the Royal Ballet people said the Little Angels school is the best in all of Asia. They could not find any better school or better students in Japan or anywhere.

It is Father's goal that when you get Blessed and have children, they will be educated in your own country through elementary school. Then they can go to the Little Angels School where they can study Korean and English. Our children are going to speak three languages, your native language, Korean, and English. You Americans and British are lucky because you already are English-speaking.

One of my children is now a ballet student under Adrienne. She was born in America and joined the Little Angels after elementary school. Now she is in the third year of middle school and is speaking English and Korean perfectly. In addition, she is getting the best ballet instruction in Korea and the best Divine Principle lessons.

EXCITEMENT WITHOUT IMPURITY

Adrienne, Father said your mission is to create the heavenly dance company for the world. So we are going to have a heavenly dance company, even better than the Royal Ballet, better than the American Ballet Theatre. It will happen, within five to 10 years it will happen. The artistic world has become so sensual, so physical, in order to excite the audience. That is the kind of feeling the artistic world has today. But Adrienne firmly believes that we don't need all this physical contact. We don't need to kiss one another on stage. We can create tremendous love and warmth and the most beautiful, divine excitement and inspiration for everybody, Christian and non-Christian alike.

I believe it, because I have been traveling with the Little Angels for 10 years. The Little Angels don't have to kiss anybody to excite people. The Little Angels excite the world, but they don't have to do any naked dances. They cover themselves from tip to toe, everywhere but their faces and hands. They don't have to shake their hips. They don't have to kiss anybody. But through their dance and music they can excite the world. That is the kind of dance company and ballet world we are going to create, and Adrienne is determined to do it. It is going to happen. This is where your children are going to be educated.

We have a special language laboratory to teach them the best Korean language, so the Korean language can become your children's native language; your children will have two native languages. Your children will do very well. They can master two languages in no time. Father already has a school ready. We are going to build a dormitory now. Everybody will sleep on the floor, Korean-style. Health experts are telling us that sleeping on the hard floor is best for our health, and the heat radiating from the floor is the best form of heat. You discovered it now; we had it 5,000 years ago. In addition to our dance department, we have the best music department, painting, all the artistic areas. So our children will study one art form, painting or music or dance.

Father takes such pride, such joy in this school. I want you all to come and see it. The auditorium will be completed soon. There the Little Angels will perform for guests, heads of state, and all the dignitaries who come to our country. Let the world come to see our school. That is the plan. So we have now from kindergarten to high school. What level do we need next? University. That is why I went this time. I laid the groundwork for the university. But according to Father's instruction, we are going to have the most wonderful university established first in Korea, then Japan, then America. We have a name for the university. Can you read this? I am sure the Japanese can read all the Chinese characters. Sun Moon University. Right. This comes out of Father's name. It translates into English and makes such a perfect name.

So we have hope, our children shall be the best in every way. Your children will be born in the direct lineage of God. Your children will be born under the True Parents' blessing. That is the number one blessing to you. That is the number one revolution we are making. We are terminating the sinful lineage. We are making a new heavenly lineage where the original sin will be eradicated. Our children will be born in that heritage. But after they are born, Father has a plan to educate them right, discipline them right, so they can be great leaders of the world. This one thing alone is worth living for. Worth dying for. Worth marrying for. Our marriage itself is sanctified and dedicated to heaven. Marriage itself is our offering to God. That is the Divine Principle way of life. But you will not lose a penny because of that. Instead you will be given one blessing after another.

Adrienne came to London this time and was Blessed with an English gentleman, Michael Thornton. I traveled together with her from Korea to London, and she just couldn't eat. She said, I must keep my stomach empty so that I am mentally alert. She was trembling. She said, I don't know what kind of husband Father will give me. I trust Father, but until that is known I will not eat. She was worried that by the time we got there all the men would be sold out and she would have no one to marry. But then she said, no, that is all right too if there is no man left for me to marry. I will greet Father, I will show my love to True Parents, I will get to see his face, and I will come back to Korea. That will still be worthwhile. Boy, what faith. I don't have to marry this time. If it is God's will I will, but if it is not God's will, I'll just look at True Father to see him, what a joy to see him in person, and I go back to Korea and await another chance. That is the way she thinks. Beautiful faith. When she arrived there was a beautiful man waiting. Father already had a plan for her. I have never seen her so happy. Absolutely shining in joy. She went back to Korea with added energy to fulfill Father's wishes in the artistic world.

The day after the Royal Ballet accepted our students to go to England, the National Ballet of Korea collapsed. They heard Adrienne's students would all be going to England. All the National Ballet ballerinas enrolled in a special class with Adrienne. Adrienne had only five adult members in our dance school, but in one day, the number of students became 35; 30 new people came. They said, Adrienne, would you take me? Amazing. With the power of God amazing things can happen. I want you to know we always hope, we always expect.

My final plea to you today is to pray for our leaders. Father assigned a special leadership representative during his absence. Reverend Chung Hwan Kwak has been delegated to lead the American movement. I want you to pray for him. Reverend Kwak will be supported by two most dynamic leaders, Mr. Kamiyama and Mr. Salonen. So this trinity is going to lead the American movement. I want you to pray for them, support them, obey them, and furthermore really, really let them be Father's living representatives while Father is away.

After I finish with the Fraser committee in Washington on June 20, I will be going back to England to see Father and fulfill my duties as his special assistant. I shall be like a shuttle between the two continents, bringing Father's message and flavor to you all the time. I will also go back to Korea to fulfill other duties. I will be in and out of America, but every time I can, I will be here with you on Sunday morning.

ACTS OF THE APOSTLES

BELVEDERE ESTATE, TARRYTOWN, NEW YORK

JUNE 6, 1978

Before delivering this holiday speech, Bo Hi Pak asked True Mother for her guidance as to its content, and she instructed him to explain to the members the Principle meaning of World Day, or Day of All Things. She also asked him to tell the members to pray for and accomplish victory in Father's absence, and Dr. Pak does his usual good job of embellishing these and other points in an inspiring sermon.

Let's face in the direction of East Garden and the sun and give a big greeting. Happy World Day, Father. Happy World Day, Mother. Look up at the sky and say Happy World Day, God. Happy World Day, sun. Now face front. How about greeting the trees and birds. Happy World Day, Mr. Tree. Happy World Day, Mr. Bird. Let's sit down.

One more Happy World Day. Now say it with a whisper, don't shout it. Say, Happy World Day, my dear grass. Happy World Day to you. And Happy World Day to our great New Hope Singers.

My dear brothers and sisters, World Day 1978 is very special. We are truly celebrating this day on a global scale, having our True Mother here and True Father on the other side of the Atlantic in London. This morning we had our World Day Pledge service and Mother presided over that ceremony and gave a profound prayer. After that we talked to London and learned that this morning Father also celebrated with 7:00 a.m. Pledge service. I asked what message Father gave to the European members this morning and I received a brief summary, which I am going to share with you this morning.

Shortly before we came out here I went to Mother and asked, "Mother, won't you give us a World Day message and let me have the honor to translate for you?" Mother said, "I will delegate the job to you." Then I said, "The members really want to hear you, so what would you like me to talk about?" Then Mother gave me beautiful guidelines. Mother said, "Just as Father this morning explained about the meaning of World Day in London, you go ahead, give our brothers and sisters the Principle meaning of World Day, the Day of All Things. That is number one." Yes, Mother, what else?

Mother said, "Tell our members let's appreciate Father while he is away and let us be grown-up children of God. We have been like little children. We have been a little bit spoiled having Father in New York all the time. Sometimes we do not really appreciate having Father in New York all the time."

What else should I say? Then Mother said, "Pray hard and tell the members this is the time for victory. This is the ripened opportunity for victory. Let us win the victory before Father's return so that we can present that victory as a homecoming gift to Father."

So these are the three main messages that came from Mother this morning, and I am going to dwell on each in a little more detail. But before I go into that, I would like to say that in a few days Mother will deliver another prince or princess. Let me ask you, how many of you want to have a prince? How about a beautiful princess? Well, you are quite spoiled in the Korean tradition. So far we have five princes and four princesses. If another prince comes, it will make it six to four, and if this is a princess, it will be five to five, making it even, then we have to wait for another opportunity. In either case, it is going to be a great joy for all of us and that is the reason Mother cannot be here with you this morning physically, but she told me her spirit is with you and she asked me to tell you that she loves you all.

IN FATHER'S OWN WORDS

I would like to read from Father's World Day message last year because that will set the tone for this World Day very well. Father said this:

All of creation, including man, was made by God for a specific purpose. He did not create all things just to look at. The specific purpose was the fulfillment of His love. Even though God exists, without his Love His very existence is meaningless. In order to be a true God, He must be a God of love, and for this reason God wants to fulfill His love in His creation.

What is a true man? He is a man who is able to receive God's true love. The desire of all things surrounding mankind is to see the day when they can receive true love from true man, a recipient of God's true love. All things of creation exist to receive true love from man, while man exists to receive true love from God.

Due to man's fall, his perfection never came about. Since fallen man was never able to receive God's love, God could never fully give His love and thus fulfill perfection Himself. Man was never perfected, and as a result all nature has been unable to receive perfect love from man. God wanted to have a reciprocal relationship between Himself and all things and men. Even though His creation was completed, no relationship of true love ever emerged. In that respect, neither God nor man has been perfected.

This explains the meaning of World Day very clearly. First of all, God created all things with a capacity to feel. We humans can be happy, we can be joyful, we can be sad, we can be excited. These are what we call emotions, feelings. But do you know that all of nature has similar perceptions and feelings? For example, to a certain degree, a tree has feeling. So does a rock to a lesser degree. You know the Holy Ground rock has feeling, emotion.

Modern science has developed a certain technique to prove this. One scientist's experiment showed that nature can respond to music. He made two separate areas in a greenhouse and played music for the plants in one area. All other conditions were exactly the same: the moisture, the fertilizer, the soil condition, the seeds. Everything was precisely the same except one room had music and the other room had no music. The scientist found that the plants with music grew much faster. Apparently plants are stimulated by music. It is an amazing experiment. Then the scientist expanded the scope of the experiment. He played beautiful Beethoven in one room and in the other very noisy rock music. The amazing thing he discovered was that the plants that were exposed to Beethoven grew very rich, full, and straight. The leaves were perfectly shaped. But there were astonishing consequences in the room with rock music. The plants were very ragged, all kinds of shapes. The plants themselves looked like rock music.

I am going to write to this scientist suggesting one more experiment. Let the scientist make one more situation: play the music of the New

Hope Singers International Chorale for the plants. This would introduce one more kind of music, heavenly music. We call it heartistic music. Father introduced a new word, heartal. The Korean word is shimjung. We couldn't find such a word in English, so Father made a new one. He said shimjung is heart plus love, so heartal, and as an adjective we say heartalistic or heartistic. Heartistic relationships, heartistic fellowship, heartistic workshop. Then the rest of America will say, what did you say, and you will have a chance to explain that this is a new word made by Reverend Moon meaning heart plus love. This will lead to a new area of witnessing. So I will say to the scientists, let's introduce one more kind of music, heartistic New Hope Singers. Then we will see if that has a different effect on the plants.

HUNGRY FOR THE LOVE OF GOD

What I am trying to say here is that all things have a heart and can appreciate love. But ever since the fall of man, all of nature, all things, never truly tasted the love of God. This morning we said Happy World Day to everything. Why? There is a meaning. All things are heart-hungry or love-hungry. Romans 8:19 says, "For the creation waits with eager longing for the revealing of the sons of God." Nature has been waiting for so long, waiting for the true sons of God so they can love them, so they can channel the love of God. Romans 8:20 says, "for the creation was subjected to futility." And Romans 8:21 says, "because the creation itself will be set free from its bondage to decay and obtain the glorious liberty of the children of God." It shows nature is not only love-hungry, but all things in creation need liberation. They have been in the bondage of Satan. That liberation can be brought only by the true sons of God.

Romans 8:22-23 says, "We know that the whole creation has been groaning in travail until now; and not only the creation, but we ourselves, who have the first fruits of the spirit, groan inwardly as we wait for adoption as sons, the redemption of our bodies." After the fall, Adam and Eve, who were supposed to be lords and masters of all creation, came under the bondage of Satan. How could nature accept love that came from fallen man?

Yes, I tell you, for many thousands of years we have looked at nature with satanic eyes. Yes, that is so true. We look at nature, at all material things, from the satanic viewpoint. How many people think of God when they see something beautiful in nature? Our fallen nature makes us, when we see something beautiful like a flower, think, I want it, I wish it was mine. When we look at a delicious-looking piece of fruit, we think, I wish I could eat it. When we look at land, we think, how can I make this land into a shopping center. When we look at the beautiful rivers, how can I capitalize on the rivers for my own benefit. When we drive through the Texas farmland and see the beautiful fat cows, we see juicy Texas steaks out there. People see in that fashion. Whenever we see a beautiful fish in the pond, we think it might make a good dinner.

But you know, God created all things as a masterpiece of His art. God is waiting for His children to say: how beautiful nature is. How glorious my God is. It is my Father's creation. Look at things from the Father's point of view, God's point of view, and appreciate His art, His creation. That is the way it should be. We look at the tree. Oh, God created the tree. When you look at the bird and hear the sound of the bird, you hear God singing through the bird.

I read a book called *Life in the World Unseen*. A man who died and went to spirit world communicated with someone here on earth and asked him to write down the message from the spirit world. It is an incredible book. We can see that spirit communication is certainly powerful. I am sure this book is telling the truth. Imagination cannot create a book like that. In it, there is a vivid description of how beautiful the spirit world is, particularly Paradise. There are flowers, trees, rivers, mountains, and sky. Everything you see here on earth is there. But one thing is different. There we can communicate with nature. You can understand the tree, and the tree rejoices and embraces you. The rivers and streams give you loving care. They embrace you. You can understand the trees, the flowers, and the grass. There is communication.

That is the way God created this world as well. This world is nothing more than a mirror of spirit world. What we see here is a reflection of the spirit world. Spirit world is subject and physical world is object. Once we truly become sons of God and daughters of God, we can communicate freely with nature. We can communicate with all things God created. We can extend to them the love of God. That was the original intention.

In order to do that, what is the first requirement? What shall we do first? You and I must first become sons and daughters of God. Without transforming into sons and daughters of God, we will never be the lord over all things. We have no capacity to communicate with and appreciate and share love with nature. God has been working for this dispensation all along. Once man fell, man became deceitful and wicked, lower than nature. Therefore, in the Old Testament we can see that fallen man had to come through nature to reach God. This is why he made offerings. All things of creation became the mediators between God and man. That was the dispensation of the Old Testament.

In the New Testament era, after Jesus Christ, we were elevated into a new phase. We were given the right to become adopted sons of God. We did not have the power to be born as sons and daughters of God, but we were adopted as God's children. That is the power of the New Testament. That is why Romans 8:22 says we wait for adoption as sons and the redemption of our bodies.

MORE THAN ADOPTION

But being adopted is not the perfection of man. It is not the design and blueprint that God originally intended for man. Mankind has been looking forward to one more gigantic leap. Now, dear brothers and sisters, I tell you, you and I, whether you accept it or not, whether you feel it in your bones, have been making that gigantic historical dispensational jump with the True Parents. With the True Parents, we are opening up a new era, the Completed Testament era. The time has come for the perfection of man. And that perfection of man was pioneered by the coming of the True Parents.

I don't really know why I have been picked for this great honor. You have no idea how great a privilege it is to be included in this celebration, talking about True Parents, greeting World Day with True Parents. This is a historical day. We should be like pioneers of the old West. We should be bold because we have no way to understand the true implications of our status here this morning. None of us comprehends the gigantic meaning of this day. So, I urge you, my dear brothers and sisters, let's have faith. Let's have commitment. Let us be bold and once we are committed, let us hang on and persevere.

What is the messiah? Father has explained the meaning of the messiah. People think of the messiah as some kind of magician, some kind of superman. But actually the messiah is an ordinary human being. I will tell you why God sends the messiah as an ordinary human being. Ordinary at least in appearance, expression, and his human way of life. The messiah has to lead the world, save all of mankind, as a guide, a champion. That is the messiah. So if God sends some superman, we will know that we can't do what he does because we are not supermen. The messiah has to come as a man and give the living example of how to become perfected. Otherwise it has no meaning to ordinary fallen humans.

Suppose Jesus died on the cross as a superman who didn't feel pain. Would the shedding of his blood be so meaningful to us? Would his pain choke our hearts?

It is very difficult for many Christians to understand Jesus. For 2,000 years a great deal of harm has been done in the Christian world by elevating Jesus to God, leaving man way down in the dungeons of hell. They are satisfied to worship and look up at God and look up at the savior. They never even imagine that this gap between God and man can be closed. This makes it very difficult for this world to accept our Father, because Father did not come as a superman or a mechanical giant. Father came as a man.

Father mentions sometimes that many people today think that Jesus Christ was such a superman. Since he is God, he doesn't need a toilet, he doesn't have biological functions, he doesn't need a staircase. Why would he need to walk up to the second floor when he can fly up if he wants to or an angel can lift him up? Why does Jesus Christ need food? He is a super-man. Could he walk on water? Why certainly he can; he is a superman, the angel is lifting him, and so forth. That is the concept of the messiah.

MEANINGFUL SUFFERING

Today, you and I must realize Jesus was so great and his suffering was so meaningful because he suffered as a man, a human just like you and me. His 40-day fast was meaningful because he did it as a human. He did it as God's true human son. His blood is so precious, and he shed it for us when he died on the cross. He suffered incredible pain without complaint, and he gave himself for the sake of the sins of the world.

So when the messiah comes again, it also has to be as a human. But I tell you, in another respect he is a superman. He became a superman in spir-it. He brought to earth the way to become a perfected human, which God originally intended Adam and Eve to be. Unless the messiah comes as a perfected man here on earth, we have no hope. All these years in all of America and all over the world, we have declared the day of hope. We have had the Day of Hope Crusade all over the world. But have you ever really thought about what is hope? That hope is him. He is the one. He is the mes-siah. The man whom God sees as one with God. The man who has no sep-aration between God and himself. The man who perfected God's love here on earth, so for the first time here on earth, all of nature can sing. Finally, the Lord has come. Finally the Master has come. Finally the Master who can share the love of God with us has come here on earth.

I want you to know that before you and I ever realized that Father had come in that capacity, nature knew him first. When he came to America, America misunderstood Father. America mistreated him, but I tell you, the American land, sky, water, trees, and grass welcomed our Father in the truest sense. Many times Father told me when he opens his spiritual eyes, he sees the trees rejoicing. Flowers are dancing. The birds are really singing the joy of God. Even the rocks want to embrace Father. This Father sees. For the first time, nature throughout the whole world is experiencing lib-eration. They see the master has come.

We are not talking about some theory or philosophy. If the Unification

Church is just talking about philosophy, some kind of beautiful theory, we have no power. We are talking about a most vivid reality. Unfortunately, the reality is hidden from our eyes. It takes the truth and bold faith and commitment to understand. But this is in a way our fortune. If everybody could understand like nature does, then you and I have no place. We have no chance to show how good we are. It takes energy. We have to remove the veil between truth and reality. That is where we come in. We come in as the champions of God. There is a need for us. That is also a great blessing. Truly we are all here to understand that we are becoming the children of God through this simple Principle.

FATHER IS THE MAGNET

You know if you take a magnet and run a small piece of metal into it, then that little piece of metal becomes a magnet. That is what the Bible describes as the grafting procedure. Grafting into the true olive tree. How can you and I graft into the true olive tree, which is True Parents, so that you and I can become another messiah? We can become the True Parents of our tribe, our nation, of all people. The grafting process is simple, and we can understand it through the theory of the magnet.

We rub into Father. Yes. That is what we are doing every day. We are rubbing into Father. More and more every day. When we say rubbing into Father, it doesn't necessarily mean physical rubbing. Then Father would disappear, be rubbed away. If everybody rubs into Father, then Father will vanish. But sometimes our brothers and sisters do want to physically rub into Father. I saw that in Europe. This time when Father went to Europe, I was there. After four years the European brothers and sisters were absolutely on cloud nine. They really didn't need a staircase to go up to the second floor. They could fly up.

When Father gave a speech, there was a massive congregation assembled from all over Europe, and Father was walking down the aisle. Everybody was sitting very close together. The brothers and sisters who were within reach of Father's path stretched out their arms hoping Father would touch their hands. Father, touch me. Touch me. So Father couldn't walk too fast. It was absolutely so beautiful to behold. It reminded me of the story of Jesus and the woman who was suffering from a long illness who had no hope to be cured, but she heard about the power of Jesus. She had faith in him. She was shy, very ill and pale, and she was sitting in Jesus' path. She quietly touched the garment of Jesus when he passed by. Jesus knew someone had touched him because he felt some power and energy go out from him. So he turned around and said, who touched me? This lady had to confess; she thought she made a big mistake or did something really wrong. She was practically trembling when she said to Jesus, yes, Lord, I touched you. Jesus knew then precisely why she touched him. What a beautiful faith she had. You know what Jesus said: "My daughter, your faith has made you well." Jesus didn't say, I will heal you, or you shall have a miracle, or why did you touch me without permission. He didn't say that. He said, my daughter, your faith has made you well. The moment he made that pronouncement, her disease was gone and she was healed. Completely healed. Yes, a beautiful miracle happened. Her faith led her to touch Jesus, to rub into him.

So today it is the job of all us Moonies to rub into Father. Like small pieces of metal, let us shine ourselves vigorously on Father. Through this process, we shall become shining sons and daughters of God when we receive the Blessing from heaven, which this time occurred in Europe. As I mentioned on Sunday morning, 118 couples were given the Blessing in Europe, out of which only 12 couples were married with someone of their own nationality. One hundred six couples were married internationally. The French were shocked to marry Germans, and the Germans were shocked to marry French people. Throughout history, they don't even like to look at each other too much. But quietly, quietly, quietly, Father on May 21 helped start the greatest revolution of all in Europe. That day, by giving the Blessing to over 100 couples in international marriage all over Europe, Father literally broke down the barrier of nationality and national boundaries. There will be no more Germans, no more Frenchmen, no more Englishmen. There will be Europeans.

The other day one of our missionaries came from Zaire, Africa. You heard his report last Sunday. He talked about a spiritual group that is prepared to accept the coming of the Lord of the Second Advent. They have almost five million members in nine nations in Africa. The founder received a revelation. His son, who is succeeding him, is also spiritually open and ready to receive the revelation from God. And they were in contact with the Unification Church. They felt they had at last found the ultimate church of the universe. So they are making a tremendous overture in trying to come to New York to meet with Father. This exciting thing is coming. But other Christian missionaries in Africa—Presbyterian, Catholic, Methodist, whatever—began making accusations against Reverend Moon and the Unification Church, spreading all kinds of rumors and slanderous remarks.

ONE FAMILY OF MAN

That is what happens to all righteous men in history. Jesus was crucified because of that kind of criticism. Moses and Abraham were attacked and criticized. All the righteous men in history know how to persevere with the truth of God. All the prophets of God have been persecuted. This African spiritual group leader listened to all the accusations, trying to convince him that the Unification Church is not the one. Finally he pulled out one picture and showed the accusers. Look, that is a picture of the 1,800 couples married in Seoul, Korea. He said, these 1,800 couples are from dozens of nations all over the world, all six continents. They came to this man and they received the Blessing. Unless Reverend Moon is a man of God, why would they come? This is the most historic thing I have ever seen. All the revelations are pointing to this one family of man and this is the way to create one family of man. There is no other way, he said.

We do not know how significant all these things are, but even those people who communicate with the spirit world know what we are, what Father is, and how great the new world is that we are bringing to this earth. Many of you have received that Blessing. But my brothers and sisters, it is our path here today to become true sons and daughters of God. Not adopted sons. Not servants anymore. Christians are calling themselves servants of God. God does not want to hear that any more. God wants to hear: my Father. God has been lonely. No companionship. God is Almighty, and He can do everything by himself except enjoy the fellowship and give and take of love.

God made the Principle in such a way that even He needs someone to have give and take with. He needs someone to love. He needs someone to love Him. The day Adam and Eve fell, God fell in a way because the hope of perfected man was not in sight. God would not find for a long time the give and take relationship with His children. God really wants to hear His sons and daughters saying, my Father. You think it is humble to say, I am your servant. Is it very arrogant to say, I am your child? It is not arrogant at all. God has been waiting, lonely, longing to hear someone say, my daddy, you are my daddy. So intimate a word, daddy.

God is really a living God. Who is God? God is just like you. God feels as you feel. God looks as you look. When we look at nature and all the animals, we see beauty. Then look at the beauty of man. Among all of creation, man is supreme.

When we were in Europe, Father made a tour of a wild animal farm with Mr. Dennis Orme. We drove through and saw many, many animals. That particular animal farm has more monkeys than anywhere else I have seen. Boy, I really enjoyed it. I didn't know much about monkeys, but I really had a chance to appreciate monkeys in two ways: how closely they resemble human beings, but on the other hand how ugly they are. Boy, they look so proud. They walk so tall, their chins up, so much like human beings. But they are also so ugly. Particularly their rear ends are so red, I don't know why that is. And they have a tail. At that moment I appreciated the beauty of man compared to monkeys, which is the closest animal to man. Even though many biological functions are the same in monkeys and man, still monkeys are in the field of animal and we are in the field of human beings, entirely different. We are created with a spirit and the monkey is not, so there is a gigantic gap.

Incidentally, this African missionary told me that in Zaire they eat monkeys. That is hard for people to accept. One of our Japanese members visited Zaire and told the cook not to show him the monkey, otherwise he would not be able to eat it after it was cooked. Incredible, isn't it? There are many stories from our missionaries and some day they will all become part of the Acts of the Apostles. Entwined with humor is the beautiful power of faith they demonstrate. Anyway, one day the Japanese missionary went to the grocery store. Something he saw there made him run out. He ran home, all pale, and he went right into his room and locked the door and started to pray: Father, Father, an awful thing is happening in Africa. God, please save these people. Gregory and his wife asked him what happened. He kept crying and praying to God, saying something awful was happening in Africa, what can we do. Here in the grocery store they are selling human meat—little babies!—they are selling babies! Actually, what the brother saw was a little monkey.

GOD'S MASTERPIECE

Anyway, my main subject is to show how beautiful we are as a masterpiece of God's creation. Recently the Royal Ballet came to Korea for the opening of a big theater, and we went to see them. I really was intoxicated with the beauty of the human form of man and woman. It is so beautiful. Divine beauty. Compare that to the monkey figures I saw at the animal farm in London. It is absolutely a contrast. We need to see each other as the most perfected part of God's creation. But how many times do we appreciate it? How many times do we say to God, thank you, God, you made me this beautiful. You made me this perfect. When you look at each other, when you look at your brothers and sisters, how many times do you think, this is God's creation? My Father created her. My Father created him. Thank God we have a chance to appreciate such beauty.

Yes, this is the concept of the heavenly Blessing. Your husband is a representative of God, man's world. When you look at your husband you are supposed to see God manifested in him. The male form of God, the plus energy of the universe, is manifested as a microcosm in your husband. At the same time, the female energy of God is manifested in the form of your wife. So husband and wife together make up the total harmonized universe, total unified form of God. How many of us really appreciate each other, particularly when we get married? When husband and wife look at each other, they can see the most beautiful manifestation of the work of God, the art of God.

I said God was lonely. At the same time, God needs to receive a compliment. You need petting, don't you? You need encouragement and praise, don't you? Isn't that true? All humans are thirsty for some kind of recognition, some kind of compliment and praise. Don't we? So does God. Why? Because we are the manifestation of God. What we feel, God feels. It is very true. So God needs a compliment. So why don't you talk to God? God, my Father, how wonderful you are to create the beautiful flowers. How wonderful you are to bring us to this beautiful Belvedere today. All of you say, God, my Father, how wonderful is your creation. Everything I see here is your creation. Perfect. Your masterpiece. But the most praise goes to God when we appreciate each other. So precious. Look at your brother as the image of God. Look at your sister as the image of God. This is the heavenly concept of the Blessing, so that we can discipline ourselves and practice and experience all kinds of love here on earth. Then we will be eligible to be admitted into the kingdom of God in heaven.

You know, even though the heavenly kingdom comes here on earth, there will be pain. There will be suffering. There will be a certain amount of agony. Sadness. Joy. Excitement. As long as we live in this physical world, we cannot avoid all these things. This earth is the training ground, God's workshop, for heaven. We live here on earth to be disciplined, trained, and experience the love of God so we can truly appreciate Him. So we can mature and be admitted to the Kingdom of God in Heaven. This is the whole purpose. Otherwise we would not need this world.

It is almost like an obstacle race. God allows certain sadness, certain pain, certain accidents, and certain unfortunate things like obstacles. Each time we race over the obstacle we experience a new feeling of God. Also, we experience all kinds of love. Love of the parents, love of the mate, love of the children. We have to get experience here on earth so that we are not crippled in the Kingdom of God in heaven.

THREE STAGES OF LIFE

It is an amazing thing. I want you to know that we all are supposed to live three segments of life. One segment of life is inside the mother's womb for nine months. We live in water. We survive in the mother's womb in the bag of water. We are surrounded by water. Our universe is water, like a fish. Then we are born to this world, and we breathe air. Our atmosphere is air. So the time spent in our mother's womb is training for the next world. The baby attends a workshop inside the mother's womb to prepare to be able to breathe air in this stage of life. But this is not all. Suppose we live 100 years. After 100 years, we are going to live one more segment of life. The real world. Eternal world. Spirit world. There we breathe, not air, not water. We breathe love. Love. If you have no capacity to breathe love, if you flunk your course and your mark is "F" here on earth, if you fail to practice the art of giving and receiving love, then in the next world you are going to choke. You can't breathe that atmosphere of love. The choking people go to that place known as hell. No light. No love. They didn't live the truth. They didn't learn to love. They cannot breathe love at all.

So, my dear brothers and sisters. It is not how many citations or how much recognition you receive from the movement, from the leaders, even from True Parents. Actually, it is up to you what grade you receive in love-breathing, how prepared you are to breathe the love of God in the spirit world. We must begin to practice breathing love here on earth. The quickest way to be able to breathe the perfect love of God is to meet the True Parents. It is like a super highway. Without the Divine Principle, you would never comprehend the truth of God, the concept of the purpose of this creation. But after meeting True Parents, we have to practice the love of God.

As our True Parents keep emphasizing, the best way to understand and know God and face His love is in the circumstances of suffering. God is coming to the jungle of Zaire. Yes. Our missionaries have met God out there. The missionaries' zeal and excitement and fervor for God is so great. They indeed met God. One time I went to the MFT captains and leaders meeting with Father. Those MFT leaders are pressed and pushed all the time, and I really expected to see a tired bunch of young people who needed Father to lift them up. But as soon as I walked into the room where about 50 captains and team leaders were waiting to see Father, as soon as I stepped into that door, powerful energy came to me with the beautiful sound of singing. Of course, our Unification singing is different. We sing from the soul. This is one thing that has always impressed me, the first thing that convinced me that the Principle is the truth. I first joined the Unification Church because of the singing of the hymns in Korea. On a cold winter day a bunch of young people were gathered together on a Wednesday night and they were singing the hymns and I saw their souls living.

PLUG INTO THE SOURCE

So, brothers and sisters, we are not going to have a long time to suffer for our True Parents. The heavenly world is closer to the physical world. Amazing things are happening. I want you to know the victory has been won in the entire spirit world. The spirit world is united into one with the power of the True Parents. All we have to do is translate that victory into this world. Every day the spirit world is pushing down, and down, and down. The power of the spirit world is available to us. All we have to do is plug into it. Like an electric wire, you can plug into the source of the power: God.

That is happening in Japan. I have heard reports so many times, particularly recently with the True Parents in London. Japan is beginning a second 40-day campaign for membership. The first campaign at the outset of this year was the fund-raising campaign like you are going through now. Normally Father's goal is very high for Japan. I have never seen in history any nation or group of people break the records even beyond Father's expectation. But this year, 1978, Japan in 40 days broke the record. Father set a goal, but Japan's record went far beyond that accomplishment. That is what the Japanese brothers and sisters did.

How can they do that? The reason is very simple. The Japanese brothers and sisters, the entire movement from the president of the church down to every member of the church, honestly accept Father 100 percent. They are not wishy-washy. They take Father's direction at face value, no discounts. There is 100 percent obedience to True Parents. Just like in the time of Noah, when Noah demonstrated absolute faith in God, God used that faith as a handle to pull the world and gave the flood judgment. It is not the number. What we are talking about is the quality. Noah's family had only eight members, but they were united through the undaunted faith of Noah. For more than 100 years nobody believed him, and they laughed at him all the time saying, what kind of flood is coming. You are building an ark on top of Mount Ararat. Incredible. People laughed at him for 100 years. But Noah's faith persevered. The Day of Judgment came. Noah received the revelation and he believed it blindly, without compromise.

So it is with the Japanese members. Father gives a mandate and they take it at 100 percent face value. No compromise. All kinds of spiritual phenomena happened. Many brothers and sisters were led to make special sales, and tens of thousands of dollars were coming in every day. Then after that Father ordered the Japanese movement to work for the restoration of man, to witness. In the first 40 days of witnessing, the Japanese membership grew by 2,500 solid members. There were hundreds and hundreds of associate members.

During that time, spirit world was pushing further down everywhere. Incredible spiritual phenomena occurred. Just as we have here in America, parents were deprogramming their children, in many cases incited by the communists. One set of agitated parents who had two children in the movement, one son and one daughter, came to our church for a showdown. The mother publicly announced, I will go to the Unification Church and talk to the leader and to my son and daughter and I am going to brain-wash them out of the church.

They came, and our leader listened to her, along with her son and daughter. All were listening very sincerely. This lady was giving all kinds of abuse, making slanderous remarks and accusations. And we didn't say a word. She gave her all; then all of a sudden, she faltered, foam came from her mouth, and she fell down on the ground and that was the end of her life. Think of the shock of our people. We didn't say a word to her. We never responded to her. We listened to her. Her children were just listen-ing. She collapsed dead. Judgment, end of the world, came to her.

It would have been even worse if the son and daughter hadn't been there. We might have been charged with murder. It was that kind of situ-ation. But there was a most beautiful witness. Her son. Her daughter. In the Bible, Acts 5:1-11 describes how Ananias and his wife, Sapphira, both lied to Peter about money they were donating from the sale of a piece of prop-erty. First the husband and then the wife collapsed and died when Peter confronted them. That happened in the first century, why couldn't it hap-pen in the 20th century? It makes us fearful.

My dear brothers and sisters, God wants to love you. As soon as you become the sons and daughters of God, you will become the recipients of the love of God. You love God and you love the universe. So there are three stages of love. Father, mankind, and all things of creation. Ever since the fall of man, the connection to the three elements was broken. There was no channel of communication. It was like a body crippled. The leg and arm don't listen to the brain. The leg and arm don't even know there is a brain. It is a sad situation. But once the mediator between God and all things and between God and man appears, all communication will be restored. All the communication shall harmonize, bringing unity with the love of God.

It is our privilege. We shall become the sons and daughters. Not because we are great or smart or have Ph.D.s, but because we met the True Parents. It is our fortune. Do you understand that?

ASK GOD FOR CONTROVERSY

Every day it is the reality of Moonies here in America and all over the world that we are hit with all kinds of negativity. Our press is not that friendly. We could sue the *New York Times* for $45 million in damages, but the dam-age the *New York Times* caused cannot be translated into money. They have really done an incredible historical crime. We are practically numb from the avalanche of negative news. So I tell you today, do not ask God for an easy life. Ask God for controversy. Troublesome situations. Crises. Crises will give you a chance to prove yourself. Missionaries suffer one crisis after another in Africa, South America, the Middle East, everywhere. If there was no crisis of the War of Independence, there would not be a George Washington. If there was no crisis of the division of the country, the Civil War, there would be no Abraham Lincoln. If the Roman Empire was not attacking the Christians with persecution, there would be very little to write about in the Acts of the Apostles. That is why God is now allowing you to take the heat. It is our chance to not complain, but thank God we have this opportunity.

Crises with communists will really prove that Father is the savior of the world. You will see. Communists will bring one crisis after another. We can translate every one into our victory because we have conviction, we have faith, we have God on our side.

So today in Washington, the Fraser subcommittee is meeting right now. They have been meeting since 10:00 a.m. I don't know what they are saying but undoubtedly Fraser is saying something negative about us. About Father. About me. He was very mad at me, and I was very mad at him too. But I want you to know I never asked God to take care of Congressman Fraser. No, I didn't say that. I said, God, you gave us the opportunity to really prove how tough Moonies are. Fraser's plan is very clear. He is trying to make Reverend Moon and the Unification Church a mockery with scornful laughter in front of the American people. He wants to cash in on that particular situation for his political advantage. I can be the subject in this fight. I told God, let me handle Fraser. You just wait awhile and sit there and listen and look at how we are doing. I told Father, "Father, don't worry about Fraser. Let me take care of it."

I am sure he is going to say the nastiest things about Father. You may read all those things in the *New York Times* again, but don't worry about it. I tell you, this is an opportunity. This is really the first century of the Completed Testament Age. We are going to write this dramatic story into the Acts of the Apostles. In order to do that, we need crises. Let us take care of the crises.

You and I, with our True Parents and God in heaven, shall be an invincible force. No force under the sun can dampen or deter or even slow down our movement. Impossible. We can turn every crisis into a great victory. I want you to know that. Every crisis we can translate into God's victory and victory for our True Parents. Why? Because, as I said last Sunday, there are no forces that have power over us. We can give our life for the sake of True Parents. Young Nathan Hale in the Revolutionary War gave his life for the sake of his country. He said before he was executed, "I have but one regret, that I have only one life to give for my country." This is precisely what we Americans feel. We Koreans feel. We Japanese feel. Every time it comes to give our life on the altar of God, all we can say is we regret that there is only one life to give our True Parents.

With that kind of commitment, without guns, without cannons, without the atomic bomb, we shall become an invincible heavenly force. You know that. We don't need an atomic bomb because each one of us is becoming a spiritual atomic bomb that can shake the entire world. Let's think big. Let's look for the big goal and ruthlessly attack that goal. We shall attain it in the name of God and in the name of True Parents.

I conclude this World Day message with the 23rd Psalm, which I recite over and over. Even at the Fraser committee, it was so appropriate. Father said in London he is opening up another frontline. We are the frontline soldiers. I want to emphasize something I said last Sunday. Some of you may not have been here. Father was in Europe, but not because America failed the mission. As Mother said this morning, Father went to Europe to open up another frontline. Father trusts the American movement, trusts you and me. He knows that we are no longer children and that we can take care of this frontline. That is why he is now ready to open up another frontline in Europe with the European brothers and sisters.

The European situation is very severe. The communist takeover is imminent in many countries. Father's presence is absolutely necessary in Europe, and it is long overdue, after four years. Father spoke until 2:30 in the morning, 5:00 in the morning. Father is acting like a young man. I was really ashamed. I am 10 years younger than Father, but I could not keep up with his energy. Father is working just like a teenager. He doesn't think about the time. He forgets meals. He is really applying himself to open up another frontline. Meanwhile his attention is always on America. America is the Abel nation. Europe is the Cain nation. Father wants to help the Cain nation while the Abel nation is standing on its own feet. Father wants you to stand on your own feet. You must show Father maturity. And when Father comes back, we don't want to greet him with empty hands. We want to offer him our achievement in terms of fund-raising and membership.

College campuses in Japan used to be rampant with communist forces, but now Japan's campuses are completely occupied by our CARP students. In Tokyo alone, 50 or more Tokyo University students were coming to our center. They are working day and night trying to increase our membership in CARP in the Tokyo center. Think of it. Tokyo University is like Harvard or Yale here. The most intellectual, in a way the most selfish, young men and women are joining our movement and moving into the CARP center. It is happening all over Japan. Why not here in America? Why not?

Our brother said that in Zaire there is no room for all the new members to move in anymore. They are fund-raising, but no matter how hard they work all month, the salary is only about $50 or $60. Eighty dollars is what a well-paid executive receives in Zaire. Think of it. How fortunate you are. Now, we can translate this fortunate circumstance into a victory. We must do that now. We cannot wait. While Father is away this is a great opportunity. When Moses went away, the Jewish people created the golden calf to worship. We learned the lesson. We are mature. We are each becoming another Sun Myung Moon. Miss Sun Myung Moon. Mr. Sun Myung Moon. So when Father leaves, many more Sun Myung Moons are coming up. Wonderful. Each one of you must act as Father. When you go and play today, look at yourself as Sun Myung Moon. Greet the trees. Greet the grass. Talk to nature like Father does.

Every opportunity Father gets he goes out to sea. He likes to go to flower gardens, parks, and mountains. Why? Because Father is welcomed by nature more than he is by mankind. Man still does not know him. Nature knows him. Father would rather go to a friend, that is nature. We must make people welcome Father here in America.

So I want to close this sermon shouting out the 23rd Psalm together with you. David said that Psalm a long time ago, but even though he was close to God, he called God "Lord" and himself "subject." Those are more distant terms than "Father" and "Son," aren't they? So I want to change "Lord" into "Father" in the 23rd Psalm. Let's do it, you follow after me.

Father is my shepherd, I shall not want;
he makes me lie down in green pastures.
He leads me beside still waters;
he restores my soul.
He leads me in paths of righteousness
for his name's sake.
Even though I walk through the valley of the shadow of death,
I fear no evil;
for thou art with me;
thy rod and thy staff,
they comfort me.
Thou preparest a table before me
in the presence of my enemies;
thou anointest my head with oil,
my cup overflows.
Surely goodness and mercy shall follow me
all the days of my life;
and I shall dwell in the house of the Father
for ever.

Thank you, brothers and sisters.

Prayer by Bo Hi Pak:

Our Heavenly Father. Such a great day of joy celebrating the Day of All Things. Father, my words and knowledge and power are not adequate to truly express your feeling and the feeling of our True Parents, but You forgive me and You substitute all the shortcomings with Your own power, Your own spirit to touch every heart of our members and brothers and sisters here in this congregation and throughout the country and throughout the world. Father, thank You very much for this privilege to know You. To know True Parents, to become true sons and daughters of God. Father, we shall never let You down. We shall accomplish Your goal. Father, our life is Yours and we are at Your disposal. Father, give us any amount of crises; we shall show ourselves that we are able to overcome not only the crises, but win the greatest victory of all. Thank You, Father. Thank You for the Day of All Things celebration. As we go through the celebration, be with us all the way. All these things we pray in the name of our most beloved True Parents. Amen.

A KOREAN DEFENDS HIS COUNTRY

BELVEDERE ESTATE, TARRYTOWN, NEW YORK

JUNE 25, 1978

*Dr. Pak brings the members up to date with regard to impor-
tant providential events since his last sermon on World Day
(June 6). First he shares about the birth of Young Jin (June
22). Then he goes into detail about the successful press conference in Washington, D.C., where he announced the $30
million lawsuit against Congressman Fraser. He reads in
full the statement he made at the press conference and the
one he made to Fraser himself, giving a clear and bold
example of how to stand up proudly for our ideals.*

How are you? It seems like a long time since we met here. When was it?
The Day of All Things, June 6. Only 19 days and it seems like a long, long
time because there are so many wonderful and great things happening.
Let's count some of those wonderful things.

First of all, do you know Mother had a baby? Not an ordinary baby.
This is a super baby. Do you know his name? Young Jin. By now you know
what Jin means: march. What does Young mean? Glory. So actually his
name means "March of Glory." It is time to glorify our Heavenly Father
and True Parents. This child brought the glory of God to the world. Truly

he did. As I said, he is a super baby. He weighed 10 pounds, 3 ounces. Think of it. A baby normally weighs 5 or 6 or 7 pounds. So our baby is about double that. That is why his nickname is super baby. The height was 22 inches, although Mrs. Choi said the doctor didn't measure correctly, didn't have the legs straightened out. So he really is 24 inches. Mother brought into this world a very extraordinary blessing.

Do you know the date of his birth? June 22. The 22nd of June is a very historical day. Father left for the European crusade on April 13, which means that June 22 is the 40th day after Father's departure. You know the number 40 is significant. Also, in Washington, we gave one final big punch to Fraser on that same day. A super punch. We had a press conference. Fraser compelled me to testify a total of five times, so for the sixth time I took the initiative in the form of a press conference. We brought all the press out, and then we declared war against Congressman Fraser by announcing a $30 million lawsuit on the grounds of deprivation and violation of the constitutional rights of me and the Unification Church.

Before the press conference began, I spoke to Father in London. I wanted to hear Father's voice before I went in to meet the press. Also, I wanted Father's guidance. I was going to call Father, but actually Father called me at that particular moment. Father knows what is going on here. So Father called and I talked to him and I was so happy and ready to go. Father's final word was, "Do you know Mother went to the hospital?" No, sir, I didn't know Mother had gone this morning to deliver a baby. I felt so grateful to Heavenly Father that on the day I was going to punch Fraser's nose that a new prince was coming into the world.

Before the press conference began at 10 o'clock, I called East Garden to see if there was good news. If there was, then I could announce that hot news to the world. But since this baby is such a super baby, he took a little time to be delivered. One hour after the press conference was over we had the good news. That was the beautiful, victorious conclusion of the battle. The glory came. That is the way it should be. Glory cannot come in the middle of the battle. Glory comes after completion. So we declare the victory and based upon the victory, the glory of God can come. It is the Principle.

A SPECIAL TACTIC

So, March 22—I mean June 22. The reason I keep saying March 22 is because that was the first day I testified before the Fraser committee. So June 22 is three months after. I would like to give more report and I have more good news to share with you, but first let me dwell on this press conference a little while. You know what the press is like pretty well by now, especially the *Washington Post* and the *New York Times*. They are a different breed from the normal human species. To deal with this difficult and special species, I needed a different tactic. So I asked for advice from the *News World*.

The *News World* staff said to me, well, there must be a solution. Press people usually work till late at night and when they have to get up and attend an early morning press conference, they are not in a good mood. They dash into the room and are bombarded with speeches and papers and they don't even get a cup of coffee. There is one way to make them more friendly. Feed them. Well, I thought that was a very good idea. Also, I thought that would be courteous. We Unification Church members always feed people. Father always feeds the VIPs. Father serves banquets. Yes, Jesus fed 5,000 people. So, I decided to feed them more than five loaves and two fishes.

The announcement the press received said, "Press Breakfast and News Conference." They didn't even have to read the words "News Conference." As long as they read "Press Breakfast," they would come. We prepared a room for about 100 people to sit comfortably at the Washington Capital Hilton. We had a breakfast buffet line, beautifully organized. As usual, whatever we Unification Church members do, we do it meticulously. The room almost looked like a banquet hall.

When the press walked in, they were so surprised; they had never seen such a press conference in their lives. They had never seen a food line like that. Then they were greeted with the famous Moonie smile. They were each given a big package, the press kit, with every kind of material neatly prepared and organized for them. One of our sisters led them into the breakfast line with lots of good food, and they had coffee and sat down at the nicely set table. Then they started to read. They loved it. Something to eat, something to read, something to drink. Perfect. By 10:00, they were very comfortable. Their stomach was comfortable, their brain was comfortable because they didn't have to work that hard since the material they received was so well prepared, already digested for them. So the hostility of the press was all gone. Almost like pulling their sharp teeth. They have no teeth to bite us.

When the representative of our headquarters, Susan Rhinebolt, who always deals with the press, came, she couldn't believe her eyes. She said, "The Unification Church has conducted many press conferences, but I have never in my life seen the wolves become lambs." They were sitting quietly, like well-trained high school students, really listening. When I read my statement, they read along, going over every page with me. It was almost like a classroom.

All right, I will make that statement now. This time I have a better audience. This nine-page statement shows our church's position very clearly so you ought to know about it. You will know clearly where we stand, what kind of fight we are in, and how we should pray about it.

> Ladies and gentlemen, thank you for coming. Yesterday I completed my fifth appearance at the Fraser hearings. It was an Executive Session...

Do you know what Executive Session means? It means secret session. In other words, the doors are closed, no press, no audience. The previous meetings were public. There was an audience, our members were there, and our enemies were there. All the press, *Washington Post*, *New York Times*, everybody was there. But, all of a sudden, because Fraser was punched three times at the public meetings, he changed to Executive Session.

I fought him with the truth. I attacked with the truth. Apparently he felt very uncomfortable. In the entire history of the Congress, no congressman got that kind of pain. One of our members attended a meeting in Washington, D.C., with many high-level people. Everybody was talking about Fraser and his subcommittee. One person casually commented, "Did you hear about the little Korean man came who came before Fraser and ripped him apart?" Apparently, that little Korean man was me. I am not that little, but to Americans I guess I am little. A little Korean man came in and tore him apart. That is what he said. Amazing, that kind of talk is going around on the Hill. Anyway, Fraser decided not to give me this opportunity again, so he closed the doors.

> However, what I have said in the three previous public hearings is not secret. What took place there is already history. Today I would like to announce that the Unification Church and I, Bo Hi Pak, have jointly filed a lawsuit for $30 million against Congressman Donald M. Fraser and his investigators, Mr. Edwin H. Gragert and Mr. Martin Lewin, on the grounds of conspiracy to violate and deprive the Unification Church and me of our constitutional rights. Through this lawsuit, we are seeking a court injunction and damages to stop the abuses and violation of civil and constitutional rights of the church, its leaders, and its members. The lawsuit was filed at 9:00 a.m. this morning with the United States District Court in Washington, D.C. Copies are available for the press.

> For the last 36 months because of the investigation on Korean-American relations, which has been more a witch-hunt than a fair investigation, my honor and the safety of my family have been greatly jeopardized.

> The constitutional rights of Reverend Moon and the Unification Church have been freely invaded and violated. His safety and the safety of his family are now seriously threatened. This has been the result

of the slander, innuendo, and the premeditated character assassination of the Fraser subcommittee.

We believe that Congressman Fraser has an ulterior, hidden motive in this investigation. He is determined to destroy Reverend Moon and the Unification Church and to undermine Korean-American relations. In so doing he violated numerous laws and rules of the House of Representatives and denied the Unification Church and me our First Amendment rights. We protested again and again to no avail. Thus we have constituted this lawsuit today.

Congressman Fraser has abused the enormous government power to intimidate the powerless. He has exploited popular and sensitive issues for personal political gain by using the technique of the "big lie" and guilt by association. I am one of these victims. Reverend Moon is another. Thirty-five million Korean people, by and large, are the victims of his plot. Many Asians in this country have suffered. Yet the Unification Church members around the world are the ones who have been hit the hardest.

In the ruthless pursuit of this end, Congressman Fraser adopted the classic formula: the end justifies the means. For example, he dispatched the investigators Gragert and Lewin to the Unification Church in Washington without authorizing and issuing a search warrant. They falsely misrepresented themselves as architects and conducted a secret search of our church. When this was discovered, one of them tried to cover up their illegal conduct.

In addition, in order to pursue his hidden goal, Congressman Fraser stacked his investigative staff with people who share his predetermined commitment to getting Korea and the Unification Church.

Also there is evidence of what has been termed a reverse Korean pay-off scandal. Congressman Fraser awarded $2,000 consulting contracts to four witnesses who had given testimony detrimental to South Korea or the Unification Church. In order to investigate influence-buying here in America, he paid witnesses to testify the way he wanted them to testify.

I do not approve of influence-buying. Several Koreans have been accused of buying the influence of United States congressmen by giving them campaign contributions. Congressman Fraser has bought the testimony of several witnesses by awarding them consulting contracts. What is the difference?

Today's action by me and our church is the only alternative left for us to see that justice is done. We have pleaded, we have protested, and

343

we have petitioned over and over again, but to no avail. We have come to the point where we have to appeal to a court of law.

I have been summoned by Congressman Fraser five times to testify in the congressional hearing room. Now, I want to meet Congressman Fraser in the courtroom. It is ironic that we must bring this civil rights lawsuit against Congressman Fraser, who is supposed to be the gallant fighter for human rights and who should be regarded as the defender and guardian of the powerless, unpopular, and oppressed. After all, America is the land of justice and freedom. We believe this is the land where the powerless, unpopular, and even oppressed can still be heard and still find justice for all.

Therefore, filing this lawsuit against Congressman Fraser today marks a day of vindication for all the powerless, all the unpopular, all the oppressed. Through this lawsuit we want to bring this gross injustice to the attention of the world and bring ultimate vindication for all those who have been oppressed by the abuses of government power. This fight is not just our fight. This is a fight for what America stands for. For the sake of God and the very sake of America, our fight must prevail.

Now I would like to take a moment to give you the reason why Reverend Moon will not cooperate with the Fraser subcommittee investigation. On June 6, 1978, Congressman Fraser in his eight-page statement regarding Reverend Sun Myung Moon indicated to the press that the subpoena issued by the subcommittee called for Reverend Moon to appear on June 13. He led the reporters to believe that Reverend Moon had been expecting the subpoena, and he implied Reverend Moon might have gone to England to avoid being served.

Yet, previously his attorney had told my attorney that there was a very good chance it would not be necessary to call Reverend Moon. They promised my attorney that the subcommittee would not make any decision about calling Reverend Moon as a witness and would not issue a subpoena for Reverend Moon until after the completion of my testimony. Then why should Reverend Moon expect that he would be subpoenaed for June 13 when I was scheduled to testify on June 20? Reverend Moon has planned to conduct an evangelical tour in Europe for a long time. Reverend Moon was also scheduled to officiate, as he did, at the marriage of 118 couples on May 21, 1978.

What really happened is this. When Congressman Fraser heard Reverend Moon was in London, he issued a subpoena and quickly held a press conference to wave the subpoena in order to make it look like Reverend Moon skipped the country to avoid being served. Reverend Moon was in the United States for a solid two years while the subcommittee hearings were being held. He actually avoided going out of the country. Congressman Fraser could have subpoenaed Reverend Moon any time. He didn't. He waited until he could make the most political capital. Korea is in the news again. Congressman Fraser's Senate campaign is under way. Reverend Moon left the country and Congressman Fraser seized the chance to make a grandstand play.

I tell you, ladies and gentlemen, honestly and openly, Reverend Moon will not cooperate with such a sordid investigation. Would Pope Paul dash to Washington to answer questions about the extent and sources of the Catholic wealth? Or the charges that Catholics in America had lobbied against abortion? Would Billy Graham abandon his evangelical schedule to answer malicious, slanderous charges after Congressman Fraser had secretly conspired against him, broken his promises to him, and tried to trick him?

Our fight is a fight for principle. Reverend Moon is not a private person. He is a symbol of our church and religion. Once a religious leader becomes prey to a political opportunist, then every religion in this country is threatened. Not just Reverend Moon's church, but other Christian churches, Jewish synagogues, and Buddhist temples. We will not permit our religious leader to be dragged through the mud and accused and humiliated by the Fraser subcommittee. At stake is not only Reverend Moon's honor, but America's honor. If Reverend Moon is made to go through with this farce, then America and not Reverend Moon will have been demeaned.

What lies before us is a fundamental constitutional question. It is not a question of the Unification Church versus Congress, but rather a question of the Constitution versus misguided Congress.

Is Reverend Moon trying to hide from giving testimony? Just reflect for a moment. Would he have voluntarily testified before the Securities and Exchange Commission if he were hiding from giving testimony? No. It is this subcommittee and its bias and intolerable abuses that Reverend Moon must oppose. We will not permit Congressman Fraser to stage his Senate campaign at the expense of our religion.

Reverend Moon just might consider accepting the subpoena under one condition: They issue a subpoena to Pope Paul, Billy Graham, Oral Roberts, Robert Schuller, the head of the Mormans, the Baptists, Jews, Methodists, Lutherans, and many others. Why? Because Reverend Moon has done nothing more to deserve a subpoena than any of these great religious leaders. If the subcommittee thinks they deserve a subpoena, then perhaps Reverend Moon will consider the subpoena of him. In fact, he would then insist on one. He would not allow these great religious leaders to be persecuted without coming to their aid.

Yet if they call Reverend Moon because his activities are political, then they must call each of these religious leaders. Reverend Moon's activities are far less political than any of these great religious leaders in this country.

You know it is so true. Look at this, I have a newspaper clipping here. *New York Times*, June 15, 1978: "Certain Baptists call for arms limit." That is political. That is really political. Then it said, "In another action, the convention adopted the declaration that urges Southern Baptists to be committed to political action on behalf of human rights." That is political. They are all doing things like this. The Unification Church is far less political. I am so mad. What kind of double standard is that?

If the subcommittee calls Reverend Moon because his church is engaged in business, then they must call each of the great religious leaders. Reverend Moon's church has invested far less in business than these religious organizations. This book is titled *The Religious Empire*. It describes church businesses worth multi-billions of dollars. In this book Reverend Moon's Unification Church received one tiny paragraph consisting of five lines, a fraction of the space devoted to other churches.

Mr. Charles A. Stillman, Reverend Moon's attorney, wrote to the subcommittee, "Does the Constitution permit any different treatment of the Unification Church because of the unpopularity of both its spiritual leader and the country which occupies a special place in his theology? If the First Amendment were only intended to protect popular causes, it would be meaningless."

Reverend Moon stands for principle which he knows to be more important than life itself. And he does not stand alone. We stand with him. We will fight with our lives. And we do not stand alone. The Constitution of the United States stands with us. The men of principle around the world are our allies. We will fight the injustices and abuses of power of this subcommittee. We will fight to protect the good name and honor of our religious leader. We will fight for the principle of religious freedom and honor of America in the courts and in the Congress. Thank you very much.

What you just heard, the press heard. About 100 people from the *Washington Post*, the *Washington Star*, CBS news, UPI, AP, of course *News World*, and the French news and *London Times*, Japanese *Osahi*. All kinds. After this statement there was no hostility. There were a few questions, but very friendly questions. I don't like to meet the press because they are always hostile. But after being grilled by the Fraser subcommittee, boy, nothing is hostile anymore. Meeting the press was like a spring vacation. I really enjoyed it.

Yesterday there was a big celebration in Barrytown for the Unification Theological Seminary graduation. In the school's second graduation, 49 wonderful brothers and sisters graduated. It was a beautiful ceremony and a beautiful day and a beautiful setting. It was really heavenly. Many parents, brothers and sisters, and other relatives came to celebrate. Father gave his commencement address over the phone to David Kim, president of UTS, who read it in a most beautiful and inspiring way. Many brothers and sisters were really tearful to hear Father's message coming through Mr. Kim. After that there was a very inspirational banquet. As usual our great group Sunburst performed and uplifted the morale of our members as well as all the families. There were also great honor students.

Many of our brothers and sisters are going on to get their Ph.D.s. Some of them were accepted by Yale University. Some have already gone to Harvard. Our seminary standard is so high. Of course, the moral standard is probably the highest. Not probably—it is the highest. All in all it was a great day.

You know, in the lawsuit I am going to win $30 million. This is a new form of fund-raising: legal fund-raising. The *New York Times* owes us $45 million, Congressman Fraser owes us $30 million. Pretty good, $75 million. But actually I spent $30 million yesterday. I pledged $10 million to the Unification Theological Seminary for their facilities. I pledged that to David Kim, and he was happy to accept it. I pledged another $10 million for the future university of the Unification Church in Tarrytown. I pledged another $10 million for the international crusade for worldwide evangelism. So I have not even a penny left. Great, that is Father's way.

So all in all, many great news. I want to read another part. This is not from the press conference, but from the Fraser subcommittee testimony. I would like you to hear this because I know how much we all love Korea, the Fatherland of our faith. So what I have said about Korea I think is very meaningful to you. So I would like to recite a few pages and later on you can read the whole 43-page booklet of my testimony called "Truth Is My Sword." Have you seen it? Father would like to have this distributed all over the country because it presents the position of our church. In a way, Congressman Fraser did a great favor to our church. God even works with Satan. In other words, God can make use of everything. Even communism is unknowingly assisting God's dispensation.

NOTHING BUT THE TRUTH

This testimony at the congressional hearing is meaningful because I did it under oath. I am sure you saw the picture. I am telling the truth, nothing but the truth. Congressman Fraser posed such difficult questions, which I answered through the guidance of our Father. It is Father's spirit and Father's philosophy, Father's way of life. So this is not actually my testimony. It is the Unification Church testimony. Many brothers and sisters have told me that through this testimony they have learned how to handle certain tough questions. We know now how to answer those. So in that respect, it is valuable. People outside can come to understand our church in earthly term. Not the Divine Principle way, but in earthly terms, their language.

The 43 pages of this fourth testimony answer many allegations that not only Fraser is making but Satan also. So Part I is the general rebuttal and the reason why Reverend Moon will not cooperate with this investigation. Part II, point by point, answers Fraser's allegations of June 6, 1978, against Reverend Sun Myung Moon. In Part III, a Korean defends his country. I would like you to read it and also use it in witnessing about our church all over the country and the world.

I would like to take a few minutes to read the following pages. This is more meaningful than giving an ordinary sermon this morning. This is my sermon actually: "A Korean Defends His Country." Actually I want to say "A Moonie Defends His Country." In Korea, this book is being distributed all over the country and what 35 million Koreans think is: boy, Fraser finally got the real taste of Korea. That is what they say. Real taste. I hope he got the real taste of Moonie, too.

By the way, the press conference was at 10:00 in the morning, and at 2:00 in the afternoon Fraser quickly called a press conference. He could not take it quietly. He has been so powerful and his nose was so high in the air. He was so scornful, not wanting to deal with us. But not anymore. It has become very hot now. So he had to respond. About six people showed up at his press conference. One of the six people was a *News World* reporter, and he really gave Fraser a hard time. I appreciate Father's wisdom in directing and building *The News World*. We have our own newspaper company. Our reporters can be good to people, they can be nasty to people. Particularly our *News World* reporters are toughened and seasoned. So frontline reporters of *News World* are really elite now.

Yesterday at the seminary I explained that in the first century "Christian" was not an honorable title. It was a scornful word. Oh, he is Christian, she is Christian. That means he is a bad person. She is a bad person. That is what it meant in the first century. Also, 100 years ago in America, having a Mormon in your family was bad news. Parents were totally embarrassed if their son or daughter became a Mormon. But Christians, by their actions in service to God, made the word Christian an honorable name. Mormons made theirs an honorable name. We Moonies didn't choose our name, it was given to us. But we are making Moonie the most honorable name under the sun. And we don't need 2,000 years or 100 years. We need 10 years. In 10 years or even less than 10 years, Moonie shall be known as the most honorable name under the sun. That is our determination.

Yesterday at the seminary graduation, Dr. Thomas Boslooper, a very good scholar and a professor at our seminary, who was the emcee, stood up and said, "Today somebody called out to me, 'Hey you, Moonie Boslooper.' If I had heard that two years ago I'm not sure how I would have responded. But today I am more inclined to say, yes, I am more like a Moonie." And he feels it to the bone. Yes, Barrytown, beautiful Moon-wash. So I am determined to make Moonie an honorable name. Right? Do you agree with me?

Now I will read my statement to Congressman Fraser.

In the 1950s there was a senator who wanted to become famous. His name was Joe McCarthy. At one time he made everyone in government tremble. Innocent people were charged with being communists. He destroyed their honor, fame, and livelihood. He bluntly asked everyone the same question. "Are you now or have you ever been a member of the Communist Party?" He imputed guilt by association. He abused enormous government power to intimidate the powerless. He exploited popular and sensitive issues for personal and political gain. In the name of fighting communism he launched his inquisition, a witch-hunt. Most people think that McCarthyism has been laid to rest. Not so. Joe McCarthy may yet have to share his place in history.

Mr. Chairman, in 1978 the pendulum has swung to the other side. The same tactics and methods are being used under a different name. Another congressman wants to make his fame. Like Joe McCarthy, he is using the technique of the big lie and guilt by association to make headlines for himself and is destroying the lives of hundreds of powerless people. He is abusing the enormous power of a congressional subcommittee. His name is Congressman Donald M. Fraser of Minnesota. Fraserism is the McCarthyism of the left. But whereas Senator McCarthy was ostensibly fighting communists, Congressman Fraser is fighting anti-communists. Now the question is, "Are you now or have you ever been an agent of the Korean CIA?"

That is why Reverend Moon and Col. Bo Hi Pak are targets. They are both Korean and anti-communist. Congressman Fraser's ultimate target is not any single person, however. Congressman Fraser wants even bigger game and Reverend Moon and Col. Pak are only stepping stones. He wants to destroy the foremost anti-communist nation—South Korea.

It has been said that when Joe McCarthy went hunting for subversives, he should have started with himself. The idea is that in so freely violating the constitutional guarantee of freedom of others, he became the real enemy of America. Indeed, America finally stopped him.

Mr. Chairman, America will stop you. For a long time I thought I was alone in this fight. But I have learned I am not alone. In early June of this year you were endorsed by your party on the third ballot for the nomination for senator from Minnesota. At the convention there were over 1,000 Minnesota residents demonstrating against you. They were shouting, "No Fraser, No Fraser." You were the only candidate to arouse such fury. A friend sent me some pictures of the demonstration. The demonstrators were carrying signs. One slogan read, "In God We Trust, With Fraser We Bust." Others said, "Tip a Canoe and Fraser Too," and one American was holding the sign, "Fraser Is the Enemy of the People." I don't know any of these people, but I understand them. You must face them in November. Good luck, Mr. Chairman.

I recently returned to Korea. I saw that my country is booming and determined. Bubbling enthusiasm and optimism are filling the land. Our people are determined to survive. They are moving toward unparalleled prosperity. It is a miracle in the making.

On the other hand, I saw that my country and people are absolutely disillusioned and disheartened by Koreagate. They are troubled and sad. They feel they have been bombarded in this surprise attack. They have no defense, especially against the distorted image of Korea which is being communicated by the media. It has been a trying time, not just for President Park, but for all Korean people. Mostly they are disheartened that the trust between Korea and America, built over these many years and sanctified by the sacrifice of many American soldiers, could be shattered so easily. They do not understand why America wants to abandon them.

Ever since 1945, when America delivered Korea to freedom and liberation, Korea has been in love with America. Korea has been faithful and steadfast. Korea has bent over backwards to comply with America's wishes. In order to thank you for defending Korea in the Korean War in 1950, we went to Vietnam and fought and died with you, even though we knew it was losing battle. We didn't want America to suffer alone. America is our lover. After a love affair of 33 years, we suddenly learned that you will not return our love. All along we thought America loved Korea and Korea loved America. Now we are told that it is a marriage of convenience. Instead of being treated as a loving partner, Koreagate made us painfully realize that we have been treated as a servant or, at best, a colony.

After Tong Sun Park testified in Congress, Koreans thought their ordeal was over. The time had come at last to heal the wounds, we thought. Then another shock came. When the House of Representatives voted on March 31, 1978, to cut off aid to Korea unless former Ambassador Kim was delivered for questioning, the Korean people were dumbfounded. This is indeed foolish blackmail. It is almost like a husband saying to his longtime faithful wife, "Unless you tell me of the plot of how you plan to hurt me, I am going to cut your throat." How can America have done this to Korea! It is unprecedented in relations between nations. It is the act of someone without self-esteem or respect for others. America's own diplomatic service, the Department of State, has reacted to this request with shock and disapproval.

Koreans can take any amount of hardship. Any amount of suffering. Yet we cannot take one thing. Humiliation. Millions of dollars of aid cannot make Korea surrender its heart. In the long run, I know the loser will be America. You seem bent on self-destruction. On the day of the vote, one of the distinguished congressmen from New York said, "We are going to move closer to war in Asia." He said precisely what all Koreans feel in their hearts. America will be the ultimate loser. Korea cannot afford to lose America. But how long can America go without Korea?

Yet Koreans do not resent the desire of the Congress and the American people to get to the bottom of Korean influence-buying. However, Koreans do resent the way some people have tried to make headlines out of these investigations at the expense of the truth. Some people have used these investigations to paint Korea as an enemy of America rather than a friend. You, Mr. Chairman, and this subcommittee label Korea "subversive." How could Korea be subversive? Korea never has and never will betray America. On the other hand, Koreans feel they have been betrayed by America. That is why the name "Fraser" has become a notorious household word in Korea. When they think of the Korean investigation, they think of you. They think you are the one subverting Korea. Why?

Let me tell you a story about a famous American whom all Koreans admire. He is John Wayne. From my very early days I have been a dedicated fan of John Wayne. Not because he is anti-communist but because of his western cowboy movies. He is my hero. He is the hero of many Korean people. I have watched dozens of his movies. For most Koreans he is the embodiment of the American character: good, rugged, and fair. He shot a lot of people, but never ruthlessly. As far as I could tell, he would only shoot someone to protect the life of others or to protect his own life. Most importantly, he never shot anyone in the back in cold blood. I always thought this was the American character.

Mr. Chairman, you betrayed this good American character. You have shot Korea in the back in an attempt at cold-blooded political murder. Korea was already wounded and staggering. Korea has been beaten and hurt by the media and other harsh critics. We can envision this nation like a person terribly wounded with much loss of blood, but still standing with what little energy he has left, trying to survive with dignity. Korea needed a Good Samaritan. You have not been that Good Samaritan. Mr. Chairman, instead you decided to take advantage of Korea's travail and shoot her in the back. How cruel you are. It is indeed cold-blooded political murder.

Let me close, Mr. Chairman, with a word of advice. Remember the fate of Joe McCarthy. Remember the virtue of John Wayne. And please remember God lives and reigns. I tell you, you will not succeed in shooting down my country of Korea. God will not let you. He cannot afford to let that fate befall Korea or America.

You have worked behind closed doors to keep the truth from getting out. Eventually the truth will win out. It may seem to you naive of us to believe this. In many places, over many long, dark centuries, lies reigned supreme. Jesus was killed by a lie. Many before and since, known and unknown, have been silenced by lies. What else is communism but lies on top of lies, lies that hold sway over half the world? But we believe the truth will triumph in the end because God is truth and God will triumph. Jesus promised that one day everyone will know the truth of God. We believe that day is at hand. That is why we oppose your investigation and everything it represents. That is why we will never cease to speak the truth no matter what the cost. God's message is clear. Jesus said: "Know the truth and the truth will set you free." Amen.

Not all Koreans feel this. Only Moonies feel this. That is why this is not a Korean's message but the Unification Church's message. Do you agree? I know one thing: any power that is trying to destroy Korea by making it into another Vietnam will not succeed. As our True Parents have taught us, no power will prevail over Korea because God cannot afford it.

Today I would like to dwell on one other thing and that is communism. Do you know Alexander Solzhenitsyn? The great Nobel Prize winner and exiled Russian author recently spoke at the Harvard University commencement ceremony. The *Washington Post* reported that Solzhenitsyn said, "This war, even without nuclear warfare, will surely destroy western civilization forever."

I tell you, Alexander Solzhenitsyn is a great blessing to America. God saved his life. Yes, he could have been buried inside Siberia very easily. But God saved his life and brought him out of Russia. He is becoming a voice crying in the wilderness. Like the prophet Isaiah, he is giving a warning to

America. The two individuals in the world today who truly understand the core of communism are Alexander Solzhenitsyn and Reverend Sun Myung Moon. Two great men.

But the differences of the two are important. Solzhenitsyn is giving a warning as a prophet. America needs it. But the warning alone does not bring the solution. The solution is something else. Who can rebuild this nation so that the warning does not become reality? Our Father. Father not only understands communism, but Father is a builder. Father is a builder of a new world and a new nation. This is why Father is the embodiment of hope. Father is the one who brought the solution to communism. Not just a warning, how terrible, how dangerous communism is. That is not enough.

The solution did not just come yesterday or two days ago or last year. The solution came many decades ago. Without the world knowing, Father is laying one foundation after another to meet the critical deadline. Solzhenitsyn is the turning point, but he does not know what will turn the world. Father will turn the world. Father's ideology will turn the world. We are the axis. We will turn the world right side up, upside down. Unless this turning point is completed successfully, the world certainly is without hope.

The future world is not a struggle between capitalism and socialism. It is not a struggle between tyranny and freedom or between communism and democracy. The simple struggle in which the world is engaged is: God or no God. God power or no God power. That is the struggle in which we are committed. Father has come as the central axis person. The future struggle is going to be the decision between communism and Moonism.

Father never used the word Moonism. But at the Washington Monument rally, Father declared so clearly that the future is going to be Godism. Absolutely God-centered ideology. God-centered individual. God-centered family. God-centered society. God-centered nation. God-centered world. Absolutely God-centered ideology. Father called it Godism. He gave us a new word. But I think that in less than 100 years that Godism will be called Moonism. Whether we like it or not, we are Moonies. The hope of the world is Moonies.

My dear brothers and sisters, this morning let us once again be inspired to be proud Moonies. We are tackling and building the new history. Compared to the population of New York, the people gathered here are just a handful. All the members put together around the world are still just a handful of people. We are a very small minority. But these people are together with Father. We have rubbed into Father, as I said on the Day of All Things. So we can become another Sun Myung Moon. That means we are the axis. Each one of us is important. Each one of us is making history. You are making history.

Yesterday morning, I said to the seminary students, we are writing a chapter in the Acts of the Apostles. We are going to have another Bible. Old Testament, New Testament, then Completed Testament. There will be an Acts of the Apostles in the Completed Testament. We are writing today and every day a chapter. When you read the Acts of the Apostles in the Bible, what do you find? Three things. Number one is suffering. Those people suffered. St. Paul suffered. St. Peter suffered. What else did you find? Martyrdom. Stephen became the first martyr. And what else did you find in the Acts of the Apostles? Miracles. One miracle after another. Suffering, martyrdom, and miracles. That is what is written in the Acts of the Apostles.

My dear brothers and sisters, that is what we are doing. You may think you are a small, unnoticeable person. You might think you are a nobody, a nonentity. Not so. You are heroes and heroines. Simply because we belong to God. You belong to our Father. Simply because our name is another Sun Myung Moon. Particularly while Father is away in England, we are Sun Myung Moons here. That is so important to realize. Each one of us, each day, is responsible for writing a chapter in the history of God. Acts of the Apostles. So our suffering is meaningful, offered without complaint to God. That is what Father is asking us to do. What else can we leave behind in 100 or 1,000 years? What will our children and our grandchildren read about us? How we suffered for the sake of God. How impossible our task was. What incredible things we did for the sake of God. That will move them.

In the 2,000 years since Jesus' crucifixion, God prepared a most formidable power for Moonies to work with, that is, democracy. That is a great blessing that God gave to us. What does democracy represent? In a way, it is the clumsiest form of government. But democracy does one thing. What is that? It guarantees freedom. In Korea I told my countrymen what I had said to the Fraser subcommittee. They were completely astonished. Mr. Pak, how can you say such a thing to a powerful congressman and still keep your neck? That is the way they think. If I said these things 2,000 years ago, I don't think I would have been able to read the whole statement. In the middle of the statement, my neck and my body would have been separated. Don't you think so? Look what they did to Stephen. Even look at English history. King Henry the VIII beheaded Sir Thomas More simply because More said to him, I cannot recant my religion. I cannot change my Catholic faith. I cannot change into the Anglican Church. King Henry VIII said, all right, if you say so, I will give you a little gift. And he had Sir Thomas' head chopped off. Neck and body separated. Look at how many people died after the reformation of Martin Luther. Look at the religious war in Europe. Over half a million people died because of religion. That was only a few hundred years ago, not 1,000 years ago.

DEMOCRACY PROTECTS US

So you know God must have worked very hard to bring about democracy. Today all the Moonies are proclaiming the coming of the Lord. Proclaiming True Parents and the Divine Principle. Proclaiming the revolution. Still, our necks and bodies are staying together. It is a miracle. Don't you see that? Oh, this is a blessing. With freedom of religion and freedom of speech, nobody can touch us. That is our weapon. God gave it to us.

We think our job is difficult today. Think about the first century. Every day the shadow of death was around them. They could not escape the danger of death. When they were caught, they were beheaded or worse. For a century Christianity was the greatest clandestine CIA operation. They operated under codes. That is why the sign of the fish was used. But today we live in an age where it is very difficult to be a martyr. That is the blessing.

So our job is not just to be beheaded. There is another way to become a martyr. Burn every ounce of your energy, give every ounce of your flesh and blood for the sake of God. That in itself is the action of the martyr. In the Bible Jesus said we must bear the cross. There are two ways of bearing the cross. One very dramatic way is to die as Jesus did, nailed to the cross. But today, our way of bearing the cross is a little different. We must win the victory without physically shedding our blood. This is a day of glory. This is the day of fulfillment. Every day we give ourselves completely to God and the purpose of True Parents. Actually, this kind of life is a slow dying on the cross. Don't you think that slow dying on the cross is more difficult than the dramatic dying? The drama is over in a few seconds.

Today we do not work in that fashion. Every moment of the day we shall have a martyr spirit. We shall die for God and True Parents. This is far more difficult. This is why you have to practice the perfected form of giving. That is what Father wants from us. We do have some martyrs. Our dear sister Christiane Coste, for example. I knew her very well. I met her in the PR center. Such a dedicated, charming, sweet girl. She was a genuine martyr. Some more people may die. But that is not the primary way we give ourselves now. St. Francis prayed that in dying we live forever. That is the Moonie way of life. It is not easy. I know some of you look very tired. Some look pale. Some of you, your hair looks a little messy. Yes, I understand where you are. But I want you to really hang on to Father and determine yourself, saying, yes, I am dying every day. I am bearing the cross every day in order to live forever. That is our battle.

Many Moonies fail and become ex-Moonies, not because they repent their faith, but simply because their God-energy runs out. Don't set your goal for the short term. If you think everything will be over next year, your energy will run out next year. You must set the goal, saying, I don't care whether it is 10 years or 100 years, I am going to give myself. I am living and dying for the sake of True Parents, the sake of God. There will be eternal life. There will be glory. There is life forever.

I want you to understand we are the champions of God, whether you like it or not, not because you are great, but because you know the name of the Father, Reverend Sun Myung Moon. That name made us champions. We are writing a chapter of history, a chapter of suffering, martyrdom, miracles. Once you have total commitment, there is a miracle. After two years of struggle against the Fraser committee, I am speaking here today. That is in itself a miracle. Only God could save me, I know. My heart is filled with gratitude. I am really giving my thanksgiving to God. I am here because of God's power, not man's power, not me, not Bo Hi Pak. I want you to be proud Moonies. Let us pray.

Prayer by Bo Hi Pak:

Our loving Heavenly Father, we are deeply proud Moonies. Each day, each moment we are going to be proud Moonies. We really understand what Moonies are. Father, we belong to True Parents. We are the only people who know the name of our True Parents. So, Father, we shall be the only people to truly rally around your central dispensation. When we know this, we know how inadequate we are, how unprepared we are. But Father, we are determined to do our job. We shall never let you down. Never. We shall keep on going and win the victory day after day and shall bring the ultimate victory here on earth. Father, may you bless our True Father in England. He is on a most important evangelical mission. And our American brothers and sisters are joining him shortly. Seminarians are going. Father, truly we are going to win the magnificent victory in the Cain world in Europe. By the presence of our True Father it can be done. Please bless Mother and bless this true child that came. We all are rejoicing over such a happy occasion. But Father, we have to work harder and really bring your expected victory here in New York. So when Father returns we shall come back to him with the most glorious outcome and result. Thank you, Father, for this most beautiful day. Beautiful sunshine. Beautiful green nature. All is part of your kingdom, but they do not know who the true masters are. We shall love them as a true lord of all things because we shall be given the title as sons and daughters of God. We will live up to that title, the greatest of all titles in humanity. Thank you. All these things we pray in the name of our beloved True Parents. Amen.

St. Stephen

NEW YORK, NEW YORK
APRIL 8, 1979

Bo Hi Pak loves to compare the lives of Unificationists to the Acts of the Apostles, and in this sermon, he does precisely this using the life, trial, and martyrdom of St. Stephen to illustrate a true man of faith.

We gather this morning to worship God. The worshiping of God consists of songs, prayers, sermons, the offering, and benediction, and another important part of service is singing hymns. You know from hearing my testimony that when I first joined the Unification Church, the singing of the hymns truly shook my soul. My dear brothers and sisters, today I would like you to sing that kind of hymn. You are as important as the person who delivers the sermon. Let us sing one more hymn before the sermon, "The Father's Dwelling Place." Let us sing from the bottom of our souls.

It is a great day shortly before Easter Sunday of 1979. The Sunday service we're now instituting will continue with vigor and enthusiasm in the weeks to come. Sunday service is our unification rally. I want you to make this gathering a spiritual volcanic eruption that will go out from this World Mission Center into the entire New York area and cleanse the city of New York, the nation of America, and the world in which we live. We have that kind of spirit and power. I want you to come every Sunday and worship together. I'm sure you will invite many friends, relatives, and home church brothers and sisters. I would like the youth to bring more friends, every Sunday, so that this New Yorker will not be big enough. Eventually the Manhattan Center will be the place of worship.

However, the place of worship is not important. The spirit is important. So today, we set the tradition of service. The Bible says, we worship God in spirit and truth. If we have only truth, it becomes philosophy. If we have only spirit, it becomes superstition. The true religion is spirit and truth. The spirit of God and the truth of the Divine Principle are the spirit of the service of the Unification Church.

When I read the Bible, the part that most impresses me is always the Acts of the Apostles. When you read Acts, you soon realize that you are reading your own autobiography, your own story. In the first century, the disciples of Jesus struggled through the streets of Rome. That is precisely the situation of the Unification members today struggling in New York, Washington, London, Tokyo, and Seoul. Same spirit.

Among the stories in the Acts of the Apostles, the one that always touches my heart is the story of Stephen, the first martyr of Christian history. I will share with you today the story of Stephen. Acts 6 tells that there was some disagreement between the Hellenists and the Hebrews. Hellenists were Jews who spoke Greek and had adopted some Greek customs. Hebrews were more conservative Jews who spoke Hebrew or Aramaic. The Hellenists were complaining that their widows were being slighted in the daily distribution of goods.

A MAN FULL OF FAITH

To set the matter straight, the 12 apostles got together and decided to appoint deacons. They selected seven men and one was Stephen. A deacon was almost like an administrator of the church. They took care of practical matters, including the fair distribution of goods to the poor, so that the apostles could more fully devote themselves to preaching and witnessing. Stephen is described as "a man full of faith and of the Holy Spirit. ... Stephen, full of grace and power, did great wonders and signs among the people." After the appointment of Stephen and the other six as the first deacons, "the word of God increased; and the number of the disciples multiplied greatly in Jerusalem, and a great many of the priests were obedient to the faith." It seems there was a great crusade in Jerusalem, almost like a 120-day witnessing crusade in New York, and many people were converted, including priests.

Then Stephen, full of grace and power, did great wonders and signs among the people. Some members of the synagogues of the Freedmen,

Cyrenians, and Alexandrians and those of Cilicia and Asia "arose and disputed with Stephen." They argued with him, but "they could not withstand the wisdom and the Spirit with which he spoke." They couldn't defeat him in argument, so what did they do? They "secretly instigated men, who said, 'We have heard him speak blasphemous words against Moses and God.' " They were jealous of the Christians' success and didn't want to see them gaining power. This happened then and it is happening now.

So they hatched a plot. "They stirred up the people and the elders and the scribes, and they came upon him and seized him and brought him before the council, and set up false witnesses." That's what Stephen went through 2,000 years ago.

When you think of Stephen, who do you think of? I think of Moonies. He would have made a good Moonie if he were here today. What are you? You are men full of faith and the Holy Spirit. Grace and power. You do wonders and signs. Yes, you do! Washington Monument! Yankee Stadium! These are wonders in America today. Turning the New Yorker into the World Mission Center, a holy place to worship God, is a miracle, isn't it? What you do in home church is a work of wonders and signs. The outside people try to dispute you. They cannot withstand the wisdom and the spirit of Moonies! Can they? Impossible. So Stephen is my idol as a good Moonie.

We in the Unification Church are as successful in every way as the early Christians were in Jerusalem. The word of God increased, the members increased, even priests joined, and many institutions were established. The work spread all over the world. Then people, as they did in the first century, became jealous, people who are not happy with our success and want to stop it. It happened then, and it happens now. But today, what do we have? We have false allegations, insinuations, innuendoes, and lies against us. Actually, Reverend Moon is the Number One Moonie. Reverend Moon is full of faith and the Holy Spirit, grace and power. He works wonders and signs, and no one withstands the wisdom and the spirit with which he speaks. Amen.

Therefore, allegations are raised against us, just as they were against Stephen. They know face-to-face confrontation will not work. They cannot challenge us squarely. Fair play with the Unification Church will not work, so they use dirty tricks. In Japan, the communists—and there are many in Japan, the Communist Party is one of the major political parties in Japan—were the first ones to try to destroy the Unification Church.

They challenged the Unification Church. We responded squarely. We challenged them to come on public television and debate fairly. You state your point of view, we'll state our point of view. But the communists withdrew. They gave up. They knew we speak the truth and lies cannot win over truth. So they never responded to our challenge or came forward in a public forum to discuss whether God exists or not.

They knew they couldn't win, so they used dirty tactics, false allegations, and violence, their favorite tactic. But the Unification Church could not be defeated, and we won campus after campus. We turned lawlessness into order. The Japanese campuses had been ruled by communists, but within two years we took control and gradually changed public opinion in the country. The communists always use the same tactics. They always accuse you of the very thing that you're against.

180 DEGREES THE OPPOSITE

Here in America, the Fraser subcommittee is a very good example. These are my own words before Fraser's subcommittee: "Jesus came to this earth as the son of God, and the world treated him as the prince of demons." 180 degrees the opposite. "Reverend Moon comes as a prophet of the living God, teaching God's highest moral principle, and now the world is trying to portray him as a man of immorality." 180 degrees the opposite.

Face it. They always use this tactic to discredit the man of God by accusing him of being that which he condemns. History proves it does not work. They could not destroy Jesus with these tactics, so what will it be with Reverend Moon? At one point I shouted out by saying, "Mr. Chairman, you are a liar. You alter this information which you created and you give the lie in the power of the United States Congress. It is the worst character assassination possible. You did this to the man who came to America to do the work of God and save, yes, save, this country from immorality. I cannot help but believe that you are being used as the instrument of the devil. Yes! Instrument of the devil! I said it! Who else would want to destroy the men of God but the devil?"

I expected him to be so mad, enraged, throwing coffee cups, and ashtrays. As a matter of fact, I expected, just as Stephen got the stones, I will get the ashtray. Good deal, I thought. And when ashtrays fly—I was fully expecting them—I would say "God, let it hit me!" Yes, I tell you between brothers and sisters, the story of Stephen, the work of Stephen was very much in my mind during the fight with the Fraser subcommittee. I'm sure Stephen's spirit has been helping me. I can feel it. You know what I really wanted? I wanted to expose the lies, the innuendoes, and the false tactics of Fraser to the whole nation. I needed a newsworthy event. The best event would be that Fraser got so mad that he threw a coffee cup at me and I started bleeding.

Then I had the best scene ever developed. I had three minutes. I wanted to stand up and expose the lies, innuendoes, and devilish tactics of Fraser to all the nation. Why three minutes? I knew the networks would never carry more than three minutes. So I wanted to keep every message to three minutes. Compact.

But anyway, Fraser was cunning and clever like all politicians. He would not dare make such a blunder as to throw anything in front of the public and the media. But then that was all right too. I had my chance to deliver the message.

Finally I would like to read one more paragraph from that day, the battle against Fraser. I said this:

> Mr. Chairman. I know that it is easy and popular in the short run to persecute new religious groups. So it was for Nero, so it was for Julian the Apostate. But does history remember them for their social reform, or foreign policy, or human rights? No! It remembers them as the great persecutors in history. So history might remember Donald Fraser, if it remembers him at all. You may get my scalp, Mr. Chairman, but never my heart and soul. My heart and soul belong to God. The Lord is my shepherd, even though I walk through the valley of the shadow of death, I fear no evil, for thou art with me.

That was my conclusion that day. I am trying to make a point here. Why is Reverend Moon being accused and criticized here in America of brainwashing and all kinds of things? Well, never mind. Jesus Christ was accused by the people in those days of preaching blasphemy.

YOU STIFF-NECKED PEOPLE

Stephen's trial began and he stood before the council, a man full of faith and the Holy Spirit. He fought bravely. Almost all of Acts 7, three entire pages, is his strong testimony. You can tell that he had studied the Old Testament well. He went down in chronological order from Abraham, to Joseph, to Moses, and showed how the people of Israel has gone against God and His prophets. They had betrayed the spirit of God, over and over. He made a long speech which led to his powerful conclusion:

> You stiff-necked people, uncircumcised in heart and ears, you always resist the Holy Spirit. As your fathers did, so do you. Which of the prophets did not your fathers persecute? And they killed those who announced beforehand the coming of the Righteous One, whom you have now betrayed and murdered, you who received the law as delivered by angels and did not keep it.

Here Stephen is saying, your fathers persecuted all those who foretold the coming of the righteous one, the Messiah, and ultimately that righteous one, Jesus Christ, came to this earth as prophesied, and now you have betrayed him and murdered him. Stephen was condemning his own people. You murdered Jesus Christ. Murder means taking someone's life against their will.

My dear brothers and sisters, this clearly shows that Jesus did not come to die. He was the victim of ignorance. He was the victim of selfishness. They, without knowing him, murdered him. That's why St. Paul said that the rulers of this age did not understand, for if they had they would not have crucified the Lord of Glory. If they had known who he was, they would not have crucified him. It was already made clear 2,000 years ago.

And what did the people do? "When they heard these things they were enraged, and they ground their teeth against him." They couldn't stand to hear the verdict. At that moment, Stephen received a vision and said, "Behold, I see the heavens opened, and the son of man standing at the right hand of God." The people went mad. "They cried out with a loud voice and stopped their ears and rushed together upon him. Then they cast him out of the city and stoned him." They stopped their ears. They dragged him out of the city. They grabbed up stones. And they stoned him to death. "Pull him out, cast him out!"

In Stephen's vision, he saw Jesus, not sitting, but standing at the right hand of God. Jesus is usually depicted as sitting next to God. But at that moment, Jesus could not sit still. Jesus stood up, ready to receive the soul of Stephen. That was also a dire emergency for God. No one can see the invisible God, but God must have been standing too.

This is the message I want to leave with you today. Stephen received a standing ovation from God. The standing ovation from Jesus. Not just applause. God was ready to receive the soul of Stephen. Now we must ask ourselves, the Stephens of the 20th century, the Stephens of the Unification Church, are we ready to receive the standing ovation of Jesus, the standing ovation of God? Our deeds every day in home church, witnessing, whatever duty we have, are they worthy of the standing ovation of Jesus? Does my life make God and Jesus feel a dire emergency so they cannot sit still but have to stand up? If your answer is yes, I admire you. You are indeed the proud sons and daughters of God. If your commitment goes that far, if that is the spirit of Moonies today, then you and I know that it is just a matter of time—we can change this world and build the Kingdom of God. There is no power under the sun that can stop the surge.

This is why Reverend Moon always says, America thinks that if they stop me, the Unification Church will collapse. Oh, they do not know anything about Stephen. They do not know anything about religion. If anybody thinks that by stopping Reverend Moon, they are stopping the movement. Wrong! How ridiculous! Stopping Reverend Moon means raising up millions of Reverend Moons, don't you think so?

FATHER, FORGIVE THEM

Stephen, shortly before his death, gazed into heaven. Do you know what his final words were? "Lord Jesus, receive my spirit. Lord, do not hold this sin against them." In other words, Stephen is saying, forgive them. Just as Jesus prayed in his last hour, "Father, forgive them, for they know not what they do." Stephen lived and died in the same tradition as Jesus. Forgive them. They don't know what they are doing. That is truly the epitome of faith. And we have such a perfect example of such a perfect faith: Reverend Moon. With this kind of faith, we shall become invincible.

Recently, someone in my office showed me a book about us—not a very kind book—written by an ex-Moonie named Christopher Edward. The name of the book is *Crazy for God*. I said, "That's a great title for a book, but I'm going to re-write it." If we ever have a chance to write this brother, I am going to quote from Matthew 22:34-40:

> But when the Pharisees heard that he had silenced the Sadducees, they came together. And one of them, a lawyer, asked him [Jesus] a question, to test him. "Teacher, which is the great commandment in the Law?" And he said to him, "You shall love the Lord your God with all your heart, and with all your soul, and with all your mind. This is the great and first commandment. And a second is like it, You shall love your neighbor as yourself. On these two commandments depend all the law and the prophets."

If you love someone with all your heart, all your soul, and all your mind, do you have anything left over to do anything else? If you love someone as yourself, is there any room to do anything else? Besides, if you love someone with all your heart, all your soul, and all your mind, you're actually crazy about that person, aren't you? In plain American English, you're crazy about them. American English is sometimes very handy. You don't have to waste many words. So the modern-day version of the first commandment is: You must become crazy for God. You know today, we are living in a mad world. A mad, mad world. Everybody is crazy about something. Crazy about money, crazy about cars, crazy about honor, crazy about knowledge, crazy about women, crazy about sex, crazy about peanuts, crazy about popcorn. If you are going to be crazy about something, why not! Why not! Our choice would be, crazy about God! Amen!

My dear brothers and sisters, we are on the right track. The Unification Church can tell us the way to become crazy about God, so that we have no time and no energy to think about anything else. This is truly a blessing. So my dear brothers and sisters, let us obey the commandment to the letter.

I want to close this sermon with a story from the international leaders conference. One leader from Austria testified that one of his members in Austria was going out and witnessing every day and met a good-looking young lawyer, a very intellectual, snobbish young man. This young sister was genuinely interested in him and kept pounding on him, insisting that he must be interested in the new truth. Well, he listened very carefully, and after a few minutes, he shook his head and said, "No, young lady, you are trying to do an impossible thing. You actually are trying to change the world, aren't you? Don't try with me. I'm not going to change, and this world isn't going to change. The Moonies can't change the world."

Amazing, isn't it? I thought we had a pretty good reputation around the world. People know by now that only Moonies can change the world. Not by defiance, not by the bullet, not by violence, but by the truth of God and the love of God and by living the truth. You and I today are living that truth. It is truly a great honor and a great glory. We must lift ourselves up to perfection. With Reverent Moon guiding us, we can. We can achieve perfection. Let us pray.

Prayer by Bo Hi Pak:

Most loving Heavenly Father, thank You very much for this special day of service. Father, we want to uplift our hearts. Father, I want You to accept this altar, this offering. Father, make us the instrument of Your kingdom building. Father, we prayed about You, prayed about Your mission. We are loving You with all our heart and soul and mind. We are acting full time for You. Father, everything we do, the things we eat, the things we make, the places we work, whatever we tackle, there is a meaning behind it. We make the holy offering of our everyday work. Father, thank You very much for the most important Sunday worship. We are going to continue the worship every Sunday. We are going to make this worship like a volcanic explosion in New York and give the city of New York, 10 million New Yorkers, hope. Reverend Moon declared this frontline of our movement. We are so honored to become frontline soldiers. We want to fulfill Your mission in the spirit of Stephen, and in the spirit of the commandments. Love God with all our hearts and minds and souls. Love our neighbor as ourselves. All these things we pray in the name of our true Father. Amen.

I AM THE RESURRECTION

NEW YORK, NEW YORK

APRIL 15, 1979

On this Easter morning, Bo Hi Pak reminds the congregation that our movement was born on Easter Sunday morning in 1936 when Jesus first appeared to Father. Using the Divine Principle as a guide, he explains the true meaning of death and resurrection.

Good morning. Happy Easter to you and to our Spanish brothers and sisters upstairs. Today the world celebrates Easter. When you read the Bible, in John 11:25-26 Jesus said, "I am the resurrection and the life; he who believes in me, though he die, yet shall he live, and whoever lives and believes in me shall never die." This is the most powerful declaration of Jesus Christ. The title of this morning's Sunday service is "I Am the Resurrection."

In the Christian world, Easter Sunday must be regarded as the greatest celebration of all, although the entire world celebrates Christmas, the birth of Jesus, in such a hectic manner. But the most important holiday is Easter because we celebrate the triumphant victory of Jesus Christ. The power of resurrection is the power of salvation. Therefore, Easter Sunday is far more than Easter bunnies or lilies or eggs.

For the Unification Church, Easter has a very special meaning. The Unification movement was born on Easter. In 1936, early on Easter Sunday morning, Jesus Christ manifested himself to Reverend Sun Myung Moon, then 16 years of age, on a mountainside in northern Korea. Jesus gave him the mission to succeed at what was left undone 2,000 years ago. Jesus promised the young man, Reverend Moon, that he would work with him all along to fulfill the task. That was the beginning of the Unification Church.

Reverend Moon accepted the challenge. Thereafter, for nine years, Reverend Moon went in and out of the spirit world and encountered the living Jesus numerous times. In the presence of Almighty God, he discovered the most formidable truth, known to us today as the Divine Principle. This is the origin of the Unification Church. So today we celebrate the beginning of our movement, the origin and the root of this church.

What the Divine Principle has given to the world is the true meaning of Easter. In the Christian world today, regardless of the denomination, there is still a lack of understanding of the true meaning of resurrection. But the Divine Principle, in black and white, reveals to the world the true and precise meaning of resurrection.

There are two common schools of thought regarding the resurrection. In the first, resurrection means raising from the dead or passing from death to life. Many people believe that someday all those who have died throughout human history will come alive again. One scientist estimated that more than 130 billion people would come back to life. That would create an immediate problem: how to feed them. The McDonald's hamburger chain boasts that in 10 years they sold 30 billion hamburgers. In order to feed 130 billion people, it would take 40 to 50 years to give each person one hamburger. I don't think President Carter could handle such a problem. It is beyond human capability.

It seems to be illogical. It seems to be impossible. But many Christians literally believe that will be the case. Why? Because they base their belief in the Bible. Read Ezekiel 37:5: "Thus says the Lord God to these bones [God is speaking to the bones]: Behold I will cause breath to enter you, and you shall live. And I will lay sinews upon you, and will cause flesh to come upon you, and cover you with skin, and put breath in you, and you shall live; and you shall know that I am the Lord." So God would put flesh back on the bones of 130 billion people. Ezekial 37:12 says, "Thus says the Lord God: Behold, I will open your graves, and raise you from your graves, O my people." So one day all the cemeteries will open up.

DEATH AND SIN

There is another school of thought that believes that once we accept Christ, or we meet the coming of the Lord up in the clouds of heaven, we shall never die. Never die, period. Again, that belief is based on the Bible. They believe physical death here on earth resulted from the sin that Adam and Eve committed. Once we cleanse the sin, we are no longer sinners; then physical death will be no more.

One denomination believes that if they wash their robes of sin, they can live here on earth for many thousands of years. Again their belief is based on the Bible. As I read earlier in John 11:25-26 Jesus said, "I am the resurrection and the life; he who believes in me, though he die, yet shall he live, and whoever lives and believes in me shall never die." And Revelation 21 promises that God "will wipe away every tear from their eyes, and death shall be no more, neither shall there be mourning nor crying nor pain anymore, for the former things have passed away." It is clearly said there shall be no more death. After Christ comes, no more death. So they literally believe that once we accept and meet the Christ, we are going to live here forever.

In fact, for 2,000 years Christians lived in that faith. But they died. Everybody dies. So today I tell you, we have confusion in our world. We have confusion in our faith. The scientific mind of the 20th century cannot be certain of what the Bible says. So we need enlightened truth. You shall know the truth and the truth shall make you free. We need liberation. We need freedom. And I tell you, the Divine Principle, revealed through Reverend Moon, given by God, has the answer.

Today I would like to share a portion of the Principle. Right in the beginning of the Bible, God Himself mentions death. Genesis 2:17 says, "but of the tree of the knowledge of good and evil you shall not eat, for in the day that you eat of it you shall die." This is the first time the Bible mentions death. Unfortunately, even though that commandment was given to Adam and Eve, what did they do? They didn't obey. They violated the commandment. They ate the forbidden fruit. And did they die? The Bible says that Adam and Eve, after eating the fruit, lived another 900 years.

Did God lie to them? No. God is truth. God will never lie. Then did the Bible record what happened incorrectly? No, the Bible is the word of God. So we need to understand the definition of death. What we think about death and what God thinks are two different things. We think of death as the destruction of the physical body. My pulse stops. We think that is death. But God looks at death as something else. The moment Adam and Eve ate the fruit, they surely died, and ever since, death has reigned.

Death in God's terms is invisible death. It does not take place in a physical or visible form. It took place quietly, but absolutely. That death is separation from God. You think you are alive. I think I am alive. But in the sight of God, we are dead people if we don't have God. The separation from God is true death. Therefore, the moment Adam and Eve ate the fruit, they were separated from God, and they died.

The Gospel of John says, "in him was life." In the universe we have only one life. The life of God. God is life. We are supposed to partake of the life source of God. I always use the analogy of an electric bulb drawing light from the powerhouse. That is God's position. We are in the light bulb position. Therefore, the moment the connection between light bulb and powerhouse is broken, no matter what, that light bulb is dead. It doesn't function. That is what happened. Adam and Eve broke that power line the moment they ate the fruit. At that very moment, Adam and Eve were no longer alive in the sight of God. That is why the Bible says the wages of sin is death. As it says in 1 Corinthians 15:22, "for as in Adam all die." So because the first forefather died spiritually, separated from God, succeeding generations were born dead. Furthermore, Romans 5:17 says that "because of one man's trespass, death reigned." Ever since the fall of Adam and Eve, death reigns.

A WORLD OF CORPSES

More than 130 billion people have lived on earth. In the sight of God they existed here as biological life. They came on the surface of the earth and vanished. They had no impact on God's life. They have been nothing to God. Think of how terrible and shocking a consequence that is. That is the real death mankind suffered. I don't know how many people live in New York today, but in the sight of Goal, not many are alive. Here in America, in the sight of God, how many people are alive? What a smelly world of corpses we are living in.

Last year in November some shocking news spread through the entire world: the Guyana tragedy. When the U.S. police landed in Guyana and went into the people's temple, they saw one corpse after another, bodies rotting in the jungle heat. But think about it, God has been walking through the Guyana jungle of this world for 6,000 Biblical years. Smelly, intolerable jungles of death. You can imagine how the heart of God has been broken again and again. The police could only pack up the corpses and send them back to the United States to be buried. That is all they could do. But God is different. In Isaiah 46:11 God promised, "I have spoken, and I will bring it to pass; I have purposed, and I will do it." I will do what? I will bring it back to life. That is why Jesus came.

Jesus came entrusted and empowered by God with the power to resurrect the death of mankind. But you don't have to die to resurrect. Not at all. We are already dead. Now is the time to resurrect. You don't have to wait for physical death to resurrect. That is why Jesus said, "I am the resurrection." Jesus did not say, I will die on the cross and I will be resurrected. Jesus said, I am the resurrection. I am the life. I am the way. In order to come to the Father, you come through me. That is the prescription God gave to mankind. All mankind has to do is accept the resurrection. God brought down to earth the walking resurrection: the living Jesus. He is the resurrection. He is already triumphant. All mankind has to do is believe in him and accept him. Jesus had the power to resurrect all mankind 2,000 years ago. He didn't have to go through the cross. He didn't have to go through three days in the tomb. He is the resurrection, and the moment people receive him and accept him as the Messiah, they are instantly given the resurrection.

However, what happened? Instead of accepting him, they crucified him. And today the Christian world believes Jesus came solely to die on the cross. I tell you, if he came solely to die on the cross and that was the only way he could save mankind, the entire New Testament is wrong. Jesus did not say, wait until I die, then you will be given salvation. No. Jesus said, I forgive your sins. My daughter, arise, walk, be saved. Acceptance of Jesus brought forgiveness of sin. Passing from death to life took place at that moment. Jesus was not issuing a raincheck. Jesus was not saying, wait until I die.

BELIEVE IN HIM WHOM HE HAS SENT

One day one of the disciples asked Jesus what he could do to be doing the work of God. Jesus did not say, wait until I die on the cross. Jesus did not say, wait until after I shed my blood. Jesus said [John 6:29], "this is the work of God, that you believe in him whom He has sent." Your job is solely to believe in him whom God has sent. All you need to do is accept Jesus. Suppose Jesus' wish was fulfilled. Suppose everybody in Israel accepted Jesus as the son of God. Who would dare crucify Jesus on the cross? Who would dare?

I want you to understand, this is a revolutionary declaration to the Christian world today. Jesus was murdered. St. Peter said it, St. Stephen said it. And St. Paul said it in 1 Corinthians 2:8: "None of the rulers of this age understood this; for if they had, they would not have crucified the Lord of glory." If they had known who Jesus was, the rulers of that age would not have crucified him. What an incredible mistake mankind has made.

369

Jesus was crucified. People saw him die. He went to the tomb for three days. God dramatically demonstrated victory by raising Jesus and letting the world see him. But if mankind 2,000 years ago accepted Jesus in the first place, that would not have been necessary. All the people needed to do was accept him.

God has given you two bodies, one for the physical world and one for the spiritual world. Your real body is encased within this physical body. You think this outer one is real. I can eat, I can laugh, I can smile, I can touch, I can see. You think, oh, I don't want to live a ghost life. You don't want it because you don't know it. Once you are given spiritual eyes, you will see the true world and you won't want to live this physical life for another 200 years. Why? You will see that this world is just a carbon copy of the real, eternal world. This is a shadow world. Upstairs is real. Of course, this physical body is important. Without the physical body you cannot nourish your spiritual body. Unless you do the will of God with this physical body, your spirit body will not grow. That is why we need this life. It is very important.

However, when the time comes to go upstairs, we won't need this clumsy body anymore. We will turn it back to nature. After all, the 180 pounds of my body came from rice, vegetables, beef, and chicken. Where are they from? They came from the soil. We borrowed 180 pounds of soil for probably less than a hundred years. But these hundred years are important. Why? Because this is the time you come to know and love God and love your neighbor. By doing so, you protect your spirit body which is inside. That is the real body you are going to live in upstairs for eternity. But you must earn it here on earth. This is a good deal. We invest for 100 years and we receive eternity.

One day Jesus took three of his disciples, Peter, James, and John, up a high mountain. Matthew 17:2-4 describes what happened: "And he [Jesus] was transfigured before them, and his face shone like the sun, and his garment became white as light. And behold, there appeared to them Moses and Elijah, talking with him. And Peter said to Jesus, 'Lord, it is well that we are here; if you wish, I will make three booths here, one for you and one for Moses and one for Elijah.' " How amazing—tired, pale Jesus, probably wearing an old garment, was transformed. They could see him shining like the sun, with a dazzling garment. They could barely look at him because there was so much light. But it was such a wonderful thing to behold. The disciples for the first time saw a different aspect of Jesus. But Jesus was not alone. Moses and Elijah, who had been dead for many hundreds of years, were standing there. Peter felt so wonderful. He suggested, Jesus, let us build three small houses, one for you, one for Moses, and one for Elijah. Let's live here. He didn't want to go anywhere. It felt so good.

At that moment, do you know what had happened? God opened Peter's spiritual eyes. He saw the spirit man of Jesus, which was shining like the sun. He saw Jesus' permanent body, which did not need any resurrection. By accepting Jesus we are all supposed to be given the same resurrection. We are supposed to shine like Jesus, with a shining body, which we call in the Divine Principle, the divine spirit. With this spirit we are permanently elevated into the future world to live there forever in the love of God.

That was the plan. But because the people crucified Jesus, that dispensation was delayed another 2,000 years. We must wait for the Lord to come a second time. It is a mandate of history. New York, America, humanity will never be perfected without welcoming the son of God once again. He will come to the earth and declare, "I am the resurrection." He will not say, wait until I die and then I shall resurrect you. Not at all. Once we receive that resurrection by knowing him, accepting the Christ, we will not only be elevated into the kingdom of heaven upstairs, but we will start to live in that kingdom here on earth. Thy kingdom come, Thy will be done, on earth as it is in heaven. Christ's coming is the resurrection. Death shall be no more. Do you know what that means? It does not mean this physical body will not crumble. It will. At a certain time you will no longer need it. But you shall fear no death. You have been afraid of death because it has been an unknown quantity. You don't know what will happen the second after death. You don't know if you will be there or if you are going anywhere. The fear of death, that is the real death. But once you accept the Christ and your spirit man receives enlightenment like the sun, you no longer live in fear of death.

I'm sure Linda is here today. Where are you? She must be here somewhere. Right there. Hi, Linda, how are you? When Linda is in her home she goes out during the day and plays all around the neighborhood. But I bet you dollar to donuts, she won't go out at night. "Oh, mommy, I'm scared." Same neighborhood, same places she plays during the daylight, but at night she doesn't want to take even one step outside of the house. Why does the night scare her? Because of the darkness. Unknown quantity. She can't see what is only one foot away from her. That is what is scary about death. We don't know what it is like. But once you now the truth, there will be light. You are no longer in darkness. You shall see the way you are going, what is your mission, where you will live after your lifetime here on earth.

FROM A CUBBYHOLE TO A MANSION

This earthly life is like living in a small, cubbyhole apartment, almost like a prison. But someday someone will invite you to come live in a mansion. This is all yours, all yours as long as you want it. It is 1,000 times better than the cubbyhole. You are more than glad to take off your old clothes and put on a new garment and move into the new mansion. That is what physical death is all about. If there had been no fall, there would be no darkness. You would know your destination, so there would be no fear of death. You will make a natural transformation from one life to another.

You are going to resurrect right here on earth. Right here, right now. The entire resurrection may not come all at once. But today you resurrect this much, tomorrow you resurrect this much more, and soon you reach your destination. That is what you are doing here. That is why you came here. That is why this service is important. That is why coming to the Unification Church is so important. That is why coming to the Unification workshop is so important. Know the truth and the truth shall make you free.

In Luke 9:59-60, Jesus said to one man, "Follow me." But the man said, "Lord, let me first go and bury my father." Jesus, my father died; let me go bury my father and then I will come back and follow you. Well, this is certainly a logical request. I want to go bury my father and then come back and follow you. Most logical. But do you know what Jesus said to him? Jesus said, No! Leave the dead to bury their own dead. Jesus was looking at the world from God's viewpoint. As far as God is concerned, your father who has physically died and the people around him were already dead. All corpses. You have no time to fool around with those people. Let them take care of their business. Leave the dead people, who are the worldly people, to take care of their own dead. Your job is to follow me. This is an emergency. I have come to bring you resurrection. Your job is be resurrected by following me and then bring the resurrection to the people.

My dear brothers and sisters, today we must heed the teaching of Jesus. Follow me. Leave the dead to bury their own dead. Today there is no more important task for you and me than to seek the coming of the Lord who will declare, "I am the resurrection." That is the first and foremost job. There is no time to do anything else. It is a wise man and wise woman who will do that. The Unification Church members are wise people. We have leaders who guide us clearly. Last Sunday I declared, "Let us be crazy for God." I want us to be proud once again on Easter Sunday, 1979, to be crazy for God. There is no moment to spare for anything else. Jesus said, love God with all your heart, all your mind, all your soul. This is my first and greatest commandment. Yes, let's act on it. This Easter you can receive resurrection. It is available to you right now. You have no time to waste your energy anywhere else. We need our strength to tackle the business we need to do. Remember once again, Jesus declared the emergency. He said, follow me. Leave the dead to bury their own dead. Let us attend to the business of life, the business of resurrection. Not for our own sakes but for the sake of New York, the sake of this nation, the sake of this world. Let us pray.

Prayer by Bo Hi Pak:

Most loving Heavenly Father, thank You very much for Your life, for Your beauty, for Your excitement, and above all for Your love. Above all we thank You for the truth which takes us out of darkness. We are saved in Your truth, in Your love, because we know the person who declares, I am the resurrection. Thank You, Father. Those brothers and sisters who came, bestow upon them the joy of resurrection. Those brothers and sisters who could not come, be with them today. Guide them into the resurrection. Thank You, Father, until we gather together again next Sunday for a most inspiring and glorifying service. Father, protect all of us in Thy bosom. Thank You, Father. All these things we pray in the name of Christ, Your Son. Amen.

Saul and Paul

NEW YORK, NEW YORK

APRIL 22, 1979

*In this sermon, Dr. Pak uses the dramatic conversion of
St. Paul to illustrate the law of indemnity and the power
of the truth.*

Good morning, our brothers and sisters. I have not forgotten you. Did you
have a wonderful, God-centered week? I pray that we will increase His
Kingdom this coming week. Here in the New York metropolitan area, we
are in a 120-day crusade and we are approaching the final week. Today we
worship together in this auditorium to renew our loyalty, love, and enthusiasm to increase his Kingdom in the coming week.

Two weeks ago I preached about an important disciple of Jesus whose
name was Stephen. Today I want to share with you about another great
individual, probably the greatest name in the history of Christianity, St.
Paul.

The title of my sermon today is "Saul and Paul." Of course, I am talking about one person. Saul was Paul's name before his conversion. The
important thing is that Paul and Saul are one and the same individual. Saul
was a very wicked man, an enemy of God, persecuting the disciples of Jesus
with all his might. In those days of the first century, he was truly a great
enemy of Jesus Christ. He was a most feared person among the Christians.

I don't think any name today is comparable to the Saul of the first century. We have notorious names such as Ted Patrick. We have infamous names like Congressman Fraser. We have unkindly statesmen like Senator Robert Dole. But all these people combined don't match the magnitude of Saul.

Saul was a great leader, full of energy and enthusiasm. He had conviction. He was capable. He was a fiery speaker, probably comparable to Billy Graham. But he was working for Satan and his power was destructive, devastating, and formidable.

But then he became Paul. After he became Paul, all the qualities he demonstrated against God, against Jesus Christ, he now concentrated and used for the sake of God, for the sake of Jesus Christ, for the sake of Christianity. He became a great soul in Christian history. Today among many theologians Christianity is known as St. Paul's religion. That is how much Paul molded the tradition of Christianity, and his sermons and letters became part of the Bible.

We can learn many lessons from St. Paul's most dramatic conversion. Please remember that Saul and Paul are one and the same person. Paul was the restored Saul. We know clearly that the work of God is the work of restoration. Today we see out there the world of Saul: New York City, the great city of Saul today. There is also the nation of Saul, the world of Saul. But there is hope when we read the dramatic conversion of St. Paul. The city of New York can be a Paul City. The nation can be a Paul nation. This world of ours can be a Paul world.

I WAS A SAUL

Also, at one time you and I were Saul. Today we are living as Paul. Before I came to God and Divine Principle, I was a Saul. Let me dwell a few moments on my personal testimony.

In 1950 when the Korean War broke out, I was studying in a military academy comparable to West Point. I was a cadet and I was looking forward to becoming a general one day. That was my hope and ambition. Not as much as St. Paul, but I was an ambitious young Korean man, 21 years old, with bubbling enthusiasm and vitality. Then the Korean War came June 25, 1950. On that very day, I was already at the frontline. In three days, two-thirds of our classmates, approximately 220 comrades in the West Point of Korea, were killed in action. That was the beginning of my military life. During the three years of the Korean War, I really learned the emptiness of human life. I became a searcher for the meaning of life.

One time I was leading a company of 200 men. We came to a river. Everything seemed clear, and I asked my men to put their gear on top of their heads and forge across the river. There was a cliff in front of us. It seemed to be a peaceful day, almost like a picnic. Then all of a sudden, when every man was in the water, a shower of bullets came right across the river from the top of the cliff. The Chinese army struck with their machine guns at this most vulnerable moment when everybody was in the water. We were absolutely defenseless. Before I could even give any orders, most of the men collapsed and the water immediately turned crimson red with their blood.

I was still on the river bank. I fell to the ground, but there was not much to take cover behind. I pulled a big stone out of the sand. I became like Samson. I don't know where that strength came from. I used the stone to protect my head. But under those circumstances, even though you may not be killed instantly, if you are hit in the arm or leg, you are finished because you have many, many hundreds of miles to retreat. With a wounded arm or leg you cannot go on. It would be better, if you are destined to die, to be killed instantly. But instinct drove me to take cover.

At that very moment, I felt God. I needed God. And in the very next split second I felt: I don't have God. I called the name of God and knew my heart was empty. I called the name of God and found that I was not ready to die. I was not prepared to die. A very empty feeling. Then I felt there is only one thing. If I survive this, God, I will worship you. I will find you. I need religion. But as a soldier, I knew what I really needed was military help. I needed United Nations bombers. They could attack the enemy and maybe I could escape. And exactly as I was thinking that, four fighter bombers appeared in the sky and began to bombard the enemy with rockets. The enemy had to take cover so the shower of bullets decreased. I stood up and checked my body. That was professional training. You have to check your body because sometimes in battle you are wounded, but you don't recognize the pain. I found myself whole, intact. Then I shouted to my men to follow me. But there were almost no men to follow. Only two men were alive and trying to follow me but they were seriously wounded. During the bombardment I escaped.

At that time I knew that Bo Hi Pak was dead. For some reason, some power saved me. I must make good on my promise. I must find God. I decided to become a religious person who will find the meaning of life and the meaning of death.

In 1952, I came to Fort Benning, Georgia, for military training for six months. I saw the Christian nation of America blessed by God. I decided to become a Christian. I was baptized into the Church of Christ in Columbus, Georgia.

MY HEART WAS COLD

For five more years, I kept searching for the meaning of God. I was search-ing for the true meaning of the Bible. I was reading. I was attending church regularly. But my heart, for some reason, was not ignited. I was not really burning in zeal or religious fervor. I still found myself very cold. God was not real to me. One day the Church of Christ minister approached me and said, "Would you like to go to the United States to finish your degree? Our church will pay you a full scholarship. Your trip, dormitory, everything." The only condition was that when I returned I would have to become a Church of Christ minister. I spent a sleepless night. The next morning I went to the minister and said in a heartbroken way, no, I cannot do it. Why? Because God is not real in my heart. I cannot preach to anyone if God is not real to me. I simply cannot become a hypocrite. It is one con-dition I cannot accept. If he wanted me to become a slave, I would have been happy to do it. But to become a church minister, no, because God is not real to me. So I gave up that opportunity.

Five years later, in 1957, I met Reverend Moon. I learned the Divine Principle. I never had the title of "reverend," but ever since I met Reverend Moon, one thing is sure: I am fired up with the zeal and fervor of God. The Divine Principle made God so real to my heart. This morning I was sitting in the chair thinking about those days. I refused to preach to anyone because God was not real to me. But now here I am willing to speaking to you brothers and sisters, even in English, which is not my mother tongue. I know I cannot convey fully what I want to convey. I know I cannot be eloquent like David Hose or Billy Graham or Oral Roberts. These are not my competitors. But here I am, genuinely trying to convey that I have found God through the Divine Principle. I have found the purpose of life and I will gladly give my life for the purpose of God. That is my testimo-ny. It is not like the dramatic story of St. Paul, but you know I was a Saul one day and became a Paul. Everyone one day is Saul and will become Paul one way or another.

Today I would like to share with you several lessons from St. Paul's dra-matic conversion. First, you might ask God why He chose a man like Paul, the worst enemy of God in the first century. There were priests and many well-educated people. But God bypassed everybody and asked Saul to serve Him. I want you to understand that Saul's dramatic conversion could not take place without Stephen's great sacrifice.

As you know, Stephen was the first martyr in Christian history. Satan took the very best member of Christianity of those days. They didn't have too many members. But Stephen was one of the best champions of God in those early days of the Christian church. And Satan claimed the best of

God's soldiers, Stephen. I want you to understand that the law of indemnity is always at work. Satan claimed the best soldier of God. Because of that condition God now claimed the best soldier of Satan. Saul was chosen.

GOD NEEDS PEOPLE OF PASSION

I want you to understand the Bible. Revelation 3:15-17 says, "I know your works; you are neither cold nor hot. Would that you were cold or hot! So, because you are lukewarm, and neither cold nor hot, I will spew you out of my mouth." This is a very important passage for us to know. God needs either a cold man or a hot man because these two extreme temperatures have something in common—passion. This is their common characteristic. Saul was extremely cold. Icy cold. Yet he was a man of passion, a man of justice. Saul went after the disciples, one after the other, because he believed that Christianity was truly evil. He believed that exterminating Christianity was the work of God. That is why he was doing it. He was a most effective destroyer of Christianity because he believed in it. His conscience, in a way, was clear. He didn't know the true aspect of Christianity. In other words, he was totally ignorant about Christianity, but he had passion, ability, leadership.

So, when God claimed Saul, he was stricken by the light from heaven and heard a great voice. He became blind. The old self of Saul was dead. He became a new man. Out of his new vision, he saw the new truth. He no longer was in darkness. He saw who Jesus Christ was. So then the cold passion turned into God's passion. From then on he was an extraordinary worker for God.

Today we are in the same boat. When you go out and preach the gospel of God, the Divine Principle, don't worry if the person you are witnessing to is negative initially. I want you to understand that the work of God is done, not by you, but by the power and spirit of God Himself. In the conversion of St. Paul, it was Jesus who directly intervened, not the preaching of any disciple. Jesus struck him down. By the same token, if you are today truly working in the spirit of God, I want you to know that the extraordinary power of God and the Holy Spirit is working with you. Do not judge that this man is hopeless or that man is of God. It does not work in that fashion. The worst enemy can become the best disciple of God. That was the case 2,000 years ago and can be true today.

Christianity itself is truly the religion of indemnity. Two thousand years ago Satan claimed Jesus Christ and nailed him to the cross. Nailing Jesus to the cross was like destroying the entire will of God because no one else on earth represented God's will. Jesus Christ was the only son of God living here on earth. The rest of the world is the world of Satan in the sight of God. So when Satan nailed Jesus Christ down on the cross, he nailed the entire world of God to the cross. This was the greatest victory Satan could claim.

By the law of indemnity, since Satan claimed the entire world of God by crucifying Jesus, now God can claim the world of Satan by resurrecting Jesus Christ from the tomb. By believing in Jesus, the entire world can be saved. In other words, God claimed the entire satanic world. It doesn't make any difference whether you are Korean or American or Japanese or Eskimo—whoever comes to the name of Jesus Christ shall be saved. Salvation was made universal. Because Satan claimed the entire world of God, now God by the power of the resurrection can claim the entire world of Satan.

MILLIONS WILL RISE UP

Today many policymakers of this country or some of our adversaries sometimes think that by removing Reverend Moon from this country, the problem of the Unification Church will be ended. But this is not how the law of indemnity operates. As Reverend Moon himself has preached: "Do you think that knocking me down or killing me or deporting me from this country threatens the Unification Church? No. If I die, if somebody destroys me, millions of Reverend Moons will rise up and continue the task."

The work of God in the history of Christianity has always been nonviolent. When Jesus' army landed in Rome and the Roman Empire, which was truly the entire world in those days, they didn't have any arms. This was a nonviolent, bare-handed army. But in 400 years, the Roman Empire collapsed in front of this feeble army through the law of indemnity. You pay the price and God can claim it. Acts 9:10-16 describes how after Saul's conversion experience Jesus instructed Ananias to go find Saul and bless him so that he would regain his sight. Ananias resisted this command, saying Saul was doing much evil to Jesus' followers. Jesus answered that Saul was his chosen instrument and that he would "show him how much he must suffer for the sake of my name."

Why does almighty God have to make His people suffer? All the disciples of Jesus suffered. Saint Paul was already ordained for suffering. Why? I want you to understand suffering has two meanings in Christianity and today in the Unification Church as well. Through suffering you can show your true loyalty to God. In an easy, comfortable way of life, there is no way you can set yourself apart as different from others. Under adverse conditions you prove who you are, whether you are sons and daughters of God. In Divine Principle we say by being willing to cope with suffering we can set ourselves apart from Satan. Satan will have no more to say about you and me. The greatest of all the tests we are going through is liberation from Satan. Satan is holding every man here on earth. We must chop that tie. We must separate ourselves from Satan and move into God's camp. That is what our job is all about today.

In order to separate from Satan you must prove that Satan has no way to accuse you anymore. In other words, Satan must surrender and say to God: this man is truly your man—you can have him. Satan must release us so that we can move into God's camp. For this reason the best way to pay indemnity is by absolute loyalty and gratitude. No matter how much great work you do or how much you suffer, if you do it with a very conditional and complaining heart, it does not bring you any good. You are wasting your energy and time. Therefore, two key words in Christianity to become a godly man are: unconditional faith and total commitment. This is very difficult to do, particularly today in the American way of life. People are always looking for excuses and protection. We want to have insurance. In business, we have contracts between this company and that company, with brilliant lawyers working to protect their interests. They like to have some loophole so that they can escape. But when you face the work of God, the wisest thing to do is to give your unconditional devotion and unconditional dedication and total commitment. That is the essence of the Christian faith. This is the one thing Satan cannot have any claim on. Satan will surrender to this attitude of absolute loyalty.

Remember Abraham. God gave Abraham an unreasonable instruction. One day God said to Abraham, I need your son. Take your son to Mount Moriah and offer him in a burnt offering. Kill him and offer him to me. This was unreasonable, illogical, even crazy. There were thousands of complaints Abraham could choose to make. He could say, "What kind of God are you? How cruel you are. Didn't you say I would have this son so that my generations will be like the stars in the sky and the sand in the ocean? You gave me this son when I was 100 years old. You know I am not going to have any more sons. If I kill him, how can I be the father of thousands and thousands of generations?"

Abraham could have complained, but he chose not to. He knew that these instructions came from God and he accepted them unconditionally. He had a willing and a grateful heart. It was a three-day journey to Mount Moriah. I know that was a painful three days. You know Isaac constantly asked him, "Father, we have a knife, we have wood, but where is the sheep?" When his father heard such questions how much his heart must have broken. He unconditionally obeyed and he went to Mount Moriah and finally bound his son upon the altar and lifted up the knife. He was totally obedient. He had not even a single trace of complaint. In that moment, what happened? God said in a loud voice from heaven, Abraham, Abraham, I know now that you fear Me. Do not kill him. You already passed the test. You have proved yourself worthy to receive My blessing.

In terms of the Divine Principle, God was saying that Abraham was free from satanic accusation. With that kind of faith, Satan had no more claim on him.

A RANSOM TO SATAN

Jesus Christ's severe test came to him when he was hanging on the cross. The Bible records that Jesus shouted out saying, "*Eloi, Eloi, lama sabachthani?*" which means "My God, my God, why hast thou forsaken me?" Jesus knew God had given up on him. God was giving him as a ransom to Satan. Why have you forsaken me? But it was not said out of a disobedient heart. It can be seen very obviously in the final words Jesus spoke, "Father, forgive them for they know not know what they do."

Jesus was dying as the messiah for the salvation of the people. As he was dying, he was asking God to save and forgive his enemy. What total faith, what total commitment, what total gratitude. Upon such faith indeed the power of God resurrected him and brought salvation to mankind.

Today let us move in this spirit. Let us not be wise men in earthly terms. Truly wise men in God's sight look like fools in the sight of the world. So we Unification Church members will accept the criticism that we look like damn fools. St. Paul himself said, "Yes, we are fools for Christ." Let us become today fools for God. In the sight of God, we will be truly wise men and women.

There is another point I want to emphasize from Acts 9. When God appeared in the power of Jesus Christ and St. Paul shouted out saying, "Who are you, Lord?" Jesus said, "I am Jesus, whom you are persecuting." Jesus did not say, "I am Jesus, whose disciples you are persecuting." Jesus said, "I am Jesus, whom you are persecuting." Actually, St. Paul didn't do any harm to Jesus. He was killing Jesus' disciples. But Jesus said, "You are persecuting me!" This is quite significant. I want you to understand. Once Jesus commissioned his disciples to preach the gospel to the four corners of the earth, every disciple's action was the action of Jesus. The disciples were walking as Jesus himself. Every single one of them was commissioned to be another Jesus. So when they received persecution, this persecution became Jesus' own. So Jesus said, "I am Jesus, whom you are persecuting."

Today we must make ourselves champions of God. Reverend Moon says that God is looking through your eyes at the world. When you use your brain, are you thinking like God? I want you to understand your two eyes are two windows for God. God is looking at the world through your two eyes. God is talking through your mouth to the world. God is listening through your ears. From God's standpoint, your heart must be broken. This world is full of so much wickedness, ungodliness. That is why if truly you are a Christian, if truly you are the servant of God and sons and daughters of God, your heart must be broken.

So Reverend Moon has brought not just a joyful religion. Before we come to rejoice over the true joy and peace we are going to have, we must first understand the broken heart of God. We look at the world from God's standpoint. We speak to the world from God's standpoint. Then I want you to understand your battle is God's battle and God's battle becomes yours. So if anybody persecutes you, the spirit of God will say: I am God whom you are persecuting.

Finally, when you read the verses right after Saul's conversion experience, before he even left the city of Damascus, Saul was already preaching to his fellow Jewish people saying that "Jesus is the son of God." Think of it today. Let us say that the great power reveals to Senator Robert Dole, and he stands up one day saying, "I saw the power of God." Maybe someday the power of God will appear to [deprogrammer] Ted Patrick and convert him and he will say, "I thought Reverend Moon's movement was wicked and evil, and now I have found that it is godly. Now I proclaim that it is the work of God." Unthinkable, isn't it?

But I want you to understand that the worst enemy of Jesus, who was killing the disciples, turned around in the city of Damascus and began proclaiming that Jesus is the son of God. Amazing. We must respect the courage of St. Paul. Paul totally repented. He turned around without any reservation and gave his total commitment, testifying and proving that Jesus is the Christ. Today when we see the truth, let us go to the world and preach boldly. It is not easy to stand up for the truth. It is not easy. People will spit at you. People will scorn you. But that is the kind of courage we must learn from St. Paul.

In Matthew 10:32-33 Jesus said, "So every one who acknowledges me before men, I also will acknowledge before my Father who is in heaven; but whoever denies me before men, I also will deny before my Father who is in heaven." Let us boldly acknowledge the work of God, have no fear, and speak the truth.

Today every one of us in this troubled world today is commissioned in the mission of St. Paul. Let us be committed and let us be bold, proclaiming to the world the truth of God.

Prayer by Bo Hi Pak:

Our Father in heaven, thank you very much that we can gather together in Your name to be Your sons and daughters. Father, we have true happiness and joy that is everlasting in our hearts. We have been given the power to overcome the difficulties, overcome the problems, even overcome the fear of death because we see your word is powerful. Thank you, Father. Bless all of the brothers and sisters gathered together in this room so that they can increase Your kingdom. We gather together to rejoice over the fellowship centered upon You. Thank You for this worship. All these things we pray in the name of Christ our Lord, amen.

Daughter, Your Faith Has Made You Well

NEW YORK, NEW YORK

APRIL 29, 1979

Using stories from the New Testament, Bo Hi Pak talks about our portion of responsibility in God's restoration and about how our love and faith are pivotal to the liberation of God's heart.

May God bless you richly this morning with grace and spirit and love. It is wonderful to see you again. Many new faces. Many old faces. Many different colors and many different races. Truly, this is a living color service. I know this service pleases God. We come from all different cultural backgrounds. Different languages. Different ways of life. Different food. Yet we are fully aware that we gather together in this auditorium on one common ground as children of God and we are brothers and sisters.

In order to truly become brothers and sisters, we must recognize one common parent: God. When God has become real in our hearts, we truly recognize him as our Father. Then we know our brotherhood will become complete. This morning I want to speak about faith.

There is one incredible story in the Bible, in the fifth chapter of Mark, that always touches my heart. We can see in this passage a beautiful example of simple faith. Visualize a very poor, suffering woman. She had suffered from a disease for 12 years and had visited many doctors, all to no avail. She was hemorrhaging blood, and she became desperate. She heard about Jesus performing miracles and healings. She wanted to be healed. She wanted to believe in the power of God that manifested through Jesus Christ.

The woman waited quietly for Jesus to pass. I know she was timid, almost trembling. Having simple faith, she touched the garment of Jesus Christ. At that very moment, the blood stopped. The hemorrhaging was healed. Of course, she was jubilant. I can well imagine her excitement and joy and happiness. But that only lasted a few seconds because she knew Jesus detected that someone had touched his garment, and he was trying to see who it was. Jesus asked, "Who touched my garments?" There was a large crowd around him, so naturally many people had touched him. But Jesus didn't mean that. Jesus meant the one specific instance that someone touched him and "power had gone forth from him."

This woman of simple faith knew that she could not escape so she, "in fear and trembling," confessed to Jesus. She thought that touching him might have been a grave mistake or some kind of sin. But Jesus turned around to her and said, "Daughter, your faith has made you well; go in peace and be healed of your disease." The key is in this sentence: "Daughter, your faith has made you well." Wasn't it God who healed her? Wasn't it the power of the son of God that healed this woman? Surely, the credit must go to God. But Jesus said your *faith* has made you well. Go in peace.

From this story we learn an incredible truth about God. God does not really heal. Why? Because the power of God's healing is always available. It is a matter of men claiming it. That is the whole point of the Bible. That is the central point about the dispensation of God. For example, in this room, although you don't sense it, there are all kinds of waves. Some rock music, some other sermon, some classical music, some television waves, all kinds of waves are here to fill up the air. In order to understand those air waves, we need a radio or television set and we have to switch it on. Then we can receive the air waves that are already here.

By the same token, the power of God is always available. It is a matter of men becoming a radio set or a television set and turning on the switch. That switch is our faith. Jesus said, your faith made you well. Jesus Christ, as the son of God, brought down from God the power to heal this entire universe and more. Many times over. But Jesus needed a response from the people. The response was to determine the outcome. This area of responsibility God cannot touch. This is why God is taking so long to restore mankind. This is why today many people claim that either there is no God, or they don't understand God, or they don't need that kind of helpless God.

Many people who come to study the Divine Principle say, "I want to believe in God, I want to know about the Bible, but truly I cannot understand. If almighty God exists, why doesn't He do anything about this suffering world?" People even believe that God is dead. If God is dead, it is useless to call on Him for help.

Communism tells believers that they are crazy. There is no such thing as God. One time on Moscow radio they pronounced on Christmas morning that their rocket was flying through space and had not discovered God yet. According to them, Christianity is the opium of the masses and Jesus Christ will be relegated to mythology. What the communists are trying to do is throw God out of this planet, and they themselves want to become the god of this world.

I FOUND THE REAL GOD

But the men and women who come to the Divine Principle brought by Reverend Sun Myung Moon find a deep understanding of the Bible and the fundamental questions of life. For example, I, myself, was trying to be a good Christian for five years before I joined the Unification Church. I was trying to understand the Bible. But the Bible didn't make sense. I thought I was awfully dumb. God was not interesting to me. The Bible was very dry. It didn't seem to have answers to the vital questions such as why a God of goodness would leave all the wickedness and evil of the world alone. Why is there so much crime, so much war and death, dishonesty, impurity? When I studied Divine Principle, it gave me the answers. This is the deepest motivation. I knew that the Divine Principle was the truth. A revelation from God. I found the real God. I understood God.

Men are born to believe. Today many people believe in science, and they say science is everything. Science will bring utopia and solve the human problems. There are great Nobel Prize winners. They invented the atomic bomb. They discovered the mighty power of atoms. It seems to me humankind is truly cracking open the secrets of the universe. They are trying to solve the problem by knowledge. But I tell you, even a million Ph.D.s and Harvard graduates or Nobel Prize winners cannot figure out the mystery hidden in just one simple green leaf. They cannot figure out why this particular flower is white and this one is yellow, what makes this one such a beautiful pink. Even in this one green leaf, there is incredible mystery.

According to the Divine Principle, when Almighty God created man, He left a certain responsibility to man. For illustration purposes, we say that God left five percent of the responsibility to us. God creates us unperfected, unfinished. We have to fulfill our five percent of responsibility to become perfect. Everything else God created 100 percent complete. The trees, stones, rivers, sun, and all the heavenly bodies are 100 percent complete. This means that all these creations, other than man, are like a gadget, like a machine, set to do certain fixed things. This watch was created to do a set responsibility. This watch does not have the liberty or freedom to deviate from its given purpose. But God did not create man like this. God created man with freedom, with choice, which is given to man as a responsibility to God.

Why did God do that? Because of that, the fall of man came about. You see, if God had set man's will 100 percent, man could not deviate from the Principle. There could be no sin. There could be no fall. For God it would have been much simpler and saved a great heartache. But men were given choice and freedom, and men made the wrong choice. For 6,000 biblical years we have suffered the consequences of Adam and Eve's choice. Why did God do that? Why didn't he save Himself the trouble? He did it with nature, the trees, the moon and sun and water and everything else.

THE ANSWER IS LOVE

When I understood the deep meaning of why God made man different, it touched my heart. I became a Unification Church member. I knew the answer through the Divine Principle. The answer is love. God loved man. God wanted man to be special. Do you know how special? God wanted man to be another God. How can you expect any more than that? God wanted us to be another God, or even better than God. I am sure some brothers and sisters might say, you, Mr. Pak, are blasphemous. How can we be better than God? Yet I learned this from Reverend Moon, so don't blame me, blame Reverend Moon, all right?

But this makes sense. In what respect are we better than God? We have form. God doesn't. In other words, God is infinite, invisible form. We are made into substantial form. We are supposed to be walking Gods. There is a phrase in the English language, a "walking dictionary." You are not supposed to be just a walking dictionary. You are supposed to be walking Gods. In order to be like God, what do you need? What is God's most important characteristic? God has many, many important characteristics. But what makes God, God? The power to create. God has the power of creation. God is ideal and He can make that ideal become real. Therefore, in the original Principle of Creation, God wanted us to be another God. We can be identical to God, except He is invisible and we are visible. We can be another creator.

We know that we are created beings. We can never imitate God 100 percent. In other words, God is Creator. We are creatures, or created. He is the manufacturer, and we are the manufactured. I manufacture the watch. The watch is manufactured. The watch and I can never be the same. In order to make this watch the same as the maker, man, it would have to fulfill a qualification. Man, also, has to qualify to be a walking God. This is the reason God created man imperfect. The five percent responsibility God left to man. If we accomplish that responsibility, then God will say that man is a joint project between man and God.

Let us say God is building a wall, and God has laid 99 stones, but the wall will never be completed without one final stone being laid on top. God is asking man to put the final stone on top of the wall. When we have done it, God will say, my son, my daughter, you and I created this wall, so we both are the creators. So when there is a stockholders meeting for that wall, God sits on one side of the table and man sits on the other. We sit together. We are partners. God wanted to give this qualification to man. If God creates 100 percent of man, we are merely robots, no different from this watch. Therefore, we would eternally remain as creatures, created, not creators. To me this is the highest love God can bestow upon man. Although God created you and me, God wants us to be a joint, common, co-creator. This is love.

Since God is our Father, we shall become His sons and daughters. We call ourselves mankind, right? I want to create a new word: Godkind. We want to be included in God's race and not the fallen human race. And God wants to lift everybody up to be side by side as father and son. How could we ask for anything more?

WE CAN DO WHAT GOD CANNOT DO

As I said, we can do more than God. We can do things that God cannot do. We can eat the steak which God cannot. We can touch things which God cannot. We can build a wall which God cannot. This is the very reason God needs you and me today. We are God's tools. Without us, God's ultimate fulfillment of the kingdom of heaven will never be possible.

When man fell it was something like the man dropping the final stone that would have completed the wall. Any parent would be able to pick up the stone and say, let me do that for you. God could easily say, let me do it. God indeed has the power to pick up the stone. But God cannot do it. Why? Once God picks up the stone and completes 100 percent of the wall, at that moment you and I would be relegated to being robots. Do you understand? Robots. God did not want to have robots as His children. God wants to have Godkind as His children. Therefore, 6,000 years have gone by already. It might take another 1,000 years. But God needs us to pick up the stone and try again and again and again, until we finish the wall, which means finish ourselves, make ourselves perfect as God is perfect. Perfect in love.

For that purpose Jesus came. Matthew 5:48 says, "You, therefore, must be perfect as your heavenly Father is perfect." It is our goal. As impossible a goal as it seems to be, it is our goal. One day God wants us to be as perfect as He is perfect and even better. And what is our responsibility? It is to pick up the stone and lay it on top of the wall. That means to have faith. Faith is our responsibility. Faith will complete our creation. Faith means willing participation. God gives us the bold choice of saying yes or no. God is waiting for us to voluntarily stand up and say, yes, Father, I am your son.

How many thousands of years God has been suffering, waiting, waiting in anguish. God cannot do things directly. The moment God does things directly, does the things you and I should do, we would be relegated to robots. A manufactured product. God does not want that, no matter how many more thousands of years He may suffer. Compared to eternity, many thousands of years of suffering is nothing. God can still wait. In the meantime He suffers without His children. This is the heart we must understand. The Unification Church brought the heart of God to the world for the first time. Reverend Moon is the prophet who revealed the broken heart of God. God's broken heart.

Many Christians think God is sitting on a throne, enjoying great power and presiding over the universe. No. He is not. God is without a smile. His heart has been broken again and again. After all, we are His children and we are either dead or crippled. Do you think any parents would enjoy a single day when their child is either dead or crippled? That has been the life of God for 6,000 years. God's situation has been a tearful one, not because He is lacking in power, but because He created us in such a way that He could not exercise His almighty power until men take initiative and say, Father, I believe, I can take responsibility, I have faith. That is the kind of children God has been waiting for for 6,000 years.

Today, the Unification Church is creating a new faith, a new breed of people who will come out and stand before God saying, my Father, now I know you finally, I believe in You unconditionally. That is what the Unification Church faith is all about.

Reverend Moon's favorite words are "the liberation of God." Liberation of God. Amazing. Who has ever talked about this in all of human history? Have you ever heard any philosophy, any religion, anybody talk about the liberation of God? Reverend Moon is the first to proclaim this in history. Reverend Moon is proclaiming that we are going to liberate God from His heartbroken sorrow, and we will comfort Him and bring

Him joy for the first time in history. In order to do that we must fulfill our five percent responsibility, which is faith.

After God created Adam and Eve, God said to them in Genesis 2:16-17, "You may freely eat of every tree of the garden; but of the tree of the knowledge of good and evil you shall not eat, for in the day that you eat of it you shall die." This is very interesting. If God is almighty, God can block any danger that would come to His children. God didn't have to give such a commandment. If any danger crept up to His children, He could stop it. He could protect them. He doesn't have to give them this warning. But there is a reason God told Adam and Eve that they would die if they ate of the fruit of that tree. He was telling them that they had a choice. They had to choose to obey or not to obey. And God could not protect them from the consequence of that choice. It is their responsibility. Therefore, to undo the consequence of that choice is also their responsibility. It is our responsibility. God is waiting.

Adam and Eve made the wrong choice. They disbelieved God. The fundamental reason for the fall of man is disbelief. Eve, instead of listening to the word of God, listened to the word of Satan. The word of Satan was more sweet to her. That was the motivation of the fall. They disbelieved in God. God cannot give you faith. God cannot make you believe.

A HORRENDOUS SCENE

During the Korean war I had an incredible experience when I was a company commander. My company of about 200 men was attacking one hill. Enemy machine gun fire was coming from the top of the hill. They were firing at us, firing and firing. Even though we bombarded them with artillery and air support, they never stopped. Every time our company tried to assault the top of the hill, they fired at us. I was thinking how brave the enemy soldiers were. I respected their courage. But finally, at the end of the day, we took the hill. When we came to the enemy trench, we found a horrendous scene. It was unbelievable what we found in that trench. The enemy soldiers were all dead. But that was not what so horrible. Every single communist soldier was chained to the concrete wall of the trench. They had no freedom to escape. They were there to die. They were forced to die.

Do you call that patriotism? Did they die for love of their country? Were they loyal even unto death? No. Forced loyalty, forced patriotism, forced death have no value. Patriotism, loyalty, love—all have to be voluntary, freely chosen, freely given. If you do things at gunpoint, there is no value in the sight of God. God will never deprive us of our five percent responsibility. We would no longer be God's children. Our return to God has got to be voluntary. God cannot force you. No one makes you worship. God doesn't call you to Him at gunpoint.

I want you to understand this is why God is taking a long, long time to restore mankind. God could restore the world in a second. Presto, finished. But God wants us to come to Him voluntarily, by our free choice, through faith. The power to re-create man and the universe is always available. We must respond to it with our faith. This is why Jesus said to the woman, your faith made you well. This is why John 3:16 proclaims, "For God so loved the world that He gave His only Son, that whoever believes in him should not perish but have eternal life." But that does not give you automatic salvation. There is a condition. "Whoever believes in Him should not perish but have eternal life." It is your responsibility and my responsibility. "Whoever believes in Him" is your job and my job.

I want to conclude by recalling another dramatic story from the Bible. One day Jesus encountered a man who had been born blind. According to John 9:6, Jesus "spat on the ground and made clay of the spittle and anointed the man's eyes with the clay." It sounds dirty, doesn't it? Spit and dirt on your face. Jesus said to him, "Go wash in the pool of Siloam." This man who was blind must have been a very righteous man and a man of simple faith. This was his test. He believed in that word and stood up and went to the lake and washed and came back completely healed. His vision had come back. Restored. Praise the Lord, he said.

Every miracle has a teaching. The teaching is this. Jesus did his part in restoring the man's vision; then the man had to do his five percent: believe. Accept the word. Unite with it. The pool of water was not important. Acceptance of the word of Jesus was important. Believing in him was important. Believe in him, obey him, and go to the lake and wash, and you will see.

HIS FAITH HELD HIM UP

Matthew 14:22-33 describes the night Jesus walked on the water. He had been alone up on a mountain praying; the disciples were waiting in a boat "many furlongs distant from the shore." Jesus "came to them, walking on the sea." Jesus told Peter to walk on the water, which Peter did, but after a moment he became afraid and began to sink. As soon as he doubted, he sank. His faith held him up; his lack of faith sent him down.

Today, let us become men and women of infinite faith. Let us accept God and Christ and the Coming of the Second Advent, the Divine Principle. Let us accept in faith. Trying to gain salvation through your brain will not work. Once the Divine Principle convinces you that the power of God is working, then you must solve your problem in infinite faith.

I remember Reverend Moon saying in the early days of his discovery of the Divine Principle that he prayed for only one thing. "God, let me believe the things that throughout history all other people said they could not believe." That was Reverend Moon's prayer. The things people could not believe, let me believe it. Let me accept it. Let me obey it. Let me do it. Because of that infinite faith, the Divine Principle is today in our hands.

Faith the size of a mustard seed can move a mountain. I see that Reverend Moon's faith is a mountain-size faith. I know that the truth and his faith and our faith together can move the world. We can move God and move God's heart. We can liberate God from His sorrowful, broken heart. Let us pray.

Prayer by Bo Hi Pak:

Our loving Heavenly Father, thank You very much for this enlightening day. Father, Your truth is assimilated into our hearts, deep down, cleansing all ungodliness of the week. Father, we truly believe in You as our Father, Almighty God as a Creator, but who because of us, suffers so much for humanity to restore us. We believe in You that You will ultimately restore all mankind. We believe in You and You will prevail. You will win. Father, we want to be Your champions. We want to be Your instruments day by day. Give us added energy and inspiration this coming week. Every one of us who bows down together in this room shall receive Your power in our infinite faith in You. All these things we pray in the name of our Lord Christ. Amen.

God Was Sorry He Had Made Man

NEW YORK, NEW YORK

MAY 6, 1979

Here, Dr. Pak compares our way of looking at the end of the world to how other people and religions perceive it. For them, he says, it represents destruction, whereas for us, it represents the end of an evil sovereignty and the beginning of a new era of hope.

Prayer by Bo Hi Pak:

Our most loving Heavenly Father. Once again, we gather together in this holy, sacred place to worship you, almighty Father. We've been through one entire week; you've been guiding us, leading us this week, so that we have much to thank You for this morning. Many have gone through burdens of the world, burdens of life, burdens of responsibility, many sicknesses, many trials and tribulations, Father, but You have been our Shepherd. I shall not want, because you make us lie down in green pastures, lead us to the running waters; our soul has been restored over and over again. Father, we empty our heart to concentrate on You this morning, nothing else. We come to receive Your spirit, Your truth, Your love. Above all, Your strength and power will carry us for another week, beginning from today. Father, we want to dwell with You in Your Kingdom, as Your sons and daughters. Father, cleanse our hearts this morning so that only Your spirit can speak and echo into our heart. We shall be better sons and daugh-

ters after this moment. It is the beginning of the hour, be with us all the way. All of this we pray in the name of Christ our Lord. Amen.

Welcome, once again, to this wonderful Sunday service. It is such a great pleasure to meet you and see your shining faces, beginning the new week. It is very wonderful that we consider Sunday as the beginning of the week. Many in our world regard Sunday as the last day of the week or as the rest day, picnic, laundry day, a day for doing whatever chores have accumulated during the week. But we believe Sunday is a day of dedication, of sanctification. So it is truly appropriate we gather together, sing hymns, pray, listen to the sermon and wonderful holy music to begin our new week.

I want you to make this Sunday service an important part of your life. Imperatively important and absolutely necessary. Without a Sunday service, you must feel the week would not go right. So let us make this Sunday service of the Unification Church, of Reverend Sun Myung Moon, an important spiritual phenomenon, a volcanic explosion in New York.

This morning, I would like to share with you the concept that we frequently hear talked about nowadays, commonly known as the end of the world. I'm sure that, not just me, but all of you frequently hear various predictions about the end of the world. No evangelical meeting in this land would be complete without mentioning the end of the world.

The phrase "end of the world" brings out a gloomy, unpleasant feeling. What comes to mind when you hear it is fear. Today, however, in this Unification Church pulpit, I want to share with you a different kind of end of the world. But, first, let us consider what people are saying.

Some time ago, a great scientist predicted that the end of the world will come in the form of heavenly bodies colliding. Two stars will collide with each other and it will destroy the earth. The scientist gave a very accurate prediction, the exact year, month, and day. Many people took it seriously because the scientist was very prominent and had data from a computer. Many people took refuge in the Colorado Rocky Mountain area, hoping they would be safe. Finally, that moment came. The moment for the collision came and nothing happened. The entire room exploded in joy! Several men had heart attacks, so at least those men saw the end of the world. The scientist who predicted the end of the world felt so bad. I heard that he killed himself, so he saw the end of the world too.

This is a very unusual story, but the common theme of all the beliefs and predictions is the expectation of destruction.

A few weeks ago there was a crisis with Three Mile Island, the nuclear power plant that almost brought the entire nation to hysteria. Within our own backyard, we were trembling in fear that we might become victims of nuclear holocaust. This country alone possesses nuclear power capability to wipe out mankind many times over. But America is not the only country with nuclear power. The Soviet Union probably has far more than this country. In nations like India, where people are starving by the millions, huge amounts of money are being spent to develop nuclear power. We know France has it, Great Britain has it, maybe South Africa has it. In a couple of decades, probably most of the countries on earth will have some form of nuclear capability.

Is that the way the world is going to end? Mny people think, well, while we have life here on earth, let us have fun today; we never know about tomorrow. That expedient way of life has become very popular.

THE STARS WILL FALL FROM HEAVEN

On the other hand, Christians have different reasons to believe in the end of the world, because they believe in the Bible. The Bible has many predictions about the end of the world—which is not very comforting to Christians and non-Christians alike.

For example, Matthew 24:29 warns, "Immediately after the tribulation of those days, the sun will be darkened, and the moon will not give its light, and the stars will fall from heaven, and the powers from heaven will be shaken." Malachi 4:1 reads, "For behold, the day comes, burning like an oven, when all the arrogant and all the evil doers will be stubble; the day that comes shall burn them up." And 2 Peter 3:10 says, "But the day of the Lord will come like a thief, and then the heavens will pass away with a loud noise, and the elements will be dissolved with fire, and the earth and the works that are upon it will be burned up."

It's not comforting. However, according to the revelation received by Reverend Sun Myung Moon, we Unification Church members do have a very clear explanation of the end of the world.

For us, the end of the world is hope—not despair. We believe in a God of perfect will. In Isaiah 46:11 God says: "I have spoken, I will bring it to pass; I have purposed, and I will do it." God will accomplish His original purpose of creation, which is perfected man. God's children will be restored and one with Him. God did not say, I may do it ... I'll think about it ... I'll sleep on it overnight. God said, "I Will Do It!" There we see God's determination and iron will.

Because of the fall of Adam and Eve we live in a world of sin. Divine Principle describes our world as the kingdom of hell on earth. The world we live in is not in accord with God's plan. Far from it. It's a broken, sickened world. It's a world that needs to be cured. So when God says "I will end the world," it does not mean He will demolish the entire creation once and for all. God is saying that He will destroy evil and Satan's sovereignty.

Many places in the Bible indicate that the ruler of this world is not God. For example, John 8:44 says, "You are of your father the devil, and your will is to do your father's desires." Satan is our father, and we have been following him, rather than God. In other words, we've been a sinful generation. John 12:31 says, "Now is the judgment of this world, now shall the ruler of this world be cast out." So God is not the current ruler of this world. And 2 Corinthians 4:4 says, "In their case the god of this world has blinded the minds of the unbelievers, to keep them from the light of the gospel." That god is not a capital "G" God.

So, when God over and over talks about the end of the world, God is talking about the end of evil sovereignty on earth. The evil era will end and the good era will begin. Talking about the end of the world is only one side of the coin. When you look at the other side, it is a beginning of a new world of hope. God rules again. His power prevails. Christlike men see the day of justice. We'll see the kingdom of heaven on earth. That's the new world.

As it says in Revelation 21:1-4, "Then I saw a new heaven and a new earth; for the first heaven and the first earth had passed away. ... and I heard a loud voice from the throne saying, 'Behold, the dwelling of God is with men. He will dwell with them, and they shall be His people, and God Himself will be with them; He will wipe away every tear from their eyes, and death shall be no more, neither shall there be mourning nor crying nor pain any more, for the former things have passed away.' "

What will pass away? All the ungodly things, satanic things, unclean things. We will see new life and a new world. "The dwelling of God is with men," which means that God is not dwelling completely with men now! We must await the dwelling of God.

Therefore, the Unification Church proclaims the day of hope, rather than the fearful last days. Hope is a key word in the Unification Church. Once we have hope, we must know a couple of important things about God. As Reverend David Hose read to us, God declared in Genesis that He was sorry He had made man. Have you thought about that? God was sorry that He had made man. Why do you feel sorry? You feel sorry when your wishes have not been fulfilled. Your will has not been accomplished. That is why God felt sorry. When God first created the world, He was not sorry at all. You can read in the first chapter of Genesis that after every thing God created, God said that it was good. "And God saw that it was good." Heaven and earth, good. The sun and moon, good. Birds and fishes, good. It was good, wonderful, exactly the way He wanted it. Then, finally, God created man, Adam and Eve. You know what God said? God said it was VERY GOOD! Total satisfaction! Then He could rest.

But in Genesis 6, God said he was sorry He had made man. We learn two things from this statement: First, something went wrong. Something went against the will of God. Something terribly disturbed God. The second thing we learn is very important: God was sorry because for some reason God Himself could not prevent this from happening. God had to let it happen, even though the consequence was grief and suffering. That is very, very important. God was sorry He had made man. God's heart was broken.

That is still true today. When God looks at America, at New York City, He is still saying, I am sorry to see New York. But God is not in despair. God is not totally helpless. But it is important to understand that God is a personality of emotion. His heart has been broken again and again by us, His children.

Many Christians describe God as a God of power and dignity and happiness. They think that God is upstairs sitting on a gigantic throne wearing a crown. He is enjoying His power, sprinkling blessings here and there. "Are you happy this morning, my children? Here, have this blessing." Smiling ear to ear, morning to night.

Honestly speaking, before I joined the Unification Church, I thought of God in that fashion. I thought that was God. The greatest revelation Reverend Moon brought to this world and brought to me and many members of this church is: God is heartbroken. Our Heavenly Father is heartbroken. And the remedy must come from man, not from God.

Last week I described how God, because of His love, wants to make man like God. God created man with free will. You and I have a choice. No matter how many thousands of years God might breathe out His love, He did not want us to become robots. He wants us to become His sons and daughters. The true relationship between father and son must be one of love, and love must come from voluntary action. So, I want you to understand that the broken heart of God cannot be remedied until man voluntarily comes out of sin and comes back to calling God "Father."

If God could manipulate us like a computer, push buttons that would cure sin and get rid of Satan, I tell you, God would have done it a long, long time ago. It does not take God 6,000 years to think of a way out of this painful situation. So many people have come under the communist ideology, which is basically atheism. They say there is no God; we shall make ourselves God, the state will become God. God is listening to all of this kind of talk, and still He doesn't bring judgment down on us. Still He doesn't use force to change us. Our hearts won't change by force. It must come from education and inspiration.

GOD NEEDS YOU AND ME

There is beauty in the Unification Church revelation. We believe in infinite, almighty God, our loving Father in heaven. But, at the same time, we believe that God needs you and me, your heart and my heart. God needs you to come forward and say, God, I love You, You're my Father, You have been suffering long enough, I want to liquidate Your suffering, I want to liberate You from Your sorrow, Your heartbrokenness. Let me do it, let me bear your burden. God is waiting for such people.

When Reverend Moon proclaims the liberation of God, some people say it is absurd or blasphemous. But think of it, if God really can do everything by Himself, He would not wait for 6,000 years. He needs you. He needs a champion. Until you take voluntary action, God's heart will not be healed, God's purpose of creation will not be completed, and the Kingdom of God here on earth will not be a reality.

So, my dear brothers and sisters, you and I have been challenged to become champions of God. God is calling you this way. God is calling you in His most sad voice. For 6,000 years mankind has been deaf. God has been calling, over and over and over. Only the voluntary action of man, the triumphant action of man, will make God prevail.

Yes, very few people in history have listened to the bleeding voice of God, the suffering, heartbroken voice of God. Most of the people turn away with deaf ears. That's why you read in the Bible, in the days of Noah, people turned deaf ears. The Bible says they were given in marriage, they ate, they drank, they did all kinds of things on earth, but never thought about the situation of God. The same in the days of Lot; they never bothered with God.

Today, what do we have in New York? The people eat, they drink, they are given in marriage. Actually, they don't even have to be given in marriage these days! These formalities no longer seem to be necessary. All kinds of crazy things are going on in the city. People turn deaf ears to God, but His voice is calling and Reverend Moon heard His voice, very clearly. For the first time in history, one man is purely representing the suffering voice of God, calling out to humanity. That is Reverend Moon. The truth of the teaching of his revelation is so clear, even a dumb person like me, once I came to understand the teaching of the Divine Principle, understood the heart of God.

Now we can listen, now we can understand the suffering heart of God. Once you understand you automatically say to God, I'm your champion, use me. This is the day of challenge. Since we now know God correctly, we have our greatest, most important, most extraordinary challenge. I want to accept that challenge. It's going to be an exciting life, for you and me. Suffering may come, because as the Bible says in Luke 17:25, "But first he must suffer many things and be rejected by his generation." There's a lot of rejection going on, because this world of Satan, this world of sin, doesn't want to change. Satan doesn't want to give up being ruler of this world. Fallen people want to protect their fallen way of life. It's not going to be easy.

God needs your commitment, your undivided, total commitment. That seems impossible, but it can be easy with the power of truth. Once you learn the power of truth, commitment becomes easy. And I tell you the beauty of commitment: you don't lose. Commitment in life is like flipping a switch. Even if you forget everything I said today, please bring back home one phrase: flipping the switch. Commitment to God is like flipping the switch. You know, before you came to this room, somebody flipped the switch to turn on the lights. If you only move the switch part way, there is still no light. You must hear that clicking sound, then click, the light is there. Once you click yourself, you commit yourself to God.

At that moment, your life begins to shine; everything will happen. You will find you are no longer you, you are part of God. Your eating becomes God's eating, your speech, your hearing, everything becomes an instrument of God, and the power of God is shining through you. Before you commit yourself, it seems like a foolish thing to do, that you will be a loser, but once you click into the "on" position, then you are really plugged into God's power. Living for God is joy. Living for God is power. Living for God is happy. And one more important thing; in living for God there is no retirement. I'm determined not to retire; I want to go on. Another fantastic thing about living for God is there's no bottom, you'll not hit the bottom. Infinite giving, infinite receiving, there's no end. You can make yourself as big as the universe. Reverend Moon frequently says, "Do even better than God, and God will love you, God will not be jealous."

Yes, we're living in the 20th century waiting for the appearance of such sons and daughters who will say, God, I'm coming, use me to build your kingdom! I've determined my life to liberate you so that You can say, once and for all, "I'm glad I made man." No longer will God say, "I'm sorry I have made man." He will say, "I'm so glad I have made man, I found my sons and my daughters; here is my heaven, my dwelling place is with you!"

Prayer by Bo Hi Pak:

Our loving Heavenly Father, thank You very much for giving this inspiration to us. Father, You want us to taste living for You. Living for God is joy, power, happiness, and spirit. Father, from this day on we want to do more every day to reach out for perfection. As You say, "You shall be like Me." Yes, one day, Father, we shall be like You. We shall be like Christ, so that we shall be proud to be Your sons and daughters in the fullest capacity. This morning, Father, thank You very much for these brothers and sisters who gather together to worship. Your sons and daughters shall come together again next week. Until then, Father, bestow upon them Your love, Your inspiration, Your truth, and Your power. Father, every moment of the day Your dwelling shall be welcome with all of us. Thank You, Father. All of these things we pray in the name of Christ our Lord. Amen.

LONELY MAN

NEW YORK, NEW YORK
MAY 20, 1979

━━━━━━━━━━━━━━━━━━━━━━━━━━━━━━━━

Dr. Pak opens this sermon in the World Mission Center ballroom by explaining that the previous Sunday's service was not held because of an historical event that had taken place there: the matching of 705 couples on May 13, 1979, by Reverend Moon. He goes on to describe the aching, parental heart of God. He calls on the membership to be willing to receive persecution on God's behalf in an effort to comfort His lonely heart.

Once again, it is so wonderful to see all of you this morning. May God be with you today and every day. I'm sorry that some of our brothers and sisters were disappointed that there was no service last Sunday. Some of our home members, our friends, and associates came to worship with us. But last Sunday, this ballroom was filled with men and women who became engaged in the name of God. Because of that extraordinary event, we could not have our usual Sunday service.

What occurred here last Sunday was a truly historical event. We know that great events in history often happen quietly, without fanfare. The birth of Jesus was one, and the arrival of the Pilgrim fathers upon the shores of America was another. Now, on Mother's Day weekend in 1979, one of the greatest chapters of American history was written in this room. It's not just that 705 couples were matched and engaged, although you have never before seen such an event here in America. More important was the commitment these 1,410 men and women made in front of God, pledging their lives together for the sake of God. That is historical.

There were many Oriental and black and white brothers and sisters, many Europeans, Japanese, Koreans, Indians, and so forth. Of course, many if not most of them are not citizens of the United States. But their engagement, their eternal commitment in front of God, is as important as the arrival of the Pilgrim fathers 350 years ago. These couples are the new Pilgrim fathers of America. It doesn't matter if they are Korean or Japanese or black or white. They are the new Americans, and they will establish a new God-centered America.

One black brother was matched to a white sister. When they appeared at the press conference Monday afternoon, the brother said, "Many of you may be thinking that the two of us have no common ground. I myself come from the Deep South of Mississippi; my fiancé comes from a sophisticated Jewish community in Yonkers, New York. But we have a common ground: the common ground of God."

I proudly announce to you that Unification Church marriages will indeed bring a new chapter of American history, because we have found the eternal common ground upon which man and woman can be united, the common ground of God. We are marrying for the sake of bettering our world, which it desperately needs now. Today, most marriages are formed on the common ground of social fame, knowledge, money, power, physical attraction, and all kinds of external things. When those external things fade away, the bonds of those marriages are weakened and break. It is no secret that here in America today families are in trouble. According to one report, almost 90 percent of the California married couples are breaking up. Nationwide, over 50 percent of marriages end in divorce. In the midst of such an atmosphere, we gather together here and pledge eternal, unchanging love. The base of these marriages can never erode, for they stand on the ground of God. These good men and women have pledged their lives to bring joy and glory to God. That's the purpose of marriage. When you truly bring joy and glory to God, naturally you can be a happy couple.

UNHAPPY 'ME' GENERATION

Think of it: if your physical parents whom you love are desperately sick in the hospital, you as their child cannot be happy. There is no way. In the same way, our Heavenly Father is suffering, and we are trying to be happy. Nowadays we have the "Me" generation who think: I don't care about others, I just want to be happy. I tell you, that will not work. That is not the way of the Principle, that is not the way that God created this world. Therefore, no matter how hard the Me generation tries, you won't find happiness. True happiness can come only after we take care of our common parent. We must care about God and bring joy and glory to Him first. He comes first. Me comes second. If this God-centered way of life replaces the me-centered way, America will be happy. America will filled with happy couples.

Actually that is the task of the Unification movement. We are trying to remedy the core problems of the universe. We are trying to remedy the problem of our common parent, God, first. God comes first. Let God be happy, let Him receive joy, let Him receive our comfort. Then we don't even have to try to make ourselves happy. It comes automatically. That is the universal principle. The Unification Church is here to perfect that way of life.

This morning the subject of my sermon is "Lonely Man." The day of the matching, you saw me working with Reverend Moon. I try to help as much as possible to make his chore easier. One brother had a scar on his face, not an old scar, but very fresh, not even healed yet. I was a little worried, and I asked him what had happened. But there was so much going on right then that he could not explain. The next day, I met him at the elevator and he explained that he had been out witnessing late one night and he was attacked and beaten by three men. He was glad that he escaped with his life.

How many of you come back to the center bleeding or with a heavy heart, discouraged. I know what you face out there: hostility, misunderstanding, violence. That has been the Unification Church member's daily life. The day does not go by without some form of persecution from the world. One of our performing arts members one day came in with blood all over him. Some months ago, our sister Christiane Coste was murdered while she was doing her duty as a daughter of God. This is what we face today.

But this morning my purpose is to comfort you. Throughout the history of God, all those who truly forgot themselves and gave their lives to God for the greater purpose, how lonely they were. Persecuted, even martyred. Do you realize how hard it is find a person like yourself who can say: yes, I've found the truth, I want to dedicate my life to God and Christ; I come second, God and Christ come first. It is very rare to find men and women like that in the world. Even among the 10 million people in New York, it is very hard to find men and women like you. This is why everyone who gathers together in this room is so precious to God and Christ.

In the Bible, we read in Genesis 18-19 that God destroyed the wicked cities of Sodom and Gomorrah because of immorality. Fornication, adultery, and homosexuality were rampant in these cities. You know that God hates sin, period. However, the sin God abhors most is sexual immorality. That is no secret in the Unification Church. God rained fire and brimstone down on Sodom and Gomorrah and they were consumed in one second. God could not withhold his wrath

Abraham was a righteous man and found favor in the sight of God. He petitioned God to save those two cities. He asked God, would you destroy Sodom and Gomorrah if you can find 50 righteous men in it? Don't you think it is unfair to destroy the city together with the 50 righteous men? And the good Lord agreed not to destroy the cities if there were 50 righteous men. Then we found how good a bargainer Abraham was and very persistent, too. God, what about 45? Would you destroy Sodom and Gomorrah if you can find 45 righteous men? God said, well, it's not like 50, but I will live with it. But that was not the end of it. Abraham kept coming back to God, asking for Him to spare the city if He finds only 40 men, 30, 20. He said to God, forgive me—he was very humble man—I am just a man of dust and ashes. I know you will be angry with me, but how about 10 men? God was really ready to get mad: you rascal! But Abraham was not asking anything for himself, only for mercy for others. So God agreed. God's heart was moved by the selfless devotion and mercy of this good man. Abraham, God said, if you find 10 righteous men, I will not judge Sodom and Gomorrah.

But history is our witness: God could not find 10. Not even 10. And judgment became reality. The only ones saved out of those cities were saved simply because they were relatives of Abraham. As you know, that was Lot and his family. God was willing to save the two men engaged to Lot's daughters, but they didn't heed his warning. They were busy enjoying life and scornfully rejected Lot's warning of judgment. Just as in the time of Noah, they drank, they married and were given in marriage, they fulfilled their carnal desires. Sometime I wonder if we were in the position of Abraham, would we petition God to save New York City? How many righteous men would we find there? I know there are undoubtedly some, but I do know that figure is unbelievably low.

Elijah was one of the greatest of all Israel's prophets. He lived approximately 900 years before Jesus. Elijah fought for God, trying to turn the wicked and ungodly nation of Israel back to God. Three times he said to God, Lord, I am the only one left. They have killed all the other prophets. He became so discouraged and said, it is enough, I am no better than my fathers. He felt discouraged even after having a great showdown with 450 of the prophets of Baal. This was a million a times greater than the showdown at the Fraser committee.

At Mount Carmel, there 450 false prophets and God had only one champion, Elijah. Elijah challenged them. He told them to prepare a bull for sacrifice but not to put fire to it. And those false prophets prayed and marched all day, and even tore their skin and bled. But their false god could not answer, and the bull was not burned up. Then Elijah prepared an altar for God and laid the bull on it with wood. But Elijah was not satisfied to ask God for an ordinary miracle of providing fire or lightning to burn up the bull. No. He soaked the bull and the wood and the altar with water, not once but three times. Then he called on the God of Abraham, Isaac, and Jacob and asked Him to consume the offering. "Then the fire of the Lord fell, and consumed the burnt offering, and the wood, and the stones, and the dust, and licked up the water that was in the trench." [1 Kings 18:38]

That was a showdown! The 450 false prophets had prayed and prayed and prayed, and nothing happened. But when Elijah called on the name of the true God, the fire consumed the offering. Elijah won. Israel saw the real God. The people even helped Elijah kill all the false prophets. But after that great victory, many times Elijah prayed, oh, God this is enough. Oh, Lord, take away my life. I no longer desire to live. I'm no better than my forefathers. Elijah, like Abraham, was a lonely man. I tell you, those who follow God's way have to follow the lonely path.

JESUS IS THE MOST LONELY MAN

Jesus is another good example. The most lonely man is Jesus. In Matthew 8:20 Jesus said, "Foxes have holes, and birds of the air have nests; but the son of man has nowhere to lay his head." The son of God, Jesus Christ, was envious of the birds in the air; he was envious of the foxes. The birds have nests and the foxes have holes, but this lonely son of man has nowhere to lay his head. You can imagine the loneliness of Jesus.

Today, Reverend Moon is a modern-day prophet. I tell you, he is a lonely man. How lonely is he? If you truly know his loneliness, you cannot stand still, you cannot sit still; you will break down in tears and cry out. This morning when I think of Reverend Moon's path, as much as I know it, it truly makes tears stream down. He is a lonely man, in the tradition of Abraham, in the tradition of Elijah, in the tradition of Jesus Christ. Since he is pursuing the same call, he is absolutely lonely. After he came to America in 1971, Reverend Moon has made history, but how many Americans truly understand him? How many?

Yesterday I met with someone very important in the field of public relations. He said to me it is incredible how maligned the Unification Church is without any reason. The media has created an incredible wall of separation between us and the public. Each day it is more and more difficult for the public to understand. But, this man said, Reverend Moon has brought hope. I deeply thanked that man, saying that he is one of our dear friends because he said that if the Unification Church fails, America will see no hope. The success of the Unification Church will be the success of America. He equated our mission to the destiny of America. I look at him as a prophet. I bowed almost to the ground and thanked him, saying, mighty friend, at least I found one righteous man who knows what Reverend Moon stands for. In that tradition we are standing on the side of God. Therefore, we are lonely people. We are beaten, we are poisoned, we are hit, we have scars all over. Even some of us will become martyrs. This is the tradition of God's people.

Why do you suffer? Why do you get this scornful treatment? You are decent men and women, well educated, good looking. There is no reason you should be persecuted. You are not persecuted because of your own name. It is because of God's name we are persecuted. We are like the armor of God. What a glory, what a joy! We can be used as the armor of God.

But this is not the deepest point I would like to make today. I would like to go a step further. I have not yet described the most lonely person in the world. That is God. God Himself. God has been scorned. Our Father in heaven has been lonely. He created all this wonderful world, heaven and earth, all things that surround us in nature. Then He created man and woman as His children, and Satan took those children away. And all of creation was also stolen by Satan.

God is not a helpless God. God is almighty. But there is a reason God cannot strike evil off the face of the earth. God loves His children. God loves us. He wants to restore His children. But He has to wait until the day we turn around and come back of our own will. We must demonstrate that we are superior to Satan. We united with Satan and now we must separate from Satan and come back to God on our own. God has been waiting for that day, hour after hour, year after year, for thousands of years. In the meantime His heart has been broken and broken, over and over. We may think we are misunderstood, you may think Reverend Moon is the most misunderstood, but no, there is one more. God is the most misunderstood.

How many people in our world today are saying that there is no such thing as God? Think of it: you are daddy and mommy but your children are mentally ill and they are saying, I have no daddy, I have no mommy. Suppose your children are saying such things and you have to listen to every word. How tragic and incredibly sad for that daddy and mommy! For 6,000 biblical years, God has been listening to that conversation every day, every moment. There is even an ideology like communism saying not only that there is no God but that we will become gods, the state is god, matter is ultimate—and God is listening to all this. Even among the Christian community there are many theologians saying that God is dead. Think of it, God is not just lonely but He is pierced over and over again by His own children. And finally one man will stop that pain. The final champion is Reverend Moon. Reverend Moon came to change all that. After I met Reverend Moon a new aspect of God came to my heart. Reverend Moon is a champion like God never had before. Most people say to God, I am lonely, God, help me. Even Elijah said, God, take my life; this is too difficult, I don't want to be here anymore. What did Reverend Moon say? God, don't worry about me. I will win. I will comfort your heart. I will liberate you from your sorrow.

The one man prior to Reverend Moon who said something closest to this was Jesus Christ. Jesus was a lonely man. When he was crucified, he did not say, God, your son is dying, can't you send down your legion of angels and take revenge on these evil people? Jesus shouted out, *"Eli, Eli, lama sabachthani?"* which means "My God, my God, why hast thou forsaken me?" But Reverend Moon told me that Jesus spoke one more sentence that is missing from the Bible. Jesus actually said, "God, even if you have forsaken me, even if you abandon me, don't worry about me; I shall live, I shall fight on in your cause."

What a great man, how noble he was. Even at the moment of his death, Jesus forgave the Roman soldiers. "Father, forgive them; for they know not what they do." That was the messiah. It was not being crucified that made Jesus the messiah. Many others were crucified, including the two thieves. At that time, crucifixion was a common method of executing criminals. What distinguishes the messiah? The messiah saying, "My God, my God, why hast thou forsaken me?" But also saying, "Father, forgive them; for they know not what they do." And Jesus saying, I will not complain.

I learned this from Reverend Moon. And Reverend Moon himself lived that way. When he was in a communist prison camp, Reverend Moon suffered under the worst circumstances. It was not a prison; it was a death camp. Most prisoners didn't live longer than six months. Reverend Moon survived two years and eight months.

During this incredible suffering, no one saw Reverend Moon sleeping. When the prisoners finished their long day of backbreaking labor, they would collapse on the floor until the prison guards whipped them awake in the morning. But Reverend Moon was always already awake, praying. When they asked him what he prayed about—did you pray for angels to come down and release you from this prison—he answered: I was busy comforting God. God already knew my suffering. I don't have to tell him. I don't want to make God suffer more by praying for help. I told God, don't worry about me. Your son is all right. Your son is going to win this battle.

Finally, the United Nations forces were bombarding the area. That prison was undergoing saturation bombing. The prisoners began to follow Reverend Moon wherever he took shelter. They followed him like chicks following a mother hen. Reverend Moon hadn't said even one word about Divine Principle in prison, but somehow everybody felt drawn to this one man. They followed him to survive. The bombs fell all around, but not on Reverend Moon.

PERSECUTION IS AN HONOR

My dear brothers and sisters, today I want to conclude by saying, let us be honored to be persecuted in his name. There is no reason for us to be persecuted, except for following him. In the past, in Christian history, many people have suffered. Let us go one step further. Follow Reverend Moon's example and say, God, don't worry about me. I want to comfort you. You are suffering more than anybody else. God, I want to liberate you from this sadness, from this heartbrokenness. And I want to give you joy and glory first before I take mine.

If you think and pray and live like that, you will become an invincible champion of God. It doesn't matter if you are well educated or young or old, or men and women; that doesn't matter. You will be unprecedented champions of God. God has been waiting for such children for 6,000 years. Can you find any cause greater than this? There have been many, many causes in America. Civil rights, helping the poor. We are all doing good. But ultimately, there is no greater cause than this one. You are giving yourself as a volunteer to heal the broken heart of God. As long as God is eternal, this cause will not diminish even one iota. This is your pleasure and joy and honor. With the guidance of Reverend Moon we shall win. Let us pray.

Prayer by Bo Hi Pak:

Our most loving Heavenly Father, thank You very much for this wonderful morning, wonderful inspiration, wonderful fellowship with You. Father, we know You more than ever. We understand Your heart, and I know that Your heart has been lonely, has been broken. Father, we do volunteer to be champions. To truly unite with You. Truly give You comfort. Truly give You joy and glory. Father, You come first, You come first. Thank You, Father, for making us aware of who comes first. Thank You, Father, for giving us this spirit today and every day. Please give us Your power to continue so that we can go on spreading the most wonderful good news, so that people in New York, all of America, all of the world can hear it. Thank You very much for this blessing. All of these things we pray in the name of the Lord. Amen.

DEATH SHALL BE NO MORE

NEW YORK, NEW YORK

MAY 27, 1979

*This is a unique and frank sermon about the real mean-
ing of death. In it, listeners are reminded about the importance of having complete knowledge of the spirit world,
so that they can overcome the power of death.*

May God be with you this morning. Nowadays in our Christian churches
ministers are very careful in preparing their weekly sermons. They seem to
have a tacit agreement not to touch upon sensitive subjects. My years in
America have taught me that, although there are many aspects of the
American mentality and culture that I admire, Americans have a tendency to avoid talking about certain things at cocktail parties or other gatherings.

One subject the good American people do not like to worry about is
death. And this topic is not fully discussed in the pulpit either. So I am very
glad I am not a trained minister. I don't know the good pulpit etiquette that
they teach in American theological seminaries. I am like an outcast, a revolutionary. I deliver my sermons as if I am tackling a bold adventure.

I understand that another tacit agreement is that a sermon should not
last more than 15 minutes. It is said that after 15 minutes no soul can be
saved. Again, I am not a trained minister, but it is my opinion that talk-

ing seriously to people about committing your life to God takes a little more than 15 minutes. So please forgive me. Even though I want to finish in 15 minutes, my English capability keeps me from competing with other ministers, so at least allow me double time.

Another important thing: the Unification Church is here to ignite a spiritual revolution. We are not here only to seek our individual salvation. Basically we gather here today and every Sunday to think about committing our lives for the sake of Christ, God, and the world. For us, world salvation comes first. We want to burn our God-given energy for the highest purpose. The Lord's prayer says: Thy will be done on earth as it is in heaven. Our job is to think how we can make ourselves available to do the work of God so that His will can be accomplished here on earth as it is in heaven.

So I want to make our service a very serious one as well as a revolutionary one. We want to talk about serious subjects and naked truth. This morning I want to talk about death. But in hope, not in despair.

MANY HEROIC DEATHS

In history, we have many examples of heroic deaths. In the 5,000 years of Korean history, there are many patriotic, heart-rending, and thrilling heroic deaths. Here in America there are also many instances of what your great ancestors did for the sake of the country. One of these was Nathan Hale.

This story touched me when I first read about him with my children. I can never forget this great man of America who lived during the Revolutionary War, serving under George Washington as a most promising future commander of the Revolutionary Army. He was only 21 years old when he was given a mission by Washington to scout the British territory. He bravely penetrated deep into British territory and he obtained important information, but he was captured while he was returning. The British officers grilled him—much like the deprogramming methods they are using today—trying to convince him that it would be to his advantage to join the British army. They would make him an officer, and then he would fight the Revolutionary Army. He was given great temptations. But their efforts were to no avail. They failed. And they set the date for his execution.

The day came. The chaplain said a word of prayer in front of the execution squad, and the British officers asked young Nathan if he had any final wishes. This is your last chance to change your mind, they said. Nathan Hale uttered only one statement: I regret that I have but one life to give for my country. And they hanged him.

In Christian history there are a great many heroic deaths, a great array of martyrs. Just a few weeks ago I gave a sermon on St. Stephen. He was the first martyr in Christian history, as you can read in the Acts of the Apostles. St. Stephen had no fear of speaking the truth. He condemned the Jewish people, his own people, for murdering Jesus Christ. The people did not want to hear this stark truth. It hurt their conscience, so they plugged their ears. They were enraged and they drug Stephen out of the city and began to stone him.

In his final moments, Stephen, full of the Holy Spirit, gazed up into heaven and saw Jesus Christ standing on the right hand side of God. Jesus is usually described sitting next to God. To me that one word difference is very meaningful: Stephen saw Jesus standing, not sitting. At the moment of Stephen's death, Jesus could no longer sit next to God. He stood up, ready to receive Stephen's soul. In his final moments Stephen echoed Jesus' final words: "Lord Jesus, receive my spirit. Lord, do not hold this sin against them." To me this epitomizes the courage of men living the tradition of Jesus Christ.

Actually, crucifixion was the most cruel way to kill a person. Killing a person slowly is most painful. You know that. If you want to be merciful, you kill them quickly. They don't suffer too much. But slow killing is the worst. Crucifixion was used during the time of the Roman Empire and that was Jesus' sentence. They nailed him down on the cross and finally pierced his heart with a spear. Even while hanging from the cross, Jesus never allowed his mind to stray to his own situation. There was no moment when Jesus was worrying about himself. He was worrying about the mission. He was worrying about his own enemies. He was worrying about the salvation of mankind. He forgot himself in this worst hour of his life. He prayed to God, "Father, forgive them, for they know not what they do." Forgive them. Stephen followed that tradition most eloquently.

The Roman Empire picked the same cruel way to execute Peter: crucifixion. When the moment came, St. Peter told the Roman soldiers that it would be too great an honor to die the same way that his Lord died and asked them to crucify him upside down. What courage. There was no panic. Just peace.

My dear brothers and sisters, today I would like to talk about the source of power that helped these brave saints overcome death. As the Bible says, He will wipe away every tear from their eyes and death shall be no more. As far as the apostles were concerned, they did not die. They did not recognize death. They conquered death.

Today, the Divine Principle makes it easier to understand the meaning of "death shall be no more." Many people today think that accepting

Christ, receiving the coming of the Lord, means that they will live forever on this physical earth. They expect that there literally will be no more death. I tell you the Divine Principle clearly reveals that that will not be the case. According to the Principle of Creation, we humans are destined to die, but that is not death in God's sight.

THE TRUTH BRINGS LIGHT

What is death? Why is death such a problem to us today? Why is death so fearful? Because death is darkness. Because we don't know the truth about death. We can't see an inch beyond death. Therefore, we are afraid. But God did not create darkness. Darkness came because of the fall of man. It is spiritual darkness. We are living today in absolute spiritual darkness. We only recognize physical things. We see only what we eat, what we touch, what we read, what we see, what kind of fun we can have with our body today. This has become the focus for people today, particularly here in America. But actually, we are missing 99.9 percent of the true reality God created. What you perceive today is not even one percent of God's creation. We are blind to the greater reality, the spiritual creation of God. That is the real world God created.

Actually, the physical world in which we live today, the planet earth, is merely a staging area for humanity. It is a trial run. While you are here on earth, you think it is your whole life. But actually God designed man's true life as a spiritual one, an eternal one. The physical world is bound by the elements of time and space. Compared to eternity, the 6,000 years of biblical history—much less an individual's 70 or 100 years—is like a sparkle of light. Eternity is a long time. How long? There is no way to describe how long eternity is. That is the real life you and I are going to live. God created that as the main world and the physical world as a pet project. Just a small pet project and staging area of man so that we can prepare ourselves for the spirit world. We are like little babies in our mother's womb, being educated for nine months to come out into the new world. The nine months is the baby's indoctrination period to be ready for this world, which is incredibly larger than the mother's womb, isn't it?

By the same token, we live here today in this physical life as an indoctrination period to be ready for the ultimate eternity. You know the Principle of Creation teaches that everything passes through three stages: formation, growth, and perfection. Gestation in the mother's womb is the formation stage. Our life here on earth is the growth stage. We have one ultimate stage to come. Perfection stage. That is the ultimate life of the spiritual world. You learn in the Bible that what you worship today here on earth is a carbon copy of the real world. You are not even living in the real world yet. You think this is real. You think the sounds are real. This microphone is real. You know your friends and family are real. Wait until you get there. You have not even opened up and tasted the real world yet. This world is a shadow of the heavenly sanctuary above us.

There are two types of people who live here on earth today: those who totally disregard the future, and those who live for the future. The first kind think they are very wise and that Christians, and we Moonies in particular, are very foolish. We are so foolish we don't know how to enjoy life here on earth and waste all our time on the fantastic, mysterious idea we call heaven.

St. Paul once said, let us be fools for Christ. To be a really good Christian, you should look like a fool. Dumb, dumb. Yes. But in reality, once we know the truth, we are no longer in darkness, and when we perceive the entire world God created, we find we are not that dumb. We are perceiving the greater reality of God.

But most people are trying to make a showdown in this life: success or failure within 100 years. That is all I have. I have 100 years to enjoy my life. Of course, people very seldom live that long, but they are trying. They jog a lot and try to prolong their life, sure that it is the only life. And while they are enjoying their physical life here on earth, the most important aspect of life has been neglected. Not only neglected, but forgotten. When that person ascends into heaven, there is not much to ascend. When the physical body decays, there is not much left to bring back to heaven.

As you know, your spiritual self lives encased within the physical body. Your spirit self is your real self, not your physical body. I like to describe the body as being like a rented car. You have to turn it back into nature when your lease is up. If your spirit self does not develop during this life on earth, when you turn in your body, nothing remains. But if you have a true passenger, meaning you developed your spirit self, then you ascend into heaven to enjoy eternity. That is the deal. But the amazing thing is so many people don't see that truth. This is such a pity.

ETERNAL SPIRITUAL FABRIC

In the same way, just as our spirit man is encased in our body, the spirit world is encased in our physical world. This particular space here in the New Yorker Hotel is occupied by the spirit world as well as the physical world. In other words, this ballroom is spiritual as well as physical. Except the spiritual part is not composed of physical fabric. It is made out of spiritual fabric, which does not decay. No matter how great the New Yorker was when it was built 50 years ago, now when you look at the ceiling you can see very clearly it is decaying. In another 100 years, we'll have to rebuild something here.

But spiritual fabric is different. It is of ultimate quality. We can live in it for eternity. In that spiritual world, our spirit men are going to enjoy eternity. That is the way God planned. So once we know the reality of spirit world, death is merely a transition from one place to another. Furthermore, when you have the absolute truth, there will be no more darkness. While you are here on this earth, you are already enjoying the spirit world. You already recognize the spirit world. You know in this auditorium there are all kinds of waves, for example, from radio and television. But you don't perceive them, do you? You need a television or radio set to perceive the electronic waves coming into this room.

By the same token, there is a spiritual reality. Our spiritual senses were darkened due to the fall so we cannot perceive the spiritual world. We are blind to it. But the spirit world was not supposed to be hidden. God originally intended for us to be able to perceive spiritual reality while we are here on earth. When restoration is complete, then you and I will no longer live in darkness. When you are not in darkness, you no longer have fear. Death shall be no more. Death is merely a move from the ghetto of New York to a mansion in Miami Beach. How do you like that? When we move to the spirit world, it will be much greater than moving from the ghetto to a mansion. It is really a heaven and earth difference.

Therefore, the Divine Principle is the first step ever taken in human history to try to mend this broken radio in human form, so that we can be eventually restored and made whole; so that we can perceive the spiritual reality as much as Jesus did. Today, the one person living on earth today who perceived the absolute naked truth of our spirituality is Reverend Sun Myung Moon. When I learned the Divine Principle, much of the darkness faded away. Still I am so imperfect. Our spiritual senses are not fully opened. We still have a long way to go, but I do have hope. I do have hope to conquer the darkness. We shall no longer suffer in fear of death. We have already been given the great power that can conquer the fear of death.

My dear brothers and sisters, you have many, many important chores to take care of today. Many things you need to do. But if anyone asks you what is your most urgent business, the answer is obvious. Solving the problem of death is most urgent. Because you have no guarantee when that particular moment will visit you. There is no age that makes a difference. There is no rule that only old people die. The other day the entire nation was shocked to read about the tragic airplane crash in Chicago. Something like 272 persons were aboard and not one single soul was saved. They were heading to Los Angeles. I am sure there were many families with children who were looking forward to visiting Disneyland for the first time. But not even one person in that plane was thinking about that darkness when it struck.

I was in the army, and one time I was under bombardment from enemy machine gunfire. I felt empty. What can I do? I found pity for myself who was not ready for death. It is a most important and urgent task now. You and I have a way to overcome death. That does not mean you will live for 100 years, or even 200 years. Maybe you would like to go past Adam's 900 years. Go ahead, do it. But compared to eternity, no matter how long you live, 900 years or 9,000 years, it doesn't make any difference, you are living in darkness. The length of your life will not make any difference.

ENTITLED TO HEAVEN

Today the number one job for us is to recognize spiritual reality. You can have spiritual perfection through the Divine Principle. You will have complete knowledge about spirit world. Second, you must overcome the power of death. You will no longer dwell in darkness. Furthermore, whenever that physical transformation comes, you know you are entitled to heaven. You know you are already in the bosom of God and you will demonstrate any amount of courage, like those saints in the history of the Bible. I tell you, think simply of two things. First, know about the spirit world. Second, make yourself a child of God today. I want you to live today, this moment, with the complete realization that I am a child of God. I am His child. I am His son, I am His daughter.

Therefore, it doesn't make any difference how long I live. I will do my best for God and humanity as long as I live. But no matter how long or how short my life is going to be, ultimately that transfer from physical life to spiritual life will come. It is like a switch. I am ready because I am already a child of God. The full meaning of my life lies in God, and my life's purpose is to serve Him and serve mankind. You don't have to wait to get into spirit world to live eternal life. Let us start eternal life today. The physical transfer from this world to the spirit world will come. Let it come. I have already started the eternal life now. What do I have to fear? My eternal life starts now. I am His child. I am with God and I am with Christ.

Therefore, I want to read from Matthew 10:39: "He who finds his life shall lose it, but he who loses his life for my sake will find it." This is a powerhouse for the martyrs of Christianity. I am sure Stephen and Peter and Paul recited this verse many, many times. Jesus said, he who loses his life for my sake will find it. There are many people who lose their lives for a good cause today. But the greatest cause is for the sake of Christ and the sake of God. It is the only way you can conquer your death and death shall be no more. An ordinary death will not serve the purpose. You must lose your life for His sake and let Him be responsible for you, your life, your eternity. Trust him. He is almighty. He certainly can be responsible for your life.

Now, I want to conclude with one more statement. You think Jesus died and came back to life three days later in the resurrection. Actually, he did not. Even if the Roman soldiers crucified Jesus thousands of times, they could not kill Jesus. Nobody can destroy Jesus. They only destroy the physical fabric, the body. But the real Jesus no one was able to destroy. Resurrection did not come three days after. Jesus was the resurrection. The Bible says, "I am the resurrection." No one can destroy him. That is a man of God. That can be you and me. Everyone here on earth. We can become indestructible people. No power can destroy us. We already started the eternal life.

This is why the Bible says, do not fear those who will kill the body. They cannot kill the soul. Nobody can kill the soul, which is the real you. Rather, fear him who can destroy both soul and body in hell. That is God. Dear God is the one entity to fear. Nothing else under the sun. No power under the sun can destroy me. They may destroy my body, but my body is not the real Bo Hi Pak. The real Bo Hi Pak is the eternal one and has started the eternal life here on earth already. Nobody, no power can destroy me or destroy you. You are the resurrection. If you live in that condition, you will see no more death. You have conquered death already. Let us pray.

Prayer by Bo Hi Pak:

Thank you, Father. Father, You are the source of life. You gave us such an abundant life. You gave us such a full truth. But, Father, it has been darkened by the invasion of darkness, known as the fall of man. Today, most of our brothers and sisters around the world, more than four billion, are suffering in darkness. Father, thank You very much for giving us the truth of the Divine Principle, which is life, which can shine in the world. We can bring a touch of light to every corner of the earth. We can have the power, we can give them power, give the world power to conquer death. Everyone shall become invincible in Your sight. They can proclaim more proudly that death shall be no more. Thank You, Father. We are deeply grateful for giving us the most wonderful truth through which we already feel liberated. You said 2,000 years ago, know the truth and that truth shall make you free. Father, we know every sense of this verse. Thank You, Father, for the truth. All these things we pray in the name of Christ our Lord. Amen

ABRAHAM, FATHER OF FAITH

NEW YORK, NEW YORK

JULY 1, 1979

When I first joined the Unification Church, one of the most moving things I encountered was the singing of hymns. Even though I had been a Christian for five years prior to joining the Unification Church, when I sat down with our brothers and sisters singing holy songs, I truly felt the singing was coming from the soul. A genuine quality of heart was so evident. I would like to preserve the tradition in all worship services of the Unification Church throughout the world. This is where Reverend Sun Myung Moon is leading the crusade about God's message, God's movement, directly from New York.

So I would like you to be very conscious when you are singing hymns that you are contributing to the service. I would like to have every guest who comes here be inspired by your singing more than anything. In order to raise our spiritual temperature a little higher, I would like to ask Brian to lead one more hymn. Let us sing "Song of the Banquet."

As you all may know, the Unification Theological Seminary at Barrytown, New York, held its third commencement ceremony yesterday morning. We congratulated about 50 determined champions of God who have been equipped in spirit and knowledge and experiences to go out into the world and build the Kingdom of God on earth. This morning I am sure some of the parents who came to congratulate their sons and daughters in

Barrytown are here worshiping with us. Perhaps some brothers and sisters of the graduates are here also. I would like to recognize them. Stand up, please. Congratulations on behalf of all the brothers and sisters of our church around the world, and thank you for coming.

GOD'S FOOTHOLD

This morning I would like to invite your attention to the crusade of Abraham, one of the most prominent figures in the Old Testament. Abraham is commonly known as the Father of Faith. Actually, God established His first foothold with the faith of Abraham. Of course, God intended to establish the foundation of faith earlier than Abraham; God's dispensation to restore man started immediately after the fall of Adam and Eve with Cain and Abel. Then God worked with Noah. But Noah, although he was intended to become the Father of Faith of Israel, failed to secure that position. Then came Abraham's opportunity.

So today I would like to dwell on how Abraham was chosen and approved and accepted in the sight of God as the Father of Faith. As you know, the human fall in the Garden of Eden mainly came about because of the failure of Adam and Eve to uphold God's word. They lacked faith in God and God's word. That was the cause of all sin and suffering. God gave Adam and Eve the commandment to obey, just as Moses brought the Ten Commandments and Jesus brought the two most important commandments to all mankind.

But the first commandment was given by God to Adam and Eve. A commandment is like a big traffic sign on the highway. It is obvious: Speed Limit 65 Miles Per Hour; Yield; Stop. But what good is it to have that road sign unless the drivers have faith and obey it? Unless drivers obey the traffic signs, those signs serve no purpose. In the same way, God's commandment is no use unless man obeys it. To obey that road sign what you need first is faith in the authority of that road sign. If you think that road sign is somebody's joke, then certainly you would not obey it.

Adam and Eve's destiny was to reach perfection, which means total oneness with God, oneness in heart and love. When you reach that, you don't need faith. God is in you and you are in God. God is fact, reality, not a matter of faith. But in order to reach this union with God, you must grow into it. During this time, you need faith, faith in God, faith in His commandment. And that is exactly where Adam and Eve failed. Instead of having faith in God, they demonstrated skepticism. That is, instead of taking the word of God seriously, they took the word of Satan seriously.

Therefore, ever since the fall of Adam and Eve, God has been seeking one man who could demonstrate absolute faith, someone absolutely faithful and obedient to God. Nothing under the sun could deter such a man's confidence in God. God was searching and Abraham was the first candidate who passed that test.

But Divine Principle also teaches that Abraham didn't pass the test with the best score. He didn't make the honor roll. Do you know why? Because Abraham did not fulfill the entire requirement of Father of Faith. Abraham was succeeded by his son Isaac, who was in turn succeeded by his grandchild, Jacob. It took three generations to meet the requirement. So that is why the Bible frequently mentions "the God of Abraham, Isaac, and Jacob."

Did you ever notice that God liked to give names to His special people? In Genesis God said, "Let us make man"; the word "man" is the generic Hebrew term "adam." Abraham's original name was Abram. God appeared to Abram when he was 99 years old, and in Genesis 17:4-5 God said to him, "Behold, my covenant is with you, and you shall be the father of a multitude of nations. No longer shall your name be Abram, but your name shall be Abraham, for I have made you the father of a multitude of nations." God gave him his new name of Abraham, which means "father of a multitude." God gave Abraham many tests to see if he qualified to be the Father of Faith.

God also changed the name of Abraham's grandson. Jacob was a central figure in the Old Testament dispensation. Actually it was Jacob upon whom the nation of Israel was born. Jacob was on his way home to a great confrontation with his brother, Esau, when he came to the ford of Jabbok. There he had a showdown with an angel, wrestling him all night. In Genesis 32:28, the angel said to Jacob, "Your name shall no longer be called Jacob, but Israel, for you have striven with God and with men, and have prevailed." So upon the new name of Israel, the Israel nation was born. Today the name of the nation of Israel comes from the name of Jacob, a God-given name.

YOU SHALL CALL HIS NAME JOHN

An angel also appeared before the birth of John the Baptist. Zechariah, the father of John, was a priest of Israel. Luke 1:12-13 describes, "And Zechariah was troubled when he saw [an angel], and fear fell upon him. But the angel said to him, 'Do not be afraid, Zechariah, for your prayer is heard, and your wife Elizabeth will bear you a son, and you shall call his name John.' " God gave John his name before he was even born.

And of course, Jesus' name came from God. An angel appeared to Mary and told her she would conceive a son and that his name would be Jesus. An angel also appeared to Joseph when he was planning to divorce

Mary because she was pregnant. "Son of David, do not fear to take Mary your wife, for that which is conceived in her is of the Holy Spirit; she will bear a son, and you shall call his name Jesus." [Matthew 1:20-21] The name was given.

Do you know that Reverend Moon's name was given by God? Probably very few people know about this. Reverend Moon's original name was Young Myung Moon. Then God revealed to him, "Your name shall be Sun Myung Moon."

Incidentally, we are building our university in Seoul, Korea. This morning we talked about it a little and the name of that university will be Sun Moon University. It comes from Reverend Moon's name. Instead of Sun Myung Moon, it is Sun Moon University. It is very providential, even prophetic. The sun and the moon are the two major heavenly bodies that give out light. We are going to create a university, which, like a mother and father, will give out light to the world. Incidentally, we are the first to create a chain university. You have heard of chain supermarkets, like Safeway, and fast food chains, like MacDonald's and Burger King, but you have never heard about a chain of universities. Harvard is not a chain, Yale is not a chain, but we are going to have one. Sun Moon University is going to be a chain. It will be established initially in Korea, Japan, and the United States and eventually in 120 countries all over the world. How do you like that?

This has become a dire necessity because we are not one family of man. We need one common true parent, regardless of where we live, what nationality we have. We are the children of God so we should live as one family. So this one family of God will have one university teaching under one concept, one ideology, one commitment to God and fellow man. It is most logical. But this kind of thought can only be possible after we have the knowledge and understanding of God and the True Father of mankind.

Remember the famous words Reverend Moon spoke at Madison Square Garden: "God is color-blind." God doesn't see you as a white man, black man, yellow man. God sees you as His child, His sons and daughters. The Unification Church is symbolic of His ideology. Isn't it truly wonderful? Look at this audience. It is far greater and more colorful than NBC's "living color." We have a living color family here. It is beautiful, a beautiful mixture of all colors and races, all languages and cultures under one love of God. Truly magnificent. This is really our own witness. Already we are showing where the Unification Church is heading: one family of man, under one common fatherhood of God.

In the Unification Church our Blessed couples feel it is a great honor for their children to be named by Reverend Moon. In fact, Farley Jones' two sons were named by Reverend Moon. Their names have a deep philosophical meaning. I won't explain the philosophy of names now, but it is a tremendous joy for our members to have their children named by Reverend Moon, just like the important people in the history of God were named directly by God.

So Abraham was given Isaac when he was 100 years old. God promised Abraham that he would prosper through his son Isaac: "I will bless him and make him fruitful and multiply him exceedingly; he shall be the father of twelve princes, and I will make him a great nation." [Genesis 17:20] God established His covenant with Abraham and gave the blessing.

Then one day, the heavenly mandate came. Abraham was told to offer his son Isaac. It was very ironic. God knew precisely what He was asking. He said, "your only son." Abraham was to bring Isaac to the land of Moriah and offer Isaac as a burnt offering. It was a horrendous request. How could anyone in Abraham's position accept that? Immediately he could have protested, God, what are you talking about? You said I will multiply generations through my son Isaac, and now you want me to kill him. But Abraham didn't say that. Abraham accepted God's direction with absolute faith.

A DARK THREE DAYS

Abraham took three days to get to the place God told him. This three-day period is a very important period for men and women of faith. Every great man has gone through three days of darkness in his faith. I am sure you have experienced that. After the crucifixion Jesus was to stay in the tomb of darkness for three days. It is a period where you can doubt God, curse Him. You can turn around and reject him. It is the best arena for Satan to come in. It took three days for Abraham to get to the place of sacrifice. I am sure those three days seemed longer than three years. Many, many kinds of thoughts came to him, I am sure. We may not talk about it, but you and I sometimes have many mixed emotions going through our hearts. This was a dark three days for Abraham.

To make the situation worse, his son Isaac, probably 11 or 12 years old then, was not that dumb. He was a very clever boy. He knew all the Jewish customs. He knew how burnt offerings were made. So he said, "My father!" Abraham answered, "Here am I, my son." Isaac said, we have wood, we have fire. In those days you had to carry fire. There was no lighter, no matches. So they carried the seed of fire with them. We have fire, we have firewood, we have a knife. But, father, "where is the lamb for a burnt offering?" Can you imagine how this question pierced the heart of Abraham? Abraham would have gladly taken the position to die himself a hundred times rather than have to kill his own son. I am sure he would rather die himself than kill his own son.

At that point normally you would expect to hear a word of complaint. That is the moment that Abraham could explode and burst into complaint. You know, my son, I don't know what this business is all about. He couldn't say, you are going to be the lamb, but there were plenty of ways to say that God was being really unreasonable. This was another test. Abraham answered him, "God will provide himself the lamb for a burnt offering, my son." He showed his absolute faith in God. He could not say to his son, you are the lamb.

Abraham built an altar and laid the wood on it. The time had come. He bound Isaac and laid him on the altar and took up the knife. If he lifted up the knife with a complaining heart, he would not pass. Abraham maintained his untiring, absolute faith in God. God will provide. That was a precious moment. It was the most beautiful moment of Abraham's life. God's will be done, period. He was ready to use the knife and offer his son.

"But the angel of the Lord called to him from heaven, and said, 'Abraham, Abraham!' And he said, 'Here am I.'" Abraham was still listening to God. "He said, 'Do not lay your hand on the lad or do anything to him; for now I know that you fear God, seeing that you have not withheld your son, your only son, from me.'" In other words, God is saying: you passed the test.

I would like to dwell on that particular statement of God, "now I know that you fear God." God is not truly a God of fear, but a God of love. Up to now, we did not know and no theologian could explain why God seems to be so cruel. Now with the Divine Principle, we do know. It is not because God is cruel, but because Satan possessed all mankind. We were united with Satan. It is absolutely man's responsibility to reject Satan and come back to God all the way. We have a duty to separate Satan from us. Satan separates from you only when you demonstrate that your faith in God is greater than your attachment to anything else, all your precious things, including your own son, your own wife, your own family. When you demonstrate that God comes first, upon that faith alone Satan no longer has a claim over you.

We are fighting a battle with Satan every day. You know, in many cases Christians are borderline. One leg is outside in the satanic world and one in the kingdom of heaven. This person suffers the most. You are torn between the two powers. The most beautiful thing about knowing God is that there are no strings attached. When you are completely, 100 percent inside of God, then you already have separated from Satan. Abraham, to be the Father of Faith, had to demonstrate that nothing came before God. He did that. That qualified him to be the Father of Faith.

Yes, that was a great faith. God did test Abraham, and he passed. This is our story too. God today is asking us to become even greater than Abraham. Do you know what is greater than Abraham? Father of Faith is not the greatest title. The greatest title of all is to be a child of God. To be a son or daughter of God. God is asking us to become His children. The greatest thing that could be written on my tombstone is, "Bo Hi Pak, son of God, lived and died for His sake." Nothing could be greater. This is far greater than Abraham's title of Father of Faith, because even Abraham could not conceive of how to become a true son of God. We can.

SHOW THAT GOD COMES FIRST

So our job is greater than Abraham's, but the method is the same. We must have absolute faith. We must demonstrate that God comes first. Actually, when you possess God, you possess everything. This is Reverend Moon's ideology. When you possess God, you lose nothing. You possess everything. You possess the world, you possess a family, you possess husband and wife, but since God comes first, there shall be an anchor and peace. This is why our marriages can work. America's modern-day system for marriage doesn't work.

In California, approximately 90 percent of marriages end in divorce. I am not saying anything unkind about divorced people. I am sorry for the heartbreak and suffering they have to go through. I know they tried to make a home. Why didn't it work? Because they need some common ground upon which men and women can be united. That common ground is the "God comes first" ground. When men and women meet based upon commitment to God, their commitment to each other cannot be broken as long as their commitment to God is not broken. This is why we know our marriages will work, and not only work but prosper. Our marriages will bring children who will fill the earth.

Yes, there are so many, many ways to live, but I tell you Abraham's philosophy is Reverend Moon's philosophy: God comes first. Nothing is ahead of God. Nothing can stop you from going to God. Nothing under the sun. By doing so you can completely separate from Satan. No more strings attached. If a string is attached to you, someone can jerk it. Who is that? Satan. That is why the person inside of God has the courage to cut all the strings.

I would like to say a word to the parents of our Unification members. Our members are trying to give their 100 percent devotion to God in order to live by the God-comes-first philosophy. I am sure you sometimes feel neglected. Forgotten. Unloved. But I tell you, my dear fathers and mothers of our members, you are owning your sons and daughters even more. Because in this ideology, the God-comes-first ideology, the parents come second to God. Isn't that true? Isn't that the way Reverend Moon is teaching? Therefore, we are not dividing the family. We are uniting the family in a permanent way.

In order to go a permanent way, you need restoration. You know we are working on restoring the New Yorker Hotel. It looks ugly at the moment. Some of you may have gone up to the fourth floor. It is torn apart and looks ugly. But that ugliness is actually beautiful because through that ugliness we are creating beauty. We are not just covering the old dirt with lots of paint. We are taking off all the layers of old paint, getting down to the original wall, and rebuilding it.

Faith is just the same. I tell you parents, you will be proud. Your sons and daughters are greater than Abraham. That is my gift to you this Sunday. I want you to go back to your homes thinking, my sons and daughters are greater than Abraham, the Father of Faith; my sons and daughters are becoming the sons and daughters of God. Direct heirs. Chosen champions. Chosen for greater things than even Abraham was chosen for. This is my gift to you today. Reverend Moon always recognizes the family as the basis for the kingdom of heaven. What Reverend Moon and God call family does not mean only husband and wife. No, Reverend Moon thinks the father and son relationship comes first. Father and son relationship between God and man, father and son relationship between parents and children. That vertical relationship becomes the anchor. Then the horizontal relationship between husband and wife will be stable. That is the way it goes in lasting homes. America will be built upon this foundation.

We learned the God-comes-first philosophy from Abraham, absolute faith. You live it. You practice it. I know you will not regret it. I know things will be infinitely better in every way. You think you will lose a lot, but actually you gain so much. That is the glory of the future of our young people and our society and ultimately the new America, the new world. The kingdom of heaven is realistic, not just some fantasy.

So this morning I thank you for listening and for coming. Let us uphold our faith in God. Let God come first. Jesus said, love your Lord God with all your heart, all your mind, all your soul. There is no room to do anything else. Love your neighbor as you love yourself. Let us live more than the standard of Abraham. We shall indeed become the sons and daughters of God because we have a couple living for God here on earth, guiding us to the goal. God is here on earth, guiding us to the goal. Our way is so brightly lit, so much brighter than this auditorium. We are no longer in darkness, we can see the goal. The great day is here. We accept the challenge of building the Kingdom of God here on earth. Let us pray.

Prayer by Bo Hi Pak:

Our most loving Heavenly Father. Thank You very much, Father. You have been searching all these years for Your children who would come up and stand in front of You unconditionally, without any condition or string attached. Father, it is very difficult to become one in the unruly, despairing, and satanic world. But we have hope because we have a guide, we have the truth, and we have light. We are not in darkness. We are not dismayed. We have a clear-cut plan to reach You and become like You, Father. To live in Your image. Father, we will live and pursue the philosophy that You come first. You come first. Nothing under the sun can come before You. Father, we want to be totally separated from Satan so only You can indulge us. So only You can use us as Your instrument to build Your kingdom. Thank You, Father, for this most beautiful morning of July 1. Keep all in Thy grace. All these things we pray in the name of Christ our Lord. Amen.

IN GOD WE TRUST

NEW YORK, NEW YORK

JULY 8, 1979

In this stirring sermon, Dr. Bo Hi Pak expresses his deep love for America and reiterates both the serious shortcomings and the providential importance of America.

Last Sunday I preached on the topic "Abraham, Father of Faith." Every Thursday night our program director for Sunday service comes to me and asks me what my sermon topic is. Last Sunday I felt I had not quite finished describing Abraham, so I said, what about "Abraham, Father of Faith, Part II"? We had the movie "Rocky II." Why not "Abraham, Part II"? Then this brother asked, "May I make a suggestion? We just celebrated July 4th, the 203rd birthday of our nation. Maybe 'In God We Trust' would be a good topic." Well, that was a very wonderful recommendation, but I didn't want to change so abruptly. I had already decided to talk again about Abraham. I left for Washington for an important meeting, but during the night, a very powerful inspiration came to me that I must speak about America. That brother was right.

Since my title this morning doesn't come from me, if something does not go too well, I have somebody to blame. But at the same time, if there is some inspiring quality in this sermon, the credit should go to him, too, not to me. I am trying my best to honor this brother this morning.

I first came to America in 1952 as a soldier. At the time I was a first lieutenant in the Korean Army, and my country was engaged in a desperate battle during the Korean War. I had been brought up in a very humble way in the Korean countryside. I entered the Korean Military Academy of the Republic of Korea, comparable to West Point here, at the age of 21, and I thought I would be a military leader. But just 25 days after entering the academy, on June 25, 1950, the Korean War broke out. My school was located at what is now the border between North and South Korea. That day, without knowing our destination, we were called to an emergency assembly and put on a truck heading north. That was my last day in the Military Academy.

From that day on, we were engaged in battle. In 1952 I was selected as one of 150 Korean officers to come to America for more advanced military training. At that time, I did not speak even one word of English. In fact, none of the Korean officers who had been selected spoke English, so we were accompanied by a group of interpreters. Just as our Hispanic brothers and sisters are listening to my sermon today through an interpreter, I was trained for six months at Fort Benning, Georgia, through an interpreter. By then I was already commissioned as a lieutenant and was leading a company in the Korean War.

FARTHER THAN THE MOON

Of course, I had heard about America, but in my imagination America was a far-away country, even farther than the moon. I thought there was no conceivable way I would ever visit here. As a Korean boy growing up in the countryside, not educated in any special way, speaking no English, how could I harbor any hope of coming to a country like America? Furthermore, everything I read in newspapers or magazines showed the beautiful, fantastic side of America. To me, America was a distant country, almost like heaven.

Then all of a sudden I had an opportunity to come to America. From where? From a foxhole at the frontline of the battlefield. I was in combat uniform. One day they gave me a brand-new uniform and said, wear this, you are going to America. I just couldn't believe this was happening to me. So I came out of the foxhole and shaved for the first time six months. I went to Seoul, but I found no capital city any more. The ravages of war had totally demolished the city. We went to Inchon Harbor, which was made famous by the MacArthur landing operation. There President Syngman Rhee, the beloved first president of the Republic of Korea, came in person to this very humble dock. He shook the hand of every Korean officer and asked us to be good soldiers. He said, learn as much as you can and come back and win this deadly war. It was an inspiring and deeply touching moment: the president of the Republic of Korea shaking hands with these 150 officers and telling them they are the hope of this country, you come back soon and win the battle.

We did not come by plane. I came to America by military ship. It took about 15 days. We were part of a large contingent of American soldiers returning from the Korean battlefield. Entering the San Francisco Bay and then seeing the Golden Gate Bridge was something like coming to a fairyland. The beauty of America was unbelievable. San Francisco was like heaven, a beautiful white city with the red Golden Gate Bridge. Everybody came on deck. The moment the boat passed under the bridge all the GIs threw their hats in the air and cheered, in tears, for their homecoming. As a Korean officer who had witnessed so many desperate battles going on in the homeland, it was an absolutely beautiful thing to behold. I truly envied the American soldiers who had a beautiful country to come back to.

Well, I cannot go on like this or the sermon may last three hours. Do you know what made the greatest impression on me? Now, after being here so many years, I am numb about the American phenomena. But coming from a foxhole, landing in San Francisco, was truly an amazing experience. The thing that was most incredible was the flood of automobiles. I thought the whole country was covered by automobiles. The second incredible thing to hit my eyes were the beautiful women drivers. Seeing beautiful, blonde young ladies sitting behind the wheel and driving was so amazing. Now, even my wife drives and in the Orient there are many women drivers. But in those days, it was virtually unthinkable. The only automobiles I saw in Korea were jeeps and trucks. Only fierce-looking men drove.

Another thing. I didn't even know what Coca Cola was. I thought it was like candy. I was introduced to the Coca Cola machine, and it only cost a nickel but I put a quarter in and—boom—the Coke came out. Then clink, clink, it gave me change. It did all the mathematics by itself and gave change. I was just amazed.

To make a long story short, I was so moved by the nation of America and seeing that God had made this nation great. At that time, I was searching for some kind of religion. I was not even Christian. I hadn't met Reverend Moon yet. But I wanted to become a Christian. I wanted to become part of these great people. I was baptized in the Church of Christ in Columbus, Georgia, a small town outside Fort Benning. I decided to be a good Christian.

The only break from our military training was the Fourth of July. It was only a three-day vacation, but the military doesn't give week-long vacations. This was the only vacation before I was to go back to the battlefield. Maybe death was waiting for me. I knew this was my first and last chance to see America. How could I come to this country again? I wanted to see this great nation's capital, Washington, D.C., and New York City. Three days was enough; you can fly there and back. But a military officer from Korea didn't have that kind of money.

So five brave officers got together, and we each put in $50 and hired a taxi. When we got in the taxi, the driver asked where we would like to go. We all said, Washington, D.C. You have never seen such a startled taxi driver. What did you say? Washington, D.C. Since we cannot speak much English, we just showed him the money. We had enough money. He was a good-looking taxi driver. Brave, too—he accepted the offer.

It took 16 hours to get to Washington. Even this brave driver began to doze, and the taxi was swaying this way and that way. Boy, all five officers were looking at each other and saying, well, the American highway is much more dangerous than the Korean battlefield. We would rather die in the battlefield. So we decided to take turns keeping the driver awake. He was a good smoker, thank God. So we kept lighting cigarettes, and he kept smoking cigarettes. We couldn't talk to him, we didn't speak the same language, so we had give and take only by cigarette. At the drug store, we stopped to get lots of coffee and cigarettes. But without accident we made it to Washington.

A GREAT MIRACLE

I don't remember everywhere we visited, but two things stand out. One is walking to the Washington Monument. I even have a nice picture taken there. Finally, I made it. This was going to be my last visit to Washington. You see how ironic, in a way, how miraculous that is. That man who in 1952 didn't speak even one word of English, in 1976 stood at the Washington Monument with the prophet of Korea, Reverend Sun Myung Moon, translating to 300,000 people. I tell you, this in itself is a great miracle of our time.

The other place I remember visiting was Capitol Hill. I am sure I went into the House and Senate chambers, but the one thing I cannot forget was the guide leading us into the small dark room they call the prayer room. There were only a few chairs. The stained glass window showed George Washington on his knees at Valley Forge asking divine guidance. The guide explained that this is the place where the great leaders of this nation, the senators and congressmen, come when they have a vital decision to make, regardless of their faith. They come and pray. The guide also explained that every meeting in Congress is opened by prayer and that the president of the United States is sworn into office by placing his hand on a Bible.

Those things struck me so hard. I felt I was an eyewitness to the greatness of America. Yes, today Reverend Moon has come to this country to make the purpose of this nation so clear. At Madison Square Garden, Yankee Stadium, and Washington Monument, he showed that this nation has a special purpose in the sight of God. Even the discovery of America is amazing. All the old world of Europe and the rest of the world was known for over 5,000 years. But until several centuries ago, this great land of America was a hidden secret, hiding until such time as God wanted His people to immigrate here from the whole world. America is known today as a melting pot. But what is the heat for this melting pot? As Reverend Moon has so clearly stated, the heat of the melting pot was God. The Christian spirit melted a nation and made it great. God clearly has a culminating purpose for this nation.

I truly became a lover of America. I went back to Korea and I met Reverend Moon. Then I discovered the meaning of America as a chosen nation of God for the consummation of teaching about God on earth. America is a melting pot for this reason. God ultimately wants to have every nation, the entire world, to be a melting pot. All people, regardless of race or nationality, are supposed to live under one God as one family. There must be some example, and God put this nation of America together to make the external example.

Externally speaking, America is truly the form of the kingdom of heaven on earth. To me, the United States of America is actually the United States of God. America externally is the U.S.A., but internally it is the U.S.G. God really wanted to see this nation, which is prepared externally, one day turn around to God. Then the kingdom of heaven would become a reality here on earth. It is so clear that America is prepared for that.

This morning my teaching aid for the sermon is American money. I have coins and dollars because I want to testify that every penny, nickel, dime, quarter, and dollar bill has the beautiful motto "In God We Trust." That expresses the founding spirit of America. The American forefathers came to this land, planted here by God. This God-trusting nation and democracy can only flourish upon that foundation, strengthened and inspired by the Christian spirit.

I tell you, American democracy would not work in any other land. Many Asian nations have failed in democracy. Many South American nations have not done it, neither have many European nations. Do you know why? Democracy itself will not work until democracy can blossom upon the foundation of the Christian spirit. Upon Christian brotherhood alone can democracy work.

But today America's democracy is in trouble. Why? Because America's Christian spirit is fading away. This nation is becoming very self-centered. If this nation continues in that direction, America will be in more and more trouble in the days to come.

AMERICA NEEDS THE WILL TO WIN

This great America needs help. It needs a solution. What kind of problems does America have? Of course, you know better than I do. Just look at the difference between America in 1952 during the Korean War, when I first came here, and after the Vietnam War. This was the first war in which America was defeated. In 203 years of America history, the first war you lost was in Vietnam. But it was not because of lack of soldiers or money or weapons. Do you know that at the close of the Vietnam War the American Army had to abandon, along with the Vietnamese, about $5 billion worth of equipment, military gear and weapons? Why, then, did we have to retreat? We had no clear purpose and no will power to win. This was the first war in which America was not united in will and purpose. The American young people, soldiers, and government could not see clearly our purpose to be there.

Communism is like a crazy dog. I sometimes give this example: When a barking dog is trying to bite you, what is your best defense? If you try to run away from the dog, no matter how fast you run, the dog is faster. The dog will get more excited and triumphant. The best defense against this crazy, barking dog is to turn around and face the dog, eyeball to eyeball, and yell at him. That dog will put his tail down and run away. You think that running away from communism will keep you safe, but America will never win the race against communism this way.

God has chosen America and made it the mightiest power on earth. If we are awakened to our true purpose, if we turn our eyes from the selfish point of view to the survival of the world, if we fight in the name of God, we will win the war against communism. When I first came to America, I wrote "My Tribute to America." I said in those days that the war against communism is not an American war. If you think you are winning for the sake of the American people, the chances are you will lose. Communism is actually a declaration of war against God. The ultimate confrontation is between a God-denying ideology and a God-accepting ideology. Khrushchev clearly stated the communist goal: "We shall bury you." Not just America would lose, but the real loser would be God. If America loses, on that day God has no instrument here on earth.

America today is summoned, like David against Goliath, to be a strong defender and fighter for freedom, to make God's kingdom flourish. That is why 200 years ago God founded what would become the mightiest nation on earth. What makes America mighty is its spiritual purpose, and this is what America is losing today. America is losing its basic purpose.

Here are some statistics about what is happening in America. I know you don't want to hear all of it, so I will only read a few examples. These are the results of the abuse of freedom and great confusion and chaos without God. Two million children are abused by their own parents each year; 5,000 children die from parental abuse or neglect each year; 700 children were murdered by their own parents in one year; in New York City there are more than 5,000 professional prostitutes and many more thousands of girls who are part-time. In 1977, 235,000 children were born out of wedlock. One out of two marriages are not successful. Each year there are 15,000 drug abuse-related deaths. About 35,000 suicides are reported each year, but there could be as many as 100,000 suicide attempts. Someone is murdered approximately every 27 minutes, raped every eight minutes, robbed every 78 seconds, and assaulted every minute. More than 10 million serious crimes are committed each year in the United States. There is a $1.5 billion sex industry in Times Square alone. Students assault 70,000 teachers each year, and some are murdered. More than five million young Americans have venereal disease. Some time ago *Time* magazine reported that a VD epidemic was second only to the common cold.

FOUR MAJOR PROBLEMS

We have a problem. We have to solve the problem. But we have to know the cause of the problem. This ugliness is not just in America but all over the world. It is more severe in America because there is so much more freedom here. The problems have four major causes: (1) dishonesty, (2) impurity, (3) jealousy, and (4) greed. None of these come from our God-given nature. All four of these come from Satan.

We know through the Divine Principle that Satan is none other than the fallen archangel, Lucifer. The archangel approached Eve. He told her a direct lie to win her. He was a liar. Jesus said the devil was a liar from the beginning. Lies and dishonesty come from Satan. The reason Lucifer approached Eve was jealousy. Lucifer was jealous of Adam's position. Furthermore, Lucifer's motivation to approach Eve was impure, illicit love. Finally, Lucifer approached Eve because of his greediness, his self-centeredness. He didn't care about God's dispensation. He wanted to make himself as high as God.

So all the problems in the world and in America today come from satanic invasion. How can we win this battle without God? Today America is trying so many ways to solve the problem without God. It will not work. America has many religions, many churches. But that is not enough. What we need here in America today is to make God's truth a way of life. There are many preachers in America. Billy Graham's sermons are beautiful words of God. A few weeks ago Oral Roberts came to Madison Square Garden. There are many others. But what America needs today is not preachers. What America needs today is a prophet.

What is the difference between preachers and prophets? Preachers inspire you with the word of God so you can be closer to God and understand the truth. The prophet has another role. The prophet is a channel between God and man to bring His new message to people. In other words, preachers expound on the Bible; a prophet writes the Bible.

At this particular juncture of history, God summoned Reverend Moon to come to America. *The New York Times* and the *Washington Post* say that he is a preacher or evangelist. Wrong. He has come to this land as a prophet.

What has Reverend Moon done for you and me? What is he doing for America? How can you sum up in one word the accomplishment of Reverend Moon? I say it this way. What Reverend Moon has done for you and me, and will do for millions of Americans and the rest of the world, is make God real in our hearts. Yes, Reverend Moon brought God to your heart. Without any hesitation, I say to you, without Reverend Moon making God real in my heart, I have absolutely no qualification to stand at this pulpit and speak to you. There are tens of thousands of people who can be more eloquent than I am. I was once asked to be a preacher; I declined simply because God was not real to me then. I could not be an unreal preacher. I could not be a hypocrite. But one thing is sure, Reverend Moon ignited me with God. He ignited you, I know it. So will he ignite millions of Americans.

Once God's truth is ignited in your heart, the true solution emerges. That we call a revolution without bullets, without fire. We call it a quiet revolution. But Reverend Moon is not the inventor of the quiet revolution. Two thousand years ago Jesus Christ ignited the quiet revolution. John 3:12 says, "If I have told you earthly things and you do not believe, how can you believe if I tell you heavenly things?" We can see that 2,000 years ago Jesus could not preach too much because good people were not ready to accept all that he could say. At the same time, Jesus said in John 3:3, "Truly, truly, I say to you, unless one is born anew, he cannot see the kingdom of God." Born again. It is a religious way of saying "revolution." Born again is a revolution. We are not talking revolution of the economy, the government, the nation, any of that kind of revolution. Revolution in Cuba, revolution in Russia. The quiet revolution Jesus Christ brought to us was the revolution of heart. This revolution has been alive for 2,000 years, carried by many torchbearers. All kinds of people have carried the torch of Jesus Christ and made Christianity a worldwide religion.

But I tell you, that race has not been finished. We must finish the race. The marathon must come to the final goal. On the final day, Reverend Moon will receive the baton of Jesus Christ and finish it. We don't have to talk about how he will do it, he is already doing it. He is already doing it for me and doing it for you. All we have to do is become another prophet. Another Reverend Moon. Go out and do the work. Expand the work. That will bring God back to America. I am still a Korean citizen. Reverend Moon is still a Korean citizen. But God doesn't care where the birth certificate is from.

Do you know to whom America belongs? Ask the flowers, where would you like to belong? The flower will say, I would like to belong to the person who loves me most. America, this great land of America, this truly marvelous land, doesn't care what is written on the birth certificate. America cares about who loves America. How can you love America until you truly know about America's mission? You cannot truly love America until you love God. Then you love America. That is real love. In this respect, Reverend Moon to me is the first citizen of the United States. He truly loves America. I want to become a citizen in that spiritual sense. I want to love this country. So do you.

NO FREEDOM WITHOUT GOD

We sang "The Star Spangled Banner" the other day at the Unification Theological Seminary graduation. I really read the words for the first time. It says, let this be our motto, In God We Trust, and the Star Spangled Banner in triumph shall wave over the land of the free and the home of the brave. You will never be truly free without God. When you try to be free without God, you are actually putting yourself in greater bondage. If you only trust in mortal strength, mortal wisdom, you cannot truly be a brave soul. When you completely trust God and His power, you can be brave. It is your job, yours and mine together, since we have the truth, since the trumpet call has been ringing. Let us become a soldier of true freedom because we know God. Let us become true brave soldiers because we trust not our power, but His power.

My dear brothers and sisters, America cannot afford to become another Roman Empire. Neither you nor God can afford it. God is definitely doing two things. First, He summoned Reverend Moon to this country, and second, He raised the young people of America—that is you—to rally around the new quiet revolution. I tell you that is our only hope. We do have hope. Let us ignite this hope and become a torchbearer. Move forward. Truly bring America to be one nation under God. And as Reverend Moon said in Washington, D.C., make this one nation under God become one nation, one world, under God. Let us pray.

Prayer by Bo Hi Pak:

Loving Heavenly Father, thank You very much for this day. For this service. Father, we are truly united in one heart. Our dear brothers and sisters are dedicating themselves to You and Your cause. Father, we want You to be real in every heart in America. Thank You, Father. We are so inadequate and not qualified in many ways, but we want to serve You because You are so real in our hearts. Father, bless everyone in this congregation and those who could not make it today. Father, be with them all the way. All these things we pray in the name of Christ our Lord. Amen.

REV. SUN MYUNG MOON: THE MAN

ARTICLE PUBLISHED IN *TONGIL SEGYE*

FEBRUARY 2, 1980

Dr. Pak sprinkles this personal account of Father's life with wonderful anecdotes demonstrating Father's love for God and his country.

I was seized with panic when I was asked to contribute an article entitled "Rev. Sun Myung Moon: the Man." Why? Because I strongly felt the subject was beyond my powers.

I have been Reverend Moon's follower for the last 22 years, and in the last 10 years I have served as his interpreter whenever he goes on a speaking tour across the 50 states of the United States and throughout the rest of the world. And yet I am completely at a loss as to where and how to begin this article about him. That's why I was panic-stricken. Perhaps I should say that although I have been his disciple for 22 years, I have just begun to understand him. Believe it or not, this is the truth.

As I've just said, I've just begun to "scratch the surface," a very apt phrase in English that accurately describes my situation. After 22 years, I have to say that I have a long way to go to really know him inside out.

If you stand at the foot of a very high mountain, you can't estimate its height. You would need an appropriate instrument to measure it. My attempt to describe Reverend Moon is like using a measuring stick that's only 30 centimeters long to gauge the depth of the Pacific Ocean. Hence, you can readily see I have great temerity to undertake this almost impossible task.

While serving Reverend Moon in various capacities for so long, I have more than once wondered to myself whether there ever was or will be another human like him.

It is almost 2,000 years since Jesus Christ came upon this earth. However, no one, in my opinion, has completely understood Jesus the man, his total personality. Many scholars have written their Ph.D. dissertations on him and yet none of them has understood him inside out. Probably, the same thing may be said of the Buddha, Confucius, Meng-tzu, and Mohammed.

Speaking of Reverend Moon, maybe I should deal with him by the same yardstick that applies to these greatest of men. Korea was founded as a nation by Tan-Goon 5,000 years ago. In those 5,000 years, Reverend Moon is the first Korean to affect world history. There is no shadow of a doubt in my mind that in the next hundred, nay, thousands of years to come, he'll continue to shake up the course of human history. His thought, his outlook on life as a whole, is already making a big difference to the lives of millions and millions of people of all races, in all cultures, throughout the world. I can confidently predict that even in his lifetime, he will transform millions of people. His impact on their lives is simply too mind-boggling to contemplate. Now it becomes doubly obvious, then, that it is beyond my powers to do justice in this article to Reverend Moon the man. Under the circumstances, I tried to decline to do this piece on him, yet as he is about to celebrate his 60th birthday it behooves me, as one of his closest followers, to accede to the request. In any case, by a miracle I can stay two days longer in Korea than I anticipated, and it is as good a time as any to do my best in writing about him.

REVEREND MOON'S "ISM": LIBERATE GOD-ISM

To put in a nutshell the teaching of Reverend Moon, it is this: liberate God. We often use the expression "liberation," but when we apply it to God, we find ourselves flustered. We readily understand expressions such as liberation of all mankind, liberation from oppression, liberation from poverty, liberation from colonialism. But if one says we "liberate" God, we don't know what is meant by it.

No philosopher or religious thinker has talked or written about "liberation of God." But very often, indeed, Reverend Moon concludes his sermons with his reference to "liberation of God." This must be a new expression, a new "ism," to put it mildly.

But what does it all mean? Liberating God from what? In whose captivity is God held?

Reverend Moon preaches that we should liberate God from His sorrow and suffering! Two thousand years of Christianity have nothing to say about God's sorrow and suffering. God is omniscient and omnipotent, all perfect, seated comfortably in heaven, bestowing His blessings now and then upon mankind.

We must say of Reverend Moon that he has gone far beyond the ordinary understanding of mankind in his concrete and practical yet transcendental knowledge of God. Reverend Moon says: "I would rather know God, see Him and feel Him than to believe in Him." To believe may imply the denial of any proof. I don't say I believe that my parents gave birth to me. I don't use the expression "to believe" when I mean "I know."

Up to the present time, Christianity has believed in God. This could mean that it has not fully understood and known God as manifest reality. But Reverend Moon is the first person in human history to proclaim that he "knows" God. We read in 1 Corinthians 13:12, "For now we see in a mirror dimly, but then face to face. Now I know in part; then shall I understand fully, even as I have been fully understood."

Reverend Moon's knowledge of God is the fulfillment of the prophecy in this biblical quote. Reverend Moon does not see God through a mirror dimly. He sees Him, knows Him, face to face.

Now Reverend Moon really knows God inside out, face to face; he knows His loving heart. As a result, he now knows that God does not dwell in joy and dignity and peace. He has discovered that God, indeed, is a suffering God. Since His Creation, this suffering God has gone through all manner of hardship and heart-rending frustration.

This discovery is a great discovery in the history of mankind. God is not a God living in glory and joy, but a suffering parent who has lost His children, who cries out in anguish over them. God sees that His children are fighting and killing one another, and His heart literally bleeds; hence, the history of God is one of sorrow and suffering. No one has given an accurate portrait of Him whose heart is broken, torn apart. Only Reverend Moon has succeeded in doing so.

And he publicized his portrait of the suffering God to every corner of the world. He started campaigning for the liberation of God from this heart-rending situation. His is the Unification Movement that spreads like wildfire all over the world. Now then, how does he propose to liberate God? What constitutes true liberation?

The only road to liberation of God consists in this: to save fallen mankind from sin and to restore them to the state of perfection. This is the teaching of Reverend Moon and also the Unification Movement. To say that one should liberate God from His suffering and sorrow is to say, in the final analysis, that we ought to realize His original plan for the kingdom of heaven on earth, so that when He looks at the earth here below, He would be filled with joy and happiness. This is the first of Reverend Moon's "ism's" and, in a word, it is "liberate God-ism," to coin a new term.

The reason why Reverend Moon is the first to proclaim this truth in human history is that he also is the first to really know God, and only because he knows Him so well, can he proclaim his new truth or "ism" and start a new movement.

CRAZY FOR GOD'S LOVE

"Crazy for God" may not sound genteel, yet I can find no better or more accurate expression. The Bible tells us, "Love God with all your mind, all your heart, and all your soul."

Suppose we use this phrase in connection with love between man and woman. Suppose, then, that a man loves a woman with all his mind, all his heart, and all his soul. Can he, then, really do anything else? Suppose, further, that a woman loves a man likewise; then we may say, aptly, that she is "crazy" about him.

For similar reasons, Reverend Moon, too, not only knows God and feels His presence, but loves Him with all his mind, all his heart, and all his soul, and is said to be really crazy about Him to the highest degree, more than anyone else. He works with God, toils and sweats with Him, dedicates all his life and heart to Him.

Because Reverend Moon knows God to be a suffering and sorrowful God, he has become a person who cries for Him, comforts Him. Throughout human history, no other human being has shed more tears for God than Reverend Moon. Now and then we hear a story or anecdote. One has it that in the early stage of the Unification Church, Reverend Moon spent many countless hours, hour after hour, in ardent prayer. Once he knelt down to pray, he continued in his prayer for 14 or even 17 hours at a stretch. Can we find anyone who cried on God's behalf like Reverend Moon? After a while, we are told, calluses developed on his knees and elbows.

Once he begins his prayer, his prayer may last one day or two days. He forgets food and drink. He forgets sleep. Some of us who were close to him observed all this. No lesson was as momentous to us.

In recent years, Reverend Moon speaks through an interpreter to the American congregation; he begins at six in the morning and may end at five in the late afternoon, speaking for 11 hours. Then, after he finishes his sermon he turns around to ask someone if it is lunch time.

He always teaches his followers to live for God, to become crazy for God. After all, they are bound to be crazy for something, whether it be money, the opposite sex, honor, learning, etc. Why not God, he says.

Two years ago, Reverend Moon proposed for our annual motto: "Let's be crazy for God." Life that is crazy for God is not only holy in itself but also worth living. Blood and sweat shed for such a life can never be washed away. And Reverend Moon lives this kind of life more intensely than anyone else.

Once a high U.S. government official came to hear Reverend Moon speak. Of course, Reverend Moon was not prepared and he and the visitor casually started in a conversation. After it was over, the official was duly impressed and concluded: "Reverend Moon is crazy for God. No matter what he talks about, he somehow manages to get back to talk about God." This is a very interesting observation. Reverend Moon's being is filled with God's words. I have seen at least one person who is truly crazy for God.

HE LIVES ON GOD'S BEHALF

Reverend Moon may be said to be a person who is willing to shoulder all the responsibilities in the world. This sense of responsibility dominates his daily life, so that it can be said he represents God in every conceivable way.

God is formless. Reverend Moon wants to dedicate his whole being to the formless God. That's why his eyes, ears, and mouth represent those of God, his body that of God Himself.

As a religious leader, Reverend Moon takes interest even in things that are not religious. He seems interested in almost everything. It matters little to him that it is economic, industrial, political, or cultural. He is a completely natural person. If, for instance, an earthquake brings disaster in a remote corner of the earth, he stays up all night praying for the victims. If famine strikes somewhere, he does the same. He tries to understand how, in these dire situations, God will think or react to these people and events.

He teaches that God as our Father takes interest in everything that affects His children. Parents are concerned over everyone and everything in their household; God is the same, concerned over everything in His creation and creatures. Hence, Reverend Moon teaches: "This God is our Father. If we are to become His true children, we should also be concerned over everything and take responsibility for all things."

Reverend Moon's sense of responsibility and mission is overwhelming. He believes that without him there may be no one who can save this world. That is why, whether he is awake or asleep, he suffers for and with his fellow men and takes responsibility for all that happens to them.

When he came to the United States, Reverend Moon wanted to shoulder the responsibility for that country and its affairs. This goes for every other country, too. He sends missionaries to every nation and through them tries to take responsibility. He knows only too well that the free democratic nations are invaded by communist ideology and they are like a house on fire. No wonder he asserts that one of the most urgent problems of this world is that of combating communism. Communism is an ideology that seeks to chase away God from this earth. If communism achieved victory all over the world, the world would be godless, God having been booted out unceremoniously.

If there is one who constantly thinks about how best to eliminate the evil of communism, it must be God. So if someone truly knows God and His heart, he must also feel the same way about communism as God does. This someone is none other than Reverend Moon.

Reverend Moon carries on his shoulders the burden of combating the plague of communism. Now, Reverend Moon and communism are engaged in a final battle. Communism has no other choice but to confront him. For this reason, Reverend Moon spread his teaching concerning Victory Over Communism throughout the world. He thus exposed the deception and unrighteousness of communism. He makes it clear to the whole world that communism is the enemy not only of mankind but of God as well.

For the first time communism is on the defensive because Reverend Moon has mounted his attack on it. There is only one sure way to eradicate the evil of communism, and that is to speak the truth. This begins with the assertion that God exists. An ideology that denies His existence must crumble when another ideology that believes in His existence prevails.

Now, for the same reason, communism is put on the defensive, too, in Japan and the United States. Up to now, communism has swallowed up one-third of the world through its effective but misleading propaganda offensive in the last 60 years. But the anti-communism of Reverend Moon has been pushing it into a narrow corner. I firmly believe this: that a new weapon is being forged in Korea to effectively combat and win victory over communism. This weapon is Reverend Moon and his new ideology. Armed with these, a country will be safe from communism. Nay, not just a country but the whole free world. Then the free world will take one step further and liberate the communist world.

Reverend Moon feels that it is his responsibility to liberate the communist world. It is then natural that he wants to stage the next big rally (similar to the one at Washington Monument) in Moscow, symbol of the communist world. It would be no exaggeration to say that in one sense Reverend Moon wants to eradicate communism from the face of the earth and erect on it, through his "revolutionary" army, the kingdom of heaven. This "revolutionary" ideology is the ideology of the Messiah.

I once accompanied Reverend Moon to England. It was about 10 years ago. There were not many English family members. When he arrived, about 25 members were there to welcome him in a large room. Reverend Moon asked them a question: "Is there anyone among you who can confidently claim that he or she will save England single-handedly? If you think you are the one, raise your hand!" The task was considered too stupendous, so that none answered in the affirmative. "Then," said Reverend Moon, "let me ask another question. How many saviors do you think God needs to save this world?" Everyone kept silent. No answer. He went on to ask, "Two thousand years ago, how many saviors did God send on this earth?" All answered in unison, "Only one, Jesus Christ." Again he said: "Now then, God needed only one savior to save all mankind. So to save this small country—England—how many saviors does He need? If you are armed with the ideology of the Messiah, possess the character of the Messiah, and carry out the mission of the Messiah, how many of you are needed to save England?" He added parenthetically that if they, 25 English family members, understood his meaning, there were more than enough in the room. Thereupon, all of them got the message and without a moment's hesitation raised their hands. Reverend Moon, looking over them, said quickly: "England has 25 Messiahs. Aren't there simply too many?" In other words, he taught them that if any of them meant to dedicate his or her heart to God's will, then he or she could be more than enough to save England single-handedly.

A PERSON OF SIMPLE HEART

It comes as a surprise to one when one is told that Reverend Moon is a person of simple heart and of human love.

On one occasion, there was going to be an open-air gathering of Unification Church members in the United States. When the news got out, the American magazine, *People*, sent its photographers and reporters to cover Reverend Moon's outdoor preaching to his own followers.

The magazine later printed a story in which the reporter described Reverend Moon's outfit in glowing but inaccurate terms: His suit was specially custom-made in England; his watch, studded with diamonds and other precious stones, was worth $30,000 or $40,000; his shoes, worth several hundred dollars, too, were not U.S. made but custom-made just for him in England; his expensive shirt was custom-made, etc., etc. In other words, Reverend Moon was supposedly covered from the top of his head to the tip of his toes with gold and jewels and other fanciful and fantastic things.

In fact, however, he then wore an inexpensive Korean-made suit, his watch was a birthday gift from his own son worth about $40, and his shoes, U.S. made, only cost $40.

Many people don't realize what simple taste Reverend Moon has in his daily life. Contrary to the newspaper account, he leads an utterly simple life. I have been with him for so long and I have yet to hear him complain about, say, food even once. He relishes his food, even if it is coarse. He doesn't care much about gourmet food.

One of the reasons why so many Americans respect and adore him is that he and Mrs. Moon often eat at very inexpensive places such as McDonald's. McDonald's is a chain of fast food restaurants designed to please children and common folks. You can eat your meal for a dollar or so, and a small Mac will cost you anywhere between 40 and 50 cents. He often takes his children there and enjoys eating with them, which looks so natural that newspaper reporters who happen to be there swarm around him to take pictures of him and his family.

When he is on a lecture tour throughout the 50 states, he makes a point of taking his hard-working followers, most of them Americans, to McDonald's for hamburgers and milk shakes. He chats with them at the same table and expresses his appreciation for their hard work. This simple lifestyle of Reverend Moon leaves an indelible impression on American members, who try to emulate him in this regard.

In 1974, he toured 50 states in 40 days on a speaking tour. He rode in a beat-up Plymouth, day and night, and one thing that really worried me was that he ate only coarse food. He often had the car stop in front of a supermarket where he bought a loaf of bread, a jar of cucumber pickles, a bowl of soup made of cow intestines; that was his meal day after day for 40 days. Even when he shops for his own clothes, he picks up a pair of pants for $9, and the whole suit costs him $30 or $40. He is very careful and strict with "public" funds. He teaches his followers that Heaven's money may not be misspent without becoming a thief before Heaven.

He practices what he teaches and preaches. But he may hold the world's record in spending money generously on other people. And I may add that when it comes to spending money on himself, he is downright stingy. He must hold the world's record in this respect also.

One anecdote deeply moves our family members. When Reverend Moon was imprisoned in North Korea, the prisoners were given so little food that he knew no one was supposed to survive on that meager diet; he realized that only God's love and grace could save his and the other prisoners' lives, so he decided, living among these hungry wolves, to give away half of his small barley-ball to another prisoner. Even the whole barley-ball would not have allayed a small child's hunger. Hunger was so real and demanding that some prisoners wrenched the chewed-up food out of the mouths of dying prisoners. Under these extreme conditions, he gave them love. He did not pray for more food but delighted only in God's words. Some say that because of Reverend Moon's unselfish, selfless, and loving way of life during this period, the Unification Church members of today receive from heaven material bounty and other blessings.

A MAN OF BIG HEART
WHO PAYS ATTENTION TO DETAILS

Reverend Moon is a Korean, but he transcends his ethnic identity. He is a cosmopolitan, a citizen of the world. Anyone who comes into contact with him and listens to him is struck with amazement about how one person can be so big and great in his heart, dreams, ideals, etc.

When he sits down with his followers, he talks about the world, the very axis of heaven and earth. He talks not only about the earth but about the invisible but real spirit world.

In the final analysis, even before he fights against the evils and sins of this world, he has already won his victory in the spirit world. He teaches that we must first conquer our enemies in the spirit world and achieve unification in that world, after which we can dispose of the straggling and exhausted enemy soldiers on this earth. He leaves us with the impression that his grand strategy covers heaven and earth, and it is too vast for our minds to imagine. After 22 years, I still hear new things in the speeches I interpret for him. In them I find inexhaustible truth, wisdom, joy, and hope. Since his heart and mind are overflowing with God's words, he cannot help but share them with others whenever he speaks.

Many people expound their philosophies or ideologies yet utterly fail to put them into practice. But as for Reverend Moon, he backs up his grand philosophy with very intense and faithful practice, even in the smallest detail. He always makes a very careful and detailed plan before he acts, and more than once I have been amazed at how he can pay attention to such minute details.

For example, I have watched him dress on many occasions, but he has never left a single button unfastened. He carefully knots his necktie and sticks a tiepin at exactly the right spot. His dressing habits demonstrate his careful and detailed mental attitude.

I once heard this incredible anecdote. Before the Korean War broke out in 1950, Reverend Moon had already spent almost three years in the hellish Hungnam prison in North Korea. Even here, under the most trying circumstances, he saved a thread here and there to sew a small bag to put his chopsticks in. Some of his followers who had been in contact with him now and then told me that it was very well made. He has an amazing gift in so many different areas. He is a born calligrapher as well as a good painter. He teaches American seminarians at his Unification Theological Seminary how to mend fishing nets and catch fish in the Hudson River. None among them could compare with him in dexterous skills in mending or casting fishing nets. When he goes on a trip, he carries with him a small bag. Once he opened it to take out a book. I took a quick look at the opened bag, and what struck me most was that everything was so neatly put in its place. His lifestyle shows even in packing his traveling bag.

Reverend Moon always sits straight. He never lets his body tilt or twist. This is another indication that in every area of his life, he never lets things go awry. His neatness without is but an external manifestation of his neatness within.

Reverend Moon always aims at the highest peak. I have heard several anecdotes about his childhood, both from Reverend Moon himself and from his close relatives. In his childhood or at the age of 60 today, he impresses us as being one who never gives up until he reaches the top, so to speak. He is always keenly aware of the flow of human history in his daily life. He thinks of what legacy he should leave to future generations. He establishes a tradition that they will continue in the days to come. This tradition is to strive to break all records, that is, to improve, to overcome, and to go beyond all that has been done before.

Reverend Moon once casually remarked, "I want to be someone who sleeps least among all those who have been born on this earth." This implies that he tries to get along with less sleep than anyone in history in order to fulfill God's will better than anyone else. I am sure that no one in history works harder for God's will. I have never seen him going to bed before midnight. In the early days of the church at Chung Pa Dong, Seoul, he stayed up till two or three in the morning, speaking to his followers. And when and if he sleeps at all, he gets up before 5:00 a.m., always earlier than anyone else. Since he came to America, he seems to have forgotten about his sleep. Many times he takes a catnap in an armchair and goes right back to start his new day.

I am 10 years younger than Reverend Moon but I cannot possibly claim to be "younger" than he is. I can't keep up with him. The greatest difficulty in serving this man is lack of sleep. If someone asks me what I want most of all, I must answer: I want to sleep to my heart's content.

Who in the history of mankind has spoken or preached more than Reverend Moon? His words, from beginning to end, are always God-centered. No one, I am sure, can beat his record in this regard. Reverend Moon always emphasizes that the road that our church must walk is a difficult, torturing and tortuous, tear-filled road, but we must be grateful to God for having the opportunity to walk on it at all. Thus he endures so much hardship and suffering of which he never speaks, bur rather emphasizes God's love, suffering, and sorrow. Reverend Moon often asks his question: If we know that God is also suffering, how can we complain? He tells us that God is now seeking people like us. He cannot help but walk this difficult road and can ill afford to get tired. He teaches us that our road is worth all of our effort, for it is the road that leads to the fulfillment of God's will.

For the last few years Reverend Moon has engaged in tuna fishing near Boston. Of course, he is no fisherman by trade, but in a few years he has emerged as a highly respected "instructor" in tuna fishing. His boat goes out before dawn and returns late at night, so that no one seems to be able to see it. Several hundred boats gather in the area for the summer; most of them happen to be millionaires who enjoy sport fishing.

Whoever who catches the largest number of tuna for the season wins a prize. But Reverend Moon, since he came on the scene, has beaten everyone, including those sport fisherman with 30 years' experience. In 1979 he broke the old record in catching the largest tuna ever caught in that area. It was over 1,000 pounds. Reverend Moon has become a legend among fishermen. They now believe that wherever he happens to be fishing, that is where the tuna gather around. Consequently, when his boat, New Hope, is on the open sea, other boats follow it. When his boat anchors, other boats follow suit in the same spot. And when a tuna is caught, other fishermen at once resort to binoculars to observe his technique of handling the giant fish. In recent years, these fishermen, who can't catch up with him, have become convinced that Reverend Moon can brainwash tuna.

But the world has no miracles. You have got to "make" them. Reverend Moon believes in the history of God's dispensation, and he knows man's portion of responsibility to fulfill that dispensation. He believes in and literally puts into practice an Oriental maxim: "Do all that is humanly possible, and await the command of Heaven."

A POSSESSOR OF STRONG WILL AND INDOMITABLE SPIRIT

Once he starts something, Reverend Moon never lets up until he finishes it. In America, he has acquired the reputation of being a born fighter. This implies that as a revolutionary he is born to win. In my opinion, God has sent him as one who will subjugate Satan. But one thing that he hates most would be to say that because he is a special person he can never get tired.

This would be equivalent to saying that because Jesus was a special person he did not feel the excruciating pain on the cross.

In 1965, Reverend Moon had to go through a physical examination before he applied for visas to various countries so that he could meet and talk with family members all over the world. The doctor who took his x-ray was taken by surprise and asked him whether he had ever had pleurisy. Reverend Moon was surprised, too, and asked why, and the doctor replied that the x-ray clearly revealed the vestige of an old pleurisy. Reverend Moon had been too absorbed in his mission to carry out God's will to be aware of this malady. It seems that the disease surrendered before the iron will and the fighting spirit of Reverend Moon. This also shows us something about his life.

No wonder his message—somewhat marred in the process of an interpreter's translation—is bound to reach his American members. His strong will and fighting spirit can't be lost in the translation. That's why a man of little faith, once he listens to Reverend Moon, suddenly summons his courage and decides to have strong faith and determination. For he feels the power of resurrection in Reverend Moon's words. I've seen many who have lost hope for themselves come and receive hope and revitalization from his words.

Once he went to speak to students at the Unification Theological Seminary in Barrytown, New York. I was to interpret for him but I was not there when he needed me. So he loudly asked, "Where is my mouth?" and broke into a grin. Afterwards, I got the nickname of Reverend Moon's mouth. Whenever I am called by this nickname, I pinch myself and wonder whether there could be anything more glorious. His real mouth is the mouth that speaks God's words. If I am supposed to be the "mouth" that interprets Reverend Moon, am I not honored with a historic, glorious mission?

But I don't just translate his words. I try my best to bring out in my translation that which lives between the lines: his spirit, his faith, his love, and his heart. That's why I pride myself on the fact that the best U.N. interpreters cannot interpret for him as effectively as I do. His words cannot be only literally translated to effectively communicate his true message. An interpretation of his overwhelming sense of loyalty and filial piety to heaven, his will to persevere as a born fighter, his iron constitution that overcomes all disease, must convey his exalted place in the spirit world, his personality, his faith and love. Hence, the first one to be moved by his words happens to be his interpreter himself.

HE LOVES KOREA MORE THAN ANYBODY ELSE

In conclusion, I would add that Reverend Moon is a true patriot who loves his own country, Korea. When he returned last year he was invited to speak to a group of prominent leaders of the nation at the Institute of Rural Community Development, he chose as his subject, "May the Fatherland Shine Forth." He is engaged in the stupendous task of liberating and restoring all mankind on a stage as wide as the world itself, yet whenever he returns to his native country he speaks of "May the Fatherland Shine Forth." He never forgets for a moment his own country. And he is constantly busy helping Korea to become a country that all the peoples of the world may look up to some day as their own country of "faith." In the future, all the peoples of different races and cultures scattered in 127 countries of the world will visit Korea as their own Mecca. It is not too far in the future, either. The time will come, too, when peoples of the world will love and admire things Korean.

The long history of Korea is not exactly a glorious history we may be proud of but one of tears, sorrow, and humiliation. The domination of her peninsula for 36 years by imperial Japan is but an example. Now 17 million Koreans are suffering under the inhuman and oppressive rule of communism in the north. This history is one of suffering and sorrow. Reverend Moon wants to put an end to this once and for all and begin the first page of a glorious future for Korea, a country that is not to be ignored or forgotten in God's history, a nation whose future generations will bear the brunt of liberating all mankind.

Some time ago, I happened to talk with the president of a leading newspaper in this country. In the course of our conversation, he said that in order to come up with a special edition on the 100 years since Korea opened her doors in the last century, he had gathered and intensively studied the relevant material on the subject. He came to the inevitable conclusion that this 100-year history has been one of shame and humiliation, except for the last 10 years. During this time, the Unification Church has come up with an ideology that proclaims to the world the Korean people's noble spirit, greatness, and all-embracing love for mankind. This, he added, commands respect and admiration from the rest of the world, thanks to the Unification Church. It also restores the dignity of the Korean people.

What Reverend Moon has done is more than to save "face" for the Korean people in the last 100 years. Since Tan-Goon, the founder of Korea as a nation 5,000 years ago, no Korean has made such an impact on world history. The world will everlastingly benefit from an ideology conceived and put into practice by a Korean leader. Korea will thus emerge as a liberator in God's history.

And the blessing of the liberation will continue as long as God's history continues.

"May the Fatherland Shine Forth!" This is Reverend Moon's fervent prayer and wish. The shining history of this nation will be realized in our generation and will perpetuate itself for 10,000 generations to come.

"Reverend Moon: the Man" is the greatest treasure that Korea has ever produced, and his name will signal of the new dawn of mankind's history. "Reverend Moon: the Man" is, above all, the liberator of God.

Wise as Serpents, Pure as Doves

UNIFICATION CHURCH ON COLUMBIA ROAD,

WASHINGTON, D.C., MAY 1, 1982

Dr. Pak reports about Father's trial and challenges the Washington membership to become exemplary in every way. As their spiritual leader, he pledges to stay accessible to every member and encourages people to write him with both problems and exciting testimonies.

Some of you may not have seen a copy of this speech from April 1 at Belvedere, exactly one month ago today. That was the very day Father and Mother entered the courthouse for the first day of the trial. Jury selection began March 22, but April 1 was the first day Father was in the defendant's seat. That morning, like today, Father spoke at Belvedere because it was the first day of the month. His subject was public life.

It is truly a historical statement, a beautiful, powerful, enthusiastic, and inspiring message. I believe this message will go down in history. Of course, any words Father speaks will go down in history, but this particular sermon, on the very day Father was going into the courthouse, is significant. People would expect Father to be very bitter and complaining about his unfair treatment. This would be normal. But Father through his public life always expresses his love for this country, his determination to go on. This is the kind of life we all should live. I made 200 copies of this speech for *Washington Times* members because this is the kind of backbone we need for our spiritual life here in Washington while we fulfill our mission at the *Washington Times*. After this meeting is over, I would like you to have a copy. If you have a little time before Father's arrival, I would like you to read it, but if you don't, never mind. Keep it as a daily inspiration. Keep it at your home and read some of it every day.

I wanted to have this meeting quite some time ago. I wish I could be with you frequently, but it simply doesn't happen. I am not only engaged in many traditional missions—translating for Father, being his assistant, running *The News World* in New York, and other spiritual and business missions, diplomatic missions such as CAUSA—but at the same time, I have been spending virtually every day, every minute of the day with Father during this special trial period. Every morning I report to Father at 7:00 a.m. on the dot. After having breakfast with Father and Mother, we talk about the day's agenda, the previous day's happenings, and the press handling of the case. At 8:30 a.m., I accompany Father to the courthouse in Manhattan. It takes us about one hour to get there. On the way, I give Father more reports with Mother listening. It is a very intimate period of conversation, mostly in Korean. Sometimes I read some English-language letters and tell funny stories and jokes and so forth, and Mike McDevitt, who is driving, can join the conversation.

Then about 9:30 we enter the courthouse. The courthouse has given Father extraordinary treatment. We have a special waiting room, a brand-new jury room right next to another courtroom on the fourth floor. The courtroom is on the fifth floor. We wait in that room until 10:00 a.m. when the day's agenda for the trial is announced. Then Father and Mother go up one flight and from the back door move into the courtroom. I accompany Father up to the door, but I do not enter the courtroom. I do a lot of important contact with the lawyers and make telephone calls. This is generally the time I call the *Washington Times* because I want to know what is going on here and I can keep Father and Mother informed.

CAN'T TRUST BO HI PAK

The reason I do not enter the courtroom is that I was reserved as a possible witness. As one of the closest people to Reverend Moon, the government was planning to call me as a witness for their side to try to prove conspiracy, which is the heart and center of this particular case. But they never called me. They gave up. They had an uneasy feeling because they said that Bo Hi Pak is unpredictable. They just didn't know how I would be on the stand—particularly after Fraser's experience. Nobody wants to be in the position of Fraser. So they had been waiting. They had a tremendous appetite to call me on one hand, but tremendous fear on the other. The fear won and they didn't call me.

Two days ago, the government rested, which means they finished presenting their case and it was now the defense's turn. Yesterday there was an oral debate between the prosecution and our defense attorneys without the jury present for at least 2-1/2 hours. It was a very heated legal battle, which will set the tone for the rest of the trial. Yesterday our lawyer presented a Memorandum of Law, which is a motion asking for acquittal or a mistrial.

The defense attorney is saying, well, you presented your case and you haven't proven anything on any of the charges, not conspiracy, not filing a false report. This motion is going to go down in history as a great legal document and a beautiful, powerful statement in support of Father.

The initial paragraph goes like this: "Defendant, Reverend Sun Myung Moon, moves pursuant to Rule 29 FRCRP for a judgment of acquittal on both the conspiracy charge and the three substantive charges. In the alternative we move for a mistrial on the grounds of prejudice."

During the whole trial, for an entire month, we listened to the most boring and incredibly tedious presentations by the government. The jurors, 12 regular jurors and four alternates, were so bored. They are housewives, regular people. The judge said, you are people who don't talk much, who don't know much, who don't read much. Those people have no idea what is going on. For one month they were almost snoring, bored to death. The judge was concerned and frequently admonished the prosecution, saying, why do you make things so complicated? You don't have to make it that complicated. I had only one fear: these jurors may not understand. They may be unbiased—we made every effort to select an unbiased jury—but at the same time there is a drawback: they are not educated and may not understand this case. The judge was constantly reminding the prosecution, but they didn't listen and presented tons of papers and one witness after another. Incredible. Hours and hours and hours.

The only part the jurors enjoy is our attorney's cross-examination of the government witnesses. Everybody is sleeping, but when Mr. Stillman gets up for cross-examination, the jurors signal each other. Showtime, showtime. Their eyes are wide open. Mr. Stillman is really a professional. A most seasoned, gentlemanly, authoritative lawyer.

THE THREE MUSKETEERS

Actually, there are three lawyers working together, and we call them the three musketeers. They represent three different law firms. One is Mr. Stillman, another is Bernard Bailor of Washington, whose Kaplan law firm specializes in tax law. The other law firm is defending Mr. Kamiyama, and their attorney is named Andrew Lawler. The three musketeers sit there, all three very tall, handsome, good looking. They are right next to Father, surrounding Father. Next to Father is Mr. S.I. Kim, who has been appointed through News World Communications as Executive Vice President. He has been translating because I could not be there; all potential witnesses have to stay outside the courtroom. Then there is Mr. Kamiyama. Mr. Kamiyama's interpreter is a very good-looking Japanese. So when you look at the defense line, it is the most beautiful thing to behold.

When you look at the prosecution line, first there is the chief prosecutor, whose name is Jo Ann Harris. That woman is a most untypical woman. She is extraordinarily tall. I tell you, not so attractive. Almost grandma. But the government chose a woman prosecutor because they knew it would be a long, long ordeal and they cannot afford to lose this case. They desperately want to win this case. In a jury trial, the prosecution must be charming to win the jurors. The prosecutor who made all these things happen is a 34-year-old Harvard graduate, a most ambitious, vicious, bitter prosecutor named Marty Flumenbaum. Mr. Stillman is a Jewish lawyer and Marty Flumenbaum is a Jewish prosecutor. So they are Abel Jew and Cain Jew. The government knew Flumenbaum could not win the heart of the jurors, so they assigned a very polished, polite gentleman named Pomeran. He conducted Father's arraignment. Then what happened? The very next day Pomeran got sick and was hospitalized. He was expected to be in the hospital for several months. Amazing. The government could not wait for him to come out so they assigned Ms. Harris. They picked a woman because most juries are predominately made up of men and they thought a woman would relate to men jurors better. Well, man is always interested in woman, right. But, totally unexpectedly, the jury turned out to be 10 women and two men. Anyway, right next to her is Flumenbaum. He is the most untypical American man. There is another prosecutor, Eveta, a very hard-looking man. Next to him is one IRS agent. He cannot even look straight. His eyes cross somehow. He is not a normal-looking man.

So when you compare the prosecution line with the defense line, you automatically know which are the good guys. Anyway, I cannot spend the whole morning on this because there are so many stories that can be told about the court trial. It is going to be the trial of the century. No question about it. Many books will be written about it. Hal McKenzie has been assigned to cover this proceeding and to write the first book.

I would like to go through at least the first day. On April 1 Father spoke in the morning at Belvedere. I commented to Mother how beautiful the sky was, not even one cloud, although we had just had some very bad weather. Look at the sky, I said, so clean and beautiful. It is a sign of great hope and great victory. I comforted Mother that way. So that is the way we entered the courthouse, beautiful day, sunshine, calm, no wind.

THE SKY DARKENED

But something incredible happened the moment the judged ordered the prosecution to make a statement. Just as Flumenbaum stood up and moved to the podium and began to utter his first words, the sky grew dark with all the signs of an incredible storm. The windows were shaking. It was so sudden, so drastic. The jurors were facing that window and were frightened. They weren't listening to the prosecutor. They were looking at the windows and looking at each other. Then some kind of storm hit. The electricity went out four times during the prosecution's delivery. This little man, Flumenbaum spoke so fast, the jurors probably couldn't understand what he was saying. It was noisy, they were frightened, the electricity was blinking.

After 40 minutes it was time for our side's opening statement. Mr. Stillman stood up. He moved to the podium and began his statement. Amazingly enough, his voice was so clear and the jurors were listening closely, not missing even one word. After 10 or 15 minutes, the wind outside was becoming calm. Mr. Stillman moved into a very emotional appeal, saying that this is injustice, there is no case, this is government fabrication. He was accusing the government of doing this to Reverend Moon, the religious leader. The wind totally died down, and when he was moving into the conclusion, speaking so powerfully in a low, emotional voice, the courtroom was absolutely quiet. The drop of a needle could be heard. Everybody was listening so intently. When he said, "Thank you very much, ladies and gentlemen," the church bells rang.

So many episodes to tell about in this trial. The government's final witness was Michael Young Warder. I know him very well. He is not just another witness; he is an ex-Moonie, and he used to be president and publisher of *The News World*. The government used him as their big gun. This was the grand finale. He had held a high position; he could say so many things; he could lie. Three times he actually said I had lied in previous testimony to the Securities and Exchange Commission. I was giving sworn testimony, but he said I lied because I was in the church. He openly said that I lied to the government.

The government was really counting on Michael Warder in this case. They met with him four times at the grand jury investigation and 10 times after the grand jury for interviews. They intended his testimony to deal the final blow in their case. But, it is amazing how God works, Mike's testimony turned out to be the strongest proof, not for the government but for Father.

They totally failed to prove there was any conspiracy. Because of Mike. One time during the court proceedings Mr. Stillman protested that the government hadn't shown any evidence to prove their charges. The judge answered that he agreed but that the government had promised that they did have proof and he was still waiting for them to present it. Their star witness was supposed to be Mike. The plain and simple fact, incredible as it may seem, is that Mike's testimony exonerated Reverend Moon of any participation in the conspiracy charges in count number 1. Even on direct examination, he testified that Reverend Moon was not part of any of the discussions he had with other church members about the tactics to adopt in the face of the investigation. Here is some of the testimony:

> Flumenbaum: Mr. Warder, now during this period of time did you have any conversation with Reverend Moon that related to the ongoing investigation?
>
> Warder: No.

On cross-examination Michael Warder completely failed to implicate Reverend Moon in any conspiracy. He made it clear that Reverend Moon had no role in any obstruction.

> Stillman: Did Reverend Moon ever tell you to lie about your SEC testimony, sir?
>
> Warder: No.
>
> Stillman: He knew you were going to testify before the SEC, did he not?
>
> Warder: I think he knew.
>
> Stillman: Did he call you and say, Michael, here is what I want you to say to the SEC? Did he do that?
>
> Warder: No.
>
> Stillman: You would have lied for him, wouldn't you? Even if pushed that far, if he had done so, you would have lied for him, wouldn't you? If he had said to you, Michael, go in and lie for me, you would have done it, wouldn't you?
>
> Warder: I think I probably would have.
>
> Stillman: The fact of the matter is, he did not, isn't that correct?
>
> Warder: You are correct. He did not.

This is a dramatic moment. Pushing and pushing, still the man could not hide his original mind, his conscience. Throughout the proceeding Michael Warder could not even look at Father. Not once. He could not. He is a pitiful man. He is a broken man. He could not lie under this probing. He just said the truth.

> Stillman: Did Reverend Moon ever come to you and say to you, now Michael, in case you are asked about Chase Manhattan Bank, here is what I want you to say about it?

> Mr. Flumenbaum objected to this question about the Chase Manhattan account. But the court said, how can you object? That is what we are all here for, to hear about the Chase Manhattan Bank account. Then Mike answered:

> Warder: Your honor, he never said that. Reverend Moon never said that.

In the motion for acquittal, Stillman wrote:

> It must be kept in mind, of course, that this was not just any witness. It was the government's best witness. It hardly needs repeating that in order to be convicted of criminal conspiracy, the defendant must be a knowing and intentional participant in agreement with others to commit criminal conduct. Neither Warder's testimony nor that of any other witness in this case provides any basis on which reasonable jurors could conclude beyond a reasonable doubt that Reverend Moon even knew about any criminal agreement by another person, much less that he knowingly and intentionally joined such an agreement and adopted this objective as his own.

> Well, the government is entitled to all reasonable inferences on the Rule 29 motion. The key word here is "reasonable." Inferences can defeat a motion for acquittal only if they can be reasonably drawn on the basis of evidence before the jury. But where there is no evidence, no basis exists for drawing an inference favorable to the government. Obviously realizing the wickedness in this conspiracy charge against Reverend Moon, the government is attempting to proceed on some unspecified theory to establish the requisite knowing and intentional agreement by Reverend Moon. The government has previously argued that if affidavits and other documents submitted by Reverend Moon's counsel to the Justice Department were false, those submissions are attributable to Reverend Moon because his lawyers were acting on his behalf. Similarly, the government may also argue that other agents of Reverend Moon allegedly gave false information to the accountant who prepared the tax return at issue and since this information was ultimately submitted to the IRS, these false statements are also attributable to Reverend Moon.

The government position is based on a fundamental perversion of the law of agency as it applies to a criminal case. Before a principal can be held liable for criminal conduct of his agent on the basis of relationship between them, it must be shown that he authorized those crimes and adopted them as his own. As the Second Circuit Court states...

I don't want to read everything here.

In conclusion, even the government must concede that there are many people who might have had the motive to obstruct the investigation of Reverend Moon and many people would have viewed themselves as beneficiaries of any successful attempt to do so. Even the government must concede that there are thousands of members of the Unification Church who view Reverend Moon as divinely inspired, as doing God's work. Each of these people would have a motive to protect Reverend Moon and their church against what they view as unwarranted harassment. It is entirely plausible and, indeed, likely, they would have made such an attempt without informing Reverend Moon. This is not just idle speculation. Indeed, Michael Young Warder admitted that he previously lied under oath because he somehow thought this would help Reverend Moon. Most importantly, he also admitted that he did this without Reverend Moon's knowledge or approval or direction.

It should also be noted that Reverend Moon is charged only with conspiracy to submit false statements and obstruct justice and not with substantive violation of the statutes violated. We submit that the government's failure to bring substantive charges against Reverend Moon with respect to these objects is a tacit admission of the wickedness of the allegation that he conspired to achieve these unlawful objects.

The conclusion follows because it is routine in the District for the government to charge a defendant not only with the conspiracy to commit an offense, but also the crime which is object of that conspiracy. Particularly where others have been charged with that offensive violation, one can be certain that if the government truly believes it has sufficient evidence to prove Reverend Moon conspired to submit false affidavits, documents, and testimony, it would have charged him with the offensive crime of obstruction, just as it did for defendant Kamiyama. That it did not do so, of course, is perfectly understandable. Why? There simply was no evidence to support such a charge. But the same lack of evidence requires the judgment acquittal today on conspiracy counts as well. Point two, the judgment acquittal should be directed on the substantive counts two and three and four. Then final point three, a mistrial must be declared as to the counts two, three, and four because the trial has been tainted by admission of evidence of a

coverup without the government having established that Reverend
Moon was a party to such purported coverup.

In other words, a lie is a lie, period. The communist lie that there is no God
will be exposed. Same thing here. They really fabricated. It was a real fireworks. Fourth of July. Big cannons here and there. They were trying to
deceive the jurors. From the beginning we said we didn't want a jury, but
the government wanted a jury. The Constitution provided the jury system
for the benefit of the defendant. If the defendant waives the jury, the government always says yes, but not in this case.

Somehow I have a great hope today. The trial will be over in the next
two weeks. Father is moving into the most crucial final two weeks of trial.
And I am honestly telling you I have a great hope today. Justice will be
done. The American judicial system may not be bad after all. Father is
being tried in the worst kind of atmosphere. Can you imagine anything
worse that this? When this type of motion is presented, the judge normally rejects it, saying, I want to go ahead with the trial to see what the jury
will say. We presented the motion, knowing it was likely to be rejected, but
also knowing it is good for appeal later. But this judge didn't reject the
motion. He said, I reserve judgment. That was an extraordinary victory
already. He said he will study the law this weekend and rule on Monday.

FATHER IS NOT ANXIOUS
So Monday maybe we will get some good news. He may not throw the
entire case out of court, but he may strike out some counts, particularly the
conspiracy count. That would be a great victory. All we need is one victory. Either at the District Court level or Appeals Court level or Supreme
Court level. We want to win at this level, formation level. If not, we want
to go to the growth stage. If not, we want to go to the Supreme Court. But
in the courtroom of the history of justice, we have already prevailed. That
is why Father has no anxiety. Not one bit. You may see him today. He
doesn't show even one bit of anxiety. He was the most jovial person in the
courthouse. He was only frustrated because he could not talk there. He
would like to get up and give a sermon for four or six hours. That would be
a lot easier for him to do. But for Father, sitting there without speaking for
hours and hours was a pain. You can imagine, right?

The first day, Mr. Stillman said, "Reverend Moon, I am sorry that I
have to bring you into this circumstance and you have to listen to the
garbage and dirt being thrown at you. I am so sorry, Reverend Moon. I don't
know what I can do." Do you know what Father said to him? He said, "Mr.
Stillman, don't worry. When I consider this as part of the providence,
nothing bothers me." Beautiful. When he looks at it as "I am doing the will

461

of God," no amount of hardship bothers him. Father said, "No amount of embarrassment will bother me." Then Father looked at Mr. Stillman and said, "Mr. Stillman, I will be Buddha. Buddha sitting and saying nothing. No Buddha talks, right?" That is the most descriptive expression I have ever heard. I will be a Buddha. But then Father added, "But I will not be a stone Buddha. I will be a smiling Buddha." He is smiling all day long.

The person most depressed was Mr. Kamiyama. Father was busy comforting him. What are you doing, Mr. Kamiyama? Come on, eat more, eat. Father gave him sandwiches, gave him his own food at lunch time. It was beautiful to behold. I just discovered another greatness of Father. Of course, in my service to Father for 25 years, I never went into a courthouse with him. This is the first time. I tell you, I am an eyewitness to another greatness of Father, another beautiful dimension of Father.

So that is my first report this morning. My conclusion is we are all children of God, children of True Parents, and we must be proud of being what we are. Let us be really proud of our True Parents. Every day I am not depressed. I am just uplifted. I am really bubbling with enthusiasm. That is what I am.

Now let's talk about the *Washington Times*. The *Washington Times* is the single most important thing on Father's mind today. This is no exaggeration. Father looks at the *Washington Times* as the most important project of our time. He asks me many questions every day, so many that I am always running out of new things to tell him, even though I read virtually every edition to Father, cover to cover. So I sneak down here to Washington to get more material from you. I come here to refuel so I can go back with a big package of news, but then during one breakfast, because he wants to hear so much, all the material is gone. By lunch hour, always I am empty. So I keep calling on the telephone to Jonathan, Joseph, Paula, Jim Gavin, talking every day. What is new, what is going on? Talking to Ted and Jenny and telling them to give me some news because Father is waiting.

FATHER SEES THE REAL YOU

So Father is very anxious to come and see you. Of course, no one is sure until the last minute what Father will do, but I feel 99 percent sure Father will be here in Washington. You want to meet him, don't you? What would Father like to see in Washington? Not the building, not the paper; you. Father wants to see you. What portion of you? Somebody said, spirit, bubbling enthusiasm. That is absolutely correct. Father comes to see your eyes. He feels exactly where you are. He knows if you have elevated yourself or lowered yourself spiritually. For that reason, serving Father around the clock, I have no moment of real relaxation. I cannot relax because Father immediately sees through me.

Now, my dear brothers and sisters, I am making a genuine appeal to you today. I wish I could have more time to speak to each one of you. After the court victory, I will spend more time in Washington and have more time to get acquainted with each one of you. Last night our leaders came out to meet me at the airport; we spoke until 12:30 or 1:00 this morning because I want to hear and know more about how you're doing.

But I tell you today, probably the most important factor for the success of the *Washington Times* is the people from outside joining the staff. They are caught up in our enthusiasm, right? Did you see it? Did you feel it? Yes? These professionals will make the *Washington Times* a professional paper, a great paper. Our job is not just to make a great paper. Our primary job is to witness to these people, not in terms of giving Divine Principle lectures, but in terms of way of life. These people who joined are stars of journalism, like Rock Hudson or Robert Taylor or—I don't know the names of the modern-day stars, they are changing so quickly. Anyway, they are like John Wayne. Pulitzer Prize winners. The caliber of the people now coming to work for us is just amazing. These people know the newspaper business inside out. We don't yet, even with five years of experience with *The News World*. Compared to these people's experience of 30 or 40 years, ours is nothing.

WIN THEM FOR GOD

So this morning I want to ask you, don't just try to be great journalists or great reporters. Our job is to win them for God, without saying God. This is the time you and I must become truly religious. It does not mean you have to preach the Divine Principle in the newsroom. It means to live Father's way of life, the true way of life. You cannot win these people any other way except by being truly religious. Truly a Moonie. In other words, let's make Moonie attractive to them. They have come here as total strangers to Moonies, almost thinking a Moonie is some kind of monster. The first time they look at you, inside they are thinking you are some kind of monster. They are literally looking for the horn or tail. The media created such a bad image of our Father and you and me. Be a humble student. Do not pretend you know everything. Rather, show you don't know much, but show how much you love God, love Reverend and Mrs. Moon, and serve this country. Being truly religious means being loving, caring, serving, dedicated. I tell you, you will win them absolutely.

Another important trial is going on at the *Washington Times*, in addition to the one in the New York courthouse. These professional journalists are the judge and jurors. You are the defendants. They are looking at you to see whether we are truly the kind of people we say we are. They are the judge. Not me and not you.

I just received a letter from Mrs. Whelan. I understand some of you have written to her. When Mr. Whelan joined the *Washington Times*, they were persecuted. Mrs. Whelan has been under extraordinary stress. Her car was vandalized, with "You Moonies" painted on it. Her fence was broken. She was frightened. I wrote her a letter of comfort. Of course, I did not expect any reply, but recently I received a letter from her. I wish I had brought the letter because I wanted to read it to you. I read that letter to Father. It was such a beautiful letter, and it moved me to tears.

She said that the day she received my letter, she was feeling desperate and really needed some kind of encouragement. Everything had gone wrong. A woman who came to her house to pick up the baby furniture Mrs. Whelan was giving away made comments that Jim is making a big mistake in leaving the *Sacramento Union* and going to the *Washington Times*. Then she got some tough telephone calls. Family members on her side and his side called, asking what is going on there, what is Jim doing. She did not want to be home to get more phone calls like that, so she went out with her baby, Heather. She bought Heather her first helium balloon and tied it firmly to her wrist so it would not fly away. Then she went into another store to buy a lot of boxes to pack for moving here to Washington. Then on the way back somehow Heather lost that balloon and she was crying. She said, I have no way to comfort her. Her very first helium balloon was sailing away, higher and higher. Then when Mrs. Whelan returned home, she found the mailbox knocked to the ground. She got out of the car and picked up the mail and went inside crying. She was so lonely and sad as she sorted the mail. Then she saw my letter. After reading it, she said, "I was so wonderfully happy. And without me knowing, I was crying, tears trickling down my cheeks. And Heather came to me and said, 'Mommy, don't worry, I don't mind about the balloon.'"

Her letter moved me to tears. I read it to Father and Mother on the way to the courthouse. Then I wrote her back at the courthouse and told her, "I read your letter to Reverend and Mrs. Moon and when I came to the end of your letter, I saw tears in their eyes. We are most anxious for you to come here and meet Reverend and Mrs. Moon. You are going to meet the most compassionate people you have ever known. Please give my best wishes to your children, particularly your daughter Heather, and tell her I promise her that when she comes to Washington a second helium balloon will be waiting for her at the airport."

This time it doesn't matter if she loses it because there will be a third, fourth, and fifth balloon, an entire world of balloons for Heather. I am sure by now Mrs. Whelan received that letter. I told her that May 17 was our launching and reception and I will be standing in the receiving line and look forward to seeing her here in Washington. All the members are looking forward to seeing her. Jim is doing a great job. I am sure she had another great day. She is really a most prepared godly woman.

GOD LED THEM HERE

These journalists are coming to the *Washington Times* for more than the money. Something is pulling them beyond the money and the job description. Yesterday our leaders were talking about why such righteous people are coming to the *Washington Times*. They must have Abel hearts, good hearts. These people are superb journalistically, but they have one of the greatest things missing. Yes, God. God can come into their hearts through True Parents.

I am looking forward to meeting Mrs. Whelan. I know her heart is God-centered and inspired, but she still needs something. There is some thirst. She is looking for some water of life. My dear brothers and sisters, have a different kind of pride. Not the pride of journalism. Not the pride of reporter. Not the pride of newspaper men and women. But the pride of being a godly man, a man who belongs to True Parents. That conviction and bubbling enthusiasm are there every day. I tell you, beautiful spiritual vibrations are coming out of you. These people will be touched by these waves and vibrations. It will create incredible miracles one after the other.

So that is your first job, your primary job. If you do that job well, don't worry about anything else. Everything will be great. The newspaper will be great. Our reputation will be great. Jim Whelan talked to me yesterday over the phone, saying we are preparing to take this city by storm. I believe every word of it.

How many of you are staying in this church building [1610 Columbia Road, Washington, D.C.]? Raise your hands. Thank you. We are preparing a house for you. We bought a very good seminary in the middle of the city. After it is painted and remodeled, it will become the *Washington Times* center. I hope you come up with a good name for that center. Anyway, we want to have one place, other than the church, where we can enhance our spiritual life by give and take, communication, fellowship, and sharing spiritual food with each other. We need one central place. We cannot do these things at the *Washington Times* building. Our spiritual life should be centered somewhere. So all the people who are staying in the church will go to our new home within the next two to three weeks. It is only 12 minutes from there to the *Washington Times* building.

So many great things are happening on Jim Whelan's side, too. He is reporting to me virtually every day. Many things are happening. Did you hear about the White House press dinner? The other day we had a White House press dinner. Jim Gavin used to do all the public relations for the church. He has met senators and congressmen many times in the past. In order to win one congressman and one senator, it takes a month. But with the *Washington Times*, in just 24 hours three tables were completely filled. Ed Meece dropped by our reception. Anthony Dolan, who is writing Reagan's speeches every day, made himself at home at the *Washington Times*. Yes, we will take this city by storm. That is no exaggeration.

I don't worry about that. I worry about you and me, how we conduct ourselves. My appeal to you this morning is that we do it truly religiously. In other words, let's enhance our spiritual side. By doing so, everything else will be taken care of. No problem. We will make things happen. Don't worry about them. Let's worry about us. Every time a finger is pointed at us, we can ask ourselves, am I doing the right thing? Am I a true representative and ambassador for our True Parents? Am I truly engaging God in my life?

GOD IS EXCITED

I am sure you are already doing that. I have heard tremendous comments from outside people, but let us not be satisfied there. No, let us pick ourselves up and move forward and really finish the task. Let us lead an exciting and enthusiastic life with God in the center. God is excited. True Parents are excited, I tell you. So when these 110 people are totally united, can you imagine what can happen? We are just 110 people, most of us knowing virtually nothing about journalism, but we can take the city by storm with the greatest newspaper. We can do it only with the power of God.

Another reason I came to appeal to you this morning is this. I don't want to repeat the News World Communications mistakes here. While working day in and day out for News World Communications, many members lost their vision, lost their sense of purpose, sense of spiritual value. Then they became most unhappy. Once you lose the central purpose of what you are doing, you become so unhappy. I don't want anything to happen to these 110 members, not even one individual. That is my fervent wish and prayer. Let us lead a holistic life, which means lead a balanced life between professional life and spiritual life. Never forget that spiritual life is subject.

Let me speak a little more about holistic life. This is exactly the kind of word that Father would chose to use. Father has always told me you should not smell like a pastor. Father says you must become a natural person. When you go to the farming village, be a great farmer. When you go to the fishing village, be a great fisherman. When you go to a factory, become a good factory man. In diplomatic circles, be a good diplomat. When you stand at the podium, be a great fiery speaker.

By that same principle, when you do journalistic work, you must become a natural journalist. Don't behave strangely. Adapt yourself to that atmosphere. You should be able to do that. What is a special characteristic of a Moonie? The Moonie doesn't smell like Moonie. A Moonie should not be one special category of people. Father does not want that. A Moonie is a natural person, a beautiful person shining with spiritual quality. That is the true way of life of a Moonie.

This is why people are amazed when they first look at you. You are so natural. You are so genuinely beautiful. Your behavior, your attitude, your way of doing things is so natural. They thought you would be some kind of robot. They can't find one robot here. Why should they? We are all natural people. We are intelligent, polished, but with a spiritual quality shining from within. That is why I say holistic. Subject and object. But the subject is the shining inner quality of the spirit. We have a great invisible diamond. We are in a position to share those diamonds with those people who come to work for the *Washington Times*.

That is the basic point I want to make. Now I want to move into the second phase. That is, let us become and feel the master and owner of the *Washington Times*. The *Washington Times* is yours. Mine. Because it is Father's newspaper and we are Father's children, we are not just employees. On paper, yes. But spiritually, no. I have never done any job in the Unification Church where I felt I was just a worker doing a job. I always felt: this is mine. It is almost like caring for children. Not many of you have had that experience but you will soon, I hope. You can imagine, when you have your own children, you don't look at taking care of them as a job. It is not a burden or duty. No, it is a way of life. It is a pleasure. It is an honor. This is how I look at the jobs in the Unification Church. That is why I have never received a paycheck. I want to be rewarded by heaven. As the Bible said, if everybody is rewarded by the secular world, there is no room for God to reward you. I don't want that situation to happen.

WISE AS SERPENTS, PURE AS DOVES

We in the *Washington Times* need to conduct ourselves as it says in the Bible: wise as serpents and pure as doves. Let us adopt this as our motto. At the *Washington Times* we must be wise as serpents. We have to deal with the wicked world out there. Wolves are out there. Hungry wolves, lions, and tigers are out there. They are ready to attack at the first opportunity. The *Washington Times* is such an incredible project for God's side that all of Satan's side will hate for us to succeed. But don't forget the second part: be pure as doves. Do not lose your purity. This is very, very important.

Jim Whelan has been given authority to run the *Washington Times*. He is your boss, your professional boss. He reports to me. You report to your department heads, who report to the top executives, who report to Jim Whelan, Jim Whelan reports to me, and I report to Father. That is the way it goes. And I want to honor the chain of command. So from the professional point of view, you are absolutely loyal to the chain of command. For example, Jim Gavin or Jonathan Slevin, I want them to be spiritually reporting to me, but I want them to be absolutely loyal to Jim Whelan. That is another way of winning your people. I want you to be absolutely loyal to the person above you. You will win their hearts. Give them loyalty, trust, warmth, and—on top of that—love.

When you receive your salary, don't just think, oh, I am worth this much. If we do, if we think like everybody else, we will lose faith, lose our enthusiasm, lose our power. This is not just a job. You have to be able to say, this is my paper. Say, I will not let my paper fail. Don't say, there's another job out there for me. Father is pouring an incredible amount of money into this project. The money goes like water, almost like Niagara Falls. We bought the building and land and machines. I have a great fear now that we don't know how much it really costs to do a great job in the *Washington Times*. Fear and trembling come to me because Father must give me every dollar, every penny I put into it, and furthermore that money comes from the blood and sweat of brothers and sisters somewhere on the face of this earth. Brothers and sisters are going out at 5:00 in the morning, working until 12:00 midnight, in order to make the *Washington Times* possible. It is not coming from Wall Street. It is not coming from bank interest. It is coming literally from the blood of our members.

When you think of it, every dollar we spend comes from a brother or sister sweating to earn that dollar. Even $1 million is big money, but spending $10 million, $20 million will give you the same feeling I have, trembling inside. Aren't you virtually trembling inside? We cannot afford to fail. I would rather die than fail. I am responsible. If I cause Father to spend $10 million, $20 million, and it doesn't work, how can I live? It is that serious. Who will share this seriousness? You. Because you are the *Washington Times*.

DISCIPLINE YOUR SPENDING

Speaking of money, money is an amazing thing. It's like time. Time and money have the same quality. You want to be idle and rest. Well, a couple of hours fly by like nothing. You can spend the day doing nothing. You can rest for one month or a year. But in two hours a marathon runner can run 26 miles with his two feet. So time is like a rubber band. You can expand it, shrink it, it can go either way. Time is elastic. Money is elastic, too. You can stretch the dollar or you can throw it away. So using money takes a great deal of discipline, and you start your discipline from using an initial small amount of money.

Let me give this analogy. I was very poor when I was your age. I was in the Korean military, an army captain, and the salary was very meager. During the Korean War I was selected for training at Fort Benning, Georgia. I went there twice, once for six months, another time for one year. I was paid in cash in U.S. dollars. How much do you think I received each month? $150. Don't misunderstand. That was not for one week, but for one whole month. With that $150 I had to pay for three meals a day, my shelter, transportation, laundry, heating, everything. Most of the Korean officers said, we cannot live on $150 a month. They usually spent all $150 in the first 25 days of the month. In the final five days, they always had to borrow money. They would ask, lend me $10 or $20.

But I had a strong motivation to save money. I had a wife at home, just married, children would be coming soon. So if I didn't have to spend money on something, I didn't buy it. I saved money so I could help my family. I lived well for one entire month in good health, and I only spent $50. I saved $100 every month. Sometimes I spent $55. But I never spent more than $60 in any month. I paid for all my meals, my housing; my uniform was always shining because I was the one who laundered it. I washed my uniform and ironed it. In the evening, dinner at the mess hall was only 60 cents. For that, you could have fried chicken, steak, anything you want. But I could not spend 60 cents, so I would go to a grocery store and buy a can of meatball spaghetti for 15 cents. I heated it in a little pan and put in a little kochichan and had a great dinner, a 15-cent dinner! I didn't drink Coke or coffee. I drank the God-given drink: good pure water.

That is the way I lived. But I had a purpose. I did it with joy, without any pain, because I knew what I saved would help my family. So from both times in the United States, I saved about $2,000. You know what I did with that money? I went back to Korea, and the government gave me a small piece of land where I could build my home. My wife and I built a brick house. Most of the labor was done by me and my wife, and my brothers helped me. We built a beautiful house with the $2,000. Of course, we had a little loan from the bank. At that time we could use the house as collateral. So after an ordeal of nine months, my wife and I moved in, and we lived there for three months. Then the Divine Principle hit me. At that point my motivation changed. My direction changed. But the same attitude and discipline were there.

Where is that house? I sold it. I sold it for two reasons. After I discovered the Divine Principle, the house was not that important any more. Listening to Divine Principle lectures was more important. So I wanted to move nearer to the church. I could not commute such a long distance, particularly with the curfew. Impossible. That is one reason. Second, at that time the church was in great jeopardy, undergoing persecution by the Korean government. We needed a great deal of money to fight the legal battle. But nobody had that kind of money. So I sold the house and the blood and sweat that we had poured into it. We got several million Korean won for it. That was a great deal of money at that time. That money paid for a victory in one court battle. That was 1958.

GOD GAVE US A GREATER HOME

Then I was without a home, but I was very happy renting two small cubbyholes. My wife and I and our children were living in those two small rooms, but I was happy because I had a higher purpose. When I returned to the United States, God gave me a better house to live in, a better house than I had built. Then in 1969, we moved into our present home for a church reason, for the service of God. God elevated me more and more. Think about it. Because of the Divine Principle, I am today an instrumental person in establishing the *Washington Times* in the nation's capital. Not the Korean nation's capital, the U.S. capital and the world's capital.

Virtually it is a miracle for a man like me from Korea to be here. What would give me the power to do this? In 1952, I didn't speak even one word of English. Not one word. The Korean war was going on. I went back to a foxhole in Korea, knowing I might be killed in action. Soldiers are killed every day. But I wanted to see Washington, D.C., and New York. Someday I want to tell you that story about my crazy, 16-hour taxi drive from Fort Benning, Georgia, to Washington, D.C. Before I died, I wanted to see Washington. I took a picture of the Washington Monument and another of Capitol Hill. But there was one more building to see, the Empire State Building. So we took another crazy ride from Washington to New York. It all happened in three days. We took another picture on top of the Empire State Building. I thought, this is it, I am really ready to die now.

Many years later, after learning the Divine Principle, I stood at the Washington Monument again, this time interpreting for the most precious man in the eyes of God, Reverend Moon. Could any power under the sun do that except the power of God? The same man who admired the grandeur of Capitol Hill, with my mouth open like this and my eyes popped out like that, stood at Washington Monument next to Reverend Moon. And in 1978 I made history fighting against one powerful congressman, Donald Fraser.

I am sharing this small testimony for a reason. You may think you are suffering, you are losing, you are poverty-stricken, and so forth. You are not. You are the richest people with Father and the Divine Principle, and you will consummate your life in a most glorious and honorable manner.

When I think of Mike Warder, I am not angry at him at all. I am not angry. Father came out of the courthouse and said, I am sorry for Mike Warder. He said so softly, I have pity on him. God grant him mercy. That is Father. Father is not angry at him at all. Father has compassion. He knows the consequences for Mike Warder. His heart aches for him. You will see. History will be the judge.

So you and I are here for the destiny of God. We are picked to live our lives as revolutionaries, like righteous men. That is why we are here. So let's do it proudly. Let's live in a most dignified way. Josette one time told me it was pride. Yes. Witness our pride when we go to the *Washington Post* or *New York Times* or other parts of the journalistic world. She is a professional journalist. She could earn much more money elsewhere. But she is voluntarily giving her life for this great task. She is proud to be different from others. She is not ashamed. *The Washington Times* is in an excellent position to show the world the model life of Reverend Moon's disciples.

I have many, many beautiful plans, beautiful dreams. As one of your elder brothers, my primary duty is to look after my younger brothers and sisters. *The Washington Times* and *The News World* are not my primary duties. My primary duty is, as one of Father's elder sons, to look after the younger brothers and sisters of the world. That is my primary duty, and I pledge to you I will live my life for it. I want to give my life for the well-being of our brothers and sisters, for their children, and for their families. In Korea I built the Little Angels School in that same spirit. We want to show the world what the ideal world is like, ideal family is like, ideal society is like. So in this Washington Times we want to create an ideal society in the nation's capital. We are imparting incredible vibrations of light, fragrance, beauty, and warmth. Each one of you will become like a magnet to pull outside people. We must do this within the *Washington Times*.

OK, now my conclusion is this. We are living in a very exciting time. We must make ourselves worthy of living with the mission that True Parents have given us. Father and Mother are so excited about the *Washington Times*. They already came to the *Times* five times. They didn't even come to the church center. Hopefully, they will come again today for another visit. Do you promise to give them comfort and encouragement, showing your bubbling enthusiasm? Would you do that?

Number two, let's really make the *Washington Times* successful by keeping ourselves strong spiritually. Do you agree that is the secret? No external activities will work. You must be genuinely what you are. Demonstrate what you stand for. By doing so, we will make the *Washington Times* a success, not by our journalistic skills alone, but by our special inner quality. Demonstrate it, be proud of it. I tell you, I demand the respect of the high-ranking people who have joined our staff, including Mr. Whelan. I told Mr. Whelan that if he does not have respect for me and respect for Reverend Moon, he should not come here. He does not need this job. He already had an incredible, well-paid job. He did not come for money. Something told him he has to come here. It is a call from God. That is why I look at Jim Whelan as a God-sent man. This is another way of witnessing. I have yet to speak one word about Divine Principle. But actually, I spoke every word of Divine Principle; I showed Father's movie, "Truth Is My Sword."

So I want you to be exemplary. Be dynamos, light-giving, heat-giving objects. Your auras, your spirits are shining strongly. When you are spiritually weak, that aura is weakened, like a fading rainbow. Keep that aura strong and bright. That is the challenge. That is how we are going to make our *Washington Times* successful.

I WANT YOUR LETTERS

Also I want to pledge one thing. I want to keep my communication channel open to every level. You have a right to communicate with me directly. A very good method would be to write me a personal letter. If you have a spiritual problem or need some kind of help, write me. I am very good at reading letters. I do not neglect them. I read a lot on the airplane flying back and forth between New York and Washington. I get one hour of reading time because no telephones are ringing. If you want to tell me certain exciting things or if you have a problem, please write me. I don't want any problem to fester inside and become rotten. So you write me.

Also write me if for some reason you simply cannot stay here, you cannot continue in this mission. I don't want even one brother or one sister to live a miserable life. I want every one of you to be sparkling, shining, bubbling with enthusiasm, and moving toward the goal with purpose and joy.

I have already heard many wonderful stories that you are encountering people in the State Department and the White House and Congress. You see they are treating us differently. We will use our power in a righteous way to bring a great victory for this nation and for traditional American values, which are parallel with Father's values. We will build the kingdom of God on earth here in Washington. We are going to make Washington,

D.C., an exciting city. Without us Washington would be pale and flat. Yes or no? We are going to make this city exciting and bubbling, and we will bring the light to the city. You are the salt of the earth. You can prevent the decay of this city.

Remember to be as wise as serpents and as pure as doves. Keep your purity. Keep your fidelity. Be proud of what you are and what you are doing. And today when Father and Mother come, show them.

Now, I want to really finish. This is such a rare opportunity to share my heart with you. At the *Washington Times*, we have our professional organization, which is headed by Jim Whelan. But we also have spiritual organization. I am your spiritual leader. I would like to be responsible. And I would like to assign Jonathan to represent me during my absence. You can convey to him all the spiritual counseling and needs. And we have seven key brothers and sisters with key newpaper roles. I would like them to be a spiritual counseling team with Jonathan Slevin as their head. They are Jonathan, Jim Gavin, Paula Gray, Josette Sheeran, Ted Agres, Denny Duggan, and Susan Bergman. This will be the initial committee. They will look after the spiritual well-being of our members. Let's give them a big hand. Those home leaders, stand up, please.

In Father's eyes, every one you is the president and publisher. Eventually we will have this many newspapers. Yes, that is the way Father sees. To be a good leader, be a good follower during your *Washington Times* life.

Thank you very much.

Prayer by Bo Hi Pak:

Our most loving Heavenly Father. We thank You very much that this morning You uplifted us all together for an even higher mission, higher dedication and purpose. Father, we thank You for hand-picking every one of us for this incredibly important mission in Your providence. Father, we have been committed, we are committed, we will be committed. Father, there is no alternative. We shall move on. Fulfill Your will. Do Your desire. Be Your representative. We shall win our people in our time. We shall win the world by the same one principle. That is the power of love, power of service, power of dedication. Father, we shall not let You down. The Washington Times is going to be an incredible victory for You. We will make it. With our blood and sweat and tears we promise to deliver the victory. Extraordinary victory. Thank You, Father. All these things we pray in the name of our most beloved True Parents. Amen.

OUR FATHER'S HOUSE

WASHINGTON, D.C.
NOVEMBER 18, 1982

---

*The Washington Times was founded on May 17, 1982. In
this talk Dr. Bo Hi Pak challenges the church members on
the staff to practice true love in their families, altruistic
love in their public lives, and to proudly represent True
Parents in their missions.*

Father has continuously emphasized the sacrificial and altruistic way of
life. Love your fellow man. There is no better way to prepare for your eternal life than to practice God-centered love in the family. You cannot go
wrong. You are so fortunate. You think you are suffering. You think you
have a hard time. Take it as a privilege. That is the best way you can prepare for eternal life. That is the real life to live. That does not mean we
abandon our hope here in this world. No. On the contrary, since we know
about the value of spirit world, this life becomes so important.

We are not just believing in the other world, waiting for utopia to all
of a sudden happen. No. We have to create utopia here. So everybody
should be practicing those two principles: God-centered family life and
altruistic life for the sake of the world. Basically that is what the *Washington
Times* is trying to do. The *Washington Times* itself was conceived for an
altruistic purpose. To create the *Washington Times*, our members all over the

world are sacrificing. When we understand this, we cannot take our job lightly. I want you to really shine among the *Washington Times* staff. Be exemplary family members, God-centered and altruistic. At this time in New York, Father announced a special 40-day condition. New York is virtually deserted. Every member is out in the street fund-raising for the yuletide season. Father exempted the *Washington Times*, not because you are very special, but because the *Washington Times* itself is a mission.

I want you to truly understand Father's heart. I want you to give everything to serve Father's purpose with the *Washington Times*. Be grateful and work with bubbling enthusiasm. Do well. Particularly, I want you to help me in a special project. When I have walked around our building, I have seen new desks chipped and dirty, coffee spilled on the floor, cigarette butts on the floor, dusty equipment buried under boxes. Things covered with dust. It almost breaks my heart. This is Father's building, Father's equipment. Our members have worked so hard to pay for this building.

I want you to bring a revolution to the *Washington Times*. Those sloppy journalists. Those sarcastic journalists. Make believers out of them by your own deeds. I am going crusading myself. I would like you to give at least 100 hours this week or next week to make this newspaper building the cleanest, the most spic and span. I am going to do it myself. I am going to clean the bathroom with my own hands. Somebody else dirties the bathroom, I am going to clean it. I did that at the Little Angels School. I taught the children and took them to the worse place, the bathroom. In front of their eyes I cleaned up their stool and their urine. I didn't hesitate to do it. It is a pleasure doing it because it is Father's house, God's house.

We can bring a new spirit to Washington merely by keeping this place absolutely spic and span. I feel like dying when I see the computers and all this intricate equipment covered with dust. They are getting old so quickly. I would rather chop off my arms than have to replace that equipment.

Let us make the *Washington Times* not a normal newspaper company, make it extraordinary, an unusual newspaper company. Let's make it an organized newspaper company. As clean as possible. Cleanliness is next to godliness. This is one way you can show appreciation to Father. Thank you. The other day I asked the production manager to make a pledge that I could come to the press area and eat off the floor. Behind the scenes I want you to be crusaders. You are the champions.

This is the one immediate thing we can do and we can do it well. We can proudly do it. From time to time the leaders will organize a cleaning crusade of the *Washington Times*. Give at least 100 hours to do it. I am going to give my 100 hours. You will find me working in the bathroom. I want to make the *Washington Times* a shrine, a temple. Josette the other day told me even those sarcastic reporters are finding God in the newsroom. Even Smith Hempstone came to her party, saying, I began to believe in Reverend Moon, God bless you. Everything is a testimony.

Also, make yourself clean-cut. It is one thing Father can be very proud of. Do not try to imitate these journalists, who are sloppy and casual. It is a disgrace when you look at the White House press conferences sometimes. Those Washington journalists are messy. They make the whole area stink. This is not Father's way at all. Shave everyday, that is mandatory. Those brothers who have a beard, make it distinguished-looking or cut it off. If you want to grow beards, grow them so they serve some purpose of God. Everything you do serves a purpose.

So my dear brothers and sisters, Washington is one place we can truly organize the kingdom of heaven. I am trying to work with Tom McDevitt, who is trying to create a Unification community in Washington as a model. We have more manpower here. More leadership here. More intellectual people here. If we are united, totally dedicated to our True Parents, we can do it.

I tell you, even though the newsroom will be finished tomorrow, in the next two or three months we are going to continue building the *Washington Times*. It will be transformed into a palace. Don't ever think Father has lots of money or that Bo Hi Pak loves to spend money doing all these things. Not at all. I am dying trying to squeeze the most out of every dollar that has to come to Washington. I am in agony. Father predicted that by the time I finish with the *Washington Times* I will lose all my hair. I am sure this prediction will become a reality. Every morning I find myself more bald than the previous day. That is all right. My hair is my offering.

But I want you to know Father wants to create a shrine, a temple, so the president of the United States can come on May 17 for the one-year anniversary of the *Washington Times*. When do secular people and heads of state come to Father's house? When? But they will all come to the *Washington Times*. By this newspaper, they will know Father. By knowing Father better, they will know God better. It is evangelism. Everything has a purpose.

So I want to do this building right. Period. I don't want to have any sloppy work in your office area. Keep Father's image high. We want to finish up 1982 so that we can move on to 1983 with conviction, loyalty, and love to our True Parents. As I told you before, there is no better life you can lead than being a member of the Unification Church, following our True Parents. I can find no better life. When you put your three lives together—your embryonic life, life on earth, life in spirit world—we have the total value, and there is nothing better. There is no better life than to give yourself as much as you can for the sake of our True Parents. Love your family. Love your husband and wife. Love your fellow man. Always be God-centered. Be ready to shine eternally in the spirit world.

It is our pleasure, duty, and joy to bring glory and, as much as possible, pleasant news to our True Parents. That is the way I live. I live to report. I work so that I can create some report that can go back to True Parents, so that I can say, Father, I have good news for you. You do it for me, and I will do it for you to Father. When Father knows I am coming to Washington for two days, he can't wait two days for a report. Father calls me: Bo Hi Pak, you are staying down there too long. Why, because he wants me to come back and bring him some up-to-date news. That is how much Father is interested in the day-to-day activities of the *Washington Times*. So let us bring victorious news to Father by giving ourselves totally to the mission Father has given us. Thank you very much.

Seung Hwa Ceremony of Heung Jin Nim Moon

SEOUL, KOREA

JANUARY 8, 1984

In this moving Seung Hwa address, Dr. Pak explains the
providential meaning of the Seung Hwa and of the Day
of the Victory of Love. He recounts the life of Heung Jin
Nim, who ascended to the spirit world on January 2,
1984, and describes his heart and desire to serve and pro-
tect True Parents. He also testifies to the greatness of
True Parents by sharing his experiences and observations
of them during this most difficult time.

Today we are standing on sacred soil. All of us are attending a solemn ceremony to commemorate Heung Jin Nim Moon's passing away to heaven.
We call this ceremony the Seung Hwa (Heavenly Ascension) ceremony.
This is a new heavenly word that can be understood and appreciated only
by those of us who are attending the True Parents.

The death of a human being has traditionally meant despair, darkness,
and sorrow because it was taken to mean eternal separation. This is why
it is called in the Korean language the "Ceremony of the Last Farewell."

We who are attending this ceremony, however, are citizens of heaven living in a very different dimension from other people. We have the privilege of being proud saints in the Age of the Completed Testament. It is a privilege that can be obtained only by those who are attending the living True Parents who have been victorious over the world and over death.

Revelation 21:4 reads: "He will wipe away every tear from their eyes, and death shall be no more, neither shall there be mourning nor crying nor pain any more, for the former things have passed away." Blessed are all of us living in the glory of the True Parents who have caused all the former things to pass away.

Heung Jin Nim is one of the sons of the direct line of Reverend Moon. He is one of the True Children born physically of the True Parents. How can there be death for such a son? Heung Jin Nim has cast off the umbilical cord connecting him to this world and has been reborn in the world of light.

Reverend Moon, our Father, consoled the brothers and sisters who cried with sorrow on the day of Heung Jin Nim's passing, saying, "This is a new birthday for Heung Jin Nim. Let us celebrate Heung Jin Nim's new birthday. Heung Jin is now marching to a new world of glory and eternity by being reborn. Heung Jin is now truly free to move in both the physical and the spiritual worlds, living permanently together with us. We must celebrate his passing in the same way as we would celebrate his wedding ceremony."

The use of the Chinese characters meaning "Seung Hwa" is new and unique to this ceremony and is not commonly used. The character for "seung" means "ascending, elevation." It is sometimes used to mean "demise" when said "seung ha," and to mean "peace" when said "seung pyung," and to mean "sublimation" when said "seung hwa." The character "hwa" has meanings of "harmony, the sun, peace, etc." It is often used to mean "peace" when said "pyung hwa" and to mean "unity and harmony" when said "hwa hap." The use of "Seung Hwa" was first instructed by Reverend Moon.

Therefore, this is the day for celebrating Heung Jin Nim's new birth into the eternal world of God. Today, we must learn from the example he set during his 17 years of life and appreciate that we are standing before a sacred altar before which we should solemnly determine and resolve to unite together, centered on Heung Jin Nim's holy ascension, which was a sacrificial offering for the unification of the world.

That is the essential meaning of this Seung Hwa ceremony. This is a holy moment for us to solemnly respond to the spirit of Seung Hwa to Heung Jin Nim, who is harmonizing both the physical and spiritual worlds, mankind and Unification Church members of five colors from 70 countries.

THE SACRED AND INNOCENT HISTORICAL SACRIFICE

It is likely that some people may ask why such an unexpected accident should happen in the family of the True Parents, and why such an ordeal had to occur to the perfected True Parents themselves.

Those of us who know the original ideal of creation understand that the power of sin and darkness has reigned over the world since the tragedy of the fall of man. Since the fall was caused by man's lack of faith and his immorality, his voluntary give and take of love with Satan, God has suffered and has been bound by the principles that prevent even omnipotent God from retaking creation and man without a condition.

We all know that God works within the principles of restoration and has to pay indemnity conditions to Satan in order to restore mankind. This principle was expressed in the sacrificial offerings in the time of the Old Testament and in the offering of Jesus Christ, His only son, to Satan in the time of the New Testament. Through these conditions man was able to receive salvation and stand before God.

True Father, who understood this principle of sacrificial give and take for the first time in human history, made himself a sacrificial offering and has devoted his life of over 60 years according to the principle of "blessing after hardship." This is why he has been suffering with blood, sweat, and tears throughout his life and is now fighting the last fight against Satan to save all mankind, broadening the foundation from individual to family, from family to race, from race to nation, and from nation to the world.

The Unification Church, which today is standing on the worldwide foundation, has its origins in the very bottom of hell, in a North Korean labor camp. The ordeals that Father went through in Hungnam for two years and eight months were the worst kind of experiences a human being can go through, and resembled the Cross at Golgotha.

Unlike the case of Jesus Christ who was betrayed by his 12 disciples, Father found his disciples in the communist prison, in the depths of hell, and was liberated in 1950, thanks to the participation of the worldwide Abel nations in the Korean War. His coming to South Korea at that time enabled the Unification Movement to begin its work toward the salvation of the world. The Unification Church was established in 1954. Thirty years have passed since that time. During this period True Parents have been unable to obtain the response and support of the Christian world, which was prepared as the second Israel, and by himself, Father has established the Unification Church in the place of traditional Christianity as a foundation for the world to receive the Messiah.

This is why Reverend Moon had to fight against all adversity and, using the principle of sacrificial give and take, has overcome all satanic persecution and is now striding forward to the imminent day of victory on the worldwide level.

Today, there is no one in the free world who dares to halt the spread of communist power. There is no king, president, or prime minister who volunteers to take the responsibility for overcoming communism. Even the United States, the leader of the free world, is at the end of its tether.

Now the only ideology that can halt communism is the messianic ideal and the thought of the True Parents, which proclaims the existence of God and the original ideal of His creation. The reason why our True Parents held the International Federation for Victory Over Communism rallies from December 14 through 23 in Korea was so that an international frontline against communism could be created with Korea as its center, and the worldwide victory of True Parents could be connected to Korea, their country of origin.

There was an absolute providential reason for holding these rallies not later than the end of 1983. In a short space of time, we were able to gain an exceptional victory, mobilizing over 250,000 people in eight cities.

The satanic powers, however, were alert to obstruct such a victory. Our strategy for the rallies was so successful that Satan suffered a desperate failure in his plans to hurt the True Parents in Korea. Finally, Satan had to demand a sacrifice from the family of the True Parents. According to the principles of restoration, Heung Jin Nim became this historical sacrifice.

The accident happened at the very last moment when the last rally was being held in Kwangju. There was not even a second's discrepancy in the timing. The accident happened in America at 11:10 Korean time, just after the final rally had begun. In America the time was 21:10, December 22, 1983.

In fact, all the spiritual people in the Church warned us that there could be danger to True Parents' security. Mother had asked if the rallies could be postponed until 1984 because she had a premonition of some misfortune. However, they were held in 1983 so that providential conditions could be satisfied.

In the end, after his failure to hurt True Parents, Satan invaded by attacking one of their beloved children. The fact that the two events happened at exactly the same time is clear evidence of the great historical meaning of the success of the national IFVOC rallies.

The regret we all share is that the sacrificial offering was Heung Jin Nim and not someone like ourselves.

We learn from history that Satan always demands the best sacrifice in proportion to the degree of his failure. True Parents' victory gained through the IFVOC rallies had a symbolic meaning for the worldwide victory. The True Parents established the basis, both physically and spiritually, for communism to totally collapse. Furthermore, we firmly believe that this basis has enabled us to start marching toward the achievement of a country for God, the providential goal.

Considering this extraordinary meaning, our own lives are not worthy payment as an offering for such an historical blow against Satan. Abraham offered his son when he was 100 years old, and Jesus Christ, God's only son, was offered as a sacrifice to save the whole of mankind. Likewise, the True Parents had to offer one of their beloved children for the restoration of the original world of creation. This is the very meaning of Heung Jin Nim's passing and the great role of his sacrifice.

In a word, Heung Jin Nim died for True Parents. God could never allow Satan to invade Father's body. Instead, he had to allow Satan to take one of Father's beloved dutiful children, even though it caused him much pain. At this point, we have to recognize the deep meaning of Heung Jin Nim's victory. The role of replacing Father's position! What greater way could there be than this? What greater filial piety and loyalty could there be than this? Heung Jin Nim has achieved the ultimate in filial piety. We cannot but be moved by his victory.

Please assume for a moment that it was not Heung Jin Nim but True Parents themselves who had been sacrificed. This would have been a day of darkness, a day of Satan's victory over the world and a day of desperation for mankind. In such an eventuality, what value could we find in our own and Heung Jin Nim's survival? We would have all fallen down to the state of being slaves of Satan.

When we think about it like this, Heung Jin Nim's death has two meanings. First, it was in place of True Parents' death, and second, it was in place of our death.

DUTIFUL SON AND A LOYAL SUBJECT

According to the providential meanings I have mentioned, we come to understand that Heung Jin Nim has carried this role since his birth. Heung Jin Nim was born in Chongpadong, Seoul, at 12:33 p.m. on October 23, 1966. His survival was uncertain for three days after his birth, indicating that he had to pass a three-day Way of the Cross even as a newborn baby.

He had a reputation for being a warm-hearted boy, and even as a child he was recognized as having a unique wisdom. He was respected by all of his friends and had that special characteristic of deeply loving his brothers and sisters. His mental and physical growth was outstanding compared to that of his siblings, and when he was only 15, he already fully comprehended and absorbed the ideology of the True Parents. We all saw that even at such a young age he tried his best to make his parents happy.

When he was 16, he already sensed the danger his parents faced from communist terrorists and was always alert to maintain his parents' security. When he visited my home with the children of Blessed families recently in New York, he asked each one of them whether they would dare to throw their own bodies in the way of a terrorist's bullet to protect Father, saying "I will, of course, do it myself," and raising both hands, he swore that he would definitely protect Father with his life.

I heard from an American family member that Heung Jin Nim told him, "I can die in place of my father. The only regret I would have would be that I could not be blessed and that I would be dying at such a young age. However, what greater thing could there be for me than dying for Father?" This conversation took place only seven hours before the accident!

Heung Jin Nim devoted himself to following Father's will completely. He was a naturally gifted artist, and when he was young, he wanted to become a famous industrial artist. After he understood Father's ideology, however, he made up his mind to major in history and archeology and later study theology and philosophy in order to become a great religious leader.

Heung Jin Nim loved humanity. He loved and was very friendly to every visitor at East Garden and shared all of his best things with his friends. He did not discriminate between people but loved everyone who was loyal to Father. On top of that, he endeavored to share his possessions with those who worked hard for God's will.

Jin Bok and Jin Gil, the two sons of Mrs. Yi Seng Yeon who were in the car with Heung Jin Nim at the time of the accident, are out of the hospital and have now fully recovered. On the day that Heung Jin Nim's body was taken from New York to Korea, they gave the following testimony in tears:

> Heung Jin Nim died in order to save our lives. The car Heung Jin Nim was driving was not at fault. A truck that was driving in the opposite direction skidded on the slippery road, crossed the central line, and came straight toward Heung Jin Nim's car. If Heung Jin Nim, who was driving, had veered to the left he would have been only slightly injured and Jin Gil would have been killed. Even though he knew the risk, he veered to the right and took the terrible impact that resulted in severe cerebral concussion.

The Bible says, "There is no greater love than this that a man give up his life for others." At the young age of 17, Heung Jin Nim already understood these profound words and realized them as the embodiment of love.

When they heard the sad news, the students of Hackley Middle School and Irvington High School, which Heung Jin Nim attended, without being instructed to do so by their teachers, put up placards expressing their condolences, lowered the school flags to half-mast, and held tearful memorial services. This is further testimony that Heung Jin Nim is a hero of love and friendship.

If we look at Heung Jin Nim's life, we can clearly see the determination he held in his young heart to sacrifice himself for Father and give his life for others if necessary as the absolute expression of love.

Deep in our hearts we should remember Heung Jin Nim as the greatest of filial sons to our True Parents, the most loyal of followers, the most glorious hero of the Unification Movement, and the saint of saints.

After Heung Jin Nim had passed away, he appeared to one spiritually open member and earnestly said, "How sad Mother must be to see my broken body after the accident. Please console her. I am fine. My only sadness is to see Mother so sad." As one who has known Heung Jin Nim all his life, I could not control my weeping when I heard these words that express his heart so well.

I am sure that all of us cannot help feeling intense sorrow and frustration when we think that Heung Jin Nim could have lived a long and successful life as a filial son of True Parents. From a human point of view, there would seem to be nothing more sorrowful and pitiful than this event. However, even at a very young age, Heung Jin Nim completed a historical, providential mission. Even if he had lived to be 60 or 100, I doubt he could have exceeded this providential achievement.

At the very moment of his passing, at 1:15 a.m. on January 2, 1984, Father's last words to Heung Jin Nim were,

> Heung Jin, goodbye. When you go to the spiritual world you will be the commander-in-chief of all young people there, from East and West, past and future. You will have the mission of making an army of heavenly workers by mobilizing all the spiritual men not only of the free world but also of the communist world and freely descending to earth and awaking in spirit all young people. Mother and I will be eternally proud of having a filial son like you.

On December 30, 1983, Father, who had been told by the doctor that Heung Jin Nim's brain was too damaged for any chance of recovery, held a special Pledge Ceremony of Unification for Heung Jin Nim in the hospital. Just as Abraham offered Isaac and just as God offered Jesus Christ, His only son, so Father decided to offer Heung Jin Nim as a sacrificial offering. Father held the ceremony of offering of Heung Jin Nim, through which all levels and kinds of unification could be accomplished.

Based on the condition of Heung Jin Nim's sacrifice, this deeply meaningful Pledge Ceremony of Unification could be held, signifying the complete unification of Father and Mother, the complete unity of True Parents and True Children, the complete unity of the True Children with each other, the complete unity of the Unification Church members and True Parents, the complete unity of the spiritual and physical worlds, the complete unity of all religions, and in particular, the complete unification of the First Israel, the Second Israel, and the Third Israel.

With the passing of Heung Jin Nim, we are now standing at a new turning point. Internally speaking, this is a turning point of unification between the members of the Unification Movement, and externally speaking, this is a turning point that marks the collapse of the communist world from an aggressive to a defensive position.

Heung Jin Nim practiced filial piety until the very moment of his passing. According to the doctor, Heung Jin Nim should have been killed instantly in such an accident. However, at the time of the accident on December 22, Father was in Korea and was planning to hold a general meeting of all the IFVOC regional leaders in the nation on December 26 and 27. Because of his public mission, Father did not want to leave Korea despite the urgent news of the accident. This is because he is the Father and has the public purpose of living for the sake of the cosmos before the world, the world before the nation, and the nation before the family. Even though he was in a coma, Heung Jin Nim persisted until the last possible moment until Father had completed his mission in Korea.

Father did not want Heung Jin Nim to pass away before God's Day even though he might have arrived in America before that time. Hovering on the borderline between life and death, Heung Jin Nim tried his utmost to survive until the very last moment when True Parents could complete the God's Day Pledge Ceremony, God's Day address, and their words of instruction to the world. He held on up to the moment of January 2 and, at 1:15 a.m., passed away peacefully during Father's prayer, surrounded by his parents, brothers and sisters, and world Unification Church leaders and representatives. This was the final act of a true filial son.

TESTIMONY ABOUT THE GREAT TRUE PARENTS

I have never before felt to the bone so strongly the greatness, sacredness, and love of True Parents as when I witnessed the occasion of Heung Jin Nim's passing.

Father acted as a completely public man from the beginning to the end. He did not move even an inch from the originally planned providential plans, even after he was informed of Heung Jin Nim's accident. He left his son in God's hands. Father flew to America to see Heung Jin Nim in the hospital on December 29, five days after the accident. During the five days Father completed all the plans that were originally scheduled and spoke to the regional IFVOC leaders here in this theater just before he left Korea.

Father was concerned about consoling Mother's broken heart at the hospital. From the time he arrived there, Father stayed awake day and night until Heung Jin Nim's death. He never showed his extreme exhaustion. He thought only of the will of God. He never shed a single tear. I can imagine, however, that he might have shed floods of tears in his heart. Father is just crazy about God and God's work, and he offered his most beloved son to God in his prayers to fulfill God's will if it was necessary.

He was very dignified and remained unchanged when he was saying that he would offer his son if it could result in the collapse of communism and could establish a way to save not only hundreds or thousands, but billions of people. He scolded, consoled, and taught the children who were exhausted with grief.

Indeed, Father is the savior of all people and the father of all people. The doctors and nurses at the hospital were also greatly astonished by Father as a great leader.

We have a great Mother also. How sorrowful she was to see the broken body of her son lying in the intensive care unit. How ready Mother would have been to sacrifice herself a hundred or even a thousand times for her son! As long as Father was only concerned about God, however, Mother was only concerned about Father. I could not stop myself from saying, "Mother is great! Mother is great!" when I listened to her teaching the children who visited the hospital. "You should not cry or feel sad. There is Father with us who is more important than our lives. Heung Jin Nim was sacrificed for Father. What if something had happened to Father! Who would have been responsible for preventing communism and saving mankind if there were no Father in the world? All of you children, please become dutiful sons and daughters who love Father by devoting your lives as Heung Jin Nim did." There have been many great mothers in human history, but I cannot imagine a greater mother than our Mother.

We who live with True Parents are happy people. I think I can understand now why God has waited for 6,000 years to have the central figure on earth. A person like him is born only once, not every 100 years, nor even every 1,000 years, but only once in human history. We met such parents who had a dutiful son—Heung Jin Nim. Now we have to follow Heung Jin Nim's example and be loyal to True Parents. We are at the happiest point in human history in the sense that we can sacrifice our own lives in the same way if necessary.

DECLARATION OF THE DAY OF VICTORY OF LOVE

True Parents declared the Day of Victory of Love at 4:00 a.m. on January 3, 1984. Earlier, True Parents announced the Day of Victory of Heaven on October 4, 1976, to commemorate the victory of the Washington Monument Rally. The Day of the Victory of Love announced at this time is to commemorate the victory of God's love. Up to this point the power of death has reigned in the world. But Heung Jin Nim's innocent and sacrificial victory of love has enabled the power of love to conquer the power of death. Now the physical and spiritual worlds have perfectly become one.

This body is not to die but to "seung hwa" and to win a victory with love. True Parents overcame the power of death through the power of love, and Heung Jin Nim has opened a gate for us to go the way of victory of love through realizing Father's teachings himself.

There have been many dutiful sons and daughters in history. There have been many loyal followers who loved their kings and their countries. But all of them were limited to this world. They had no chance to be loyal to an eternal country and to eternal parents. We have, indeed, the eternal heaven and eternal True Parents, a central figure in this world. This is the time for eternal dutiful sons, dutiful daughters, and loyal followers to be born. The model for such figures is Heung Jin Nim.

Father made a calligraphic drawing for Heung Jin Nim ascending to heaven. It reads in Chinese characters as follows:

CHUNG HYO JI SHIN (The incarnation of loyalty and filial piety)
CHON SONG BONG HON (Offering to the world of heaven)
CHON UN DAE HAE (Ocean and heavenly blessing)
YONG WON AN SHIK (Eternal rest)

It means that Father offered Heung Jin Nim, an incarnation of loyalty and filial piety to the world of heaven so that Heung Jin Nim can enjoy eternal rest in the ocean of heavenly blessing.

Before closing my Seung Hwa address, I would like all of us to swear and pledge before the True Parents to become another Heung Jin Nim by taking example from his spirit.

Dear God, our Father, we celebrate the victorious way of Heung Jin Nim, a uniquely loyal and dutiful son. And we pray for Heung Jin Nim on this occasion of his Seung Hwa (heavenly ascension) that God's glory and True Parents' love can be eternally and forever with him. Amen.

BLESSING BANQUET

MANHATTAN CENTER, NEW YORK, NEW YORK

FEBRUARY 20, 1984

================================

At the Blessing banquet of In Jin Nim and Heung Jin Nim, Dr. Pak shares his heart of gratitude to True Parents at having two of his children join the True Family. He gives a description of the character and accomplishments of both Jin Sung Nim and Hoon Sook Nim and then explains the purpose for celebrating the completion of 50 days after the ascension of Heung Jin Nim.

Today we are not only celebrating great weddings in history. The most important thing to remember today is that we celebrate the ascension of Heung Jin Nim. As you know, Heung Jin Nim passed away on January 2, 1984, at 1:15 a.m. Today is exactly 50 days later. Christianity began from Pentecost. When Jesus was crucified, there was a great deal of dissent among the disciples. They were weak and cowardly. Even the chief disciple, Peter, fled and denied Jesus three times. No single major disciple of Jesus Christ was there to die either in Jesus' place or together with him. Jesus' army was broken, dispersed, helpless, of no courage. During the first days after Jesus' death, none of the disciples worked together. However, on the 50th day, about 120 disciples assembled in Mark's upper room and prayed. All of a sudden, the Holy Spirit descended from heaven like a whirlwind. Every single one of them received the Holy Spirit and spoke in tongues; they received revelations. Incredible power and spirit over-whelmed Mark's upper room.

This morning at breakfast, Father stated very clearly that Christianity began on the 50th day after the crucifixion of Jesus Christ: the day of Pentecost. Today we are marking our Unification Church Pentecost. The sacrifice of Heung Jin Nim carries far greater importance than the cruci-fixion of Jesus Christ, because the True Parents are still on earth. Jesus did not have True Parents on earth after he ascended into heaven. Not only do we have the presence of True Parents on earth today, but also the foun-dation which they laid on the clan, tribal, national, and worldwide levels. The ascension of Heung Jin Nim to heaven is upon this foundation of True Parents on earth. No one in all of human history has ever ascended into heaven having received the true love of God conveyed through the True Parents except Heung Jin Nim. Of course, there are many Unification Church members who have gone to spirit world, including the late President Eu. However, Father has stated that even though True Parents' family has already paid the sacrifice in the past, nothing can compare with Heung Jin Nim's sacrifice. The reason is that Heung Jin Nim is the only one who ascended into heaven on the foundation of the True Parents' vic-tory. The Victory Over Communism rally in Korea during December 1983 particularly signifies an incredible foundation for the victory of True Parents on earth. It laid the national foundation to win the hearts of the people in Korea. Ever since Father won that victory in Korea, the entire spirit world has been mobilized.

Dr. Durst just read us news about the important victories of our church going out even through the UPI news service. There is now a united effort of Christian churches of America standing up for our church.

The national emphasis has been changing. This is the reason that Father won the foundation in Korea. In addition, Heung Jin Nim gave his life on behalf of Father. This is why today is so significant. The natural death and ascension of any member of the True Family could not ever compare. The reason is that only Heung Jin Nim served the providential role most important in our Unification Church: to safeguard the life of our True Parents. That is precisely what Heung Jin Nim did. That is why his death, his passing, is so significant. It moved the entire history of heaven and earth. That is why he is the king in spirit world, the commander-in-chief in the spirit world, and why there were incredible things happening here on earth these last 50 days. Heung Jin Nim has also appeared in the London church and churches in Africa and South America. Of course, he also appeared in our Korean churches. Heung Jin Nim is working everywhere. His spirit is with this celebration today. His spirit is with his bride today.

LET ME DIE WELL

The Unification members are the people who will conquer death. Death will be no more. There is no such thing as death on earth. Today I pledge in front of our True Father and Mother that I have no more blessings to wish for. I have already received too much. One child becoming a part of True Parents' family is already extraordinary. But two children joining the True Parents' family is too much. I just don't deserve such a blessing. I pledge only one thing. Father, give me courage, inspiration, and power. Let me die well when the time comes. When you need a sacrifice, please call upon me. That is the only thing more I want to request tonight.

Heung Jin Nim does not stay up in the spirit world all the time. Father said that Heung Jin Nim is totally free to come up and down all the time, any time he desires. The spiritual and physical worlds are now one world, no longer two. We live in both worlds right now. I can only expect great things to come to you, to every nation in which our Unification movement is working because the Holy Spirit has descended. We have True Parents on the earth and our king in the spirit world, Heung Jin Nim. God sent Jesus to the earth as savior. True Parents, in a way, dispatched the most important special ambassador to heaven. It is an amazing kind of parallel. God sent Jesus to earth. True Parents, the king and queen of the whole world, sent their best soldier to the spirit world so that he could perform the True Parents' duty there.

Because of that, True Father said our dispensation will advance far more quickly than before. Father told us this morning that the work Heung Jin Nim will do from the spirit world was only to happen after True Parents ascended into heaven. What joy we can celebrate today! Father and Mother are still with us here on earth. But the king who has been loyal and faithful to True Parents, and who will do exactly what True Parents would do when they ascend into heaven, is now working in the spirit world. This is the meaning of this day of celebration. It is a victory for Heung Jin Nim and a victory for True Parents, the True Family, and the Unification move-ment. We all want to share in their joy.

ABOUT IN JIN NIM AND JIN SUNG NIM

I would like also to share the great joy of In Jin Nim as a bride today. In Jin Nim is one of the beautiful children of our True Parents. She is gifted, charming. During our meal, I sat next to her brother Hyun Jin Nim. Since I know they are very close, I asked him what he would say was the single most important fact he could offer about In Jin Nim. Hyun Jin Nim said, "My sister is a wonderful person. So warm-hearted, soft-hearted, pure, and kind." What more could anyone ask of a person? She has blossomed into such a beautiful woman. Today, Father Blessed her. She was given in marriage today to a young man who used to be my son. Jin Sung Nim, this is a great day for you, too.

Jin Sung Nim is a student at the University of Pennsylvania in his senior year. Before he was born in 1962, my wife received a great dream. In it, Father came down with a basket from heaven and placed a male child in my wife's arms. Everybody landed on green pastures full of flowers and there was a great celebration. In that same dream, she saw that Father was a conductor, conducting the entire world.

Jin Sung Nim has been an obedient son, very faithful to Father and Mother. Last summer he faced a great test. Father summoned him to Ocean Church for the entire summer. He was to spend 85 days in Gloucester. In fact, he was the first one True Parents selected. At that point, I, as his physical father, admired my son deeply in my heart for the first time because, I honestly confess, that I could not do that. I could not spend 85 days on the sea. During that summer, Jin Sung Nim told me that he wanted to follow the example of Father. He told me that he did not want to take any naps during the day. He wanted to rise earlier than Father and go to bed after Father.

Jin Sung Nim is American-born and his Korean is not as fluent as that of the other Blessed children. But he told me that when he really concentrates and listens hard to Father, he understands deeply what Father says. He feels incredible inspiration listening to Father's words. And now God has Blessed him today. That summer he caught probably the biggest tuna in all of last year's tournament: 1,040 pounds. I feel it was not by accident. When I look back on his life now, such incidents tell me something.

Currently he is doing very well at the University of Pennsylvania. He is a straight "A" student. He even received an "A+" in one particular subject, and by doing so, set a precedent in that one subject. At the same time, he is also involved in many campus activities. He is president of the Korean Cultural Society at the University of Pennsylvania. He is founder and publisher of the college campus newspaper called The Red and Blue, a conservative newspaper that opposes the liberal campus newspaper. He is the chairman of the Finance Committee of the Student Activity Council of the University of Pennsylvania. He is also chairman of the United Minority Council, the governing body of all minority students at the University of Pennsylvania. He is also a member of Sphinx, the senior honor society. He is among the top 20 of 2,000 senior students, the top one percent of his class. I do not know where he will go. That depends on Father's order. I know he is ready to follow Father's footsteps and set the tradition of our Unification movement.

ABOUT HOON SOOK NIM

I would also like to say a word about Hoon Sook Nim. She is now a professional ballerina. She was a member of the Little Angels of Korea. Father initiated the Little Angels in 1962. By 1965 the Little Angels traveled from Korea to the United States. Their first performance here was at Gettysburg, given in honor of the late President Dwight D. Eisenhower. During the last 20 years, the Little Angels have given over 2,000 live performances and 200 television performances. They have met over 30 heads of state. At one point the Little Angels performed in New York at the United Nations Assembly Hall. True Parents attended that particular benefit performance for UNICEF. The Little Angels are Father's cultural ambassadors to the world.

Hoon Sook Nim toured the world three times throughout the United States, Canada, and Europe. At that time, she was the only English-speaking child in the group, and when they traveled to the United States and Canada, she was the only one who introduced them in English. This little Korean child came out as emcee and spoke perfect English. Even before they danced, she had won the audience.

She went back to Korea to attend the Little Angels Junior High School; she won the distinguished honor student award five times and was one of the top 10 students in the entire school. Four times she won the Artist Scholarship Award and the Little Angels Award. Three times she won the Meritorious Service Award. After graduation, instead of going on to college, she joined the Royal Ballet Academy in London. She moved on to the Princess Grace Academy of Dance in Monte Carlo, Monaco, for advanced professional training in ballet. She participated in the Lausanne Junior Ballet Competition in Lima, Peru, at the International Dance Festival. After that, she joined the Ohio Ballet Professional Company. Later she joined the Washington Ballet Company and has been performing with them all over the world. She won the Gold Medal at the National Dance Competition in Korea. She was one of the finalists of the Lausanne International Dance Competition and was awarded the Certificate of Appreciation by the Peru International Dance Competition. In fact, she was in Hong Kong doing a tour which had not ended when she was called to participate in the matching. She knew that the Blessed children were assembling at East Garden and obeyed the order to come. She flew here without knowing anything, arriving at East Garden on February 12. Many people have commented that there is some quality of heavenliness in her dance. It is spiritual. Even the *Washington Post* implied that. I bet you, dollars to donuts, they did not know she was my daughter!

The most important thing is not how well she dances. The most important thing is that she understands True Father, True Mother, the True Family, the Unification movement, the Unification goal, as well as our way of life. She has proved it to me so amply during this time. I am ready to bow down to her one thousand times, even one million times. My gratitude and love for her will never end.

My dear brothers and sisters, this is a great day. But this is not just a day for these two Blessed couples. It is your day. It is my day. True Parents' day. True Family's day. Spirit world's day. Father said that there is a great celebration going on in the spirit world right now. A spiritual whirlwind, a spiritual storm is taking place. We only have to capitalize on it.

In front of our True Parents, tonight we are all blessed. The marriages of In Jin Nim and Heung Jin Nim become our marriages.

When I visited the *Washington Times*, many staff members came up to me and said that they felt as if they were getting matched and Blessed again. The excitement spreading all over the world is incredible. Please capitalize on it.

Sermon on the Mount (Airy)

MT. AIRY, NEW YORK

JANUARY 25, 1985

═══════════════════════════

All members with a mission at News World Communications gathered together in upstate New York for a weekend workshop. The purpose of the meeting was to enrich their lives spiritually and professionally, to share creative ideas, and to renew their commitment to God and their mission. Dr. Pak begins the meeting by sharing Father's vision for News World *and for all the Unification Church businesses. He also shares his personal experience of being kidnapped to illustrate how we can always bring victory and glory to God through absolute conviction and determination.*

In the last year, many of our News World Communications family members were given to many other missions, such as the IOWC, state missions, and spiritual missions. So right now, from roughly 200 or more original members, we have roughly 65 brothers and sisters working for the company. They are the most precious backbone of the company. In a way this is our stockholders meeting because we are the ones who can say, yes, I own this newspaper because it belongs to God and True Parents, and I am a child of God and True Parents.

So this is a heavenly stockholders meeting of News World Communications. I am glad that you have the entire day tomorrow to discuss the success of our company. I'm sure that's the number one topic. Number two, we will discuss how we can enrich our lives spiritually as well as professionally. Our movement is maturing, we are no longer teenagers, and we are having children. So we and our company are growing to maturity. We want to find spiritual enrichment inside, but we also want to become productive, creative components of the company and of society. This is what we've been thinking about and what you are going to discuss all day tomorrow.

Therefore, I really want tomorrow, January 26, 1985, to be the beginning of a turning point for News World Communications. For that reason I put aside everything to come here because I feel it is so important to set the tone for tomorrow. Also I'd like to share with you a wider vision, Father's vision, particularly in connection with News World Communications. That is the purpose for this gathering. Tomorrow you can bring it down to the nitty gritty, working level and discuss and share creative ideas. Then we will go home with a renewed spirit and a renewed commitment. I'd like you to stay on Sunday and enjoy some more of life so you can have a very rewarding conference. I won't be with you because I have another important duty tomorrow morning. You go ahead and have a wonderful day with Nick Buscovich, the vice presidents, and team leaders. I'm very glad to be here tonight, particularly coming directly from Danbury, which has a special meaning. I am linking you directly to the True Parents.

Most of you have been surviving in the News World mission for many years and have had many times when you felt burnt out, almost extinguished, just hanging on with the day-to-day mission. In some cases you were just functioning mechanically and that was not your fault. But those periods were definitely necessary. Everything was in God's plan and you endured and you survived.

Of course, some new people joined recently. News World Communications is not going to just accept anybody who wants to come. No more. That day is over. We're going to carefully select each individual for the mission. Unless you can find the way to contribute meaningfully and offer this service to God and humanity and unless you are working toward your own self-perfection, you shouldn't be here with the company. We have no intention from now on to run the company like a charity. We are going to be running this as a vibrant, forward-looking, and aggressive company. Each component and each individual has a very special, dynamic, creative mission and position. Each one will become a light-giving object, a dynamo. Each person is moving the company forward, so that you can have self-respect, satisfaction, and enthusiasm in your mission so that our company can move forward. When you unite those creative energies, they become a dynamic force that will really move the company.

WE ARE GOD'S CHOSEN CHAMPIONS

I do not use the word "rebuild," because we never really built a company, but I feel in this year of 1985, the opportunity has come. We are going to build our company. The opportunity is here, and I want to give you an ultimatum: unless we make it this year, we'll never make it. God has bestowed upon us an opportunity, and it is passing by. We've got to grab it and make use of it. When that opportunity has passed by, it will be no more. Like in Divine Principle, if one person fails the mission, then the mission remains, but a new champion will come and take on the mission. That is the Principle. We are like the chosen champion and God has given us that opportunity. So we must grab that opportunity and make use of it. Then we can bring glory to God and True Parents. But if we fail and the opportunity goes by, it should not be me and you who is responsible. Probably we will not be there anymore because God will choose someone else and try again in the future. That failure would make things 10 times, or 100 times, more difficult because more indemnity would have to be paid. Because of the indemnity that our members, our church, our movement, and our company as a whole have paid over the last several years, I believe the time has come that we can cash the indemnity in for glorious success and power.

First of all, let us share our common heritage. What is it? What is our identity? What are we? We've got to find our identity. We always renew our identity every day. How are we different from the millions of people streaming down Fifth Avenue every day? How are we different? What is our pride? What is my prestige? Our prestige is that we are children of God in the name of our True Parents. This is very important. This is the most important thing. There are many people out there who will say, "I am a child of God." Many Christians will say, "We're children of God." But not many will say, "I am a child of God in the name of the True Parents." Only we can say that. That is the heritage. That is our real classification, our identity. Commonly they call us Moonies. But really in the spiritual heritage we are saying, "I am a child of God in the name of the True Parents." The children who are sitting here are Blessed children. How are they different from other children? These children were born as potentially sinless. That is the difference of our children. We still have a perfection stage to go. We have to provide our children with a sinless environment to grow up in.

We didn't give them that yet. We are still living in a sojourners land, enemy land, enemy territory, hostile, polluted ground. So these children can go wrong. Don't be mistaken—they can go wrong. But that is why we have got to work to change the environment for our children. They are born with a heritage that has never before been given to mankind in human history. Only by the True Parents are our hereditary sins eradicated. It's really a matter of claim or a matter of recognition. None of us here is yet perfect, including myself. The important thing is that we've been claimed by our True Parents as members of their family. Here is a dollar bill. What is its value? It's just a piece of paper. Why is this paper important? Because it has been given certain recognition by the authorities. Everyone has to recognize the authority that says this is a one dollar bill. That is where the value exists. Otherwise it is just a piece of paper. Authorities gave this bill the value of one dollar.

By the same token, True Parents claim Luis as their son and Vicki as their daughter. True Parents have that authority. No government has permanent authority. The only eternal authority is borne by God alone. So True Parents with that authority claimed Richard, Nick, and Tony. He claimed you and told Satan, don't touch them. The price we pay is faith and loyalty and love. Satan cannot claim you back. But when you fail to give faith, loyalty, devotion, and love to our True Parents and Heavenly Father and you fail to profess that you are a child of True Parents, then Satan says, "Come here. You are my child, not the True Parents' child." This is why our condition is absolute loyalty and faith in the True Parents. This is our identity. This particular recognition and value God bestowed on us has been priceless.

None of us in this room really deserve it, and nobody in this room has earned it. Nobody in this room can say, "Yes, I'm clean enough, I deserve that blessing." None of us. It is really given freely. For that reason, we are the recipient of such a blessing, but we cannot claim such blessing and this is priceless. You've found such a priceless blessing, and we really don't understand the full impact of it until we get to spirit world. This is the problem. What a priceless prize in heaven we've won already. We just don't know. That is why when your focus becomes dimmer and dimmer and dimmer, you can become an ex-Moonie, just completely blinded. One day you saw a flare of hope and great vision but lost it while doing so many missions and paying so much indemnity. Your spirituality gets worn out, becoming weaker and weaker, and then one day is totally extinguished. On that day, you ask yourself, "Why should I be here?" You totally lost the vision, and at that point you became an ex-Moonie. We do not know how much incredible blessing has come upon us already. This is the reason we need fellowship and testimony. This is the reason we need prayer and we need to listen Divine Principle to help us to always renew ourselves to the priceless blessing we've already received.

WE NEED MATURE MEMBERS

This is particularly difficult in a business mission. In a spiritual mission, you always walk with the truth. The person who reads the Divine Principle every day never can become weaker because there is no time when Satan can infiltrate that person. So I was happy when I was teaching Principle every day in Korea. Father said that only mature members should go into business missions. In dealing with business missions like News World Communications, you have to deal with the secular world, money, promotion, all kinds of procedures, regulations, legal affairs, and so forth. Every day you've been dealing with those matters and you seldom have a chance to meditate and renew yourself. This is why Father said this mission is not easy. Sometimes this mission becomes a curse. Only mature members can tackle the business mission. Only mature members can tackle News World.

When you look at Father, he is really a super dynamo, super engine, super star, and super sun, light-giving object, spiritually. But at same time, I've never seen anybody so acute in business judgment. I've never seen anybody who has more political vision than Father. In terms of business vision or political vision, no one can compete with Father. I see Father has two sides. The spiritual side is a shining sun. Really Father is the spiritual sun of the world. But at the same time, Father's mind is so quick to understand the reality of the world, whether it is business, social, political, or economic. We all imitate Father so that we are always spiritually vibrant and alive, but at the same time we are mature enough to have a clear vision in a business sense. We can deal with the world. As Jesus said, "Behold, I send you out as sheep in the midst of wolves; so be wise as serpents and innocent as doves." [Matthew 10:16] That is what mature members should be like. And we are moving into that stage.

So tonight the first thing I want to impress upon you is that I am a child of God in the name of the True Parents and therefore I belong to the True Parents' family. I am a son and a daughter of True Parents, and True Parents claimed me. This is my most important identity, which will remain as a blessing for eternity. When you lose this identity, it becomes a curse for eternity.

You know I was once kidnapped. I didn't have a chance to share that experience with you yet. Probably I should write a book about it. Now that all the kidnappers have been captured and the trial will be this spring, probably I'll wait until all that is done. But I was in captivity for 40 hours, and the first 12 hours I was absolutely convinced that I was going to die. Throughout my life, my prayer has always been that I want to live for the glory of our True Parents and I want to die for the glory of our True Parents. That has been my prayer. Then all of a sudden my final opportunity was approaching and I asked myself, "How can I die in the glory of True Parents?"

I was thinking two ways. The first was that I wanted to give some meaning to my death. I wanted my death to be a ransom so that Father could be freed from Danbury prison. I wished that somehow it could be incredible news that Reverend Moon's special assistant, and one of the members of the 36 Blessed couples, the president of News World Communications, had been kidnapped and killed. I wish that public opinion would say, "Gee, that is too much. That is really too much. Reverend Moon is in jail and his disciple has been kidnapped and been killed. What is America doing?" Some kind of incredible public outcry would be created so that public opinion would say, "Free Reverend Moon." I really prayed because I felt that my lack of faith and lack of devotion caused the imprisonment of True Father. So upon my death God can use my life to create some kind of condition so that Father can be freed. That is my first prayer.

Second, I wanted to prepare myself so that when the final moment came, either by dagger or by pistol, I didn't know what method they were going to use, I could end my life here on earth with True Parents' name on my lips.

"CHAMBUMONIM, MANSEI!"

That was a difficult 12 hours. They said they were going to kill me at 1:00 in the morning. So they were saying "Now it's 12:00, now it's 12:30." They were preparing something. I knew the time was coming. I was bound to two chairs, blindfolded, handcuffed and everything, but I picked up the two chairs and shouted, "Mansei!" Three times I shouted. The kidnappers rushed toward me and pulled me down and got the electric shocker to shock me. They thought I was trying to call for some help, neighbors or police. But I really wasn't trying to call for help. Then I was tormented and tortured. My mouth was completely bloody. From that point on they gagged me. My eyes were already blindfolded, and everything but my mouth had been gagged. But they gagged me so I could not even speak a word. So I kept speaking inside my mind, even though I could not voice it. I'd say, "Chambumonim, Mansei! Chambumonim, Mansei!"

Well, apparently God gave me my life. That was not my last moment, as I had thought, and a miracle happened. They changed their plans. The one who masterminded the kidnapping, who confessed to the FBI, has said that their plan was to kill me, to shock the Unification Church and to shock the world. But somehow that night, among those men, a vision came. One person said, "Let's kill him." The other said, "Well, let's get the money first." In that battle God was working. Something made them change their course.

The second night that I was in captivity, they bound me to some kind of metal bed and told me to sleep a few hours. I was absolutely physically and mentally exhausted. I was trying to be alert, but it was virtually impossible and I was falling asleep. I had a dream. In my dream Mother appeared shouting at me, "Bo Hi! Bo Hi!" Very urgently she shook my body. Now this is in a dream, not real, but I saw Mother and she shook me saying, "You've no time to sleep here. Unless you get out of here in the next 10 hours, you'll be dead. Do everything, use your imagination, your wisdom to get out of this place in the next 10 hours. Otherwise, you'll be dead."

I woke up and remembered what had happened in the dream, so I was sitting and thinking how I could get out of this place in the next 10 hours. The next morning there was a meeting and they were asking for ransom money. If I hadn't had that dream of Mother, I would not have had enough courage. But because of that dream I had the courage to say to the kidnappers, "OK, you want money. All right, you will get the money, but you won't get a penny as long as I'm here. No one can bring you the money, even if you ask me to call the bank or call the Unification Church headquarters. It won't work because you know I've been missing already 36 hours. Don't you remember the FBI is all over the place? It won't work. Let me out of this place. Let me go to the bank."

Because of that dream experience, I was very determined, completely subjective, not passive. I didn't say, "Can I do this?" No! I said, "You can kill me, but it won't help you get any money. The only way you'll get it is to let me go. It's 10:30 now. I must go to Washington by 12:00 sharp." I was virtually commanding them. They were completely flabbergasted. I was a captive, and yet I was commanding them. "Bring me my neck tie! Bring my eyeglasses! Take these handcuffs off! You want the money, don't you? Handcuffs won't get you money." I was absolutely determined to get out, one way or another. I had to make a showdown with these people. I just had to take command of the situation.

A GOOD SIGN

They were completely persuaded by my commitment and my attitude. You can't be wishy-washy, looking this way or that way without commitment. I had learned if you want to get something done you've got to be committed. I had that kind of energy because of Mother's revelation. She said, "Get out of this place in 24 hours." So I began to give them orders, and they had to obey me. One person brought me my glasses. Another person brought me my jacket. Another brought me my tie. When they had taken off my tie, I was particularly upset. The tie clasp I was wearing had been given to me by Mother on a very important day. Mother said that Father had been wearing this tie clasp for many years, and she was giving it to me because Father wanted her to give me something that he had been wearing, so that I could wear it all the time. So it particularly upset me when they took off my neck tie. Of course, they hadn't asked me to take off my neck tie. They just took it off. So this tie clasp was hanging from the tie and it could fall off very easily. So during my captivity I had been worried about it. But I still have it. When I saw it, I knew it was a sign from God, because when they took off my tie they just threw it away somewhere. I was thinking in my mind that if the tie pin still stays there it's a good sign. If it's not there, I must face my destiny. So I was enthusiastically asking them to bring my tie. And when they brought me my tie I looked at it and it was still there. It was hanging there, unhooked, with no support but still there. I said, "Thank God." I knew I could make it.

So then I was even more forceful, saying "You're wasting time! You have already wasted 10 minutes. I've got to go to La Guardia airport. Have the car ready!" So one guy said, "Look! Get up! Get the car." At that point I had virtually brainwashed them or hypnotized them. How had I hypnotized them? With conviction. I told them, "Your option is to kill me. Go ahead, you know everyone has to die once. I don't care. I'm going someday. But you guys will be killed too. Why should you do such a foolish thing? Why should you be so foolish? You want to get something out of me. Let me out."

Since then it has become a sort of a joke. In Washington there is a very important minister, and I testified about Father and the kidnapping and so forth. Ever since he heard this story he has said, "Well, I'm not going to deal with you because you are the man who talked the kidnappers into releasing you. You can sell ice to the Eskimos. How am I going to debate with you?" But it was not debating skills really; it was conviction.

I said, "Are you going to kill me? I'll let you do it. Or if you want to get some money, let me out." So they took me to La Guardia. I walked out of that kidnap place like a king. Everyone virtually bowed down and was shaking hands with me, like giving me a VIP sendoff. Two guys, one guy driving and the other guy sitting right next to him, took me to La Guardia. At La Guardia they said, "We apologize for hog-handling you. Forgive us." I said, "No problem. Get out of here." Then I ran onto the plane.

When I told Father all these things, he said that God saved me. "If you had tried to survive any other way, you would not have made it." Today I do not know whether I could do the same. Can I really hold myself up until my last breath here on earth? This is something you cannot really test. You have no way to test yourself in advance, because you have only one death to go through. But even this day my total confession of faith is that I want to live my life for the sake of my True Parents. And I want to die in the name of our True Parents. Aboji, mansei. This is my identity. Yours and mine, the same. I am a child of God in the name of our True Parents. No one out there can even come near me. No one can even come near in terms of value.

Today Reverend Kwak came with me to Danbury and reported to Father about the things that are happening. You know, we are sending out so many videotapes and books. You have to always do your spiritual duty. We have 300,000 ministers receiving our videotapes, Divine Principle books, and Father's letter and book from prison. There are many incredible stories. Many ministers are now preaching the Divine Principle as part of their sermon, without telling their congregation that it is the Unification Church's Divine Principle. That's all right.

The wife of one of the ministers confessed to one of the state leaders, "You know my husband has been preaching as a minister for so many years. But I could tell his spiritual life and spiritual power were virtually dead. Ever since he saw the Divine Principle tapes, and he watched them five times over, his sermons on Sunday have become powerful. He was always saying, 'I've run out of topics, I have to get a guest speaker from somewhere.' But after he saw the Divine Principle tapes, he couldn't wait for Sunday to preach."

One Sunday our member was so surprised when walking into the church service of another church. The minister who was preaching had a big chart in front. The chart said, "Formation, Growth, Perfection." Our member was flabbergasted.

A PLEA FOR SPIRITUAL CLEANSING

Also there was a very arrogant minister in Detroit, Michigan. He was absolutely negative and nasty. He was just a no-good minister. But one day he had heard our state leader explain about holy salt usage, practices, and traditions. This minister heard that the meaning of the holy salt was to spiritually ward off all the bad luck and the bad spirits, etc. Two months later this state leader got a call from the very same minister, and the minister asked if the state leader would come to his house and holy salt it for him. The state leader was totally flabbergasted, but he said, "Of course, I'd be glad to." He went with holy salt to the minister's two-story house. He told the minister, "We have to do a special prayer, so could you get all your family together?" So all the minister's family gathered and they prayed and our state leader led the service. They sang a church hymn and prayed in the name of True Parents.

"Just follow me while I holy salt this house. In the name of the True Parents, I'm going to holy salt this house, the first floor and then the second floor." After the second floor was holy salted completely, they prayed again and the state leader prepared to go back home. The minister asked, "Can you leave the leftover salt with us?" The state leader replied, "We normally don't do that unless you accept the True Parents," but he left the holy salt.

A few days later this minister called the state leader and said, "I must confess that the reason I asked you to holy salt my house is that every night when my children were sleeping they'd be haunted. They couldn't have a peaceful night. Incredible spiritual phenomena came every night and the children were so scared that they couldn't sleep peacefully. So I thought about you for two months, but finally I thought that I had nothing to lose, so I had better try Unification Church holy salt. From that night on, the children are sleeping like a log, every night." This minister was convicted. Now he is not only listening to Divine Principle, but he has become an important CAUSA member and is trying to promote the CAUSA movement.

This is just one of the many things happening like this. You know, if holy salt does that much, how much more can you who have the True Parents do? We not only have the holy salt but we belong to the founder, the origin and source of the holy salt, True Parents. Aren't you proud, aren't you grateful, aren't you happy, aren't you really glorified that we are part of the True Parents?

For two hours Reverend Kwak was reporting many stories. Another minister was listening to Divine Principle 20-hour tapes. He listened to the 20-hour tapes five times, 100 hours. On the final day he was looking at the TV screen, he saw a vision of the spiritual world. He was looking into spiritual world. There he saw Reverend Moon doing the matching in the spiritual world and he was one of the candidates being matched. After that vision, this minister had just no question who Father is. Now many ministers are virtually converting their entire church into Unification Church teaching. So the age of one-on-one restoration is over. Entire churches are turning around and joining with Father.

There was an accident between a mobile home and a car in Florida. A very wonderful sister and brother were killed and other members were injured. One brother had worked at *The News World,* and the sister had been a team mother. There was a very beautiful Seung Hwa ceremony for them that Reverend Won Pil Kim officiated in Alabama. The husband of the Japanese sister who died came from California with their two children. They completely inspired everybody. He wasn't shedding even one tear and was absolutely centered upon the True Parents and always smiling. "My wife is in the highest place. She was martyred for the mission and I am proud of my wife and I'm taking care of my children. Why worry?" It inspired so many members.

FATHER NEEDS YOU

This team mother who died and is in spiritual world has appeared to the church members, state leaders, and others so many times it's incredible. One member was still in the hospital because his concussion had not healed. She appeared to him, asking him, "What are you doing? This is an emergency period, and Father needs you every minute. What are you doing here? Get out and work." She always appears with a happy face, a most glorious, beautifully shining face. She always appears to members saying, "What are you doing? This is such an important time. No time to waste. Get out there and work. Father needs you."

In that state there are three sisters all 26 years old and nearly the same spiritual age whom the state leader was educating to become team mothers. This sister who is in spiritual world appeared to them and said, "I'm having trouble because I need to work through my successor, another team mother, but because the state leader has not appointed a team mother, I have no one to work through. So please tell your state leader to appoint a team mother right away. Out of the three I recommend this one." The state leader heard that report and immediately appointed a sister to be team mother. Now that Japanese sister comes and helps that team mother.

One thing that the Unification Church is doing is bringing the spiritual and physical world into oneness. Heung Jin Nim is all over the place. We can write already a dozen books of Heung Jin Nim's appearances. There was a testimony in the CARP magazine that some of you may have read. There are 12 things that Heung Jin encourages us to do. One is to bring unity, another is that the American church needs tearful prayer. The reason I'm telling you this is that during the seminar tomorrow, I'd like to encourage you to make that meeting prayer-oriented. We need to pray, particularly when we're out in nature like this. At least one time before you go back to New York City, go out in the snow and unite with nature and pray, if at all possible a tearful prayer, a prayer of repentance. Cleanse yourself completely.

You know that while we live here on earth we are not cultivating this body; we are building our true body, our eternal body, our spiritual body. Within you now, right now, is that spiritual body. This physical body is sort of a case for the spiritual body. This physical body is like a rented vehicle for my spiritual body. When the time comes, the car rental company will say to turn it in. In our case, nature will say to turn it in. But the real body is being grown right now. You have no time to waste. You must grow your spiritual body every day. With Divine Principle and True Parents, you can reach perfection. That perfection means becoming a divine spirit. Your spiritual body will glow like a sun. That is our goal. We are investing our physical life for the perfection of our eternal life. That is what the Divine Principle is all about. We are practicing this; it is not a theory. We are doing it and we have a physical central figure, True Parents, who will cover millions of miles in one second. This is the kind of spiritual heritage that we have. I want to talk about other things, but this is the most important thing. You and I are the children of God in the name of our True Parents. We have this kind of privilege that no money can buy. In order to have this kind of spirit, you have got to live a vibrant, very happy, rewarding life here on earth.

Your newspaper mission is a good mission and a very important one. We are the Unification Church air force. The media is like an air force. The CARP mission is like a naval fleet. And church centers and IOWC and city centers are like the foot solders. They will actually face the hill and take the hill. But unless we have air superiority we will not win the naval and ground battles. This is why Father said one time in East Garden, "The important thing is the ideological, internal warfare." These battles can be won more effectively by the communications media than by any other means. Father is building what people commonly call a media empire. I tell you we really need a God-centered media empire—no question about it. It is my absolute determination to achieve that media empire for Father and for God. The name of that media empire is called News World Communications. We are going to do it from New York, Washington, Los Angeles, Miami, San Francisco, Texas, Boston, and eventually all the 50 states of the United States.

WE WILL BE THE BACKBONE

If we can effectively create a strategic air force, Father's mission will become incredibly easier. Our mission is to build a God-centered air force. This is your mission and my mission. I told you at the outset that I'm going to absolutely make a turning point in the year of 1985. With you and me as a backbone, we've got to do it. This year we are going to make history with News World Communications, Inc.

I talk a great deal about spiritual heritage because this is central. You and I understand what comes first. I want you to be spiritually enriched, well, happy, and vibrant—not barren, devastated, dried up, burnt out. And, second, you must find meaning and position in your News World duty. I want you to find your purpose and your position, how and where you can serve the best. You've got to find your professional position. If you don't have one, then develop one. You can do it. Our company is going to strive for excellence in everything we do. Never will we do patchwork. We've got to be professionally organized, professionally executed, professionally evaluated. Your job and your achievement will be evaluated professionally, and you will be rewarded and punished professionally. That is only fair. I want you to compete with outside professional people.

At the *Washington Times*, Alex Hunter, a 23-year-old brother, has become a star of the arts department. He is destined to win awards and eventually the Pulitzer Prize. Our designer for the *Washington Times*, Gil Roschuni, has become a celebrity in the country in terms of newspaper design. He was invited by the *New York Times* to give a seminar because the *Washington Times*, in terms of overall newspaper design, was chosen as number one in the entire country. Another brother, Tim Elder, was a missionary in Korea. When Father brought him to the *Washington Times*, he didn't do too well at first. Jim Whelan came to me and said, "Get this member out. He is no good. He is dead wood." I begged him, "Can you let him stay three more months? Let him have one more evaluation." Soon Tim's true abilities came out. To make a long story short, he is now the best foreign correspondent the *Washington Times* has ever had. He is the kind of brother who will eventually not only win the Pulitzer Prize but can become an editor, international editor, national editor, managing editor, editor-in-chief of the *Washington Times* and be recognized by the world.

We at the *New York Tribune* have won many awards. Our paper is striving for excellence. We must try even more. I want you to understand that for many years our company has virtually existed to survive or survived to exist. Always we hung in the balance, always a shoestring operation, always we had no money. I stopped that this year. Although we don't have a fat budget, we have a budget. At least every leader knows how much money they have and can decide how to spend it. It's not Richard Jones, not Mark Wilenchek, not Mr. Kim who will spend it, but you who will spend it. Each one becomes a responsible manager in your area. Do what you can with your amount of money. We want to give you that kind of opportunity. We want to have that kind of creative and autonomous leadership. You'll not always be held down to minimum pay because you are a Moonie.

I'll change that, too. If you are valuable to the company, you'll be rewarded according to your value. Then you get your money and you have your own funds to contribute to the church and our movement. If you deserve $100, then that's what you get, but if you deserve $50,000, then that's what you get. I don't want you to misunderstand, the Unification Church is not trying to create a socialistic economic system. CAUSA teaches that socialism will never work. Communism is baloney. It contradicts human nature. Therefore, it can never win. Human nature will always win. What is human nature? Creativity. Human nature is creativity. This is why one person can make $100 and another can become a billionaire. The value of creativity is immeasurable. Therefore, we have to bring out that creativity. How? We have to give each person a purpose, because God gave man a nature to develop himself or herself. That is human nature. We all want to strive to better ourselves.

This is why the communist system does not understand God. In the eyes of communism, Einstein would look like a laborer, a $50 laborer. Put him in a labor camp and give him $50 for labor, and Einstein would not have come up with the theory of relativity. You have to give freedom, room enough for creativity to blossom, and a proper incentive. That is the law of human nature, and any system that goes against that human nature will fail. What is the difference between the Unification Church and the outside world? We are a different kind of men and women. That's why I talk about our identity. The outside world is blinded to God's creative reality. They can only see the material reality, but they are completely blind to the true reality, which is the spiritual reality. We can't afford to be blind.

We've got to be a new kind of man and woman, a new creature. We see the spiritual reality and the material reality. We work with them both, spiritual and physical. That's the difference. For example, I would never become a millionaire because that is not my motivation. If that was my motivation from the beginning, then I could be rich. I could be a rich man many times over in my life. But my life goal has been to truly serve God and humanity and bring good news and victory to our True Parents. So in True Parents' lifetime I want to see this world turned into the kingdom of heaven on earth.

For that purpose I must win not only the spiritual battle but the physical battle. I must be a good businessman. I must build News World Communications into a billion dollar corporation. I want to achieve that kind of goal. I don't think God will say, "Oh, you are praying for a billion dollars." Not at all. God made the material world for what purpose? The important thing is that I'm trying to form a billion-dollar corporation to serve God and transform our world into a God-centered world. So we are not denying the material world. On the contrary, we must give it even greater value than anybody else. But our ultimate goal will be service to God and humanity and not just to serve my physical body. That is the worst incentive, trying to serve the physical body, because the time will come when nature will say to turn it in. Then what do you have? Nothing. You, however, accumulate your value in your spiritual self.

This is where we are different, but at the same time, our running of the company should be the same as any other good company. Up until now, the mentality has often been that our employees are members, and they can just hang in there to survive and we need only pay them a few dollars. This kind of attitude we've got to weed out. Either you are a creative part of the company or you should get out of the company. I want you to be a creative part of the company. I hope I'm inspiring you tonight—you are stock-holders. Your burning desire is just like mine. We must build a billion-dollar corporation. God is not a small God. God is never limited, but we limit ourselves. We want to be a gigantic business success so we can command the respect of the people. You as an individual must command the respect of society as a professional, whatever your duty. Never become a burden to the company or to anyone else. You must be creative, a dynamo, giving energy to other people.

This year we must create what will probably be the most modern printing house in the New York area. We bought a $3.7 million press, and it's already paid off. It will be able to do color production. We should be able to print our three newspapers on one machine, as well as many other outside jobs coming though satellite. Since we have a satellite system, if some outside journal on the west coast wants to publish in New York, they will come to us. They'll transmit to our satellite and print with our machine.

We are going to have a lot of that kind of business. The *Washington Times* in the last several months made several hundred thousand dollars in outside printing jobs. We now have it in Los Angeles and soon will have it in Miami. Then we will have *Noticias del Mundo* in the three cities with the largest Spanish populations in the United States. *Noticias* has the capacity to become a money-maker in a way that will support the corporation economically.

We've also become a politically powerful and influential people. We are going to have our News World Communications corporate headquarters updated into the most modern corporate headquarters and newspaper facility. The *Washington Times* equipment is already three years old. We will be ultra-modern and the most effective system in operation. Father will complete it by the early part of next year. The company that will build our newspaper building will go into high gear. It will be absolutely beautiful and organized into the most effective and productive newspaper operation. We're looking into an opportunity that will get the *New York City Tribune* a spot to evolve itself into a newspaper that can truly be a contestant of the *New York Times*. Ultimately the *New York City Tribune's* mission is to win over the *New York Times*. That is its ultimate mission. The *New York City Tribune* will be better than the *New York Times*, and it will have more credibility than the *New York Times*. Its readership will be more than the *New York Times*.

I tell you the kingdom of heaven has come within your reach. It's come down that low, and all you have to do is jump up and get it. Our movement is making many other investments. I see 1985 as the turning point. For example, our fishing business is really growing. We have 80 shrimp trawlers working part-time in three different places: Colombia, Surinam, and Brazil. They are the largest shrimp trawlers in the area. For example, in Colombia, other boats are catching 150 pounds of shrimp every day, and our boats are catching 300 pounds every day. So we are bringing our ship from Surinam to Colombia. In Surinam one gallon of oil is $1.19 while in Colombia it is cheaper. So we are really searching around the whole world to find the best fishing area. Colombia is right here in our own back yard, but also we are moving into the African coast. In Alaska we already have a fishing business and have an incredible opportunity to export bass. We caught $10 million worth last year and this year. This is just one of our many areas of development. Our members are becoming professional and learning the businesses, and 1985 will become the turning point all the way around. In terms of political or spiritual aspects, 1985 will become CAUSA year, and 3,000 ministers will become full-time CAUSA preachers.

MOUNT DANBURY

BELVEDERE ESTATE, TARRYTOWN, NEW YORK

FEBRUARY 3, 1985

═══════════════════════════

In this brief yet informative speech, Dr. Pak describes Danbury as the Mt. Calvary of the 20th century and shares how Father is proceeding with the process of salvation from there. He also explains the meaning of Father's recent Day of the Opening of Heaven declaration and testifies to the victory of the four-day CAUSA seminar in Washington, D.C.

This morning I have only 50 minutes to be here because I am going to Danbury with Mother to see Father. This morning I want to talk about the Day of Opening of Heaven, which Father declared on February 1, just two days ago. Mother and I were at Danbury and Father brought us all small prison towels, and on them he had written "The Day of Opening of Heaven, February 1, 1985, 3:35 a.m." At that moment Father declared in prayer, in heaven and to the world, and then he looked at his watch and wrote down the time. This is probably the final clearing of the way to heaven. Father declared the Day of Victory of Heaven on October 4, 1976, and now Father is declaring the Day of Opening of Heaven. What does it mean? God is now opening up a big highway from heaven to hell, a highway of salvation. Think of it as a highway of truth and light, the opening of a big door that has been closed up in spiritual world. Now the door is open and the spirit people can get on the highway and go to heaven. Father has cleared all the obstacles.

Today Danbury is the 20th-century Mount Calvary. By being crucified on the cross, Jesus set the condition for the salvation of mankind spiritually. In this age, by suffering with the living flesh on Mount Danbury, Father has completely set the condition for the salvation of humanity, spiritually and physically. The amazing thing is that when you go up to Danbury prison where Father is, there is a hill. Very unusual. Prison facilities are almost always on flat ground, but Father's camp is on the highest hill in that area. When Mother arrives, Father is standing on that hill, and when Mother leaves, Father is standing on that hill waving. So that's going to be a famous hill in world history. So Mount Danbury is going to be the source of power for the salvation of humanity on a spiritual and a physical level.

Father is now proceeding with the program of salvation from Danbury. Father is thinking, what else can I do to set the condition before I leave here? While Father is in Danbury incredible miracles have been happening. The Christian community has been turned around, which I'll talk about more a little later. America has been awakened; religious unification has become a realm of reality. All these great things have been happening because Father has been setting conditions. And on February 1, 1985, Father has cleared the way to salvation. No more obstacles, none whatsoever. Everyone who comes to the Divine Principle and accepts the True Parents is going to be streaking down the highway at 100 miles an hour. That is the kind of condition Father is setting. Imagine a highway that starts from the worst part of hell and goes to heaven.

Father is now making things go easy for everybody. For the last 2,000 years, the price of salvation was very high. Since Jesus was crucified, his followers also have had to suffer and go the way of the cross and shed blood. The standard for salvation was so high that it was virtually impossible for ordinary people to go through Jesus. Father knew it was very difficult to attain even just spiritual salvation.

Now Father would like to completely flatten the condition by suffering for mankind himself. He is thinking, I'm going to suffer more for humanity, and by doing so I'm going to let humanity come the easy away. I will work hard on that highway; I will sweat so that the rest of mankind can come easily. Once the super highway is created, all you have to do is get on it. You don't have to worry about bumps or curves. Even a clumsy driver like me can drive it. Speaking of driving, my whole family is scared of my driving. When we drive together, mom drives. Mom has better credibility than daddy, because while I am driving I am always thinking of something else, of going to Danbury or the *Washington Times* or CAUSA, so the car wanders this way and that way. But even my kind of driver can drive on Father's highway.

So this Day of Opening of Heaven is very important. It's not a crooked road, not only a country road, not only a West Virginia road. They say West Virginia roads are almost heaven, but they can never actually get there; they are always almost there. We don't want to be almost in heaven, but all the way. That's the meaning of the Day of Opening of Heaven. Father erected that highway, sweated and suffered, so that all the rest of humanity and all future humanity can travel that highway to heaven. That is the role of the messiah, and Father is doing it right now. This time that Father is in Danbury is absolutely the most important time in Unification Church history.

Father has suffered on many other occasions, such as in the Republic of Korea, particularly in North Korea, but this is the most important period. Why? Because even though Father suffered in Korea and North Korea, that was not the cosmic age for universal salvation. That was not the worldwide level. Today here in the United States, which is the microcosm of the world, whatever Father does has a universal impact. For that reason, this particular period of suffering of our True Parents is very important. What Father has accomplished at Danbury is the restoration of Christianity and the unification of Christianity. Father brought Christianity into one with the Unification Church. Christians began to understand Father and accept Father and Father's dispensation.

One good example is Dr. Tim LaHaye's visit to Danbury. Dr. LaHaye is a very famous minister. On that day, it was snowing. He was coming from Washington, D.C., and his plane was an hour and a half late. It was the only flight that got out; everything else was canceled. So I met him at the airport and took him by car to Danbury, which normally takes an hour and a half. But that day it took three hours in the snow, and several times our car was dancing on the highway, very dangerous, so we really slowed down. Nobody else was on the road.

During the drive, Dr. LaHaye said, "It is incredible what our government did to Reverend Moon, to confine Reverend Moon in this kind of place." When we got to Danbury, he met Father, who was wearing humble prison clothes. He held Father's hands and the first words Dr. LaHaye spoke were, "Reverend Moon, I apologize on behalf of my government." Mother saw that Dr. LaHaye's eyes were red and he was crying. What a beautiful union, a beautiful union of brothers, like Esau and Jacob. Father and Dr. LaHaye were embracing. Then Father said, "No, Dr. LaHaye, you have nothing to apologize for. It must be God's will, and God's will brought us together. You know, because I am in Danbury, you came all the way from California to meet me here. If I were in East Garden, you would not come there to see me. Now you came here. So you see, God works in mysterious ways."

Another great victory took place over four days during a great seminar in Washington, D.C., from January 28 to January 31 for Christian ministers. From the 50 states, 300 ministers gathered together in Washington at the invitation of CAUSA International, which is known to the world as Reverend Moon's organization.

I have never seen a lecture so noisy. The ministers were not just listening, they were saying, "Amen! Amen!" I can tell if the lecture is going well or not by the sound of the amens. Sometimes it was just a few people saying amen, sometimes it was the whole 300 saying amen, sometimes amens and hand clapping, sometimes black ministers standing up and saying "Hallelujah!" It was not a seminar at all—it was an evangelical meeting, Pentecost in a way. All in all, during these four days, there was an incredible harmony and inspiration and enthusiasm, and most important, unity was created.

By the way, we published a new book, the CAUSA lecture manual. The name CAUSA comes from the Latin word "cause," the first cause. So CAUSA is the movement of the first cause, which is God. Therefore, we declared Godism.

The communists took the color red for their book, so we published the blue book. Blue represents heaven and peace; the golden frame and golden lettering represent unchanging quality. The Principle never changes, truth never changes, so that is the purpose. This text presents an examination and critique of Marxist-Leninist ideology and a critique of the confusion in the Western system of values. It presents the new worldview based on the affirmation of God inspired by Reverend Sun Myung Moon, founder of CAUSA International. Divine Principle is Sung Sang (internal), and CAUSA is Hyung Sang (external). What CAUSA has done comes from Divine Principle. It created a weapon to smash the enemy ideology, which is godless communism, which is Marxism-Leninism. That is what the CAUSA manual is all about.

Since I don't have much time, I would like to read several comments of the ministers from the CAUSA workshop. Here is one, "The ecumenical approach of the movement is a big plus. CAUSA does not waste time on theological nonsense, but gets down to the basic beliefs necessary to be a child of God here on earth to prepare oneself for eternal life."

Here is one from a minister from Utah named Willoughby:

I felt desperate to educate Americans about the value of God, family, and country. I am so grateful to have the opportunity to come to this conference and listen to the fantastic messages that are being given here. I thank Reverend Moon. I have had a new rebirth of opinion of Reverend Moon. I heard through the smear tactics of the news media about the Moonies and Reverend Moon, and I was down on them. I tell you, now I hold them in the highest esteem there is. The principles here are something that we can all work for. I have finally found an organization that is really serious about communism. Most Americans are asleep. This organization can wake them up. God or no God. I want to be counted. I want you to know that I want to be counted in the number when we go to the Soviet Union. So let us set the date and get over there to Russia and be heard, declare the truth. Four days ago many of us descended from our planes with hesitant steps. I sense that most of us will be leaving today with firm steps.

There was one Mexican-American minister whose name is Reverend Albo, a very tall and handsome minister. He was always in the front row listening to the lecture. So we asked him to speak. He went up to the stage and said to the 300 people sitting there, "Everybody stand up." So everybody stood up. He said, "I want to give you a simple Spanish lesson. Repeat after me, 'Viva la CAUSA, Viva la CAUSA, Viva la CAUSA,'" which means "long live CAUSA." Then he said,

CAUSA has been the great inspiration in my life. It is certainly a wonderful thing that Reverend Moon had this revelation from God. For the word of God says that without vision men shall perish. Thank God for this man who has vision and is bringing together all different kinds of faith and different colors of skin.

I am pledging before you that with the help of God I will go back to my community fighting communism until the day I die. I came here with some fear and trepidation about what was going on. I wasn't sure if the purpose was to make me a member of the Unification Church. But I realized that my vision was too low. Their ambition is far greater. Actually what they are trying to do is to unify the whole world fighting against the enemy of God and men: communism. Brothers and sisters, it is not a question of whether you are Assembly of God, Methodist, Baptist, Catholic, or whatever. Rather we are going to maintain faith in God and in our world today. Because we are in a real crisis. I praise God that this organization is reviving interest and rekindling the flame. I want to tell you that they are rekindling it in my soul. Although I am a Baptist, and as such I may not accept everything, I believe in the universal Fatherhood of God.

Brothers and sisters, it doesn't matter whether you believe in Baptist water or the Pentecostal fire. Why don't we put it together? When you put water and fire together, you make steam and put the power into solving the crisis we have today. If you live in a community where there are people of all faiths and poisonous snakes come into your community and start biting your children, you wouldn't ask the person next to you if he is a Buddhist and then tell him that he couldn't fight the snakes. The most poisonous snake of all is godless communism. You and I need to pull together no matter what our religions are so that we can save this world. I have been stirred and motivated. I am going back to the television station which I preach over each week and I am going to do more than I ever did before. God is helping me. I am 76 years old. I pray that I can live another 100 years so that I can keep on fighting communism, and I want to join with you in that parade into Moscow.

I could go on and on with these testimonies, but I must go to Danbury and I am already late.

Thank you very much.

TRUE PARENTS SAVED MY LIFE

WASHINGTON, D.C.

MARCH 20, 1988

═══════════════════════

At the time of this Sunday sermon, True Parents had just visited Washington to see the Washington Times facility and left again for Belvedere. Dr. Bo Hi Pak assures the membership that on the foundation of the indemnity paid in 1987, 1988 will reap many miracles. He then shares his own personal miracles, of how his life was saved by God and True Parents, explaining his more recent and serious illness and recovery.

Yesterday at the *Washington Times* Father said that the providence is such that Father's entire efforts are now dedicated to the homeland of Korea. The goal is the reunification of our country, and incredible things are happening. So for that purpose I am also mobilized, almost more than anybody else, and that is the reason that I must get on an airplane and take off for Korea the day after tomorrow to attend a Korean leadership seminar. The full name is the National Leadership Seminar for the Preparation of the Unification of the Fatherland. The leaders attending are comparable to your State Department leaders, secretary of state, secretary of defense, and so forth. The Korean general elections are coming up on April 26, and we're educating many of those congressional candidates at seminars.

Three seminars have been conducted already. Father and I left together for Korea on March 17. Then I came down here and opened the seminar on March 18. The doctor had ordered me not to exceed 80 percent of my workload. But Father is giving me 800 percent, and I'm doing it and I feel fine. It is truly the power and grace of our True Parents and the power of God. More than anything else, I'm very happy to see you. I missed you, the leadership of our ACC/AFC, CAUSA International, but I especially missed our state representatives. You know how lonely it can be to be a soldier, commander, commanding general, everything in one person. Fighting for one state, no matter how small the state, is still a big job for one person. I really prayed for you and missed you, especially since we have not met for several months.

Good to see you, truly wonderful to see you. Even though I went to Washington, I did not even have a chance to go to my home to change my underwear. I had so many plans yesterday to meet different groups, and then I got the word that True Parents' family of 16 are on their way. I was virtually paralyzed. I simply didn't know where to start. But to make a long story short, Father came, Mother came, True Children came, they went to the new *Washington Times* facility and *The World & I*, and then we went to the Washington guest house. Jefferson House was prepared for Father and Mother's use, so that when they come to Washington they always have their own place to go and have meetings. So Father came to dedicate that building and we had a meal. Father and Mother left about 7:30 last night for New York.

One sure sign of the success of the True Parents' visit to Washington is that Father simply didn't want to leave. He would have stayed longer if today hadn't been Sunday, and he wanted to speak at Belvedere this morning. And still Father wanted to stay. Knowing Father's heart, Mother said, "Father, time to go now, could you kindly get up?" And Father said, "Mom, somebody glued the chair to my body and I can't get up!" And he stayed and stayed and stayed, until they absolutely had to leave. I felt very good about it. And I had reported about this particular conference to Father and Mother over the phone on the previous night. Although they have not come to this place, they were fully aware of what is going on here, and they are really looking forward to seeing you in New York.

Now I want to give the personal side of my story. You know most of the history that happened in this country. Before I left for Korea we had a meeting, didn't we? I had just come out of the hospital, and you carried me up on the podium and I conducted the conference. I really squeezed out the last ounce of energy to do the job right. I was even more powerful in that conference because I felt that it might be the last American Leadership

Conference in my life. Something tells me this may be my last. I want to have a grand finale.

Although I was not well, I thought somehow I could recover; but as you know, after that particular conference, something was terribly wrong. I entered the Georgetown University Hospital again and tried to find out, but at that time True Parents were already in Korea, and they wanted me to come there as quickly as possible. So I said to the doctor, "You don't need to operate on me or anything like that. I just cannot stay here for a slow recovery. I'd rather go to Korea and recover." So I took off. Our dear brother Jim Gavin came with me simply because I needed someone to support me physically. When I landed in Kimpo, the airline people could tell something was wrong and they brought me a wheelchair. It was the first time in my life I arrived in my country in a wheelchair.

I WAS FEARFUL

Then I went to see Father and Mother, pretending that nothing was wrong. I was absolutely exuberant in giving my exciting report about ACC/AFC, the television program by Global Images Associates, CAUSA International, and Father and Mother were overjoyed. But at this time, the same indemnity ceremonies were going on in Korea. Honestly speaking, I was very fearful. It's human nature. Even if I have faith in True Parents, I would personally, privately be very fearful in my heart to encounter the ascended Heung Jin Nim in Korea. I simply did not know how to face the situation. I did not have a solution to it.

On one occasion the ballet company was performing at the Little Angels School. The True Parents and their families were invited, and that included Heung Jin Nim. I was the host, and during the performance I fell twice, because I did not have my balance, and Heung Jin Nim saw me. He immediately sensed that I was not recovered. The next day I got a call early in the morning from the church to come there and meet with Heung Jin Nim. That was one moment in my life that I just didn't know what to do, whether to go or not. I didn't want to aggravate the situation further, but at the same time I had the deep desire to reconcile, harmonize, support whatever are the wishes of heaven. My wife and I decided to go. It was a very tense morning. There was no advance warning for the first encounter—it just simply hit me without any preparation. So, if this was a repetition of the other time, I knew I would be a dead man. But if that is God's will, I didn't want to say no to that. Furthermore, I didn't want to continue the very tense relationship with him. So I went.

To make a long story short, it was a good meeting, an hour and a half. He talked, I talked, he questioned, I answered. After that we had such a beautiful prayer together, all tearful, and sang a holy song together. At that time, upstairs in the main church sanctuary, about 1,600 young Korean Blessed children were gathered. Heung Jin Nim told me, "Let's go up, I want to speak to them." I said fine, and since I was wobbling, he supported me and took me upstairs. True Parents' picture was up front with seven large candles, 1,600 people in front of us, holy songs going on, all night fasting and prayer going on for three days. The youngsters gathered there were very tired, but still going, and Heung Jin Nim put out all the candles and gave me a match to relight those candles, so I did. Then he asked someone to bring a big glass of water. He drank half of it in front of True Parents, then gave it to me to drink, so we shared one drink together in front of True Parents, in front of our 1,600 brothers and sisters. Together we bowed three times to our True Parents. I felt very peaceful inside, almost beautiful and powerful. There is such beauty and harmony in union and reconciliation.

Then Heung Jin Nim introduced me and asked me to speak; of course, he had spoken the previous night to the audience. I spoke about an hour, standing with the microphone at the podium on the stage. Several times I could not control myself and almost fell into the audience. That fall would be fatal, because it's almost like hitting a concrete floor. Everybody was listening, and the fatigue was gone in the 1,600 youngsters. Their eyes were shining, everybody was hoping that nothing would happen to Bo Hi Pak. They could see something might happen at any moment. Heung Jin Nim at that point provided me with a chair and asked me to speak sitting down. He was very kind. So I sat down, continuing to speak. Even on a chair I fell twice to the floor.

I spoke basically about the Unification commitment, how a Moonie should live. There's nothing else I can talk about. I told them God has been gracious enough to give me three lives to live. First, I was supposed to die during the Korean War for the sake of the country. Many hundreds of thousands of young Korean men my age died during that war. Two-thirds of my 330 classmates died in the first three days of combat. After we were commissioned, even that number was reduced down to 50 or 60. It is only the power of God that preserved my life. Although I was not a member of the Unification Church at that time, now in hindsight I know that God prolonged my life to use me for a certain purpose because three times during the war I was miraculously saved.

One time almost a whole company of 200 men was annihilated. Only three were left alive, myself and two others. We didn't do anything cowardly to stay alive, not at all. All 200 men were crossing a river when the Red Chinese Army machine gun fire came. Where can you hide? The entire company went into the water. There was no chance to defend ourselves. Furthermore, we were holding our weapons up high, because we didn't want them to get wet, so we had no way to respond to the firing. We were sitting ducks. And I was one of them. When the United Nations fighter bombers swooped down firing their rockets, the Red Chinese machine gun unit stopped firing, and I commanded my company to retreat behind a rock. Only two could follow me, and they were terribly wounded. I was the only one without a scratch.

THE KOREAN WAR PREPARED ME

So that was the first grace of God. I felt that was the end of my first life, and I wanted to give my life for the purpose for the Creator. I felt humble and that, from now on, my life does not belong to me. Then my search began. And, to make a long story short, that is the reason I became a Christian. I was not satisfied after several years and continued my search for the meaning of life and death. That is how I found the Divine Principle and met Father. If I did not have that Korean War experience, I would not have been in the Unification Church.

My second life seemed to be expiring in 1984 when my enemies kidnapped me for 40 hours. I was tortured, and at that time I also felt I must give my life as an indemnity for fallen Adam's world because I was in fallen Adam's position. In the 36 Blessed couples, there were three groups of 12 couples, representing Adam's family, Noah's family, and Jacob's family. The youngest group would be Jacob's family, the middle group would be Noah's family, and the married group was Adam's family, and I belonged to Adam's family. I was chosen as elder brother for the Adam's family group. So in other words, I represented the fallen Adam restored. That was my position.

So if anybody has to pay indemnity for Father going to Danbury, because this is the work of Satan, if somebody has to give his life, that is me. That was my Divine Principle reasoning. And I was ready. It was the most incredible experience to be kidnapped. I was absolutely sure that the end of my life was coming. How cruel it would be I did not know, but I did know one thing: this is it. I was sure that no one had a reason to kidnap me except communists, because I'm not a millionaire, my parents are not even alive, my wife does not have money, my children don't have money, so I was a bad choice for a target. The grandson of David Rockefeller would be a lot better choice than me. The only reason for someone to kidnap me is that I'm close to Reverend Moon, his special assistant, and we're fighting all-out against communism. In other words, this must be a political kidnapping. If that was the case, there would be no chance for me to come out alive. Their goal is not money, so how could I come out alive? They just followed orders from a higher authority, that was exactly the feeling. Tony Colombrito here was having an awful time. All of a sudden he was left alone. I had disappeared, and he didn't know what to do. I had never, never thought that I had any need to be protected.

Exactly 40 hours later I was miraculously alive and released. There are two reasons. First, True Father's prayer in Danbury. As soon as Father heard from Mother that I had disappeared and might have been kidnapped, Father told Mr. Kamiyama, I want to pray, and don't disturb me. Forget about meal time, just don't touch me. And he went up to the top bunk, and sat there, head down, hands down. Mr. Kamiyama said he prayed the entire night without ceasing. For 40 hours he was alert spiritually, defending me, saving me. For 40 hours the spiritual power of True Father was guiding me. How do I know that? Forty hours after I was kidnapped, Mother called Father with the joyful news that Bo Hi came back! And came back in one piece. Not two pieces, not three pieces—in one piece! Father at that moment said, "Fine. Now, Mr. Kamiyama, I want to rest a little bit." And he laid down and immediately was sleeping and began to snore. Mr. Kamiyama said that in his entire life he has never heard anybody snoring that loud, like thunder! This is Mr. Kamiyama's testimony. It's an absolutely true story. That shows you what a concentrated effort Father made to save me!

During 40 hours of captivity, they told me nothing. They didn't reveal anything. They just said, "We are agents, we are professionals, we are working under orders from some governmental body. We are supposed to kidnap you and kill you. Then your body will be put in a drum can with stones and sunk in a lake." They told me that not even the FBI would ever find my body. They said they would execute me at 1 a.m. I was kidnapped at 7:00 in the evening. I had no watch, and I was blindfolded and tied to three chairs, naked. I had no way to know the time, and I was desperately trying not to faint, but I thought a long time had elapsed. I wanted to die like Father's son, True Parents' child. And I wanted to die shouting out "True Parents, mansei." I asked the kidnappers to grant my final requests. I felt like Nathan Hale, but the British in that case were gentlemen. At least they gave Nathan Hale one wish to say his final words. I was following Nathan Hale's pattern, but it didn't work, because my kidnappers were not British. They were savage.

The first request I made was to let me make one telephone call. Not to my wife or my children, but to Mother, Mrs. Moon. I wanted to leave my final words with her. They said no. All right, I said, give me a piece of paper and a pencil. I want to write down a few words of determination and farewell to our True Parents. They said, "No, you don't have that kind of luxury. You're going to be dead in a couple of hours."

NOT THE POLICE—BUT GOD

The last option left was to say somehow before my death "True Parents, mansei" three times. So I measured the time in my brain; my physical body was failing after so many hours in captivity. I squeezed out every ounce of energy and stood up and shouted out the three cheers with my entire body: "Aboji, mansei!!" Three times I shouted. All the captors were not in the same room at that time. Everybody came running in. They rushed into me, hitting me and knocking me down. They tortured me with electric shock. All hell broke loose because they thought I was calling the police. Actually, I was calling God, but they thought I was calling the police. Boy, that was incredible.

They bound me even tighter and gagged me so that I could not yell out any more. They completely immobilized me; I could not move an inch. I could hear a noise downstairs, the rattling of a drum can.

So I thought, boy, they are really getting ready for me. When they had taken me out of the car I was without shoes, and I said, "Where are my shoes?" They bound my feet and one of the kidnappers said, "You need shoes? A dead body doesn't need shoes."

My mouth was gagged and cut inside, but in my mind I kept saying,"Aboji, mansei, Aboji, mansei." When they killed me, I wanted my final word to be "Aboji, mansei."

They also used psychological torture. They were professionals, and they knew how to do it. They had an empty gun. I could not see it because I was blindfolded, but I know what a pistol sounds like when it's being loaded. I could hear the loading sound, then they pulled the trigger. They were doing it to scare me, doing it again and again and again. It was making me crazy. The kidnappers kept saying, "Just one bullet, no matter how important you are, no matter how great a man you are, no matter how much work you have done, no matter what belief you have in God, it doesn't make any difference, one bullet will finish you."

Eventually I was sure that 1:00 a.m. had past, but the execution hadn't come. I was desperately trying to remain conscious, trying not to sleep. They said they were waiting for a message, the final order, to execute me. The night passed. The kidnappers said that someone was coming at 8 o'clock in the morning, and he would decide my fate.

That man came at 8 o'clock and stood in front of me. I could not see him but, through his voice, I could see him. He was none other than one Korean I knew very well, who had even tried to be a member of the Unification Church. He was trying to exploit the Unification Church. He thought the Unification Church had a money tree somewhere, that he could squeeze money from our church. He thought he could do it through me.

At that point, I was a little bit comforted knowing my kidnapping was not a political game for communists, that it was a money game. I had a little hope, but not much, because I had no way to deliver the money, that is for sure. And I wouldn't deliver the money, even if I had it.

MOTHER WARNED ME

The next night, I was physically and mentally exhausted. They let me lie down on the floor, bound and gagged, and have a little rest. That moment I had a dream, and this is the second reason I came out alive. Mother appeared, shaking me and waking me up. Mother told me in a clear voice three times, "Bo Hi, unless you get out of this place in the next 10 hours, you will be killed. Do everything you can and get out of this place in 10 hours." That was Mother. I was shaken up and somehow my energy and power were coming back. So I started planning. Like a good military man, I started strategizing. What can I do? What is the strategy? You know, the best strategy is always the bold strategy. It is the same for you and me and for ACC and AFC and CAUSA International. The bold strategy is always the best strategy.

At 9 o'clock the next morning they took me to another room and began the negotiation for money. They had a telephone on the table, and they told me to call my bank and ask the bank to deliver $1 million cash to this place. I told them—I was very bold, because of the dream Mother gave me, knowing that Father and Mother were with me—I told them, "Are you guys kidding me? I will not call the bank. I'd rather be killed. You can kill me now and bury me, because that is a lot easier. There's no way you can get $1 million out of me, because first of all, it is physically impossible. I have no money of my own." My captor said, "You have a big company, News World Communications, all kinds of newspapers and businesses; they have all kinds of money." I'm head of the Unification Church International and they thought the church has millions of dollars. "Even if there is money," I told them, "if I asked the bank to bring $1 million, you know the FBI is everywhere right now. I disappeared 40 hours ago. Give the FBI a clue through a telephone call where I am and where you are, and they will surround this house. I know you're going to kill me first before you run away, isn't that true? So why should I do it?"

I was very bold. I said, "Go ahead and kill me, let's finish this whole episode." I was very powerful and bold at that point. The tables were turned; I was the master, commanding the situation. They were like helpless children, not knowing what to do. I told them again that if I called, they would be captured and in the process I'd be killed. So they began to negotiate with me, asking, "Dr. Pak, please help me. What can you do?" I said, "There's nothing I can do." Then they said, "What about just a little money? You could ask for a bank transfer to a Swiss bank."

Well, at that point, I remembered Mother saying, "Get out of this place within 10 hours, otherwise you'll be killed." They were trying to negotiate with me, but I took the upper hand. I knew that a bank transfer takes three days. And during that time the FBI would stop it. In my mind I figured that out.

I agreed to transfer some money but not $1 million. They said, "No, $1 million." I said, "No, probably $250,000." They said, "No, no, at least $500,000." "All right, $500,000." Not a lot of negotiation, but I told them, "Still I will not call the bank." That was my ultimatum. I will not call because when the bank receives my call, they would not obey my instructions. They know that I have been kidnapped. Bankers are not that foolish. So he asked, "What are our options?" "There's only one option." "What's that?" This was really bold—I said, "Let me go to the bank myself. The bank is in Washington. Another condition: nobody will follow me. It's 10:30. There is a 12:00 flight from La Guardia. It takes one hour to Washington. If I get to the bank by 2:00, I'll be able to do what you want before the bank closes at 3:00."

At that point they had no choice. So they started ordering their little boys, saying, "Boys, get his jacket. Where are his eyeglasses? Where's his watch!" Everybody was worrying about me now, trying to put clothes on me. My watch and eyeglasses were given back, the handcuffs were taken off. They said, "Go now. Your car is ready." I walked out of the kidnappers' house like a commanding general. They all came out to say goodbye to me. Just the driver and one escort drove me to La Guardia. I got out of the car there and told them to leave, otherwise I wouldn't leave. So they said goodbye, and I took off.

Incredible. I wanted to be a man of my word. I didn't want to be a liar. Later on I didn't want to be accused by these people, because they could kidnap me a second time and say, "You lied to us. What did you do to me—BANG!" They could kill me any time. I knew that, right? So I did not call anybody at the airport. I came to Washington and went to the bank and ordered $500,000 transferred to a Swiss bank, thinking that the FBI would stop it. That happened exactly as planned.

After I made that order, I went home to McLean, Virginia, and the FBI were there, listening to all the telephone calls, with two men posted outside and two men inside. My wife was in New York, but my children were there. I knocked on the door and walked in. They said, "Who are you?" I said, "Who are you?" "We're from the FBI!" "Why are you here?" "Because the man of this house has been kidnapped." "That's me." They were completely flabbergasted. Then I made a call to Mother and said, "Mother, thank you, Father and Mother, you saved my life." Then two FBI men escorted me to East Garden. They took me in a special car and special plane to East Garden from Washington. I met Mother, and Mother was absolutely, completely pouring out love. She was crying, rejoicing, almost like a dead son had come alive.

What I'm trying to say is that my second life is over. I have to pay it as a ransom. Love of True Father and his prayer and the intervention of True Mother saved my second life.

NEW DISPENSATIONAL WORK

This is the third time. Up to 1978 the Unification Church has failed. Members have failed many, many times, including myself. Father already predicted that 1988 would be an important year, that something very important should happen in 1988, that a new unity must be made, and that's why this entire new dispensational work of Heung Jin Nim came. In each country the leaders were the worst treated; in Japan, Mr. Kuboki is not well, he is still recovering in hospital; in Korea, Rev. Young Whi Kim was the hardest hit; here in America, somehow Bo Hi Pak was chosen. Now I feel honored, but when I was facing that ordeal, my only prayer was that I wouldn't die there. No matter how difficult the ordeal, it's OK, so long as I come out alive. It wouldn't be good for anybody, the church, Father, Mother, you, me. I didn't want to become a problem for the church.

In any case, when I went back to Korea, I thought I could recover. But on the contrary, there was blood in my head. A vein was broken and blood was leaking every day, accumulating inside my skull and putting pressure on my brain. That's why my brain could not function and I could not handle myself.

That night I suffered the most incredible headache of my entire life. The next morning my brother, Jim Gavin, and my wife took me to the hospital, Seoul National University Hospital, which is supposed to be the best hospital in Korea. After examining me, the doctor didn't waste a moment. He said, "You've got to be operated on at once, because each hour is critical. Once the blood penetrates the brain, you will be a vegetable." But I didn't want to be operated on without Father and Mother's permission. So we went to the East Garden of Korea, but Father was away. We were waiting and waiting and waiting without knowing when they were coming back. I know now that if Father and Mother had returned even one day later, I would not be here today.

But thank God, they came that evening at 7 p.m. While we were at the dinner table, I told Father what the doctor said, and Father said to go immediately to the hospital and have the operation. Father and Mother were so serious to give protection, like a guarantee, so Father asked Mother to bring some money to pay in advance. I told them that wasn't necessary, but Mother said to pay something in advance, that it would be like a heavenly guarantee. She said, "Don't even go home, go directly from here to the hospital." Father took me out of the room, helped me into the car, shook hands with me, and waved until my car disappeared. That was very special.

The next day, December 30, I had a full examination, x-ray, blood test, in preparation for the operation. At 7:30 a.m. on December 31, the last day of 1987, an Il Jung candle was lit and I was lying on a hospital gurney. My wife saw on my hospital gown True Parents' pictures and Heung Jin Nim's picture. I don't remember, but later on members told me I demanded one final prayer before I went out. I didn't remember doing that, but someone recorded it.

At 5:30 that morning they came to shave my head. Oh, that was painful. In one minute I became a monk. So I need my hair to grow; this is the best so far. I was on the hospital operating table for three hours, with many members praying outside. Jim Gavin, my wife, and my brothers suffered more than I did, because I was unconscious. I had no way to suffer, but they suffered.

The operation was critical. They were supposed to open up four holes in my head, with two in my forehead. Can you imagine me having two holes in my forehead for the rest of my life? The doctor reconsidered. Although they had never done so before, they reduced it to two holes instead of four. They made a hole right here. As soon as the surgeon opened up one hole, blood shot out like a fountain, two feet. The surgeon's gown was completely wet with my blood. The doctor later told me, "When I saw the blood shooting out like that, I knew you would have been dead if that operation had been delayed 24 more hours."

FATHER PRAYED FOR ME

It was the final day of 1987. The next day, January 1, 1988, was a holiday. In Korea, January 2 and 3 are also holidays. The earliest I could have been operated on was January 4. I would not have been alive by January 4. It was that close. The day before my operation Father took the disciples to the holy ground at Chung Pyung Lake, at the top of the mountain, and had a special prayer for me. Mother came back and called me at the hospital, letting me know that Father had said a special prayer for me. How grateful I was.

On the day of the operation, a spiritual lady was praying all three hours and she saw a vision from heaven. She saw two birds, cranes, come down and land on my head, healing the entire wounded area, taking out all the rotten blood. Immediately the entire wounded area was made whole. The crane represented Mother. So what I'm trying to say to you is this: My life was saved because of the True Parents. My testimony in our church has always been that I am living and dying for the sake of True Parents. That one line is my life. Over and over because of their love and power and prayer and the Holy Spirit, I was restored.

Yesterday, after dinner Father asked me, "How do you feel? Are you OK? Are you strong?" I answered Father by saying, "Father and Mother, I wanted to say this on the plane and at East Garden, but I didn't quite have the courage to say it, but now I say it, because you asked me: Father and Mother, thank you, because so many times in Korea in the hospital I felt, this is the end of it, I will never come back to America again."

So that's the story. I'm very happy to stand before you, and I feel fine. I'll be busy, I'll be even more dedicated for the sake and mission of our True Parents. Join with me. That is my testimony to you. In 1988, because of such incredible indemnity we all paid in the year of 1987, we're going to make a miracle. A political miracle has come in the Honduras situation, as well as Ollie North's indictment. Father saw that this would be an opportunity to influence public opinion in America. And we're going to launch an incredible offensive at this time.

I would like to have all the regional directors and some state leaders ready to report to Father. In one year the ACC/AFC made a miracle. If Father gives us another six months, this country will never be the same. We're going to create an entirely new atmosphere, new power, new influences. The political system in this country will never be the same because of us, our presence. Already many people in Washington conservative circles are saying: The most influential group to move America is ACC and AFC. I'm not saying it, those people are saying it. Because no other organization is in 50 states, systematically organized and sacrificially serving. You're growing every day, you're becoming a leader every day, you feel so tall. I look at you as tall men now. Tall political saints, not political animals. We all are supposed to become political saints, that's what you are. That's going to be happening, that has happened. This year we want to do the job that would take other people probably 10 years or 100 years. Amen? Amen!

This time when we go to New York, I want you to dress up well, comb your hair nicely, shave yourself well, show Father and Mother how much you have grown spiritually in political savvy and acumen, and still maintain your purity like an innocent dove. That's what I want you to do at East Garden. We'll really shout it out: we shall bring the total victory for our

True Parents. Remember that. That's all I ask, show Father confidence. The mobilization soon begins: throughout the world 7,000 Western members and Japanese members will be coming to Korea. But I do not think ACC/AFC members will be affected, because you are the only ones in the state. All our churches will be affected.

So what I'm saying is that America is upon your shoulders. What you do or you don't do will affect this country. Father trusts you for America. You are going to be the ones to take responsibility for America. You're the main players and Father knows that. That's why Father leaves you alone in America, lets you do your work. In the meantime many, many other members will be mobilized for Korea. Maybe some of your spouses will be going. Thank God in that case. Don't hesitate to accept any order from the True Parents. That guarantees you the greatest success. Don't worry about anything, don't worry about any order. Know that your Father trusts you, and you are responsible for America, and Father will leave you alone to do the work to change the destiny for this country and, by doing so, change the destiny for the world. In order to do that, you've got to win the True Parents' favor. Trust, credibility—that's the mission of tomorrow. That's what you're going off to New York for. That's all I can say. I know what you do. You are children, you are mature leaders, you know how to report to Father, you know the Bo Hi Pak style. Do it and exceed my expectations. Give Father confidence, saying, "Father, we'll do it, we'll take care of America, America will not be the same."

That's what I'm asking you to do. The details are up to you. That's all I can say. I don't know what time it is now, I don't have a watch, but it's just about time to break, so go ahead, have a great breakfast, be good soldiers. Go to service and then go to the lectures, attend every lecture, do not escape or be absent from the lectures. You are renewing yourself in those lectures, it's very important. That's why every time, as much as I can, I listen to the lectures. Tom Ward's lectures, Bill Lay's lectures, I've heard 100 times, but I'm still doing it. Maybe not today though. I have so much to pin down this morning. But you, don't miss the lectures. Show your most incredible dedication and concentration that will affect the rest of the leaders who came here.

I would like you to have the opportunity to fellowship with the regional directors, but I promise I will try to come back next month. In April Father will already be in Korea. I would like to have two days of beautiful fellowship with you and the opportunity to listen to each one of you. But this time, look forward to seeing Father, give him confidence, let him trust you, let him feel that his providence is winning here in America. That's all I ask you.

So, prepare your tie, shirt, clean hair, eyes shining, with your voice full of power, coming out of your gut. Thank God we have this opportunity. This is a miracle in itself for me. Let us pray.

Prayer by Bo Hi Pak:

Our Heavenly Father, we thank You for this most beautiful opportunity to share this testimony with our dear brothers and sisters. Those are the people, Father, who are responsible for America. By doing the mission here in America, they are responsible for the world. Father, we can do it, we can do it. The disciples of Jesus, 12 of them, turned the world upside down. Father, children of our True Parents, 60, 70, 80 of them assigned to this very special so-called African mission, will turn this nation upside-down and right-side up. By doing so, we do it for the rest of the world. God, Heavenly Father, and the True Parents, rest assured, we will be Your children, we will be Your proud children, we will do Your will, we shall be victorious, we will become, each one of us, somebody Heaven and True Parents can be really proud of. All of these things we pray in the name of the most precious True Parents. Amen, amen, amen! Thank you.

A VICTORY OF TRUE LOVE

NEW YORK, NEW YORK
AUGUST 20, 1988

In honor of the third anniversary of Father's release from Danbury, the New York members gathered at the World Mission Center to celebrate, beginning with a special message from Dr. Pak. In his sermon, Dr. Pak explains how much Father accomplished providentially while in Danbury and how many victories were won despite his incarceration.

Good morning. This third anniversary of Father's release from prison is a great opportunity to gather together for this most meaningful celebration. I know that you already know most of the facts concerning Father's incarceration in Danbury. But this is our great tradition—we must remind ourselves of the meaning of this day.

What does Danbury represent? Danbury represents a victory over gross injustice. Father responded to this injustice not with revenge or retaliation, but with true love. Danbury is our symbolic cross, and upon that cross, resurrection took place all over the world.

Let me elaborate on how the United States government worked its injustice upon Father. First of all, Father was indicted on very dubious fabricated charges. Father's indictment came on October 15, 1981. At that time Father was in Korea. Our lawyers' unanimous recommendation was that Father should not have to come back to subject himself to humiliation by the United States government. He is a Korean citizen, and there is no extradition treaty between the United States and the Republic of Korea. After all, they were trying to keep Father off United States soil. But when I conveyed this message to Father, he immdiately said, "I did not go to the United States for my own comfort. I went there by the order of Heavenly Father, and I have a mission in America. Whatever cross I must bear, my mission comes first." Father volunteered to come to America immediately, knowing his path was going to be arduous and painful.

I AM NOT GUILTY

On October 22, 1981, Father was arraigned in Foley Square in Manhattan by the District Court of New York. I was there, translating for Father when Father stood before the judge. Father kept his dignity and only spoke one sentence: "Your honor, I am not guilty."

Then the trial began on April 1, 1982, and lasted for 48 days. This trial was not justice. It was almost like the communists' style of court. Using the public's biased opinion, the United States government was determined to send Father to jail. Finally, the judge asked Father if he wanted to speak to the jury in his own defense. Father declined, saying, "I am not here to defend myself. I am here for a mission." That was Father's stand.

During that whole time, during the break hours at the trial, Father was sitting in a back room with a few staff members making plans for *The Washington Times* building. He did this while the United States of America was trying to destroy his reputation and the honor that he had built over his whole life.

Father entered Danbury on July 20, 1984. That day the members were all sobbing. Father was the only one who was not sobbing, and he scolded the members, saying, "I am now leaving for Danbury full of hope. God has prepared something extraordinary for me there. I am looking forward to discovering the miracle of Danbury."

Senator Orrin G. Hatch, chairman of the Senate Judiciary Committee's Subcommittee on the Constitution, conducted a special investigation about Father's case. He came up with this conclusion: "I do feel strongly, after my subcommittee has carefully and objectively reviewed Reverend Moon's case from both sides, that injustice rather than justice has been done."

I will give a few simple facts that Senator Hatch found. First, consider the following: Three Justice Department attorneys, who each undertook a review of a possible criminal action against Father, agreed unanimously and independently of each other that there was no case for a trial. This was the Justice Department's own conclusion, by three different levels of government attorneys. Yet even though they came to this conclusion, Father was still indicted.

Second, the Justice Department's own guidelines state that criminal tax cases will not be tried if the alleged tax deficiency is less than $2,500 a year; three times $2,500 equals $7,500. According to the Justice Department's review, Father's tax liability was only $7,300 for a three-year period. So who broke the law? The Justice Department broke their own law in order to indict Father.

Third, despite the government attorneys' recommendation not to prosecute, and despite the fact that there was no evidence of any kind to establish that even a single cent of the money in dispute was spent by Father personally and not for the sake of the church, the Justice Department was pesuaded to seek an indictment by government attorneys in New York, who built the case entirely on supposition and innuendo.

Fourth, Father wisely asked for a non-jury trial, knowing already that the government was trying to destroy him through public opinion. Normally the Justice Department welcomes this, because it's a much cheaper, much easier trial. However, the prosecutor refused, insisting that Father be tried by a jury.

THEY ARE AFTER BLOOD

This is the skeleton truth about the injustice that the United States government worked upon Father. That's why the lawyers recommended that Father not come to America, saying to him, "They are after blood! Why should you subject yourself to such a bloodthirsty Justice Depatment?" But Father came because he loves America. He loves his mission and he loves Heavenly Father. Even though he knew he might end up in jail, he came.

When Father entered Danbury, he got a very cool reception. Because of the work of the American media, even the inmates thought, "Oh, no! That monster Reverend Moon is coming here!" But Father did not even bother with that; he didn't lose a bit of his composure. He just began to love all the inmates from day one.

Father was not allowed to preach at all in Danbury, but Reverend Graham, the chaplain of Danbury prison, agreed to let him pray in the chapel for two hours every Sunday. Reverend Graham asked Father, "What time would you like to have?" Father simply said, "Three a.m." Reverend Graham looked at Father, puzzled. "What do you do at three a.m.?" Father said, "That is my prayer hour. I pray at three a.m. every day, whether in a chapel or not. I love to pray at three a.m. because at that hour, the hotline between God and the earth is open. I can monopolize it!" The first inmate who joined Father to pray in the chapel at three a.m. was Bill Sheppard. Father had told him, "You don't have to come because I pray in Korean." But Bill said, "The reason why I want to come, with you is because of the spiritual atmosphere. I want to be with you." So Father became known as a man of prayer in prison.

He also became know as a father figure. Within a couple of weeks, very quickly, Father began to be respected, even without preaching one word. That is why I say he is the personification of the Principle. Father doesn't have to preach to convey the Principle, because his entire life is the Principle. His twinkling eyes are the Principle; his laughter is the Principle; every action, every step he takes, is the Principle. People feel it to the bone.

Father was given the job to scrub the floor of the kitchen and clean the toilets and feed the inmates. Father did it with joy and gratitude to Heavenly Father. Father thought, "This is my greatest honor. I am cleaning up America. I am cleaning up the fallen world. I'm feeding these children of God who are, in a way, the most unfortunate children of God on the face of the earth." Soon respect among the inmates of Danbury prison toward Father was not only growing, but became unquestionable.

WILL YOU BE MY FATHER?

Once a young man approached Father and said to him, "Reverend Moon, I have a personal request. You know, I never had a father. He died before I was born. I've always wanted to have a father. Reverend Moon, you are that father to me. From this time on, can I call you Father?" This occurred without his even hearing one word of the Principle! Father embraced this young man, patting him on his back, saying, "Son, I'm honored to be your father."

Father had one deep regret in prison. One morning a young inmate hung himself from a tree. Father was stricken. He said, "If only I had met that young man three days earlier, I could probably have saved his life." He did not complain about the food; he did not complain about the bunk or the hard work. His only regret was that precious young man who had killed himself.

I want you to know that the spirit Father kept in Danbury was proclaimed in the United States Congress. When Senator Orrin Hatch invited Father to the United States Senate on June 26, 1984, to give his testimony, Father said:

I am honored to dedicate myself today to the preservation of religious freedom in this country. If I can raise up a beacon warning Americans of the danger which lies ahead, then my sacrifice will serve a great purpose. The issue today is the very survival of America and the free world. To assure this survival, I'm willing to suffer any indignity, to go any distance, to do any labor, and to bear any cross. I'm even willing to give my life if that will insure that the nation and world survive and do God's will. ... I have no hostility toward the United States government. Instead, I pray for this country. I thank God that He is using me as His instrument to lead the fight for religious freedom and ignite the spiritual awakening of America in this most crucial hour of human history.

Yes, a miracle came in Danbury. Public opinion changed. The attitude of established Christianity now has been changed. When Father's court case was brought to the attention of the Supreme Court, 40 prominent organizations and individuals petitioned on behalf of Father. These individuals and groups represent over 160 million American people. Thus, in this sense, through Father's court case, Father won 160 million American people to his side.

On this day, I would also like to note that this was the period of growth for everybody, including the True Family. Hyo Jin Nim just mentioned that a tremendous transformation took place in him during Father's incarceration. The True Family joined side by side together with Father in his suffering. While Father was in prison, Hyo Jin Nim initiated a 40-day prayer vigil during the cold nights of winter. But then after 40 days, Hyo Jin Nim thought it was not enough, and he initiated another 40-day condition, and then another—120 days in all. Hyo Jin Nim's courageous example was willingly followed by all the True Family and the East Garden staff. We are celebrating this and many other victories today.

FATHER IS NOT ALONE

Two thousand years ago when Jesus was crucified, he was all by himself. But 2,000 years later, when True Father was crucified in Danbury, he was not alone. It should be a source of pride to us that during that time our movement sprang into action and spread out. Many of our greatest projects were conceived by Father in Danbury: The *Washington Times*, *Insight* magazine, *The World & I*, the ICC program, and dozens of others. Our movement prospered more than ever during Father's incarceration.

Furthermore, Father was not alone even in Danbury. He was with a most trusted disciple, Mr. Kamiyama, who bore the cross together with Father. Two thousand years ago, even Peter denied Jesus three times. If the 12 disciples had rallied around Jesus and hung together with Jesus on the cross, an entirely different Christianity would have been born. But instead of denying Father during his incarceration, we united and worked together and created an even greater victory. This is your pride and my pride and True Family's pride.

Mr. Kamiyama has been a faithful follower of True Parents for a long, long time. He was the one to walk alongside Father in Danbury. He was Father's secretary, chief-of-staff, bodyguard, errand boy, liaison—everything in one person. I'm so glad God's dispensation worked in such a way that Mr. Kamiyama could stay with Father. And after Mr. Kamiyama's release, men like Bill Sheppard and Larry Evola followed Mr. Kamiyama's pattern exactly, and so a tradition of serving Father in prison was established. God prepared people everywhere. At the halfway house there was a most dedicated man with whom Father shared a room. All night this man stayed awake in front of a small television with the sound level turned down, sitting in a chair placed against the door to prevent anyone from coming into that room while Father was sleeping. How can you say God does not work in mysterious ways?

AMERICA, YOUR TIME HAS COME

WASHINGTON, D.C.

NOVEMBER 13, 1988

―――――――――――――――――――

*Dr. Pak speaks intimately and with great pride to all the
American Freedom Coalition and American Constitutional
Committee leaders after pledge service. He reports that
Father asked the members at the recent leaders conference
to lecture Divine Principle eight hours a day as a condition
to increase the membership. He asks each of the AFC/ACC
leaders to give brief reports from their states in preparation for reporting directly to Father and congratulates
them on the effort they all made toward the victory of
George Bush's election.*

When I ask Father about having only one AFC/ACC representative in
each state, Father always replies, "God sent only one messiah to the entire
globe." I can't win, you know. I am trying to get more people, so I always
emphasize, Father, only one in a state, but Father says, one messiah for five
billion people. So what can I say? You are the messiah of your state.

This morning I really do not want to talk for hours. I want to hear
from you. Also I want to give the regional directors a chance to practice
your reports before you give them to Father and Mother. That will definitely happen unless some emergency occurs. Father and Mother are most

anxious to have you in East Garden after the conclusion of the Washington activities. Father arrived on November 7, the election was on the 8th, Children's Day the 9th, then the leaders' conference on the 10th. I did not ask Father to include you in that conference. On November 9, you had to take care of your flocks, your spiritual children. After the election you had to organize many things. But I have a separate ambition, to have all of you be invited as a single group to East Garden so that Father and Mother can concentrate on your activities only.

You know membership is so scarce, particularly after so many members went back to Japan and Europe, and the numbers are decreasing in this country. Father was deeply concerned. His message in that meeting can be summed up in only one sentence: America, your time has come. The American movement must increase membership. So Father expounded for five and a half hours on the importance of witnessing, bringing spiritual children into the center. Father said we should go back to the original tradition of the Unification Church, that is, 16 hours lecturing. Mr. Eu, the late president of the HSA-UWC in Korea, lectured every day for 16 hours. Sometimes no one came to listen and Father was a student, sitting there for 16 hours listening. He said, this is my Divine Principle and this is my expression of the truth. I am the center of the Divine Principle, but I was like a student sitting in front of Mr. Eu listening for 16 hours a day. That is the way the Unification Church foundation was laid. You do the same.

So at the end of the day our members pledged to Father and Mother to lecture at least eight hours a day, no matter what. Each week two cycles of Divine Principle shall be taught. If there are no listeners, speak to the wall, speak to the trees, cry out. God will send you children. That was the message.

Twenty-one day workshops will begin in every center. That means everybody will hear six cycles of Divine Principle in 21 days. That does not mean one person has to be on staff 21 days. The lecturers can change. Anyone can come in any day at any hour and start 21 days. After 21 days is successfully completed, that person will become a member. Thus, we can increase our membership.

The George Bush victory was seen by Father, and together with Father I explained how the election was going, state elections and so forth. Father's expectation and complete faith was that the George Bush/Dan Quayle team could never win that kind of victory without you. So Father did it because you did it. That was the confidence and joy and satisfaction Father has in his heart and we returned that glory.

Now I would like to have the 10 regional directors come up here in front and one by one give a report. Each one will have exactly five minutes. Who is going to be our chime? Bob Spitz, you have a good watch. Every five minutes you lift your finger and signal. They cannot speak more than five minutes. Five minutes is up—out. This is good training. You have to give a certain message within so many minutes. It doesn't have to be perfect today. Make any mistakes now, so you won't make a mistake in East Garden. I just need to know the impression of how your region has done in this election, what things are happening. Of course, already two or three phenomena were reported by Michael Beard, Michael Leone and Gary Jarmin, and all these I already reported to Father. Father was delighted to hear several extraordinary things that happened. But now I want to hear a little bit more deeply from each region, and you can all hear what is happening in other regions. That is very, very important.

[After all the reports, Dr. Pak continued.]

I wish we could have more time, but the service is beginning right now. We have to go out right away. However, I suggest a couple of things. Mike, you did a beautiful job in presenting all this, but especially I am happy you prepared the gold cup for Father and Mother. That is the most important thing. When I receive something, I always feel uncomfortable because I would rather have Father and Mother receive it. I hope that is genuine gold.

Mike Leone, you discussed with Bob Grant one of those sessions with the Board of Governors. I would like to invite Tom Ward and Bill Lay and Rick Swarts to present those plaques once again in front of the Board of Governors. I will be there too to receive mine. That is one occasion I will show up, because this kind of thing is so important and I don't want it to be done casually.

Finally, all the regional directors, when you report to Father and Mother, you are right. Absolutely Heavenly Father and True Parents made the difference for victory. Jim, I would like you to take this chart with you and add something to it. This shows that without our help George Bush could not win. Those states with close votes, about 10 of them, could have gone the other way. Those 168 electoral votes could have gone to Dukakis without us. If Michael Dukakis got those 168 votes in addition to the 112, he would have gotten 280 votes, more than the 270 he would have needed. That means victory would have gone to Dukakis. This is the kind of thing that really shows we are making a difference. Not just a loud voice, but substantial results.

But I want you to know, as many of you already said, it is God and True Parents who made this victory this year. Father said, behind every bush is a Moonie. Father also said a bush has no trunk. George Bush is all bushes. We are the trunk, Father said. It is another way of explaining how Father's incredible mind is working. Bush has to be molded into a trunk. If he stays a simple bush, he has no power, no energy. In any case, you regional directors, everybody, report in my tradition: give all the glory, all the commitment to the True Parents, period. Because that is what brought the victory. Begin with the glory of True Parents, and close with the victory of True Parents. That is the way you report. Attribute everything to the True Parents. That is the way I feel. If you did not win this time in certain cases, fine. That doesn't matter. We are laying a tremendous foundation. We won a most incredible victory.

I want you to go and help the great service this morning. Have a great breakfast and a great day. I will see you later on today and tomorrow. God bless you, great brothers.

STAYING ALIVE

MIAMI, FLORIDA

DECEMBER 11, 1988

Here, Dr. Pak encourages, inspires, and compliments the hard work of the American Leadership Conference and expresses great confidence in what they can and will accomplish in the future.

This morning I want to share just a few things with you, and I want to hear state leaders this time instead of regional directors. I want to hear five-minute reports from those state leaders who brought the most state legislators. Most of all, I want to see your spirit. Remember the last time we saw Father at East Garden? He said, "You all look good, shining." Father said your eyes were shining. With those two sentences I knew that conference was very, very successful because Father seldom says such a thing. Father does not give complements for just anything. You know that, right? Father does not pay lip service. If Father says it, he means it. So when Father said that, I was jubilant. I almost could not hear what Father said next.

In any case, that was a historical conference. We never had that kind of conference before. That was the most smooth, most comforting, loving conference at East Garden. After that experience, after Father's talk at that time, I do not have too much to share today. You have that impact still alive in your heart.

This morning what I want to share is this: America has more and more come into the hands of American leadership. Father is spending more time in Korea; many old Japanese members had to return to Japan; and Reverend Kwak, who has been leading the World Missions Department, has now been given a more primary assignment in Korea. For that reason most of the responsibilities Reverend Kwak was fulfilling with the church organization have been transferred to Dr. Durst. That means American leadership. That cannot be done without Father's permission. Father ordered that transfer to happen. American leadership is now the central point of the American movement. That means ACC/AFC and CAUSA International, you are truly, truly the center of the American movement because most of the American seniors, elders, leaders are all here. Father gave ACC/AFC and CAUSA International the best, the elite of our movement, the veterans, seasoned soldiers of our movement.

I know your shoulders are more heavily burdened. You are responsible not only for the mission of ACC and ALC, but also for indirectly assisting America's spiritual movement. That is the implication. For that reason, more than ever, I want you to be exemplary Unificationists. You are more than ever required to become political saints and spiritual saints of the American movement. 1989 is going to be a fantastic year. A lot of work needs to be done. That year is going to be your year: ACC/AFC, CAUSA International, Global Images Associates. It is your year. 1989. We are going to make a truly substantial advance in every direction.

In 1988 we laid the groundwork. In 1989 we will physically bring the achievement so that we can become 10,000-pound gorillas. We choose where we stay. We choose where we sleep.

SPIRITUALLY ALIVE

That is the year that is coming up. As I always said, unless you become an exemplary Unificationist, you cannot become a political saint. Nor can you become a political leader. It has always been my principle and that principle you now know is working. Nothing pleases me more than when members come to say to me that, after tackling the ACC/AFC mission, you have become more spiritually alive. You are more spiritually alert, you are witnessing more and teaching the Divine Principle more. Nothing is more pleasing to me than hearing that kind of testimony. I know that person will succeed, not only in their spiritual life, but in their political mission.

In many, many cases our members get burnt out because they forget their roots. They pursued their mission as a political, PR mission. Soon, their energy sags, they are confused. Their spiritual reservoir has dried up.

I saw many members leave, even after 10 or 15 years of great service to our True Parents.

You can do that. I cannot afford to do that. After 31 years of service, I simply cannot burn out. You must have more spiritual liquid inside. With spiritual fluid abundantly flowing in your body, you will never dry up. You will be deeply ready to be touched, moved to tears. Those people who do not have the experience of being moved to tears are not true Unificationists. Tears, sweat, blood. Those are an integral part of the Unification movement.

So allow yourself to be moved, inspired. When you are in that state, you can move other people. Amazing. No matter how beautifully you have written your speech, if you have no spiritual fluid lubricating your body, you will not move people. You will not inspire people. What is leadership? The quality of inspiring power. That is leadership. You have the quality of inspiring power. Yesterday, after I gave testimony to our True Parents, several state legislators came to me and said, "I have listened to your testimony several times, but tonight it was almost like hearing you for the first time. So refreshing, so touching. I heard it before, but it came to me as brand-new information."

That is the way it should be. Divine Principle, CAUSA material, Godism, can never be stagnant. It is flowing water, not stagnant pond water. Still water becomes smelly, dark green, not pure. Unless water is flowing, it will stagnate. I am always amazed by True Father and True Mother. After listening to Father for 31 years, today is no exception. When he begins to speak, he forgets himself. Forgets time. Forgets eating. Forgets the surroundings. He is full of endless energy and power and the message of resurrection that revives people.

I was at the science conference in California, and Sunday morning we went to Fish House. All the members gathered and Father began to speak. I thought Father would speak probably two hours, or at the most three hours. Father reached the conclusion at three hours. I knew it. I had been translating, and I had the feeling that Father said it all. But Father just could not stop. He had so much love flowing, energy and spirit flowing. Father just kept pounding, going, going, going—for six hours. There I saw the difference between Father and me. After six hours Father looked more energetic. After six hours he was just as fresh as the first moment. He had energy, even after a six-hour sermon, standing and moving around for six hours. He had gotten into the car to return to the hotel, but then he got back out and spent another 15 to 30 minutes looking around that gigantic factory. I confess, I couldn't. My legs wouldn't listen to me anymore. So I stayed in the car. That is the difference between Father and me.

Although we are each a mini-Father, we have a long way to go. But we are doing very well. You are winning. You are winning handsomely. So, be sure to be good Unificationists. Read the Divine Principle every day. When we read the Divine Principle, it is almost like reading it for the first time. If you are really reading it, that is the way it should be. You always do Pledge Sunday morning at 5:00 at home, with your wife and children. Even the little baby does Pledge. This is all the True Parents' tradition. Also do Pledge the first day of the month and do the Il Jung prayer. Always have the candle ready. Take time to pray. Then you will have that reservoir of spiritual fluid. Spiritual liquid will be abundant in your body, so your character will turn out to be very tasty. People will see it. Almost like juicy fruits, not dried fruits, but juicy fruits. Human beings should be like juicy fruits. People feel it through you; the vibration goes out from you.

If we all had spiritual eyes, we could see our spiritual auras. Everybody has an aura, like wearing a hat. Some people have a more intense aura, more shining. Some people have a less intense aura. I know every one of you wears a good aura, no question about it. But Father and Mother wear an aura like the sun in heaven. In the spiritual world, you cannot stare straight at Father and Mother. You cannot see them because your eyes are blinded by the light, just as Jesus' disciples could not see too well when Jesus transformed into shining light on the Mount of Transfiguration. That is what Father and Mother are spiritually. And we all can be like that. We are spiritual beings; this body is merely a case, a vehicle to carry your spiritual self while you are living here on earth. While on earth your spiritual self can grow more intense and brighter every day through your commitment, practice of true love, connection to True Parents, study of Divine Principle, and doing good actions in accordance with the truth.

TRUE PATRIOTISM

This is why this ALC conference is so important. People can feel that it is not a dry, business-like, anti-communist conference. Yes, we critique communism. No question about it. But we critique communism in order to bring Godism out brilliantly. Communism is like a black backdrop. Then the Godism lectures write white letters on top of that black backdrop. That is why it shines out brilliantly, and that is why it makes an impact. Many people will be motivated when they come here and for the first time in their lifetime experience true patriotism, love of family, love of humanity.

Yesterday I listened to AFC presentations after not hearing them for a long time. The speakers are becoming one of us now; they sound like one of us. I am overjoyed. There is a bigger commitment, more clear direction. Later in the evening one of the speakers was very apologetic, saying he was sorry they didn't do a great job. But I told him he did a great job because I felt the spirit, not only in him, but in every single speaker. Wendy Flint, for example. At dinner she told me the NEA already had a plan to cut her out in the next election to the school board. Do you know what she said? "Wendy Flint must die so that a thousand Wendy Flints will come into being." That moved me to tears. She wanted to be a Joan of Arc of the United States, and as the Bible said, the barley seed must die for new barley to come up. You must feel exactly the same. By dying, we never die. This is the secret. By dying, you become an undying dynamo. You never die. You become a saint. That is all there is to it.

I want you to know clearly that recently I feel my physical limitation. I start to feel that I am not like Joe Tully, Tom Ward, or Matthew Morrison. I am not like big man Mike Leone. For the first time, I am starting to feel I am a little older man than you are. But I am really pushing myself to the edge, because this is not the only mission I have. I have many dozens of responsibilities, especially the China initiative.

Father called me here to the conference. When Peter Kim calls, I know who is calling so immediately that ignited me. I just asked Peter Kim one question: where are you? He said East Garden. Then Father got on the line and I gave a really good report to Father, at least 30 minutes. Father was very, very, very inspired. Father needs to have give and take too, just as much as God needs give and take of love. That is why He created us. God needs give and take of love, and True Parents need give and take of love. You must realize that. We had wonderful give and take with Father and reported all about this conference, all the speakers, and how all of you look. So Father's spirit is here.

You know a secret of our movement. When Father's interest focuses on a project, that project succeeds. When Father forgets a certain project, that project will die. Isn't that true? As long as Father's active interest is with AFC/ACC, CAUSA, American Leadership Conference, we shall be booming. So my role is to become a good mediator between all of you and our projects and Father. That is my mission.

So, spiritually you are more pure every day. Your spiritual liquid is flowing. But politically you are also becoming wiser. Learning, experimenting, experiencing, working. You are becoming better leaders. Initiate, create, fund-raise, so that each state becomes autonomous. Joe Tully told me he visited the Florida AFC headquarters and was impressed. Each state will become a vibrant operating center as much as Washington headquarters. Each state is a nation. The 50 nations in this one United States of America. In that respect you are like a national leader. Vibrant, autonomous, organized, with stamina, planning, execution.

ONLY ONE MESSIAH

I try to emphasize to Father that AFC has only one person in a state, trying to get you some more support. But I never win that game with Father. Father answers that God sent only one messiah on the planet earth. I have nothing more to say after that. So one in each state, in Father's eyes, is too many. Father thinks big, you know. He sees you as the messiah in that state because you are the only link that state has with True Parents. You are the link to the political life of this nation. You are the link.

Because of AFC this nation will be blessed politically. The hands of God are now on all 50 states. You as individuals are the vibrant, most independent, autonomous, creative, dedicated, showcase of leadership in every state. For you regional directors, it is almost like being responsible for one continent. You must feel that way. It is always my conclusion that never before and never after will you meet any person like True Father and True Mother. You always come to the poignant realization that the True Parents are here one time in the entire human history. We are sharing life together in the same time with our True Parents. It is the greatest honor and the greatest responsibility as well.

So, that is all I have to say. You figure it out. I am not going to give you any minor details. You are vibrant, dynamic, creative individuals. By now you know what needs to he done. You figure that out. That is your responsibility. I am just giving you the basic, fundamental core of truth. I am not dealing with the nitty gritty too much anymore—except money problems. Those money people harass me, saying please help me. Those brothers harass me. Hitoshi Nagai always calls me and says, "Dr. Paaaak, how are you, sir?" I tell him I don't want to hear you; don't call me. Hitoshi is very obedient. Yes, sir. He hangs up. He never argues. The problem is I am always the loser and he is always the winner. Sooner or later he catches me somehow. Tom Ward is smart. He never calls about money—he always puts Hitoshi in the hot spot.

In terms of money, ACC/AFC is never that fortunate. Working within the parameter of the budget never happens. You state leaders, regional coordinators, you know that very well. There is no such thing as a budget. I am trying to work always for the best but I always prepare for the worst. If Father does not give us one penny for 1989, is that the end of AFC/ACC? No. Be ready. That is why I am trying to make this organization as autonomous as possible.

So far we have not succeeded completely. We are going to do more. I would like to see at least one million dues-paying members. Not 300,000, 400,000, 500,000. One million. That will happen in 1989. We are going to organize the Ollie North World Freedom Project, a program on SDI, and anti-pornography programs. During the non-election year, those kinds of projects must be promoted. So we will have different kinds of people associating with AFC. The Ollie North project won't be there forever. His trial will be go on for six months or a year. Eventually, however, I want to have Ollie North vindicated and become a hero, become a candidate for political office.

AFC will do different kinds of projects. We will work against pornography, child abuse, free sex, child molesting. All these are the core evils of American society today. We will hit the root.

The bottom line is we want to be autonomous. Even if Father does not give one penny budget, we shall overcome. Father does not give you a budget just to maintain the current level. No. Not at all. Zoom! Grow! When Father sees that possibility, it is more likely we can get that budget. Just maintaining at the same level will never get you the budget. Father invests where miraculous success can be obtained. When AFC shows that kind of potential, then we will have a budget.

We have Pierre Ceyrac from France here. He came here to copy. Be careful. He is a spy now, coming from France trying to duplicate AFC's success in France. I want him to succeed so I want him to be a good spy. Learn everything we have. We are not that stingy. We are going to teach him. France politically is very important. Pierre is going to have a great future in that country. He was the first Blessed brother who served as a National Assembly congressman, and he will again in the future. He is an example of what you could be in this country.

I am using up all your time. I want to hear from two or three people who brought the most in terms of legislators. Which states brought the most? Iowa. OK, Iowa stand up. Come here, please. Give us a five-minute report.

David Payer has been very successful from day one. Many successful things are happening in Iowa. This never happens by accident. It is so important to have dedicated people at the local level leadership. If you have the right person at the top, 90 percent of the work is done. We are people, not machines. This is how we differentiate ourselves from the Marxist point of view. Marx looks at the human being as a machine, a chunk of dirt. But we see ourselves as the image of God, co-creators. So we can have infinite energy and creativity. Human beings are incredible. Each one of you is the image of God, with creativity and endless energy. God's supreme creation.

Also, yesterday at the invitation committee breakfast, someone said that the campaign strategy he used to get elected came from the AFC manual, 12 points. They were his campaign pledges. So, knowingly or unknowingly, you can influence and impact these people. They come here and listen several times. They start to speak like one of us. And they get inspired and win the election.

OK, next state. Mississippi. Then I would like to prepare West Virginia. Tom, make sure that when we take a picture, that an 8x10 print and a cover letter are sent out automatically. This should be our standard operating procedure.

OK, one more report, very quickly. Missouri.

I felt very sorry when James Meredith was so Republican, so anti-Democrat, almost to an embarrassing degree. I respect him as a person. He is a truly godly man, no question about it. He is a spiritual man, a dedicated man, a great American, but his delivery is somewhat embarrassing. Just hitting the Democrats so hard. So we have a problem, of course, getting more Democratic senators and congressmen as speakers here. However, you are bringing a lot of Democrats. But to make sure, tell them Dr. Pak loves Democrats. How can you know? Because he quotes only two presidents, John F. Kennedy and Thomas Jefferson. I am not quoting any Republican until I start quoting Abraham Lincoln some day. But I am quoting only two presidents, Democratic presidents, so tell them Dr. Pak seems to be more Democrat.

You don't hear me using words liberal and conservative too much. Their definitions are also quite difficult. More important is to recognize and fight against the movement that is anti-religion, anti-America, anti-humanity, anti-God. Atheistic humanism is so dangerous, as dangerous as communism. ALC and the CAUSA movement will continue because our job is to make America pro-God, getting back to our roots.

THE BLESSING IS LIBERATION

WASHINGTON, D.C.

APRIL 16, 1989

*Dr. Pak gives a beautiful testimony during morning service
for the staff of the 15th American Leadership Conference,
describing the Holy Wedding of 138 Couples and stress-
ing the incredible power of our individual conscience.*

April 7 we had a beautiful celebration of a Holy Wedding in New York.
There were three tiers of the wedding: those matched couples who could
not go to Korea to attend the Holy Wedding; then we had a married couples Blessing, which was the second or third in the United States and the
largest in our history, 138 couples; and we had an elderly single Blessing,
which was unique in American history. So a lot of history was made.

The day of Blessing started out as hell, an incredibly difficult time. I
am sure those sitting there listening to Father for three hours really felt they
were in hell. Father showed us how unworthy we are to stand before our
True Parents to receive the Blessing. About 400 brothers and sisters, candidates for the Blessing, were in that room listening to Father talk about
the meaning of the heavenly Blessing and True Parents. Not one, I am sure,
felt worthy of sitting in that room. In secular language, I have to say that
all hell broke loose.

This is Father. This is what common people could not do. Father did not hesitate to completely open up the wounds. He didn't hesitate to shake us down to our naked, inner selves. He made it so clear how unworthy we are. He explained absolutely the meaning of the Blessing. Even elder Blessed couples like myself attended that sermon. We rededicated and reconnected through knowing the preciousness of the Blessing and lineage transfer, of changing from one root to another, completely belonging to a different lineage, coming back home to Heavenly Father's blood lineage.

Some members who were not worthy of sitting there were kicked out. The uncompromising standard of selection and judgment came down from heaven. It was hard for everyone, and it was hard for me to translate. But Father gave an uncompromising standard of how important the Holy Wine ceremony and Blessing are. Each Blessed couple can stand before God and True Parents now. Ambassador Phillip Sanchez and his lovely wife went through all that hellish fire.

A little after 10:00 a.m., the ceremony took place. The Holy Wine ceremony was very meaningful and beautiful. Then we had two separate weddings: a matched couples Blessing first, then the married couples Blessing and the single individuals, mostly those over 60 years of age. One lady has served Father for 25 years. One came in a wheelchair.

I want you to know that never before anywhere in the world has the married couple Blessing been conducted in that formal way. Father and Mother wore the ceremonial gowns with their crowns. The setting was beautiful, everyone all lined up, and the sequence of ceremonies was absolutely prepared. We had never before gone through that perfect and most dignified wedding for married couples. In Korea there were several Holy Weddings for married couples, and they were conducted in a simple way, completely different from the matched couple ceremony. They just got together and Father gave them a short talk and then lifted up his hand and Blessed them. That is all. Finished. There was no master of ceremonies, no formal ceremonial gown for Father and Mother.

I had always had the impression that the married couples Blessing is secondary, but this time it was not. Father really gave a tremendous gift to the married couples, making a formal proclamation of the Blessing. In the name of God and True Parents, before the world and humanity and the cosmos, he granted the Blessing to these 138 married couples and 57 single individuals. That was beautiful. This was liberation for many of them. Many of them waited for 10 or 15 years, and all at least seven years. At that point they really felt liberated.

That evening there was a most beautiful banquet that True Parents and True Family attended. This had never happened for married couple

Blessings in the past. But this time everybody got together at the Manhattan Center and had a beautiful celebration, songs, dancing. But most important of all, each one was dedicated to the True Parents and each one had a special testimony to make. A Japanese professor, Kyoshi Natsu, is an old journalist who wrote the two books *The Messiah Appeared* and *The Messiah in Prison*. He and his wife were another celebrity couple Blessed along with Ambassador Sanchez and his wife. They gave a beautiful testimony and a grand bow to our True Parents. Absolutely beautiful.

OUR LINEAGE IS DIFFERENT

You and I simply don't realize, even now, how precious is the Blessing that we have received. But this is what sets us apart from others. Our lineage is different. We are dealing with original sin and with the basic surgical operation to get rid of that original sin. True Parents came to this world empowered to do away with original sin.

AFC had some members who had not been Blessed and went to Korea and received the Blessing. Those who went to Korea, stand up, please. They had extraordinary experiences. All the state leaders are Blessed now. Pamela Kuhl, your husband came or not? [Yes.] God bless you. Where is he? Come, stand beside her. What a good-looking couple. Your husband is really a handsome man, isn't he? Do you truly deserve such a beautiful wife? OK, sit down, right there together.

The spouses of some of you who were Blessed in Korea have not yet come to join you. Does anybody have a problem? Where are they? Korea. Your wife is in Korea? Is she doing well? [Very well.] Good. In that respect we are so fortunate and more solid because we have the most incredible, powerful spiritual bond through the Holy Wedding. That is actually our ultimate secret, and this time our dear Ambassador Phillip Sanchez and Juanita Sanchez found that out and enjoyed it. Let's give them a big hand.

The Unification Church life is almost like the study of tae kwon do. You start out with the white belt, novice level, then you can achieve a blue belt, yellow belt, green belt, brown belt, and finally go for the black belt. People who get a black belt can advance to second-degree black belt, third-degree black belt, etc. The reason I am saying this, Phillip, is you have got them all. You have a black belt now. There are no more surprises. All you have to do is advance in black belt status, second degree, third degree, fourth degree. That is all you need to do. The experience you went through, all of us went through, including myself and my wife, everybody. Normally we do not speak about it, but inside we know what we received and that becomes an unbreakable bond.

Many people throughout the history of the Unification Church have tried to say that the church is a clandestine organization. They criticize us, saying that we are brainwashed and zombies and mind controlled and so forth. You know and I know what we all have gone through. We are not controlled by any brainwashing. We are not controlled by any unholy or immoral or peculiar mechanism to mold a person in a special way and put us in a prison that we can't get out of. Actually, the Unification Church door is wide open, probably more so than any other church in the world. Our doors are open 24 hours a day, and you have every right to walk out that door any time. And you have the privilege to walk in.

WE STRUGGLE LIKE PAUL

This is the reason we have so many ex-Moonies. That is one proof that we are free people. In a way we are really free people in that respect. We have the freedom that St. Paul was seeking. He was seeking true freedom and he agonized over the bondage of sin. Oh wretched man that I am. I can't get rid of these shackles of sin. Inside of me two selves are fighting. One is following the law of the devil, the other is following the law of God. What an agonizing life. That was the confession of St. Paul.

This is exactly what is really binding us and controlling us. It is not Father, it is not even God, it is not even the regulations of the church or a piece of paper or any law in the church. No. What is really controlling us and makes us remain here, what inspires us day after day to do our best— our own conscience. Father recently described conscience as your vertical self. Your body is the horizontal self. Your mind is the vertical self, which is directly connected to the vertical giant self, who is God. So your vertical true love self, your conscience, is supported by your horizontal true love self, your body. We are seeking harmony and unity between the vertical and the horizontal. The conscience always hurts when this crossing point is not 90 degrees. That is why 90 degrees is so emphasized by Father. What comes down from God is always vertical. If the crossing is 90 degrees, your conscience is perfectly clear. You become perfectly satisfied. That will make you exhilarated.

This is what is driving me. Nothing else. No whip is driving me. No threat is driving me. No pressure is driving me. If any pressure is coming from somewhere, it is from within me: my conscience, which is united with Heavenly Father, God. Your conscience becomes your vertical self. Your vertical self has homing devices; it knows where to go, where God wants you to go. That is the secret.

THOSE WHO LEAVE, SUFFER

This is why many ex-Moonies are suffering. They thought they could leave the Unification Church and be freer and happier than they were in the church. When they severed the relationship with the church, they thought, now I am free, I can grow my beard and I can smoke cigarettes and I can drink. Oh, I can do anything. Usually they get out of the church and do that for three days. Grow beards, drink beers, thinking, I am free. But what happens? Day after day they become more imprisoned. Who imprisoned them? Their own conscience. Their own vertical self keeps saying, no, no, you are wrong. Their homing device is saying you are going in the wrong direction. And they begin to suffer. Even if you are high on drugs or liquor or whatever, trying to forget and enjoy, you can't do it.

More than 20 years ago I was pioneering in Washington, D.C., like a state leader. At that time one member who joined was Joe Badra. Joe was here in 1965 when Father came to America. He was like the head of the church in Washington area. He was a powerful senior member of the church and is the one who fund-raised and donated the money so that we could welcome Father. Today, we have the New Yorker and East Garden and Belvedere, and in Washington we have Capital Gardens and Jefferson House. But in those days, we had 3421 North Utah Street, a small house. My house, actually, and at the same time the church center and the regional headquarters. And that became Father's quarters when he visited in 1965. Joe Badra was there attending.

To make a long story short, some years later Joe Badra left the church and married outside. That happened about 20 years ago. But he couldn't get away from the church. His vertical self took him to task and punished him. He was literally in hell for 20 years. Joe is a very good businessman, and he made a lot of money. But nothing satisfied him until he came back and was accepted by the True Parents. He was dying to be Blessed this time as a married couple. He was waiting and waiting. Of course, his wife was ready, too, after she came to know the Principle.

Joe and his wife were one of the 138 couples in New York this time. Father was looking around, walking around; Father's eyes were everywhere. He said, "Joe." "Yes sir." Father gave him a very hard time. "Your wife was like the serpent in the Garden of Eden, like the archangel. She was responsible, wasn't she?" He really gave him a hard time. They went to the bottom of hell. Father scolded both of them, yet Father approved them. That is the beautiful thing. In other words, they were not just quietly included in the 138 couples. No. Father actually questioned them and scolded them and then Father accepted them. This gave them such a liberation. So after they were Blessed, I talked to Joe and he said, "My wife and I are floating six feet high. I am so liberated." You see, this is how things work in the Unification Church. Nobody is governing you except your vertical self, your own conscience, which is the dwelling place of God. This is the way it works.

LIBERATE THEM AND WELCOME THEM

During that 20 years of suffering, how many times did Joe try to get out of it and completely forget it? He couldn't do it. Many other ex-Moonies are suffering today exactly the same suffering that Joe Badra went through. But they do not have a way out or the courage or momentum to come back and renew themselves. Therefore, the time has come to become a tribal messiah. If you become a tribal messiah, you can liberate them. You can bring them in. This is the time for ex-Moonies to come home. They are like the prodigal son coming home. We are the ones to welcome them. They are not cursed. They should not remain cursed. No. They should be liberated. This is very, very important. Don't hesitate to do that. Give your embrace, your warm embrace to these ex-Moonies out there in your area. Communicate with them. This is very, very important.

So if we have any secret power, this is it. It comes from the Divine Principle. Once you know the Divine Principle, you cannot get the Divine Principle out of your brain cells for eternity. You cannot. This is not an ordinary book. This is not fiction. This is what Kyoshi Natsu said: "When I read Divine Principle, I think how in the world could any man's brain come up with this kind of principle? It's impossible. God must be speaking to this man." Kyoshi Natsu testified, "I came to the conclusion that Reverend Moon is half God and half man." What a beautiful expression. He must be half God and half man. Otherwise, we could not have the Divine Principle.

Divine Principle gets inside your bones. You cannot get it out of your body. There's no way to take it out. The best way for you to succeed in the Unification Church, therefore, is to commit all the way. This is my way of life. My wife and I are doing it every day. It gives your vertical self such freedom. That is where you feel exhilaration, joy. That is where you can sleep at night. Even if your body is tired, your spirit says, you are OK.

Your conscience is like a compass. No matter what, the compass needle always faces north. Wherever you turn, your vertical self always points due north. So when you contribute more, dedicate yourself more, sacrifice more, you know you are going in the right direction. Your vertical self says yes. You are now due north. Everybody has a compass. We are sailing north together now.

It is such a long time since we gathered together. We have not seen each other for five months. That worries me. Not because anything is going wrong, but because I want to see you. You reassure me and I reassure you. We are mutually pledged to each other. That is the meaning of our gathering. If you see me and think, oh, Bo Hi Pak looks weak somehow, then I have failed. At the same time when I see you, simply shaking hands tells a lot of stories. Don't try and tell me all the stories by your mouth. Tell me by your handshake. It is amazing. Your spirit is reflected everywhere. Just look at you, look at me, look at your behavior. Just one word reveals so much. You reveal where you are.

We are gathered here this morning, mutually pledging together our lives, our fortunes, our sacred honor for the mission given by the True Parents. That is all there is to it. That is all the sermon I can give you. Nothing more. Nothing is more important or powerful. I am reassured by you and I reassure you. We are unique, chosen people, special brothers and sisters. We are going to renew ourselves and go forward pledged to help each other fulfill the mission given by God through the True Parents. That is the purpose of this service.

Some of you look almost too good. Like Bob Spitz. Stand up. What have you been doing? It is almost like you are trying to become an 800-pound gorilla, not physically, but in power and influence. You are a big man now so you can cover more territory. Thank you. You can sit down.

Don't allow me to get too heavy. That is no good. Mike Leone is always making the effort to look a little smaller, but it doesn't work too well. Father likes strong, tall, big people. No question about it. This is one thing Father likes about America. Tall, big, and heavy. But not this heavy. Really solid and tall, with a lot of muscle, no fat anywhere. As the Marines say, "lean, mean fighting machine." That is what we are. Lean and mean fighting machines. We are really heavenly soldiers. So this AFC, top to bottom, is complete now. More blessing is coming to the American Leadership Conference this year because look at what we have here: the number one chairman, Ambassador Sanchez, who is now a Blessed couple.

Therefore, from top to bottom, everything is conducted by Blessed people. Isn't that special? So outside people can't help but recognize what wonderful people you are. What a well-organized conference. We are doing such a professional job. You cannot find any better emcee in all of the United States than Phillip Sanchez. Heavenly Father is working through him. More and more spirit is pouring upon him. God is giving more inspiration. Every loophole has been plugged. No more loopholes in ALC, ACC, AFC, Global Images Associates, all these organizations.

In your daily life, where is the leak that dissipates energy? When energy goes the wrong direction, you lose energy. You have to plug the hole. In this respect ALC and AFC have completely plugged the hole. The ambassador opens the conference. I will give the keynote speech and testimony about Father. You are winning the people in your state and region. Then they are being connected to two great lecturers, Tom Ward and Bill Lay. Their lectures are getting better and better, more inspiring. Father instructed them not to teach intellectually. Don't try to teach them by the brain. Teach the heart. Look at it as evangelical speaking. Tears must come out. That is the only secret for success we have. We plug into the spirit of God. God's reservoir of true love. True Parents' spirit. That is where the power comes from. It will never fail you.

I understand that one brother resigned from his AFC post. When he was appointed we were already worried because he is a young member. It takes a black belt to be able to stand up in the lonely battle. Unless you yourself become a dynamo, you cannot deal with the lonely battle. Only one member in each state. Very lonely. When you are together, you can compensate for a lot of things. But when you are all alone, it is entirely different. You have to be a dynamo, an energy-producing, light-giving, heat-producing entity. You must become a small sun. Not a moon. A moon is a reflecting entity. The moon does not give out light. It does not give out heat. The sun does.

Unification Church members always start out as moons. They receive light and reflect it. That is the way it starts. In the moon era, you cannot be an independent leader because when the sun disappears, the moon has no light to give. You run out of energy. The American term is "burned out." You burn out unless you have a constant source of energy by yourself. In the Divine Principle we call that a divine spirit. You have to become a life-giving object. Then you can be successfully independent.

This is why this kind of reunion is so important. We renew ourselves. Even if we are a small shining sun, we sure still need refilling. We need to come to the filling station and refill ourselves. That is the power of True Parents. We always get that from True Parents.

The morning service will start soon, so I will not speak too long. This morning I wanted to pour out to you my heart and my feelings and tell you how precious you are and how wonderful you are to look at and give congratulations to you all.

Celebrating the Victory

WASHINGTON, D.C.

APRIL 16, 1989

During the evening celebration following the 15th American Leadership Conference, Dr. Pak pours out love and compliments to Ambassador Sanchez and his wife and several of the ALC leaders, and introduces some Japanese and Korean sisters who have been taking care of the many VIPs who have been visiting Washington. He also reports on the victories that occurred at the World Media Conference.

AFC, ACC brothers and sisters, after six months of being separated from each other, this is a great occasion. We seldom get together in a hotel like this, and we want to make the most of it. Those whose birthday is in April, raise your hands. All of you come forward. Look how many people were born in the great month of April. Do you know why these great brothers were born in the month of April? Because April is my wife's birthday month too.

So, I am going to have a little cake and ice cream for dessert. But somebody has to cut the cake. Let's have our birthday brothers and sisters and my wife do it. Don't you think it is a great idea?

But I want to use this cake for another purpose. You know I believe that in the Kingdom of God we will put things to good use. All those who were in the recent Blessing, please come forward also.

[Dr. Pak continued speaking after picture taking and after some remarks by Ambassador Sanchez about his Blessing.]

Ambassador Sanchez was talking about the separation period. He told his wife, I will be here in New York and you will be in San Francisco. He is very serious about it. And Juanita said, what's new about being separated?

When I talked to Father about Ambassador and Mrs. Sanchez being candidates for the married couple Blessing, he did not ask any questions, what about this qualification, what about that qualification. Father simply said, of course, I will Bless them. I have been walking on cloud nine since then, no question about that. I knew that Ambassador Sanchez's Blessing is a very special one. It is a providential one.

When the Blessing came, Father asked one couple to come forward to represent the 138 couples on the stage and to have Father and Mother place their hands on the head. That usually is not done. So I recommended Ambassador Sanchez and his wife, and Father and Mother immediately approved. I brought them on the stage in front of Father and Mother. By the way, in Unification Church history, Father and Mother never wore formal attire at a Blessing of married couples. This is the first time. Father gave the full measure of Blessing.

So not only has the ambassador been Blessed, but his couple was chosen for Father and Mother to put their hands on their head, Juanita on Father's side and Ambassador Sanchez on Mother's side standing in front of them. Father had already put his hand on Juanita, but Mother was a little bit shy and hesitating to put her hand on Ambassador Sanchez's head. Father looked at Mother, saying he is our son, put your hand on him. So Mother did. That is how the invocation of Blessing was given. It was absolutely beautiful to share.

Later on, Ambassador and Juanita Sanchez presented the flowers to Father and Mother, and that was beautiful as well. All in all, it was a wonderful occasion, and I want you to recognize that the ambassador's life has been exemplary according to all the standards of the Unification Church. They have been moral and pure throughout their lives. Father knew, Heaven knew. That is why the dispensational Blessing was given to them. This is a great tribute to them. The Kingdom of God has been enriched by having Ambassador and Mrs. Sanchez in our ranks. Let's give them one more big "thank you."

[After other testimonies, Dr. Pak continued speaking.]

Speaking of birthdays, there is something I want to share. Some of you may not know that Father fasted on his birthday up to the age of 40. Until 1960 when the Holy Wedding was conducted, Father fasted on every birthday. So that was the early tradition of our church, and my wife and I fasted on our birthdays until the age of 40. (By the way, every Sunday morning we fasted, no breakfast before service when I was in Korea.) So you can say Mrs. Pak did not have many birthdays.

In 1961, Mrs. Pak and I were in the United States on Embassy duty and her birthday came. Of course, this was after Father's Blessing and after we were given the honor to be chosen as one of the 36 Blessed couples. So then we could eat on birthdays. There was no fantastic birthday party, no cake, no cake cutting, nothing like that. Mrs. Pak and I decided to go for a picnic in a nearby park. Our meal was barley—no meat, no chicken, no fish, just barley. In America today barley is known as a health food, but in the Korean tradition only poor people eat barley. So our picnic consisted of barley with kim chee and a couple of other vegetables. The two of us enjoyed the picnic and took some pictures. We still have those pictures, and that is the way we celebrated our early birthdays.

Truthfully speaking I have not celebrated many birthdays with her. In the last several years if I happen to be here in Washington, we remember her birthday. That is all we did. So I have not been too good a husband in that respect. But that has been our tradition. That is the way we have been trained, and we have been more than happy to live Father's tradition. I am so glad. There used to be so much fasting. So much self-chastisement. Cold showers and early morning prayer vigils, for example.

All these things have been in a way liberated because of True Parents' victory, particularly Father's victory in America at Washington Monument. That was the peak of Father's victory. Father declared that the Moscow Rally would be next. At that time everybody was completely flabbergasted and totally taken aback at the idea of a Moscow Rally.

THE UNBELIEVABLE IS HAPPENING

But now what has happened? Just recently we had a very successful World Media Conference in Washington, and Father and Mother came from Korea to attend that conference. Believe it or not, 12 high-level Soviet journalists attended. Why? They came to meet Father. How do I know? At the receiving line we had a metal detector, and they were worried they might not pass the metal detector. They said, do you want me to take off my watch? I want to shake hands with Reverend Moon. I have got to meet Reverend Moon.

In 1976 when Father declared the Moscow Rally, could you imagine that happening? No way. But it has happened. The whole Soviet delegation, all of them in the receiving line, cordially shaking hands with Father and Mother. Boy, can you imagine. And in addition to the 12 Soviets, there were six delegates from Red China. At the conference this time, we had a Korean flag in the center, the United States flag, the Japanese flag, the German flag, then we put the Soviet Union flag next. This never happened in our history. And next to it the Chinese flag. They immediately noticed. They were so glad that we treated them fairly and cordially.

On the first day of the media conference, the Soviets all sat together, 10 at one table and two at the next, 12, like the tribes of Israel. Somebody said they acted like the Japanese, who always stay together. But that was only the first day. By the second day everybody was relaxed, and one of them went out and bought blue jeans. That was the thing he wanted most in the United States. He was walking around wearing them very proudly.

During this conference, the Soviets were hit very hard by the conservative media, saying we cannot trust Gorbachev or glasnost and perestroika. The Soviet and Chinese delegations concluded that the only people who said a kind or sympathetic thing about the Soviet Union and Red China was Father. By the time of the farewell banquet, they felt like Reverend Moon was their savior.

This is really Father's Headwing ideology. That does not mean Father compromised the Principle one iota. Not at all. Father talked about God and a free, responsible, and moral press. But Father embraced them. The basic difference between communism and Godism is that communism's fundamental power comes from a sense of hatred. Our Father's basic power stems out of love. True love. That is the difference. Father truly demonstrated the Headwing spirit, without compromising the Principle.

Father was really a parent. I asked Larry Moffitt to see if we could have a media conference in Moscow next year. I wanted him to move very carefully though, to just feel them out. But an amazing thing happened. Before we ever opened our mouth, they said, can you hold the media conference in Moscow next year? Incredible. The next day the Chinese people came and said, no, no, next year can you bring the media conference to Beijing? So there was a tug of war going on, trying to pull Father to their side. Amazing. In 1976, could you even imagine these things?

Later I had a special dinner with the Chinese delegation, and I asked them, what would you say if we decide to go to Moscow first before Beijing? Would you be offended greatly? The Chinese people smiled, and said, we are a big people, we are not going to be offended by it. But we know that Reverend Moon is our Oriental cousin, closer to our race than the Soviets.

So there is competition between Red China and the Soviet Union in a good way. This is the kind of news I want to share with you.

Father now has an exchange program with the Soviet Union delegation. We sent them out to Montana and Seattle, Washington. They were received by the *Washington Post, New York Times, Wall Street Journal*, and that nasty *Seattle Times*. They were guests of many famous people, governors, trade union leaders. They have been treated like VIPs everywhere, and everywhere the TV people came and news coverage was incredible. These are rare guests: 12 journalists from the Soviet Union. In Montana at the television station, they were asked why they were here. Their representative answered: we are the guests of Reverend Sun Myung Moon. Oh, boy.

Furthermore, they were guests at Matthew Morrison's house, and they fell in love with Matthew's children. A lot of incredible things went on. Matthew can report better than I can, so I would like to turn the microphone over to Matthew for a five-minute report.

But first I want to tell a CAUSA joke. Actually, it is a true story. The Soviets were in New York, and Larry Moffitt took them for lunch to the Russian Tea Room, which is a very famous restaurant right next to Carnegie Hall. I thought that the Russian Tea Room would serve good Russian food, but all they have is American food: American salad, American beef, nothing Russian about it. Then one of their guys said, if you really want to see the Russian aspect of this restaurant, go into the kitchen. The dish-washing machine is broken—that is the Russian aspect of this restaurant.

Another CAUSA story, and I witnessed this one. I was having a farewell dinner with the 12 Soviet journalists at Windows on the World, on top of the World Trade Center. Larry and Domingo and myself went there to treat them. I asked them to order scotch or whatever drink they wanted. They love American scotch. They ordered the most expensive scotch called Chivas Regal. I don't know why that is so famous, but they all drink Chivas Regal. The cocktail always comes out in a glass with so much ice. They drink it in one gulp, gone, period. They kept ordering scotch on the rocks, scotch on the rocks. It was absolutely time-consuming. So I had to make a special arrangement with the restaurant manager to bring two entire bottles to the table so they could drink as much as they want. That is the only way we could get out of that restaurant. OK, Matthew come on up.

[Dr. Pak continued after Matthew Morrison's report.]

Everything that Matthew said is not only true, but much more. All of them signed the Montana picture album, and they wrote, "Reverend and Mrs. Moon, thank you for inviting us to America." Furthermore, they all sent postcards from Montana to Father. Can you imagine? Not one person of the American media who has attended World Media Confernces sent a postcard to Father, but all 12 Russians sent a postcard of thanks to Father and Mother. Amazing things are happening.

BEAUTIFUL, DEEP QUESTIONS

One of the delegates is editor-in-chief of a weekly magazine known as *Abroad*, which has a circulation of 900,000. He said all the Russian intellectuals and party members read that magazine. This editor presented five questions to Mother to answer in writing. Of course, he wanted to do a direct interview with Mother but that was not possible. So we drafted five answers. Each one is like one chapter of the Divine Principle. You know the authors of those answers: Tom and Bill. I read every page, every paragraph, to Father and Mother to get their approval. Father amended them in several places. The basic questions were, what is Reverend Moon's ultimate goal, spiritually and physically? What is Reverend Moon's idea about ecology? How can we eliminate the suffering of people? Is there any way the Unification Church and the Soviet Union can cooperate? What great questions! The Western press would never ask those questions in a million years.

So we answered them all, and Father added a few paragraphs. He said, it is not so much a contest between East and West; it is not so much communism vs. the free world. Father answered in the CAUSA way. It boils down to God or no God. So you are not too late. If you really accept God and absolute values, God-centered freedom and moral free enterprise, you could even be a winner in the world. In God's providence everything is possible. Father is really motivating them. America is good but not perfect. Many things are going wrong in America too. So why don't you be challenged by the United States and become the good guy this time and compete with the United States? If you do these things well, then in God's providence you may even be ahead of the United States. Father is telling them, you have been wrong because you denied God. You have been wrong because you thought a human being is merely a chunk of dirt.

So Iordansky got that answer. So much God. So much Divine Principle. So much about Reverend Moon and so much about Mother's life. How many children you have, and what they are doing, and so forth. It is virtually a little book. Iordansky said, I like this last paragraph. If we do this, we might even have a chance to beat the United States. I like that. Well, just let them be good guys and compete with the United States. Come on in the ring and let's play the same game. Do well and you may be rewarded. That is exactly what Father is saying.

PURE DOSE OF PRINCIPLE

So, 900,000 people will read Father's words through Mother's words. Father's ideology, the truth of Divine Principle and true love, are explained by Mother. We answered the questions unabashedly. We didn't compromise anything. Isn't that right, Tom and Bill? It is a 100 percent pure dose of Divine Principle. And these journalists accepted it gracefully.

I want you to know that these 12 people are not nobodies. They flew here on the Soviet Union airline. We did not pay their airfare except for their domestic flights. Four of them are so important the government paid for them to fly first class. That means they are very, very high in rank. One of them is a very close friend of Gorbachev. He will accompany Gorbachev to Beijing next month.

And all of them openly admitted that the Soviet Union and Marxism-Leninism are over. They said, we have got to change. The question is how. I bluntly asked them, do you think Gorbachev will finally be successful? Will the hard-liners come to power and change the goals pursued by Gorbachev? They said the possibility exists, but they said that the genie is truly out of the bottle. And they said the media is becoming very, very strong in the Soviet Union.

So who knows what will happen next year. The possibility of a Moscow Rally is real. We are working on that. Instead of an American Leadership Conference, maybe we'll have an American-Russian Leadership Conference. Why not? A Chinese delegation of 40 professors already came to Japan and studied Unificationism. So it is just a matter of time when Russian professors and KGB will be in this room hearing all about Godism and Reverend Moon.

That time is here and my conclusion is this: Father is the only hope for Russia and for China. We have been saying it, but at this time it has come to my heart. That is the only way they can survive.

Tonight we invited our Japanese and Korean sisters for good reason. Father has blessed us in the Washington area because of the World Media Conference. During Father and Mother's stay in Washington, the Washington Church was greatly blessed. Many other organizations such as the Washington Times Corporation, *World & I*, and the Universal Ballet all have been inaugurated and really had a great blessing from Father. During this time the Japanese and Korean sisters were really united in serving Father and Mother with a sacrificial spirit and bringing them great joy.

Mother even gave them money so they can buy something for themselves or their children. Mother was deeply touched, I could see that.

I invited several Japanese sisters. Mrs. Michael Runyon is the head of the Japanese team. Michael Runyon is the president of One Up Enterprises. I would also like to introduce Mitsuko Nagashima, whose husband is with Happy Group. Yuichiro Watanabe is a very famous man in Washington. He was the editor-in-chief of *Sekai Nippo* in Japan and is now a special correspondent in Washington. His wife is Hisako Watanabe. And Shigenobu Inoue works for the *World & I*. His wife is Emiko Inoue.

Mrs. Runyon is working to organize baby-sitting so the Korean sisters can take care of the many groups coming from Korea, VIPs and professors and religious leaders. It is incredible cooperation. The Japanese sisters are behind the scene demonstrating sacrificial spirit. I am so deeply grateful to you all.

I would like to have all the Korean sisters come out here and sing a song. My granddaughter is here, and she already said good night to mom. Here is a top gun wife, Yun Ja Tobkin. She has been with us in New York. She came down here when her husband was called upon for AFC. A wonderful team. The Tobkin team is always the top gun team. No question about it. And Do Soon Maketa is married to an American husband. Frank is not here because he is working late. Frank is my family member. He is really special to me, and she is a wonderful Korean sister who is helping the professors.

This is Soon Ja McDevitt. Beautiful, isn't she? I understand she is wearing the jacket that Mother gave to her. Soon Ja has four sons. Soon Ja didn't have four sons alone, you know. A little credit goes to Tom, of course. Just a little. She used to be a staff member at East Garden helping Mother and Father. She knows Father and Mother's taste exactly, so it is a great help to have a sister like her in Washington.

Here is Eun Hi Smith, or Mrs. Mike Smith. Tall Michael Smith is my brother-in-law. Yes, she is my sister. Many of you may not know because I never publicized anything. She is just one of the members. That is the way I always treat her. She has gone out witnessing and fund-raising, but she happens to be here in Washington now. She is doing a great job helping the many Korean groups that are coming here.

Many people also don't know, but Chung Hee Lee is my wife's youngest sister. Her husband is Marc Lee, who used to work for the *Washington Times*.

And this is my daughter-in-law, Sun He, my son Jonathan's wife. They gave us the pleasure of having one granddaughter. Now, as you can see, another grandchild is coming. I prefer a grandson this time, but whatever

God gives will make us happy.

These Korean sisters have been very busy witnessing to all the visiting VIPs. They have been the best tour guides, ready to deal with any situation. Michael Smith learned for the first time the real meaning of the Declaration of Independence; his wife is teaching him because she has to teach Korean professors. Through their wives many American husbands are learning about American history. Isn't that ironic? One day I am going to rent a bus and ride around and relax, and I want them to guide me throughout Washington, D.C., where I lived more than 25 years, and I will learn about Washington and American history. That will happen. I think they have a lot to tell me. But the important thing is that every other sentence they speak is a testimony to Father. Whether they talk about Washington Monument, Congress, or the Jefferson Memorial, there is a story to tell about Father.

Also, during Father's visit many blessings came to Washington. For two years we have had a guest house prepared for Father and Mother, Jefferson House, waiting for the day when they would come and stay there. The man who really worked on that house is our dear brother Bruce Johnston, so I invited him to be here to celebrate this victory. How successful that house has been with Father and Mother. Reverend Yu was trying to entice Father to visit other places, like Upshur House and Capital Gardens, but Father and Mother were so comfortable and relaxed at Jefferson house that Father said, my house in Washington is Jefferson House. We know exactly what we need to make it perfect for their next visit. We are looking forward to their next visit. This house is dedicated for Father and Mother and True Family.

THE MAN WHO THINKS HE CAN

SAN DIEGO, CALIFORNIA

MAY 28, 1989

━━━━━━━━━━━━━━━━━━━━━━

In this sermon to ALC leaders following pledge service, Dr. Pak's innate ability to inspire and encourage is clearly evident. Full of spiritual insight and nourishment, he reminds his audience of the power of their thoughts— telling them, "the real you is what you think."

Once again we gather together in the beautiful city of San Diego. I didn't know so many brothers came. We have a big force here. How are you doing? You look great. We are having a piece of banana as holy communion. It is True Parents' tradition after Pledge Service to have some drink and a little food, cake or fruit or something. It is not just to fill our stomachs. Father feels it is very important for a family to pray and do Pledge together, then eat together. This is a very important part of the Pledge service. So you can do it in your home too.

When we went back to Korea, when Father and Mother were there, Mrs. Pak and I went to Hannam-Dong, Father's residence. We pledged together with Father and Mother, and then we had this communion afterwards. The brief moment of fellowship at that time was very, very precious. So we have our own precious time now. New York is three hours ahead of us, so Father must now be speaking at Belvedere and may be at the most passionate moment of his speech. We never know, it might go on another 10 hours. Do not discount the possibility.

Father spoke 13 hours in Washington. The first six hours I translated. The next seven hours I was just standing. But after six hours I was badly in need of going to the bathroom, but I simply couldn't ask to leave the stage. Father was so intense that I did not want to interrupt him. I did not want to break his chain of thought. So that was my time of indemnity. I was standing and supporting Father without disturbing him one iota. I waited and endured for seven hours. It was terribly painful. After seven hours, I was able to relieve myself and it was like heaven. Then I told Father about it after we came back and had breakfast. Not breakfast actually. It was dinner. We gathered at 5:00 in the morning and Father began to speak at 6:00 and it was a whole day and the evening. We had a late dinner as a matter a fact. A very late dinner. We spoke about it in fellowship, and Father laughed and laughed. He said, why didn't you tell me. I said, Father, I could not interrupt you. I could not break your chain of thought. Father felt sorry for me and had a little mercy upon me.

FISHING FOR THE WORLD

So, this is an exciting life. Even after serving Father for 31 years, in the 32nd year you still learn. You still don't know what to expect from one day to the other. Father is now fishing in New York. You know that when Father is fishing, fishing is not just a sport or fun for him. It is Father's battle. Father is fishing for the world, fishing for China, fishing for Korean unification, fishing for Japan, fishing for the AFC and the United States. When Father is fishing, his concentration is absolutely incredible.

On some days, Father struggles for many, many hours in the small boat, without a bathroom, without anything. He goes out in a small boat and may have a raincoat on a rainy day, but his whole body gets soaking wet. Father spends 12, 13, 14 hours and more on the water. Sometimes Father catches nothing. Peter Kim told me, before I went out with Father, that Father has said that sometimes when unholy men are in the boat the fish are disturbed and the whole day goes by without a catch. Well, that sounds right, except that day Bo Hi Pak was going out. If Father didn't catch anything, he was not going to blame anybody, but I was going to blame myself, knowing that I was the reason Father had no catch that day. So I offered a special prayer: Heavenly Father, it is OK for me not to catch anything. That is all right. But, Heavenly Father, please let our True Father make a tremendous catch today. That was my prayer.

Also I was thinking, I represent AFC, ACC, CAUSA International, *Washington Times*, and so forth. If Father does not make a catch that day, it will reflect on all these missions. They won't receive a great blessing. So I was trembling inside. In any case, Father had the biggest catch that day. Father caught 11 fish, In Jin Nim caught two fish. All together 13 fish: striped bass, the largest catch in 40 days. We took pictures of Father with his fish. I wish I could have brought one picture to show you. It was wonderful. Other members have gone out with Father for 40 days and never had the opportunity to take a picture with Father with a fish. I just went out one day, and not only was I there for the biggest catch, I got to take a picture with Father. That is going to be a historical picture. So that shows that the destinies of AFC, ACC, and CAUSA International are going to be great. We are going to have the greatest catch in our mission. That is what that particular day's fishing symbolized on your behalf.

This conference is one of the greatest catches. Very, very successful. I feel very comfortable with this conference because the spiritual atmosphere is so beautiful. It is almost like I have already known the people here for 10 years. I have never had so many people come to me and say, your message was so deep, inspiring, and I am deeply moved, almost to tears. Our American Leadership Conference is maturing. The American Leadership Conferences are history-making events.

IGNITE A REVOLUTION

Father changed the priority from the western hemisphere movement to the Orient. You know that. However, Father did not reduce the budget for the American Leadership Conference. We will soon have the 17th conference, the 18th conference, and beyond. This is quite significant. Why did Father cut all the other budgets, but not ALC's? Father sees that the ALC is the instrument of God, igniting the new American revolution. This is the fruit of Father's 17 years of toil, sweat, labor, and imprisonment for this country. This quiet revolution is igniting hearts to change from selfishness to unselfishness. Yes, that will make America great. That will make our nation of America great.

Father is leaving this nation to you now. The AFC mission has grown tremendously in less than two years. AFC is the external instrument that Father uses, and the AFC is backed up by the ALC conferences. AFC could not shine that brilliantly. AFC is like a physical body, flesh and blood. But the ALC is like the soul. It is like every creation. In the Garden of Eden, God made men out of dirt. The body first. Then, God put in the spirit that became men and women. In the same way, we are building America. God and Father built the AFC as an instrument and container. Father is putting the true spirit into the body of this nation to complete the revolution.

It is important that you understand that the AFC is the external physical body of our True Parents for furthering the American revolution, and the ALC is the soul of that body because this is where Godism is given. This is where the True Parents' testimony is given. Last night, in front of all these current leaders and future leaders of our nation—state senators, representatives, assemblymen, former congressmen, mayors, admirals, generals, colonels, civic leaders, future political candidates—True Parents' testimony was given. This is amazing.

So where do we go from here? From here we go to the electronic means of doing ALC. That is the goal. No matter how often we hold a conference in one year, eight times, 10 times, still we are confined to reaching several thousand people. It takes much longer to change the atmosphere of the entire nation. To quickly change this nation toward our True Parents, we have to use electronic media.

When the 10th World Media Conference was conducted, Father's opening address and the beautiful introduction by Ambassador Douglas MacArthur II were given in Washington, D.C. C-SPAN carried over two hours of the beautiful opening session. William Rusher spoke and testified beautifully about Father and our movement, and it was televised throughout the country. It is the first time that happened in Unification history. Father's entire spoken message was televised. Ambassador MacArthur's testimony was televised. William Rusher's testimony was televised. The former president of Peru, Fernando Belaunde, spoke. All this was televised for two hours. It is so difficult to get even 30 seconds on the news.

Normally when the networks mention anything about us it is negative. They instill hatred in people. You know the media's crime is incredible in this country. They instill hatred toward Father in the innocent and beautiful minds of the American people. America is going to pay the price. But C-SPAN televised Father's message. Ambassador Phillip Sanchez was there, and it was a beautiful, beautiful morning. Father's message was so beautiful.

I realize C-SPAN is not the most watched television network. Nevertheless, when the airwaves carried Father's message throughout the country, leaving out no corners of this nation, what happened? More people than you imagine listened, and many of them were moved to write to Father and the World Media Association. We received numerous pledges, letters of praise, and requests for the text of Father's speech. We had to print more copies to meet those requests. Many people were astonished at the scope of Father's work, saying, I didn't know Reverend Moon is doing such a great work and giving such a great message. Father spoke about the free media, responsible media, and, going a step further, a moral media. Father spoke about God, freedom, and the media's responsibility to God and humanity. He also welcomed the Soviet and Chinese media delegations. This was an incredible demonstration of the beauty of Father's work. People could not help but be impressed.

USE ELECTRONIC MEDIA

So, electronic media is the direction to go. We are now researching the way and the time will come. The World Media Association, we are the ones. We are the ones who will give the correct testimony about Father, as we did last night. This entire conference in itself is a testimonial. The lectures are a testimonial. The ideology they are hearing is a testimonial. Your presence is a testimonial. You are the fruit. Through you, they know Father. Through you as the fruit, they know the tree, Father.

Think about it. With the 430 people here, including you, we have now held the largest ALC conference. And judging from the quality of people participating, this is the greatest conference. They come from virtually all 50 states. They are the microcosm of the United States. When the atmosphere is this good, people change quickly, becoming so inspired and friendly. By the end of this day, they will be committed to the cause of a God-centered America. Think about it. If this congregation can change this much in two and a half days, we can do the same with the entire United States of America by electronic means. The time will come. I predict that time will come.

The American Leadership Conferences will continue. By the time we go to the 20th, 25th, 30th, 40th, 50th American Leadership Conferences, ALC will become an institution in America, the backbone of this country. This is as vital as George Washington's battle at Valley Forge. Our weapon is the truth. The theme of this conference is "the truth shall prevail." Truth shall make you free. This is the conference of truth. Truth about God, truth about freedom and light and America. Most important of all, the truth about True Parents shall prevail. Amen!

The message to you this morning: become political saints. I can see the maturity in each one of you. You look and behave mature. That does not mean you look arrogant. That does not mean you just put on the pounds. On the contrary, I am asking you to reduce the pounds. Dan Fefferman has done it. Bob Spitz made a special effort, and Patrick Hickey testified to me he was trying to reduce because I urged him to do so at the last conference. When I say you look mature, I don't mean you should put on pounds. I made a deal with someone yesterday. You cannot go beyond my belly. Mine is going to be your comparison. I have to reduce too. But I am 50 years old, and when you are beaten by me that is no good.

Ambassador Sanchez always exercises. I saw him many times in the gym during this conference. Congressman Ichord exercises. I have been admiring that man because he is so fit. He told me he flew to Paris, attended a conference for five hours, and flew back. He stayed on American time. The trip didn't bother him even one iota. He is absolutely fit. He is over 50 years of age. I need to go much further to keep up with the fitness level of Congressman Ichord.

I wish that I could have started my fitness program 10 years ago. But in those days, serving Father, can you imagine, one trip after another. Going to one city after another for the Day of Hope tours. It was like a whirlwind. When you stay with Father, you are always awake until 1:00, 2:00 in the morning. Then Father promptly gets up at 6:00 in the morning. I could not manage to go on any fitness program. Now I have done a little bit.

A strong spirit can only dwell in a strong body. I am a believer of that. So go on a fitness program. It is not that expensive. It is will power more than anything else. You don't have to join a fitness club. All you have to buy is less than a $100 investment: Buy good sneakers. Period. That is your fitness club. The best thing you can do is walk for 30 minutes or, better yet, jog. Jim Gavin is always going out jogging. It is a matter of discipline, habit. I am saying all this for your benefit. But generally speaking, you all look good.

DO MORE THAN SURVIVE

The important thing is to not look defeated and never feel defeated. I know that budget cuts put a strain on you. Just struggling to survive is no good. One way or the other you will be defeated. You have to take survival for granted. You have been trained by True Parents. No problem, I can survive. My family is not going to be hungry or naked. You have got to have confidence in those things. But you have to worry all day long how you can raise more money for your state and become autonomous. I know some states are succeeding. Some regions are better than others.

I told you three years ago when we started at the Princeton conference—that was a historical conference—that it is almost like a marathon. Everybody starts out the same, but one year later, two years, three years, there will be a winner and there will be a loser. I don't want you to be a loser. That was my statement. Now I began to see each state, each region running faster and ever faster; some are behind and nobody dropped out yet. Good! But I want to see everyone victorious.

Confidence reigns in your life. You have a plan. You are not nervous, you are not jittery, not arrogant, but confident. You know why. Because

True Parents are with us. As I prayed this morning, I was thinking that your greatest asset and greatest power is the True Parents. God is depending on True Parents' success here on earth. So God is investing energy in them, and True Parents in turn invest in you and me. Our success, therefore, represents True Parents' success. True Parents' success represents God's long-awaited victory. So you are the extension of our True Parents. Having this consciousness is not enough. It must go deep into your subconscious, into your spirit mind. Your oneness with the True Parents must be in your subconscious. How can you tell if True Parents are the center of your subconscious? When someone is suddenly hit in the dark, some people say, ouch. Some people shout in fear. Some people say, oh no. When a mortal blow comes, some people say, oh my God. But we should be able to say, my True Parents. We should be able to say Aboji, Mansei. That is our code word.

WITH EVERY BREATH

When the greatest inspiration hits you, Aboji, Mansei. When the worst fear grabs you, Aboji, Mansei. It has to be automatic. It has to come out of your subconscious. This is because Father is the personification of God, God's feeling, heart, and truth. Father doesn't have to prepare a sermon. He opens his mouth, and God's words come out. When he is angry, that is God's wrath coming out. When he is really laughing and full of joy, God's joy is coming out. I see that so vividly. So if you think you are doing things by yourself, you are wrong. You will fail. You will be defeated. Always say, all things are possible in our True Parents who strengthen me. All things are possible in our True Parents who strengthen me. Say it. Strength comes from them. It is almost like a ritual. Ritual is sometimes very necessary. If you say it only from the lips, ritual has no meaning. But when you say it from the heart, ritual becomes very, very important. How can you put certain concepts into your subconscious if not by ritual? Repeat it again and again and you are pushing it down into your subconscious.

Father is giving you this blessed opportunity to become autonomous. Become a man. Become an independent man. Become a confident man. You cannot be confident alone. When God is with you and True Parents are with you, then you can be confident.

I have been given a mission in China. Father is telling me not to try to do it by myself. He will be with me, and God will be with me. When you go with that spirit, you will always meet someone who is prepared, who will automatically help without them knowing why they are doing so. It is true. Incredible allies will show up. The most incredible things are possible. When Father spends 12 hours on the ocean, he is not fishing for a particular fish. Father is fishing for the sake of China. His support is always with me. Yes, you are our True Parents' fishing rod. Father is fishing symbolically, spiritually. Somebody has to be the physical fishing rod of our True Parents. I always put myself in that position. I am fishing like Father. But my fishing pond is Washington. My fishing pond is in Tokyo, Seoul, and now Beijing. I am fishing over there. That is my pond. You see. It is simply incredible. That is the way you can win. Do not be defeated. That is the most important thing.

I want to read a poem that Tom Cutts gave to me:

The Man Who Thinks He Can
If you think you are beaten, you are.
If you think you are beaten, you are beaten.
If you think you are not, you are not.
If you like to win, but you think you cannot,
   it is almost certain you won't.
If you think you will lose, you are already lost.
For out in the world we find success begins with a fellow's will.
It is all in the state of mind.

Your subconscious is like a homing device, a computer system. The greatest computer system is within you. But when your mind gives your homing device an order saying "you failed," then your homing device delivers failure to you. A woman who always thinks about traffic accidents is issuing an invitation to have a traffic accident. And she will have one. Do you know why? Because the most perfect homing device or computer system is the one God gave man. You ask for an accident, and it will be given to you. The Bible says, ask and it shall be given. Knock and it shall be opened.

So the poem says: "If you like to win, but you think you cannot, it is almost certain you won't. If you think you will lose, you are already lost." This is beautiful. If you think you will lose, you are lost. "For out in the world we find success begins with a fellow's will. It is all in the state of mind."

KEEP YOUR VEHICLE STRONG

It is all in the state of mind. So what is eternal life? What is the real you? The real Paul Yasutake is not what you see here. The real Paul Yasutake is what he thinks, every minute of the day. That is the real you. And that real you is going to go on for eternity. The carnal body, the corruptible body is only sustained as a vehicle for your soul. Your vehicle will not go on forever, but it has to be maintained and that is why I am recommending physical fitness. You need a strong vehicle to support you while you create something that does go on for eternity—your spirit.

If you think you are outclassed, you are outclassed. You have got to think high to rise. You have got to be sure of yourself before you can win a prize. Life's battles don't always go to the stronger or faster. The man who wins is the man who thinks he can win. But there are two kinds of thinking. You deliberately think "I win." But your subconscious thinks "I fail." Yes, you sometimes find contradictions within yourself. Feelings of guilt come when your subconscious is saying one thing, and you try to justify wrong actions. The division between conscience and subconscious creates a guilty feeling.

The subconscious responds only to the truth. The truth is inscribed in the subconscious as a permanent memory. So each day we have to put more good things into the subconscious. Communism is based on the emotion of hatred. The system is deliberately designed to engender hatred in the human heart and to spread hatred. That is destructive. That is poison to eternal life. What is the opposite? Love. Altruistic love. True love. Always Father says, true love, true love. True love cleanses your subconscious, and it will lead you to one victory after the other.

The other day I was attending an award ceremony for Tom Ward's grandfather-in-law, Congressman Fish. He is 101 years old. This is the first time in my life I met anybody older than 100. He is an incredible orator, and he gave a little advice on how to live long. He said it is not that difficult. Everybody can live to be over 100 years of age. Then he gave us very simple advice. He said, watch what you eat. Watch what you drink. Watch what you smoke. Of course, it is best not to smoke. Then finally he said, watch out, don't hate anybody. That was the advice. Hatred doesn't bother your opponents. Hatred bothers you. It is a poison to you. You are poisoning your subconscious with hatred. Don't hate anybody.

That is precisely Father's teaching. Father hates no one. Even people from the Soviet Union came and shook hands with Father. Father embraced them. People from the Soviet Union expected that Reverend Moon was going to hit them hard. But Reverend Moon only embraced them. The people who hit them hard were the ultra-conservative journalists during the three days of the conference. Then on the final day Father came and said, I welcome your efforts for glasnost and perestroika. I hope you will succeed. In the meantime I will give you a fact-finding tour of America. I want you to go to Montana and see the beautiful mountains. I wish you good fortune.

TRUE LOVE: THE GREATEST WEAPON

They all felt like, oh, we met the messiah, we met the savior. He is the only one comforting us. Nobody else is comforting us. Father hates no one. In that tradition, I hate no one. I have no enemy. Even Donald Fraser is not my enemy. I can sit down with him, I can talk with him, I can eat with him, I can drink with him, I can joke with him. No problem. Hatred is the worst enemy of humanity. And true love is the greatest weapon God gave us. You are the personification of true love. Then you become like True Father and True Mother.

As the poem says, "Success begins with a fellow's will. It is all in the state of mind." The man who wins is the man who thinks he can. And people live a long life if they think they can. So I was learning from Congressman Fish. I was exactly 59 years old standing before the 101-year-old man. I looked at myself. I am a little boy. I am going to declare my new life at the age of 60. Up to 60, my life has been a dress rehearsal. Ambassador Sanchez is just 60 now, and he is now truly living the real life. That is why he was Blessed this year.

One of the reasons this conference is going so well is because the key organizers of this conference—Ambassador Sanchez, Tom Ward, and myself—have a spiritual bond. That makes the difference. So we truly are very, very blessed people. We have everything we need. Money always comes and goes, Father says, but real men and real women are the most precious commodity. God made you and me. That is the way you inspire yourself. That is the way you go on. Discipline your life. Become a political saint. Do not act like a politician. Do not even use the word politician. We don't have that word in our vocabulary. You will become political saints and statesmen.

I predict that many of you will become prominent. As you go this path and endure, you will prosper in your mission and God will make you prominent. Many of you will be elected to public office in local, state, and federal government. When Michael Leone presented to me the roster of each region with your pictures, I saw each one of you looking mature, beautiful, handsome. I said that this picture album is far better looking than the roster of the United States Congress or the United States Senate. I told Mike to prepare a beautiful album inscribed to True Parents so I can bring it to Father and Mother. They feel the same way. So your pictures will always stay in East Garden. Amen! A good link between East Garden and you.

I want to conclude with a very simple, familiar conclusion. Be a good Unificationist first before you think about becoming great leaders or political saints and statesman. Study the Divine Principle. Do Il Jung prayers. Kneel down in front of Father's picture. Just like Abraham Lincoln showed his humility before God, you can declare your day of fasting and humility. After the Blessing, I told Ambassador Sanchez that tradition requires a seven-day fast to qualify for the Blessing, but at the age of 60 you can break it into two parts, three days and four days. For a man of 60, a seven-day fast is not easy. Do you know what Ambassador Sanchez said? "I don't want to be a second-class citizen in heaven." Beautiful. And he fasted for seven days. It doesn't even show in his face. The only difference is that his belt is a little bit looser. Then a couple of days later, he came to East Garden and had dinner with True Parents. He was given an additional mission. He is not only the publisher for *Noticias del Mundo*, but the *New York Tribune* as well. The *Tribune* people said, it's the first time we got an English-speaking publisher. When Ambassador Sanchez was told about the separation period, he took it literally. So he called Juanita, and said, we have to separate for a while. Juanita answered him, saying, what's new about that? It is actually a beautiful story all the way around. You can see that True Parents love him more and trust him more and give him more responsibility.

GOD LISTENS TO THAT PRAYER

You are truly citizens of the kingdom of heaven. Your names have been inscribed in the book of life. Under your name is True Parents' name. Nobody in spirit world will pay attention to the name Bo Hi Pak. They will ask, who is Bo Hi Pak? But when they see Bo Hi Pak with the title "Son of Our True Parents," the entire spirit world will jump, trying to get on the bandwagon and reap the benefits. You are like Abraham, spreading the blessing to all here on earth and in spirit world. That is why we pray in the name of True Parents. That prayer in the True Parents' name will be accepted. God listens to that prayer.

If you pray in your own name, God and spirit world could care less. Who is that guy murmuring down there? There is no meaning to those words. But when the words are accompanied by the name of True Parents, they are all of a sudden so powerful. That is the beauty of our lives. You have to pinch yourself to realize what a great life we are living. How lucky we are. How fortunate we are. Out of five billion people, we are hand-picked by True Father and Mother. Blessed by True Parents. Here we are with citizenship in the kingdom of heaven. Your name is inscribed in the book of life. Your children are born without original sin. So when you have all this, you can never be defeated by the mundane things. You don't worry and suffer over day-to-day things. Problems will never overtake you.

Do not be beaten. If you feel and think you are beaten, then you are beaten. It's as simple as that. The AFC is going to be powerful, no matter what the media says. Look at the people. When they hear the truth, they are so inspired. It is almost like skeletons putting on flesh again when they hear the words of love and life. That is the power you have. AFC is going out with that kind of power. This is such a beautiful and invincible movement we are spreading in America. You need only one of this kind in all of history. And we are going to be winners, we are going to be bubbling enthusiasts.

FATHER INVESTS IN YOU

Without enthusiasm nothing can happen. Do each of you feel that way? Amen! Shall we do it! We can. We can do it. This is why this conference is so important. When we come here and see other people getting inspired, you get inspired, I get inspired. I tell the same testimony, but each time I get more inspired and mature. I am growing up every day. So are you. Do not be defeated. We are doing it. We are winning. The major victory is won. We are harvesting Father's victory. We are the most important people for True Parents in America because Father invests his most precious time, energy, blood, sweat, and tears in you. He is praying for you. Think about the fact that you have that kind of backing. How can you not be inspired, not be strong, not be confidant? Money or no money, that is secondary. You are abundantly rich.

So I want you to become a true leader. People will come to you for advice. Political leadership will come to you. Who in the world would ever have thought that I would become a principal speaker and give the opening address? But that is happening not because I can do those things, but because of whom I represent. So do you. Nobody else, no political leaders will have this kind of training over and over and over. Who else has had this kind of training? Nobody.

REMEMBER YOUR ROOTS

MIAMI, FLORIDA
NOVEMBER 18, 1989

As the providence turns to the Soviet Union and China, Dr. Pak acknowledges with pride the victories accomplished in North America and Central and South America by the ALC, ACC, and CAUSA leaders. At this 18th American Leadership Conference, as always, he encourages them to get their strength and power by going back to their roots: the roots of True Parents, the Divine Principle, and the Unification Church.

I'm sorry for not meeting you for so long. I missed you very, very much. Basically, you have been on your own. You are like astronauts, but nowadays even astronauts go into outer space in teams. But you are on your own. You have grown into mature adults and leaders. Yet we do need Father. We need fellowship. We need brothers and sisters. Our leaders need to gather in fellowship. This chance to get together is very precious. That is why church is needed. Church is nothing less than an assembly of the people of God. The reason we assemble is absolutely from the Divine Principle. Divine Principle explains that energy is created when subject and object have beautiful give and take.

So when you are alone, I know you are trying. But Father knows and you and I know that we need a team effort. We need fellowship. So these three days here in Miami are very precious. Now we can see all our brothers and sisters. State coordinators, please raise your hands. About 25 or 30 states are represented here. The next conference will be in December in San Diego, the final conference for this year. We are going to have the largest possible conference, and Father is looking forward to having a great conclusion to the year.

This is a very important gathering. I am concerned about what happens after we leave here and go out into the secular world. How can we maintain our pure enthusiasm all by ourselves? That is my concern. I would like for you to show me your spirit, so I would like to turn the microphone over to the regional directors to give five-minute reports. We all need to hear from them.

[After the reports, Dr. Pak continued.]

I am very, very happy to see you. You all look good. You look very prosperous, like leaders, congressmen and senators. I must tell you honestly, though, that all of you are getting a little heavier. I don't mind you get a little bigger and heavier, but I would like you to get taller at the same time. I want us to get taller spiritually. You have got to be shining in spirit. Yes, I can see you in spirit. So you must be single-minded going forward in the mission. Maintain your purity. Keep the absolute standard. At the same time we get wiser. Even though we mingle every day with the secular world, we don't belong to the secular world. Jesus said we are not of this world. That has a deep meaning. We belong to heaven. Heaven on earth now, later in the spiritual world. But we have a job to do, to build heaven on earth.

HE IS THE SEMINAR

I am especially grateful to have Jesus Gonzalez here from Central America. He is the first CAUSA missionary to Honduras, but he is working also beyond Honduras. He has many CAUSA spiritual children and has organized an incredible network of people. He is recognized as a great teacher in the entire region. He is a good example. Just one man thrown into an alligator pond, but he swam and swam. He is tackling Nicaragua. He was all by himself, alone, but he is a champion. We had several seminars in Honduras, but not any more—he is the seminar. He has single-handedly taught teachers, politicians, professors, political leaders, civic leaders, you name it. From north and south, east and west, and all of Central America. Let's give him a big hand.

Jesus Gonzalez is our kind of hero. I don't have to go to Central America any more. I don't have anybody to meet. I used to go to those countries and meet heads of state, ministers of foreign affairs, university presidents, and so forth. But Jesus is meeting everybody, so my going there would only be redundant. This is exactly what Father has been predicting. He told us to meet the governors, mayors, congressmen and senators, the president of the United States. So the only place I have to go is China and the Soviet Union. Father assigned me these territories because you have taken over all the rest.

I am concentrating now on how to bring Father to the Soviet Union. The real historical thing is not that the Berlin Wall came tumbling down. The real history is going to be Father meeting with Gorbachev. This is really Jacob and Esau meeting in the modern day. In 1976 when Father announced the Moscow Rally, nobody took it seriously, including myself. I repent. But now it's just a matter of working out the details. Incredible things are happening. So that is my job. You are doing your job very, very well. True Parents and Heavenly Father are proud of you.

We have one other brother I would like you to meet, Cesar Regalado. He is doing a marvelous job in the Dominican Republic. Cesar graduated from the Unification Theological Seminary and the Go World Brass Band. He used to play the piccolo. That is all I knew about him. I thought he was just a member of the Go World Brass Band. Then he graduated from the seminary. He is Blessed, of course. He went back to his home country, the Dominican Republic, as a tribal messiah. Martin Bauer, a member of CAUSA, was martyred. A big price has been paid in that country. Martin Bauer was murdered in a most incredible fashion. Cesar and I are not going into all these stories.

ANOTHER HERO

But I would like you to meet Cesar. He is another kind of hero. We have the Dominican Republic contingent here. In accordance with Father's wishes, we have a flower farm in the Dominican Republic and import flowers into the United States. Another Dominican brother is Publio De La Rosa. Stand up, please. His good wife, Maria, comes from Austria, and this one pair is doing a marvelous job. He is single-handedly building what is probably the largest flower wholesale company in Miami. All the flowers you see in this hotel came from his company.

Cesar is a musician and a scholar, but he must be more than that to be assigned to the business responsibility. He is doing very well. He had no problems after Martin Bauer was martyred. The whole business was incinerated, but he picked it up and put it together and made it work. Father's original ideal for the Dominican Republic is now flourishing. It is a beautiful country with so much potential. It is a beautiful location, very strategically located, and is important in dealing with Cuba and Haiti. This is why Father has his eye on the Dominican Republic. It is the Abel country to save the Caribbean nations. Cesar is responsible for that nation and reports directly to Antonio Betancourt, who is vice president of special projects for CAUSA International. And AULA [Association for the Unity of Latin America] is one of our projects. The Summit Council for World Peace and the International Security Council are our projects. CAUSA International has given birth to many, many sons and daughters. All those children of CAUSA International are growing wonderfully. CAUSA has become a worldwide movement.

Why are Jesus and Cesar doing so well? Because we have True Parents. We have the truth. The participants come to this kind of conference where I testify about Father. For them it is very, very important because they can take this model home with them and do the same. Of course, they can adjust it to the regional character. It is very important for them to come and see the model. And for you, too. Each time you regional directors and state coordinators come, you learn something new.

We also have a Canadian contingent here. Dan Stringer, stand up, please. We have our dear brother from Canada. Give him a big hand here.

Peter Brown's baby was born today. I would like to reveal the name: Shin Young Grace Brown. Shin Young means God's glory. Grace happens to be my daughter's name as well. I am working on so many names. I have got to pray harder to get more inspiration because I am running out of all the good names. When I put a big order into heaven, the answers come down. We will make sure that our babies are all wonderfully named. Normally, you choose the American name and I select the Korean names and they become American/Korean babies. That is our tradition.

The time has come to conclude this meeting, but I want to have my five minutes. I don't need to talk to you too much because I have said so many things in public. You read between the lines. You know my spirit and where I stand. I want you to know we began in 1987, and 1989 comes to an end in just a few weeks. This is a most crucial three years for AFC, ACC, and all the other organizations.

This marriage between AFC and ALC is absolutely perfect. Without the sponsorship of CAUSA and CAUSA's work over the last 10 years, we would not be here today. We have the miraculous educational format. We are educating American leaders, and more and more young people are coming, which is very good. They are the future leaders of America. And we would like to go on even further in 1990 with AFC and ALC in strong partnership. There was a serious recommendation that in 1990, from the San Diego conference on, ALC should be cosponsored by CAUSA International and the American Freedom Coalition. I think there is a great deal of merit to the idea, so ALC will become your instrument in the field. Make a list of people and win them. As soon as they are educated, bring them into the ranks. I would like to have more power in your hands to select the guests and bring them to the conference, nourish them, bring them back, and put them to work.

Also, from this conference on, there is a $75 registration fee. This is good. Let them know there is no free ride. Let them invest something and not be able to think, these people have so much money. The ALC is a prestigious conference that is worth paying money for. This will be discussed this evening with the regional directors and the leadership of CAUSA, AFC, and ACC. My basic principle would be to give each state leader more leeway and more control.

OUR ROOT IS TRUE PARENTS

Just like America needs to go back to its roots, we always go back to our roots. Our root is True Parents. Our root is Divine Principle. Our root is the Unification Church. So I am repeating again and again that you will never be successful unless you operate out of your roots. Become model Unificationists. Without this spiritual unity and harmony, you have no energy. The well of energy comes from our spiritual foundation, which is our True Parents. Do not become a secular politician. You are political saints. I have probably said it 100 times already, and I am saying it again: You are going to be political saints. Period. You are not ordinary political activists. You are God-given, God-chosen, True Parents-chosen ones.

You are now maturing in every way. You can deal with the world and create your own funds and your own projects. The year 1990 is going to be a great leap forward. Next year we are going to have congressional elections. And then two years later we are going to have another presidential election. Between the two elections there is AFC, the second-to-none national organization, which has the real power in grass roots. We are going to be the real power and the only power who can save America. I say to you: save America. That is the basic message of my opening address. Communism needs to be liberated. America needs to be liberated. What can do that? Godism, our True Parents' ideology.

You are True Parents' representatives. Unless we do it, nobody else out there can do it. America will decline. We don't want this great nation to decline. No. We are going to be the personification of our True Parents. America must be strong. The moral fiber of this nation must be restructured by you and me and like-minded people. Pray that the next World Media Conference will be held in Moscow in April of next year. I am praying and organizing, trying to prepare the way. Father will go to Moscow and declare Godism in the capital of Moscow. Can you imagine the power that will have? That is how the entire spirit world will be opened up. For that reason I am leaving for the Soviet Union next month. I never in my life thought I would go to Russia. I was sure I was a target of the KGB and that the first day I entered Russia, I would disappear.

Now we have high-level friends in the KGB. In the past they were so destructive to our movement, but they have been transformed into body-guards for our True Parents. You know the world has really changed.

This is the time you will be pioneering your home front. When you really make up your mind, focus your iron will, and move forward with strong conviction, you can win the victory. It will be done. There is no such thing as something we cannot do. For example, look at the Moscow Rally. In 1976, it seemed to be impossible—except to True Father. But within a little over 10 years, we are arranging for the True Parents' trip to Moscow. That is incredible. You can do the same thing. Shoot high. Meet the governors. Meet the lieutenant governors. Meet the mayors. Meet the police chiefs. Meet all those important people. Deal with them. Buddy-buddy with them.

Because of AFC they will respect you. AFC is going to be a household name in America. This is the salvation name for America. The American Freedom Coalition is Father's action arm. You are the ones who will be tribal messiahs as well as political messiahs to America. Be sure to become political saints. Be sure to become model Unificationists. Be sure to say Il Jung prayers. Be sure to say Pledge at 5:00 every Sunday morning, pray in tears with your wife and children. Even the little babies. Let them participate in the Pledge services. Do not say, my baby is too little. No, that is not True Parents' tradition. You must pray more tearfully than ever. Read the Divine Principle more heartistically than ever.

Everything I said in my opening remarks yesterday came from the Divine Principle. God is the answer to America. God is the answer to the Soviet Union. God is the answer to the free world and the communist world. Both need liberation, and Godism will do it. We are preparing our world for the 21st century. Everybody will be taken care of, including the Soviet Union, even though economically they are desperate right now. All these problems will be resolved in the next 10 years.

The ultimate 21st century challenge is the challenge of men and women. The challenge of heart and true love. That is solved only by the truth, Divine Principle and Godism, period. The 21st century will be a spiritual century. Any country or individual who lives up to True Parents' ideology, Divine Principle, will prosper. Without it, this world cannot survive. This is why we shouldn't rush into the Soviet Union with tons of dollars and aid packages. What they need is God, freedom, a true value system. A revolution of heart is the topic of the 21st century. Without true love, it doesn't make any difference how great an empire is, it will crumble. It will tumble down like a burning wall.

You and I are embryos for the 21st century. We will hatch ourselves. I predict that state legislators, congressmen, senators will do Pledge service with us. That day is not too far away. In 1976 the Moscow Rally was unimaginable. I repent. I did not believe it would happen. We believe unbelievable things. That is Father's creed all the time. Believe the unbelievable things. Believe when all others say no.

So we will keep marching on. I feel pretty confident when I see you, look into your eyes, and hear your voice. Especially your voice at Pledge service and during prayer. I can tell where you are spiritually. This conference is like a revival. Every American Leadership Conference is a revival of our leadership of ACC, AFC, Global Images Associates, CAUSA International. You can shoot yourself to the moon now.

Be sure to attentively attend the lectures. Listen to every lecture, every testimony. You will learn much more. Become a lecturer. Become an eloquent guest speaker like Jesus Gonzalez. You will be so much in demand that you won't even have to organize the meeting. People will just ask you to come to speak. Once they taste you, they cannot get away, because the taste is so good, so powerful.

I was with True Parents in Korea for two months and it was incredible. Finally, Sun Moon University became a reality in Korea. The government has issued a license. The satanic world is attacking, attacking, and attacking. Trying to prevent, prevent, and prevent. But they cannot stop us. The entire Christian world in Korea was completely flabbergasted. They tried to stop our university for so many years. No longer. Public opinion has said, you Christians are crazy. Reverend Moon needs a university. He will produce better leaders than anybody else under the sun. You Christian churches, you Christian ministers are crazy. This is what public opinion said. That is why the government gave us the license. A major building has been built, and I was there when Father dedicated that building. We had a great celebration for kicking off our university.

In these next year let's keep marching on, full of hope, full of enthusiasm, and full of excitement. God bless you and keep going. Let us pray.

Prayer by Bo Hi Pak:

Our Heavenly Father, we thank You, Father, for this most precious opportunity to share with brothers and sisters. They have given us the most incredible fellowship. Father, we have True Parents' spirit dwelling with us. The entire spirit world is governing us. They are opened up. Father, so many things are happening. People don't know. They only look at the horizontal thing. But, Father, True Parents already mobilized the entire spirit world. All the saints in the spirit world. They are all coming down now. They are on our side. We are truly the majority. No matter what, we are the greatest majority. No power under the sun can come against the power of True Parents, the power of God. You and Father, we are Your instruments. Let us be Your great and powerful instruments. Faithful instruments. Obedient instruments. And most wise instruments. Effective instruments. Father, we pledge we shall be that. Just exactly that. Thank You, Father, for this conference. All these things we pray in the name of the most precious, beloved True Parents. Amen.

A Deeply Emotional Experience

BELVEDERE ESTATE, TARRYTOWN, NEW YORK

APRIL 22, 1990

━━━━━━━━━━━━━━━━━━━━━━━━

On the foundation of years of prayer and preparation, Dr. Pak delivers an emotional and personal testimony of the Moscow Rally and True Parents' providential meeting with Mikhail Gorbachev on April 11, 1990.

I would like to read several excerpts from a newspaper article that illustrates how even non-members view Father's trip to the Soviet Union. This particular article is a column written by Ms. Georgie Anne Geyer that was printed in the *Washington Times.* Her column is distributed through the Universal Press Syndicate and appears in 250 newspapers around the United States. Ms. Geyer has attended many World Media Conferences and fact-finding tours. She attended the Moscow World Media Conference, and afterwards wrote an article entitled "Most Unlikely Moscow Meeting." She writes:

> Of all the impossible events that have occurred in the Soviet Union in the last five years, probably none has been as unlikely as the happy meeting in recent days between Mikhail Gorbachev and the Reverend Sun Myung Moon. The *Moscow News* called Mr. Moon the "most brilliant anti-communist and the No. 1 enemy of the state"—and then added, please, that it was "time to reconcile." For his part, Reverend Moon said that he loved the Soviet people and that now the "Soviet

Union was going to play a major role in the plan of God to construct a world of peace." To crown the new era, Mr. Gorbachev on Wednesday hosted Mr. Moon in the bowels of the Kremlin. This was after Reverend Moon, the head of the Unification Church, had lectured the Soviet people on Adam and Eve. If this meeting did not cap the new era, one wonders what would.

Father is beginning a new dispensational era. So, horizontally speaking, historians will also see it as a new era. At the conference, a full gamut of former heads of state surrounded Father, from Marxists from South Yemen and a former leftist president of Mexico to royalty and moderate and conservative leaders. Fifty people were seated at the head table, 40 of them former heads of state invited by the Summit Council.

GOD'S MESSAGE TO THE KREMLIN

Father's plenary address [to a joint assembly of the World Media Association, Summit Council for World Peace, and the Association for the Unity of Latin America conferences] was given on April 10 and concerned the Principle of Creation, the Fall of Man, restoration, and most importantly, the vertical and horizontal True Parents. They got the whole message, lock, stock, and barrel.

Ms. Geyer continued, "The highest level Soviet officials present—atheists all—listened impassively. When Albert Vlasov, chairman of the Novosti Press Agency, spoke afterward, he simply said that 'the Reverend Moon has really crossed a long way to come to the Soviet Union, and not only miles.' "

Father brought the message of God, as Ms. Geyer put it, right into "the bowels of the Kremlin." That was Father's purpose, and he did it without hesitation. I was the one sweating next to Father because his words were so strong. I looked around at this Russian face, that Russian face. I was worried they might stand up and walk out, which sometimes happens in the United Nations when an ambassador disagrees with someone. So I was watching everyone carefully, but it didn't happen. Of course, the Soviets don't know how to say amen, so they clapped a lot.

Father can now show the world that he has, in a spiritual sense, completely conquered Soviet atheism. This is the true victory, and it is this victory that will hasten the unification of North and South Korea. This next goal will only happen through Father.

Harvard professor and world-famous Sovietologist Richard Pipes attended the World Media Conference. Previously, when we had invited him to a conference, he brusquely turned us down. This time, he came and listened attentively, particularly after Father's meeting with Gorbachev. He commented: "The man of the hour today is not George Bush or Mitterand or Kohl, and not even Walesa. The man of the hour is Mikhail Gorbachev." Mikhail Gorbachev is at the pinnacle of popularity in world opinion. *Time* magazine gave him the title of "Man of the Decade," when they normally only use the title "Man of the Year." The time will come when *Time* magazine will say that Reverend Sun Myung Moon is the "Man of the Century" and "Man of the Millennium."

SEARCHING FOR GOD

Gorbachev personally invited Father and Mother to meet with him. He first spoke about one and a half hours in the conference with True Parents and the other presidents. Afterwards, he cordially escorted Father into his own personal office to a private meeting for 30 minutes. This is totally extraordinary!

Father is respected by the Soviet Union for several reasons. Now that communism is crumbling, the anti-communist is a hero for the intellectuals of the Soviet Union. Because Father was an unflagging anti-communist his entire life, it follows that Father is the number one hero of the Soviet Union. Second, he always stands up for God, wherever he goes and with whomever he meets, whether that person is a Soviet journalist or a Soviet politician.

The people of the Soviet Union are now God-hungry. They know that this anti-communist who stood up for God his entire life, even during incredible torture by communist forces, is an avatar of their country. Responding to that sentiment, President Gorbachev had to invite Father and Mother into the Kremlin.

On the day Father landed in Moscow, Mr. Albert Vlasov, the chairman of the Novosti Press Agency, which cosponsored the World Media Conference, and many other Novosti officials were at the airport. There are two VIP rooms, one for regular VIPs and the presidential VIP room, which is used only for Gorbachev or people on the level of presidents. The presidential reception room was reserved for us. Mr. Vlasov and Ms. Natalia Yakovleva, the editor-in-chief of the North America Department of Novosti Press Agency, presented Father and Mother with flowers.

There was a national television interview in which Father was asked for a few words about the meaning of his coming to Moscow and how he felt, to which he graciously responded: "I am very happy to be here in Moscow." We then entered the VIP room, where they had prepared a toast. Mr. Vlasov lifted up his glass and said, "Reverend Moon, welcome to the Soviet Union." Then Father responded, "Now let me return the toast. I would like to toast to the great people of the Soviet Union and your great leader, President Gorbachev." In Father's toast, the "great people of the Soviet Union" came first.

A ROYAL WELCOME

There was a VIP car waiting for us, a Chaika. We had a BMW police escort. I thought the Soviet Union was treating Father very well. Later I asked about it and their response was, "Yes, this kind of escort is only used for presidents." The sirens were on and the lights were flashing as we rode from the airport to the city. We traveled the traffic lane usually reserved only for the president and special officials. There were stop lights, but our caravan never stopped from the airport to the hotel.

Father's hotel was the Oktobraskaya Hotel. It is the Central Committee's hotel reserved for the highest communist officials. There was no better hotel in which Father could be accommodated. Father was escorted to the 12th floor, where he could see the Kremlin towers and the Russian Orthodox Church buildings from his balcony.

Every time we traveled we had a police escort. The first policeman who arrived at the Oktobraskaya Hotel said to me, "Representing the entire police force of the Soviet Union, I want to salute Reverend Moon. Could you allow me to do so?" So I invited this police officer, a very bulky man, to meet Father, explaining, "He wants to represent the Soviet police to you." He then saluted. Father smiled and shook his big hand.

At the April 9 reception there were participants from all over the world, including many former presidents and prime ministers, as well as the incumbent vice president of the Philippines and several incumbent prime ministers. There were two presidents' representatives standing in the receiving line, through which about 700 people came. Approximately 1,000 people attended the reception with each one receiving a name tag. The Soviets had never seen such beautiful name tags; everyone was so proud to wear them.

During the reception Father and Mother shook hands with many Russian journalists. Mother was especially beautiful. Mother wore Korean clothes on three occasions: at the reception, on the visit to the Kremlin, and at the Little Angels' performance. As soon as one Soviet photographer saw Mother, he forgot everyone else. He confided that he had never seen such a photogenic woman in his entire life. Each of Mother's Korean costumes were photographed, so Mother became a one-person Korean fashion show on Soviet television.

TEACHING THE PRINCIPLE

Before the opening session speech on April 10, the conference participants found the special book we created, *Reverend Sun Myung Moon, Peacemaker and Unifier*, in Russian and English, on their tables. This book is Father's life history and of its 225 pictures, the most important one of all is a beautiful grand finale picture of Father's and Mother's happy faces. By the time they finished looking at all the pictures and reading about Father's life, everyone was ready to hear Father's message. At that time Father could have said anything and everyone would have said "Amen."

Mr. Yuri Ossipyan, an influential member of the Presidential Council, attended the conference and gave the first speech, greeting the participants on behalf of the government. Father was then introduced; everyone was so absolutely attentive that you could have heard a pin drop. Father taught the Principle for 45 minutes. Although this was not a religious conference, Father was speaking about Adam and Eve. Logically, it didn't make sense, but Father is so well respected that everyone listened deeply. The spiritual atmosphere was building and heightening every moment. Father's message was an immortal one: good for today, good for 100, even 1,000 years in the future. Father left a declaration in the Soviet Union that the Moscow Rally is also a world rally. This message was translated into English, Spanish, Russian, Korean, Japanese, and French.

The next day, April 11, was True Parents' 30th wedding anniversary. We had a humble but very heartwarming celebration with all of our members. Father and Mother were very happy, very energetic, and very beautiful.

MEETING WITH PRESIDENT GORBACHEV

That same day, President Gorbachev invited Father and Mother to meet him at the Kremlin. At 4:30 p.m. we entered the Kremlin and were seated. Father was first, Mother was second, and I, as the translator, was third. Other presidents were seated on both sides of us. Gorbachev entered and sat down. In that formal meeting, President Gorbachev spoke and listened for an hour and a half. In his opening remarks, he stated formally: "I am here to welcome the presidents of various nations, and especially Reverend and Mrs. Moon. I welcome you to our country. Your conference is a very important and special one. I am happy that it has been very successful so far."

Father was the first speaker; Ambassador Chaves introduced him as the founder of the Summit Council for World Peace and the World Media Association. Father can always capture the heart of the other person in his first sentence. He said, "Mr. President, this is my first time to see you. You look very young and handsome." President Gorbachev didn't need a translation for that. The ice was broken and intimacy was created. He replied, "Thank you, Reverend Moon. I was forgetting that I am a young man because my job is so tough. Thank you for reminding me."

Father thanked him for the opportunity to come to Moscow and for being a good host. He explained that all the heads of state at the table were supporting Gorbachev: "Therefore, you must utilize these powerful people by sending the message to your embassies to work with them. Let us make perestroika and glasnost known all over the world immediately. This assemblage has the capacity to do it; it is your asset."

Father said, "Mrs. Moon and my family are very pleased to come to Moscow. This is truly a deeply emotional experience. We are learning about this great country, and I think we can do a much better job in the days to come. I brought a special gift for you." The gift was a white marble vase, carved with a dragon, a beautiful masterpiece. Father said, "I want to present this special gift of South Korea to the Soviet people in the name of Mikhail Gorbachev, for your museum. This vase has a special meaning. You and I are working for world peace. The white marble represents peace. This graceful shape represents art. The dragon in Oriental philosophy means power, good health, and good fortune. I think you and the Soviet Union need these three things the most at this time."

When Gorbachev heard that, he came to Father and received the marble vase. Mother was standing right there while Father and Gorbachev shared a firm handshake. After this meeting, everyone was leaving. But I escorted Father and Mother, Ambassador Chaves, and Reverend Kwak in a different direction. Everyone wondered, "Where are they going? I thought the meeting was over." We entered a secretarial office, then another door opened, and Gorbachev's aide came out to say, "Reverend and Mrs. Moon, please come this way."

We entered another office where Mr. Gorbachev and a couple of aides were standing. Gorbachev said, "Reverend Moon, this is where I work." We were in his personal office where usually no one is invited except his own staff. Usually, a person from a country without diplomatic relations with the Soviet Union can never enter that room. But Gorbachev invited True Parents there. Outside this office, Gorbachev was rather formal because he was dealing with other presidents, but inside he was completely free, embracing, and talkative. It was the most incredible fellowship—truly the moment when the universal Jacob met the universal Esau. Father gave him a big hug.

There was a lot of publicity in the Soviet Union. The *Moscow News*, with eight million circulation, did a great interview with Father. Another interview was published in *Family* magazine, with five million circulation. In *Izvestia*, Father's meeting with Gorbachev was carried on the front page. *Pravda* also carried a big article, publishing Father's words in detail. The greatest thing was the Soviet national television's interview with Father. On April 20, a one-hour special aired in the Soviet Union. The central themes were the journalists' visit to Korea, Father's meeting with Gorbachev, and the World Media Conference in Moscow. The show was carried on Channel One and seen by 300 million viewers!

LITTLE ANGELS IN MOSCOW

Another one-hour special will broadcast the Little Angels, who came to Russia as cultural ambassadors. They really live up to their name. Father and Mother were deeply pleased. The Little Angels brought an anniversary cake from Korea to Russia to celebrate True Parents' anniversary. The First Lady, Raisa Gorbachev, came for the second half of the program. She had a state function that evening but left early to come. She really enjoyed it. At the end when the Little Angels sang a Russian folk song, many Russians cried. It melted Koreans and Russians into one.

Can you imagine if 2,000 ago Jesus Christ had gone to Rome, visited the Senate, and been welcomed by Caesar and his wife? The kingdom of heaven would already be on the earth. This is exactly what happened in Russia. Raisa Gorbachev came to greet Father and Mother. Father gave a speech, in front of the First Lady, who was sitting there listening. Father said:

> Yesterday, I had a remarkable meeting with President Gorbachev. I respect and admire his courage and leadership. I assured him that I would cooperate in every way I can to support his program of peace. I told President Gorbachev that the secret for the success of the Soviet Union is to place God at the very center of every endeavor. Throughout my own life, this has proven over and over again to be essential. Mr. Gorbachev's burden is great and his mission difficult. It is only with God at his side that he can win the victory. I am leaving the Soviet Union with great hope in my heart. This nation will play a central role in God's providence in the coming decade. I know that in my every prayer I am going to include the Soviet Union and her great people.

> In my opening remarks, I spoke about the importance of a God-centered worldview. Many of you commented about that point. As a religious leader, I firmly believe that a God-centered worldview offers the solution to all problems. Atheistic theories centered only on man bring disaster and self-destruction in the end. This is the universal principle, true in both the East and the West. I sincerely hope that all the dis-

tinguished statesmen and journalists who have been attending this conference will unite with this principle. Let us work together to support glasnost and perestroika in the Soviet Union; let us work for lasting world peace.

GREATEST VICTORY WON

Then the Little Angels brought out the wedding cake. In front of the First Lady, True Parents blew out the candles and cut the cake while the Little Angels sang "Happy Anniversary." I could not imagine anything more beautiful. The First Lady was absolutely charming. Finally, they sang "Moscow Night," and the First Lady sang along. She came back to congratulate Father and Mother, and let us take a picture of her embracing the children. She completely forgot about the time. She finally stood up and said in English, "My Little Angels, bye bye." On the way out she spoke to the Korean press and said, "I have never seen such disciplined beauty in my life. It's almost like my girlhood dream coming true."

My dear brothers and sisters, I want to conclude by saying that Father and Mother won the greatest and highest victory ever imagined. You and I doubted that the Moscow Rally would ever take place. Father and Mother attained the worldwide mountain peak. All we have to do is expand it. Father is going back to Korea to have a True Parents' welcoming party throughout the country. After a once-in-a-lifetime experience you sometimes feel that you can die with no regrets. After this Moscow rally, I feel that if I were to die any moment, I would have nothing to worry about.

This great victory could occur because the dispensational time was correct. The True Parents' preparation was fulfilled spiritually, even kingship was declared. Father's most incredible strategy and wisdom accomplished this. So we thank True Parents and are grateful for True Father's wisdom. Once again I could witness the greatness of our True Parents. God is working every minute of the day.

When we work with the mind of the victorious Moscow rally, we can score a Moscow victory in our home church areas and our workplaces, day after day. We have the greatest blessing to have True Parents. Today we are all Moscow victors. The victory of True Parents' celebration is going to reverberate throughout the entire year, but today is the beginning. Let's pray for the Soviet Union and Mr. Gorbachev, and for the next dispensation: an even bigger summit conference in North Korea. It's going to happen. Believe it and pray for it. Amen.

PAVING A TRUE SON'S PATH

SAN FRANCISCO, CALIFORNIA
AUGUST 18, 1990

True Parents invited Dr. Pak to celebrate his 60th birthday with them in San Francisco during the Assembly of the World's Religions Conference. Following is Dr. Pak's testimony.

I began life on August 18, 1930, in a simple village in South Korea, Jung Byong Ree, which lay 100 miles south of Seoul. I was born the oldest son into what is referred to as a family of "Yang Ban." There is no correct English translation for this, but it is similar to "noble family" or "elite family of society." Those families whose ancestors had served in high government positions would call themselves Yang Ban. My grandfather, for example, was born during the Yi dynasty. During that time, a Yang Ban person had to be born in the family tradition of Confucianism, because the Yi dynasty's state religion ("religion" may not be the correct word; it may be more correct to say "way of life" or "tradition") was Confucianism.

My grandfather and also my father were prominent Confucian scholars in the community, while my mother was a good worshiper of anything if she were told that it would help her son's success. In a way, her son (myself) was her religion. She would do or believe anything once she believed that it would be good for the future of her son. I was born from such a parental heart.

My family was closely knit and intimate. My father was stern, yet loved me a great deal. My mother, Pyung Chun Han, was absolutely loyal for the sake of her son. I felt tremendous love from my mother, as did my brother and two sisters.

My parents lived in very harsh conditions, and as a result, I grew up in near poverty. Traditionally, the Yang Ban were always landlords. But during the 40-year rule of the Japanese government, the Land Distribution Act was enforced, which deprived us of all the land we owned. The Japanese gave it to the farmers who had tilled, but not owned, the land. Since we had not tilled the land ourselves as the landlords, we became virtually penniless overnight. My father and mother had to begin working in the fields in their middle age of 40. Certainly they could not become farmers overnight, so we barely survived with such a small amount of land to cultivate. Because of these dire circumstances, they could not afford to send me to a good junior high or high school after elementary school.

Instead, I entered Chun-an Agricultural School and commuted daily almost 30 miles via train from my home village. This caused extreme suffering to my mother and to myself. After three years of study, I decided that I could not continue my higher education. I told my father that I would become a good farmer in order to take care of my parents, so they needn't work so hard anymore. I then settled at home as a farmer.

Shortly after this, Japan was defeated in World War II by the Allies, liberating the Korean peninsula. Now a farmer, I was asked to become a local country school teacher. That is how I began to do both—a farming career to serve my parents and a teaching career at the local elementary school I had attended in my childhood.

So you can see that I don't have any formal religious education, except Confucian teaching, but somehow I strongly believed in the existence of God, although not a Christian God as yet. I began having strong urges to be very prayerful. Early in the morning and in the evening I climbed up a mountain and prayed during the sunrise and sunset. Of course, at that time my prayers were not in the name of Christ and I prayed especially for longevity for my parents and good fortune in my farming so that I would be recognized as a man of success.

THE KOREAN WAR

That peaceful life which I thought would be my lifetime career was abruptly ended when North Korean forces crossed the 38th parallel. I was 20 years old when I was drafted into the army. Since I had to go into the army anyway, I decided to become a military officer and applied to the Korean Military Academy, equivalent to the West Point of the United States, for advanced study. Luckily, I was accepted. On June 1, 1950, I entered the Korean Military Academy to begin four years of the best training available for the future military leaders of the Korean Army. I was burning with zeal and hope as a young cadet that "one day I will become a general." This dream, however, only lasted 25 days.

On June 25, as a young cadet, I found myself in the middle of the Korean War without even knowing how to handle an M-1 rifle. Communist North Korea attacked that day and the Military Academy cadets were the first troops committed to stopping this overwhelming invasion, which was an impossible task. Within three days of battle, our 330 classmates were reduced by two-thirds. Of my classmates, 220 died without ever receiving even a rank or serial number.

Soon afterward we were sent to Pusan for more training. My religious search began during my military service, especially during the war. After only eight weeks of training, I was commissioned as a second lieutenant and immediately became a frontline platoon leader. War is always horrible. People were dying every day. My superior died; my men died. The shadow of death was always around me. Under those circumstances as a young officer, I had to think, "What is death? If I die tomorrow, what happens to me after my death?" Certainly, there were no easy answers.

In 1951, the Red Chinese Army entered the war. They launched what has come to be known as the Spring Offensive of 1951. One day during this time, my company was moving across the Chang Chon River. All of a sudden, when 200 men were in the water with all their gear, including rifles, on their heads, enemy fire came from the other side of the river crossing. Bullets showered down on virtually everyone in the water. I was still on the other side of the river. When the bombardment of bullets came, I immediately threw myself down on the sand, although there was absolutely no cover. In this dire emergency I shouted out, "God, save me. You are the only one. If you do, my life is yours."

Suddenly U.S. fighter bombers appeared and began firing rockets at the enemy position, stopping them from shooting at us. I stood up, and called my men in a desperate voice, "Follow me. This is our chance to escape." Only two men followed. Even those two men were terribly wounded. I was the only one without a scratch. At that point I felt my life was no longer mine. I must give my life for the purpose of God.

Most of our Division Combat Team had no time to escape and were left behind enemy lines. I and the two other wounded soldiers were hiding in enemy territory and knew that the end had come. It was just a matter of time before we were found and killed. I saw no hope. As I struggled to pull my two comrades behind a rock for temporary shelter, I prayed. The prayer was a promise. If I lived, I would dedicate my life to God. Unlike most "foxhole conversions," I meant every word of it.

We were hiding in the mountains without food or a means of communication for many days. Then one day we saw a long line of enemy soldiers retreating back to the North; many of them were wounded and limping. Gradually, we learned the U.S. Third Division had been pursuing the enemy to the North with tanks. God had saved our lives!

When the U.S. soldiers greeted us, I literally kissed their tanks. I thanked God and thanked our U.S. comrades-in-arms. This was my first personal encounter with the United States of America. America had saved my life.

After that experience, my religious search began. I first picked up the Bible. I also went to the temple to hear Buddha's teaching. I was chosen by my superiors for further training in America and assigned to Fort Benning, Georgia. In those months in America, I became attached to this new country. I really felt the Christian faith was the reason for America's prosperity. Knowing I would be going back into battle again, I wanted to be a Christian because I had seen God in action in America. I wanted to believe in the Christian God and keep my promise made at the river crossing in that desperate moment.

The Korean War continued taking more and more lives—Korean and American. But before I returned to the conflict, I wanted to learn more about the United States. So I and other Korean officers pooled our money and journeyed to Washington, D.C., and New York City, visiting such sites as the U.S. Capitol Building, the White House, and the Empire State Building.

Trained and prepared for the first time, we returned to the war. With the help of the United States and the other United Nations' forces, the new South Korean army beat back the Northern invaders and their Chinese ally. I fought with Americans in subsequent battles until the war ended in 1953. I prayed to God, asking that someday He would give me the chance to repay America for saving my life.

FREE TO SEARCH

When the war ended, I married Ki Sook Yoon, who was brought up as I had been in the Confucian tradition, which emphasized loyalty and piety. My wife also came from the same province and county as I, and her parents and family were also of strong Yang Ban tradition. Her father was scholarly and had briefly been a government official. Her family had very strict ethics and tradition. We were matched by our own parents in accordance with our customs. Without even seeing each other, we were obedient to our parents, totally trusting their judgment. It was not until the engagement was finalized several months later that we were introduced to each other for the first time. From that point on, we were exchanging letters—first getting to know each other, gradually developing mutual understanding, and in the end growing in love. Our marriage ceremony was conducted six months after the engagement. This is a very traditional Korean way of getting married.

At the same time, I began intensive study of the English language in Korea and eventually returned to Fort Benning for an advanced infantry officers' course in communications. I did so well in my studies that I impressed the American officers. Now a captain, I was assigned as an interpreter to the staff of General William Matthews, who then served as Chief of the U.S. Advisory Forces in South Korea.

But even in light of such a promising military career, I could not forget my promise to God, who had protected me from harm during the Korean War. I began attending churches of all denominations—and there were many represented in South Korea. But I could find no religious faith that made God seem as real and immediate to me as He had the day He saved my life.

While a 24-year-old captain, I was serving as an instructor at the Korean Military Infantry School at Kwang-ju when my mother died. I felt as if heaven crumbled and the sun darkened; there was no longer a purpose for living. I was so attached to my mother. She was not ill for a long period. She just simply collapsed one day from hard exertion, and probably malnutrition. A brain hemorrhage had occurred. She died almost instantly with her final words being, "Do not call a doctor." Knowing how poor she was, she did not want to burden the family even at her death. When I think of that kind of mother's devotion even now it brings tears to my eyes; it is very difficult to suppress my deep sadness. My mother died in such a horrible condition, without taking even one medication. I really adore my mother's devotion to the family. I feel guilty that I left my mother in such a condition. It is very difficult to suppress endless tears even at my age of 60. I always say I have the greatest mother who loved me more than the whole world, more than life itself.

THE HOMECOMING

Before I met Professor Young Oon Kim in 1957, I had been a Christian for five years. But I must confess that even after I converted to Christianity, my heart was still empty and my religious fervor was not ignited. There were so many questions in the Bible which no minister was able to answer for me, such as: What is the meaning of the Tree of Knowledge of Good and Evil? How could man's eating of a fruit become a hereditary sin? Is Christ God or man? When would Christ return? And a million others.

One day in the cold month of February, Professor Kim, who was working in the same military compound as I, wrote to me about a "new truth" that would answer all the questions that I had. She didn't mention Father's name; she didn't even mention the church's name. She simply invited me to come one night to hear about this great truth. I was so thirsty for truth that I immediately accepted. I listened to the Divine Principle lectures for two nights. At that time I didn't even know that it was Divine Principle. But the important thing was that I learned more in two nights about the Bible than ever before, and all my deeply held questions were answered. It was liberation and a joy. This was a powerful truth. I had absolutely no hesitation to say to Professor Kim, "I have found the truth. Please bring me to your leader. I want to become a teacher of this truth. I want to learn more."

Dr. Young Oon Kim introduced me to Father two days later in a humble church where there were no chairs and no stove in winter. But I was moved by the fervent devotion of the members. I automatically became a member without even questioning whether I should join or not. No such question ever came to me. I was only thankful to God that He had led me to the truth; my search was over. Now only the job was ahead of us. I thanked God a million times.

As soon as I realized I had found the truth, I told my wife that I was a member of the Unification Church. She replied, "Then I'm a member of the Unification Church, too. Wherever you go, I will go." We then began to study the Divine Principle together. From day one, my wife was an exemplary member. From that day in 1957 until now, over 34 years later, both my wife and I have been completely one; we have not had even one conflict over religion. Father said of my wife: "She can be more sensitive in the spiritual senses. She will be faster in understanding spiritual things than you." My character emphasizes the intellectual or logical side, whereas hers is more on the intuitive side.

We were Blessed as one of the 36 Couples, but on March 1, 1961. The other 36 Couples' Blessing came on May 16, 1961. The reason was that on that day, March 1, my wife and I were to leave for Washington, D.C., to assume my duty as military attache to the Korean Embassy. On the morning of our departure, Father and Mother gave us the Blessing and then came with us to the airport to send us off. That was one of the greatest honors of my life.

SERVING IN AMERICA

In 1961 I returned to America with the rank of lieutenant colonel to serve as the assistant military attache. Simultaneously, I wanted to serve as an emissary of our True Parents. I became the first missionary in the eastern part of the United States while serving at the embassy. So at night, I taught Divine Principle in the basement of my home, establishing the first Unification Church in our nation's capital. As hard as my wife and I tried, there never seemed to be enough time to help our little congregation grow more quickly.

Three years later, in 1964, I retired from active military service. As much as I appreciated my duty to the Korean Army, I wanted to serve my church full time, which was now starting to grow more rapidly. I had been trained in communications while I served in the military, and I was determined to use this knowledge to help True Parents.

The Korean Cultural and Freedom Foundation was the first project where I poured a lot of my creative energy. The KCFF brought Korea's rich cultural heritage to the world through the Little Angels Folk Ballet. The Little Angels soon became world famous as cultural ambassadors of good will for Korea. They performed before the queen of England, two American presidents, and 30 other heads of state around the world. They appeared at the United Nations and at the Hague to raise money for UNICEF. The KCFF also established Radio of Free Asia, which beamed news and hope to the people of North Korea and Mainland China.

In 1965, True Parents came to America for the first time. During their three-month stay, they made an arduous tour of all 50 states to establish at least one Holy Ground in each state. When they weren't traveling, they stayed at our family's home in Arlington, Virginia. That was again a very special time and honor.

In 1971, Father and Mother came to the United States permanently. You know the history more than I do from that point on; I acted as Father's interpreter in all official and private functions, traveling together all over the country. During that time on many occasions we went into a McDonald's for a McDonald's party. All these things are such pleasant memories.

TRIALS AND TRIBULATIONS

When Father and our church were hounded by the American government, the Congress, and the media, I felt it was my duty to defend True Parents, my brothers and sisters, and my faith:

I do not know how or why God has put me in this position, but if this is my destiny, I will not shirk my responsibility. I will speak what I know to be true. Then let the world decide what it must do. Reverend Moon stands for principles which he knows to be more important than life itself. And he doesn't stand alone. We stand with him. We will fight with our lives. And we don't stand alone; men of principle are our allies. We will fight the injustices and abuses of power of this subcommittee. We will fight to protect the good name and honor of our religious leader. We will fight for the principle of religious freedom and for the honor of America in the courts and in the Congress. We will take our case to the American people if we have to. Even then, if the law and the good will of our fellow men fail us, we will fight on until God Himself comes down from His throne in Heaven to vindicate us. My final plea to all the people of this chosen nation of America is this: Do not throw away this nation's heritage or fail your God-given mission. It is a plea we must heed for the sake of our children and all future generations. [From "Truth Is My Sword"]

Congressman Fraser's hearings were unsuccessful, and he was subsequently defeated in his bid for election to the Senate.

I came to the United States, particularly to the nation's capital, to be an ambassador of God and of True Parents. I came representing fallen Adam, paving the way for the True Adam, so that when True Parents came they would receive great glory and victory in this country. When they arrived in America on December 18, 1971, True Parents began working tirelessly for the salvation of this country. In fact, this nation owes its life to our True Parents. Instead of repaying that debt with gratitude, America put our dear Father into Danbury Prison.

As you know, when Father testified before the Senate Judiciary Committee's Subcommittee on the Constitution, he concluded with a most noble and remarkable statement. I quote:

> The issue today is the very survival of America and the free world. To ensure this survival, I am willing to suffer any indignity, to go any distance, to do any labor, and to bear any cross. I am even willing to give my life if that will ensure that the nation and world will survive and do God's will.

> Today I carry no animosity toward anyone. I long ago forgave my accusers. I have no hostility toward the United States government. Instead I pray for this country. I thank God that He is using me as His instrument to lead the fight for religious freedom and to ignite the spiritual awakening of America in this most crucial hour of human history.

> Mr. Chairman, I once again thank you for this opportunity. I would like to conclude by saying "God Bless America."

On July 20, 1984, when Father was heading for Danbury, I felt like a dead man, a man with no purpose to serve in the future; I felt I was totally responsible for Father's imprisonment. I was really miserable. Riding in the car together with In Jin Nim that day, I could not stop weeping from the moment we began the journey from East Garden to the gates of Danbury. In Jin Nim comforted me so many times, saying: "This is not quite the end of it, so do not cry so much." But I could not stop. How could I live, how could I eat another meal or sleep another night?

I fully expected Father to reprimand me or show us his discouragement or dissatisfaction, his grief, his pain. But on that day, Father was absolutely a new champion. I had never seen Father's face glowing as brilliantly as the sun. "You never know," Father said, "beyond the hill of Danbury, what great blessing from Heavenly Father is waiting. I'm jubilant, I'm exuberant and looking forward to the new chapter that is going to be opened beyond the hill of Danbury." It was that statement and seeing the great hope and determination on Father's honestly joyful face that really prolonged my life and lightened the burden I felt in my deepest heart.

THE VIRTUE OF FORGIVENESS

While Father was in Danbury, I was kidnapped by North Koreans. When Father heard of it, he began to intensely pray for my life. He continued to pray the entire 40 hours I was gone. Like the battle at Chang Chon River, I thought my final moment had come. I did not want to die in shame or dishonor before our God, our True Parents, and our church. Nor did I want to give shame or dishonor to them. At that time, I desperately called out to God declaring that if I have to die, I want to die in glory and victory, reaffirming and proclaiming this as if I were standing in front of the True Parents. I wanted to die with my final word calling out to True Parents, "Mansei." I received God's help so definitely and manifestly. Because of His grace and the grace of our True Parents I was saved. I owe God and True Parents eternal gratitude.

Father's 18-month sentence was shortened to 13 months because of his good behavior. He was a model prisoner under these unpleasant and undignified circumstances. This is just one beautiful example of Father's entire life. I learned from Father the virtue of forgiveness. Any grudge or embedded animosity toward someone, or any hatred, is poison that does not hurt anyone except oneself.

Therefore, my life credo is to hate no one, to have no embedded animosity toward anyone. If someone does work malevolence on you, pray for him and forgive him. If someone misunderstood you, drop everything and go talk heart to heart to end the misunderstanding and bring harmony between you.

Honestly speaking, I have no enemies, just as Father said he has no enemies. I have no one to hate. Yes, I may like someone better than another, but I have hatred toward no one. I never tried to hurt anyone. I want to try to see the goodness in each heart and bring that goodness out and praise it. I love to praise and applaud others. On the other hand, if someone is trying to praise me, I feel very uncomfortable because I always feel success and credit belong to God and True Parents. I never want to keep it as mine.

Another credo of my life is to never speak ill of anyone, especially in the absence of that person. Yes, I have given a lot of advice and counseling to many brothers and sisters, but I do it face to face, out of genuine love and strictly for their benefit. One time a brother broke down in front of me and said, "You truly love me more than my own father ever did." Nothing pleases me more than when someone feels that way.

To my wife and me, Father and Mother are not just our spiritual Father and Mother. In our minds they are absolutely our physical Father and Mother as well as the Eternal True Parents. Being close to True Parents is also a grave responsibility. It is not always a "fun time" with them. Sometimes we do have serious moments together. Father has many times scolded me and still does without any reservation because he trusts me and I am his son. As a son, you have to suffer heavenly wrath many times. You will be scolded and spiritually spanked.

THE THREE STAGES OF PRAYER

My prayer life in the church has always been in three stages. First, I pray in repentance because I genuinely feel I am not worthy of receiving True Parents. Furthermore, by being close to our True Parents I must remember that I have a great responsibility representing all the members of the world. Yet I many times either forget about this or relax too much. The struggle between mind and body is always there. Sometimes I have done things which I later regretted greatly. Simply speaking, I am not worthy of being a son of True Parents. I was chosen truly by mere grace, not because of my doing. So when I am thinking of myself and the grave responsibility I have of being where I am, there is so much to repent for. Repentance is probably the only and best way to get rid of your feelings of guilt. God is a good Parent. When a son or daughter comes to Him and truly asks for forgiveness, wouldn't He, as the Parent, forgive His son or daughter? You must trust God as your True Parent. So the prayer of repentance will make you revive, cleanse you, give you energy, and make you a new person.

The second stage in my prayer is always a prayer of gratitude. It is my lifetime goal to live a life of gratitude, being grateful for everything. Even in my suffering there is something to be grateful for. I always believe my suffering will turn into a great blessing. If you are willing to suffer, welcome it when it comes. Many times I have told people that complaint is a disease. If you have an attitude of complaint or a complaining mind, you will never be satisfied or make yourself happy. You will always make your life miserable. Even if you become a king or a millionaire, you still will have a thousand things to complain about. It is a disease like cancer. External things will never heal this disease. I decided a long time ago that I would never complain under any circumstances. I would always find something to be grateful for. I am simply grateful to God for my life, my mission, my health; grateful to True Parents that I am their son, that they love me, that they are my savior, that they rid me of my original sin, that I have eternal life, that I am so close to them. No amount of suffering in any circumstance under the sun can compare to these blessings. So I am grateful in my prayer.

The third stage of my prayer is to give my pledge to God and True Parents. I pledge my life, my fortune, and my sacred honor. Every ounce of energy I have I dedicate to the victory of True Parents and Heavenly Father in bringing the kingdom of heaven on earth. How could we not be victorious with God and True Parents on our side? If we do everything in the name of True Parents, there is no way we can fail. When I am in danger or have a sense of failure, I call out to God, saying, "Thy will be done." I know that His will must be victorious. Don't let Bo Hi Pak prevail, but let God and True Parents prevail. This kind of discipline of prayer life gives me lasting energy, power, wisdom, spirit, and most important, the presence of God.

Yes, I am facing incredible challenges of furthering God's providence in everyday life—as we all are. I always believe in victory and I expect it to happen, not with my power. So many miracles have happened in my life. I always expect them and I receive them—it is that simple. Some might call it positive thinking, while others might call it my faith. Whatever definition you choose is fine with me. I believe and expect a glorious victory for our True Parents. When victory comes, I never consider that it is my credit or my victory. It is the victory of God and True Parents. I simply kneel down to be grateful, many times in tears.

LOVE ONE ANOTHER

While we are here on earth it is our duty to fervently love one another and love humanity. Let us not judge anyone, as judgment is for God, not man. The work of man here on earth is to love: to love those closest to you, your brothers and sisters, and all people around you—even the person who thinks of you as his enemy. Of course, I am far from reaching that level of perfection. Thank God we have True Parents—the greatest blessing of all for me, for all members of the Unification Church, and actually for all humanity once they realize it. Love heals; hatred is poison and hurts you more than anything else. Let us be like Father every day, more and more and evermore.

There have been many glorious, victorious, momentous, unforgettable moments with True Parents in my life. But I have to say that my 60th birthday was a special moment for me. Unexpectedly, they gave me a very extraordinary party from their own initiative, including an offering table and laying their hands upon me and my wife in a prayer of blessing. That was like a dream come true. Only my seeing a picture of it tells me that it was real. I still can't believe that it really happened. It was an extraordinary honor for an unworthy man like myself, and I said in my testimony that day that I am eternally indebted to our True Parents. No matter what I do for the rest of my life, I can never repay my debt. I own them my physical life, my spiritual life, and my eternal life.

Dr. Bo Hi Pak's 60th Birthday Celebration

WASHINGTON, D.C.

AUGUST 26, 1990

Dr. Pak uses the occasion of his 60th birthday celebration to give his heartfelt thanks to several people in attendance, including Congressman Ichord, Dr. Bob Grant, Ambassador Sang Kook Han, Ambassador Phillip Sanchez and his wife, and Gary Jarmin.

He introduces members of his family and asks everyone to join him in thanking his wife. He concludes with an honest confession of his fear of failure in front of God and True Parents and expresses his gratitude for their constant support.

I am totally unprepared. My elder brother, Ambassador Han, Congressman Ichord, Dr. Bob Grant, Mrs. Grant, Ambassador and Mrs. Sanchez, distinguished guests, my fellow brothers and sisters. If today is the last day of my life, I couldn't be any happier. But knowing that tomorrow will come, next week will come, next month will come, and next year will come, tonight the beautiful tribute you have given me is a tremendous spiritual and physical burden and I feel totally humbled. I consider every word you have spoken as an act of love, and these words carry with them the promise of forgiveness; so in the days to come, when you will discover many, many more of my shortcomings, imperfections, sins of omission, unwise decisions, I am sure you will forgive me. That is a comfort to me.

I want to express my heartfelt thanks to a few people, starting with Congressman Ichord. I have never seen a man of integrity like Congressman Ichord. He is a genuine American character, the epitome of a great American. But the reason I truly love and respect him is that he loves and respects our dear Father, our True Father, Reverend Moon. I have had some humbling experiences with him that made me feel that I, a veteran of some 30 years of Unification Church experiences, was far behind Congressman Ichord in loving, respecting, and carrying out Father's wishes. You know that Congressman Ichord led the delegation to China as a mission given to him by True Father. He not only fulfilled that mission to the fullest degree, but he did even more when he came back and sat down with the president of the United States, George Bush.

George Bush had a reason to see him because Congressman Ichord had a message for him from the secretary general of the Communist Party of China. Congressman Ichord probably spent 15 or 20 minutes reporting about China and conveying that confidential message to the president, but the remainder of the time, far more than his China report, he testified to the president of the United States, face to face and eye to eye, about Reverend Moon, why he is an associate of Reverend Moon, why he is working for Reverend Moon, why he respects and loves Reverend Moon.

I don't think anyone, member or non-member, in the United States history has ever done that. Usually any American of great fame, when they are invited to the Oval Office, would think of promoting their own work and trying to be looked upon by the president more favorably. That is human nature. But Congressman Ichord could care less what George Bush might think. He was telling the truth and telling it squarely. To me that deed really humbles me. As one of the principal disciples of Reverend Moon, I humble myself before Congressman Ichord. I truly mean it. You are a great man to me and you love Reverend Moon more than I do. I respect that. Let's give a great big hand for Congressman Ichord. Thank you.

It is not a coincidence that Congressman Ichord is the chairman of the board of this great organization, the American Freedom Coalition. It is not a coincidence. It is providential and truly a great fortune for all of us.

Now I want to speak about Dr. Bob Grant. Dr. Grant's primary mission nowadays is not leading AFC. His primary mission is to speak to visiting Korean groups, day in and day out. The other day I joked with him, and I told him, the Korean public is waiting for you, Dr. Grant. There is no presidential timber in Korea. They want you to come to Korea to run for the presidency. You have created a big constituency. There is a certain truth to it. Dr. Grant is becoming very popular among Korean intellectuals and leaders of Korea. But the more important thing is this: Dr. Grant never once complained or excused himself, never once. Speaking to these groups is an additional duty. He knows Reverend Moon wants him to do it, and that is good enough for him. He is giving his heart and soul, day in and day out, pouring out his message, teaching about America to these Korean people. No one is telling the truth about America like Reverend Bob Grant does. But he loves America. He is confident. He is a man of positive thinking. He is a man of love.

Now when the regional directors come, you usually come to his home. His basement has become a conclave of our AFC regional directors. He loves to have our people come into his home and use it and occupy it. The other day I said, bless him who understands that the kingdom of God is the kingdom of use. He is using every bit of everything he has for the sake of goodness. Of course, Judy, his lovely bride (I know she is still a bride because I was at their wedding in Palm Springs, California), supports him completely.

GREAT EXPECTATIONS

Bob Grant knows Reverend Moon loves him and expects him to accomplish great things. Reverend Moon knows he is a a great leader and even wants him to become president of the United States. Dr. Grant said, no, no, I was born in Canada. Impossible. The Constitution does not allow me to run for the presidency. Reverend Moon simply said, let's change the Constitution. My only birthday plea to Dr. Bob Grant is this. I know Dr. Grant loves Jesus Christ. He is a tremendous man of God and man of Christ. But I want to tell him I used to think that way too. I was already a Christian for five years before I became a Unification Church member. I thought joining the Unification Church was in some way a betrayal of Jesus Christ. I am sure all those Jesus-loving ministers have that instinct.

But in my life of Divine Principle over 30-some years, I have come to the realization that Jesus and Reverend Moon are one. Jesus in heaven is sweating and laboring to see to it that Reverend Moon's mission here on earth is successful. That is the way Jesus' mission shall be fulfilled. This most poignant realization came to me: Jesus and Reverend Moon are one. As much as Elijah and John the Baptist were one. They have one mission under God. And in my years of service to Reverend Moon, I have come to the absolute conclusion, over and over and over, that if Reverend Moon is not the son of God, if he is not the true one, then I have an answer for you—there is no God. That is my conviction.

From the secular point of view, it is very difficult to understand Reverend Moon as a great man, a great religious leader. Ambassador Han knows that very well. But when you know Reverend Moon deeply enough, he is the one. If he doesn't do it, nobody else can. God and Jesus, and all the great saints in heaven, are coming down to see to it that Reverend Moon's mission in the 20th century here on earth becomes a reality. It is not only Reverend Moon's victory, it is the victory of Jesus, the victory of God, and the victory of the saints in heaven. That is my conviction. That is my source of power, energy.

Last night a 20-minute film was shown to ALC. I allowed that to happen, but that was the mistake of a lifetime. I want you to know that will never happen again. It is a good film. Jim Gavin poured his heart and every ounce of his energy into it. It took a lot of sleepless nights to make it. But the reason that particular film embarrasses me in the depth of my heart is not because the quality is poor or the editing is poor, but because it is my lifetime duty and conviction that every credit, every good thing or every achievement that has occurred is not by my own merit. It is to Father's credit. True Parents' credit. God's credit.

When I give credit totally to True Parents and God, it makes me happy. It makes me peaceful. But if I am given credit for something, even a little bit, I become uneasy. I become restless, nervous, and embarrassed.

Bo Hi Pak has to be a no-name person. Bo Hi Pak wants to be just a shadow of the greatest man who ever walked and who ever lived on the face of the earth. I want to be the shadow of my dear Father and Mother, True Parents. The Little Angels, *Washington Times*, Panda Project, whatever that film mentioned, I should be given credit for none of it whatsoever. All the credit goes to Father. It is true. I am not just humbly saying it. It is his power, even the Fraser battle itself. I was scared to death. I was feeble. I was weak. Also, I felt very guilty because at that time I thought this investigation was begun because of my wrongdoing and that it would embarrass our True Parents. I really had a guilty feeling. It brought a burden on the leaders of our Unification Church. I wondered, what can I do, how can I apologize?

DAVID BO HI PAK

For that reason I was a guilt-ridden person during the investigation, and I didn't have the courage to stand up. I didn't know what to do, even though I was preparing the answers. I did not worry about my destiny; that matters very little to me. I never worry about my tomorrow. I worry about the shame that might come to Father or the Unification Church. This was unbearable to me. I went to East Garden and really broke down before Father and Mother and apologized. I begged for their forgiveness for my shortcomings, my mistakes, and so forth. Father at that moment, in a most incredible way, in a loud voice, shouted and scolded me. I was so shocked. Just like an electric shock. He scolded me by saying, Bo Hi, how can you be so weak? This is a God-given opportunity. God is trying to use you as a David, going against a Goliath. If you are so weak and feeble, with no power, no energy, you are going to fail God.

This is the way Reverend Moon scolded me. Immediately I wiped away my tears and wrote down on my script for the first day of testimony, "David Bo Hi Pak." I still have it. I came out of East Garden as a new man. I was so peaceful, I was ready to die joyfully in the halls of Congress. From that point on, nothing could shake me. Yes, I am a David going against Goliath. If I ever become a martyr, this is the place to be a martyr. When you make up your mind, nothing can make you tremble. In a way I was the subject during all the sessions. Fraser was trying to be chairman, but spiritually he was overpowered. He finally gave up. He gave up, I didn't give up. So who won that victory? It was not Bo Hi Pak. It was Father. Father won that victory. So in the Fraser battle, even though it seemed that Bo Hi Pak fought that battle, actually the power and energy, the conviction, the strategy, the bold and strong character, all came from Father. So that victory is attributed to True Parents.

So anything said in that film is not really real. I want to please God and praise True Parents. Anything that is not pleasing to God, I don't want to have. I am very, very honored by such a tribute. But I want you to know, I want to give total credit to our True Parents and God.

I really love each one of you. Although I am one individual, I am trying to be with you all the time. The work of the *Washington Times*, for example, is not really Bo Hi Pak's doing. Father is doing it. Furthermore, without Ambassador Sang Kook Han, the *Washington Times* would not be here in that great glory. Ambassador Han, as you know, is my elder brother. He is my military senior. He is a man of impeccable honesty and integrity. He made his name in Korean diplomatic circles, and he served in the highest level of the Korean government, serving Korean President Park Chung Hee.

For the first summit conference between the Korean president and John F. Kennedy at the White House, President Park searched all over Korea for someone to translate. Although the Blue House has lots of Ph.D.s, Park Chung Hee was not satisfied with those people, even those who had earned their Ph.D.s in the United States. He begged the United Nations' commander and borrowed Ambassador Han, at that time Lt. Col.

Han. He came to the summit, in uniform, with President Park, and he is the one who translated. That summit conference was a total success. Communication between the two was impeccable, just an absolutely computer-like translation. The American people respected Ambassador Han; they knew from their own interpreter what a great job he did. U.S. relations with Korea, at that time, were shaky because the U.S. government didn't support Park Chung Hee's military coup d'etat.

When Ambassador Han first joined our True Parents, I remember very clearly his first seven-day fast. He was on active duty in the military. We drink water during the seven-day fast, but some people also drink weak barley tea. But the impeccable Ambassador Han never allowed himself to drink any barley tea, only water, because barley tea has some barley in it, which is grain, and, therefore, a brownish color. He said, I don't want my spirit to become a brown color. He was that strict. I took my hat off to him.

In the last five years his proficiency in English has become so high that he can lead men like the *Washington Times* reporters. They are really arrogant, independent minded, selfish individuals, but even they have to take their hats off to Ambassador Han. He is virtually running the *Washington Times*. He was asked to ask Father for permission for the *Washington Times* to honor Dr. Pak's 60th birthday. And this splendid party was meticulously organized. I already had tremendous respect for him, but now I am even more indebted to Ambassador Han. Would you kindly join me in giving great thanks to Ambassador Han.

I now want to thank you, Ambassador Phillip Sanchez. You and your lovely wife, Juanita, are very special to me. You are a jewel. The American Leadership Conference would not be at the level it is today without your charm, poise, diplomacy, beautiful personality, and absolute faith and conviction. You have such an incredible way of dealing with people and a precious capability for peacemaking. I always think that when we have a television station, Phillip Sanchez is going to be the host of a big television show. What a great man. He rejected a cabinet post with Ronald Reagan and joined Reverend Moon's cabinet. So, my amigo Sanchez and Juanita, stand up and we will give you applause.

I have to make a long story short, even on my birthday, but I just want to mention one more couple. His wife may not be here tonight, but I want to talk about Gary Jarmin. Many people may not know Gary as I know him. He truly loves our True Parents, and he is someone who can do what Father needs. He is a political strategist like I have never seen. He has a precise and most acute mind. He makes things happen. I would like to give you a couple of examples. Many of you may not know about them because these things happen behind the scenes.

GARY GETS THE JOB DONE

On August 31, the Universal Ballet Academy will be inaugurated, another victory for Father. Without Gary Jarmin, this school would not be there. What do I mean by that? Oleg Vinogradov is an important Russian citizen, a great artist who had won the Lenin Cultural Award, the highest honor in the Soviet Union. He could not come to America to work without his government's permission, and to get that, he needed an invitation from the United States at the highest level—he needed a letter from President George Bush. The Soviet Union was still an adversary in terms of diplomatic relations, and it was very difficult for the president of the United States to write a letter to an individual, even the artistic director of the Kirov Ballet. So I brought this matter to Gary Jarmin. To make a long story short, that request went to the State Department to the Security Advisor's desk, to get clearance. Finally, thanks to Gary's tenaciousness and doggedness, his strategy and influence, everything worked out. Gary is the one who made that happen. Now Father is coming to honor that opening, and I want you to know that it is Gary who did it.

You know the president of the United States does not just sit down and write a letter to anybody. It is not that easy. But the president wrote me a beautiful birthday letter. He recognized the work of the *Washington Times*, but there was a personal part too. Unless you have the right connection, that kind of thing cannot happen. Again, Gary pulled it off. I have asked him to reserve that strategy and power, so that someday he can pull off something very big for the sake of Father's great providence. For this reason, I would like to show my respect and love for Gary Jarmin. Gary, stand up, please.

There are many members of my family here. I have three sons and three daughters. I am very proud of them. They are all grown up, and they are educated better than their dad ever was. Most important, however, all our children are obeying the True Parents' commandments. That is the greatest lesson God has given me. In the last few days at the *Washington Times* I talked about my own parents. You saw their picture. We lived in poverty because of the Japanese rule. My parents worked desperately hard on a small farm. I have one brother, No Hi Pak. Many of you know him. Stand up, please, No Hi. His wife and son are here. We have two sisters, one elder and one younger. One younger sister, Eun Hi, is sitting right here. Stand up, please. My parents' religion was their children. Anything that was good for the children, they did. If somebody said that if they went to a particular tree and prayed their children would get better, they would go to the mountain and find that tree and pray in front of that tree.

I vividly recall the love of my mother and father, especially my mother. She did not live too long. When she passed away, I was an adult, but I was like a little child, so helpless. I had never felt so helpless, and the whole of heaven and earth seemed to be falling apart. I will never forget that experience. It was the saddest and most desperate experience when my mother died. I was told her final word was, do not call the doctor, because she knew we had no money. She didn't want to burden the family with a doctor's bill even though she was dying.

My wife and I have been married for 37 years now. Our first daughter is Na Kyung, whom we also call Grace. She was born, as you could see in the picture, in a very humble situation. While my wife was pregnant, she did not have enough nourishment. Not even enough rice, and of course no meat or fish. So my wife was very feeble. I told her she should go to the obstetrician, but she said, no way, I will deliver the baby myself with the help of the midwife; my neighbor says she will come to help me. I had no experience, this was my first child, so I trusted that word. When the time of delivery came, my daughter was born, and the umbilical cord had to be cut and things had to be cleaned. But my wife completely fainted. She had no more energy. I was so shocked, and I jumped up and ran out, calling, where is the doctor. But she heard me. Her feeble hand pulled me down and said, do not call the doctor. Just like my mother.

But I could not take the chance of my wife dying. So I dashed to the hospital and about an hour later I brought the doctors in. That one hour was like a million years. She might have died. When we got back, she seemed like she was dead. The doctor said the pulse was OK. An urgent operation was conducted, and she recovered. That was the first child, the beginning of our family life. I thank God who gave me such a devoted wife who has supported me all the way. She has two religions. The Unification Church is one religion, her husband is another religion. She never said anything like that; that is my observation. Of course, she loves True Parents dearly.

I have concentrated so much on my mission that many times I neglected her. I have to repent so many times. When she is not around me and I am traveling alone, that is the time for repentance. Oh, I wish I could have done better for my wife. But when I come back, I come back the same old bad boy. She forgives me again and life goes on. At this time I really give my thanks and apology and ask her forgiveness on my birthday. Will you kindly giver her one applause.

I want to conclude with one more testimony. The 60th birthday is a long time coming, and it will never come again. So please be patient with me so that I can share one more, very important thing. Tonight is my only opportunity to share this with you.

Tonight you have talked about my faith and spoken so many wonderful words about me. But I have a confession to make. I am not that strong. I do not have that iron will. I am not hard like a rock. I am, as Dr. Godwin said, fragile. I know myself very well. Although I preach about positive thinking, the optimistic way of life, and so forth as the secrets of success of human life, and although I am convinced I have to be a man like that, I am a man who trembles every day.

I CANNOT AFFORD FAILURE

I tremble because of fear of failure. The last thing I want to do is bring failure to our True Parents. Even unto my life, unto my death, I cannot afford failure. But as the Divine Principle says, if you have faith in Almighty God, everything will happen. No problem. Faith is the deciding factor. Everything can happen with faith. Then, my life would be simpler. But that is not all the Divine Principle teaches. Yes, you need faith. However, the greatness of Divine Principle is that it teaches, more clearly than ever in history, that there is five percent human responsibility. The messiah brought that message. That is why it took God 6,000 years. Why does it take Him so long? Because of human failure. One failure after another has prolonged the accomplishment of God's will. Not because God is weak, or God is unable to do anything. God is almighty. It is that humans have not fulfilled their five percent responsibility. The Divine Principle teaching is so clear. So even though I have faith, I never know whether I am doing my five percent responsibility or not. There is always room for failure.

I am trembling now more than any other time. I cannot afford to fail with the Panda project. Father's honor rests upon it. I cannot fail. I would rather die. I want you to know the real Bo Hi Pak. If you see inside of me, I am a very feeble, weak, trembling person, spending sleepless nights, with my heart palpitating. That is why I always have pills with me. I could not get through some nights without a pill. I have to bring myself down. I am not as strong or healthy as you think.

For that reason, I put my destiny in the hands of God. How many more years God will allow me I do not know. No one in this room knows. Only God knows. But I want to try my absolute best and try to make myself strong, even physically. But I feel that agony, that restlessness, that pressure, of Father's expectation. I don't want to betray that expectation. I want to bring success. Success hinges upon the human five percent responsibility. All that makes me really cry and tremble. That is the real me, the real Bo Hi Pak.

This is why I need your prayers. Another thing I want you to know. I can never be confident that I have carved up a good cloud right next to

True Parents in heaven. Not even for one moment am I sure of that. I do not know if I will go to heaven or hell. I don't know if God sends the judgment. I see the example of Reverend Moon's way of life. When I compare his way of life and mine, and there is a difference between night and day and heaven and earth. Compared to him, I am not there. I am not even near.

For these two reasons I am humbled. As long as I can draw breath, I will do my utmost, invest my last ounce of energy. Until that moment I will give my full measure of devotion. Also, as I did during the time of my kidnapping, I want to live and die with the name of True Parents on my lips.

LISTEN TO MY CONFESSION

This is my honest confession. You are like priests today, listening to my confession. I never do this. I am not trying to show off. I want to show the honest me, the trembling Bo Hi Pak, anxiety-ridden, always thinking, always agonizing. But one thing is sure. When I put concentrated effort and deeds and prayer into it, I know God works with me. That is for sure. Everything that has happened, it is God who has been doing it, particularly the most recent victory of the meeting with Gorbachev. No one ever even imagined that could happen. Yet God did it.

Therefore, I have mixed emotions. I am always relying on God, but at the same time, I am always unsure of myself. Therefore, I have to put my 1,000 percent into whatever I do. That is my way of life, my philosophy. My duty here on earth is to love our fellow man. I am far from doing it, but I am trying. I want to love the Russian people as my fellow man, brothers and sisters. I want to love Chinese people as my fellow man, brothers and sisters. Especially, I want to love you, my brothers and sisters, because you are trained by the hands of True Parents. You are the best fruits of America. I told you so many times. If you do not win the victory here in America for the True Parents, nobody will. That is your responsibility. Sometimes you must tremble too because you have your five percent responsibility. I love you, I am proud of you, I am always on your side, I will never let you down. As long as my last breath is there, I will never let you down.

So let us make history. I am just a simple, ordinary man. When I look at Father, Father is a very special man. I always said God custom-made Father. I am just mass-produced, one individual. But Father and Mother are really custom-made. You know they have the same birthday. Don't you think that without God's custom-made system that would not be possible? Father and Mother, born so many years apart yet on the same day.

The only comfort is that we have True Parents. That is the only comfort to Bo Hi Pak. It doesn't matter if Bo Hi Pak lives 10 more years or 50 more years. It doesn't make any difference as long as True Parents are strong. As long as men and women like you, my dear brothers and sisters, are growing in True Parents' spirit, it doesn't matter if Bo Hi Pak is there or not.

So, I thank you from the very bottom of my heart. I am sorry for speaking too long. Forgive me. I didn't ask for this birthday party, you did, so you have to pay a little indemnity. Anyway, it is once in a lifetime. This is all recorded, so my children and grandchildren will someday see it. I spoke without any notes, just going back and forth, so I don't know if I made any sense or not. I hope I have not offended anybody. That is not the spirit at all. I want you to know I love you. More important, True Parents love you and they are with you. God and the entire spirit world are ours. That is for sure. That is the power of Divine Principle. For that reason, let's finish this particular 19-minute 45-second speech. Thank you and God bless you.

The Dispensational Meaning of Father's Visit to North Korea

NEW YORK, NEW YORK
JANUARY 1, 1992

True Parents visited North Korea from November 30 to December 7, 1991. This historic visit to Father's hometown culminated with a private meeting with President Kim Il Sung, leader of North Korea. After Father embraced Kim Il Sung, he said, "This is the personification of true love— the moment God's dispensational history has been fulfilled. This one event is that important." Behind the scenes working tirelessly was Dr. Pak. He invested countless hours in shuttle diplomacy between Beijing, Pyongyang, and Seoul to bring about this providential event. Here is the story in his own words for future historians to ponder for a thousand years!

I feel like I returned not from North Korea, but from a very far away place like the moon. We had wonderful experiences. Father and Mother have been absolutely brilliant in their manifestation of true love. Since Mr. Peter Kim gave an hour-by-hour kind of report, I would like to emphasize the dispensational meaning of True Parents' visit to North Korea.

The victory of Jacob and Esau, particularly Jacob, was the one time God was truly satisfied, beaming from ear to ear with joy. Jacob completely fulfilled God's expectation, and from there, the Israel nation emerged. But few before or after Jacob in the history of the dispensation have achieved victory. God felt joy when He created Adam and Eve, but He has been absolutely brokenhearted ever since they fell.

Through all this time, God has not had any good days until now when Father, as the universal Jacob, went to North Korea and embraced the universal Esau. Kim Il Sung is the only world leader whom the citizens call father, and as the false father or Adam, he represents the entire Hellenic ideology and all the satanic and communistic forces. The entire evil history is personified in one man, Kim Il Sung. Jacob was courageous enough to go into North Korea and meet Esau. That he could be welcomed by Esau is the most incredible accomplishment in the history of God and man. You will have no idea how significant this is until the entire history is unfolded. Even I only have a glimpse of it.

THE FALSE PARENTS SURRENDERED

The natural subjugation of Kim Il Sung, who symbolizes all the evil, satanic qualities, including false parenthood, means false parents have finally surrendered in front of the True Parents. Father has completely fulfilled God's dispensational history. From today on, January 1, 1992, he is much more relaxed, confident, and happy. Father knows now that both the spiritual and physical worlds will be different.

Kim Il Sung tried to kill Father three times that we know of. Once his government tortured Father almost to death in Pyongyang. The members, like Reverend Won Pil Kim, picked up Father's body and prepared for his burial, but miraculously Father survived. Then he tried to kill Father in Hungnam prison. The third time, in 1987, this man sent out two squads of the Red Army, headed by a Japanese man, Mr. Kikumura, with powerful explosives to blow up Father's Morning Garden in Boston. In the nick of time, they were discovered and captured by the FBI. I could spit at Kim Il Sung. However, Father said, "I forgive you, I love you as my brother, and I unite with you." In pictures, you can see Father and Kim Il Sung looking at each other almost like brothers who have been separated for 10 years. This is the personification of true love—the moment God's dispensational history has been fulfilled. Because of this, your job gets easier, my job gets easier, the spirit world is happy, and all kinds of miraculous things will happen. This one event is that important.

Father said he met Kim Il Sung as a friend, then after lunch they came out as brothers, and next time, Kim Il Sung will be as Father's son. I told Father that he should be in the center between Mother and Kim Il Sung in the photographs, but Father said, "No, my future son should be in the center; we must surround him with true love."

Kim Il Sung is 80 years old and many people wondered, "Why has God let such a dictator survive that long?" Father said, "Good reason." I realized he must be in the providential position to meet with True Father and be subjugated by true love before he dies.

The only newspaper in North Korea printed a picture of Father's entire party on the front page, and every day they reported everything Father was doing. All North Korean people read this, like a Bible. They know who Father is now, what Father has spoken, what Father has been doing. But most importantly, Father's welcoming speech was published in the newspaper the following day. Father gave that speech the night he arrived.

A KNOCK IN THE NIGHT

Then at 3:00 a.m. somebody knocked on my door. I did not know if it was the North Korean equivalent of the KGB. The man out there was very nervous, and he apologized saying, "I am sorry to disturb your sleep. Great Leader called me. He just read Reverend Moon's speech that he gave last night. He liked it so much he wants to put the speech in the newspaper. We have never done this before but this time Great Leader would like to do it. I need Reverend Moon's approval." I said, "Reverend Moon is in bed and sleeping. I cannot get his approval." He said, "What about your approval?" I wondered whether I had the authority or not. But most important, what if they changed and twisted the words? That would be a problem. So I said, "Okay. I will give approval if you sign this copy of Reverend Moon's speech and promise you will print it exactly as it is written." So he signed it. Father spoke about God in his speech many times, and they printed it reluctantly but each time they put quotation marks around the word "God." This was the first time in 46 years that the word God in a context of love appeared in a North Korean newspaper.

The second day we had a meeting in the Mon Su Da congressional hall. Chairman Yoon and many professors attended. They tried to persuade Father to accept their juche ideology. Yoon Ki Bok is a great orator. He gave a 30-minute speech about juche ideology, saying that it can save the entire world. When the briefing session was over, they expected just a couple of questions, but instead Father said, "Bo Hi, give them a report of what I have done in the past 25 years in the United States." Pounding the table, I spoke politely, but forthrightly, and explained Godism, headwing ideology, true love, and all our projects. They politely applauded but thought that was the end of it. Then Father stood up. The officials said, "You don't have to stand up, please sit down." Father said, "No, Bo Hi, give me a glass of water." He drank the water and began preaching exactly as he does to us. I was scared to death. After that Father said, "Juche ideology is wrong because there is no God in it, so it cannot be a unified nation's ideology." I died even more.

Finally, Father said, "In a unified Korea, I will become supreme chairman of the unified Korean peninsula. Kim Il Sung will be the vice chairman, and the central ideology will be Godism and headwing ideology." I thought we were finished and probably by the next day we would be in jail. Father said, "Since you heard this, I do not think you will want me to meet with Kim Il Sung, but no matter what, I came here for a historical purpose—to testify to the truth."

I WAS DYING INSIDE

I knew that without meeting Kim Il Sung, Father's visit to North Korea would be very much diminished. I was dying inside. But when they tried to discourage Kim Il Sung from seeing Reverend Moon, Kim Il Sung laughed and said, "What an interesting man we have, who wants to become the chairman and make me vice chairman. Well, that intrigues me, and I want to meet this man more than before."

The big man recognized the big man. Father knew Kim Il Sung, and Kim Il Sung knew Father. For that reason the petty recommendation of the lower staff would not be accepted. Kim Il Sung said to Father very proudly, "I invited you, sir." In other words, those people are so afraid of you, they do not even want to see you. But I want you to come here.

The amazing thing is that Father acted so beautifully and politely with Kim Il Sung. Kim Il Sung was so happy, from beginning to the end. Later he scolded his people, "What do you mean Reverend Moon is bad? He is a good friend of mine. Why did you report lies to me?"

Later on Deputy Prime Minister Kim said to Father, "Reverend Moon, I really respect you because at the meeting with President Kim I saw another side of you. After meeting you, I cannot say there is no God."

Kim Il Sung just happened to invite Father to meet him at Hungnam city, although Prime Minister Kim Dal Yan tied to avoid having the meeting there. Prime Minister Kim told me on the plane, "Dr. Pak, I just simply cannot deny God is there. We desperately tried to avoid having the meeting in Hungnam, but it happened our leader wanted to meet Reverend Moon there." Kim Il Sung's inviting Father to Hungnam in a way symbolically apologized for his wrongdoing. This is the way history will be written.

A normal meeting with the president at the White House is only 15 minutes, in which time you can still conduct a lot of business. But we met with Kim Il Sung for an hour and a half! From time to time, Father said, "Bo Hi, you explain." I had a good reason to shout because Kim Il Sung is hard of hearing. He gave Father a standing ovation three times. Our Father gave such a frank but loving and constructive talk. It was a historical meeting. Also unprecedented was that he spent two and a half hours with Father in the dining room. Mother is not so much a drinker, but Kim Il Sung kept saying, "This is a special wine that was especially brewed for you, Reverend and Mrs. Moon. You must taste it." What could she say but, "Yes, I will taste it." This man seldom does this kind of thing. He was like a child.

After dinner, Father and Kim Il Sung walked down a 100-yard hallway holding hands. They were no longer friends, they were brothers. Father completely embraced him. There was no animosity or hatred. Father was incredible. Father said:

> This was for me a historical opportunity to return to North Korea. I received severe persecution from the government because of my position as a religious leader and my unswerving anti-communist principles. I was tortured harshly and imprisoned for nearly three years in a labor camp. There I witnessed the death of many who had also been imprisoned without cause. The fact that I am alive today can only be described as a miracle and as a result of God's special blessing and protection. Now I have visited North Korea. For someone in my position to love those who really cannot be loved is the essence of true love. I was not entering the house of my enemy, but rather I was returning to my homeland to visit the house of my brother. I carried with me to North Korea the principle that I have always lived by—to forgive, love, and unite.

Father signed two important documents while he was there: one is a joint communique with the North Korean government and the other is an economic joint venture agreement. This communique is an act of the president. The Korean government will say that Reverend Moon as a private individual went to North Korea to make an agreement, but what God says is more important. God will say, "You are my son, my representative. Go and communicate with these people, open their hearts, testify, heal them, solve the differences between North and South, and sign the joint communique." This joint communique is really the first step toward the unification of the Fatherland and is very important. There are 10 points, like 10 commandments coming from Pyongyang. Right now South and North Korea are having talks. Father pushed Kim Il Sung to meet with Roh Tae Woo, the South Korean president, in the same way that he told Gorbachev to meet with Roh Tae Woo to open up diplomatic dialogue with South Korea. The South Korean government should be grateful because Father laid the foundation to accomplish their goals.

As a first step, the two sides decided to establish in 1992 a place where members of separated families can meet and mail can be exchanged. Father passionately appealed to Kim Il Sung, "How can I go back to South Korea after meeting my family without having permission for all families to meet each other?" Kim Il Sung said, "Reverend Moon, I am moved by your statement and passion. Let's do it."

FATHER'S FAMILY

Father met with 47 relatives but could only recognize his elder and younger sisters and his sister-in-law. Some relatives died during the war and some died of disease, but none of them were persecuted or sentenced to death by Kim Il Sung. Father respects that big-mindedness of Kim Il Sung.

Father's only elder brother, who is now deceased, loved Father very much. He knew his younger brother had a special revelation and mission and instructed his wife to completely serve Father. When Father was attending school, she truly took care of him. So at the reunion with his sister-in-law she was ready to collapse in tears. But Father said, "Don't cry. I did not come for tears. I came for God's mission. We have much greater things to do." This is how Father lifted up the spirit of the women. Father never showed tears.

Father's house is 100 years old and big by Korean standards. In one conversation with Kim Il Sung, Father said, "Thank you, I went to my hometown. My birthhouse was intact. I have paint all over my body because the paint was still wet." They were laughing and laughing. Kim Il Sung said, "We have to preserve your birthplace in an important way, as a shrine." Can you imagine? North Korea, an atheistic and totalitarian country that opposed Father, now wants to preserve his home as a shrine! So we already have a Holy Ground at Jung-ju, North Korea. Kim Il Sung, as a prodigal son who came back, fulfilled a most wonderful filial son's role.

At his parents' tomb, Father and Mother touched the tombstone the government had put there and prayed. Father's elder sister could not contain her emotions and shouted out, "Mother, you wanted to see your son so much at least once before you died. Now your son, Young Myung (which Father was called as a boy), has come here. Mother, wake up and meet your son." Father said, "My dear sister, Mother is up in heaven. Please be comforted. Do not cry." I was crying and crying. Mother cried. But Father did not shed a tear.

Father's mother truly loved him, but because of his mission, he didn't pay much attention to her, which broke her heart. When Father was in Hungnam prison, his mother prepared clothes and barley rice powder, which was very rare and precious at that time. She put it on her head and journeyed about 30 days to Hungnam to see her son and to help him survive. Father welcomed her, of course, but then immediately distributed everything to the other inmates in front of his mother. She thought, "I gave every ounce of my blood to make this and bring it here. How can you treat me like this?" Then she left and cried and cried. But two or three months later, she would go to Hungnam again, and the same thing would happen. She did not understand Father's position: I am not here for my own survival; I am here as the messiah. I have to save these people. So Father now said, "I did a harsh thing to my mother, but I am sure she understands by now." Father never preached one word of Divine Principle to his mother.

BACK TO PANDA COUNTRY

When our plane landed in China after leaving Pyongyang, the North Korean ambassador to China was waiting in the rain to personally welcome Father and Mother, the friends of his king, Kim Il Sung. Father and Mother went to Tiannamen Square and then to the Panda site. The mayor, local secretary of the Communist Party, and local officials came to welcome Father and Mother. Father spoke with them for about an hour. It was a beautiful visit. Then Father and Mother went through all the Panda facilities and walked miles and miles. Mother said it was "awesome." Father asked Josette Shiner, a *Washington Times* reporter, "What do you think about the factory?" She said, "Father, this is 10 times bigger than I imagined it." This factory is the biggest factory in the Republic of China, so all the top leaders of Beijing are coming down to look at it. This year, 1992, we are going to have a Panda car rolling off the assembly line.

Many newspapers printed headlines about Father's visit and published pictures of Father and Kim Il Sung. One quoted Father, "I entered North Korea as an apostle of peace." Even in Hong Kong, the *Sunday Morning Post*, December 22, 1991, said, "How Reverend Moon Slowly But Surely Took North Korea by Storm." The article concluded by quoting Father, "I visited North Korea in the spirit of true love. I did not feel that I was entering the house of my enemy, but rather that I was returning to my homeland to visit the house of my brother."

The prime ministers from North and South Korea met. This meeting is nothing but the continuation of Father's meeting. There is incredible euphoria in all of South Korea. One English newspaper said, "New Era Dawning in Korea."

My dear brothers and sisters, this was a great victory for Father. It is so big and we are so close to it that we cannot fully realize its significance. But Father's visit will impact all your lives in a good way. The spirit world has changed. In the Korean peninsula peace is coming. Father spoke about the unification of the new nation. That is a nation that comes under Father's principle. Korea will become a new nation. It is a matter of time. This is a great time we are living in. Father has accomplished a most extraordinary success in 1991. This year, 1992, shall be even greater, because the momentum from 1991 will be carried out. I see Father so relaxed, so happy, and today I am very happy too.

THE BLESSING CEREMONY—
A UNIVERSAL, HISTORICAL EVENT

AUGUST 25, 1992

SEOUL, KOREA

─────────────────

Dr. Pak explains the providential difference of this 30,000 Couples Blessing compared to all the previous ones. He shares his profound experience as the emcee of such an important event and concludes with exciting news about creating new Holy Grounds in Korea.

This Blessing of 30,000 couples was the first since the proclamation of True Parents. Of course, it is true that the previous Blessings were also given by True Parents—this is the tradition we have observed since the Blessing of the 36 couples. But this International Holy Wedding was the first major Blessing ceremony to be held since True Parents proclaimed themselves as messiah in front of all the world. Until this time, the Blessing ceremonies were Unification Church affairs, held within the church. This one, however, had tremendous significance. Following the proclamation of True Parents in front of all the world, it was a universal, worldwide, historical event. It was fundamentally different.

There were more than 1,000 journalists in the Olympic Stadium covering this Blessing ceremony. Some press people were using helicopters from the day before the ceremony. This had never been seen before: American and Japanese television filming the Blessing from the air. This Blessing was a world-shaking event that turned the whole world upside down. I think that is the special meaning of this Blessing.

And then there was the historical proclamation that gave special meaning to this event. Every 30 minutes throughout the day, the American CNN television network broadcast the scenes of Father and Mother coming down the stairs wearing their crowns and of the brides and grooms lined up in the stadium.

As you know, I was the emcee for this Blessing, and it seemed to me that a heavy weight I had been carrying for 35 years was lifted from my shoulders. Whenever I finished a sentence, it was with the proclamation, "...presided over by the Reverend and Mrs. Moon, the True Parents of mankind!" In Japanese this is "makodono kokosama," and when I pronounced this phrase I thought to myself. "Wow, now the whole of Japan, 120 million people, are listening to this!" I could not have felt better. And then I said it in English. The Americans have heard the words "Reverend Moon" a lot, but they probably heard the expression "the True Parents of mankind" for the first time. I proclaimed this in front of the five billion people of the world! It was received over the airwaves throughout the world.

Having made this breath-taking proclamation after each verse—"the Reverend and Mrs. Moon, the True Parents of mankind"—I can die any day and not have any regrets. I emphasized in every paragraph, "Now there are 30,000 couples including those in 10 other countries who are participating in this Blessing simultaneously via satellite." This was to make it absolutely clear that this was a historical Blessing for the whole global village.

Then there was the scene when the brides and grooms bowed to True Parents and everybody thought, "Well, now they are honoring the True Parents; they are paying respect to the officiators," but then the emcee said the words, "Brides and grooms who are participating in this Blessing via satellite, stand facing Korea!"

This is a small digression, but when I was a child during the time of the Japanese occupation, we had to bow every morning toward the palace of the Japanese emperor. This was called "Eastward Worship." The time has now come when the world performs "Northward Worship" and "Westward Worship." The time has now come for the world to bow toward the place where the True Parents are.

I told the world to officially bow to True Parents—Africa, Brazil, the Philippines, everywhere. "Brides and grooms who are participating in this Blessing via satellite, stand facing Korea!" After these words, when I gave the command to bow, I was telling the people of the whole world to bow to True Parents! What a grand feeling! It is hard to put this into words. This was a ceremony when the brides and grooms from all over the world, representing all mankind, bowed toward the fatherland of their faith, Korea, and received the Blessing of True Parents.

We printed all these words in the *Segye Times*. We even mentioned the point about the participants in the Blessing bowing toward the nation of True Parents. I talked about this earlier; the elder generation still remembers the "Eastward Worship." But because True Father was born in Korea, the people of the world are now bowing toward Korea. Whether they are Unificationists or Christians or Buddhists, no matter what their religion, all who belong to the Korean race could not help but get excited at this moment. It was an occasion to instill great patriotic pride in all the people of this nation.

All the other newspapers carried stories about the Blessing this time, but the *Segye Times* gave it front page coverage. The press and the government were shocked that such a ceremony could have been held. Even though our ceremony was the greatest, only seeing is believing. The scale of this event had to be shown, and that is what our *Segye Times* did. We had a picture of True Parents giving the Blessing and above it, in large type, the Chinese characters of Father's name: Moon Sun Myung. The opening paragraph began with, "Four hours of splendor and emotion, on the day of the greatest ever international joint wedding of 30,000 couples; the rain stopped and the sky turned brilliant clear, the Blessing of God, the Blessing of God..."

As we found out later, many Christians had prayed to God for it to pour with rain on that day. Elders, deacons, and pastors prayed in all-night vigils. But on the day, although it was raining all over Korea, in Seoul the sun was shining brightly. On the day before the ceremony during the rehearsal, I announced, "Whether it rains or snows, even if a storm blows up with thunder and lightning, we will hold the Blessing ceremony!" But Mother said as she left: "Tomorrow it will not rain. Don't worry. Father prayed for God's special intervention." After I heard these words I fully believed them and didn't prepare even one umbrella. The rain kept pouring until 4 o'clock in the morning, but when I awoke it began to clear and it became a really beautiful day. Father's prayer was answered so well that my face even got sunburned. All the brides and grooms had red noses the next day.

More than a thousand journalists reported on this Blessing. The major newspapers and magazines from America and other nations sent their correspondents. Something like that would never have been possible in the past. I have the editorial page of the *Segye Times* here with me. It carries the headline: "The World Is One Home, Mankind Is One Family." This editorial was not written by Dr. Son Tae-oh or one of our family members. The editorial department decided to carry such an editorial because "this event gives our newspaper's president the greatest victory of his life; therefore we agreed to unite with the purpose of our founder." This is a fundamentally different newspaper now compared to six months ago when 130 people resigned from the paper in protest against Father's decision not to allow them to establish a labor union. I am truly grateful to God and True Parents.

THE WEDDING VOWS THAT SHOOK MY SOUL

There is nobody on earth who could have achieved such an amazing feat. No religious or political organization could have done this. Only the messiah, True Parents, armed with the Divine Principle and its power, are able to bring about a unified world. Breaking down sectarianism and racism, overcoming national and ethnic barriers, and bringing all mankind together in this grand union of world peace—who else could have accomplished that? Could the king of one nation have done it? Could the president of the United States or the prime minister of Japan have done it?

On the day before the Holy Wedding, Father gathered more than 700 VIPs from all sectors of society and from all over the world and, in front of them all, proclaimed himself as the messiah. The next day all of them came to the Blessing ceremony and witnessed the event. There were 22 former presidents; about 100 prime ministers, ministers of state, and ambassadors; 114 leading representatives of the world's media; religious leaders; scholars and experts in various fields from all over the world. Do you think they could get much sleep after Father had proclaimed his messiahship the day before? There were many who stayed awake all night, and when it was time to go to the Blessing ceremony, they were getting on the bus one hour before departure time! Usually when there is an international conference, about half of the participants do their own sightseeing rather than join the officially scheduled tour. Because there were 114 media people we had ordered only three buses, thinking there would be plenty of room left. But finally we had to order another bus. The reason was that foreign ambassadors to Korea, embassy counselors, and foreign media representatives residing in Korea came and wanted to ride along. After all standing room on the buses was filled, we had to order an additional bus.

Also all the former heads of state who stayed at the Lotte Hotel came. There must have been many among them, too, who could not sleep the night before. But they all felt that they had to participate in this event no matter what. They had breakfast early, and some of them put on their gala uniform with black bow tie and everything, just as if they were the bridegrooms.

The former Egyptian prime minister, Aziz Hegazy, came as the chairman of the Summit Council. This person was so impressed by the dignity of the ceremony that he said to his wife: "Let's go out and join in the ceremony. How can we just sit and watch such a solemn celebration!" He was so astounded by the event. Later, some journalists who had heard him say these words told us the story.

Then there was the prayer, and the atmosphere in the stadium elevated. Then the bridesmaids and groomsmen entered. This was truly a sight not from this world. The 30,000 couples lined up, and after one holy song, during which the bridesmaids and groomsmen walked down to their positions, the announcement was heard, "The officiators, the Reverend and Mrs. Moon will now enter!" But they didn't come out. It is not an easy thing for the Lord to appear on the earth. The Christians have waited for 2,000 years, but some in the VIP seats just could not wait anymore and were staring impatiently up at the sky. But finally, Father appeared, walking solemnly in his white gown, through the golden gate with its blue backdrop. The very second the True Parents appeared, a thundering applause blended with the sound of the holy music. It was an exhilarating experience.

Usually True Parents step up to a podium, but this time they came down from heaven. All of these things completely captured the hearts of the people in the stadium. When Father read the four wedding vows, the 30,000 brides and grooms who were there in Chamshil Stadium responded in Korean by shouting "Yeh." When this "Yeh" soared from the bottom of their hearts, resounding throughout the stadium, it took everybody's breath away; it was just so overwhelming. My soul was completely shaken. I was literally trembling. When Father gave the Founder's Address at the opening of the Media Conference, he spoke of "the creation of God's army of peace." When our guests saw this scene, they felt it to their bones that this was in fact the "army of peace" Reverend Moon had been talking about.

THE CONSECRATION AND PROCLAMATION OF THE HOLY WEDDING

After that came Father's Consecration Prayer for the Holy Wedding. The VIPs may not have understood the words of this prayer, but they felt as if, for the first time in their lives, they were hearing the voice of God coming down from heaven. Father's words touched their heartstrings. The words of Father's prayer washed away all the dark and dirty things in the hearts of all the people present. He made them pure like snow. And then Father made the Proclamation of the Holy Wedding. Father first made the proclamation in Korean, but because these words were so important, they were repeated in Japanese for all of Japan to hear, and then in English too. The Japanese people heard it in Japanese, and the Western people heard it in English. At that moment, all the people who were there other than the brides and grooms felt: "Next time it's my turn, next it'll be my turn!"

All the presidents and former prime ministers and ambassadors there felt like that, including the lady ambassador of Ecuador. She said that she had been thinking that she would never be able to marry in her life, but now she had met a man who would Bless her and find a husband for her. She had heard that Father also matches by picture, so she would start preparing her pictures that same day. That's what the atmosphere was like there.

Brothers and sisters, this was a gathering of the world media people, of top world leaders, all the top representatives of mankind were there. These people were all so positive, so inspired. They were shaken by something to the depth of their souls. They were completely drawn into it. It made them think: "Now we have to study the Divine Principle!"

In the evening of that day, we had a special meeting back at the hotel. The participants wanted all their questions answered. So, for over eight hours, we explained to them. They also asked why it was necessary to have such a proclamation at this event. So we explained it to them.

This proclamation of Father actually came 40 years late. Because Christianity did not receive Father, and because we, who are following him, were not able to prepare a sufficient foundation for him earlier, the proclamation, which should have been made 40 years ago, regretfully came so late. This is how the explanation session went.

THE CONFUSED STATE OF
SEXUAL MORALITY IN JAPAN

This time, the Japanese media covered the event in amazing depth, with live broadcasts. Especially because the famous actress Sakurada Junko was among the brides who were Blessed to grooms Father had chosen, the scenes of the Blessing were broadcast live in Japan. The hearts of 120 million Japanese were turned upside down. Do you know why? Japan has been courting the materialistic civilization, immersing itself in the philosophy of the supremacy of materialistic values. This is blatant hedonism, and this hedonism has brought about a collapse of sexual morality.

There is a really evil American preacher going by the name of "Father David" who established a new religion in Japan called the "Family of Love." The teaching of this "Family of Love" is this: God did not give man his sexual capability merely for the purpose of making children and multiplying the human race, but as a way for men and women to find pleasure. They are preaching that for this purpose it is all right to enjoy sex with any man or woman one likes. This movement, which has been spreading in Japan since 1987, was written about in a very popular magazine called *Munyechoonchoo*, and when the young people of Japan heard about this they thought, "Well, look at that; that is an exciting religion!"

In this atmosphere of sexual permissiveness, the famous Japanese actress named Sakurada Junko called a press conference. She is the Elizabeth Taylor of Japan. The American Elizabeth Taylor has been married six times. The minds of the Japanese people are full of concepts about actresses. So all of Japan thinks that if someone is an actress she is like that.

Japan has so many good things, doesn't it? But because the Japanese like Western things too much, they don't discriminate and take on the bad customs together with the good ones. The bad tendencies from America are invading Japan.

But the Elizabeth Taylor of Japan said during her press conference, "Reverend Moon is matching the couples this time, and I don't know if I am worthy to get a partner from him. But if I am given the glorious opportunity to participate in the Blessing, I will do so." That was what she proclaimed. The reporters had come to the press conference expecting that she would merely confess to being a member of the Unification Church, so as soon as they heard this bombshell announcement—that this famous young woman would participate in the mass wedding—they ran to their telephones and told their news desks at their newspapers, their magazines, or broadcasting stations, "Hold everything, we have a top news article coming for the front page." Then they went back to the press conference to get the full story.

In Japan, where sexual immorality is rampant, this woman, who is like an idol in that society, said that she would do "*Mee Ai*," which means "find a spouse through a matchmaker."

TRUE PARENTS CAN RESTORE THE FALLEN WORLD

They say that in California 75 percent of couples who marry get divorced. All over America there is a divorce rate of 50 percent. Many children born in America now can't use the names of their father and mother. That is because they don't know who their father or mother is. Almost half of the children in America come from broken families. Japan has not gone that far, but it is no doubt going in that direction. It is such an immoral society. So what's the use in meeting a hundred or a thousand potential spouses, having dates with them, and trying to choose one's husband from among them? One can only see the present. One can see neither the future nor the past. But Reverend Moon, whom I follow, not only sees a person's present state, he sees their past ancestors as well. He matches people in this way. What method of choosing one's spouse is more ideal, more scientific, than that? After a press conference like that, you can imagine how shocked the Japanese were. They must also have felt a sense of shame.

The True Parents are the only ones who can restore this fallen world. Sakurada Junko was God's instrument. Dozens of Japanese TV cameras were focused on her at the Holy Wedding ceremony. From the time she joined, God used her like this, and in the future Sakurada Junko, as she understands Father's purpose, will be able to spread the Principle to all of Japan and even proclaim it all over the world. This tremendous worldwide victory shows that the completion of Father's providence is in sight. We are in the era of perfection! What good fortune for us that we are able to live together with, and be disciples of, the substantial representatives of God in the society of men, our perfected True Parents. From now on we have to lead the world, beginning with the 40 million Koreans.

PILGRIMAGES TO JUNG-JU HAVE BEGUN

We have the responsibility to lead all of them to the Blessing. The final thing I want to report to you is the fact that with this Blessing, Father has laid the cornerstone for the unification of North and South Korea. Father selected those members with special merit from among the brides and grooms and sent them on a pilgrimage to Jung-ju in North Pyongan Province.

This is a symbolic beginning. On August 31, at 9:30 a.m., they will gather in Nagoya and from there they will fly to North Korea. The Unification flag will truly fly toward Pyongyang. Father has named our brother Hideo Oyamada as the leader of the group. I think he was chosen because he can understand Korean and he speaks excellent English. So even though he is Japanese, he is a leader who can record all the details of this trip and report them accurately. Of course, the overall leader of the members in Japan is Takeru Kamiyama, but because President Kamiyama has a mountain of work to do in Japan, Father made this decision.

Nine months ago, Father met Kim Il Sung and the vice prime minister, as well as Chairman Yoon Ki Bok, and when he spoke at the Assembly Hall, he said: "The way for you to survive is this: designate Jung-ju and Hungnam, and in the future also Anju, as Holy Grounds and open them up. For us these places are Holy Grounds, but you may also call them tourist sites. When the members of the Unification Church come here on pilgrimages, and worship at these places, your country will have a way to survive."

In fact there was an economic conference planned, but, brushing that economic conference aside, Father said, "This is economics. If you do this, your economy will also survive. So hand over Jung-ju!" Kim Dal Hyun turned ash grey and could not open his mouth. This is something only Kim Il Sung could decide. Kim Dal Hyun or Yoon Ki Bok are not the people to decide such a thing.

When Father met Kim Il Sung, this conversation took place at the table: "Ah, this time you visited your hometown, I heard." Father answered: "Yes, I went there." "I hear that the house you were born in is well preserved. How did you like it?" Then Father said: "I really had not imagined that my house would still be there, but you have preserved it like that. I am very grateful that you have made all this effort and had the house repaired and newly painted and even had new sand spread in the courtyard." Kim Il Sung was smiling: "That house is a very precious treasure. I have already ordered our people to preserve that house well."

Chieftain Kim Il Sung had already heard and seen what Father had said the day before, and had decided to designate this as a Holy Area and to present it to Father as a gift of love. Kim Il Sung said this during the talks with Father.

HOLIEST OF HOLY GROUNDS

Before Father visited Jung-ju, there was no paved road to his home town. The people of that village and district must have worked for one whole week without sleeping to construct the road. The paint had apparently been applied the night before Father went into the room in which he had been born and prayed. When he came out, the paint on the doorpost stained his coat. They had been in such a hurry to please Father. Kim Il Sung did not say this, but, according to his aides, he had warned them not to make it look better than Man Kyong Dae, the place where he himself had been born. He said that Father would understand that, but because Father looks a hundred and a thousand years into the future, he doesn't think it important how these things are done now. History will decide which place is more important. Will it be Man Kyong Dae? Or will it be the home of Father in Jung-ju? Think about that.

There are plans to make the grave of Father's parents into a place where everybody can worship and pray. The spot where Father received the call of God on Easter Sunday at the age of 16 will become the holiest of holy grounds. This was not possible on this occasion, but in the future, when our members leave donations there, a museum can be built there, where pictures of Father can be shown. All the people of the world can visit.

Unification Church members who go there will leave donations. We hear that they have already prepared a collection box. They say it is made from marble and weighs two tons. It reportedly took the strongest truck in all of North Korea to get it there. Do they have cranes or good machinery like that in North Korea? It seems it took hundreds of people to shoulder it and lift it down from the truck. So they put this collection box in front of Father's paternal home and it seems they are preparing to make this into a holy area with the donations of the Unification Church members. When Father went there somebody was still living in the house.

There are also three houses where his relatives used to live. They made one of the relatives the manager of the area, and he is supposed to be the guide for the visitors. But more important than that, because it is impossible to go by helicopter every time from Pyongyang to Jung-ju, a bus route had to be prepared. The roads used to be very bad, but in the last few months they made enormous effort to build a road. Now the Moon family in North Korea has been raised to the status of nobility. In their thinking, Kim Il Sung is the great chieftain, the "Sun of the East," and now that the great Sun has joined in brotherly ties with Chairman Sun Myung Moon, right after the Chieftain's own family Father's relatives are treated like "family."

The last time I went there, I met a man who had studied much about Father's family. He asked me about the origins of the Unification Church. So I talked about Father's life from his birth and so on, but he said that I flunked the test and that he was more of a Unificationist than I was. Then he told me what the origins of the Unification Church were, and what he said I heard for the first time. Before Father was born, a pair of yellow cranes came to his home town, and whenever they came to roost some tragedy struck the village. Always somebody died. But then when Father was born, the birds disappeared without leaving any trace, and from that time on there were no more tragic deaths or accidents. This, he said, was the origin of the Unification Church.

The second story he told I had heard from Father before. After Father was born, there were no more tragedies concerning people, but a series of misfortunes with animals began. Dogs died, cows died, pigs drowned where it seemed impossible for a pig to drown. Father had told us that these kinds of things happened in his village. But as this man told the story, he added that this series of misfortunes to animals continued for 16 years—until after Father had accepted the call of God on the Easter Sunday when he met Jesus.

When Father met Kim Il Sung in Hungnam, the very place where Father had gone through unspeakable trials in the prison camp, it was as if the process of restoration through indemnity was made absolutely clear. The people there had tried to avoid a meeting between Father and Kim Il

Sung in Hungnam, but the place that Kim Il Sung chose to receive Father was, strangely enough, precisely Hungnam. So on the way to Kim Il Sung's residence, Father drove past the Hungnam fertilizer plant where he had spent his prison camp days. The North Koreans also know about the Hungnam story. During the Korean War, B-24 bombers attacked Hungnam, and people were being killed in the bombardment. After running back and forth to escape the bombs, the prisoners realized that the place where Father stayed was never in danger. So, although nobody told them to do so, whenever the sirens sounded, the prisoners all gathered at the place where Father was standing. Father spoke about this already this morning. Within a radius of 20 meters of Father, nobody was hurt at all. The North Koreans also knew this story.

In this way the North Korean people already know the origin of the Unification Church. This man told me to tell this story after going back to the South, and that he would tell it also to the Unification pilgrims who would come to the North.

This time our tour group will not go all the way to Hungnam. However, some members of our church have been to the Hungnam fertilizer factory before. The local government is now thinking about building a special monument there commemorating the history of Father's indemnity at that time.

This man told me that the people of North Korea have heard these facts by word of mouth. Truly amazing things are happening there. This time President Oyamada thinks it might be good to take photos of Father and this Blessing Ceremony along and give them to the important people there. Actually, would it be possible to hold such a historical Blessing as this, with people from 131 countries participating, under the "Juche" ideology? Short of listening to Principle lectures, there is nothing that can testify to Father more than this Blessing. I wanted to finally emphasize the fact that this event is connected directly to the unification of North and South Korea.

This time, many newspapers carried our story, and they reported the facts without distorting even one word. Father said that the *Segye Times* had put pressure on the other media. He proclaimed the formation of a moral media that is able to exert pressure on the media in Japan and around the world. On the day when a moral media proclaims Father's words to the world, Father's kingdom will appear in front of our eyes. I will end my report with profound gratitude, and a passionate round of applause, to Father and Mother.

IN GRATITUDE TO THE TRUE PARENTS

EAST GARDEN, TARRYTOWN, NEW YORK

APRIL 25, 1993

Mrs. Ki Sook Yoon Pak was the first woman in-law of True Parents' family to reach her 60th birthday. The True Parents honored her with a special celebration at East Garden. Father explained that this was not just a celebration for one day, but a new tradition. On the 60th birthday of all Blessed members, the combined families should celebrate together and every 10 years after that. Father said that based on Dr. and Mrs. Pak's "standing as an ideal couple, this kind of unified and united family involvement, family standard, is set today and will continue forever."

INTRODUCTION BY PETER KIM

I would like to introduce Mrs. Ki Sook Yoon Pak's life briefly. She was born on April 25, 1933, which makes her 60 years old. Before she joined the Unification Church, she had married Dr. Bo Hi Pak on November 29, 1953.

In 1957, they heard Divine Principle and accepted Father and Mother as their True Parents, and in March 1961, they received the Blessing as one of the 36 Couples (Dr. Pak was in America at the time). Since their marriage and Blessing, they have had three sons and three daughters. They all got Blessed and some of them have children. As you know, out of the six, Jin Sung Nim and Hoon Sook Nim joined the True Family. Mrs. Pak has one brother and six sisters. They all joined the Unification Church, and some of them are Blessed. All of them are still in the movement. Mrs. Pak has a special message this morning to show her special thanks to God and True Parents and everybody here.

[The morning included Father's explanation of the event, cake cutting, pictures, and gifts. Mrs. Pak read her thanks in Korean.]

This must be a dream. How could this occasion be real? Father and Mother, when I heard from my husband that you instructed him by saying, "Bring Ki Sook to East Garden; we shall celebrate her 60th birthday," I was absolutely shocked, to the point of almost fainting.

At that moment my heart began beating fast, and tears of overwhelming disbelief and gratitude for such great fortune began to run down my cheeks. That stream of tears continues at this moment. Father and Mother, I thank you from the very depths of my soul.

However, I know that no matter what I do to express my gratitude to you, our True Parents, I could never thank you enough for this most extraordinary heavenly blessing and for the honor you are bestowing upon me today. Even if I gave my thanks to you every moment of my life for the rest of my life, until the last day of my existence here on earth, it could not be enough. Even when it is time for me to go to the spirit world and I give you my thanks for the rest of eternity, still I would not have responded enough to the true love you have bestowed upon me, this meager, humble daughter. Today, I must confess, I am eternally indebted to you, and it can never be repaid.

In the Unification Church there are many outstanding leaders and members who are absolutely loyal to you and serve you with unconditional filial piety. There are also many heroes and heroines in our church, who served you from the very early days of our church, and whose impeccable record of upholding the tradition and whose spirit of dedication are unparalleled.

Then, who am I? I do not even feel near to those great forerunners and great members of our church. Yet I am receiving today a most extraordinary honor from True Parents, which was not given to anybody before me. When I think of the significance of this occasion, I am completely overwhelmed. My heart is filled with gratitude. I do not have a sense of how to respond properly to this occasion. Only these ceaseless tears running in a helpless way can express the most honest feeling of my heart.

SERVICE BEHIND THE SCENES

My husband and I have been in the Unification Church for almost 38 years. During this relatively long period of time, I have had no notable accomplishments. Therefore, I have always felt I am not worthy of coming before the True Parents.

Furthermore, since I am not that healthy, I have simply taken a passive role behind the scenes, silently enduring all the difficulties, obeying our True Parents, helping my husband, who is serving beside our True Parents in a very important role, and simply bringing up our children so that they will live up to our tradition and True Parents' expectation. I have always felt that this is nothing special or spectacular, just the normal duties of any good wife in the Unification Church.

Yet, miraculously and to our great surprise, two of our children have been chosen to become members of True Parents' family. In my entire life I could never imagine, nor would I even dare consider, that such a blessing would be possible. I know that this extraordinary blessing did not come by our merit, but came solely to us as a gift from God and through the mercy of our True Parents.

Father, I pledge I shall cherish and value this unforgettable honor for the rest of my life. Father and Mother, you often ask my husband, "How is Ki Sook's health? Is she doing all right?" Whenever my husband would relate to me your concern and remembrances of my health and that you frequently asked such questions of him, I would be totally overwhelmed and tearfully thankful. Each time I heard of your concern for me, I would feel revitalized and gained new energy to go on. Father and Mother, I am convinced that the fact that I am even living today is solely because of your love and your blessing.

Dear Mother, this time, in order to arrange for this celebration, you called Korea to prepare for me and my husband these beautiful Korean gowns. You also had custom-made for me this golden double ring which is a symbolic gift of good health. Then, today you prepared my 60th birthday celebration with an amazingly beautiful offering table. These are all beyond me and beyond anything that I deserve.

Father and Mother, you have breathed into my life and into our family new life, energy, and resurrection. Today we feel like we once again became a bride and bridegroom. Again, how can we repay you for such immense blessings?

Father and Mother, today I am beginning a new life. Although I am not worthy, still I pledge upon this monumental occasion to be most obedient to you, to become your pious daughter, and, to the best of my ability, to serve you until the last day of my life.

Long live our True Parents! Long live our True Parents' family, which shall be prosperous and fill heaven and earth.

Father and Mother, I thank you once again from the very bottom of my heart.

GIVE AND TAKE OF LOVE

NEW YORK, NEW YORK
JANUARY 2, 1996

══════════════════════════

On the day after the 29th True God's Day, Dr. Pak speaks at an International Leadership Conference. Following Father's instructions, he recounts a detailed report of his year in Japan as a missionary, including his Day of Hope tour and the historical five-city tour of True Mother and President and Mrs. Bush.

Good afternoon. Father is preparing instructions for you, and he asked me to give you a report of my one year in Japan as a missionary.

First of all, I would like to congratulate the missionaries who are attending this 29th True God's Day conference, especially those people who received a most incredible award from Father as well as those nations and continents that received an award for being number one in the Unification Church community. Let's give a big round of applause to Africa and Asia for being the most outstanding continents.

Congratulations to all who received awards and to all who have attended this wonderful historical conference. I'm so deeply moved by the hard work you have put into your missions. My heart is with you.

I am now also a missionary. I have been a special assistant to Father and Mother for 38 years. I was one of the first missionaries who came to the United States. The first one is, of course, Dr. David Sang Chul Kim. Let's honor him as the first missionary to the United States, a great missionary, a great elder brother of our movement. Another great missionary to the United States was Dr. Young Oon Kim, who is my spiritual mother.

I have been working in Japan for one year. Father called me in December 1994 and asked me to go to Japan to celebrate True God's Day 1995 with the Japanese movement. January 2 is the Day of Victory of Love, so I also celebrated the Day of Victory of Love while I was in Japan. Then I packed to come back to the United States. I was to take a flight on January 3 at 9:00 a.m. That night Father called me from Korea. Father's voice was very wonderful; I was so glad to hear Father at the beginning of the year. Father asked me, "Bo Hi, have you packed?" "Yes, sir. I'm all packed and ready to go tomorrow morning at 9:00." Then Father said, "Bo Hi, you have no place to go; you are homeless now. You stay in Japan and make your home in Japan." I virtually fainted, because it was totally unexpected. I unpacked, of course.

One year from that day, I have come back to report to Father and Mother that I am so deeply grateful to them for sending me to Japan to share the heartbeat with the Japanese members and to experience their way of doing things. It is a learning experience.

I rejuvenated myself. My faith was revitalized while I was revitalizing Japan and the Japanese church. It was truly a give and take of love, true love. I gave Japan my entire soul and being, all my sincerity, heart, and love, representing Father and Mother. At the same time the Japanese church gave me such an incredible gift and hospitality and love. So it was mutual give and take.

Father always taught that give and take of love produces not only 100 percent return, but 120 percent or 200 percent return. It was absolutely true in my experience this last year in Japan.

After I was ordered to stay in Japan as a missionary, I studied Japan. Japan, as you know, is the Eve nation, while Korea is the Adam nation. Korea is the Fatherland of our faith, and the Adam nation needs the Eve nation as the mother nation. Father chose Japan to be the mother nation, the Eve nation. Japan's role is to become the mother of the world, and today Japan is doing that. To make this happen, Father has given his entire heart, energy, and love for Japan.

THE FIRST MISSIONARY

The Japanese mission was established in 1958. Even before anybody came to the United States, Father sent a missionary to Japan. At the time, the Korean mother church was suffering. There was no money. There was persecution from the government, from the police, from everywhere. Korea was not in a position to send out any missionaries. However, under those circumstances, Father picked the missionary, gave him all the money he could muster, and sent him to Japan. He was kicked out of Japan three times. The first and second times, Father instructed him how to deal with the Japanese government to be successful in his mission. He followed those instructions the third time. This is how our Japanese church began.

Ever since, Father has given more attention to Japan than to any other country in the world. Father and Mother have continued to give Japan their love. For example, because the Japanese government is one of the satanic governments that does not allow Father an entry visa, Father brought 160,000 Japanese women to Korea in 1994 and 1995 under the name of the Women's Federation for World Peace. Father taught 160,000 Japanese women. Five thousand people sat down in one room for two nights and three days. Father never slept, really. He probably slept in the car traveling back and forth from Hannam-Dong to Sutaek-ri. You have no idea how much Father poured out his sweat and blood and love for the sake of Japan.

In addition to the 160,000 women, 15,000 Japanese men were invited to Korea. They were given the same training by Father, at the same time. Why so many women and so few men? Because Japan is the Eve nation. It's Eve's country. But men were given the mandate by Father: "You are going to educate 320,000 Japanese men." This is happening now.

The success of the Korean-Japanese sisterhood conferences is being expanded through the sisterhood conferences between American and Japanese women. The United States is a difficult country for mission work. They never really opened up their hearts to Father. Americans never accepted him from the bottom of their hearts. Americans are arrogant and rational and very proud, and they consider the Unification Church an Oriental religion. It has never really been accepted by high-level people, the movers and shakers of this country. Young people, yes. College students, yes.

Nora Spurgin told me that Father's sisterhood conferences have completely overwhelmed the American leading classes, including the president, congressmen, senators, future presidents, ministers, educators, you name it. Hollywood stars, Christopher Reeve, Charlton Heston, Barbara Walters have come to speak. And Coretta Scott King. Think about it: what can move Coretta Scott King? Nothing under the sun can move such people, because they consider the Unification Church too conservative.

This time American women really opened their hearts, crying, genuinely crying, having seen hope for world peace. They said, "Who masterminded this kind of project?" It was Reverend Sun Myung Moon. Some of the missionaries had no idea that 83 top-level people have been involved with the conferences. George and Barbara Bush and Rosalyn Carter head the list. Those people are the movers and shakers of this country.

The United States is the only superpower under the sun now. No longer are there dual superpowers. There is one superpower, the United States of America. The leaders of the United States have been mobilized; it is an incredible success.

The American women shed tears from the heart. This is the first time they learned how to cry. Yes, they didn't know they had tears. This time they realized they had tears. They poured out their hearts.

For the first time since Father came to America, he is moving and shaking the entire country through two major forces: one is the Women's Federation, through the sisterhood conferences, and the other is the *Washington Times*. These are the victories of our True Parents. These are the two victories in America to remember on this, the 29th True God's Day.

In 1994, Mother toured 27 cities in Japan. Mother visited virtually every city of Japan. I was there. It had the most incredible impact on Japan.

MOTHER WAS NUMBER ONE

Last fall Father organized Mother's tour of Japan accompanied by Barbara and George Bush. Can you imagine a U.S. president, whether an incumbent or a former president, doing anything in a secondary position? They are always number one. A U.S. president is always number one. But this time who was number one? Mother was number one. Their respect for Mother and Father was incredible.

The Japanese people could not believe such a thing was happening. Why? Japan is probably the number two country in the entire world. (Actually, I think Japan is number one, but I am a little prejudiced in favor of Japan.) They are a superpower in a real sense. In economic and military power, the U.S. is number one, but in people power and money power, Japan is number one. The United States today is about to face bankruptcy. The U.S. government has so much debt, while Japan has so much savings. All the savings accounts in the world cannot compare with the Japanese savings. It's like a drop in the bucket compared to Japan. The real power is Japan.

The Japanese people are proud of their accomplishments. They are afraid of nothing. They are not going to bow down to anybody, except one country, the United States, because for 50 years Japan has come under the U.S. defense program, the nuclear umbrella. The United States has protected Japan for 50 years, during which time they built up their economy.

Japan knows that the United States is the one country they have to watch out for. This is why Japan respects the United States.

The Japanese also respect anybody with a big nose and blue eyes who speaks perfect English. This is where the Japanese have somewhat of an inferiority complex. In language, English is number one for them.

The U.S. president, therefore, is like the king of the world. The king of the world comes with Mrs. Moon? Impossible, they thought. This must be some kind of trick. When 50,000 people gathered in the Tokyo Dome and the program announced George and Barbara Bush, there were hundreds of people from the media outside and inside. Their palms were sweating as they wondered: Has George Bush really come? There must be some kind of trick. There will probably be a message on the video screen saying, "I'm sorry I couldn't be there in person, but I am there on video."

When George Bush's name was announced, there was wonderful applause. The media said, "No, no. It couldn't be true. It's too good to be true." When George and Barbara Bush, smiling from ear to ear, showed up on the stage, everybody was dumbfounded. They thought it must be a phantom, or maybe somebody put makeup on to look like George and Barbara Bush. They still didn't want to believe it.

Then George and Barbara Bush spoke, supporting Mother's idea for true family and world peace. The audience could not deny that they were George and Barbara Bush. They then thought, "Oh, the Bushes must have been deceived." The opposition was incredible. In the middle of the tour, people wanted to hear George and Barbara Bush say, "Well, we've been tricked. Now we are packing up and going home." They were waiting for that news.

Never in history has a U.S. president traveled to more than two cities in Japan. This time George and Barbara Bush traveled to five cities. No U.S. president has ever set foot on the island of Hokkaido. George and Barbara Bush went to Hokkaido. The citizens of Hokkaido bowed down to Father and Mother, because Father and Mother brought an American president to Hokkaido, the northern island. No president of the United States ever went to Kyushu, the southern island. Then George and Barbara Bush went to Fukuoka, the capital of Kyushu. The people of Kyushu were flabbergasted at Father and Mother's power to tell a U.S. president what to do and plan his schedule. Incredible. This completely changed the attitude of the Japanese government and media toward the Unification community.

INTENSE PERSECUTION

Our Japanese movement has undergone the most incredible persecution because of the Aum Truth Church, Omo Jilikyo. That was the most incredible kind of cult. The Aum Truth Church believes they can wage the war known as Armageddon. They planned to destroy the entire Japanese population, except those who are converted to the Aum Truth Church. It would be much more fearful than a Third World War. Without Father and Mother, the Japanese population could have been cut in half last year. Out of 120 million people, maybe 50 million would have been killed.

The Aum Truth Church was trying to create a powerful poison gas, viral weapons, and chemical weapons. They were buying helicopters. They were creating physical weapons. On March 20, they released poison gas in the subway. Sixteen people were killed immediately and 5,000 were injured. This was incredible. The Japanese thought that theirs was the safest country in the entire world, but this happened in Japan, in the middle of Tokyo.

This brought even greater persecution to the Unification Church. Our enemies took this opportunity to say, "Another religious movement will be more dangerous than the Aum Truth Church, and that is the Unification Church. Because the founder is a Korean, we have no idea what they could do. They only follow the orders of Reverend Moon. Therefore, the Aum Truth Church is like a peanut compared to the Unification Church. We've got to do something about the Unification Church."

A large number of Japanese brothers and sisters participated in the 30,000 couple Blessing in Seoul in 1992. Among them were several famous people, particularly the famous movie star Junko Sakurada and an Olympic champion, Hiroko Yamasuki. The media did a most incredible smashing job on this event. For three years the Japanese church has been bombarded by the media. Day after day, they demolished our church in the eyes of the public. Public opinion already looked at the Unification Church as something unhealthy and dangerous.

The Japanese members truly suffered. They were trying to regain strength so they could move forward offensively, but they did not know what to do. On top of that, the Aum Truth Church incident exploded like an atomic bomb. It added to the persecution.

The Japanese members are so grateful to Father. Father instructed me to proclaim Divine Principle truth and clearly reveal Father as the Second Coming of the messiah, the True Parents.

The Japanese church and the members were suffering so incredibly. I wanted to help, but I didn't know where to start. One night I collapsed at Hiroshima, where the atomic bomb fell. I was suffering in bed. All of a sudden, the telephone rang. I picked up the phone and heard Mother's voice. Mother seldom calls me but that night, it was truly true love. I don't now how Mother discovered I had collapsed.

Mother called and in her kind voice said to me, "Bo Hi, you are a big man. Why are you so weak? You are a big man, you should have a big, strong mind." Then Mother said the most incredible thing to me: "When you face difficulty, think of Father, what kind of path Father walked, what kind of difficulty Father faced, what kind of incredible persecution Father received. When you have a difficult time, then think of Father. That will give you courage."

That was a revelation to me. Really the Holy Spirit was healing me. So I thanked Mother and moved to Tokyo and entered Isshin Hospital, our church hospital in Tokyo. For one week I held my own workshop, preparing myself for Japan. The fourth night Father called the hospital and said, "Bo Hi, what can you do? You are sick in the hospital. You may die in Japan that way."

At that point I was ready to go all the way for Japan. I interrupted Father's conversation because I was afraid Father would say, "Bo Hi, you come back to the United States." I didn't want that. So I immediately said to Father, "Father, I'm ready to die in Japan. If I collapse in Japan while proclaiming the True Parents in Japan, it would be the greatest honor for me to die in that fashion. You told me when I went before the Fraser committee in 1978, 'If you make up your mind to die for the sake of God and True Parents, you will win and you will live.' Father, didn't you say that to me? You told me that, and with that kind of strength I attended the hearings at the U.S. Congress and fought the battle and won. Father, I am going to do the same thing. This is my second Fraser battle. Please give me an opportunity." I eloquently testified from my heart.

Then Father said, very comfortingly, "Well, I heard very comforting words from you, didn't I? You go ahead. I will let you do it."

I was in heaven at that point. During the remaining three days in the hospital I prayed and prayed, "God, give me an opportunity to die for the sake of Japan." That's the way my mission started.

BEGINNING THE DAY OF HOPE TOUR

Then the Aum Truth Church attacks began, and I reported to Father. Father immediately told me to start the Day of Hope tour. "Proclaim the truth all over Japan." These were Father's instructions. I knew these instructions were most proper. I asked myself, how can I win Japan? What is my weapon? Two things: first, the truth, the most powerful truth of Divine Principle; second, Father's accomplishments in the United States for the sake of the world. None of the Japanese has ever heard what Father actually accomplished for the sake of the world in the United States. These are the two greatest weapons for changing public opinion in Japan. In the meantime, since the Japanese government was stopping Father from coming into Japan, I was ready to give myself for the sake of Japan on behalf of Father.

I came to love not only the Japanese members but the Japanese culture and the Japanese people as a whole. I want to love them because Father loves Japan. I have to do it for the sake of Father, on behalf of Father. That was my complete commitment.

On March 26, 1995, six days after Aum Truth Church bombed the subway with poison gas, we began the Day of Hope lecture in the middle of Tokyo. Two thousand people came, and half of them were new people. Those who were most surprised were the Japanese members. They didn't believe they could bring in new people. We invited professors, media people, police officers, and Korean residents in Japan. Throughout the entire lecture tour we invited everyone to see and hear for themselves.

Father told the Japanese leaders, "Bo Hi Pak knows all True Parents' secrets for 40 years." I'm so grateful to God and True Parents that I was given the opportunity to serve Father as a special assistant when Father's mission began in the United States on December 18, 1971. Father landed in America permanently on that date. During the 25 years since then, I have been with Father, side by side. I was like a shadow of Father.

I interpreted more speeches for Father than anybody else. Yesterday I commended Peter Kim for his eloquent translation. I know the value of translation. He did a great job, and I really congratulated him. The translator has beautiful give and take with Father. I had that for 25 years. Father banged my head probably several hundred times, but Father kissed my cheek about a dozen times. For every 100 bangs I got one kiss. It's a good deal, isn't it? You never had that, did you? Father embraced me, turning me around; we danced and waltzed together. That was my life.

More importantly, what is the greatest work Father has done in the United States? The liberation of communism. Who liberated communism? Father did. True Parents did. The problem is the world does not know about it.

Who knows really what Father did? Me. I was there when Father met with former President Richard Nixon in the Oval Office at the White House. I translated for Father. I translated for Nixon. Father prayed together in the Oval Office with Nixon. Father said that day, "President Nixon, when you were sleeping in the White House at 5:00 this morning, I was circling your White House already, praying for you." Father did so at 5:00 that morning. Who in the world knows that kind of secret? When I translated that statement for President Nixon, he turned pale. He couldn't believe it. He must have wondered, "Who has loved me that much?" It's an incredible report.

I have a very important message to share with you. I want to give you guts, hope, and power to do the same in your mission countries. You can do it. The power of True Parents and the Divine Principle is so great. What Father has done in 40 years is so powerful. Nothing under the sun is impossible. The 3.6 Million Couples Blessing in 1997 is peanuts when you people in this room make up your minds. This is the purpose of my report.

In Japan, one of the most incredible things I did was to testify to Father as a liberator. The world has been under the bondage of communism. Father is the messiah, anointed by God. Father and God worked together to destroy the Soviet empire and bring liberation to the communist world. I testified line by line. I showed the Japanese people 200 slides. One picture speaks louder than words, louder than a book in many cases. I showed 200 slides, including Father's meeting with Nixon, Father speaking to Congress, and Father's most incredible prediction of the Reagan landslide.

PREDICTING THE REAGAN LANDSLIDE

Who knows as much as I do about the Reagan landslide? I was instructed directly by Father what to do. It seemed impossible, but I obeyed Father and miracles happened. Who at that time really believed Reagan could be a winner? No one. *The News World* was Father's newspaper in New York in 1980. The *Washington Times* did not start until 1982. Compared to the *New York Times*, *The News World* was a little paper, but with *The News World*, Father accomplished a miracle; he changed public opinion in the United States in favor of a Reagan victory.

I told Father, "Reagan cannot win, Father; I am sorry, Reagan cannot win because he has four incredible handicaps. He is an old man, 71 years old. He is a Hollywood movie star, so nobody takes him seriously. He is a hard-line conservative, and American people don't like hard-line conservatives. Furthermore, he campaigned for president in 1976 and failed, and Americans don't like someone who is a failure. Finally, President Jimmy Carter is the incumbent, and incumbents tend to be elected to a second term. Reagan is very unpopular; it is impossible."

Father asked me to meet with Reagan. So I went to Ohio and met with Reagan. I showed the Japanese people the picture of our meeting. I said to Reagan, "Reverend Moon sent me to you. Are you ready to liberate communism? If that is your mission and you realize it, you shall be the next president."

Reagan said, "Who said that?" I said, "Reverend Moon said it." "How does Reverend Moon know?" "He has a hotline with God. He got a revelation from God. You'd better believe it." Reagan and his wife were so happy that somebody came to boost them up. However, when I came back and reported to Father about this substantial conversation, I still said, "Reagan has no chance." Father replied, "He has no chance? That's good, because God's miracle will be more visible that way. I will make that miracle."

Of course, Father did many things. Finally, the day before the election, Father said, "*The News World* should go ahead and print a big prediction. Announce a Reagan landslide." I said, "Father, we don't know if Reagan can even win. How can we announce a Reagan landslide? It is foolish; it's a joke." Father said, "Just listen to me. Go ahead, draft the article and show it to me."

So I went to the newspaper and said, "We will print 'Reagan Landslide' tomorrow morning." Everybody said, "Oh no. No." Then we wrote a draft article that said, "Reagan may be winning."

I showed it to Father and Father said, "Bring me that wastebasket." He threw it in the wastebasket. Father said, "What would you do if World War III broke out? What kind of headline would you put in the newspaper?" All of a sudden Father was asking a funny question. I didn't know why that question was coming, so I said, "Boy, World War III would be a big thing. We would have a banner headline and big letters."

"Do it just like that. This is my third world war." Father's statement was so true. It was the third world war. That one fateful prediction of *The News World* prevented a third world war by electing Reagan to office.

We set "REAGAN LANDSLIDE" in huge type. Our *News World* staff, even though they are brothers and sisters, couldn't understand Father, so they said, "No, Col. Pak." (At that time I was known as Col. Pak.) "Father will be laughed at. We couldn't do this. Reduce the size and we will put it on the second page."

I said, "No. We are going to be a newspaper of martyrdom. We may not publish any more papers. This may be the final issue. Go ahead and do it." We predicted that Reagan would win even in New York, but I yielded a little bit in terms of electoral college numbers, because our editorial staff was so strong. "It is so laughable, we couldn't do this," they said. We reduced the numbers but basically we announced, "Reagan Landslide." I regret now that I yielded a little bit. Then I showed it to Father. He said, "Good."

We delivered that newspaper to Reagan. When Reagan saw *The News World*'s prediction of a Reagan landslide, he was jubilant. Josette Shiner, who is now a very big woman at the *Washington Times*, took it to Reagan. He was so happy that he brought the newspaper into the news room and held a press conference. That was the morning of election day, November 4, 1980.

The News World's prediction of a Reagan landslide was broadcast coast to coast by all the television networks: NBC, ABC, CBS. The amazing things was, on top of the page were small letters saying, "News World Prediction" before the banner "Reagan Landslide." But television viewers could not read the small type. They could only see the words "Reagan Landslide."

People must have thought, "Oh, Reagan won already? The election is over?" West of the Mississippi, there is a time zone difference of two to three hours. In California, 95 percent of the people voted for Reagan, because all day long they saw the words, "Reagan Landslide." It was incredible. American people want to join the winner. You don't want to be on the side of the loser. They saw the announcement that Reagan was winning, so everybody voted for him after seeing the newspaper's proclamation. Californians voted 95 percent for Reagan. This is Father's miracle. Who else can tell these stories except me?

PROCLAIMING FATHER AS THE MESSIAH

I gave the straight talk to the Japanese people. Normally we give the Divine Principle first and at the conclusion we say, "You see, Divine Principle is so clear about who the messiah is. Reverend Moon is the messiah." We whisper: "Do you know that Reverend Moon is the messiah? You know now." The general method has been to teach the Divine Principle, and in the final lecture reveal about the messiah.

In Japan, I reversed this because of Father's own declaration about the messiah and True Parents in 1992. When I took the stage, within 15 minutes I declared proudly that Father, Reverend Sun Myung Moon, is the second coming of the messiah. Furthermore, I announced that he is the True Parents, together with Mrs. Hak Ja Han Moon.

Then I said, "This messiah loves Japan. Even though Japan persecuted Father, Father loves Japan. How do we know? Here is one evidence. Look at me. A man like me who has been serving Father for 38 years would not come here to Japan unless Father loves Japan. It is great evidence. I come here pouring out my heart to you because I love you. Do you know why I love you? Because my Father, Reverend Moon, loves you. He loves Japan. True Parents love Japan."

When the declaration of the true messiah is made, normally some people close the window of their minds. But not in Japan this time. For two and one-half hours I precisely recited what the Divine Principle content is all about. I covered the Principle of Creation, Fall of Man, Restoration, the first messiah, and the second messiah. Then I talked about what Father has done in the United States for 30 years. "I am the eyewitness," I announced. "I saw it. I was there. I was translating for Reverend Moon." How could they not believe me?

I stressed how much Father, Reverend Moon, my Father, True Parents, loves Japan. This is the mother's country, Eve's country. I really conveyed this love to the Japanese people.

A lot of opposing people came to hear what I had to say, but after one hour their hearts were melted. Within two hours they got excited. At the conclusion, everybody shouted out, "God is blessing us." The hearts of the Japanese people were melted, and they responded beautifully with tears.

Parents of members came, and they were completely melted. They wrote testimonies on response cards, such as "I believe in God, I believe in Reverend Moon. I apologize to my children. I didn't know my children were following such a great man. I'm proud that my children are disciples of Reverend Moon."

Many parents had tears in their eyes. They changed their attitude immediately, and they apologized to their sons and daughters and said, "Whatever you need, tell me." The Blessing fees are coming in; contributions are coming in.

Parents ask, "What do you need? More money? Oh, I heard there are Japanese sisterhood ceremonies in the United States. You should go there." Parents are glad to pay now. About 5,000 have asked to go to the United States for the bridge ceremony.

Yesterday I saw the videotape, and today I listened to Mr. Dong Moon Joo's report on the sisterhood conferences. I have come to the conclusion that Japan must respond to Father and send more people to the United States. This is Father's greatest victory for 1995. We will make 1996 victorious. We are so inspired by Father's great victory.

So far I have spoken to roughly 100,000 Japanese people. What is most gratifying is I have spoken throughout Japan—north and south, east and west—73 times. Total attendance at the meetings was 91,491. Of these, 47,000 were new people and around 43,000 were our members.

When Japanese people are moved, their hands go into their pocketbooks. They are amazing people. I really respect the Japanese. We include an envelope in the program. Amazingly, 43,000 people donated $4.7 million after the program. This is on top of the 2,000 to 2,500 yen admission which they paid; thus their contributions totally roughly $1.8 million.

About 14,000 people promised to send a contribution every month. "I am an old man," one person wrote. "I cannot do anything else except give you money." Well, we need that kind of people.

Normally the rallies started at 12:30 or 1:00, so people came without eating lunch. When it was an evening program, they always came without eating dinner. They listened and listened and prayed and prayed. I have never seen such a phenomenon anywhere.

About 2,000 people came to the Blessing because of the lectures, and we gained about 6,000 members. More amazing is the number who want to study about True Parents; 11,767 people said they want to know about Reverend Moon; 5,900 want to attend a seminar; 8,500 joined the Unification community; 5,429 joined the Unification Church. In some cases they signed membership right at the door, so now we are including a membership form in the envelope. (This doesn't include the students, which brings the total to roughly 6,000.) Those who want to go to the United States for the sisterhood conferences: 5,691. If each person pays 620,000 yen, that is a potential of $35 million. It's good, isn't it? Those who want information about the Blessing: 2,164. Already 2,100 of those people were Blessed. When we get back we are going to sign people up for the Blessing in Washington. At every lecture, people will sign up for the Blessing in Washington. Many tens of thousands of people will do this.

HEALING FAMILIES

I am moved when members come to me and tell stories like this: "I brought my father and mother who kidnapped me from the movement twice. They opposed Father and the Unification Church for 10 years. After listening to one of your lectures, my mother was crying and holding my hand. Then I was moved and began to cry. My father was sitting next to me and said, 'Today is the Day of Hope. Let's not cry.' But as he was speaking he was crying too."

Father healed so many families in Japan; he brought so much harmony in Japan. In particular, many wives were saved. There are 5,000 or more women whose husbands have been adamantly opposed to the church. These wives have been suffering for eight, 10, 12 years. This time those wives struggled to bring their husbands to the lecture. They created a showdown, not by fighting, but by fasting, taking cold showers, praying, serving, and just saying, "My dear husband, do me one favor. Come to just one lecture of the Day of Hope."

One wife was very discouraged. Her husband had refused to come. She came to the event and was sitting in her chair and crying. Then she looked beside her and was amazed to find her husband sitting there. Husband and wife were seated side by side in an auditorium of 1,000 seats. Her husband said, "I was heading toward work. My tram car had to pass the auditorium, but in front of the auditorium the tram car broke down. I was so fearful. I thought God was going to punish me if I didn't come into this auditorium. So I came."

This is how incredibly the spirit world is working. Such testimonies occur one after another. Incredible things have happened.

OTHER PROJECTS

On October 1, Father directed me to speak to the university students. Mr. Tokuno is the leader of the Japanese CARP movement. CARP and the church youth department together created 13 youth groups. Under their sponsorship, I spoke to about 10,000 young people. Among them, roughly half were new people. University students, high school students, and even middle school students came and listened to a two and one-half hour presentation without moving. This I saw is the hope of Japan. The youth movement will be greatly successful in Japan.

Father emphasizes the pure love movement, so I proclaimed Father's teaching about pure love. The young people responded to the pure love movement. The promiscuity in Japan is incredible. Many parents worry about their children and don't know what to do with them. Now there is an answer. More and more, the Japanese public recognizes that Reverend Sun Myung Moon has the answer for their children.

CARP is now growing. Every week there is a workshop, and membership is growing. The Japanese CARP membership will be doubled soon. Father gave us the initial goal of 5,000 members, which should ultimately be doubled. If the Japanese CARP obtains 10,000 members, it will shake all Japan. This will open up the road for Father to come to Japan, because 10,000 young people are very powerful.

The Japanese media will no longer be able to say bad things about our church, because there are no bad things, only good things. They fabricate the bad things. Suppose 1,000 university students march into a television station and have a sit-down demonstration for 24 hours, 72 hours, or even one week. There is no television station in Japan that would not surrender. This is how we are going to teach the Japanese media. We need youth power.

On December 14, the Youth Federation for World Peace in Japan was formulated. Ichiro Kaicho has been appointed the chairman and president of the Youth Federation of Japan. He is a good man. He reported to Father. The Youth Federation will be a nation-saving movement in Japan. Mr. Bong Tae Kim, president of the Youth Federation of Korea, came to Japan and made a great speech. He felt great hope for Japan. Together the Korean and Japanese youth movements will change the entire picture. Mother changed the entire picture of the college youth. This year, the Japanese college campuses will be different due to the pure love movement. I assure you it will happen.

Another incredible area of breakthrough in 1996 will be with the Korean residents in Japan. There are several million Korean residents in Japan, from both North Korea and South Korea. They have lots of money.

Father instructed me to win their hearts so they can unite with Father and do something about the unification of the Fatherland. This is the year of breakthrough, because the groundwork has been laid. All of the leaders of the Korean residents came to the Day of Hope lectures. They are overjoyed and proud to be Korean. They are very proud of Father. They call this the hope of Japan, and they asked me to come and speak to the Korean residents association this year. This will happen in 1996. All these wonderful things are going to happen this year.

This year I'm going back to Japan for the second round. The time will come when Father will sign this map of Japan, which shows all the places I have lectured. When I go back this year, I want to touch all the Japanese islands through Day of Hope speeches and True Parents' declaration. I would like all the Japanese people to hear about True Parents and how great a man Father is.

One 11-year-old school boy who listened to my lecture said, "Well, Dr. Pak is good enough to be a disciple of the messiah." Approval came from an 11-year-old boy. I cherish this more than anything else. If anybody says to me, "You are good enough to be the disciple of the messiah," I am happy.

LIVING FOR TRUE PARENTS

Finally, I would like to testify about the Japanese church. The Japanese brothers and sisters are truly great people, heartistic people. They are absolutely obedient to Father. Father loves them. They want to reciprocate for what Father has given to them. They are dedicated, ready to give their lives for Father.

From Mr. Takeru Kamiyama on down, everybody is focused on living for the sake of True Parents. They are willing to die for True Parents, in order to be able to live. Otherwise, they realize that they will collapse and the whole nation of Japan will collapse. Right now, Mr. Kamiyama, Mrs. Erikawa (the first vice president of the Japanese Family Federation), and Mr. Sakurai are totally united. They are going around the country. I gave 73 speeches on the Day of Hope Tour, but they gave 77 speeches. They are giving one-day seminars in each church, reviving people, challenging people to live up to Father's expectations.

Japan has been suffering, but Father has given Japan such hope. Mother's tour of Japan accompanied by George and Barbara Bush gave them an enormous boost. They have received the most incredible revelation of Father's love for them. Father sent me as his representative. The Japanese people are so grateful to Father and Mother for never abandoning Japan, never giving up hope in Japan. They knew this before, but now their courage is renewed and their cup is running over.

The Japanese church has experienced incredible persecution. During 1996 we will completely chop off the old persecution, double the membership, and double it once again. The current membership will increase four times.

Then I won't have to stay in Japan, and I hope Father can call me back. The work in Japan is too hard, but I decided to give my life for the sake of Japan. That is the heart of the missionary. I am doing the same thing you are doing. You are giving your life for Africa, for Asia, for everywhere. That's why Father loves you.

I am joining you, offering my life for the sake of Japan. I may die for the sake of Japan and God's will, but if True Parents' will is fulfilled in Japan that will be more than enough honor. Yesterday I was given an award for serving True Parents for 33 years. I don't deserve it. I want to pay it back by giving my life for the sake of True Parents and Heavenly Father.

I want you to know that Japan is going to be strong in 1996. It will live up to Father's expectation. In 1996, we pledge to bring Father and Mother to Japan and have them be welcomed by the Japanese nation. Thank you, Father.

HEAVENLY DANCERS

WASHINGTON, D.C.

DECEMBER 10, 1996

Dr. Pak speaks to the students of the Kirov Academy of Ballet with a deep parental heart. He talks about the importance of beauty and self-discipline and implores them to strengthen and purify their spirits as well as their bodies. The Kirov has gained international recognition since its founding in 1990, and its dancers regurarly win prestigious awards. Its graduates are sought after by dance companies around the world.

Good afternoon, ladies and gentlemen and students. I have so much to tell you that I don't know where to begin. It is true, as Michael Beard said in his kind introduction, that I was involved in creating the Kirov Academy of Ballet. However, I am not a founder. The founders are Reverend and Mrs. Sun Myung Moon. They are religious leaders who founded a religious movement that has spread all over the world. Out of their religious conviction, they were motivated to promote artistic excellence.

I have always been very careful in handling this academy because I don't want it to be regarded as a part of the church or the church work. I do not want to impart that image because that is not the case for the student body or the faculty. I have wanted to meet all of you for a very long time, but I didn't want to be in a position to be criticized that we founded the school with some ulterior motives, which is not the case.

The school has been in existence for five years now. That is a very short time for any major institution. In this five years we have proven to the world what the Kirov Academy is all about. This is an artistic school, educating and training the future stars of the dance world. We have already won several medals, including two gold medals in Varna, Bulgaria. Many graduates are joining the major companies around the world. And in the future among you there shall be great medal winners and future ballerinas and danseurs. It is my greatest honor to speak to you and to your distinguished teachers.

I come today to speak to you to share the founding spirit of this school, to establish a dialogue with you, and together create a vision of the future of the Kirov. In just a short span of five years, the Kirov has become the number one ballet school in the entire world, including even Russia. I want to give my heartfelt thanks and appreciation to our artistic director, Mr. Oleg Vinogradov, our deputy artistic director, Yelena Vinogradova, and the members of the faculty, both academic and artistic. That is my first order of business today. Let's join together to give our director and our deputy director and our teachers a resounding round of applause.

A LOVER OF BALLET

Where do we go from here? What kind of dancers would you like to become? I am not an artist, I am not a musician, I am not a dancer, but I am a lover of ballet. Why do I love ballet? I don't know even myself. I love ballet, period. Therefore, I love you because you are ballet dancers. Yesterday I went to the shopping center to buy some Christmas cards and I was trying to find a 1997 calendar. There are many, many beautiful calendars, but the one I bought was of ballerinas. In looking at these pictures, I came to a deep realization. I am looking at something very heavenly. Next year we are going to create a ballet calendar by the Kirov Academy, I promise you. We will make an even better calendar than this one.

What is ballet to me? I am not an artist; basically, I am a military man. I fought in the Korean War. For three years I was in battle. Many times I was on the verge of being killed, but miraculously I was saved, and ever since I have been a believer in God. I know I could not have survived unless God exists and unless He helped me. That is my experience. That is my background.

After that kind of desperate experience in war, surrounded by death, I came to think about life. What is life? What is death? What is the best way to live? That is what I was thinking about at the age of 21. I was at war when I was 21. Some of you will be 21 soon. At that age I was thinking deeply about life. I am not trying to give you my whole life story; that is not the purpose of my talk today. But I was pursuing something truthful, something wonderful, something pure and beautiful and moving. I was aspiring for those things as a young man. Then I came to the poignant realization that the very famous Russian writer Dostoyevsky expressed as "beauty saved the world." Especially God-centered beauty. The most beautiful things were created by God. Everything that God created is beautiful. In my life, I try to appreciate God-created beauty.

MANIFESTATION OF BEAUTY

Among the many things that God has created, what is the most beautiful? Do you know the answer? You. Men and women. Human beings. Men and women are God's highest, most beautiful creation. And where is that human beauty most completely manifested? In ballet. When I see ballet performed on the stage, I see the most beautiful form of man and woman. That is what made me fall in love with ballet. When I look at pictures like this, and when I see you performing, I feel only one thing: heavenly. Pure and heavenly, beautiful and heavenly. I give praise to the Creator. That is the basic and the fundamental reason I have fallen in love with ballet.

You are in the process of creating that beauty. You are being trained in this school to manifest the ideal form of man and woman as God intended in the Garden of Eden. That is the kind of role you as ballet dancers are going to play. You didn't know that, right? You didn't know why you liked ballet so much, why you have to sweat so much. But you now know you are really trying to manifest to the world the most beautiful thing that God created.

You know human history has not always been a beautiful one. There is a lot of ugliness, lots of suffering, war, disasters, human tragedy, blood, fighting. Even today, all that is going on in the outside world. Why? What is the reason for this? Simply because man has forgotten God, our Creator. That is why all these terrible things are happening. We left God, sinned, and human beauty and purity was lost. Human history is nothing more than the history of restoration, trying to reach out for God. All of humanity is reaching out for the God we lost.

So everything we do, the ways we express ourselves—in beautiful writing or movies or dance or music—come from the human desire to reach out for God, longing for His love and wanting to be embraced by the Creator. The best artistic expression of this longing is ballet. That is my conviction. When I watch Swan Lake for example, or Giselle, or the Nutcracker, something in the ballet hits me, deep inside, the real me.

All you young women, what do you do? You are learning what? To stand on point. This is very painful. Your foot was not designed to walk on point. If God had designed the foot for you to walk on point, it would be shaped differently. You know how painful it is, and you never let others see your feet. The worst thing for a ballerina is to have to show your feet. But you just swallow that ugliness, swallow that pain. Why? You want to be taller. Why do you want to be taller? You want to reach out for God. Isn't that true? Isn't that beautiful? Isn't that a beautiful interpretation? You are always reaching out with your arms, your neck, your whole body. What happened to your arms? They are getting longer, always reaching higher and higher. And your necks are getting longer. Look at pictures of all the great ballerinas. Your desire for God makes you reach out, getting longer and taller.

JUMP FOR GOD

What are you men trying to do? You want to jump higher and higher and higher. Rasta Thomas, why are you so famous? You jump and stay in the air for a while before coming down. Why do you do that, you men? Because you want to get close to God. You jump and reach out for Him. Your hands and arms are up. When I see all this beauty on stage, I see all of humanity reaching out for our lost God, desiring His love. This is what ballet means to me. It is the perfect art form that engenders tremendous beauty and is so very moving and soul-shaking. It tries to bring human beings closer to perfection, close to the Creator. This is why I love ballet.

And this is why in my life I invested myself into the children's ballet company known as the Little Angels in Korea. Our founder, Reverend Moon, created them, and I became a sort of project officer. I helped the Little Angels project materialize. Over the last 33 years, they have performed more than 4,000 times as ambassadors of peace around the world. Why a children's ballet? Because children represent innocence and purity. When the Little Angels perform, it doesn't matter if the audience is in America, Russia, Germany, England, South America, or any corner of the world, the people cry because it is so beautiful and so pure, so innocent. It touches their hearts. Every human being has that craving for the purity and beauty and innocence. The Little Angels set off that inner desire of human beings, and that is why all of a sudden tears come.

So you manifest two qualities: purity and beauty. Also in ballet the struggle between good and evil is very, very clear. No other art form makes that distinction as clearly. You immediately know who is the good guy and who is the bad guy. On stage, the bad guy often wears black or some special mask. So good and evil are very clear on the stage. Usually good triumphs, but not always.

Classical ballet engenders incredible sensations in the audience. This is why I like classical ballet better than modern ballet. I enjoy modern ballet, but I love classical ballet more. You have to learn both. You have to be professional on both sides. Because of the reasons I have already explained, the classical form of ballet is to me the real ballet. The reason I love the Kirov Ballet is because it is the classic of classics. It is the pacesetter of the entire ballet world. Throughout the 250 years of ballet history, the Kirov has set the standard for the entire ballet world. That is why I am very, very happy to be associated with Oleg Vinogradov, the artistic director of the Kirov Ballet for 20 years, with Yelena Vinogradova, the deputy artistic director, and with the many Kirov dancers and teachers.

We are good enough to be given the name Kirov. We are the Kirov Academy of the West. The Vaganova school is the Kirov Academy of the East. We have the best of the both worlds, east and west. We have the Kirov tradition, the Vaganova tradition, and the best possible teachers you can imagine. We also have the western conveniences, western facilities, and the western style of management. So the best of the two worlds have come together to produce this Kirov Academy. In the future, the Kirov Academy is going to be the best in the entire world, even surpassing the Vaganova. That is my conviction and my pride.

What is our next goal? For me and our founder our next goal is to create a ballet company. We already created the Universal Ballet Company in Korea, the UBC, 11 or 12 years ago. It has become the number one company in Asia and one of the best in the world.

You have petitioned to create a company here in Washington. I tell you, I have a master plan to create a ballet company here in the nation's capitol. You know that the Washington Opera Company is going to build an opera house. The Kennedy Center is so crowded, we could not become the resident company in the Kennedy Center. When the opera company creates their own theater, it will almost be like the Maryinsky-Kirov Theater in St. Petersburg. I want to create a company that will become the resident company of the opera house here in Washington. I know you want that too. Our school is second to none in the world, and our company will be the same. That is going to be our goal.

But as you know, the creation of a company is an enormous undertaking. It cannot be done overnight. This school has been in existence for six years, and a company will take about the same amount of time to grow. The Opera House will be finished around the year 2000 or 2001. By that time we will have our company totally ready.

However, it takes a lot of work, a lot of preparation, and a lot of budget. All of these things have to be considered. So until then I am concentrating on the Universal Ballet in Korea. They are making a U.S. tour next year. Both companies, the Universal Ballet and the new Washington ballet company, are in the Kirov tradition. Both come under one directorship, Oleg Vinogradov, and his deputy is always Yelena Vinogradova. This company will be created under their leadership. The students who are graduating next year should consider joining the Universal Ballet. It is almost like a preparation for the Washington company. Eventually the Universal Ballet will supply a lot of trained, experienced dancers to the Washington company.

YOU WON'T WANT TO LEAVE

You will be very well treated in the Universal Ballet, which is already touring the world: America, Europe, and Asia, of course. This year we are performing in Japan, Thailand, and Formosa. After a year you might want to join some American ballet company. However, after being with the Universal Ballet, you may not want to leave. Why? It is so good. Unlike in other companies, the Kirov students and graduates are specially treated in the Universal Ballet. You won't get that kind of preferential treatment anywhere else.

I am very glad that many Korean students are here being trained by the Kirov Academy. You will be able to join the UBC with pride. Eventually your stage is the world stage. You won't stay in Korea but will have the opportunity to tour the world and join the Washington company. I promise you that will be the case for all the good, qualified students. There are no bad ones in the Kirov Academy, so I have no problem.

Now I want to dedicate the last 10 minutes to a most important subject. I want you to listen to me. Look at me, because you don't listen to somebody with your ears alone. You also listen with your eyes. We need eye-to-eye contact. That is real listening. I will prove it to you. When you sleep, nobody stops up your ears, but when you close your eyes, you don't hear anything. So you see, your ears are open but your eyes are closed so you can't hear anything. I have come to the conclusion that you hear with your eyes. If you aren't looking at me, you are not listening to me. That is for sure.

What is the most important quality you need to succeed as ballet dancers? It is discipline, self-discipline. Without self-discipline, none of you will be good dancers. You have to push yourself, exercise and train constantly, and you have to watch your diet. You can't go out for ice cream every night. You can't fill your body with junk food. No—you have to have discipline. You know what to drink and what not to drink and what to eat and what not to eat and how much to eat and when to eat. You have a disciplined life.

DISCIPLINE YOUR BODY AND SPIRIT

I have a daughter who is a ballerina. She is now in St. Petersburg. We almost gave up on her becoming a ballerina, because her mother strongly objected. Mama is mama. When Thanksgiving came and there was turkey and pumpkin pie with lots of ice cream—boy, you would be drooling. But Julia would say, "No, I can't eat." My wife would say, "It is too cruel to my daughter, you cannot do that, you cannot push her to become a ballerina. She will suffer." Her mother's love doesn't want her daughter to become a ballerina, because the discipline is so strict and her life seems painful and even pitiful. To make a long story short, Julia kept up the discipline to become a ballerina. I really admire and respect her because of her spirit of self-discipline. She made up her mind to become a ballerina. If she thinks she shouldn't do certain things, she just doesn't do them—period. Nothing can change her. I am sure every one of you are like that. Otherwise you would not be here in the Kirov Academy.

Now self-discipline does not apply just to your body. Self-discipline applies equally to your mind and your spirit and your intellect. This is why you have to study the academic courses and not just dance. You need the academic teachers to give you knowledge and experiences and intellectual development. Furthermore, you have to polish your mind and soul so you will become the owner of a great character. Art is nothing more than the expression of the inner character to the audience. If you don't have a noble, polished, beautiful inner character, you really have nothing to show on the stage. Moving your foot and your leg is not ballet. You have to convey your soul; you have to convey your mind, your heart. That is ballet. You have to polish that part too. That is why we have academic as well as artistic training. Both parts are equally important.

You know there are physical laws you have to live by. You have to breath air. You have to eat food and drink water every day. Furthermore, when you violate physical law, it will bring you to destruction. For example, if you climb to the 17th floor of a building and jump off, what will happen? You better know. You will be dead. Period. Why? You violated physical law. You are not supposed to jump off a building. If you violate physical law, it will destroy you. For example, you are supposed to breathe air. If you go under water and try to breathe water, you will be dead. It is a violation of the physical law.

At the same time there are equally important spiritual laws. You are all spiritual beings. Everyone has a spirit, your soul, your mind. There are invisible laws governing your spiritual behavior. It is equally important you live in accordance with spiritual law. Otherwise you will go the way of self-destruction. I am not happy with the artistic community, especially the ballet community, about one thing. There is a lot of broken discipline, both physical and spiritual. Let me speak very frankly to you. For example, everywhere today, not only in the artistic community, there is a lot of homosexuality and lesbianism. You know all of this, I don't have to explain to you.

But you also have to know that this is absolutely against physical law and spiritual law. What does that bring? Self-destruction. It is very important that the Kirov Academy stay far from that kind of influence. The Kirov Academy should have nothing to do with that kind of ungodly thing. I trust you. I believe you. I trust our leadership, teachers, directors, and staff, all of you. I want to make the Kirov Academy the best by not only promoting good ballet but also by promoting a good educational atmosphere. These illicit, impure things should not infiltrate into our academy, into your minds. Purity and beauty are the highest qualities, but they can be lost. Your minds can be made ugly, impure, and no longer beautiful.

Another evil enemy in our society, not only for dancers but for all young people, is drugs: cocaine, heroin, marijuana. I don't know how marijuana tastes, and I never want to know. Millions of young people in America today have become victims of those drugs. There was a beautiful ballet danseur, a principal from the American Ballet Theater, whom we invited to come to Korea to perform with the UBC. He was tall, handsome, a great dancer. I really respected and admired him. He was my hero. He had a great future. Every year we invited him, but then one year his company said, no, we cannot send that man. What happened? He is dead from drugs. Just like that, that young man, probably 26 years old, dead from drugs. I was shocked. You know all these things may seem far from your situation, but you must be realistic and know that these things are in your environment, including ballet companies.

Furthermore, it is no secret today that many famous personages in the ballet world have died from AIDS. Sad, is it not? I don't have to name them. Here in America, in France, in Russia, and all over the world, this is happening. The Kirov Academy, especially the Kirov students, will be the exception. I tell you one very important thing. This has to become your philosophy of life. You all chose ballet. You must think of yourself as being married to ballet. Before you are married to a man or woman, you are married to ballet. Until you find your husband, until you find your wife, stay faithful to ballet. Don't monkey around with anything else. Make all your dates with ballet. Day in and day out, put your heart and soul into ballet. Then when the time comes and you meet a good candidate for your wife or husband, then get married. I will congratulate you. You should have nothing to do with AIDS. Nothing to do with promiscuity. Nothing to do with homosexuality. Nothing to do with lesbianism. This is my most direct, honest, important parental recommendation for all you young people. You are married to ballet. Put your heart and soul into it. Otherwise you will not succeed.

You know, Michele Wiles wouldn't have won that gold medal if she hadn't given her total self to ballet. And she must do so until she gets married. Even after she marries her husband, she is married to ballet. All the men and women should do the same. You will become wholesome, pure, genuine people of character. This is very important.

HAVE DATES WITH BALLET

For this reason, I admire the Russian system much more than the U.S. system. This is one reason I am bringing Russian teachers and tradition to America. Of course, academically, we have the best here in American, no question about it. But artistically speaking, the Russian tradition is better than the U.S. tradition. There is much less monkey business among men and women. In the Russian tradition, yes, you touch each other physically when you are on stage, but that is for the sake of art. But off stage, you are gentlemen, you are ladies. You act like gentlemen, act like ladies. The Russian system is far closer to the ideal. That is why I brought the Russian system to our school. This is a good environment for all of you. Have dates with ballet. Your boyfriend is ballet, your girlfriend is ballet. This is a most positive slogan. You live it. Go for a date at the studio, get completely sweaty. Maintain your self-discipline. Maintain the purity and beauty of your body and soul and heart. Grow up in that fashion. You will be a great dancer. But more important, you will be a great character. You will become a great human being. I want you to become that kind of men and women. That is my final plea today. That is my Christmas gift today.

Our founders, Reverend Moon and Mrs. Moon, have given millions of dollars to this institution. No one under the sun can equal their philanthropy. They are doing this to support the growth of this great ballet school. It is the founders' desire that graduates of the Kirov Academy be leaders of the dance world, not only the best artistically, but also spiritually. In other words, our founder is investing money to create great human beings who are also great artists. Beautiful dancers who are pure and beautiful in spirit and character, who are respected not only on stage but off. If you are genuine and pure, people will love you and respect you. Toward that purpose, our founder is giving money to us. If you go in the wrong direction and do wrong things, this school will not be continued. A new company will not be created. Reverend Moon does not want to create just another company. No. We want to have something unique, different, which will lead the 21st century, a new, healthy, God-centered company. That is the kind of company we are forming. That is the kind of school we have today.

Our founder has invested from the beginning more than $30 million. That comes down to an investment of $400,000 or $500,000 for each of you. Why would we do this? We would like to see you become wholesome men and women of great character, great human beings, with purity and beauty and at the same time total concentration. It is a very expensive investment, and I want it to pay off. We don't ask you anything else. I am not asking you to pay back a penny. You give back to the people of the world. Isn't that great? Aren't you glad you are in a great school? There is nothing like this anywhere else in the world. You can look everywhere and you won't find it. I want you to be serious.

I am telling you all this not as the president of the Foundation. I am speaking to you with a parental heart. I have sons like you. I have daughters like you. I have grandchildren growing up like you. I really look at you as my daughters and sons and grandchildren. How do I want them to grow up? I am telling to you that aspiration today. I want you to be successful. Not just great artists but whole human beings. Become a great human being first. That is very, very important. I am glad you and all the academic staff are here. It is equally important that you polish their minds and their spirits as well as their dance talent. Let them become great men and women. We want to produce a different kind of artist. Not the conventional artist, a different kind of artist, to represent the Kirov. If we don't, no one else will. Did you understand my message? You got it, didn't you? Yes or no? A little louder please. Yes or no? Great.

LET US MOVE MOUNTAINS

TEMPE, ARIZONA

JANUARY 1, 1999

═══════════════════════

In an unusual departure from the norm, Dr. Pak finds himself "not" translating for Father on God's Day. Instead, he is celebrating God's Day with his wife and family in Arizona and, thus, gives the God's Day address to the members, after reading Father's speech from South America. He describes 1999 as the year for the "final clearance" of our lives, our sin, and our shortcomings, before we enter into the new millennium. He cautions that this year could bring doubt and confusion, and inspires members to absolute faith. He reminds us that our only true asset is True Parents.

I really do not know how I ended up in Arizona on God's Day. You are right, it is providence. This is really amazing. I have been in the church for 41 years—that is quite a long time—but on God's Day I have always been with Father. Not only that, but for probably 30 years, particularly after Father came to the United States, I have been translating for Father on God's day. God's Day for me was—what shall I say?—incredible hard work, actually. My physical energy could not keep up with the work. Father speaks at midnight. The summary is about four pages; however, the actual speech is three to five hours. Right? You know it. So from 12 o'clock to five o'clock I have to translate. Then at seven o'clock pledge service I have to translate, and then again at the nine o'clock main service. Sometimes the speech would last six or seven hours. Then on God's Day evening the conference would begin and sometimes last 17 hours. I would have to translate. For a change, this is my heavenly God's Day in Arizona.

You know I really appreciate this modern age. This morning we already had the great blessing of receiving an excerpt of Father's message directly from Uruguay. This is wonderful. Already the midnight address has been delivered by the True Parents, and the motto of this year is "The Cosmic Expansion of the True Blessing and the Rooting Out of Satan's Blood Lineage." Father is determined to root out satanic lineage. This is the first time Father has used the word "cosmic" in the annual motto. This means our dispensational stage has come to the cosmic level. This is really wonderful. So this morning, instead of delivering a sermon, I would like to give you a testimony to our True Parents and our lives together with our True Parents.

How did I come to Arizona? I was a great admirer of Arizona and this beautiful sunshine that you take for granted. We from the East Coast don't take it for granted; the weather there is terrible now, snow and cold and ice and slippery roads and a lot of accidents. The sunshine here is heaven; it is incredible. Arizona is known to be heaven for asthma patients. One of them is my wife. She has been suffering from asthma for more than 30 years. She kept saying we must go to Arizona. I said, yes, of course we will. Even though I promised all the time, that never happened, year after year, because I had duties in Washington and New York: the Washington Times and AFC and ACC and so many other duties, assisting Father and translating for Father at conferences and meeting VIPs and so forth. I just had absolutely no time. My wife said to me, before I die I must go to Arizona— even without you. So she left me behind and came all by herself to Arizona. Boy, she is courageous. I was so guilty that I could not come because of these things. That was five years ago already. She came to Scottsdale and settled in a small rented apartment. That is how Arizona entered into our lives. So what did I have to do? I had to follow her; she is my queen; there is nothing else I could do. Since then Arizona has become our second home. We still have a main home in McLean, Virginia.

Ten days ago I met Father in Washington for a religious conference. True Parents came to Washington, and I had a wonderful time of fellowship with True Parents as usual. I have graduated from translation, because Father now knows so much English. Furthermore, Father does not need a translator any more. The conference and everything is just in Korean. Either you know it or you don't know it. If you don't know it, you just listen to Father spiritually. This is the type of conference Father is conducting, so I am not needed. I am out of a job. I am unemployed. [Laughter.]

This God's Day was going to be in Uruguay. I begged Father's permission to spend God's Day with my wife in Arizona, so here we are. I am at God's Day in Arizona, a rare, rare opportunity. Yesterday my sister-in-law and brother-in-law joined me for God's Day. I would like to introduce to you Mr. Sung Kil Yang, my brother-in-law from Korea, and my sister-in-law, my wife's sister, Ki Oh Yoon Yang. They have two lovely daughters who are studying in the United States. The elder one, Chung Hwa, is at Brown University in her third year. The second one, Chung In, is a freshman at Yale University. This is their entire family. They flew to Phoenix and joined me for two years vacation—in two days we already have two years, right? 1998 and 1999.

GOD CONTROLS HIM

I am so happy to see this wonderful gathering. You all look well. You are getting more mature and wise-looking. You even look rich. Why not? I am also very, very happy to meet with Mark Anderson. Mark has been an Arizona state representative for two terms. When we had lunch together yesterday, he showed me this Tribune newspaper article. Look at the picture. What a sharp-looking, handsome gentleman. The headline says "Anderson Ties With Reverend Moon in Question." This is what they are trying to say. "Lawmaker Denies Claims That Church Controls Him." But this is true: only God controls him, not the church. Right? Absolutely right.

But I am impressed by one statement in the article by representative Winifred "Freddy" Hurshberger. She said, "Mark Anderson has got definite moral standards that he feels everybody should have. I don't know if it is religion so much as idealism or his philosophy or exactly what it is. I'm sure it perhaps arises out of his religion." To me, Anderson is a living testimony to our True Parents. You know I used to lead the American Freedom Coalition and the American Constitutional Committee. We had many CAUSA seminars in Washington, D.C., and one here in Scottsdale. I always told my dear brothers of the AFC and ACC that they must become political saints. Every Sunday morning I preached: you must become political saints, not junky politicians.

After many years I have come to Arizona and found Mark Anderson living that credo and virtually becoming an example to other politicians. He is gaining the recognition of the community He fought back very strongly in the face of this kind of criticism. Religious tolerance is essential to America. Absolutely. He stood up for his church firmly, strongly, and won respect. I understand the last time he ran, the race was uncontested. I wish I could run that kind of race, uncontested. Even after the publicity, nobody dared come against Mark Anderson. He will definitely win a third term. Why not? Yesterday I gave him a mandate. I am still AFC's leader. I told him to become the speaker of the House of the state of Arizona. He said, amen. Everybody say amen for him. But that is not the end of it. He will become a state senator, a congressman in Washington, a senator in Washington. Why not? Amen. Why not? Even a presidential candidate.

Arizona already has had two presidential candidates. Goldwater was the first one. I really respected him. I knew him personally and he was a great man. Now John McCain has announced his candidacy, making him the second Arizonan to be a presidential candidate. He was a great soldier I respect. Whether he will succeed, I don't know. God knows. But at least the third one will succeed. You know formation, growth, and completion. Mark Anderson will succeed as the third candidate for the presidency of the United States. Why not? Will you say amen?

Another reason I love Arizona is it is the Grand Canyon state. Dr. Mark Barry used to be my assistant. He has been promoted to be my special assistant. He has become my speech writer and he provides all the research backbone papers for Father's policy for the unification of Korea. Mark Barry has a Ph.D. in foreign affairs with a specialization in U.S.-North Korean relations.

Who is going to unite the Korean peninsula? Father. Father is the central person who will bring about unification. There is a very significant providential reason behind the unification of Korea. I am now spearheading that particular mission in Korea and in Japan, and Mark has been my special assistant. Wherever I am, in Korea or in Japan or in Scottsdale, my fax machine is busy printing out page after page about the North Korean situation. He always brings me up to date. Mark Barry is now a professor at the University of Phoenix and is working with Mark Anderson at the state house. His wife, Kim, is my dear sister.

HOW GREAT THOU ART

Arizona is a great place. What a grandeur in the sunrise in Arizona. Absolutely splendid. You automatically exclaim "how great thou art" when you go to Sedona and the Grand Canyon. God's nature is truly, truly great. When you look at Sedona, the Arizona plain, and the Grand Canyon, you are really struck by an awesome feeling before God.

Today it is God's Day 1999. How wonderful we are giving this first day of the year in honor of our Creator, Heavenly Father. On the way here, there was a big accident. We saw a lot of police cars and an ambulance from Scottsdale. I said to my wife they must have been out drinking last night, crazy, jumping up and down and drinking, and trying to drive home early in the morning. Boom—the accident occurred. This is how the world is trying to celebrate the new year. When you go to Times Square in New York, the crowd is absolutely crazy. I have never been among the crowd; I just see the craziness on television. At 12 o'clock I have always been with Father, listening to His prayer, welcoming the New Year. At the same time, the world is crazy in Times Square. What a different way to welcome the New Year.

I understand you have a block party here, a gigantic party for New Year. I am sure there is a lot of joy and shouting and fireworks and so forth. However, I wondered whether God was there at the party. Probably not. On the other hand, on January 1, we gather together in honor of Heavenly Father, giving this day in honor of Him and giving Him our new commitment for the coming year. What a wonderful way to celebrate the New Year. Amen? Amen.

Today I want to talk to you about this story in the Bible from Matthew 17:14-20.

> ... A man came up to him and kneeling before him said, "Lord, have mercy on my son, for he is an epileptic and he suffers terribly; for often he falls into the fire, and often into the water. And I brought him to your disciples, and they could not heal him." And Jesus answered, "Oh faithless and perverse generation, how long am I to be with you? How long am I to bear with you? Bring him here to me." And Jesus rebuked him, and the demon came out of him, the boy was cured instantly. Then the disciples came to Jesus privately and said, "Why could we not cast it out?" He said to them, "Because of your little faith. For truly, I say to you, if you have faith as a grain of mustard seed, you will say to this mountain, 'Move from here to there,' and it will move; and nothing will be impossible to you."

This is what faith does. Faith the size of a mustard seed will move a mountain. As Jesus said, nothing is impossible to you. I always try to live by this quotation. This is why True Father added number eight to the Family Pledge: "Our family pledges, as we enter the Completed Testament Age, to achieve the ideal oneness of God and humankind in love through absolute faith, absolute love, and absolute obedience, thereby perfecting the realm of liberation of the Kingdom of God on Earth and in Heaven, by centering on true love."

THE FINAL CLEANUP

Through Pledge number eight God wants to emphasize very powerfully, as the Bible says, that with absolute faith, nothing is impossible to you. Now we call it absolute faith, absolute love, and absolute obedience. Mark Anderson said 1999 is the final year of the 20th century. It is amazing that in our lifetime we are passing through the year 2000. It is really miraculous when you think about it. What is the meaning of the year 2000? First of all, it is not only a new century but a new millennium. A new thousand years is starting, not just the 21st century. Many Christians believe that the new millennium will bring the kingdom of heaven on earth. So 1999 is the year for the final cleanup, the final sale. Everything has to be sold out completely, clean, ready to go into the new millennium. But there is even more meaning to the new millennium. Through the Divine Principle we know every thousand years is important. Yet every 2,000 years is more important Something gigantic always happens, ever since the fall of man.

I would like to recount the teaching of the Divine Principle. When the fall came, the world, instead of turning into the kingdom of heaven on earth, became the kingdom of hell. That began a spiritually dark period of 2,000 years, absolutely pitch dark. God could touch nothing, but God was working very hard trying to kindle the seed of faith. God tried through Noah but it didn't work too well. Finally God was successful in kindling the candle of faith on the face of the earth. That was the faith of Abraham. One man was on God's side. Everything else was satanic. As you know, Abraham was the son of an idol-maker, really from the satanic realm. Among that family God restored Abraham, and Abraham demonstrated absolute faith. God ordered him to leave his home town, and Abraham obeyed. God ordered him to give his son Isaac as a burnt offering. Abraham never hesitated. He was completely on God's side. He won with complete, absolute faith.

Father is talking about absolute faith. Abraham's son Isaac was spared through his absolute faith. God had worked for 2,000 years to find that one man. Yet, Abraham also made mistakes; therefore, the dispensation centering on Abraham was extended down to Isaac and Jacob. Jacob's victory gave God his first foothold on earth. So the greatest event in the first 2,000 years was Abraham. God claimed Abraham from the satanic realm. This created the base for the chosen people. The second 2,000 years of history was from Abraham to Jesus. So biblically speaking Jesus came 4,000 years after the fall. The 2,000 years from Abraham to Jesus was the period of preparation for the coming of the messiah. The chosen people were Jacob's descendants. Finally Jesus came 2,000 years later. The greatest event in the first 4,000 years of human history was the birth of Jesus. On that day, history came back to a new starting point, and a new history started clicking.

From year one, we are now in the year 1999, with only one more year to go to the year 2000! Amazing. However, what God intended with the birth of Jesus was not another prolongation of the dispensation. God wanted to have done everything at the time of Jesus. He did not plan for the second Christ to come. He wanted to have the ideal of True Parents accomplished at the time of Jesus. If there had been no disobedience of the chosen people, there would have been no crucifixion. We would not be having this service today. God's Day would have been established 2,000 years ago.

However, the crucifixion came about because of the disobedience of the faithless people of Israel. This prolonged the dispensation of the will of God another 2,000 years. There is only one year to go to the year 2000. This is an incredible time we live in. What is the meaning of the year 2000? The year 2000 is like the inauguration of True Parents. The messiah has come to become the True Parent. That didn't happen 2,000 years ago. It is being done in our time with the Second Coming of Christ.

Father was born in 1920. In the year 2000, Father will celebrate his 80th birthday. During this 80 years Father was completely vindicated and victorious over Satan. All the indemnity has been paid. The True Parents were given the power to eradicate original sin. That is the meaning of the year 2000. In the year 2000, everything will come to zero. God will recognize no one except those who are with the True Parents; that is the only distinction. That is why Father is pushing so much with the cosmic expansion of the Blessing. Blessing means what? Recognition by the True Parents. No Blessing means no recognition by the True Parents. That will be the judgment.

'I NEVER KNEW YOU'

This year is the final year of our life, of our sin, iniquities, and shortcomings. We have to get back to total innocence, come back to zero. The only asset we have is our True Parents. No other assets are important to us. The second coming of Christ makes a world zero, zero, zero. Nothing is important except you are with the True Parents or you are without the True Parents. With the Blessing or without the Blessing. That is the difference. Even the Bible says, in Matthew 7:21-23: "Not everyone who says to me, 'Lord, Lord,' shall enter the kingdom of heaven, but he who does the will of my Father who is in heaven. On that day many will say to me, 'Lord, Lord, did we not prophesy in your name, and cast out demons in your name, and do many mighty works in your name?' And then will I declare to them, 'I never knew you; depart from me, you evildoers.'" Jesus will say, I don't know you. We need True Parents' recognition. All of us should become like a child, innocent, zero, zero, zero. All we need to have is purity of heart and recognition of True Parents.

In the eyes of the world, this gathering in this YMCA building in Tempe, Arizona, is humble, not magnificent. This is not a state house, not an assembly of congressmen. This is not an assembly of scholars. You are ordinary people, ordinary men and women, but I want you to know that you people gathered on New Year's Day at the YMCA in Tempe, Arizona, are the most blessed people, the most fortunate people, because, even if we have nothing else, we have True Parents. The most precious thing for you and me is True Parents. Hallelujah! Among the billions of people in the world, we are the handful of people chosen by God to know the True Parents first in Arizona. Several million people live in this state, but this handful of people have come here to celebrate God's Day in the name of True Parents. We heard the True Parents New Year's message. Who else in Arizona has this privilege? The greatest thing that happened in history is the coming of True Parents. True Parents came in 1920, but the year 2000 is the culmination or inauguration of True Parents on the universal and cosmic stage. That will happen next year. So this year is important because we have to prepare for the inauguration of the True Parents ourselves.

This year is not going to be an easy year. We have to get rid of all the iniquities, all the ungodly things to be ready to enter into the kingdom of heaven on earth next year. Therefore, this year the entire world is going to be on trial. The United States of America is on trial. In fact, the president of the United States is literally on trial this month. The head of state is on trial. That means America is on trial. On what charges? Moral charges. Not financial charges, not violence, but moral charges. It is symbolic of the United States going down morally. In the last several months, the United States has been shamed before the world. Proud America is no longer a proud nation. There was a phrase, "ugly American," but now the whole world is talking about the ugly president of the United States. America's question is a moral question.

AMERICA IS ON TRIAL

That is most important in the sight of God. That is the only thing that God counts. Everything else is secondary to the moral question. America is on trial. America is coming under tribulation, from the White House all the way down to every level of society. Among so many iniquities the worst that God can see is immorality, especially within men and women, all kinds of perverse acts, permissiveness, all kinds of sins are permitted in this country. Financially, everybody says this is the greatest nation and the richest of all. That is absolutely true. I love this country. You know I love America.

I have been in America for more than 30 years of my adult life. I love America. AFC/ACC people, Unification Church people all know I love America. This is why I don't want America to go down the drain.

America is deeply wounded at the moment. In the year 1999 we have to liquidate all the iniquities from our society and especially from our family. God can forgive many sins but God cannot forgive one sin, adultery or immorality. So we would like to build a proud America in 1999.

But more important, each of our Unification Church members is on trial in the year 1999. Our faith shall be tested. True Parents will ask us: Do you know me? Do you love me? You can squarely look in the eye of True Parents and answer: Yes, Father and Mother, I know you, and not only do I know you, I love you. I live for you. How else can we say that in the year of 1999; that is the question.

All kinds of trials and tribulations will come in this year to the Unification Church. This year the Unification Church will not prosper. We are being internally tested. Our spiritual faith is being tested. After the year 2000, the Unification Church will blossom, cover the entire universe, but not this year. We have to reorganize ourselves, rebuild ourselves, test ourselves, pass the test. That is our agenda in 1999. Korea too, Japan too. A lot of people all of a sudden have certain doubts. Am I doing right? Is he the Messiah? What happens if he is not the Messiah? Yes, this is the test. This test is not only for you and me, but for everybody, Korean members, leaders, from the top all the way down to the local leaders and members. Many things are going on around True Parents and True Parents' family, but I tell you I have come to the conclusion. Abraham passed the test; he had absolute faith. Jesus Christ, no question, he passed the test. When he was crucified, he was not complaining to God. He said, "God, accept my sacrifice, forgive my enemy who is piercing me with a spear."

I tell you after 41 years of following True Parents, I cannot imagine that anybody can have greater faith in God than our True Parents. Forty-one years of my life in the Unification Church. Forty-one years of being an eyewitness to absolute faith. Even in Father's God's Day message we read today, he said: there is not even one second that I was not thinking about Heavenly Father's well-being and His grieving heart; no one here on earth has ever tasted and expressed the grieving heart of God. I never even imagined that God was grieving before I joined the Unification Church, but even after 41 years of following our True Parents, I was still not feeling the grief of God, not even one-tenth, not even one-hundredth, one-thousandth, as much as the True Parents. It is so obvious. There is such a distance between me and True Parents. I surrendered myself completely to our True Parents, before their absolute faith.

LIVE BY ABSOLUTE FAITH

I am not asking that only you to do something. This sermon is a sermon to Bo Hi Pak. I am telling myself what to do in the year of 1999. God tested with absolute faith. As Jesus said, I don't want you to be cast out because of your little faith. As Jesus said, "For truly, I say to you, if you have faith as a grain of mustard seed, you will say to this mountain, 'Move from here to there,' and it will move; and nothing will be impossible to you." I want to obtain this kind of faith in the year of 1999. This is the culmination of my faith. I want to reorganize myself completely going straight forward, absolute faith. I want to live by absolute faith. Let us move the mountains

We have to learn the warning in the life of John the Baptist. The Christian churches have described John the Baptist as the greatest man in the Bible. Wrong! Divine Principle reveals John the Baptist as a man of failure. The main person responsible for the crucifixion of Jesus Christ was John the Baptist. He did not do the job that God was asking him to do, the job of Elijah. He did not even know that he was Elijah.

Today I would like to conclude my sermon by saying we must not repeat the mistake of John the Baptist. When Jesus was beginning his ministry, he asked for baptism from John the Baptist. In John 1:29-34 we read,

> The next day he [John the Baptist] saw Jesus coming toward him, and said, "Behold the Lamb of God, who takes away the sins of the world!..." And John bore witness, "I saw the Spirit descend as a dove from heaven, and it remained on him. I myself did not know him, but he who sent me to baptize with water said to me, 'He on whom you see the spirit descend and remain, this is he who baptizes with the Holy Spirit.' And I have seen and borne witness that this is the Son of God."

You know the "Battle Hymn of the Republic." I like the verse, "I have seen the glory of the coming of the Lord." Here John witnessed to Jesus as the Son of God. Amen. He was correct. He was absolutely correct. But less than three years later, John the Baptist's mind changed.

How long have you been in the Unification Church? I am sure you all have been members for more than three years. I am warning you that in three years the mind can change. It doesn't matter if you follow the True Parents for 41 years. In just three years the mind can change. How John changed is shown in Matthew 11:2-6. John the Baptist was in prison for criticizing Herod and his concubine. This was not John's job. He was supposed to be concerned with the dispensation. He sent his disciples to Jesus and asked, "Are you he who is to come, or shall we look for another?" That means, are you the Messiah or shall we look for another person as the Messiah? Three years earlier, he himself had witnessed to Jesus as the Son of God, but now he says, "Are you he who is to come, or shall we look for another?" Jesus was shocked. He did not answer directly. Jesus simply said, "Go and tell John what you hear and see: the blind receive their sight and the lame walk, lepers are cleansed and the deaf hear, and the dead are raised up, and the poor have good news preached to them. And blessed is he who takes no offense at me." [Matthew 11:4-6]

THE LEAST IS GREATER THAN JOHN

In Matthew 11:11, Jesus said, "Truly, I say to you, among those born of women there has risen no one greater than John the Baptist; yet he who is least in the kingdom is greater than he." The least in the Kingdom is greater than John the Baptist.

So with this teaching, on God's Day 1999, let us reaffirm that we have True Parents. Everybody say amen! Amen? Amen! Let us not ask this question like John the Baptist. Is he the one who is to come? Is Reverend Moon the one who is to come or shall we wait for another? Let us not ask this foolish question. Affirm the Son of God has come, and through True Parents, we will all become God's sons and daughters. What great blessing we have.

There are some young people here looking forward to the Blessing. Second generation, I want you to listen. You are not fully aware of the fortunate position in which you were born, because you are born with it. American people do not fully appreciate how great a country you are living in. You take it for granted. I suffered in my childhood; I grew up in abject poverty, so when I came to the United States, I said this is heaven. But for you: oh, not enough, not enough hamburger, not enough coca cola, not enough ice cream, not enough free time, too much homework, and so forth.

Furthermore you have great parents. Your parents have brought you by birth the greatest blessing. In your body, you don't have any trace of original sin. All you have to do is affirm the True Parents, and you will be in Heaven automatically. We shall live True Parents' moral standard and be able to say: I regret nothing. Hallelujah!

In American history, the person I admire in the War of Independence, in George Washington's army, was a very young officer whose name was Nathan Hale. He was courageous. He went on reconnaissance missions. Reconnaissance is always dangerous; you have to go behind the enemy lines to get the information and bring it back. On one mission, he was not successful—he was captured by the British army. They brought Nathan Hale to their commanding officer, who looked at this handsome, young, innocent man, and he did not want to kill him. The British officer said to him, "Nathan, all you have to do is surrender. Then we will let you live and you can join the British army and we will let you become an officer." Nathan said, no, thank you. Three times they begged him, three times he refused. So he had to be executed. The British officer asked what would his final words be. Nathan said, I have only one regret that I have but one life to give for my country. If I have 10 lives, I will give 10 lives. If I have 100 lives, I will give 100 lives to my country.

What a great patriot. We shall be better than Nathan Hale. Why? Because we serve the True Parents. We regret we have only one life to live for True Parents. We have only one life; therefore, we must do our utmost with this one life. Use it up completely, completely for the sake of True Parents. God bless you. Thank you for listening. I think my time is up. So let us have a wonderful God's Day celebration.

APPENDIX

PERSONAL TESTIMONIES

THOMAS J. WARD, ED.D.

Founding member and former academic director, CAUSA International; currently, Visiting Professor of International Studies at the University of Bridgeport.

I first encountered Dr. Bo Hi Pak in March, 1972 when he accompanied Reverend and Mrs. Sun Myung Moon on a visit which they made to in Paris, France. What first struck me about Dr. Pak was his amazing capacity to translate both the words and the heart of Reverend Moon in a way that Westerners could grasp. A linguist by training, I was astonished by his proficiency in American English, especially given that he had only begun to study the language at the age of 28.

When I returned to the United States in 1973 to join the Unification community's activities there, I had the opportunity to participate in Reverend Moon's 21-city, 32-city, and 8-city speaking tours in the United States. Later I joined the first Global Team and participated in an evangelical tour with Reverend Moon and Dr. Pak in Japan and in Korea. We usually only saw Dr. Pak from afar. I never could have imagined back then that I would later be provided an opportunity to work directly and personally with such a remarkable individual.

In 1980 Antonio Betancourt, burning with the vision of addressing Latin America's spiritual, political, and social plight, approached Dr. Pak and shared his views and what he perceived as unique opportunities. Dr.

Pak immediately understood the validity of Antonio's observations. Together they went to Reverend and Mrs. Moon and this resulted in the creation of CAUSA International, an internationally based organization which played an important role in exposing the fallacies of Marxist doctrine in the 1980's to a wide variety of audiences. Aware of my ability to speak Spanish, Antonio recommended that I along with several other seminarians come to CAUSA upon completing our graduate studies in religious education at Unification Theological Seminary. Reverend Moon assigned me along with Bill Selig, Juan Sanchis, Peter and Beatriz Steeghs, Mark Willenchek, George Allen, Roger Johnstone, Frederick Swarts, Jean Rondon, Paul Perry, and Bill Lay to multiply CAUSA's educational efforts.

For the next thirteen years, I was afforded the amazing opportunity to work closely with Dr. Pak. It is an experience which has shaped my life of faith and my understanding of what it means to be a public person. There is not space here to enter into all of the details of that experience. Because Dr. Pak sees thirteen as his lucky number, I have decided to summarize what I learned in thirteen points, many of which I hope the reader may sense while enjoying the reading of Dr. Pak's speeches in this volume:

1. To strive to live up to one's word and commitment.
   When a person makes a promise or a commitment, one must do absolutely everything to live up to it. Over and over I saw that once Dr. Pak made a promise, he did everything to fulfill it and he usually did.

2. To see the world in a more complex fashion.
   Before working with Dr. Pak, I was inclined to see things in a very simplistic world of the saved (Unificationists) and the unsaved (non-Unificationists). Through him I learned how God loves and respects people of all faiths and backgrounds. I learned to respect the spiritual accomplishments of those outside the Unification tradition. I came to value their ideas, their input, their sacrifices, and their many contributions which far exceeded my own. I came to appreciate and recognize the many things which all believers have done and continue to do for God and humanity.

3. To work to achieve the standard set by the founder, Reverend Moon.
   Working with Dr. Pak, on literally hundreds of conferences as well as on numerous publications, I saw that his absolute desire was to demonstrate an unparalleled standard of excellence in the preparation and execution of all that he pursues. I have rarely seen his standard equaled elsewhere even though I participated in numerous programs held in conjunction with or under the auspices of heads of state in Latin America, Eastern Europe, Asia, and the United States. If the Chiefs

of Protocol of the United Nations and the Big Seven spent a week with Dr. Pak, they would not go away unimpressed.

4. To love America.
   In 1987 a group of battlefield-wearied Unification Church leaders came to Dr. Pak to form the American Freedom Coalition. My wife and I commented over many years how each of those leaders became revived under Dr. Pak and the vision of Reverend Moon. Indeed they became like new members. Today several of them have even been invited to fulfill important official roles in state and city government. Almost all of them having become significant community leaders. Through the CAUSA conferences, I also came to recognize that the most maligned groups in the United States were those who vocally opposed communism. On one occasion after another, I saw how Dr. Pak appreciated this constituency at CAUSA conferences and in other encounters. He had the remarkable ability to lift their spirits and remind them of the nobility of their cause. What explains this? Dr. Pak helps others to feel God's and Reverend Moon's love for America, which has its roots in a respect for this nation's Christian heritage of sacrifice and self-denial in the pursuit of "one nation under God with liberty and justice for all."

5. To be a good listener.
   Dr. Pak has a warm, generous, and embracing nature. Though he can be strict and demanding, there is a remarkable brotherly aspect in his character, which allows one to unburden one's heart with him in a way one might not elsewhere. When he welcomes someone to his office, he devotes himself totally to that person. Those touched by him walk away in peace with a profound sense of having experienced forgiveness, renewal, and the love of God.

6. To seek inspiration and hope in even the most dire circumstance.
   I do not know how many times I saw Dr. Pak in a hopeless situation and witnessed how even there he found a cause for hope and exhilaration. Perhaps this was best manifested in 1984 when he was kidnapped, blindfolded, gagged and beaten by thugs and even given the hour of his announced execution. Even in that situation, Dr. Pak's attitude was, "How can I die so that my last words render honor to God and to the work of my Teacher?"

7. To be uncompromising in pursuing a positive result, even in the midst of the most adverse conditions.

Dr. Pak's positive attitude and total commitment explain how he could reach the highest levels of leadership in the United States, Europe, Latin America, Asia, Oceania, and Africa. Reverend Moon once said that he is thinking about Dr. Pak every second of the day. I believe that this was because Reverend Moon could sense Dr. Pak's total devotion to realizing the Founder's vision.

In 1985 I was with Dr. Pak in Montevideo. I received a phone call that there was a bomb under a podium where Dr. Pak was speaking. I was told that it would be detonated in 10 minutes. I brought a note to Dr. Pak, warning him that his life was in danger. He read the note, nodded, and then enthusiastically continued with his lecture. The bomb threat turned out to be a hoax.

8. His tearful devotion to his teacher and his desire to vindicate the ideal of True Parents.

   I cannot begin to count the many times when I witnessed Dr. Pak in tears because of the difficult conditions Reverend Moon suffered in the United States, particularly during the dark days of Danbury. The purity of his devotion deeply impressed me. I believe that this helps to explain why he has served as such an effective bridge between Reverend and Mrs. Moon and those who have expressed interest in their views and activities.

9. Never speak ill of others.

   In my thirteen-year experience of working with Dr. Pak, I almost never heard him speak ill of anyone, even those who had clearly mistreated him. He chose to remain silent or even to praise those who had taken advantage of him.

10. His desire to share his good fortune with others.

    Although our contribution to his efforts were minuscule, I saw how time and again, he gave us credit for successes which were not ours.

11. To create an exemplary family life.

    Never can I recall a time when I called Dr. Pak and reached Mrs. Pak that she said to me "Why are you calling here? Now is family time." She always called Dr. Pak to the phone. I found in the Paks' family life a beautiful devotion between husband and wife and parents and children and at the same time an exemplary manifestation of the teaching that the individual must live for the family, the family for the clan, the clan for the nation, the nation for the world, and the world for God.

12. To inspire others to follow the path which he has chosen.
    Dr. Pak always emphasized that if people are inspired by his personality and his lifestyle, they needed to understand that he was not always as he is now. He explained how he had gone through a profound change once he had met his Teacher. Later, when I had the opportunity to pursue a few projects directly with Reverend and Mrs. Moon, I realized that because of having worked with Dr. Pak, I had learned so many things that were pivotal to understanding the ideal of True Parents.

13. Never to forget what we all aspire to be.
    Dr. Pak has so often said that on his tombstone, he dreams of only one epitaph: Bo Hi Pak—A Child of God and True Son of True Parents. From my thirteen years of working with Dr Pak, I can testify that he lives as a public person, constantly pushing himself to realize that ideal and, like the Bodhisatva, he helps us to do the same.

ANTONIO BETANCOURT

Founding member and former secretary general, CAUSA International. Currently, Executive Director of the Summit Council, the Federation for World Peace, the Association for the Unity of Latin America; and president, World Institute for Development and Peace.

"You create a position by creating value. Leave a legacy of genuine value behind in whatever you do, then any position acquired in life can never be challenged." These were Dr. Bo Hi Pak's words in the beginning of 1980, and they have served as my motto ever since.

For me to reminisce about Dr. Pak is to ponder practically all my years in the Unification Church. It gives me the opportunity to publicly express my gratitude to someone who has played a critical role in my life. In reality, my 23-year association with Dr. and Mrs. Pak is integral to my relationship with my spiritual parents, Rev. and Mrs. Moon, my wife, my children, my mission, and my entire outlook.

From a singer in an international choir (the New Hope Singers International with Dr. Pak in charge) and then a missionary for the Unification Church in upper Manhattan in the 1970s, to my present position as an international consultant and director of several humanitarian international organizations—my life and my missions have all developed together with my relationship with Dr. Bo Hi Pak.

In November 1979, Rev. Moon directed Dr. Pak to prepare to go to Latin America. He felt that the Unification Movement urgently needed to support the Latin governments facing a fate similar to Nicaragua at the hands of communist-led insurgents. Along with Argentine journalist Antonio Rodriguez Carmona and Celia Fraga Roomet, I accompanied Dr. Pak in the capacity of special assistant and translator.

The direction from Rev. Moon came as a result of a project for Latin America presented to him after my brother Michael and I met Mr. Rodriguez as we were doing missionary work in upper Manhattan. Mr. Rodriguez came to the United States for a "mission from God," which he called "Crusada Argentina USA" (CAUSA). Initially its purpose was to improve relations between the United States, especially the American media, and Argentina and Latin America.

Mr. Rodriguez believed that news about that part of the world was so distorted that the United States had to be awakened to the real dangers of communist work in Latin America. After we taught him Divine Principle and Victory over Communism (VOC), Mr. Rodriguez realized that the Unification Movement had the power and mission to educate America about its responsibility regarding the totalitarian menace in Latin America and around the world.

Our first approach would be to show Latin America that The News World, the New York daily newspaper founded by Rev. Moon in 1976, could provide accurate, objective, and sympathetic coverage of the plight of the people suffering from communist aggression. To help with our project, we thought it essential to create a Spanish newspaper in New York that would serve as a tribute to and harmonizer of all Latin America.

Our champion for this historical enterprise was Dr. Bo Hi Pak. He could inspire Rev. Moon to support these efforts. Dr. Pak had just completed a historical match with the U.S. Congress defending our movement, which was under heavy attack from far left forces in America. Dr. Pak was inspired and understood our strategy very well. When these ideas were presented to Rev. and Mrs. Moon, they completely agreed with the formula. They said that the road to Washington is through the Latin American capitals. Dr. Pak wanted the United States to be indebted to Rev. Moon for fighting the forces of communism. America was advocating military and security solutions, while Rev. Moon was promoting victory over communism based on the ideology of Godism and democracy.

The first order was to recruit professional journalists who would help us launch Noticias del Mundo in New York. We toured Argentina, Uruguay, Paraguay, and Chile where we found first-class journalists who volunteered in the launching of our newspaper, which began publication in 1980.

As president of News World Communications, publishers of the New York City Tribune and Noticias del Mundo, Dr. Pak was welcomed by the heads of state of many Latin American countries: Rodrigo Carazo in Costa Rica, our first country; Napoleon Duarte of El Salvador; Aparicio Mendez of Uruguay; Alfredo Stroessner of Paraguay; Suazo Cordova of Honduras; Jorge Blanco of the Dominican Republic; Augusto Pinochet of Chile; Belisario Betancourt of Colombia; and many others.

Our detractors said we made contacts with only the right-wing dictators of Latin America, whereas the truth is we visited every head of state who would receive us with our message of peace and hope from Rev. Moon.

We never gave financial or any logistical support to the arms struggles led by anti-communist forces. We had enough responsibility in dealing with the ideological and philosophical education programs. Our fight was "mind to mind" from a theological perspective.

Over and over, we heard pleas for assistance. The heads of state wanted help in the ideological struggle. We offered them our strength, which was education on an idea that is superior to communism—Godism. With this the nations could regain their most valuable resource, their youth, who were being lost to communist idealism.

Just as Caleb reported to Moses, Dr. Pak would bring news from the field to Rev. Moon. Upon this assessment, Rev. Moon decided to establish the Confederation of the Association for the Unity of the Societies of the Americas (CAUSA International). Dr. Pak became the president and I the secretary-general. Rev. Moon also selected a group of Unification Theological Seminary graduates to develop the CAUSA Institute with its educational programs. A mighty work began that expanded from Latin America, eventually covering the five continents of the world.

We established a base in Montevideo, Uruguay, where Dr. Pak negotiated on behalf of the Movement the acquisition of a hotel (number one in the country), a bank, and a new newspaper, Ultimas Noticias, which later became the second most important daily in the country. Tens of thousands of Uruguayans from all walks of life were educated with the CAUSA worldview.

We could literally write many books about our experiences with CAUSA International and working side by side with Dr. Pak about the projects that we developed together over the past 23 years. In the early days of CAUSA, we traveled to nearly every country in Latin America. Our team taught academicians, journalists, scientists, political leaders, union workers, soldiers, doctors, lawyers—everyone. We had the honor to meet many heads of state and religious leaders, including His Excellency Archbishop Antonio Plaza, chancellor of the Pontifical University of La

Plata and archbishop of La Plata in Argentina. It pleased our hearts to hear the Archbishop praise our work.

He said, "Dr. Moon chose to challenge the ideological cause of such violence in what Pope Leo XIII alluded to as the 'obsolete theory' of Marxism itself. Rev. Moon's and Dr. Pak's activities are significant in that they constitute not only an exposé and a critical analysis of Marxism, but bring in a counterproposal to Marxism."

On November 15, 1984, while Rev. Moon was serving a term in Danbury prison on trumped-up charges of tax evasion, honorary doctorate degrees from the Catholic University of La Plata, Argentina, were presented to Rev. Moon and Dr. Pak at a special ceremony at the United Nations. Mrs. Moon received the honor on behalf of her husband. This was a demonstration of courage and moral support by Archbishop Antonio Plaza and the president of the University, Dr. Nicolas Argentato, for the efforts of Rev. Moon and Dr. Pak for the struggle of democracy under God in Latin America.

In January 1984, Rev. Moon founded the Association for the Unity of Latin America (AULA). The primary purpose of AULA is to foster activities that will articulate a route to greater unity among the Latin American countries. It takes its inspiration from the ideals and purposes of the liberator, Simón Bolívar, as well as the great patriots of the Hispanic-American world. Working with Ambassador José María Chaves, we held many programs throughout the Western hemisphere, but certainly the most memorable include audiences and recognition of our work by His Holiness John Paul II (1985), Mother Teresa (1985), and King Juan Carlos I of Spain (1986).

Recognizing the Soviet totalitarian threat and its effect upon the security and stability of the free world, Dr. Pak, along with Dr. Joseph Churba, supported the idea of the establishment of the International Security Council in Washington, D.C., in September 1984. It was founded as a rallying point for top intelligence analysts from around the world in academia, government, and the military to analyze the threat and propose solutions to problems of Soviet expansionism. It was thanks to Dr. Pak's enthusiasm and endorsement that this project received direction and generous patronage from Rev. and Mrs. Moon. By personally bringing it to their attention, we were able to create a very serious think tank with an outstanding quarterly journal, Global Affairs, offering to advise and educate leaders and enlighten public opinion on important issues such as terrorism, the radical entente, the threat to NATO, and the growing Soviet threat in the Middle and Far East.

From 1985-86, we developed the CAUSA International Military Association (CIMA) as an educational association committed to the cause of freedom around the world. This organization was geared to a membership of senior retired U.S. and foreign military officers.

In 1987, under Dr. Pak's direction as president, the inaugural conference of the Summit Council for World Peace was held in Seoul, Korea. The Summit Council, in many ways, represents the pinnacle of Rev. Moon's efforts to reach out to the world's most influential and respected leaders. Dr. Pak spared no expense to embrace incumbent and former heads of state and government and tap this rich reservoir of wisdom and experience. At each event, Dr. Pak shared the vision of the founder to challenge the participants to use their expertise as statesmen for the work of peace, unity, and harmony among the nations of the world. Former Presidents Kenneth Kaunda of Zambia, George Bush of the United States, Mikhail Gorbachev from Russia, Fernando Belaunde Terry of Peru, Julio Turbay Ayala of Colombia, and Mario Echandi of Costa Rica; former Prime Ministers Sir Edward Heath from England and Aziz Sidky of Egypt; former Governor General Edward Schreyer from Canada; and many others have helped to advance the cause of peace proposed by the Summit Council thanks to Dr. Pak's undying dedication to build that institution.

I remember the period 1990-93 as being particularly busy and hectic years. In February 1990, we held a Summit Council conference in Seoul and simultaneously celebrated the 70th birthday of Rev. Moon. In April 1990, Dr. Pak oversaw the conference in Moscow and meetings with President Mikhail Gorbachev in the Kremlin. The Summit Council brought 40 former heads of state, government, prime ministers, and many world leaders from 60 nations for a total of more than 1,000 guests. Along with the World Media Association, the conference discussed the "Global Implications of Glasnost and Perestroika." It was a gala, phenomenal event. Then on April 11, Rev. and Mrs. Moon led the delegation of heads of state for an engrossing private session with Mr. Gorbachev. For the Unification movement, this was one of the most historical providential activities of the end of this century.

In August 1991, the inaugural conference of the Federation for World Peace was held in Seoul with former U.S. Secretary of State General Alexander Haig as the keynote speaker. The Federation was initially conceived as an umbrella coalition of many organizations founded by Rev. and Mrs. Moon. An enormous amount of organizing had to be done. Dr. Pak had his finger on every detail. Within days of returning to Washington, D.C., in September 1991, Dr. Pak addressed the International Commission for the Reunification of Korea, a newly launched project of the Summit Council.

That year in November, thanks to the work of the Summit Council and its Commission on Korean Reunification, we pulled off the biggest coup in the history of the Movement by bringing Rev. and Mrs. Moon to their hometown in North Korea. How this happened is truly one of the greatest stories to be told. At the time, I honestly felt like Dr. Pak and I were true disciples of Christ. Many late night meetings took place in Beijing; quiet, intense negotiations with the North Koreans were held involving protocol, schedule, and a million other details.

Finally, a delegation of about 30 people was brought to Beijing, including Church elders and members to record and chronicle the trip. Then at the last minute, North Korea said only Korean nationals could enter the country. That meant, Rev. and Mrs. Moon, Dr. and Mrs. Pak, Peter Kim, and two assistants. The rest of us stayed behind. For us, it was like Rev. and Mrs. Moon were going to another planet; one can't imagine a more surreal atmosphere than seeing them leave on a North Korean jet, not knowing if they would be taken captive or whether their lives were in danger. We could only pray and hope they were in God's hands.

On the sixth day, a member came back to Beijing with a roll of film. It was like Alexander Graham Bell and the first telephone. We gathered around the development of that film like it was the birth of our first baby. Slowly the picture came into focus: it was Rev. Moon and Kim Il Sung embracing. The man who had imprisoned, tortured, humiliated, and abused our spiritual leader was embracing him like a long-lost brother. It was the most beautiful, tearful sight I'd ever witnessed, the embrace of the historical Jacob and Esau.

The Segye Ilbo and Sekai Nippo newspapers were on hand to transmit the photos to wire services around the world. By the next morning, the entire world saw the photo and had to acknowledge that Rev. Moon had done the impossible! When Rev. and Mrs. Moon returned to Beijing a few days later, it was total pandemonium. We gathered in their suite and heard Dr. Pak give the most amazing testimony about Rev. and Mrs. Moons' relatives, visiting Rev. Moon's birthplace, and embracing Kim Il Sung.

The result of the historical encounter between President Kim Il Sung and Rev. Moon was expressed in a 10-point communiqué, one of which was an agreement to have prime ministerial talks between North and South Korea. This opened the door to a new era of relations between the DPRK and South Korea. This occurred a few days after Rev. Moon's departure from Pyongyang. Another area negotiated included North Korea's desire for light-water nuclear reactors to replace their old ones that created the so-called controversy of the DPRK nuclear weapons program.

In the following months and years, the Summit Council, under the direction of Dr. Pak, has effectively used back-door diplomacy to promote dialogue between the United States and the DPRK in order to resolve this potential nuclear buildup in northeast Asia. The Summit Council was responsible to nourish the process of diplomatic rapprochement between Washington and Pyongyang. This led to the final signing of the "Framework Agreement" on October 21, 1994, between the United States and the DPRK that froze the weapons-grade plutonium-producing reactors in exchange for light-water reactors.

Dr. Pak was instrumental in bringing The Washington Times to conduct Kim Il Sung's first interview since 1972. He was also responsible for bringing in international cable television companies, CNN, NHK of Japan, and BBC of London. This enabled the DPRK to have international exposure and to bring them out of their self-imposed isolation.

The scope of Dr. Pak's ground-breaking work for permanent peace and the eventual reunification of the Korean peninsula deserves far more space than what can be dedicated in these pages; certainly it would be enough to fill several books.

In 1992, at the second Federation for World Peace, the keynote speaker was Mikhail Gorbachev. At the time, no Russian president, incumbent or former, had ever visited Korea, so his coming represented a major event in the country's history. There were many logistical nightmares to contend with, but like he was executing a precise military maneuver, Dr. Pak made sure every item was attended to. He left nothing to chance. The result was a wonderful, warm, and friendly encounter between Mr. and Mrs. Gorbachev and Rev. and Mrs. Moon. It was a visit filled with symbolism; the whole country watched as these two former archrivals embraced in a spirit of forgiveness and harmony.

In July 1994, Dr. Pak and I attended the funeral of Kim Il Sung in Pyongyang. He was the only South Korean citizen and I the only U.S. citizen in attendance. Upon his return to Beijing, Dr. Pak received enormous persecution from Seoul. Although we attended as representatives of Rev. Moon, Dr. Pak underwent derision from conservatives in South Korea and the threat of arrest and imprisonment from the ROK government for violating its national security decrees. Dr. Pak had to fight for his reputation and his legal rights. He had to call on his tremendous inner reserves and strength, as I watched him weather this storm that kept him from returning to his beloved homeland for three years. During that time, Dr. Pak worked tirelessly to promote family values and to help rebuild and fortify the Unification Movement in Japan.

I have only described my personal experience with the external course followed by Dr. Pak of mostly 18 years. Each step required enormous work, mastery in planning, and diplomacy, but most of all prayer. Each project has a story behind it and someday volumes will be written.

For me Dr. Pak has been a role model, a teacher of diplomacy with a heart of gold. As an example, a brother in Washington, Bruce Williams, narrates the following story. When he was assistant pastor of the Unification Church of Washington, he witnessed an event that even Dr. Pak has no knowledge of. Bruce says that one night, "Bo Hi Pak arrived outside with an elder Korean gentleman who may or may not have been a member. It was snowing heavily. I was watching from the window without being seen when the guest slipped and fell while getting out of the car. Dr. Pak looked around to see if anyone was watching, then he suddenly slipped and fell down in the snow. They were laughing about how slippery the ground was and helping each other to get up." I have never seen a man who tried so hard to make people feel at ease and who sees God in everyone as much as Dr. Pak.

He is a man I can approach, someone I can speak with honestly and forthrightly. Wherever we went, whether China, Japan, Korea, Latin America, Europe, he always went out of his way to involve me and the staff around us and to make us part of the big picture. When he visited Rev. Moon, he gave us credit for the achievements. He values the opinion of his staff and others. He genuinely and truly is interested in people. He is a good listener. Those are important qualities for a leader.

I always felt that, among all the leaders in America serving under Rev. Moon, Dr. Pak is the most approachable, the one who can understand Western thinking, our feelings and way of doing things, but more fundamentally, the one who knows how to extract the best of Western members for the sake of God's will.

Dr. Pak has this quality of taking the best from everyone. He doesn't impose himself, he listens carefully, evaluates, meditates, then acts. If it's not working out right, he's not afraid to admit his shortcomings, cut his losses, and start again. He sets a standard. We always called it "DP standard." It means doing it right. Sometimes it means spending more, but with an eye toward history, he always seemed to be right. The Washington Times, the Little Angels, the Kirov Ballet, Atlantic Video, the Summit Council, these are all Dr. Pak's legacy of doing it right. He always said we are representing Heavenly Father and True Parents, and our lives have to be absolutely True Parent-centered. Therefore he encourages us to give our best.

Dr. Pak is a passionate speaker and caring person. I saw this in November 1997 when he was asked to deliver the eulogy of our dear friend,

Ambassador Douglas MacArthur II. He brought the whole audience to tears at the Christ Church in Georgetown packed with blue blood Washingtonians. It was from the heart that he recalled the great deeds and kindness of Ambassador MacArthur.

Recently, at an international conference of the Federation for World Peace, he was asked to sit at the dais next to Mrs. Moon. He apparently had no title or position to be introduced and he asked me, "What title can I use? I have no position here in America anymore." I told him, "You have created a position and a title for yourself by creating genuine value through service to humanity, assisting and serving our True Parents, so your best and indisputable title is 'special assistant to Rev. and Mrs. Moon.'" That night Dr. Pak was introduced with the title he loves the most, "Dr. Bo Hi Pak, special assistant to Rev. and Mrs. Sun Myung Moon."

We have walked many miles together. If it is Heaven's will, I hope to walk many more. If I have to ask the simple question: where would I be if Dr. Pak had not entered my life? I would philosophically answer, I am what I am today because of Dr. and Mrs. Pak, their living faith, their selflessness, and the spirit of total attendance to God and True Parents. Dr. Pak gave me his heart and soul, and everyday and forevermore I say, thank you.

PIERRE CEYRAC

Founding member, CAUSA Europe; former Member of the French Parliament (1986-88) and European Parliament (1989-94).

When Dr. Pak came to Europe to set up the CAUSA movement in 1983, Europe was in the midst of a major ideological struggle. The communist movement was still very strong, and there was a great deal of confusion particularly among the intellectuals. At the same time, France was at the center of the new ideological resistance to Marxism. Many writers and philosophers who had previously held a creative criticism of Marxism and communism were beginning to take a tendency toward a strong spiritual vision.

After a careful and competent analysis, meetings with political and intellectual people in France and Europe, Dr. Pak decided to concentrate his activities in France in order to bring a new God-centered vision able to inspire the final battle against Marxism and communism in Europe.

He was welcomed and assisted by many important personalities, including Alain Griotteray, deputy and editor-in-chief of Figaro magazine;

Louis Pauwels, director of Figaro; Jacques Toubon, future minister of Culture in the Chirac administration and minister of justice in the Balladur government; Jean-Francois Revel, a well-known philosophical and political writer and chief editor of L'Express magazine; and Georges Suffert, a well-respected figure in the French media.

Another very notable personality that met with Dr. Pak was Dr. Jacques Soustelle, former vice prime minister of France and one of the main collaborators of De Gaulle during the Second World War and the French resistance. Soustelle was also a great intellectual, member of the French Academy, eminent specialist in precolumbian civilization, and author of books about the dangers of communism and Marxist strategy in Latin America. I was present at the first meeting between Soustelle and Dr Pak. I could see that they were on the same wave length and had an immediate mutual respect and friendship for each other, I would even say a camaraderie!

The CAUSA movement, under Dr. Pak's leadership, organized in France many seminars on Marxism and communism and proposed a new God-centered vision for the future, called Unificationism. I would estimate about 3,000 to 4,000 people among the nation's elite attended these seminars within a three-year period.

For the French, one very important seminar was held in Washington with the participation of numerous dignitaries, including ambassadors, deputies, and writers. A significant program was held in Geneva and another in Marseille with the presence of many personalities from this influential French region. Others symposia were held on the French Riviera and in Paris.

In addition to these educational roundtable discussions and outreach activities, Dr. Pak initiated a monthly magazine directed by a very competent thinker and journalist, Mr. Jean-Pierre Gabriel. The magazine immediately gained the respect of France's intellectual elite and other French-speaking countries, including Switzerland, Belgium, Canada, Africa, etc. The influence of this magazine was significant among the political leaders and opinion leaders.

A few years ago in 1988, I remember visiting a very important political figure in northern France, the former minister, mayor, and senator of this town, Roubaix, Mr. Andre Diligent. He knew that I collaborated sometime with the CAUSA magazine, he immediately went to his desk and showed me the entire collection of CAUSA journals, and said this publication was a constant inspiration for him.

Dr. Pak had a deep and genuine concern for the development of the National Front, the political party of Le Pen. In many ways, his influence on this anti-communist party was very positive at the beginning, but unfortunately Mr. Le Pen himself did not have the character to resist his old demons and his closest friends' and advisors' racist tendencies. Dr. Pak was deceived by that, but his progressive influence still affected many members of this party. His attitude helped to keep them away from extremism and racism and surely had a good impact on their future development as well as upon France's conservative parties, in general.

I have to say that the impact of Dr. Pak's activities in France and in Europe were very important because they helped ignite the awakening of the conscience of the intellectual elite in Europe about the danger of communism and the necessity to find again and renew the true roots of France and European society, which are spiritual and Christian in nature. This impact deeply affected French socialists and encouraged their progress towards a more centrist and even anti-communism direction, thereby helping France to lean to a more peaceful and headwing vision.

LARRY R. MOFFITT

Associate Publisher and Vice President of Tiempos del Mundo, an intrahemispheric Spanish-language newspaper for the Americas, headquartered in Buenos Aires; he was Executive Director of the World Media Association (1979-1997).

Whenever people discuss the life and work and ongoing contribution of Bo Hi Pak, there is generally mention of him as a genuine war hero and the consummate diplomat; and rightly so, for he has always been an excellent leader, a motivator of people, a fighter, and a healer.

His many accomplishments are what the world calls results, and though important, are eventually not as important to Dr. Pak as the vision behind the results. For Dr. Pak, ground is something gained and lost daily but vision goes the distance. Vision writes the final chapter. He could accurately be called a driven man, pushed by the energetic and capable engine of a good and worthwhile vision. A complete picture of the person must include abundant discussion of this aspect.

Many of us who have had the honor of working with him consider his genuine warmth and humanity to loom at least as large as all his other good qualities combined. There is a considerable group of us, most of us now in our 40s, for whom he remains one of the most genuinely nurturing leaders we have ever worked with.

In several of the speeches contained in this book, Dr. Pak will say that of all the titles and professional positions he holds (and they are legion), the work most dear to his heart is that which he performs as a special assistant to the Reverend Sun Myung Moon. It is the teachings of Reverend Moon, their capacity to heal conflict and serve as a guide for a moral lifestyle, that are the wellspring of both the vision that motivates Dr. Pak and his elevating leadership style.

Accompanying that vision is an epic frame of mind, an astuteness that includes an understanding that the struggle between good and evil in the world occurs with equal ferocity between the most powerful nations and ideologies as it does within the confines of each individual human heart.

Dr. Pak embraces a pliable sense of destiny, which allows infinite possibility for human initiative to alter the world's fate for the better. Quite simply, he wants goodness to win. This sense of the man comes through in this collection of speeches.

On a number of occasions he has been called upon to put his idealism and his personal safety on the line; to put up or shut up, ethically speaking. He has demonstrated the courage and willingness to face down the U.S. Congress and the government of his own country of South Korea when he felt it was necessary. On these occasions, he aligned himself with principles of honesty and unity and achieved a measure of victory and, later, the respect of those who opposed him.

For Dr. Pak, who has been handed the responsibilities of starting The Washington Times, Panda Motors, the World Media Association, the Summit Council for World Peace; establishing business ventures with North Korea; and dozens of others, his life has been the job of architect, enactor, overseer, and troubleshooter of many of Reverend Moon's projects. Thus the epic descriptions of Dr. Pak are not without merit for a man of Moses-like determination, parting the Red Sea over and over again, project after project.

His has not been a charmed life by any stretch of the imagination. There have been regrets and failures along the way to be sure, all of them useful in the instruction they have provided. More than in the successes, however, it is through observing how a person deals with failure that one can know the mettle of another. It is not falling down that makes a failure; it's staying down. Dr. Pak's "active soul," as Emerson termed it, is what gives him his value and makes it impossible for him to countenance staying down as a response to any setback.

Winter lasts a long time in Moscow and I remember the cold rain blowing outside the window of his hotel room in April 1990, as he conferred with his staff on the evening before Reverend Moon's meeting with

President Mikhail Gorbachev. In the contingent led by Reverend Moon were the former presidents and prime ministers of 60 countries. The collection of former national leaders were there to encourage President Gorbachev to keep the faith and stay the course, regardless of the cost, for political and social reform which the Soviet Union so desperately needed.

This was not long before the events that would bring an end to the Soviet Union, and the meeting in the Kremlin would be a significant historical footnote if it were allowed to happen. The question was, would it happen or wouldn't it? Many forces opposed the meeting.

The chill of the air added to the uncertainty we all felt late that evening as Dr. Pak conferred with his staff and we waited for the phone to ring, hoping for positive news from one of the channels through which we had initiated contact with the Kremlin. We went over the possible scenarios for the tenth time, to see if there might be some approach we had overlooked. Dr. Pak's resolve never flagged and he kept our spirits buoyed, though we were all fighting the effects of too little sleep and too much coffee.

At one point he looked at each one of the half-dozen of us gathered there, in a manner he would occasionally do, as though taking our temperatures. "You know this meeting has to take place," he said. Then he added quietly, understated, as though he gave us credit for already knowing it, "We must determine history."

To encapsulate the worldview of Bo Hi Pak, those last four words are as fitting a description as any.

WILLIAM D. LAY

Founding member, CAUSA International and former editor-in-chief, CAUSA magazine; currently, attorney practicing in New York City.

This collection of speeches spans some 30 years of the most taut drama ever played out on the international stage: the cold war between communism and democracy. In the midst of this drama, Dr. Bo Hi Pak, the author of these speeches, stood as the interpreter, and in many respects the liaison to the Western world, for Rev. Sun Myung Moon, the founder of the Unification Church. In each of these speeches, given in a variety of venues around the world, Dr. Pak attempts to condense and weave together three interrelated strands: first, the theological content of Rev. Moon's new religious message; second, the wisdom gained by Dr. Pak in large measure through his discipleship with Rev. Moon on the value of integrity, honesty, love, and family; and third, for those speeches given prior to the early 1990s, an urgent warning that the free world must gain its footing and stand resolutely against communism.

I had the great fortune to work closely with Dr. Pak during that time, and I carry many treasured memories of him and our times working together. I observed that Dr. Pak as a matter of course makes it a point to engage himself on many fronts. In other words, he stays busy, and he does so on a very high dimension. In one day, he might be involved in financial decisions relating to a variety of business concerns, editorial and journalistic ideas involving a breaking news story, questions about the architecture of a new theater or school, the choreography of a dance production, and situations involving the lives and families of the many people that he loves and helps. He consistently brings enthusiasm and intensity to each of these tasks. (As Dr. Pak often reminds us, the word enthusiasm is derived from "en theos," which means "God entered.") However, it always appeared to me that the thing he most enjoyed doing was preparing one of his CAUSA lectures with slides, or writing up a speech for an upcoming event. At those times, there could be no intrusion. Both business and relaxation had to wait, because Dr. Pak regards conveying the truth as the highest calling and most noble undertaking.

I remember, for example, one evening in El Salvador in the early 1980s. At that time, the people of that extraordinary country were striving to establish a working democracy literally under the gun barrel of communist terror. Weapons were everywhere on the streets of San Salvador, and Dr. Pak required an armed escort in his travels around the city. When we were safely installed in our hotel one night, after a particularly stressful day of meetings, a number of us on Dr. Pak's team were sitting on a balcony of his room, watching a musical show that was taking place in the hotel courtyard below. We had hoped that he would join us and relax a bit, but he never came out. When we later went to look for him, he was sitting at a conference table covered with books, notes, and research materials, creating a new set of slides with a felt-tip pen and a notepad. The slides he drew up that night became the core for the CAUSA lecture series for many years afterward.

As president of CAUSA International and of the News World Corporation, Dr. Pak maintained a suite of offices on the fourth floor of New York's Tiffany Building at 401 Fifth Avenue. My office, functional though smaller, was on the seventh floor. I recall that on more than one occasion, Dr. Pak would look at his watch and announce to a crowd that had gathered in his office and in his secretary's office, that he could not deal with any further matters because he needed to prepare his remarks for an upcoming event. He would then leave his office, come upstairs, take off his jacket, and settle in behind my desk with a batch of red pens to work and rework with loving care a speech draft that was waiting for him. There was something about the smaller office, removed from many of the other pressing concerns, that allowed him to focus on the message he was preparing to give. Invariably, by the time he was finished, the speech had been extensively transformed and had become closer to the expression of his heart and soul that he longed to convey.

The speeches in this volume span from the time when the early Unification Church began to reach out from Korea to the world, to today when a great number of people who have been touched by Rev. Moon's message are challenged to apply that message to their lives and in their families on a daily basis. Dr. Pak, of course, has been a part of that process and of that history. Over and over again, Dr. Pak has found a way to take elements of Rev. Moon's message and translate them into the idiom and life fabric of America and the West. This is only possible, I believe, because he has such a deep love of, on the one hand, Rev. Moon, his spiritual father, and on the other hand, the Western world, and particularly America. The speeches themselves, I'm afraid, can go only so far in showing this aspect of Dr. Pak. There is so much that cannot be put into words the spoken word is limited, and much more so, in many ways, the printed word.

Still, as the speeches in this volume make clear, Dr. Pak is never content in his speeches to recite dry facts, or to separate the ideological conflict of the cold war from the deeply personal meaning that God, and true love, and patriotism, and the dream of world peace, have for each one of us. There are literally thousands upon thousands of people who were personally touched by the words contained within this book as they were spoken. I only hope that as you read them, you can feel something of Dr. Pak's heart, and through him, the heart of Rev. Moon, and through him, the heart of God.

ROBERT MORTON

Managing Editor of the National Weekly and Internet Editions of The Washington Times; former Editor-in-Chief of The News World (later renamed the New York City Tribune).

Dr. Pak has the gift, like Presidents Reagan and Clinton, of walking into a room and being able to greet by their first names everyone present—

even those he has met only once and not seen in years. But he is able to remember more than names. He seems capable of grasping the unique gifts of those he encounters and reinforcing in his exchanges with them their very reason for existing on this planet. That is one reason why Dr. Pak has been able to readily command the loyalty, even devotion, of those with whom he has worked at *The Washington Times* and the myriad other projects he has been involved with. His persona never fails to reinforce in his coworkers the knowledge that their value transcends their salary—that they contribute in unique and priceless ways to an undertaking far greater then their own livelihood. In such an environment, labor unions are irrelevant.

The national characters of Korea and America have much in common. The peoples of both nations hate to lose and tend to be intensely competitive. Generally speaking, Koreans and Americans both want to achieve respect and prestige on a global scale, and to earn that status by matching and surpassing the highest standards, both qualitative and quantitative. Dr. Pak has an eye for detail and demands 100 percent of himself and others in most aspects of projects with which he is involved. He also understands that he cannot reach those goals by himself but needs a great "team" to deliver the result. Again, it is this spirit that helped launch The Washington Times and establish it almost immediately as a force to be reckoned with in the nation's capital. Most of the best people at The Times, still to this day, are not working primarily for money but for the indescribable satisfaction that comes from devoting their talents and even their lives to a higher calling.

The image of Dr. Pak that vividly endures in my memory is of him late at night, in his shirt sleeves, leaning over the pages of the prototypes of The Washington Times in the composing room of the newspaper in New York where they were produced. That is where you would find Dr. Pak when he was at any newspaper company—he would be where "the rubber meets the road." Not in the editorial board rooms or the newsroom at deadline time. It is in the composing room where the final fine-tuning takes place. Everyone —photographers, artists, page designers, and editors—was on hand and each one of them contributed to the creation of what has become a great newspaper. They all had an indispensable role to play, and it was Dr. Pak who both encouraged and challenged them to give their best.

DR. MARK P. BARRY, PH.D.

Research Fellow at the Summit Council for World Peace and a legislative analyst with the Arizona House of Representatives. He is also an adjunct faculty member at the University of Phoenix.

I have known Dr. Bo Hi Pak since 1972, when I first met him as a young member of the Unification Church. My first opportunity to work with him was in helping arrange a gala benefit performance for UNICEF by the Little Angels Folk Ballet at the United Nations General Assembly Hall in 1973. I then worked closely with him preparing promotional materials for three of Reverend Moon's major American speeches in 1974-76: at New York's Madison Square Garden and Yankee Stadium, and at the Washington Monument. From 1979-85, I worked directly under Dr. Pak as an executive assistant, helping with the founding of two daily newspapers, Noticias del Mundo and The Washington Times, the establishment of CAUSA International, and supporting his coordination of Reverend Moon's defense in his court case with the federal government. From 1987-97, I served under his leadership in the American Freedom Coalition, the International Security Council, and lastly, the Summit Council for World Peace, where I was Director of Research.

My most memorable moment with Dr. Pak occurred in 1981 in New York, when he was on the phone with another Unification Church elder, Rev. Chung Hwan Kwak, in South Korea. Rev. Kwak was telling him that Reverend Moon, who at that time was also in Seoul, would return to the United States to face his indictment on charges of tax evasion just issued by the federal government, despite the fact that, at that time, there was no extradition treaty between the two countries. Reverend Moon was voluntarily choosing, at the risk of imprisonment, to return to the U.S. to defend himself. Dr. Pak was in tears and speechless, having tried with all his effort to prevent the indictment, and now deeply sorrowful that Reverend Moon and his family would have to undergo a treacherous course with an uncertain outcome. Dr. Pak felt personally responsible for not preventing the indictment; he did not blame defense lawyers or anyone else.

Only a few people were in the room to witness Dr. Pak on this fateful overseas call, but I was among them. Indeed, the following year, despite his voluntary return and profession of innocence, Reverend Moon was convicted, and after unsuccessful appeals, served 13 months in federal prison. The injustice of Reverend Moon's court case was tellingly evident by the presence of dozens of Christian ministers who greeted Reverend Moon upon his release from prison in 1985. They saw the government's actions against him as a distinct threat to religious liberty.

A second very memorable moment for me came when Dr. Pak returned from attending the funeral of North Korea's president, Kim Il Sung, in Pyongyang in July 1994. He was the only South Korean citizen invited to attend an event closed off to most of the world. However, upon his departure from the North and arrival in Beijing, he learned that the South Korean government — his own country — had stripped him of his license to be publisher of a Seoul daily newspaper, his main occupation at that time, and of his legal residency in South Korea. If he returned to South Korea, he was threatened with arrest and imprisonment for violation of its National Security Law by attending the funeral of North Korea's president. Despite this effort to turn him into a man without a country, Dr. Pak went ahead and held a press conference in Beijing, which I helped arrange, to discuss his trip and share about his rare meeting with Kim Jong Il, the son and heir of Kim Il Sung. Dr. Pak handled the press conference with great dignity and eloquence, despite suggestions from the Seoul press corps that he was unpatriotic to go to the funeral. He defended his actions as highly patriotic, an effort to use this special opportunity to reach out to North Korea for the sake of reconciliation and a more constructive relationship for the future.

This was in Reverend Moon's spirit of playing the role of peacemaker and unifier. Unfortunately, from that day, Dr. Pak was unable to return home to Seoul for nearly three years until the government finally agreed not to press charges against him. Then in May 1998, he led a highly successful visit to the North by the renowned Little Angels Folk Ballet, a South Korean children's dance troupe founded by Reverend Moon. The visit won hearts in both Koreas as television viewers could see children from North and South performing together and embracing in tears. This historical trip more than vindicated Dr. Pak's visionary actions four years prior and helped smooth the way for future exchanges and cooperation.

Although Dr. Bo Hi Pak is a man of many external accomplishments, from my experience, it is his unforgettable quality as a human being which stands out most in my mind, and is indeed a reflection of his living Reverend Moon's teaching. Because of his genuineness and purity of heart, he has been a great instrument of God and foremost witness to the life and work of Reverend and Mrs. Moon.

PIERANGELO BELTRAMI

Award-winning graphic artist and packaging designer; gold, silver, and bronze medalist on the U.S. Disabled Cycling Team.

It was a rainy afternoon that September 15, 1974. As I looked out the window, the plane was circling Manhattan and making its final approach to Kennedy Airport. Suddenly I realized why they call New York City the Big Apple. I was traveling with a few other Italian volunteers selected to help with the final days of preparation for the "September 18 Could Be Your Rebirth Day" rally. The big event was to be held at Madison Square Garden on September 18.

That day still holds a very special meaning for me because, on that day, two of my closest friends joined the church in Italy, and it marks my first encounter with True Father and Dr. Pak

From the airport we were driven directly to the Unification Church center on 71st Street where Col. Pak (as we have affectionately called him at that time) was already busy translating an impromptu speech for True Father. As we walked in from the noisy streets of Manhattan, we could hear True Father's and Dr. Pak's voices echoing from the main hall.

At that time I did not speak much English, and I had little knowledge of any cultures outside my own and a zero understanding of the Oriental culture, language, and customs. Nevertheless as True Father spoke, we could sense a certain seriousness in the air for the impending event, but also I could feel True Father's love and concern for our safety and well-being.

When True Father finished speaking, Dr. Pak came onto the stage to welcome us. He welcome all the Japanese and Europeans who had arrived that week to help out with the Madison Square Garden campaign. I did not know Dr. Pak at that time and had no idea that he would became my leader and mentor for many wonderful years.

Sitting on the floor and looking around, I found myself surrounded by people from many different cultures gathered in small groups, each translating the speech into their own language. I felt that a miniature United Nations was being assembled there. Dr. Pak's speech made everyone feel very welcome.

The Madison Square Garden Rally was an extraordinary event in many ways. That evening, as I stood in the middle of the packed stadium, I realized I was witnessing an intense struggle. Reverend Moon, God's messenger, was trying very hard to deliver one of the most important and prophetic revelations of our time. I was amazed to see people of all walks of life sitting there listening to the speech. The sheer power of those thundering words sent chills down my spine and struck a note of urgency in my very bone marrow. I felt I was witnessing history in the making.

While Father at times walked around the podium, speaking from the top of his lungs, agitating arms and legs to make a point, Dr. Pak remained at the podium translating Father's every word with conviction in the deep voice that became his trademark from that time on.

A few weeks after the Madison Square Garden speech, Father embarked on a 21-city tour across the United States. I joined Rev. Vincenz's IOWC team that went to every city to witness and prepare for the event. At every city, Dr. Pak translated for Father at the speech and the victory celebration afterwards. It was a difficult time for True Parents and for everyone involved, but it was also a time of deep discovery of God's suffering heart.

I always wonder how Dr. Pak could manage to be with Father day and night, attending and translating, as well as taking care of the Little Angels tour, making sure that every city was ready for True Parents' arrival, organizing the "Forgive, Love, Unite" campaign, plus a myriad of activities that True Father was initiating every day.

For the longest time I did not know if Dr. Pak had a family. He seemed to be by Father's side every minute of the day.

Through the years I observed Dr. Pak fill many roles: An evangelist with the Celebration of Life speaking tour. An architect designing the intricate interior of historical landmarks such as the New Yorker Hotel Grand Ballroom. A publisher who started successful newspapers. A businessman. A skilled diplomat who arranged for high-level VIPs to meet True Father. A fighter against bigotry when True Father entered Danbury. At that time, Dr. Pak mobilized the entire movement to demonstrate for religious freedom across the United States with religious figures we could only have dreamed about meeting a few months before.

But whatever Dr. Pak did, he did it for True Parents. He followed True Parents' many challenging directions with absolute faith, he uplifted True Parents in every setting and with all people. And when he reported to True Parents, he always gave recognition and credit to the members who worked with him. This is one of his most precious qualities.

Perhaps Dr. Pak's biggest coup was a political one: the Fraser hearings. People in the United States who were close to the event remember it well, but this struggle was especially appreciated in Korea. His fight against the harassment orchestrated by then-Congressman Fraiser vindicated not only True Father but every Korean living in this country and abroad. The unfair attack against True Father pitted Dr. Pak against one of the most powerful congressmen of his time. I still remember Dr. Pak's testimony and his fiery responses. He defended True Father with all his heart while strongly denouncing the leftist bias of the congressional inquiry. Dr. Pak's pride in True Parents moved thousands of members worldwide to tears and showed us how a heavenly general fights evil.

For many years Dr. Pak attended Father at Belvedere at holy days and Sunday services. As customary at the end of Father's speech, after having done a tremendous job of simultaneous translation for four or five hours, Father would invite Dr. Pak to give a report on activities overseas. "Mr. Bubbling Enthusiasm," as he defined himself at one of the earlier pep talks before Washington Monument, would get himself ready to report by rushing to the pile of newspaper clippings and other material sitting on a nearby chair, quickly sifting through and organizing them.

Dr. Pak would look out from the stage, and with papers under his arm, he would first offer a full bow to True Parents. Then with a big smile, standing in front of the microphone, his thundering "Good morning, everyone, how are you today?" would signal the end of the break. Dr. Pak would tell compelling stories that he would back up with exhibit A and article B from his stack of papers. His reports were so interesting that it was practically impossible to doze off. Who in his right mind would want to miss the latest development of Father's work around the world or hear what a world leader had to say about Father? Who would want to trade such a moving experience for a few minutes of numbing sleep?

I would be up there on the edge of my seat capturing every word. As Dr. Pak got warmed up, I would soon find myself laughing with Father and Mother and applauding the report. At some point he seems to be wrapping up the report with the now famous phrase, "to make a long story short..." But the excitement was still building and so was the story. By the end of his report, Dr. Pak was always able to bring together the entire audience and resurrect even the most tired and low-spirited member.

Even on more private occasions, Dr. Pak's reports reflected his enthusiasm, which was contagious, and his words always uplifting. He more than anybody I ever knew was capable of talking to each person exactly at his or her level with dignity and respect, inevitably triggering mutual respect for Dr. Pak. Whether he was meeting President Reagan or former heads of states from other countries, Dr. Pak, through his many years of experience in the diplomatic world, would find himself always at ease with them or other VIPs.

Whatever he was doing—reporting, listening, giving directions, translating for True Father—his behavior was always remarkably consistent: strong in voice and action but humble in spirit.

Some of the guests who came to the many conferences organized by True Father were not necessarily relaxed at first. Some had doubts or personal questions while others would express the hope to meet Rev. Moon in person. After going through the receiving line where Dr. Pak would introduced them to Father, they would change. They would feel more relaxed and happy. Dr. Pak would mingle with the guests afterwards, listening to their comments and testifying to them about True Father.

The movement in the 1970s and exuberant 1980s was involved in major campaigns and conferences around the world. Dr. Pak was always in the forefront of the battlefield.

At the joint conference in Moscow in 1991 (World Media Association, Summit Council, and AULA), which was a great victory, I saw first-hand how hard Dr. Pak was pushing himself. After the conference was over, we got word that True Parents would be visiting Red Square. We quickly got in a taxi bound for Red Square. We didn't want to miss the opportunity to see True Parents and to be with them. True Parents walked the Square hand in hand, visited Lenin Mausoleum, prayed in the chapel inside the Kremlin, and granted us a rare photo op right on the Square. After we bid farewell to them and started to walk back to the hotel, we realized that Dr. Pak was not his usual self. At one point he stopped for a deep breath, but rather then feeling better he got worse. Antonio Betancourt and Bill Selig had to literally carry him to the nearest taxi. Dr. Pak was ready to collapse in their arms.

Many times Dr. Pak would return invigorated from an early morning meeting with Father. He would then proceed to tell us about that meeting. He would pause for a few seconds with his head slightly bent forward, almost like a bow, reflecting for a moment, then he would say something like: "I'm telling you, every time I meet True Father, he never stops amazing me! Or, "Time and time again he shows me the living God." Or after a very intense conference he would say: "True Father is just too much for these people. No one really understands Father, no one, no one!"

I and other members of Dr. Pak's so-called team always appreciated his special relationship with True Parents. By observing their interaction, I've come to understand the meaning of absolute faith, absolute love, and absolute obedience—even before these words became the slogan of the '90s.

Together with Dr. Pak we shared laughter, sweat, and even tears. To this day he remains for me and many others who had the privilege of working closely with him, one of the most influential and effective people who helped shape True Father's work in the last 30 years. Because of the nature of my work, I had the good fortune to work with most of the Korean leaders here in America. I spent a good part of my 25 years-plus in America with Dr. Pak. In all these years, I have never found a more inspiring and devoted leader, or anyone more dedicated to God and True Parents, than Dr. Bo Hi Pak.

JAMES GAVIN

James Gavin, special assistant to Dr. Pak from 1982 to 1982, is currently president of the Minnesota Family Federation for World Peace and Unification.

I came to know Dr. Bo Hi Pak over the years in a number of ways. He is a man with many hats: special assistant and translator to Reverend Sun Myung Moon, father, mentor, diplomat, teacher, businessman, supporter of the arts, spiritual leader, defender of the faith, friend, husband, ambassador of goodwill, gentleman, and in every way a man with a heart of gold. Dr. Pak has the rare gift of uplifting everyone he meets and works with, whether it is the president of a country or a young man or woman just starting out in life. He leaves people feeling good about themselves and motivated to give more to life.

I first spoke with Dr. Pak when the Little Angels performed at the state fair in Minnesota in 1973, although I had seen him with Reverend Moon at various events before then. At that time I was the director of the Unification Church in North Dakota. My father and mother, along with members of the church from Minnesota and North Dakota, watched the performance and then met the performers and Dr. Pak after the show. Dr. Pak spoke to everyone about the Little Angels and Reverend Moon's vision for young people and the arts. What struck me most about him was his enthusiasm and the appreciation that he gave to everyone. Afterwards he mingled with the guests and, in what I would come to know as his way of being, made everyone feel important; he listened to them. Dr. Pak made a lasting impression on my parents by being the gracious person that he always is. After he met my Mom and Dad, my Dad said to him, "Please take good care of my son Jim." Dr. Pak looked at my Dad and said, "Oh, he's going to take good care of me." As it turned out, he took better care of me than I ever took care of him.

I first worked directly with Dr. Pak in 1975 when I moved to Washington, D.C., to join the Capitol Hill Ministry. One of the first projects I helped with was to invite members of Congress to hear Reverend Moon speak in one of the Senate committee rooms. As usual, Dr. Pak accompanied Reverend Moon and interpreted his speech. Since Reverend Moon is very demonstrative and enthusiastic when he speaks, and Dr. Pak always tries to match Reverend Moon's energy, the members of Congress got the one-two punch from Reverend Moon's speech and Dr. Pak's translation.

Each time Reverend Moon spoke on the Hill, he was invited to meet privately in a senator's or congressman's office. Dr. Pak was always there to translate Reverend Moon's words, passion, and warmth to the leaders in these meetings, whom Reverend Moon encouraged to stand up to atheistic communism and revive the moral fabric of America. Reverend Moon and Dr. Pak made a great team. Dr. Pak would always show the greatest respect and love for Reverend Moon, and anyone who witnessed his attitude had to respect Reverend Moon more. Dr. Pak hung on every word Reverend Moon spoke; his concentration was 100 percent. He wanted people to understand not only the words but the man himself.

In the 1970s, Reverend Moon spoke at Madison Square Garden, the Washington Monument, and in every state over and over again with Dr. Pak at his side. During the campaigns preceding these speeches, Dr. Pak motivated and encouraged the members. His warm and generous spirit made it easier for people to work hard, and his translation and assistance to Reverend Moon made for a closer relationship between Reverend and Mrs. Moon and the members. I'll always remember the day after Reverend Moon's speech in 1976 at the Washington Monument where hundreds of thousands of people had come to hear Reverend Moon. The next day the members got together on Roosevelt Island in the middle of the Potomac River to celebrate the victory. Reverend Moon proclaimed in his speech that day: "Let us now march to Moscow." Dr. Pak's translation of those words raised everyone to their feet, and even though it was hard to believe anything like the liberation of communism would ever take place, we believed in Reverend Moon and were ready to follow him anywhere. Dr. Pak's enthusiastic translation brought Reverend Moon's words to life for all of us.

In 1978, Congressman Donald Fraser, a Democrat from Minnesota, decided to investigate Reverend Moon and his associates through the Subcommittee on International Organizations. Reverend Chung Hwan Kwak invited me to assist Dr. Pak, who had become the main target of Fraser's investigation. Dr. Pak's staff consisted of Judy LeJeune, Elena Decker, Gerard Willis, and myself. Judy and Elena were already working with Dr. Pak with the Korean Cultural and Freedom Foundation, Gerard was the editor of the Rising Tide newspaper, and I was working with the director of the Capitol Hill Ministry. We worked out of a small suite of offices on Connecticut Avenue in Washington, D.C., the office of the Korean Cultural and Freedom Foundation, which represented the Little Angels Korean Folk Ballet, the Sung Hwa Performing Arts school, and Radio of Free Asia.

Dr. Pak met with Congressman Fraser and his staff and arranged to make a statement at each session for the record before he answered questions. Judy and Elena worked primarily on preparing for the question-and-answer part of the testimony, while Gerard and I assisted Dr. Pak with his opening statements. Dr. Pak is a tireless worker; he left no stone unturned in preparing his testimony to the subcommittee. Congressman Fraser had nearly $1 million and a huge staff to assist him—Dr. Pak had only us. However, he always told us that God plus one is a majority, so if we would do all that we could do, God would do the rest.

In the office behind his desk was a large picture of Reverend Moon. Before he started work each day, Dr. Pak prayed for God's guidance and then he would start writing with his black felt-tipped pen, putting his thoughts down on paper. I have never met a person who worked so hard or prepared so diligently for anything. More than any of us, he knew just how much was on the line. He told us that Reverend Moon was praying for us and that God would be our shield in the days and months ahead.

Congressman Fraser really didn't know what he was letting himself in for. Dr. Pak is a warrior at heart. He survived years of fighting during the Korean war, he has lived a very disciplined and spiritual life as a follower of Reverend Moon, he has a spirit that never gives up, and he believed God was on his side. Each day Dr. Pak came to the hearing with a well-prepared, lengthy statement, which many times left Congressman Fraser red-faced and muttering.

We did extensive research on the time Congressman Fraser's committee had spent investigating the human rights violations taking place in various countries. Dr. Pak pointed out in his opening statement that Fraser had spent months investigating and criticizing the human rights records of our allies, such as Taiwan and South Korea, while ignoring the genocide in Cambodia and the atrocities in other communist bloc countries. Congressman Derwinski from Illinois told us later that he felt like cheering during Dr. Pak's statement because, as a member of the committee, he was frustrated by Fraser's extreme leftist tendencies. Dr. Pak also explained in his statement that Congressman Fraser's father, who was a dean at the University of Minnesota Law school, was nicknamed the "Red Dean" because of his political beliefs. He quoted sources from an FBI investigation that accused Fraser of being an agent of influence for the USSR. Dr. Pak was fighting fire with fire. He let the world know where Congressman Fraser was coming from and why he was investigating and attempting to destroy the pro-democratic, anti-communist work of Reverend Moon and his people.

It got nasty. The subcommittee did everything in its power to discredit Dr. Pak, even suggesting that he had been an unfaithful husband. Fraser's staff had planted the story in the Chicago Tribune, citing a diplomatic colleague of Dr. Pak's as saying Dr. Pak had an inappropriate relationship with his wife. Back in our office Dr. Pak told us that Fraser must think he was losing the battle to stoop so low. Dr. Pak prepared his heart with prayer and got down to work.

The next day a bombshell hit Congressman Fraser. The arrangement Dr. Pak had made with the subcommittee was to submit his prepared statement before he read it publicly. Well, that was one statement Congressman Fraser didn't want the press to hear, so he tried to change his own rules and told Dr. Pak they didn't have time for him to read it. It was tense; the two men went back and forth on the time needed. Dr. Pak wanted 19 minutes and 45 seconds and Congressman Fraser didn't want to allow him to speak. Finally Dr. Pak said, "I'm prepared to stay over all night. Just let me have my 19 minutes and 45 seconds." Amazingly, Fraser relented and let Dr. Pak speak.

Dr. Pak made it clear that he lived by God's law and the teachings of Reverend Moon. He challenged Congressman Fraser to call Dr. Thomas Chung, the man who had purportedly accused Dr. Pak and who was standing by in Korea, ready to refute the lies that were printed in the paper. Dr. Pak challenged Fraser to call Dr. Chung to restore his good name. Fraser's eyes continually went to the clock, waiting anxiously for Dr. Pak's time to elapse. Dr. Pak had to rein in his emotions to conclude his testimony, saying, "I am a proud South Korean, I am a proud anti-communist, and I am a proud follower of Reverend Sun Myung Moon. And I will remain so, all the days of my life." He then recited the 23rd Psalm: "The Lord is my shepherd…" After reciting the Psalm he broke down in tears with his head on his arms.

Dr. Pak's 19 minutes and 45 seconds had a tremendous impact. Fraser turned bright red and was visibly shaken by Dr. Pak's powerful statement. Dr. Pak took the high ground and kept it from that point on. Fraser had probably thought Dr. Pak would be like a sheep being led to the slaughter, but Dr. Pak was never meek or timid, and he was always well prepared, always speaking eloquently, with passion, straight from the heart. However, after the testimony, it still wasn't over.

Congressman Fraser took time off to run for the U.S. Senate seat for the state of Minnesota. His wish was to pursue the investigation further once he was elected to the Senate. I was born and raised in Minnesota, so I went back there to observe the race and assist Fraser's opposition any way I could. On Election Day Dr. Pak was flying back from Korea and called me in the evening to check on the early results. I told him it didn't look good; Fraser was ahead, but it was still early. When he got to California, Dr. Pak called again, and I told him the votes from Minneapolis and St. Paul were all counted and Fraser was still way ahead. Dr. Pak said, "Jim, you'd better start praying," and I said, "I haven't stopped." Dr. Pak took the redeye to Washington, D.C., and called me when he arrived. I told him Fraser was still ahead by a few thousand votes, but the outlying counties were coming in, and it looked like Bob Short, Fraser's opponent, might overtake him. Within an hour Short bypassed Fraser and ended up winning by a few thousand votes.

One paper's first headline the next morning was "Fraser Beats Out Short," but the follow-up, revised headline was "Short Victory Took All Night." When Dr. Pak heard the news, his elation could be heard all the way to Minnesota. At that moment he was probably the happiest man on earth. The voters in Minnesota had put an end to Congressman Donald Fraser's misuse of power. Unfortunately, the government investigations and persecution of Reverend Moon didn't stop with Donald Fraser.

They say you really get to know the character of a person in the heat of battle. Dr. Pak was unflappable. He is the type of person who sees the glass as being half full, very positive and very hard working. Thomas Jefferson once said, "The harder a person works, the luckier one gets." If that is so, then Dr. Pak is very lucky indeed.

Dr. Pak has always been a family-oriented person. Even when we worked very late he would go home and have a little dinner with his wife. He and his wife are very close; it's easy to see that they really love each other. Through it all, she was always there for him, and her love and care gave him strength. Also, Dr. Pak was always in communication with Reverend Moon. They have a special relationship, and the spiritual strength Dr. Pak received from that relationship made him strong. Dr. Pak would pray with us and ask us to pray with him. God's spirit was always with him. Throughout the Fraser ordeal, he never got down; in fact, he was always lifting up other people through praise and encouragement. He is a very positive person to work with.

I continued to see Dr. Pak and work with him throughout the next few years, but it wasn't until 1982 that we worked together again on a full-time basis. In 1981 the Washington Star, Washington's oldest newspaper, closed its doors. On that day I called Dr. Pak in New York where he was heading up The News World, a newspaper founded by Reverend Moon in Manhattan. When I told him about the Star, he immediately seized on the idea that Washington, D.C., needed a second voice. Reverend Moon was excited by the idea and asked Dr. Pak to explore the possibilities. Dr. Pak undertook this mission with a passion. When the Washington Post outbid everyone, including Reverend Moon, for the old Star building, Dr. Pak went on to find a new site and under Reverend Moon's direction built the paper from the ground up. News World staff members and people like myself who lived in Washington, D.C., formed the nucleus of the new paper. Dr. Pak was in the middle of everything, from hiring seasoned newspaper people for the editorial side to bringing on a general manager and circulation director to run the business side.

Reverend Moon was very much involved in all of this and was frequently in Washington, making decisions and giving final approval to all the important aspects of this huge project. Reverend Moon wanted a newspaper in Washington that would stand up to communism, something that the Washington Post had never done. In fact, more often than not, the Washington Post was an apologist for the Soviet Union and its allies.

I first worked as the public relations director for the Washington Times, helping Dr. Pak with the first advertising and promotion campaign to launch the paper and later on our first direct-mail effort to build our subscriber base. The first people to endorse the paper were friends Reverend Moon had made on Capitol Hill over the years, and we used their endorsements in our direct-mail campaign. These people were grateful that Reverend Moon and his church were willing to put their fortune on the line to take a stand for worldwide freedom and democracy.

Within a year Dr. Pak asked me to be his special assistant. I worked with Bruce Brown to assist Dr. Pak and Col. Han, the senior vice president of the paper. Politics in a paper with several hundred employees was always interesting, to say the least; however, Dr. Pak was respected by the business side as well as the editorial side of the paper and ran a pretty smooth ship. The editorial people liked the fact that Dr. Pak just let them do their job and didn't meddle in the content of the paper. His door was always open, and people would visit him to make suggestions or give their opinion on issues of the day. He made periodic rounds of the various departments and was appreciated for his warmth and interest in all areas of the paper. Pressmen, photographers, reporters, circulation people, and those in the advertising department all had contact with Dr. Pak. Reverend Moon periodically visited the paper, and it was his custom to visit every department, meeting everyone each time he visited. Dr. Pak and Reverend Moon were always like that. People saw them, spoke to them, knew them, and liked them.

Dr. Pak could be tough when he had to be. The paper's first editor-in-chief came to think of himself as indispensable, that the paper rose and set on him like the sun. He demanded a big raise and memberships in expensive clubs and other perks from Dr. Pak. He thought quite a bit of himself. To make a long story short, Dr. Pak would not give him what he wanted, so he resigned, stating that most people would leave that "Moonie" paper with him. It's funny but he was the only one to leave, and even though he voiced his dissatisfaction loudly at a press conference, no one paid much attention. Dr. Pak went out and found Arnaud de Borchgrave to replace him and the paper grew stronger. Threatening Dr. Pak didn't work. Congressman Fraser found that out and so did the former editor-in-chief.

Church members on the Times staff all loved Dr. Pak. He spent time with the members and knew everyone by name. They were his people and he loved everyone. People would come to his office or house to speak to him about all kinds of things. He always listened and helped many people, as a spiritual counselor, a family counselor, a job counselor, etc. He was there when people needed him, and it wasn't just people from the Times. People came to him from Atlantic Video, the Universal Ballet Academy, and other enterprises he had worked with Reverend Moon to create, as well as members from the local church. Although Dr. Pak had an enormous workload, he always made time to talk to and help out members. When Reverend Moon visited Washington, D.C., Dr. Pak often publicly praised church members' work and made it possible for them to report to Reverend Moon about their achievements. Dr. Pak was a living bridge for many people to Reverend Moon, and people deeply appreciated his efforts.

Dr. Pak in his capacity as president of the Washington Times Corporation met important people within and outside government all the time. People from the Reagan White House, heads of government departments, members of Congress, business leaders, various well-known religious leaders, and foreign VIPs would visit Dr. Pak. He held people's respect not only because he was Reverend Moon's special assistant and president of the Washington Times Corporation but because of his character and his charm as a person. He always treated everyone with dignity and respect. He listened to everyone very attentively and helped others whenever he possibly could. Dr. Pak often made it possible for many of these people to meet with Reverend Moon to express their gratitude to him for upholding freedom and democracy through the Washington Times.

While an officer in the South Korean Army during the Korean War, Dr. Pak came to America for special training, and during the war U.S. tanks saved him and his comrades from near-certain death. Dr. Pak always spoke about his love for and deep debt of gratitude to the people of America. In many ways he is more patriotic toward America than many Americans. At CAUSA conferences (an organization founded by Reverend Moon and led by Dr. Pak), he taught local and national leaders the counterproposal to the communist doctrine and pro-democracy principles that upheld those of America's founders. Dr. Pak motivated Americans to be better citizens and stand up to the threat of international communism. At the Washington Times he often spoke to visitors about these ideas and garnered their respect and admiration. Because of his passion for these ideas, people came to understand why Reverend Moon had established and continued to support the pro-democratic, pro-God, and pro-American Washington Times.

Actually Reverend Moon launched the Washington Times while defending himself against charges relating to the first tax return he had ever filed in the United States. Over the years Reverend Moon and our church had been persecuted by certain elements within the U.S. government and other institutions. Reverend Moon had enemies in and out of government that wanted to put him out of action because of his strong stand against communism and his unorthodox theological teachings. Reverend Moon's attitude was that there is nothing you can do about bigotry and persecution; you just have to keep on doing what is right and let God take care of sorting it all out. Dr. Pak and other members of the church just kept on working and prayed for the lawyers and the judicial system.

Dr. Pak dropped everything else when Reverend Moon was convicted. Since the justice system had failed to uphold justice, Dr. Pak and members of our church went to the people of conscience, the religious community. Dr. Pak bridged the gap between the Unification Church and other churches in the United States and launched a religious freedom movement that was unlike anything our country has ever seen. The Religious Freedom Coalition was made up of every faith, every race, and every culture in America. The outcry was "today they jail Reverend Moon, tomorrow it will be us." The undeserved conviction of Reverend Moon made many friends and allies during this period, and Dr. Pak was in the forefront of this new movement.

There were theological disagreements but no disagreement on how unfairly Reverend Moon had been treated by the government. Because of the CAUSA work over the years, Dr. Pak and the CAUSA staff had educated thousands of church leaders from every denomination. Many of these ministers were civil rights leaders like Reverend Ralph Abernathy and Reverend Joseph Lowery, and they knew what racial persecution was all about and could see that Reverend Moon's case was one of racial and religious persecution. Dr. Pak also made new friends from the religious right like Dr. Tim LaHaye and Reverend Jerry Falwell, as well as civil libertarians like former Senator Eugene McCarthy from Minnesota.

Thousands of these Americans marched and demonstrated on behalf of Reverend Moon in every major city of the United States and thousands more marched on the White House, demanding justice for Reverend Moon. Dr. Pak was everywhere, meeting with key leaders, building relationships, and desperately working to keep Reverend Moon out of jail. When Reverend Moon went to prison, Dr. Pak continued to lead the religious freedom movement. Behind the scenes he worked with political and religious leaders to petition for a presidential pardon. From seeing Dr. Pak in private, I knew how tortured he was that Reverend Moon was in prison. Nothing mattered to him other than the safety and security of his spiritual father, Reverend Moon.

I accompanied Dr. Pak to Danbury prison many times to visit Reverend Moon. Whenever possible Dr. Pak brought a congressman, a religious leader, or other prominent American to meet with Reverend Moon. It broke Dr. Pak's heart to see Reverend Moon in prison, and he wanted to do anything possible to inspire him during that period. One minister broke down crying in front of Reverend Moon as he apologized to him for what our government had subjected him to. Reverend Moon ended up comforting the minister and challenging him to love America more and work harder for the salvation of his country. Dr. Pak always wanted to lift up Reverend Moon, bring him a good report or another visitor to inspire him during that time.

Senator Orrin Hatch was a ranking minority member on the Senate Judiciary Committee whom Dr. Pak went to for advice and assistance. Dr. Pak spent hours briefing him on Reverend Moon's case and Senator Hatch took action. As chairman of the Senate Subcommittee on the Constitution, he launched an investigation into the Justice Department's treatment of Reverend Moon. After his investigation, Senator Hatch held a hearing on religious freedom, July 25, 1985, shortly after Reverend Moon had been released from prison. An hour before the hearing began, Senator Hatch, Reverend and Mrs. Moon, Dr. Pak, and I met privately in his office. Senator Hatch apologized to Reverend Moon for the treatment he and his family had been subjected to by our country.

WILLIAM P. SELIG

Founding member, CAUSA International. Currently, administrative director, Summit Council for World Peace and the Federation for World Peace; and project director of Dr. Pak's collection of speeches, Truth is My Sword.

When I was first asked to oversee the collection and production of speeches by Dr. Bo Hi Pak, I jumped at the opportunity. For me it was an immense blessing to attend a man who in my estimation has accomplished many great deeds for God and the building of His Kingdom on Earth.

As the principal assistant and translator for many years to Rev. Sun

Myung Moon, Dr. Pak was in a unique position to guide numerous providential missions around the world. By studying the speeches and works of Dr. Pak, we are in essence seeing the work of Rev. Moon in America since he first arrived in this nation in the early 1970s.

I felt that by supporting Dr. Pak in this endeavor, I was also helping to create a record and model for others to emulate. Within the next 25 years or so, most of the first generation to follow Rev. Moon and his teachings will have ended their time on this earth and will have passed into the spirit world. If I could lend my expertise to develop a working model for the acts of the early disciples, then we could leave behind a treasure store of information and facts about the time when the True Parents walked the earth.

Imagine if an accurate record could have been kept at the time of Jesus, rather than the disjointed and heresay accounts created 100 years after Christ's crucifixion by the writers of the New Testament.

I have always wanted to serve the Providence in this way and have always felt that God was preparing me for such a task. My education and experience since joining the movement in 1975 have always given me the confidence and sense that I was being groomed for such a mission. With Dr. Pak's speech collection as a model, I am sure that many other early disciples will begin the arduous but necessary steps towards similar memoir projects.

For me, it was a labor of love to work closely with Dr. Pak, a man who always demanded a high standard of production, whether it was publications, stage decorations, planning, whatever, and who maintained the highest degree of personal comportment. Ever since the early days when we worked together in CAUSA International, then through the International Security Council, the Summit Council for World Peace, the Association for the Unity of Latin America, and the Federation for World Peace, whenever something had to be done, whether a book design, a conference stage, or whatever, there was only one standard to aspire—DP standard. DP standard meant the best.

With gratitude to Dr. Pak, I wholeheartedly offer up these volumes to future historians, the Second Generation and beyond, as a testimony to our True Parents and their love for the family of mankind.